ELIZABETH'S BEDFELLOWS

BY THE SAME AUTHOR

Mary Tudor

ELIZABETH'S BEDFELLOWS

An Intimate History of the Queen's Court

ANNA WHITELOCK

BLOOMSBURY

LONDON · NEW DELHI · NEW YORK · SYDNEY

Bloomsbury Publishing Plc
50 Bedford Square
London
WC1B 3DP

www.bloomsbury.com

Bloomsbury Publishing, London, New Delhi, New York and Sydney

A CIP catalogue record for this book is available from the British Library

(hardback edition) ISBN 978 1 4088 0880 1
(trade paperback edition) ISBN 978 1 4088 3661 3

10 9 8 7 6 5 4 3 2 1

Typeset by Hewer Text UK Ltd, Edinburgh
Printed and bound in Great Britain by CPI Group (UK) Ltd, Croydon CR0 4YY

For Kate

We princes, I tell you, are set on stages in the sight and view of all the world duly observed; the eyes of many behold our actions, a spot is soon spied in our garments; a blemish noted quickly in our doings.[1]

Elizabeth I

He did swear voluntarily, deeply and with vehement assertion, that he never had any carnal knowledge of her body, and this was also my mother's opinion, who was till the XXth year of her Majesty's reign of her Privy Chamber, and had been sometime her bedfellow.[2]

John Harington, the Queen's godson,
on her relationship with Sir Christopher Hatton

The state of this crown depends only on the breath of one person, our sovereign lady.[3]

William Cecil, Lord Burghley

CONTENTS

Author's Note

The dates in this book are all, unless otherwise specified, Old Style – that is, according to the calendar introduced by Julius Caesar in 45 BC. In February 1582 a new calendar was established by Pope Gregory XIII in a bull which prescribed that the day following 4 October 1582 should be 15 October, and that the new year should begin on 1 January instead of on Lady Day, 25 March. England, having repudiated papal authority, ignored the new calendar and, until 1751, English time continued ten days behind that of the Catholic states of Europe.

All quotations are in modern English spelling.

PROLOGUE:

Shameful Slanders

At thirteen, Elizabeth was serious yet striking, with fair skin, reddish-gold hair, a slender face and piercing coal-black eyes. A portrait from the time shows her in a crimson damask gown with long, wide sleeves and a magnificent underskirt richly worked in gold embroidery.[1] A tight bodice faintly outlines her breasts and offers the slightest hint of her burgeoning sexual maturity. Her face is framed with a French hood which, together with her necklace, dress and girdle, is trimmed with pearls – a symbol of her virginity. Her long slim fingers, adorned with rings, clasp a book of prayers with a ribbon marking a page within. She is standing in front of a bed; her body is thrown into sharp relief by the dark curtains which are pulled back on either side.

It was here, in Elizabeth's Bedchamber, that one of the most formative incidents of her early life took place. For the first of many times, Elizabeth's chastity became a subject of gossip, her body the object of rumour and speculation, and her Bedchamber a place of alleged sexual scandal.

———◆———

Following the death of her father Henry VIII in January 1547, the teenage Elizabeth made her home with her stepmother Katherine Parr at the Old Manor in Chelsea, situated near the River Thames. Katherine and Elizabeth had grown close in the few years before, and shared similar intellectual and religious interests.[2] But their relationship was soon tested. In April, just four months after Henry's death, Katherine married Thomas Seymour, uncle to the young King Edward VI and brother to Edward Seymour, now Lord Protector and Duke of Somerset.[3] He was a youthful and attractive forty-year-old bachelor. Tall, well built with auburn hair and a beard, Seymour was flamboyant, ruthless and insatiably ambitious. He had hoped initially to marry either the Princess Mary or Princess

Elizabeth as a means of gaining power, but when he realised he would never secure the Privy Council's consent, he turned to the next best thing, the queen dowager Katherine Parr. Katherine was reported to have been in love with Seymour for years, even before she married Henry VIII, and so responded enthusiastically to his advances. They married, in secret, in mid-April 1547 and Seymour now became Elizabeth's stepfather, moving in with the princess and Katherine at Chelsea.

It was here that on many mornings during the next year, Thomas Seymour would go to Elizabeth's Bedchamber, unlock the door and silently enter. If the princess were up he would 'bid her good Morrow', ask how she was and 'strike her upon the back or the buttocks familiarly'. On other days, if Elizabeth was in bed, he would pull back the curtains and 'make as though he would come at her' and she would retreat to the furthest corner of the bed. One morning when he tried to kiss Elizabeth in her bed, her long-serving governess, Kat Ashley, 'bade him go away for shame'.[4] Yet the encounters continued.

On one occasion when the household was staying at his London residence, Seymour made an early morning visit to Elizabeth in her Bedchamber, 'bare legged', wearing only his nightshirt and gown. Kat Ashley reprimanded him for such 'an unseemly Sight in a Maiden's Chamber!' and he stormed out in a rage.[5] On two mornings, at Hanworth in Middlesex, another of Katherine's residences, the queen dowager herself joined Seymour in his visit to Elizabeth's Bedchamber and on this occasion they both tickled the young princess in her bed. Later that day, in the garden, Seymour cut Elizabeth's dress into a hundred pieces while Katherine held her down.[6]

The involvement of Katherine here is even more puzzling than that of the others. She had fallen pregnant soon after the marriage, so perhaps this made her jealousy more intense and her behaviour more reckless; maybe she was seeking to maintain Seymour's affection and interest in her by joining in his 'horseplay'. Perhaps she feared that Elizabeth was developing something of a teenage infatuation with her stepfather. In any case Katherine soon decided that enough was enough and in May 1548, Elizabeth was sent to live with Sir Anthony Denny and his wife Joan at Cheshunt, Hertfordshire. Denny was a leading member of the Edwardian government and Joan was Kat Ashley's sister. Before Elizabeth left her stepmother's house, Katherine, then six months pregnant, had pointedly warned her stepdaughter of the damage malicious rumours might do to her reputation.[7]

Elizabeth was kept in seclusion at Cheshunt and this led to whispers that she was pregnant with Thomas Seymour's child. Kat Ashley reported that the princess was only sick, but still the gossip continued. A local midwife claimed she had been brought from her house blindfolded to assist a lady 'in a great house'. She came into a candlelit room and saw on a bed 'a very fair young lady' in labour. She alleged that a child was born and then killed. The midwife had assumed that it had been a lady of importance because of the need for secrecy. Knowing that Elizabeth was close by at Cheshunt, her suspicions were raised.[8]

On 5 September, Katherine Parr died having fallen ill of puerperal fever a week after giving birth to a daughter, Mary.[9] Showing little grief for his wife's death, Thomas Seymour began to pursue his political ambitions with renewed energy and revived his original plan to marry the Princess Elizabeth. Kat Ashley, after her earlier disapproval of Seymour's behaviour as a married man, now became an enthusiastic supporter of a union between Seymour and her young charge. But when Protector Somerset became aware of his brother's treasonous ambitions, Seymour was arrested and accused of plotting to overthrow the protector's government and marry the King's heir.[10]

Days later, Kat Ashley and Sir Thomas Parry, Treasurer of the Household, were taken to the Tower and questioned by Sir Robert Tyrwhit, Master of the Horse in the household of Katherine Parr, as to what they knew of Seymour's plotting and his plans to marry Elizabeth. When the princess was told of the arrests she was 'marvellously abashed and did weep very tenderly a long time'. Whilst the interrogations went on, rumours intensified that Elizabeth was pregnant with her stepfather's child. In a spirited letter to Protector Somerset of 28 January, she refuted the claims and urged the Privy Council to take immediate steps to prevent the spread of such malicious gossip: 'Master Tyrwhit and others have told me that there goeth rumours Abroad, which be greatly both against my Honour and Honesty . . . that I am in the Tower and with Child by my Lord Admiral.' These were, she continued, 'shameful slanders' which the council should publicly denounce. Elizabeth urgently petitioned the Lord Protector to allow her to come to court so that she could put pay to the accusations and show that she was not with child.[11]

In an effort to crush her spirit and force her to confess, Kat Ashley was now taken to one of the darkest and most uncomfortable cells in the Tower; she begged to be moved to a different prison: 'Pity me . . . and let me change my prison, for it is so cold that I cannot sleep, and so dark I cannot see by day, for I stop the window with straw as there is no glass.' She remained loyal to Elizabeth, however, and revealed nothing of the goings on in the household or the princess's relationship with her stepfather. 'My memory is never good,' Kat told her interrogators, 'as my Lady, fellows and husband can tell, and this sorrow has made it worse.'[12]

Whilst Elizabeth and her governess remained silent and loyal to one another, Sir Thomas Parry succumbed to the pressure and a month after his arrest began to tell Tyrwhit everything that had taken place between Seymour and Elizabeth:

> I do remember also, she [Ashley] told me, that the Admiral loved her but too well, and had so done a good while; and the Queen was jealous of her and him, in so much that, one Time the Queen, suspecting the often Access of the Admiral to the Lady Elizabeth's grace, came suddenly upon them, where they were all alone (he having her in his Arms) wherefore the Queen fell out, both with the Lord Admiral and her grace also.[13]

It was this incident, it seems, that led to Elizabeth leaving Katherine Parr's household.

Kat Ashley now had little option but to give up the details she had sought to withhold. Seymour had 'come at' Elizabeth in her Bedchamber, tickled her and kissed her and, yes, Kat had latterly 'wished both openly and privately', that Elizabeth and Seymour 'were married together'.[14] She acknowledged her 'great folly' in speaking of such a marriage and promised, if returned to Elizabeth's side, that she would never do any such thing again.

A messenger was swiftly despatched to Hatfield, the red-brick palace some thirty miles north of London where the princess was then staying. Elizabeth was shown her governess's confession.[15] She was horrified that the details of her relationship with Seymour had come out, but still she would not implicate Kat Ashley or Parry. 'In no ways she will confess that our Mistress Ashley or Parry willed her to any Practise with my Lord Admiral, whether by Message or Writing,' Tyrwhit reported.[16] Elizabeth refused to either corroborate or deny rumours of the romps with Seymour and insisted that she would never have married without the Privy Council's consent. Tyrwhit remained unconvinced: 'I do see it in her Face that she is guilty.'[17]

The council ruled that Ashley was 'unmeet' to oversee the 'good Education and Government' of Elizabeth, and she was replaced as governess by Lady Tyrwhit, wife of Elizabeth's interrogator.[18] Elizabeth was devastated at Kat Ashley's dismissal and, 'took the Matter so heavily, that she wept all that Night, and loured all the next day'. Sir Robert Tyrwhit added in his report to the council, 'the Love that she beareth her [Kat Ashley] is to be wondered at'.[19] In early March, when Elizabeth received the news that Seymour had been found guilty of treason and condemned to death, she wrote to the Lord Protector pleading for Kat's release, fearing her former governess was to suffer the same fate. She asked the Lord Protector to consider Kat's service to her: 'She hath been with me a long time, and many years, and hath taken great labour, and pain in bringing of me up in learning and honesty.' She pointed out that whatever Kat had done to promote the match between Seymour and Elizabeth, Ashley would have told the council. Finally she argued that the continuing imprisonment of Ashley, 'shall and doth make men think that I am not clear of the deed myself, but that it is pardoned in me because of my youth, because that she I loved so well is in such a place'.[20] Elizabeth's tactic paid off and both Ashley and Parry were released from the Tower, though Kat and her husband John would not be permitted to return to Elizabeth's household for another two years.[21]

Kat's absence was always keenly felt. Elizabeth had grown up with Ashley and during what was a motherless childhood, following the execution of Anne Boleyn when she was two, Kat cared for Elizabeth with a deep maternal concern. Elizabeth relied on her governess for support and comfort as she grew older. Despite their temporary separation, the bond between them endured and Kat Ashley would remain a constant and ever-faithful figure in Elizabeth's life, dying eighteen years later, when Elizabeth was at the height of her powers as Queen.

The vulnerability of Elizabeth to gossip and scandal, even at this early age, had been thrown into sharp relief by the lurid suggestions of sexual intrigue with her stepfather and the intense questioning of the princess and her household illustrates the seriousness of the accusations.[22] For an unmarried woman, chastity was everything. Juan Luis Vives, author of *The Instruction of a Christian Woman*, commissioned by Catherine of Aragon for her daughter Mary in 1523, wrote expansively about the dangerous suspicions that a tarnished reputation could produce. Once a girl loses her virginity, he wrote, everyone continually gossips about her and men who might otherwise have offered to marry her 'avoid her completely'. Chastity was the equivalent of all virtue. Parents, Vives advised, should pay special attention to their daughters at the beginning of puberty and keep them away from all contact with men, for during that period, 'they are more inclined to lust'. Vives's guidance went as far as the preparation of a young woman's bed. It should be 'clean, rather than luxurious so that she may sleep peacefully not sensuously'.[23] The goal of female education, Vives argued, was also to protect chastity, to school young women towards virtuous conduct and away from the temptations of the flesh.[24] As such their curriculum should include the study of 'that part of philosophy that had assumed as its task the formation and improvement of morals'. Vives therefore recommended the Gospels, Acts 'and the epistles, the historical and moral books of the Old Testament', the Church fathers; early Christian writers such as Plato, Seneca and Cicero and Christian poets such as Prudentius. Women should also write down and learn by heart 'wise and holy sentiments from the Holy Scriptures or ... philosophers'.[25]

Whilst Roger Ascham, who became Elizabeth's schoolmaster in 1548, would extol Elizabeth's chaste, feminine virtues, he would also celebrate Elizabeth's more 'unfeminine' accomplishments: her learning and scholarship 'exempt from female weakness' and her precocious intellect 'with a masculine power of application'. She was a skilled translator and linguist, speaking French and Italian fluently, and developed interests in science, philosophy and history. In short, Elizabeth had a 'manly wisdom' and intelligence encased in a body which was held to be physically inferior and morally weak and in need of the guidance of men. Regardless of her intellectual accomplishments, her standing would always be subject to her ability to preserve a chaste reputation.[26] Alongside her schoolroom lessons, the experience of 1547–48 with her stepfather had taught Elizabeth that her sexual reputation was an important political currency and the ladies who attended on her were the key custodians of her honour.

I

The Queen's Two Bodies

At the heart of the court lay the Queen's bed. Here the Queen might finally rest and retire from the relentless pressures of the day. Yet it was more than simply a place of slumber. The Queen's bed was the stage upon which, each night, the Queen would lie. Hers was no ordinary bed; it was the state bed, and at night as by day the Queen was surrounded by all the trappings of royal majesty.

As Queen, Elizabeth would have a number of beds, sumptuously furnished in bright colours and luxurious fabrics, all ostentatiously decorated and individually designed, each fit for a queen. At Richmond Palace, Elizabeth might sleep in an elaborate boat-shaped bed with curtains of 'sea water green' and quilted with light-brown tinsel. At Whitehall her bed was made from an intricate blend of different-coloured woods and hung with Indian-painted silk. Her best bed, which was taken with her when the court moved from place to place, had a carved wooden frame which was elaborately painted and gilded, a valance of silver and velvet, tapestry curtains trimmed with precious buttons and gold and silver lace, and a crimson satin headboard topped with ostrich feathers.

In her Bedchamber, Elizabeth could de-robe, take off her make-up and withdraw from the hustle-bustle of the court. Here she was waited upon by her ladies who had the most intimate access to the Queen, attending on her as she dressed, ate, bathed, toileted and slept. Elizabeth was never alone and in or adjacent to her bed she also had a sleeping companion – a trusted bedfellow – with whom she might gossip, share dreams and night-mares, and seek counsel. We know Elizabeth was both an insomniac and scared of the dark. All her worries were magnified in the darkness of her Bedchamber at night. It was here that she might have second thoughts about decisions made in the light of day, be haunted by fears of her enemies and plagued by vivid nightmares. Sharing a bed with a sleeping

7

companion of the same sex was a common practice at the time, providing warmth, comfort and security; but being the Queen of England's bedfellow was a position of the greatest trust, bringing close and intimate access to Elizabeth.[1]

The Queen's Bedchamber was at once a private and public space. The Queen's body was more than its fleshly parts; her body natural represented the body politic, the very state itself. The health and sanctity of Elizabeth's body determined the strength and stability of the realm. Illness, sexual immorality and infertility were political concerns and it was her Ladies of the Bedchamber who were the guardians of the truth as to the Queen's and thus the nation's wellbeing.

An unmarried queen heightened fears. Women were expected to marry and Elizabeth's decision to remain unwed ran counter to society's expectations. It was generally believed that women were inferior to men and so subject to them by divine law. Women who ignored religious precepts and did not submit to male authority were potentially a source of disorder and sexual licence. Medical discourse regarded women's bodies as being in a constant state of flux and so possessing dangerously unstable qualities.[2] Such medical axioms were influenced by theology, with the belief that Eve's moral and intellectual weakness had been the primary cause of the Fall of Man and succeeding generations of women were similarly flawed.

Whilst for her male predecessors sexual potency might be a sign of political power, the corruption or weakness of Elizabeth's body would undermine the body politic. Women were to preserve their honour not only through chastity, but also by maintaining a reputation for chaste behaviour. For a woman to be thought unchaste, even falsely, would jeopardise her social standing. Moreover, Elizabeth was the daughter of Anne Boleyn, 'the King's whore', and so the living symbol of the break with Rome.[3] For Philip II of Spain, the Guise family in France, and the Pope, Elizabeth was illegitimate by birth and by religion. For them Mary Stuart, Queen of Scots, was the rightful queen.[4] Mary was the granddaughter of Henry VIII's sister Margaret, who had married James V of Scotland and was daughter of Mary of Guise. The Guise was one of the most powerful, ambitious and fervently Catholic families in France. In April 1558, just six months before Elizabeth's accession, this Franco-Scottish alliance was cemented by the marriage of sixteen-year-old Mary Stuart and François of Valois, the Dauphin of France. From the day Elizabeth became Queen, Mary Stuart claimed the English throne as her own.[5] The stakes could not have been higher; the Queen's body was at the centre of a drama that encompassed the entirety of Europe. In the war of faith which divided Europe, Elizabeth's body, with her bed as its stage, was the focal point of the conflict.[6] Throughout her reign rumours circulated about her sexual exploits and illegitimate children. Her Catholic opponents challenged her virtue and accused her of a 'filthy lust' that 'defiled her body and the country'.[7] The reason Elizabeth was not married, they claimed, was because of her sexual appetites; she could not confine herself to one man. Some alleged that she had a bastard daughter; others that she had a son, and others that she was physically incapable of having children. By questioning the health, chastity and fertility of the Queen's natural body, opponents in England and across the continent sought to challenge the Protestant state. For half a century the courts of Europe buzzed with gossip about Elizabeth's behaviour. The King of France would jest that one of the great questions of the age was, 'whether Queen Elizabeth was a maid or no'.[8]

Over the five decades of her rule, Elizabeth changed from being a young vibrant queen with a pale pretty face, golden hair and slender physique, to a wrinkled old woman with rotten teeth, garishly slathered in jewels and cosmetics to distract from her pitted complexion, and wearing a reddish wig to cover her balding head. As she passed through her twenties and thirties, unmarried and without an heir, and on to middle age and infirmity, the country's fears intensified. With no settled succession it became increasingly important for Elizabeth to try to disguise the signs of ageing. The physical reality of the Queen's decaying natural body needed to be reconciled with the enduring and unchanging body politic; only in the Bedchamber was Elizabeth's natural body and the truth laid bare.

Access to the Queen's body was carefully controlled, as were representations of it in portraits. The Queen's image was fashioned to retain its youthfulness, which necessarily obscured the reality of her physical decline. In paintings she needed to appear as she did outside her Bedchamber, enrobed, bejewelled, bewigged and painted; creating this complex confection as she aged was the daily task of the women of her Bedchamber. Such was Elizabeth's desire to preserve the fiction of her youth that she sponsored the search for the 'Philosopher's Stone', the elixir of life which would ensure eternal health and immortality.

Beyond the rumours and the sexual slander, the Queen's body and Bedchamber were also the focus of assassination attempts, as disaffected religious zealots plotted to kill Elizabeth. The preservation of the Protestant state depended upon the life of the Queen, and the Bedchamber was the last line of defence for would-be assassins looking to subvert the regime. One plan aimed to plant gunpowder in her Bedchamber and blow up the Queen as she slept; others sought to poison her as she rode, hunted or dined. Not only did Elizabeth's bedfellows, the women who attended on the Queen when she was in bed, help protect her reputation for chastity; they also protected the body of the Queen from attempts to assassinate her; they would check each dish before it was served, test any perfume that had been given to her Majesty and would make nightly searches of the Bedchamber.[9] Their presence was for both propriety and security. While the loyalty of her ladies was assured, the families of some of these women sought to use their privileged access to the Queen to serve their own traitorous or licentious ends.

The Queen's body was the very heart of the realm and so its care and access to it was politically important. By sleeping with Elizabeth and dressing her, the Ladies of her Bedchamber could observe any bodily changes in the Queen, attend to her if unwell, share her night-time fears, her good humour and her confidences and defend her against hostile rumours. Foreign ambassadors managed to bribe the women on occasions for information about the Queen's life, and despatches reported intimate details, such as Elizabeth's light and irregular periods, and supposed secret sexual liaisons with individuals such as Robert Dudley, Sir Christopher Hatton and the Duke of Anjou, the alleged 'bedfellows' who 'aspired to the honour of her bed'.[10]

2

The Queen is Dead, Long Live the Queen

In the flickering candlelight of her Bedchamber at St James's Palace in London, in the early hours of the morning of Thursday, 17 November 1558, Queen Mary I lay dying. She had been confined to her bed with influenza since her arrival from Hampton Court three months earlier and each day had grown progressively weaker.[1] She had made a will earlier in the year, but believing she was then pregnant, had provided only for an heir of her body to succeed her. In late October, now seriously ill, Mary was forced to add a codicil to her will which acknowledged that she was 'sick and weak in body', would bear no child and would be succeeded by 'my next heir and successor by the Laws and Statutes of this realm'.[2] Still she could not bring herself to identify her half-sister Elizabeth as her heir. Two weeks later, and under pressure from her council, Mary was forced to bow to the inevitable and name Elizabeth as her successor.[3] Jane Dormer, a devout Catholic and one of the Queen's most trusted women who had 'slept in Mary's bedchamber many times with her', went to Elizabeth at Hatfield and, as a token of fidelity, gave her a number of Mary's jewels from the Bedchamber. Mary asked for Elizabeth's assurance that she would be good to her servants, pay Mary's debts and maintain the Catholic religion in England.[4] In carrying this message to Elizabeth, Jane Dormer performed her last significant act as Mary's bedfellow. Now the country waited for news from the royal Bedchamber of Queen Mary's death.

On 16 November just before midnight, Mary received the last rites. A few hours later she heard mass as a small group of her most trusted ladies gathered round her bed, sobbing throughout the service. A little after six o'clock in the morning, Mary died. Her ring was removed from her finger and Sir Nicholas Throckmorton carried it to Hatfield where he informed Elizabeth that she was now Queen of England. By late morning the announcement had been made in Parliament and by mid-afternoon bells were rung in churches across London, and bonfires lit, 'amid scenes of great rejoicing'.[5]

———·———

The new twenty-five-year-old Queen was radiant, slim, and nubile – and strikingly attractive – with her father's trademark Tudor red-gold hair, a long oval face, thin lips and a pale complexion, and the dark, penetrating eyes and slender fingers of her mother.[6] She was about five foot four inches tall. After the barren reign of her sister Mary, Elizabeth's accession raised hopes of youth, health and fertility.

Three days later, Elizabeth made her first public speech in the great hall at Hatfield. It was moving, and struck a perfect note between humility and authority. She expressed sorrow for her sister's death and amazement at the great burden which had now fallen to her. But she was 'God's creature' and it was His will that she was now called to this royal office. Elizabeth would now have 'two bodies': whilst having the 'natural body' of a woman subject to error, infirmity and old age, she also acknowledged that she was to become the 'body politic to govern'.[7] With the ritual anointing in the coronation ceremony, her 'natural body' would be fused with the unerring, immortal body politic.[8]

Among those listening to the new Queen's words was William Cecil, whom Elizabeth had appointed Principal Secretary earlier that day. He was astute, loyal and hardworking, and whilst he had conformed during the Catholic reign of Mary I he was undoubtedly a Protestant. He would be one of the men upon whom Elizabeth would rely for most of her reign. Cecil, like all of Elizabeth's privy councillors, swore to 'give such counsel to her Majesty's person as may best seem . . . to the safety of her Majesty's person, and to the common weal of this realm'.[9] It would be a promise William Cecil would honour for the rest of his life.

Elizabeth also favoured those who had opposed the Catholicism of Mary's reign, had proved their loyalty to her, or were relatives and former allies of her mother, Anne Boleyn. Lord William Howard of Effingham, her mother's first cousin, was appointed Lord Chamberlain, whilst Sir Edward Rogers, a staunch Protestant who had been imprisoned for a time during Mary's reign, became Vice-Chamberlain. Sir Francis Knollys, Elizabeth's second cousin by marriage and also a committed Protestant who had gone into exile during Mary's reign, was appointed to the Privy Council and later replaced Rogers as Vice-Chamberlain. Nicholas Bacon, another Protestant and brother-in-law of William Cecil, became Lord

Keeper of the Great Seal. Nicholas Throckmorton, a cousin of Katherine Parr who met Elizabeth during the time she lived with her stepmother, rose to become Chief Butler and Chamberlain of the Exchequer. Shortly afterwards he was appointed ambassador to France. Thomas Parry, Elizabeth's adviser when she was princess, became Treasurer of the Household, having been restored to favour after his revelations during the Seymour scandal. As the Count of Feria, Philip II of Spain's envoy, reported, 'the Kingdom is entirely in the hands of young folks, heretics and traitors, and the Queen does not favour a single man whom her Majesty, who is now in heaven, would have received'.[10]

Whilst many in England celebrated Elizabeth's accession as the promise of a decisive break with the Catholic past, not all were of the same mind. Henry VIII's will had named Elizabeth as Mary's successor, however Roman Catholics regarded her as illegitimate because of Henry's unlawful marriage to her mother Anne Boleyn, after he had spurned Catherine of Aragon. Instead they held that Mary Stuart, the granddaughter of Margaret Tudor, Henry VIII's sister, was the legitimate heir to the English throne.

The French, to whom Mary was bound through her mother Mary of Guise and her marriage to François the French dauphin, immediately questioned Elizabeth's right to succeed. As Lord Cobham, then Elizabeth's envoy in France, wrote in December, they 'did not let to say and talk openly that Her Highness is not lawful Queen of England and they have already sent to Rome to disprove her right'. As soon as the French King, Henri II, heard of the death of Mary I he proclaimed his Catholic daughter-in-law, Mary Queen of Scots as 'Queen of England, Scotland and Ireland'. The royal arms of England were now blazoned with those of Scotland and France on her silver dinner plates and furniture.[11] Meanwhile, the Cardinal of Lorraine, Mary's uncle, lobbied the Pope to excommunicate Elizabeth and urged Philip II of Spain to join a combined invasion of England.[12]

Philip's position was, however, less clear cut. France and Spain were still at war. Whilst he instinctively supported Mary Queen of Scots as the Catholic heir to the English throne, this was tempered by the fact that she was the daughter-in-law of his great rival, Henri II. However, when Elizabeth moved to end England's involvement in the imperial war with France, Philip feared that she might end up agreeing to an Anglo-French alliance which would threaten Spain's interests. Therefore, while he took no overt action against Elizabeth, he began secret intrigues to support an alternative candidate for the English throne.

In the event of Elizabeth's death without heirs, Henry VIII, having excluded the entire Stuart line of his elder sister Margaret Tudor – who had married James IV of Scotland – settled the crown on the descendants of his younger sister, Mary Brandon, Duchess of Suffolk: Lady Jane, Katherine and Mary Grey. After the execution of Lady Jane Grey for her attempt to usurp the crown in 1553, Katherine Grey became Elizabeth's Protestant heir and was soon courted by foreign princes and English noblemen for her hand in what would be a politically significant marriage. It was to her that Philip now turned as Spain looked to counter the threat of Mary Stuart and her French family.

Unsurprisingly perhaps, Elizabeth could not abide the sight of Katherine and made it clear that she did not wish her to succeed even if she died without an heir of her body.[13] On her accession she demoted Katherine Grey and her sister Mary from being Ladies of the Bedchamber, as they had been under Mary I, to maids of honour, largely confined to service in the Presence Chamber. Katherine complained bitterly to the Spanish ambassador Feria, and was 'dissatisfied and offended' that she had not been accorded the appropriate honour due to her rank.[14] In the summer of 1559 and again the following spring, it was widely reported abroad that the Philip II was planning to smuggle Katherine Grey out of England, marry her to his son and from there assert her claim to the English throne.

On 30 June, King Henri II of France, Philip's great adversary, was fatally injured in a jousting accident. François and Mary became King and Queen of France and power in the French court passed to her Guise uncles. In an effort to offset the threat Mary Stuart now posed, Elizabeth resolved to court Katherine Grey's favour and by the new year of 1560 restored her and her sister to their former positions in the inner sanctum of the Queen's Bedchamber, alongside old friends like Kat Ashley, in a kind of protective custody.[15] At least here Elizabeth could keep a watchful eye on them. One of William Cecil's agents reported that the Grey sisters were 'straightly' looked to and their movements closely observed.[16]

In the days immediately following Elizabeth's accession, a number of Catholics were arrested in London. Six men were accused of 'conjuring' to calculate 'the Queen's life and the duration of her Government'.[17] It was the first of a series of conspiracies against the Elizabethan regime in which horoscopes would be cast or spirits consulted to predict the Queen's imminent death.[18] The French Catholic seer Michel Nostradamus had also foreseen imminent catastrophe for Protestant England and his prophecies were widely circulated on both sides of the Channel, fuelling mass anxiety. As one contemporary put it, 'The whole realm was so troubled and so moved with blind enigmatical and devilish prophecies of that heaven-gazer Nostradamus.'[19]

To counteract Nostradamus' prophecies, Elizabeth called on the services of mathematician, astrologer and necromancer Dr John Dee, who had been a keen supporter of Elizabeth during the years before her accession.[20] Dee performed an electionary horoscope about the day that had been appointed for Elizabeth's coronation. The configuration of the heavens on Sunday 15 January, would, he determined, presage a long and successful reign.[21] As the traditional procession on the eve of the coronation passed through the City of London, en route to Westminster, pageants lined the streets heralding the new reign as a decisive break from the Catholic past with tableaux depicting 'pure religion' treading upon 'superstition and ignorance'.[22] At the Little Conduit in Cheapside, Elizabeth took the English Bible proffered her by an allegorical figure of Truth, kissed the book, held it aloft, and then clasped it to her breast.

Once she was crowned, Elizabeth moved quickly to end the years of uncertainty over her royal title and establish her legitimacy to the throne. In the first Parliament of the reign, which met ten days after the coronation, a statute was passed which declared the Queen 'rightly, lineally and lawfully descended from the blood royal', and pronounced 'all sentences and Acts of Parliament derogatory to this declaration to be void'.[23] She was no longer a royal bastard.

Elizabeth's very existence was a result of England's breach with Rome and therefore, as Queen, and not acknowledged as such in many parts of Catholic Europe, she was bound to restore the royal supremacy which her sister Mary had repudiated. While she had outwardly conformed to Catholicism during her youth, in her prayers Elizabeth thanked God that he had from her 'earliest days' kept her away from the 'deep abysses of natural ignorance and damnable superstitions'.[24] She later confirmed her longstanding devotion to the reformed religion: 'When I first took the sceptre, my title made me not forget the giver, and therefore [I] began as it became me, with such religion as both I was born in, bred in, and, I trust, shall die in'.[25] She had also absented herself from mass at the opening of Parliament and when greeted at Westminster Abbey by the abbot and his monks carrying lighted torches she exclaimed, 'Away with these torches, for we see very well.'[26]

All the religious legislation of the previous reign was swiftly repealed and the Act of Uniformity imposed a Book of Common Prayer, which was essentially the 1552 Edwardian book with a few significant alterations designed to reconcile confessional differences. Most notably the words of the communion had been altered to allow a Catholic interpretation of the real presence of Christ in the bread and wine. Nevertheless the celebration of the mass was now illegal and all subjects were to attend the services of the new Church on Sundays and holy days on penalty of a shilling fine for every absence. By the Act of Supremacy which was passed on 29 April 1559, Elizabeth was proclaimed Supreme Governor of the Church of England, not Supreme Head in deference to objections because she was a woman. All office holders – clergymen, judges, Justices of the Peace, mayors and royal officials – were now required to swear an oath acknowledging Elizabeth as Supreme Governor of the Church. Refusal to do so would result in loss of office. Anyone writing, teaching or preaching that Elizabeth should be subject to the authority of a foreign power (including the Pope) would lose all his or her property and moveable possessions. Repeated offences would be judged high treason and incur the death penalty.

3

Familia Reginae

The coronation marked the first ceremonial outing of Elizabeth's new court. One witness described how, as the snow fell, it seemed 'the whole court so sparkled with jewels and gold collars that they clear the air'.[1] Before the Queen, who was carried on an open litter surrounded by her ladies and gentlewomen, processed her household, her bishops, the peers of the realm and foreign ambassadors. Directly behind her rode Robert Dudley, her newly appointed Master of the Horse. The procession was flanked by a thousand horsemen and by royal guards in crimson jackets, each adorned with Elizabeth's initials and the Tudor rose.[2]

The court as a whole was a vast institution of more than a thousand servants and attendants, ranging from brewers and bakers, cooks, tailors and stable hands to courtiers and ambassadors. Whilst it was a place of provision, patronage, power and display, it was also, of course, Elizabeth's home, albeit an itinerant one. The Queen and her court would regularly move between the royal palaces which lined the Thames – Whitehall, Hampton Court, Richmond, and Windsor – so that each could be cleaned, 'sweetened' and aired. Some three hundred carts of furniture, tapestries, gowns and ornaments would be moved with meticulous organisation. The court generally followed a fairly regular pattern in its movement between royal palaces, spending six weeks or so at Whitehall in the winter, then moving between Richmond, Greenwich, Hampton Court and Nonsuch in Surrey, and then perhaps to Windsor or Whitehall for Easter. Each summer, when the plague was often rife in London, the Queen and her entourage would venture beyond the capital on a series of visits to towns and aristocratic homes in southern England.

In whichever residence Elizabeth found herself she required a suite of rooms – the privy lodgings – where she would be largely secluded from the hustle and bustle of the main court. The privy lodgings consisted of a series of rooms – a Presence Chamber, a Privy Chamber and a Bedchamber

– which led off from the great hall. Entry into each room denoted greater intimacy with the monarch's natural body. The Privy Chamber formed the frontier between Queen's public and private worlds; whilst the outer rooms of the palaces swarmed with courtiers, the inner rooms beyond it were closely guarded and only few would have access. The Presence Chamber, a large reception room with a throne and canopy of state, was accessible to anyone entitled to appear at court. A throng of suitors, foreign ambassadors, bishops and courtiers would regularly gather there hoping to catch the Queen as she passed through. The Privy Chamber was where Elizabeth would spend most of her day, surrounded by her favoured ladies, transacting government business, listening to music, dancing, playing cards, sewing or gossiping. It was heavily guarded with 146 Yeomen of the Guard.[3]

Elizabeth had two to three Gentlemen of the Privy Chamber and between five and ten grooms, who supervised the outer chamber, and four Esquires of the Body, who took charge of the whole chamber through the night. There were two rooms which led off from the Privy Chamber. The first of these was the Privy Closet, a small private chapel and the second, the Queen's Bedchamber. This was the very centre of the court and the most private place in the Elizabethan realm. Here the Queen's natural body would be laid bare and Elizabeth's trusted women would take it in turns to sleep either with the Queen or on a truckle bed adjacent to her.

During the reign of her father Henry VIII and brother Edward VI, the privy lodgings had been an exclusively male preserve. However, for Elizabeth, as for her sister Mary, these rooms were principally staffed by a small group of women.[4] The first women to serve Elizabeth in her privy lodgings are listed in the coronation account book. Here the women are divided into groups of different status denoting the different kinds of cloth for their coronation clothes; purple tinsel for the more senior ladies, crimson velvet for the others.[5] There were four women who served specifically in the Bedchamber, three women identified as 'Chamberers', seven women who served 'in the Privy Chamber without wage', and six young, unmarried girls served as maids of the Privy Chamber under the supervision of the 'mother of the maids', who would be solely responsible for their care and conduct. Under the heading 'Ladies and Gentlewomen of the Household', eighteen women are listed.[6] In total twenty-eight women served in Elizabeth's private chambers at some time during her reign. It was a small number and this meant there was fierce competition for places. Ultimately it was the women and their individual relationships with Elizabeth that mattered most and those most favoured might even find themselves in bed with the Queen. The friendships and intimacies between Elizabeth and her women underpinned her reign.

＊

In the years before she became Queen, Elizabeth was surrounded by the 'old flock of Hatfield', a tightly knit group of loyal female attendants who were now drawn to the heart of the new court.[7] Some were Boleyn cousins; others had been appointed by her father and had since become old friends and political allies. Now on Elizabeth's accession their loyalty was to be rewarded with positions of intimacy and trust in the new royal household. Other women returned from having been in religious exile and took up positions in the queen's entourage.

Katherine Carey was first cousin to the Queen through Anne Boleyn's sister Mary Boleyn Carey.[8] She was born around 1524 and had served as a maid of honour to Anne of Cleves, Henry's third wife, before marrying Sir Francis Knollys in 1540. Katherine and Francis's adherence to Protestantism led to them, with their five children, leaving England during the reign of Mary Tudor and moving to Frankfurt.[9] A letter dated 1553 from Elizabeth to Katherine may have been written in response to the news that Katherine was leaving the country. Perhaps Katherine had already spent some time in the Princess Elizabeth's household, as the letter suggests a close relationship and the promise of favour to come. Elizabeth then signed her letter *cor rotto,* or 'broken heart'.

> Relieve your sorrow for your far journey with joy of your short return, and think this pilgrimage rather a proof of your friends, than a leaving of your country, the length of time, and distance of the place, separates not the love of friends, nor deprives not the show of good will ... when your need shall be most you shall find my friendship greatest ... My power but small my love as great as those whose gifts may tell their friendships tale ...
>   Your loving cousin and ready friend *cor rotto.*[10]

As soon as Elizabeth succeeded to the throne, Lady Katherine Knollys and her husband returned to England and they, together with their daughters Lettice, then just fifteen, and Elizabeth, then only nine, were appointed to her household.[11] Lady Katherine became one of the Queen's most senior ladies-in-waiting and for the first ten years of the reign combined this with motherhood to thirteen children. Less than a year after Elizabeth's coronation Katherine temporarily withdrew from court to give birth to her thirteenth child, before returning to the Queen's side weeks later, having left her baby in the care of a wet nurse. Her nieces, Katherine and Philadelphia Carey, were also appointed to the Queen's entourage shortly after her accession.[12]

Beyond her mother's kith and kin, Elizabeth also had strong emotional ties with a number of women whom she had known almost all her life, and certainly from her earliest infancy. Blanche Parry, a no-nonsense Welshwoman from Herefordshire, had 'rocked' the cradle of the young princess, and was twenty-five years older than Elizabeth. Unusually for the time, Blanche never married and for the rest of her long life remained devoted and unswervingly loyal to Elizabeth.[13]

Kat Ashley was Elizabeth's other longest-serving and most-trusted woman. She had taught her, defended her honour against the scandalous talk of her relationship with her stepfather, and had on two occasions found herself imprisoned for her loyal devotion to the princess. Ashley was now appointed First Lady of the Bedchamber, the most prestigious position in the royal household, while her husband, John, a cousin of Anne Boleyn's, was given the important post of Master of the Jewel House, which he retained until his death in 1596.[14]

A number of Elizabeth's other trusted women were themselves of royal blood or had distant claims to the throne. Elizabeth Fiennes de Clinton, known in her youth as 'Fair Geraldine' and considered one of the beauties of the age, was one such woman. Her mother Lady Elizabeth Grey was the granddaughter of Edward IV's queen, Elizabeth Woodville, and first cousin to Henry VIII. After her father Gerald Fitzgerald, 9th Earl of Kildare, was imprisoned on corruption charges and then died in the Tower in 1534, Henry had taken pity on his cousin Lady Elizabeth Grey and invited her youngest daughter Elizabeth, then about eight years old, to join the household of the Princesses Mary and Elizabeth at Hunsdon in Hertfordshire. Elizabeth, who was just two or three years old at the time, became particularly fond of her older cousin and their relationship lasted into adulthood. In the weeks immediately before Mary I's death, Elizabeth Fitzgerald married Edward Fiennes de Clinton, 9th Lord High Admiral, rejoined Elizabeth's household and became one of the leading ladies of the new Queen's court.[15]

Dorothy Stafford, the Protestant daughter of Henry Stafford, a Catholic nobleman, also returned from religious exile on the continent soon after Elizabeth's accession.[16] She had married her cousin Sir William Stafford, widower of Elizabeth's aunt Mary Boleyn, and together they had fled

England for Geneva during Mary's reign as the persecution of Protestants gathered pace.[17] Dorothy returned to England a widow with six children and entered Elizabeth's service in the Bedchamber where she would remain until the Queen's death more than forty years later.[18]

It was women such as these who formed the close entourage that surrounded Elizabeth and each, richly clad in specially ordered clothes, proudly formed the train behind Elizabeth in her coronation procession and attended on her during the various changes of robes in the ceremony itself.[19] For the Ladies of the Privy Chamber and Bedchamber their duties were to wash the Queen, attend to her make-up and her hair, choose her clothes and jewels and assist her in putting them on. They would also help serve her food and drink, to monitor it for poison or other harmful substances. The Chamberers would carry out more menial duties, such as cleaning the Queen's rooms, emptying her wash bowls and arranging her bed linen, whilst the young unmarried maids of honour provided companionship and entertainment. The maids of honour were girls of good birth who, generally dressed in white, attended the Queen in public, carried her train, sat and walked with her in the Privy Chamber and kept her entertained with dancing.

The women received only modest payment for the myriad of duties they had to perform. Some, like the maids of honour, were rarely paid at all. The Ladies of the Privy Chamber and Bedchamber received an annual salary of around £33 6s.8d (about £5,600 today). Whilst the wages were not large, the women received board and lodgings for themselves and their own servants, together with clothing for day wear and for special occasions and sometimes even received the Queen's own cast-offs. The size and quality of the lodgings varied enormously from palace to palace; space was at a premium and privacy unusual. Privy Chamber staff generally slept where they worked and only when they were off duty did they have the luxury of private lodgings. The maids of honour all slept together in the Coffer Chamber, which was very often cramped and uncomfortable. At Windsor their apartments were so primitive they had to ask 'to have their chambers ceiled, and the partition, that is of boards there, to be made higher, for that the servants look over'.[20]

Elizabeth expected all her women to be in constant attendance and to put her needs above any personal concerns. Illness, unless it was severe, was no excuse for absence; neither were marriage or children. Elizabeth required complete loyalty and commitment. If any of her married ladies fell pregnant they were expected to continue to attend the Queen until very late in their pregnancy, when they could retire for the 'lying-in', and then return to court as soon as possible after the birth, leaving their children in the care of wet nurses and governesses. In an age where motherhood and marriage were deemed to be the highest state to which a woman could aspire, here was a group of ladies in attendance on an unmarried queen who defied convention without losing status.

Together these were among the most favoured women who would be at the very heart of the court day and night. Whilst they were valuable companions, sleeping alongside the Queen in the dark or candle-lit Bedchamber, they were also bodyguards who played an important role in attending to and protecting the body of the Queen. As long as Elizabeth had neither husband nor successor, her life always would be in danger. Across the reign the risk of assassination was greater than the Queen being killed in open rebellion. Similarly, the women of the Bedchamber were closest to the Queen's thoughts and moods, and courtiers and ambassadors continually looked to curry favour with this elite group of women in order that they might promote their interests and present their petitions. Indeed Robert Beale, then a clerk of the Privy Council, later prepared a memorandum of advice about the post of Principal Secretary to the Queen and explicitly acknowledged the importance of the women: 'Learn before you access her Majesty's disposition by some in the Privy Chamber, with whom you must keep credit.'[21] To know the Queen's mood would prove vital for her ministers.

4

Not a Morning Person

When Elizabeth left Hatfield to begin her journey to London, she ordered that her best bed with its gilded bedstead, six yards square and carved with 'eight beasts', be delivered to Whitehall. It was undoubtedly a bed fit for a queen. The valance of purple velvet laced with gold and 'garnished with a thin fringe of Venice gold', was surrounded by thirty-four silk tassels hanging down from curtains of purple damask with a bedhead of purple velvet to match.[1] It became the very heart of Elizabeth's new court and a stage upon which her life and reign would be played out.

The palace at Whitehall, the Queen's chief London residence, covered a site of twenty-three acres. The hall and chapel, the royal lodgings, galleries and privy garden stood on the east side and were connected with the river by a flight of privy stairs. To the west were many extra lodgings grouped around a cockpit, tiltyard and tennis court. The palace was a labyrinth of narrow, winding corridors and some two thousand rooms. It had been built by Cardinal Wolsey and then extended by Henry VIII and altered to receive Anne Boleyn as Queen in 1533. When in residence, Elizabeth occupied what had formerly been the King's lodgings and left vacant the rooms intended for a consort.[2] All the rooms were furnished with great splendour, with a multitude of statutes and pictures, including a bust of Attila, King of the Huns, a genealogical table of the Kings of England, a sundial in the form of a monkey, an astrolabe that calculated the rising and setting of the sun, and many fine instruments.

Elizabeth's Bedchamber overlooked the Thames. The room was very dark and, with only one window, had little fresh air. The walls were hung with rich tapestries for warmth, comfort and decoration, and the ceiling was painted gold.[3]

The Queen's day began with the great curtains of her bed being drawn back by her ladies. Elizabeth was not, as she said of herself, a 'morning person'.[4] Sometimes she rose early in order to be ready to grant an audience at eight o'clock, but more usually she was still in bed while the rest of her household went about their duties, lighting fires and sweeping the chambers. The Bedchamber would have been draughty and so its fire had to be stoked to entice the Queen from her bed. Elizabeth rarely dressed immediately but, clothed in her 'night stuff', would be served breakfast in her Bedchamber – manchet bread, meat, pottage, ale or wine – before taking a fast walk in her privy garden.[5] She was an 'inveterate walker' whatever the weather. She generally walked with a 'stately gait', unless she wanted to 'catch a heat in the cold morning' or wander through her gardens for pleasure and recreation.[6] Sometimes she might walk accompanied by her ladies, but very often she preferred to be alone, with her guards at a careful distance. On other occasions she would begin the day sitting in her nightgown, reading by the window in her Bedchamber.[7] One morning a carter remarked how he had seen her only partly dressed at her window and now 'knew the Queen was a woman'. Elizabeth sent him an angel (ten shillings) to 'shut his mouth'.[8]

When the Queen was ready, her ladies would help her as she washed, assist as she dressed, brush her hair and apply her make-up. It was, even in the Queen's youth, a time-consuming process. Most commonly Elizabeth would wash from a basin of water with face cloths and Castile soap made of olive oil, shipped in great quantities direct from Spain.[9] She kept her ivory forehead virtually wrinkle-free for many years by cleansing it with posset curd. Her long golden hair was washed with lye, a compound of wood ash and water, and then rubbed with a warm coarse cloth to remove grease and dandruff before being combed. Toothbrushes were unknown, but toothpicks would be regularly used and are recorded in the lists of gifts Elizabeth received each year. She also had numerous Holland 'tooth cloths' which were also used for teeth-cleaning together with a mixture of white wine and vinegar boiled with honey.[10] Despite such efforts, Elizabeth's teeth in middle-age would be yellow, badly decayed and foul smelling, eventually becoming black, due to her love of sweet-meats such as marzipan and candied fruit.[11] She attempted to mask her bad breath with mouthwashes of rosemary, myrrh, mastic and cinnamon.[12]

Once washed, Elizabeth would be made-up. She relied on cosmetics to produce her famous ivory complexion. A meringue-like concoction of eggwhite, powdered eggshell, alum, borax and poppy seeds mixed with mill water and beaten until a froth stood on it three fingers deep was applied to her skin.[13] The mixture would apparently keep for a year and be used three times a week to whiten, smooth and soften the skin – in fact it served only to blanch it. There were many other whiteners: mercury sublimate might also be used or 'liquid pearl' to give a translucent glow. Elizabeth would also use rouge and lip salves, the main ingredient of which was ceruse, a white solid mix of lead carbonate and lead hydroxide which was made by exposing plates of metal to the vapour of vinegar. Crayons or 'pencils' (the word lipstick was not used then) were made by grinding down alabaster calcinate or plaster of Paris into a powder, which was then coloured, mixed into a paste, rolled into shape and dried in the sun. Face powder could be similarly obtained from ground alabaster. The pounding and grinding of ingredients for cosmetics, face washes, tooth powders and remedies was a daily labour for her ladies, and one involving great trust, given fears that poison hidden in cosmetics could be absorbed through the Queen's skin to fatal effect.

Not long after becoming Queen, Elizabeth steadily began to lose her hair and so John Hemingway, her apothecary, made pomades and salves to apply to her scalp. When these did not stop her hair loss, Elizabeth changed her hairstyle and wore curls to cover the bald crown of her head, each of which had to be carefully styled each day.

Regular bathing was not the norm, although Elizabeth was described as having a bath every month 'whether she needs it or no'. Nevertheless, in a world of pungent body odour, perfumes were used greatly and considered more than simply a luxury. Many women would hang a pomander, an intricately carved metal or boxwood ball filled with a paste of aromatic spices such as cloves, nutmeg or cumin, from a cord around their waist. This was considered both a means to ward off bad smells and a preservative from infection. Her physician Dr Huick regularly presented her with a flagon of orange-flower water. The following recipe was said to have been used to prepare Elizabeth's favourite toilet water, which was made from marjoram: 'Take eight spoonfuls of compound water, the weight of twopence in fine powder of sugar, and boil it on hot embers and coals softly, add half an ounce of sweet marjoram dried in the sun, and the weight of twopence of the powder of Benjamin.' The resulting toilet water was said to be 'very sweet and good for the time'.[14]

'Sweet bags', impregnated with perfume, were sewn into dresses and gloves, and stockings and shoes were also perfumed with fragrances derived from animal sources such as ambergris, a waxy substance secreted or regurgitated by sperm whales which as it aged acquired a sweet, earthy scent; civet produced by the perineal glands of the mammal of the same name, and musk, glandular secretions from animals like the musk deer. Floral oils extracted from orange, jasmine, lily and other blossoms, as well as spices like cinnamon, nutmeg and cloves would also be used. Perfumed gloves prepared by mixing ambergris, musk or civet with a fatty base and then smeared on the inside of the gloves to keep the skin soft, were a favourite gift item for those perhaps unsure of the Queen's more personal tastes.[15] She often wore gloves for warmth in the palaces on cold days as well as for travelling.

Having been made-up, Elizabeth was dressed. It was an elaborate ritual and took several hours as Elizabeth's ladies painstakingly laced and pinned her into her clothes; hundreds of pins would be needed each day.[16] The Queen wore fine linen shifts, as well as linen ruffs and wrist ruffs to protect her unwashable gowns from the damage caused by perspiration. Linen worn next to the skin would, it was believed, cleanse the body by absorbing excess moisture and dirt. Surprising though it may seem there is no evidence that the Queen wore knickers.[17] When she was menstruating she would use a length of washable linen, which would have been used as sanitary towels; Elizabeth's household accounts record long and short 'vallopes of fine holland cloth [linen cloth]' listed by the dozen with other plain linen items, and likely to have been a term for menstrual cloths. Queen Elizabeth also had three 'girdles of black Jeane silk made on the fingers garnished with buckles hooks & eyes whipped over with silk', which may have provided the necessary sanitary belt for use with the 'vallopes'.[18]

With her shift on, a 'pair of bodies' or corset stiffened with whalebone, would have been laced up on top, then her petticoat, and then her stockings. In 1561, Mrs Alice Montague, the Queen's 'silk woman', gave Elizabeth her first pair of knitted silk stockings. Elizabeth was delighted and asked Mrs Montague for more: 'I like silk stockings well; they are pleasant, fine and delicate. Henceforth I will wear no more cloth stockings.'[19] Elizabeth would then be pinned into her heavy gowns of velvet or satin, each covered with yards of gold braiding and myriads of little jewels and densely embroidered with images such as fish, flowers, birds and foliage. It was a slow and painstaking exercise during which Elizabeth would have plenty of time for relaxed conversation with her women. The colour, cut and style of these gowns changed over the course of her reign and reflected the fashions of France, Spain or Italy. Often Elizabeth would follow a particular style when courting a political alliance with one country or another. For the great occasions of state there were hefty robes of ermine and velvet to wear and in the winter furs and muffs of swansdown. She would then have some of the jewels and pearls for which she was famed pinned to her or placed around her neck. Many of the Queen's gems were from her father's coffers and had been worn by him, his six wives or her half-brother and sister. The jewels were kept in the Bedchamber in coffers covered with velvet and embroidered with gold.[20]

Finally Elizabeth's shoes would be eased on to her feet with a steel shoehorn specially made by her blacksmith.[21] At the beginning of her reign the Queen's shoes were mostly made of velvet, but as she grew older, she increasingly favoured shoes of Spanish leather.[22] Initially the shoes were flat but in 1595, at the age of sixty-two, the Queen ordered her first pair of 'high heels'.[23] When she was in the privy lodgings Elizabeth often wore slippers which could be slipped on and off without fastenings and allowed the Queen to rest her feet in comfort. Elizabeth usually had about a dozen pairs made in plain velvet each year.

Once enrobed, bejewelled, her hair dressed and styled, and with her face painted, the Queen was ready to face the public gaze of the court.

———

Elizabeth would spend the greater part of day in the Privy Chamber, where she transacted government business with her secretaries, met with councillors and received ambassadors. In the evening, when the business of state was over, she would relax with her ladies and other favourites, enjoying the music of the court musicians and singers of the chapel royal, dance, read or play cards. Gambling was a popular pursuit with the Queen and her ladies, with each regularly recorded as having gambling debts owing. Elizabeth was a very accomplished musician and sometimes relaxed by playing her virginals and harpsichord. As she carried out her duties, the Queen's women would spend many hours sewing and embroidering in the Privy Chamber making her Majesty's shifts and nightclothes and edging and embroidering sheets and pillowcases. They would also prepare the drinks, possets and sweetmeats of which Elizabeth was particularly fond, in the privy kitchen, adjacent to the private apartments.

Elizabeth would eat most of her meals in the Privy Chamber as, apart from on feast days or at special banquets, it was thought unbecoming of the Queen's dignity for her to be seen eating except by her ladies. Usually she ate around midday and then had supper at six in the evening, although she preferred to eat 'when her appetite required it' and so rarely kept exact mealtimes.[24] Food would be brought from the privy kitchen by the

Gentleman Ushers of the Privy Chamber, their arrival heralded by the sound of drums and trumpets. One of the ladies would then rub the gilt plates with bread and salt and give the Gentleman Ushers morsels from each dish as a precaution against poison. When the table had been laid out, the dishes would be carried by the ladies into the Queen's Privy Chamber so she could make her choice.[25] Whilst Elizabeth would be offered countless dishes at any one sitting, she preferred chicken or game to red meat, and always sweet things, particularly rich cakes made from Corinth currants and imported especially from Greece. She was not fond of the strong beer – 'March ale' – commonly drunk at court and named after the month in which it was brewed and which was then left for two years before it was served. Elizabeth preferred to drink light wine, 'mingled with water, containing three parts more in quantity than the wine itself'.[26] When the Queen was hosting ambassadors or other prestigious guests, banquets would be held in the great hall. Afterwards the tables would be cleared away and there would be dancing, plays or other entertainments.

At the end of each and every day, her ladies, among them Kat Ashley, Blanche Parry, Katherine Knollys and Dorothy Stafford, would help the Queen from her gowns and out of her veils and jewels and gloves. The Queen then washed her face and feet by the light of beeswax candles, renowned for their pleasant odour and clear flame. Disrobed, Elizabeth would put on her nightgown. This was a loose, comfortable gown which was made of rich fabrics like satin, silk velvet and taffeta and trimmed with gold and silver lace and lined with shag, plush or fur.[27] Elizabeth sometimes chose to wear her nightgown during the day, when she remained in her chambers among her women, and she frequently received them as New Year's gifts.[28]

Finally Elizabeth would climb into her bed beneath silk sheets embroidered with her royal arms and Tudor roses. Her bed comprised a number of mattresses containing straw, flock and feathers, each more luxurious as they got closer to the top, and each night was made ready by her ladies with warming pans of hot coals, to remove the chill from the bedding. They would check it and the straw and feather mattresses for fleas or bed bugs, or anything more sinister, lest any would-be assassins had hidden daggers or other deadly items to do harm to the Queen. The Bedchamber would also be searched every evening by the women to prevent intruders. Night-time was a time of fear and vulnerability, when noxious airs were meant to circulate and moonlight was thought to cause rheumatic diseases. Walter Bailey, Elizabeth's physician, believed it was therefore important that the Queen avoid sleeping in a moonlit room and advised that the

Bedchamber windows be closed at night to prevent dangerous air from the Thames being inhaled.[29]

After the 9 p.m. ceremony of the 'Good Night,' when the fires were banked and lodgings secured and security handed over to the Queen's personal guard, the Esquires of the Body, one of her women would climb in alongside Elizabeth or lie on a truckle bed nearby. Insomnia was a recurrent problem for Elizabeth and a number of medical treatises from the time gave advice on how to get a good night's sleep.[30] The physician and author Andrew Boorde believed that to procure sleep one should take a little camphor, mix it with woman's milk and anoint the temples with the mixture or use rosewater mixed with vinegar to aid sleep. 'To bedward be you merry,' Boorde advised, 'or have merry company about you, so that to bedward, no anger nor heaviness, sorrow nor pensiveness, do trouble or disquiet you.'[31] 'Mirth' and merriment was, it seems, the final task of the day for the women who served in Elizabeth's Bedchamber.

As some of the candles were blown out, Elizabeth would prepare for slumber by giving thanks, praying for forgiveness for her actions of the day, and appealing for divine protection from nocturnal harm. The curtains would be drawn to ward off dangerous cold drafts and night airs and the Bedchamber locked and guarded from the outside by the Esquires of the Body. Elizabeth demanded quiet in her Bedchamber and there was to be no unwanted noise near it.[32]

5

Womanish Infirmity

Elizabeth lived under intense scrutiny. All aspects of her body and behaviour, however intimate, were the stuff of ambassadorial dispatches and the subject of prurient interest on both a national and international level. On her accession to the throne, the Count of Feria, the Spanish ambassador, claimed that Elizabeth was 'not likely to have a long life'. Her constitution, he told Philip of Spain, 'cannot be very strong'.[1] The French ambassador billes de Noailles agreed; 'those who have seen her do not promise her long to live'.[2]

Since puberty she had regularly suffered from poor health, ranging from indigestion and occasional fainting fits, frequent and intense headaches which often lasted for weeks at a time, and insomnia and eyestrain.[3] She was extremely short-sighted, which must have made even the simplest daily tasks, not to mention the great occasions of state, a real challenge. Given her love of sweet things she very often experienced painful bouts of toothache.

It was generally believed that the body was made up of 'humours' – blood, phlegm, yellow bile, and black bile. In a healthy person all four humours were balanced, but any imbalance was believed to cause ill health. In her early twenties, during the reign of her sister Mary, Elizabeth was described by one of the royal physicians, Dr Wendy, as having 'many cold and waterish humours, which will not be taken away but by purgations mete & convenient for that purpose'.[4] 'Dropsy', or water retention as we would describe it, would be one symptom of an imbalance of humours as would the irregular menstruation with which Elizabeth also suffered. Amenorrhoea might in turn cause further ills such as 'hysterical fits' and 'melancholy'. Her surgeons would regularly open a vein in her ankle or her arm from which to draw blood and so bring her humours back into line.[5]

It was not just the health of the Queen's body, but her fertility and ability to bear children that was also at issue. Women at the time were thought to be more voracious in their sexual appetites than men. Contemporaries found it hard to believe that any woman past puberty could remain chaste of her own free will, especially if she lacked a husband to provide an outlet for her sexual energies.[6] The security of the Protestant state rested upon Elizabeth's ability to produce heirs. Rumours circulated about the Queen having a 'womanish infirmity', meaning she was incapable of having children and would therefore never marry.[7] When, in the very earliest days of the reign, the Scottish envoy Sir James Melville was asked to deliver a proposal to Elizabeth from the Duke of Casimir, son of the Elector Palatine, he refused the commission, saying, 'I had ground to conjecture that she would never marry because of the story one of the Gentlewomen of her Chamber told me ... knowing herself incapable of children, she would never render herself subject to a man.'[8] Had this information come from Kat Ashley or Blanche, or perhaps Katherine Knollys; or was the ambassador simply passing on court gossip? In April the following year, Feria reported similar intelligence that he had gathered: 'If my spies do not lie, which I believe they do not, for a certain reason which they have recently given me, I understand she will not bear children.'[9]

When in June 1559, Elizabeth was 'blooded' by her physicians this too was taken as proof that something was wrong with her 'natural functions'. 'Her Majesty was blooded from one foot and from one arm, but what her indisposition is, is not known,' reported the Venetian ambassador; 'many persons say things I should not dare to write.'[10] Even the papal nuncio in France had a view on Elizabeth's menstrual cycle: 'She has hardly ever the purgation proper to all women.'[11]

Such rumours were politically toxic. For the European balance of power and for the Queen's own safety, she needed to be, and be perceived as being, healthy and fertile. Only by Elizabeth's marriage and the birth of an heir could the line of Tudor succession and Protestant Church be made secure. It was a fact acknowledged both at home and abroad. 'The more I think about this business,' wrote Feria four days after Elizabeth's accession, 'the more certain I am that everything depends upon the husband this woman will take.'[12] A German diplomat, Baron Pollweiler, writing to the Emperor Ferdinand around the same time pronounced, 'the Queen is of an age where she should in reason, and as is woman's way, be eager to marry and be provided for ... For that she should wish to remain a maid and never marry is inconceivable.'[13]

When the first Parliament of the reign met in January 1559, the Queen's marriage was the focus of much attention. 'Nothing can be more repugnant to the common good, than to see a Princess, who by marriage may preserve the Commonwealth in peace, to lead a single life, like a Vestal Virgin,' pronounced Thomas Gargrave, Speaker of the Commons.[14] Yet Elizabeth's response to Parliament's petitions was careful and deliberately ambivalent: 'whensoever it may please God to incline my heart to another kind of life, ye may well assure yourselves my meaning is not to do or determine any thing wherewith the realm may or shall have just cause to be discontented.'[15]

Elizabeth was one of the most eligible women in Europe, 'the best match in her parish', and from the earliest months of her reign was never short of suitors, among them Philip II of Spain and Erik XIV of Sweden; the Archdukes Ferdinand and Charles of Austria; the Dukes of Savoy, Nemours, Ferrara, Holstein and Saxony, and the Earls of Arran and Arundel. Each was looking for an all-important English alliance to counter the threat of the other. The Habsburgs needed to keep England pro-Spanish at a time when the menace from France was particularly potent, given the threat of the French King's daughter-in-law Mary Queen of Scots's claim to the English crown. Whilst Philip of Spain deplored Elizabeth's return to Protestantism, strategic considerations dictated the need to maintain an English alliance. In the earliest days of the reign, and with great reluctance, Philip offered himself in marriage to his former sister-in-law on condition that she would embrace Catholicism and that he would not have to live in England.[16] It was never likely to be a match that Elizabeth would accept, but, as Feria presented the proposal, Philip described himself as 'a condemned man, awaiting his fate'. He later added, 'If it was not to serve God, believe me, I should not have got into this . . . Nothing would make me do this except the clear knowledge that it would gain the Kingdom [of England] for his service and faith.'[17] It was doubtless something of a relief when Elizabeth rejected his offer,[18] and another suitable Habsburg candidate was quickly sought.

Many in England favoured a marriage to a natural-born Englishman. The dangers of a foreign match were manifold, and the marriage of the late Queen Mary to Philip of Spain had left a bitter taste in the mouths of many. If Elizabeth married a foreign suitor, a tract (*Dialogue on the Queen's Marriage*) by young diplomat Sir Thomas Smith argued, she would be taking 'a pig in the poke', whilst an Englishman 'is here at home, not his picture or image, but himself. His stature, colour, complexion, and behaviour, is to be seen face to face'. And not only that, Smith argued, 'but his education and his bringing up, his study, exercise, and what things he hath a delight in, what things he doth refuse, every fault, imperfection, deformity and whatsoever should be to his hindrance, is apparent and clear'.[19] Among those thought to be suitable English candidates were the Earl of Arundel and the Duke of Norfolk, both leading peers of the realm, and Sir William Pickering, a handsome unmarried forty-three-year-old courtier and minor diplomat.[20] Pickering and Elizabeth were old friends and when he came to London to see her in May 1559 he was warmly welcomed by the Queen and given rooms at Whitehall. Feria reported that the Queen saw him secretly and then 'yesterday he came to the palace publicly and remained with her for four or five hours. In London they are giving twenty-five to a hundred that he will be King.'[21] But it came to nothing.

The other English candidate, Henry Fitzalan, 12th Earl of Arundel, went to considerable lengths to woo Elizabeth but, as Feria reported, the Queen had joked about what was being said of a match with the earl and added in his dispatch, 'she does not get on with him'.[22] Arundel was a staunch Catholic, twenty years older than Elizabeth and, in Feria's, view 'a flighty man of small ability'.[23] Yet Arundel had high hopes for his suit. In December it was rumoured that he was borrowing money and had spent £600 on jewels with which to bribe any of Elizabeth's ladies who spoke well of him.[24] Yet, to no avail. Elizabeth's sights were set firmly on another Englishman: Robert Dudley.

6

Disreputable Rumours

Within days of her accession, Elizabeth had appointed Robert Dudley as Master of the Horse, one of the most senior positions in the royal household.[1] This made him the only man in England officially allowed to touch the Queen, as he was responsible for helping Elizabeth mount and dismount when she went horse-riding. Whenever she hunted, went on progress or rode in a procession, Dudley would accompany her.

He was tall and strikingly attractive with dark skin and blue eyes. Dudley later told the French ambassador that 'they had first become friends before she was eight years old'.[2] He had been condemned to death after his father, the Duke of Northumberland, led the plot to put Lady Jane Grey on the throne in the summer of 1553, although after eighteen months in the Tower, Dudley was released and pardoned and thereafter worked to regain favour at court particularly in the service of Mary I's husband, Philip of Spain. Elizabeth and Dudley had both been imprisoned in the Tower at the same time, during Mary's reign, where their shared torment doubtless forged close bonds. However, Robert Dudley was married. On 4 June 1550, four years before he was taken to the Tower, he had married Amy Robsart, daughter of Sir John Robsart, a powerful Norfolk gentleman.[3]

William Cecil, Elizabeth's Principal Secretary, had in the early days of the reign proposed that Dudley might be sent overseas as an envoy to Philip of Spain, but Elizabeth quickly overruled him. She needed Dudley to remain close by her side.[4] He had arrived at Hatfield on a snow-white horse as soon as he knew of Elizabeth's accession and from that moment on he rarely left court. Dudley's position in charge of the royal stables gave him a salary of a hundred marks a year, four horses and his own suite of rooms at court, where for most of the time he would live away from his wife. Husband and wife therefore seldom saw one another; given Elizabeth's love of riding and hunting, the Queen and Robert Dudley

– whom she called her 'sweet Robin' – were rarely apart. As a friend of his once remarked, Dudley could claim to 'know the Queen and her nature best of any man'.[5]

From the very earliest months of Elizabeth's reign, courtiers were exchanging scandalous gossip about Dudley's relationship with the Queen and rumours of their night-time liaisons. The Count of Feria, on the eve of his departure from England in April 1559, wrote to King Philip of the extent of Dudley's intimacy:

> During the last few days Lord Robert has come so much into favour that he does what he likes with affairs and it is even said that her Majesty visits him in his chamber day and night. People talk of this so freely that they go so far as to say that his wife has a malady in one of her breasts and that the Queen is only waiting for her to die so she can marry Lord Robert ...[6]

Weeks later, the Venetian ambassador Il Schifanoya reported that Dudley was 'in great favour and very intimate with her Majesty'. Although Il Schifanoya stopped short of making any accusations of improper behaviour that could damage diplomatic relations, he did allude to the shocking rumours that were circulating at court: 'On this subject I ought to report the opinion of many, but I doubt whether my letters may not miscarry or be read, wherefore it is better to keep silence than to speak ill.'[7] The ambassador realised that his letters might be intercepted and was therefore unwilling to openly state what everyone was whispering: that Elizabeth and Dudley had become lovers.

Despite suspicions as to the nature of Elizabeth's relationship with her Master of the Horse, the Holy Roman Emperor, Ferdinand I, was keen to secure an English alliance and in May 1559 sent his envoy Caspar Breuner, Baron von Rabenstein, formally to open marriage negotiations on behalf of the emperor's nineteen-year-old son Charles von Habsburg, Archduke of Austria.[8] When Elizabeth quickly rejected the proposal, explaining that she intended to remain single for the foreseeable future, Breuner was undeterred:

> There is no princess of her compeers who can match her in wisdom, virtue, beauty and splendour of figure and form ... Furthermore I have seen several very fine summer residences that belong to her, in two of which I have been myself, and I may say that there are none in the world so richly garnished with costly furniture of silk,

adorned with gold, pearls and precious stones. Then she had some twenty other houses, all of which might justly be called royal summer residences. Hence she is well worth the trouble.[9]

English amity was crucial to the strategic interests of the Habsburgs and so the emperor was quick to dismiss the significance of the scandalous talk surrounding Elizabeth. Writing to his older son, the Archduke Maximilian, he acknowledged the danger and ubiquity of the rumours but argued that they were typical of the gossip targeted at chaste women: 'The slander proceeds from many persons, the harm done is great, and even though it be granted that it very often happens that a woman of good repute is spoken ill of, I do not wish to waste words on such.' However, he added, 'when the outcry is so great, and come from so many sides and always has the same tenor, it is indeed an awkward matter and very dangerous ... All this must be deeply pondered.'[10]

Believing that Elizabeth could be tempted to consider a marriage treaty, Cecil instructed his agent in Germany, Christopher Mundt, to discover all he could about the archduke's appearance, temperament, religion and attitude towards Protestantism.[11] Having talked with the Queen's ladies, the new Spanish ambassador Don Alvaro de Quadra, Bishop of Aquila, was soon able to report that Elizabeth favoured the Archduke Charles's suit because, 'her women all believe such to be the case'.[12] However, Emperor Ferdinand was beginning to have doubts of his own, considering the Queen's very obvious affection for Dudley, and soon was no longer sure he wanted 'to give her my son, even if she asked for him'.[13]

In August 1559, Baron Breuner decided to launch an investigation into whether or not Elizabeth was still a virgin or had indeed consummated her relationship with Dudley, as many suspected. As he reported, 'since the Queen was crowned he has never been away from court; moreover they dwell in the same house and this it is which feeds suspicion'.[14] He told the emperor that he had employed an agent, François Borth, who was on 'friendly terms with all the Ladies of the Bedchamber', to find out the truth behind the gossip. Breuner's investigations revealed little. Writing in cypher to the emperor, he reported that the Queen's ladies 'swear by all that is holy that her Majesty has most certainly never been forgetful of her honour', however they agree that the Queen 'shows her liking for him more markedly than is consistent with her reputation and dignity. But otherwise they have not noticed anything.'[15]

It was only Elizabeth's women who knew the truth of the Queen's relationship with Dudley. Only they could vouch for her chastity. But whilst they would always be quick to defend her publicly and could be relied upon to protect the Queen's reputation, they might very well censure her in private.

———•———

In August, Kat Ashley fell on her knees before the Queen in the privacy of the royal Bedchamber at Hampton Court and implored her mistress to marry and put an end to the 'disreputable rumours' of her relationship with Robert Dudley. No doubt drawing on her experience of the Seymour scandal ten years before, she believed Elizabeth was now behaving in such a way that would sully her 'honour and dignity' and would in time undermine her subjects' loyalty, and so be 'the cause of much bloodshed in the realm'. Ashley declared that rather than see this happen she would have 'strangled her Majesty in her cradle'. They were the words of a woman who regarded Elizabeth with a deep maternal affection. The Queen told Kat everything and had once said, 'I know nothing but that she shall know it.'[16]

Elizabeth responded graciously to her gentlewoman's blunt words, recognising them as the 'outpourings of a good heart and true fidelity'. She assured Kat that she would consider marrying in order to dispel the rumours and reassure her subjects, but added that, 'marriage must be well-weighed' and that at present she had 'no wish to change her state'. When Ashley suggested that Elizabeth should end her relationship with Lord Robert, the Queen angrily retorted that she had given,

> no one just cause to associate her with her Equerry or any other man in the world, and she hoped that they never would truthfully be able to do so. But that in this world she had so much sorrow and tribulation and so little joy. If she showed herself gracious towards her Master of the Horse she had deserved it for his honourable nature and dealings ... She was always surrounded by her ladies of the bedchamber and maids of honour, who at all times could see whether there was anything dishonourable between her and her Master of the Horse. If she had ever had the will or had found pleasure in such a dishonourable life ... she did not know of anyone who could forbid her; but she trusted in God that nobody would ever live to see her so commit herself.[17]

Elizabeth was nonetheless shaken by Kat's chiding and when Breuner visited her days later, he found her 'somewhat dejected' and 'daily pestered with petitions to marry'. She would, she told him, 'rather be dead than that her realm should suffer harm or loss' and so was prepared even to marry 'the vilest man in the Kingdom rather than give people occasion to speak ill'.[18] The Bedchamber women told Breuner that the Queen had been 'quite melancholy' and had slept little more than half an hour at night and woke 'quite pale and weak'.[19] Shortly afterwards Elizabeth succumbed to a burning fever.[20] The French ambassador described it as a *'fiebre quartre'*, a quatrain fever that appeared on every fourth day, and reported that the Queen's doctors had 'great doubt about her convales-cence'.[21] Already false stories had begun to spread. 'I have punished several,' a leading Devon gentleman wrote to the Earl of Bedford in mid-August, 'for bruiting the death of the Queen's Majesty and so hath others been in other parts of the shire as I hear.'[22]

De Quadra, the Spanish ambassador, soon came to the conclusion that Elizabeth was being disingenuous. She had, as de Quadra added, 'just given £12,000 to Lord Robert as an aid towards his expenses'. He believed that Elizabeth was 'astutely taking advantage of the general opinion to reassure somewhat the Catholics who desire the match and to satisfy others who want to see her married and are scandalised at her doings'.[23] But then, days later and to the ambassador's surprise, he was given renewed hope. De Quadra received an unexpected visit from Robert Dudley's sister, Lady Mary Sidney. Mary was a highly educated, pretty and politically accom-plished young woman with distinctive reddish yellow hair, who was about the same age as the Queen. The two women had known each other as chil-dren and had recently become particularly close given Elizabeth's relation-ship with her brother.[24] Mary had joined the Privy Chamber as a gentle-woman 'without wages' on the day of Elizabeth's coronation and would attend thereafter on the Queen, in between the births of Mary's five chil-dren, the running of the family estate in Kent, Penshurst Place, and support-ing her husband Sir Henry Sidney in Ireland and the Welsh Marches.[25]

Mary now sought out de Quadra to tell him that Elizabeth had changed her mind, that she had decided to marry and wanted the match with the Archduke Charles 'speedily settled'.[26] Speaking in Italian, a language in which Mary was fluent, she assured the ambassador that she was acting with the Queen's knowledge and would never say such a thing if it were not true for fear for her life. She urged de Quadra to broach the matter with the Queen and warned him not to be put off by Elizabeth's reticence, because 'it is the custom of ladies here not to give their consent in such matters until they are teased into it'.[27]

Mary Sidney's message was confirmed by Sir Thomas Parry, Treasurer of the Household, who told de Quadra that the Queen had summoned both him and Lady Sidney the night before and told them 'that the marriage had now become necessary'.[28] Elizabeth's change of heart, they told him, had been brought about by the recent discovery of a plot to poison the Queen and Lord Robert at a banquet hosted by the Earl of Arundel. As de Quadra described, 'the Queen was much alarmed' and this plot 'together with the French war preparations for Scotland, seem to have decided the Queen to marry'.[29]

With high expectation, the ambassador went by barge to Hampton Court Palace but was disappointed to find Elizabeth ambivalent about the match. 'The only answer I received,' he reported, was that she had not yet decided to marry, but should she ever do so, I might be quite sure that she would marry only the highest and the best.' When he found Mary Sidney and expressed his surprise that, 'her Majesty had not spoken more explicitly' of her renewed interest in the archduke, Mary quickly reassured him and urged him to persist.[30]

Elizabeth appeared worried by the growing scandal of her relationship with Dudley. She had learnt a painful lesson from the Seymour episode, and had witnessed how salacious stories could gather momentum and spread at home and abroad. In a later conversation with de Quadra, Elizabeth told him she feared he 'might be dissatisfied' with what he had heard about her, and that 'there were people in the country who took pleasure in saying anything that came into their heads'. The Queen said all this 'with some signs of shame', de Quadra noted earnestly.[31] He reassured her that, 'if there were anything which the archduke should not hear or learn, the idea of his coming would not have been entertained by us'. Elizabeth was anxious, she said, that if negotiations were broken off, the archduke might use the 'idle tales' that were told about her to the detriment of her honour. But, de Quadra wryly observed, 'from this point of view I was not sorry, as the fear may not be without advantage to us'.[32]

By mid-October, the Spanish ambassador felt confident enough to write, 'She really is as set on this marriage as your Majesty is', and advised that the archduke be sent to England immediately.[33] But it was too late. The Holy Roman Emperor had lost interest in the negotiations and refused to allow his son to leave Austria when the likely success of the mission was so uncertain.[34] Even Mary Sidney's enthusiasm for the Habsburg marriage appeared to have waned. In November, de Quadra said he believed that Dudley, 'had had words with his sister because she was carrying the affair further than he desired'. When the ambassador met again with Elizabeth, she protested that the match had been encouraged by someone with 'good intentions but without any commission from her'. As de Quadra wrote afterwards, 'I am obliged to complain of somebody in this matter and have complained of Lady Sidney only, although in good truth she is no more to blame than I am, as I have said privately.' In fact it was Mary Sidney's changed demeanour that had tipped him off: 'When I found Lady Sidney was doubtful and complained of the Queen and her brother, I thought best to put an end to uncertainty.'[35]

There had been no plot to kill the Queen and Dudley at Arundel's banquet; the story had been concocted to convince de Quadra of Elizabeth's desire to marry. After the death of Henri II in July 1559 and the succession of Mary Queen of Scots's fifteen-year-old husband François to the throne, the threat of a Franco-Scottish alliance loomed large. French forces in Scotland were increasing day by day and Elizabeth feared war on the Scottish borders. In October, de Quadra had warned his counterpart in Rome to, 'take care the French do not get at the new Pope and cause him to proceed against the [English] Queen on the Scotch Queen's claims. It would do much damage here and elsewhere before the marriage.'[36] By the pretence of marriage negotiations, encouraged by the unwitting Lady Sidney, the Queen had hoped to maintain the goodwill of the Habsburgs in the face of French aggression, and at the same time divert attention from her scandalous relationship with Robert Dudley.

Elizabeth had taken advantage of Mary Sidney's political prowess as well as her family connections to the Spanish court; Sir Henry Sidney had been sent on a number of missions to Spain in recent years and such was King Philip's relationship with him that he stood godfather to Sir Henry and Mary's first-born son, Philip Sidney, in November 1554. Mary had been used and when she discovered the truth she demanded to see the Queen. Despite being warned of Elizabeth's 'ill humour', Lady Sidney remained defiant. She was not, she said, 'asking anybody's opinion and would go to the Queen just to spite them all'. She told de Quadra that even if she was sent to the Tower 'she will not cease to proclaim what is going on, and that her worst enemy is her brother [Lord Robert]'.[37] She would defend what she had said, even if it 'should cost her her life'.[38] Frances, Lady Cobham, whom de Quadra described as 'the Queen's Mistress of the Robes', had also 'favoured the suit of the archduke', Mary Sidney explained, and she too had lobbied in favour of the Archduke Charles.[39]

The Spanish ambassador now saw through Elizabeth's charade. 'She is not in earnest,' wrote de Quadra, 'but only wants to amuse the crowd with the hope of the match in order to save the life of Lord Robert, who is very vigilant and suspicious, as he has again been warned that there is a plot to kill him, which I quite believe, for not a man in the realm can suffer the idea of his being King.'[40] This time it was no mere rumour. 'A plot was made the other day to murder Lord Robert, and it is now common talk and threat', wrote de Quadra. Thereafter, Dudley was known to wear beneath his clothes a 'privy coat', a doublet, made by the armourer at Greenwich – suggesting that he was taking very seriously the threats against him.[41]

De Quadra had learned 'some extraordinary things' and said Dudley's enemies in the Privy Council were making no secret of 'their evil opinion of his intimacy with Elizabeth.' There were mutterings that Dudley intended to poison his wife so he would be free to marry Elizabeth. 'It is generally stated that it is his fault that the Queen does not marry and his own sister and friends bear him ill-will.' Elizabeth had been repeatedly warned to 'exercise more prudence and not give people cause to suspect her in connection' him.[42] De Quadra was growing tired of Elizabeth's protestations of innocence; she was for ever telling him that she yearned to be a nun and pass her time in a cell praying. He had heard 'great things of a sort that cannot be written about' and in a letter to the Count of Feria, described Elizabeth as having 'a hundred thousand devils in her body'.[43]

By the end of January 1560, the marriage negotiations with the Archduke Charles formally ended and the malicious talk that Elizabeth had tried so hard to stave off now engulfed the imperial court. Sir Thomas Challoner wrote from Brussels of his shock at how far, 'these folks are broad mouthed . . . of one too much in favour, as they esteem. I think ye guess whom they named . . . as I count the slander most false'. But as Challoner warned, whilst the rumours might be untrue, Elizabeth should nevertheless be careful of her behaviour in order to prevent tongues from wagging:

> A young Princess cannot be too wary, what countenance or famil-
> iar demonstration she maketh, more to one, than another . . . this
> delay of ripe time for marriage, besides the loss of the realm (for
> without posterity of her Highness what hope is left unto us) minis-
> treth matter to those lewd tongues to descend upon, and breedeth
> contempt.[44]

7

Ruin of the Realm

As Elizabeth approached the first anniversary of her accession to the throne, Sir Nicholas Throckmorton, the English ambassador to France, wrote repeatedly from Paris of the dangers to her crown. 'We have great cause to suspect the French meaning towards us; and the suspicion thereof on this side doth daily rather increase than decrease.'[1]

In November 1559, Anthony Browne, Viscount Montagu – a renowned Francophobe – reported to the Queen a conversation he had had with the emperor's ambassador Gaspar Pregnor about new dangers facing her. Pregnor warned that 'the Queen and all England is in no small peril' and that there was a French plot to kill her. He spoke of 'talks and devices' in 'no small places' that Elizabeth 'shall be slain'. Pregnor advised that to guard against the French threat the Queen should 'please the King of Spain and lose him by no means' and so be 'temperate' in those matters 'which may and do' offend him. Elizabeth also needed to ensure 'fidele satellitium' – faithful companions – for the guard of her person.[2]

In a memorandum to Elizabeth in March the following year, William Cecil confirmed the threats. 'We do all certainly think that the Queen of Scots and for her sake her husband and the House of Guise be in their hearts mortal enemies to your Majesty's person.'[3] Weeks later, Throckmorton wrote warning of a 'pestilent and horrible device of the Guises' to poison Elizabeth by means of a 'burly Italian man with a black beard' called Stephano. He had come to England on the pretence of offering his services to the Queen as an engineer. Throckmorton reassured Elizabeth that being forewarned of this danger she 'need not fear, but in lieu thereof give good order that he may be taken, to the Guises' confusion and example to such hirelings'.[4] It was one of the first of many threats against Elizabeth, in her own court, that would be intercepted over the course of her reign.

With warnings of plots coming thick and fast, Cecil now took action to tighten security around the Queen herself and drew up a memorandum entitled 'Certain Cautions for the Queen's Apparel and Diet'. More care should be taken, he noted, to preserve the orderly guarding of the Privy Chamber and Bedchamber. Too often the back doors of the chambers where the Queen's gentlewomen were quartered were left open and unattended; little notice was taken of the stream of 'laundresses, tailors, wardrobers, and such' that came and went through them; anyone could slip in and attack the Queen or introduce into her chambers a poison, slow-acting or immediate, that could be ingested by mouth or through the skin. From now on, no meat or other food prepared outside the royal kitchens should be allowed into the Privy Chamber without 'assured knowledge' of its origins. Perfumed gloves or sleeves or other garments were to be kept away from the Queen unless their hazardous odours were 'corrected by some other fume'. And in future even the royal undergarments – that is 'all manner of things that shall touch any part of her Majesty's body bare' – would be 'circumspectly looked unto'. No unauthorised persons besides Elizabeth's trusted women were to be allowed near them, lest some harmful substance be hidden in the folds of the linen to menace the Queen's person.[5] As an extra safeguard Cecil strongly advised that the Queen should take some medicinal preservative 'against plague and poison twice weekly', just in case some evil attacked her unawares. Elizabeth was reluctant to be guided by these rules, and would remain stubborn about such matters throughout her life.[6]

Having introduced tighter controls in an attempt to safeguard the natural body of Elizabeth, Cecil also urged the Queen to shore up the body politic by offering direct support to the Protestant lords in Scotland who had taken up arms against the French presence in Scotland. Mary of Guise, Mary Stuart's mother, had remained in Scotland following the death of her husband, King James V, so she could protect the throne of her then baby daughter who, having been betrothed to the French dauphin, had been taken to be brought up in the French court. Yet Mary of Guise had become increasingly unpopular with the Scottish lords due to her attempts to enforce Catholicism and strengthen French control. When more French troops were sent to Scotland to assist her, Elizabeth's councillors feared that the northern kingdom would become a military base for an invasion of England on behalf of Mary, Queen of Scotland, and Queen Consort of France.[7]

On 29 March 1560, English soldiers crossed the border and besieged the French garrison at Leith. The campaign proved to be a disaster, culminating in the failed assault of 7 May, but the French also made little headway with their campaign. After two French relief fleets were driven back by storms, and following the death of the regent Mary of Guise on 11 June, peace was sought by both sides. As Cecil left for Edinburgh to negotiate terms he feared what might happen between Elizabeth and Dudley in his absence.

———•———

Cecil was right to worry. The Queen and Dudley were spending all their days together, dancing, feasting and hunting throughout the summer progress of 1560.[8] The story that Elizabeth and Dudley were lovers and that Elizabeth was pregnant had spread across the country that year. In the spring, John White from Devon confessed that 'Drunken Burley had said to him in his own house that the Lord Robert Dudley did swive the Queen'.[9] In June, a sixty-eight-year-old widow from Essex, 'Mother Dowe', was arrested for 'openly asserting that the Queen was pregnant by Robert Dudley'.[10] The local JPs were charged with investigating the case and wrote to the Privy Council with details of Dowe's outburst. They sought to try the case *in camera* in order to prevent the scandalous tales from spreading 'amongst the common people', but it was already too late. Around the same time, the Earl of Oxford wrote to Cecil asking direction concerning Thomas Holland, vicar of Little Burstead in Essex, who was told by a former vicar that a man had gone to the Tower for 'saying the Queen's Majesty was with child'. Oxford wanted to know whether he should follow usual punishment for rumour-mongers and cut off Holland's ears.[11] De Quadra's dispatch to King Philip of Spain underlined the seriousness of the situation and the threat to the Queen of such persistently slanderous talk: 'If she does not marry and behave herself better than hitherto, she will everyday find herself in new and greater troubles.'[12]

———•———

It was a summer of births for Elizabeth's women. Dudley hosted a banquet for the Queen at his house in Kew, during which time his sister Lady Sidney, then in the later stages of pregnancy, withdrew from service in the Queen's privy lodgings to take up residence at Kew in advance of the birth in October of her third child, named Elizabeth most likely in honour of the Queen.[13]

In late July, Isabella Harington, one of the Queen's Ladies of the Privy Chamber, was delivered of her first-born son, John, at Kelston in Somerset. On 4 August he was baptised in the church of All Hallows in London Wall, with the Queen standing as one of his godparents.[14] Isabella was six years older than Elizabeth and had been in her service for a number of years. She was a loyal servant and indeed it is likely that she was one of the maids attendant on Elizabeth when, in the wake of Wyatt's rebellion against Mary I in 1554, the princess was imprisoned in the Tower. In 1559, she married John Harington, a courtier and a writer who had become a favourite of Henry VIII. His first wife was Etheldrada Malte, supposedly the illegitimate daughter of the King by Joanna Dingle, but passed off as the illegitimate daughter of a tailor named John Malte in exchange for grants of land and revenues. By the spring of 1546, Harington had entered the service of Sir Thomas Seymour. After Seymour's arrest in January 1549, Harington was imprisoned and questioned about his master's relationship with the young princess. However, Harington remained loyal to Elizabeth and revealed nothing to compromise her honour under questioning. He was later rewarded with a position in the Queen's household. Following the death of his first wife, Harington married Isabella Markham, the daughter of the Lieutenant of the Tower of London, Sir John Harington, in 1559.[15]

Now, little more than a year after their marriage, Isabella and John celebrated the birth of the first of their five children. John, or 'boy Jack' as Elizabeth would affectionately call him, was among the first of Elizabeth's godchildren and doubtless she accepted the role as a reward for the couple's fidelity in the years before Elizabeth's accession.[16] The young John later described how, 'till the XXth year of her Majesty's reign', his mother Isabella was the 'queen's bedfellow'.[17]

Whilst in Edinburgh working on the peace negotiations with the Scots, Cecil wrote regularly to the Queen expressing his anxiety for her reputation and the unsettled succession, and offering his 'continual prayer that God would direct your heart to procure a father for your children, and so shall the children of all your realm bless your seed. Neither peace or war without this will profit us long.'[18] On his return to London, having successfully secured the French withdrawal from Scotland, Cecil told de

Quadra his franks views on Robert Dudley. He had 'made himself lord of all affairs and of the Queen's person, to the extreme injury of all the Kingdom, intending to marry her and that he led her to spend all day hunting with much danger to her life and health'.[19] He 'foresaw the ruin of the realm' through Elizabeth's intimacy with him, and such was Cecil's despair that he told the ambassador that he planned to resign his position.[20] 'So great is the common dissatisfaction with the Queen and her mode of life that it is quite marvellous that so much delay should occur without some disaster happening to her, and it will not be from any fault of the French if it be not attempted,' de Quadra reported.[21] And matters were set to get worse. Cecil had made the startling revelation to the Spanish ambassador, that 'they intended to kill the wife of Robert and now published that she was ill, although she was not but on the contrary was very well and protected herself carefully from being poisoned, and that God would never permit that so great an evil nor could a good result come of an evil business'.

'I was certain that he spoke truly and was not deceiving me,' wrote an astounded de Quadra.[22] The following day he added the dramatic postscript, 'After I wrote this the queen has made public the death of M.Robert and has said in Italian – *Que si ha rotto il collo* – that she has broken her neck and must have fallen down a staircase.'[23] On Sunday 8 September at Cumnor Place, a manor house in Berkshire, twenty-eight-year-old Amy Robsart was found dead. Murder, suicide, accident; all were possible. On the day she died, Amy had sent off her servants to the fair at Abingdon, and she was later discovered dead at the foot of a flight of stairs.[24]

Gossip had long centred on rumours that Robert Dudley planned to kill his wife so he would be free to marry the Queen, and now urgent questions were asked. Was Dudley involved? Might Elizabeth be implicated?[25] Having written a letter to Dudley consoling him on the 'cruel mischance late happened to my lady your late bedfellow', the ambassador Sir Nicholas Throckmorton wrote to William Parr, the Marquis of Northampton, of his alarm at the slanderous talk which now circulated at the French court and across Paris. 'My lord, I wish I were either dead, or that I were hence, that I might not hear the dishonourable and naughty reports that are here made of ye Queen's Majesty my gracious sovereign lady' that made 'every hair of my head' stand on end 'and my ears glow to hear. I am almost at my wit's end and know not what to say; one laugheth at us, another threateneth, another revileth her Majesty,' and bewailed, 'my heart bleedeth to think upon the slanderous bruits I hear, which if they be not slaked or that they prove true, our reputation is gone forever, war followeth and utter subversion of our Queen and country'.[26]

Upon learning of his wife's death, Dudley immediately withdrew from the court to his house at Kew: Amy was buried in the chancel of the Church of St Mary the Virgin, Oxford; the funeral cost Lord Robert £500, though he did not attend nor erect any memorial to her. Less than a month later he returned to the Queen's side and, it appears, resumed his courtship of her.[27] 'The Lord Rob in great hope to marry the Queen,' one courtier observed, 'for she maketh such appearance of good will to him.'[28] For some this was an inevitable outcome. Even Thomas Radcliffe, the Earl of Sussex, Lady Sidney's brother-in-law, who had an increasingly acrimonious relationship with Dudley, had come to the conclusion that the most important thing was for the Queen to produce an heir and that therefore the union with Dudley might be a necessary evil:

> I wish not her Majesty to linger this matter of so great importance, but to choose speedily; and therein to follow so much her own affection as [that] by the looking upon him whom she should choose, *omnes ejus sensus titillarentur* (all the senses being excited) which shall be the readiest way, with the help of God, to bring us a blessed prince which shall redeem us out of thraldom. If I knew that England had other rightful inheritors I would then advise otherwise, and seek to serve the time by a husband's choice. But seeing that she is *ultimatum refugium*, and that no riches, friendship, foreign alliance, or any other present commodity that might come by a husband, can serve our turn, without issue of her body, if the Queen will love anybody, let her love where and whom she lists, so much thirst I to see her love. And whomsoever she shall love and choose, him will I love, honour and serve to the uttermost.[29]

Sussex alluded to the contemporary belief that sexual activity was necessary for the health of women and of men.[30] Virgins were believed to suffer from disorders associated with the accumulation of unfertilised seeds which were thought to cause hysteria and illnesses known as 'mother fits', 'suffocation of the womb' and 'greensickness'.[31] Such disorders might be cured by marriage and a wife was therefore thought to be in a more healthful state than a virgin or a widow.[32]

Many did not share Sussex's view and believed marriage between Elizabeth and Dudley would spell disaster. Hubert Languet, a Burgundian diplomat, reported that the English leaders had 'made it plain to her that her too great familiarity with my Lord Robert Dudley displeases them and that they will by no means allow him to wed her'.[33] 'I know not what to think,' wrote Throckmorton from the French court, 'the bruits be so brim, and so maliciously reported here, touching the marriage of the Lord Robert, and the death of his wife, as I know not where to turn me, not what countenance to bear.' The prospect of their marriage had to be stopped, 'the matter succeeding, our state, is in great danger of utter ruin and destruction. And so far as methinketh I see into the matter, as I wish myself already dead, because I would not live in that time.' Throckmorton begged Cecil to do all he could 'to hinder the marriage', otherwise the consequences were unthinkable. 'The Queen our sovereign discredited, condemned and neglected; our country ruined, undone and made prey . . . the Commonwealth . . . lieth now in great hazard.'[34]

Throckmorton resolved on direct and decisive action. He would send his secretary Robert Jones to England, to warn the Queen in person of the scandalous tales that were making her a laughing stock in the French court, and to underline the risk to her reputation if she chose to marry her favourite.

On the evening of Monday 25 November, Robert Jones arrived at the riverside palace at Greenwich, the place of Elizabeth's birth and one of her favourite residences.[35] Mullioned bay windows adorned its river frontage and in the protruding tower lay the Queen's privy apartments. Elizabeth would often receive ambassadors at Greenwich, given its position close to the docks, wharfs and custom houses.

Upon his arrival, Jones visited Cecil with the latest news from the French court. Mary Queen of Scots had heard the gossip surrounding the death of Amy Robsart and responded that Elizabeth 'would marry her horse-keeper'. The situation had got out of hand; Cecil was furious.

The following evening Robert Jones dined with Dudley and the Privy Council at the Scottish ambassador's residence. Halfway through the meal, Dudley excused himself saying he had to return to court. Minutes later, a gentleman appeared at the dining table requesting that Jones go outside where he was informed that Dudley wished to meet him in secret later that evening. After the meal had finished, Jones made his way to Dudley's chambers at court. He found him in a foul rage; the news of the French court had reached Elizabeth, then at Eltham Palace: she had been told of Mary's malicious remark.

On Wednesday evening, Jones was finally granted an audience with the Queen, in the Presence Chamber of Greenwich Palace. He described the meeting in a dispatch sent to Throckmorton in Paris. When he told Elizabeth that the Spanish and Venetian ambassadors were spreading the rumour that she was to marry Robert Dudley, Elizabeth was dismissive. 'By my troth,' she replied, 'I thought it was such a matter, and he need not have sent you hither, for it had been more meet to keep you still.' The envoy decided to persist nonetheless and explained that Throckmorton felt duty bound to inform her 'of such things as might touch her' in person, rather than risk them becoming further public knowledge. When Jones told her plainly what was being said about her relationship with Lord Robert, and their possible involvement in the sudden death of Amy Robsart, Elizabeth moved restlessly in her chair and covered her face with her hands, then broke into nervous laughter. She insisted that the circumstances of the death of Dudley's wife should 'neither touch his honesty nor her honour'.[36]

Still, Elizabeth looked strained and ill in the weeks that followed Amy Robsart's death. Jones thought the whole business 'doth much perplex her' and noticed a definite change in her mood; 'the Queen's Majesty looketh not so hearty and well as she did'.[37] Jones's visit had little effect on cooling relations between Elizabeth and her favourite, and weeks later Throckmorton was reporting rumours that the Queen and Robert Dudley had secretly married. The Spanish ambassador in France had told him that Elizabeth had shown 'she hath honour but for a few in her realm, for no man will advise her to her folly'. In a letter to Cecil, Throckmorton anxiously petitioned him to take firmer action and curb the passions of their headstrong Queen. 'Remember your mistress is young and subject to affections; you are her sworn councillor and in great credit with her.'[38]

It was not only Elizabeth's countrymen that were petitioning her to amend her 'mode of life'. In December, Adolphus, Duke of Holstein and uncle of the King of Denmark, one of Elizabeth's early suitors, wrote of his alarm at the continued reports from England of her conduct.[39] His letter horrified the Queen, which she treated as humiliating testament to the ubiquity of the licentious rumours. In her reply to Holstein written in the New Year she thanked him for his concern for her honour and assured him that she would 'never forget what is due to herself in this respect'. She would 'consider it a favour if he will believe none of the rumours which he hears, if they are inconsistent with her true honour and royal dignity'. Finally she assured him that in all her actions she sought nothing but 'the glory of God and the preservation of her own dignity'.[40]

Elizabeth's enemies soon began to use charges against her mother as inspiration for further attacks. She was the daughter of Anne Boleyn, Europe's 'great whore'; what more could be expected of her? In August, Throckmorton wrote to Cecil that one Gabriel de Sacconay had devised and printed a defamatory tract, which denounced Elizabeth's mother as a 'Jezebel', and compared her to the 'heathen wives of Solomon' for persuading Henry VIII to turn his back on the true Church of Rome. Their 'foul matrimony' was a result of lust and Anne had met with just punishment for her wickedness. Cecil was horrified: if Elizabeth found out about the publication it would jeopardise the fragile alliance with France that was crucial to England's security. While Cecil procrastinated, hundreds of copies of de Sacconay's book were printed and disseminated across Paris and beyond. Finally, in mid-September, more than a month after receiving Throckmorton's letter, Cecil broke the news to Elizabeth. She wrote immediately to her ambassador ordering him to go 'with all haste' to Catherine de Medici, mother of the young King Charles IX, and demand that the 'lewd' book be immediately suppressed. But whilst the queen mother expressed her shock and disgust at the slanderous publication, Catherine did not move to prevent further copies of the book being published. Instead she promised only to look at a copy of the book so that she 'might cause it to be so considered, and thereupon give order for the matter'.

Catherine and her son Charles had every reason to delay taking action. Their support for Mary Queen of Scots's claim to the English throne was well known and this salacious tract played to their hand. Eventually an order was issued in Charles IX's name to, 'alter the offensive passages' from the book until which time no further copies should be sold. Elizabeth was far from satisfied and in letter after letter to Sir Nicholas Throckmorton demanded that *all* copies of the book be destroyed.

Finally, in the second week of October, the ambassador was able to report that the French King had at last issued a command that all the books should be confiscated. By then the damage had been done. Elizabeth's resentment towards Catherine and Charles simmered. Throckmorton urged her to thank them for agreeing to suppress the publication, but she refused even though, as Throckmorton pointed out, the queen mother would be highly offended by the lack of courtesy. When in late November Elizabeth did reluctantly forward a note of thanks, she did so through her ambassador in Spain. It was a deliberate discourtesy that made it clear she had not forgiven the French for slandering her mother.[41]

8

Carnal Copulation

Whilst Elizabeth was repeatedly urged to break off relations with her favourite, Dudley appeared to be committed to a marriage with Elizabeth and began to offer political favours in return for decisive foreign support to win the Queen's hand. Marriage to Elizabeth would bring unrivalled power and security for him and his family; the ultimate rehabilitation after the nadir of the execution of his father and brother by Mary I. Undoubtedly Dudley had strong feelings for Elizabeth but it is hard to separate his love and devotion to Elizabeth the woman, from the favour and riches he sought from Elizabeth the Queen.

As for Elizabeth, one wonders what her true feelings and desires were. Did she ever imagine she might marry Dudley? Did she really want to? Was she in love with him? He was certainly a man whom she trusted, and she described him as 'her only source of happiness'. On another occasion she wrote that if she wished to marry, she would prefer him 'to all the princes in the world'.[1] That Elizabeth adored Dudley was painfully obvious. Together they danced, hunted, shared private jokes and were rarely out of each other's company; it was their easy familiarity and affectionate displays which spawned the rumours as to the nature of their relationship. Even Cecil acknowledged that 'on account of his eminent endowments of mind and body', Robert Dudley was 'so dear to the Queen'.[2] Rather than avoid such gossip, Elizabeth seemed to delight in the attention it brought her. Certainly she was playing a dangerous game in not heeding advice to change her behaviour. But in truth she must have known, particularly after the death of Amy Robsart, that marrying Robert Dudley would never be possible.

———•———

In January 1561, Sir Henry Sidney approached the Spanish ambassador on his brother-in-law's behalf with an offer for his master: if King Philip supported Dudley's marriage to Elizabeth he would find Dudley ready to obey him and 'do service as one of his vassals'.[3] He would 'procure the banishment of the Gospel' and secure the Queen's agreement for the papal nuncio, Abbot Martinego, to enter England with an invitation to the Council of Trent, the reforming council of the Catholic Church.[4] Sidney was a well-known and highly favoured supporter of the Spanish and so was an obvious choice as Dudley's go-between. However, he was also the husband of Mary Sidney, one of the Queen's closest confidantes and he might therefore have, or be expected to have, particular insight into Elizabeth's thoughts and feelings. Sir Henry told de Quadra 'how much inclined the Queen was to the marriage'. He acknowledged that that they had 'a love affair' but assured the ambassador that 'the object of it was marriage' and there was 'nothing illicit about it or such as could not be set right by your Majesty's authority'. Did he have particular knowledge of the Queen's relationship with Dudley and her desire to marry him? Certainly it served his interests to promote the match of his brother-in-law to the Queen and to defend the charges of Dudley's involvement in his wife's death. Although Sidney said that there was 'hardly a person who did not believe that there had been foul play', and even 'preachers in the pulpits spoke of it, not sparing even the honour of the Queen', he was 'certain it was accidental'.[5]

When in April, Robert Dudley was given an apartment at court adjoining Elizabeth's own, the gossip inevitably intensified.[6] 'The Lord Robert is in great hope to marry the Queen,' one observer noted, 'for she maketh such appearance of good will to him. He giveth her many goodly presents.'[7]

———•———

In mid-April 1561, Father John Coxe, a Catholic priest and chaplain to Sir Edward Waldegrave, formerly a great favourite of Mary I, was arrested by customs officials at Gravesend en route to Flanders. Coxe was carrying a rosary and breviary, some money and letters for Catholic exiles. When examined before Hugh Darrell, a local Justice of the Peace, he confessed to having said mass in the homes of Sir Edward Waldegrave, Sir Thomas Wharton and Lady Carew, with five other priests, all of whom were subsequently arrested and imprisoned.[8] Seized papers revealed a plot to ensure a Catholic succession based on the prophecies of sorcerers, who were also Catholic priests. An anonymous source at court had said soothsayers had 'conjured to have known how long the Queen should reign, and what should become of religion'. Elizabeth was convinced, the

Spanish ambassador reported, that they were 'conjuring and conspiring against her'.[9]

To Cecil this all seemed to amount to another Catholic plot to overthrow Elizabeth and was clear evidence that the Catholics could not be trusted. Even Lady Waldegrave was subject to harsh interrogations and asked what she knew of the invitation of the Queen to the Council of Trent; what she knew of the coming of a papal nuncio to deliver this invitation; what she knew of the Queen's marriage plans, and what of the succession to the Crown, 'if God should not send her issue'. She was questioned as to the help she and her husband had given Catholic priests and where she had heard mass.[10]

Within weeks Cecil had evidence of what appeared to be a Catholic plot to kill Elizabeth and restore the 'true faith' in England. A letter found in Sir Edward Waldegrave's house about the imminent arrival of the papal nuncio gave Cecil, who feared a return to Rome and the eclipse of his influence, the opportunity to claim that the prisoners had conspired with the Spanish ambassador in seditious political activity aimed at restoring Catholicism in England. As Cecil wrote to Throckmorton, 'The Bishop of Aquila [de Quadra] had entered into such a practice with a pretence to further the great matter here, meaning principally the Church matter and percase, accidentally, the other matter also, that he had taken faster hold to plant his purpose than was my ease shortly to root up.' Cecil suggested that the arrests had therefore been deliberately timed:

> When I saw this Romanish influence towards, about one month
> past, I thought it necessary to dull the papists' expectations by
> discovering of certain mass-mongers and punishing of them, as I
> do not doubt but you have heard of them. I take God to record that
> I meant no evil to any of them, but only for the rebating of the
> papists' humours which, by the Queen's Majesty's leniency, grew too
> rank. I find it hath done much good.[11]

Cecil had achieved exactly what he had intended. The Privy Council refused entry to Martinengo, the papal nuncio; negotiations for England's attendance at the Council of Trent were immediately broken off and Dudley's hopes of marrying Elizabeth with Spanish support decisively thwarted. A full account of the supposed conspiracy to kill the Queen and reintroduce Catholicism was widely distributed across the country.[12]

Despite Cecil's investigations having frustrated Dudley's plan to secure Spanish backing for his suit, rumours that Elizabeth and Dudley would marry continued unabated throughout the summer. At the end of June he organised another banquet and river party for the Queen. When Elizabeth, Dudley and de Quadra found themselves together on a barge, Dudley suggested that since the ambassador was also a bishop, he should marry them there and then. As the ambassador reported, 'They went so far with their jokes that Lord Robert told her that, if she liked, I could be the minister to perform the act of marriage, and she, nothing loath to hear it, she said she was not sure whether I knew enough English.' De Quadra added that if Elizabeth got rid of her Protestant advisers and restored Catholicism, he would be delighted to marry them whenever they liked.[13]

In November 1561, in an attempt to quieten the gossip-mongers, Elizabeth went as far as disguising herself as the maid of Katherine Knolly's niece, Katherine Carey, in order to watch Dudley shoot at Windsor.[14] Katherine Carey, the eldest daughter of Henry Carey, Lord Hunsdon and the Queen's second cousin, had been appointed a Gentlewoman of the Privy Chamber on 30 January the year before and had quickly become one of Elizabeth's most trusted intimates. Two years later she married Charles Howard, son of William Howard, and later Baron Howard of Effingham, and 1st Earl of Nottingham. Howard had reaped the benefit of his father's support for Elizabeth during the years before her accession and became a loyal servant to her. He was sent as an emissary to the French court and became keeper of the Queen's house at Oatlands in Surrey. His marriage to Katherine Carey served only to reinforce his already close ties to his monarch. Together Katherine and Charles now became mainstays of the Elizabethan court and high in the Queen's favour and trust.

Later in the same month that the Queen watched Dudley at the shoot, Lady Fiennes de Clinton, another of Elizabeth's ladies, helped to arrange for Elizabeth to secretly dine with Dudley at his house. As the Spanish envoy discovered and reported, Dudley 'came from Greenwich to the Earl of Pembroke's house on the thirteenth, the rumour being that he was going to his own home. The Queen was there the next day disguised to dine with them, accompanied by the Admiral [Lord Clinton] and his wife.'[15]

———•———

Whilst talk of the Queen's trysts with Dudley continued to engulf the court, Katherine Grey, her Protestant heir, had been recklessly conducting her own secret affair with Edward Seymour, the Earl of Hertford, another claimant to the English crown.[16] When Elizabeth left Whitehall to go hunting the previous December, Katherine had remained behind, complaining of toothache. It was then that the couple took their opportunity and secretly married in the earl's bedchamber.[17] One closely observed testimony describes how Katherine and Hertford 'unarrayed themselves' and 'went into naked bed in the said Chamber where they were so married', and once in bed they had 'Company and Carnal Copulation'.[18]

In the weeks that followed, and still without the Queen's knowledge, Hertford came regularly to Katherine's chamber at court. Before long Katherine was pregnant and for the next few months disguised her growing belly from Elizabeth as she continued to attend on the Queen in the privy lodgings. Meanwhile, in May, Hertford was sent to France on a minor diplomatic mission with the intention that he would go from there to Italy.

In mid-August 1561, while the court was on summer progress in East Anglia, the Queen discovered Katherine's marriage and pregnancy. While attending a communion service with the Queen and the other Ladies of the Privy Chamber at Ipswich, Katherine saw 'secret talk amongst men and women that her being with child was known and spied out'.[19] That Sunday evening she went to Dudley's lodgings, and 'by his bedside' confided the secret of her marriage and pregnancy and begged him 'to be a means to the Queen's highness for her'.[20] When Dudley told Elizabeth the next morning, she was horrified. Edward Seymour was a descendent of Edward III, and any son of such a union would become Elizabeth's de facto heir and a possible rival. Moreover, it was treason for a person of royal blood to marry without the Queen's permission. Katherine Grey was ordered to the Tower under armed guard and messengers sent to France demanding Hertford's immediate return.[21] Elizabeth feared the marriage was part of a larger conspiracy involving some of the other women of her Bedchamber. Her anxiety is clear in the letter of instructions she sent on 17 August to Sir Edward Warner, Lieutenant of the Tower:

> You shall ... examine the Lady Katherine very straightly how many hath been privy to the love betwixt the Earl of Hertford and her from the beginning; and let her certainly understand that she shall have no manner of favour except she will show the truth, not only what ladies or gentlewomen of this court were thereto privy, but also what lords and gentlemen: for it doth now appear that

sundry personages have dealt therein ... It is certain that there hath been great practices and purposes.[22]

While the investigation revealed no wider plot, the stress of discovering Katherine's pregnancy clearly took its toll on the Queen. She was 'becoming dropsical', reported the Spanish ambassador, and had 'begun to swell extraordinarily'.[23]

———•———

Following the death of her husband François II at the end of the previous year, Mary Stuart, then only eighteen, returned to Scotland in August 1561 after an absence of thirteen years to take up residence in Edinburgh.[24] Weeks later the French, Scots, and English signed the Treaty of Edinburgh, in which it was agreed that all foreign soldiers, French and English alike, would withdraw from Scotland. In August, the Scottish parliament passed legislation making the country officially Protestant. Without her French family and away from the Catholicism of the French court, Mary was to find finally securing her position on the Scottish throne an intimidating prospect.

On her arrival in Scotland, Mary expressed her desire 'to be a good friend and neighbour to the Queen of England', and stressed the solidarity which she and Elizabeth shared as female rulers: 'It is better for none to live in peace than for women: and for my part, I pray you think that I desire it with all my heart.'[25] Many, however, still distrusted Mary's true intentions. Thomas Randolph, the English ambassador to Scotland, articulated such fears:

> Of this Queen's [Mary's] affection to the Queen's Majesty, either it is so great that never was greater to any or it is the deepest dissembled, and the best covered that ever was. Whatsoever craft, falsehood or deceit there is in all the subtle brains of Scotland, is either fresh in their women's memory, or can she fett [summon] it with a wet finger.[26]

In early September, while Elizabeth was considering what further action to take against Katherine Grey, William Maitland of Lethington, Mary Queen of Scots's adviser, arrived at the royal castle of Hertford where the court was then staying. He found Elizabeth looking depressed and ill, and described how 'to all appearances she is falling away, and is extremely thin and the colour of a corpse'.[27] Having paid his respects, and offering her cousin's messages of affection and goodwill, Maitland explained how Mary was determined that Elizabeth name her as her successor to the English crown.

This was not what Elizabeth had expected; she had hoped Maitland had come to report Mary's acknowledgment of Elizabeth's right to be Queen. Nevertheless her response to Maitland was cautious, though extraordinarily candid. 'I have noted,' Elizabeth told him,

> that you have said to me . . . that your Queen is descended of the royal blood of England and that I am obliged to love her as being nearest to me in blood of any other, all which I must confess to be true and I here protest to you, in the presence of God, I for my part know no better [claim than the Queen of Scots] nor that I myself would prefer to her . . .[28]

Here Elizabeth made clear that Mary was her preferred successor and she acknowledged her claim to the throne. How Maitland must have rejoiced to hear her words and looked forward to reporting the success of his mission to Mary. But Elizabeth was not yet finished.

In her final audience with Maitland before his departure, Elizabeth made clear that she would, however, never name Mary Queen of Scots as her chosen heir for fear of the unrest it might cause.

> The desire is without example to require me in my own life, to set my winding sheet before my eyes . . . Think you that I could love my own winding sheet? Princes cannot like their own children, that that should succeed them . . . How then shall I, think you, like my cousin, being once declared my heir apparent? . . . And what danger it were, she being a puissant princess and so near our neighbour, ye may judge; so that in assuring her of the succession we might put our present estate in doubt.[29]

Elizabeth was all too aware of the 'inconstancy of the people of England, how they ever mislike the present government and have their eyes fixed upon that person that is next to succeed, and naturally men be so disposed: *plures adorant solem orientem quam occidentem* [more men worship the rising than the setting sun]'. As men had looked to her during the reign of her sister, so men might look to Mary now as a focus of their hopes.[30]

Maitland did not have the successful mission that he had hoped for.

Elizabeth offered only the consolation that she would yield to the Scottish Queen's request that they meet face to face.[31] This too proved to be an empty gesture when shocking events in France weeks later forced Elizabeth to change her course. On 1 March 1562, hundreds of Huguenots were murdered in an armed action by troops of François, Duke of Guise, in Vassay in north-eastern France. All thoughts of a meeting between Elizabeth and Mary, the duke's niece, were quickly dropped. Emnity and suspicion undermined their relationship once more.

With growing fears that the Guises had now embarked on a long-feared Catholic crusade which would be brought to Protestant England, Elizabeth received the news that she had dreaded. On the afternoon of 24 September, Katherine Grey had given birth in the Tower of London to a son, Edward Seymour, Viscount Beauchamp. By the terms of Henry VIII's will and English law he now followed his mother in the line of succession.[32] England simultaneously had a Protestant heir and the promise of a 'masculine succession'. Elizabeth immediately announced her intention to have the young Edward Seymour 'declared a bastard by Parliament'.[33]

———— ·•· ————

In late September, Sir Nicholas Throckmorton wrote to Elizabeth from Paris warning of another plot to assassinate her. An Italian, calling himself Jean Baptista Beltran of Lyon, had come to the ambassador's lodgings to inform him that a Greek called Maniola de Corfeu had been instructed by a 'great personage' to 'make a voyage into England to poison the Queen'. Beltran had recently been in England where he had revealed the plot to Dudley and Cecil, described the would-be assassin and told them that de Quadra, the Spanish ambassador, was also privy to the plot. On his return to France, Baptista told Throckmorton that Maniola had arrived in Paris ready to cross to England to commit the deed. If he could be assured of a 'good recompense for the charges' that had been incurred and the danger he had put himself in by 'discovering the matter', Baptista said he would accompany Maniola to England, 'and there apprehend him and all his boxes with the sundry sorts of poison'. Throckmorton assured Baptista that he would be well rewarded if he foiled the plot and apprehended Maniola, although he could not assure him of any certain sum for his trouble.[34]

A fortnight later Throckmorton wrote again to the Queen, warning her that Maniola de Corfeu had departed secretly on 6 October and was going via Dieppe to England. Throckmorton described the assassin as being about the age of forty, having a black beard, a mean stature and corpulent, and with a cut on the left side of his nose.[35] Cecil had the plot investigated but was satisfied it was a false alarm.[36] Nevertheless, as de Quadra subsequently reported, Cecil had spent 'many hours' watching out for the two men described by Beltran and, 'this would not have been done, at least by Cecil himself if they did not take the thing seriously'.[37]

9

Arcana Imperii

On the afternoon of 18 January 1562, *Gorboduc* or *The Tragedy of Ferrex and Porrex,* a play written by Thomas Norton and Thomas Sackville, two lawyers of the Inner Temple, was performed before the Queen at Whitehall. It took its name from the mythical British king who unwisely divided his kingdom between his sons. By presenting the Queen with a vision of a realm thrown into chaos by an unresolved succession, it sought to spur her to marry and produce an heir.[1] *Gorboduc* counselled the Queen not simply that a royal marriage was necessary and desirable, but that it should be to Robert Dudley and not to Erik XIV, King of Sweden.[2]

An Anglo-Swedish marriage, which had been keenly promoted by Erik and his ambassadors from the earliest days of the reign, was increasingly favoured by those hostile to Dudley. After the sudden death of Amy Robsart and Dudley's rather dubious efforts to obtain Spanish and papal support for his suit to the Queen, support for the Swedish match had been building. In July 1561, wedding souvenirs had begun to circulate in London and when Erik's ambassador, the Swedish chancellor Nils Göransson Gyllenstierna, arrived in England to negotiate terms, he received a grand official welcome.[3] Elizabeth had initially resisted the Swedish overtures but as rumours reached England that Erik XIV was making advances to Mary Queen of Scots, Elizabeth began to respond with greater enthusiasm.[4]

Upon his arrival in England, Gyllenstierna was first instructed to investigate the truth about Elizabeth's morality and sexual conduct. 'I saw no signs of an immodest life,' he reported, 'but I did see many signs of chastity, of virginity, of true modesty; so that I would stake my life that she is most chaste.'[5] By September, after the assurances of the Swedish chancellor, the King himself was 'hourly looked for' and preparations made at court for his arrival.[6] Erik began his journey from Sweden to England in November but soon had to turn back because of bad weather.[7] He was not now expected until the following spring.

Whilst in the intervening months the Swedish ambassador continued to press his master's suit, Dudley and his supporters mounted a concerted campaign against it. The performance of *Gorboduc* had dramatically made their case.[8] As one member of the audience explained, the play, and particularly the dumbshow which formed part of it – in which the King was offered an ordinary glass of wine which he refused and then a golden chalice of wine which he took – showed how 'men refused the certain and took the uncertain', meaning 'it was better for the Queen to marry with the L[ord] R[obert] . . . than with the K[ing] of Sweden'.[9]

By March 1562, Erik had still not arrived and, believing any match was increasingly unlikely given that 'the Queen maketh so much of the L[ord] Rob[ert]', Gyllenstierna prepared to leave for home. Whilst Elizabeth tried to detain him for fear that he would go straight to Mary Stuart, he finally left England in early April 1562.[10]

With the Swedish suit effectively over, Dudley and his supporters grew ever more hopeful that he might finally win the Queen's hand.[11] Elizabeth told de Quadra that she was free of any betrothal, 'notwithstanding what the world might think or say', but that 'she thought she could find no person with better qualities than Lord Robert' if she was obliged to marry in England. De Quadra joked with her 'not to dilly-dally any longer, but to satisfy Lord Robert at once'.[12]

But then, on 28 April, Borghese Venturini, secretary to de Quadra, made a statement which changed everything. He revealed de Quadra's secret communications with Dudley, his contact and relations with the English Catholics, and unflattering comments he had made as to Elizabeth's indiscretions with her favourite.[13] Cecil got what he had been after. For some time he had been bribing Venturini to spy on the ambassador, in the hope of learning something that would discredit de Quadra with the Queen and put an end to his dealings with Dudley over the marriage and restoration of Catholicism.[14] According to Venturini, de Quadra had even alleged that 'the Queen was secretly married to Lord Robert' and had composed a sonnet 'full of dishonour to the Queen and Lord Robert'.[15]

The Spanish ambassador was immediately confronted by Cecil and accused, among other things, of turning his residence Durham House into a hotbed of Catholic conspiracy against the crown. De Quadra wrote of the 'disaster' that had happened in his house and how Venturini had 'been bribed by the Queen's ministers' and 'has laid more on to me than he could truthfully do'.[16] In response to the charge that he had written to Philip of Spain describing how the Queen had secretly married Lord

Robert at the Earl of Pembroke's house, de Quadra argued that Elizabeth herself had admitted that, 'on her return that afternoon from the earl's house, her own ladies-in-waiting when she entered her chamber with Lord Robert asked whether they were to kiss his hand as well as hers; to which she told them no and they were not to believe what people said'. Two or three days later, the ambassador claimed, Dudley had told him that the Queen had promised to marry him.

Elizabeth and Dudley had hitherto believed that de Quadra was sympathetic to their relationship, but now they learned that he had passed on gossip that dishonoured them both and had advised Philip II to withhold support for the match for fear of alienating the English Catholics. The ambassador denied any duplicity but neither party could trust him again.[17]

———•———

Desperate to save their mistress from a scandalous marriage to Dudley, two of the Queen's ladies, Kat Ashley and Dorothy Bradbelt, now took matters into their own hands, in the hope of reviving the Swedish match and enticing Erik to come finally to England.[18] Whilst we know Dorothy Bradbelt was at the very heart of the Queen's court and was even acknowledged in the diplomatic correspondence of the Venetian ambassador in the 1560s to be 'oftentimes' the Queen's 'bedfellow', we know very little of her.[19] She was not of noble origin and there is no evidence that she had served in the royal household during the years before Elizabeth's accession. Yet, as her involvement with the Swedish match reveals, Dorothy was a determined woman who would do what she thought necessary to defend the honour of her Queen.

On 22 July, Dorothy together with Kat Ashley wrote to the Swedish King's chancellor, Gyllenstierna, suggesting that the King's suit might now be successful if he came to England.[20] Two English adventurers seeking profit from contact with the wealthy Swedish King named John Kyle and James Goldborne (a former servant of Ashley's) also wrote a number of letters to their friends in Sweden encouraging a marriage with Elizabeth.[21] It was not the first time that Ashley had acted covertly in favour of the Swedish suit. Earlier in the year, John Dymock, a London jewel merchant, came to see her before travelling to the Swedish King's court to sell some gems.

Now in July 1565, as he prepared to leave, Dymock met again with Kat in her chamber at Whitehall and asked whether the rumour that Elizabeth was to marry Robert Dudley was true. Kat 'solemnly declared that she thought the Queen was free of any man living, and that she would not have the Lord Robert'. To add further weight to their cause, Kat and her husband John, Master of the Jewel House, concocted another scheme to convince the Swedish King of the Queen's favour, this time involving Dymock. Elizabeth had taken an interest in a large ruby that the jeweller had shown her, but she claimed she could not afford it. At John Ashley's instigation, Dymock suggested to the Queen that he show the same ruby to Erik and see if he would buy it for her, as a token of her affection. Elizabeth laughed off the idea saying, 'If it should chance that they matched, it would be said that there was a liberal king and a niggardly princess matched . . .'

Dymock suggested that maybe the Queen might like to send a ring from her finger to the Swedish King, as a sign of her favour? Elizabeth would not give up a ring but did agree to send some other less personal gifts, including a pair of black velvet gloves, a 'fair English mastiff', and a French translation of Castiglione's *Il Cortegiano* (*The Book of the Courtier*). Upon receiving the gifts, Erik reciprocated with two gems and a portrait of himself. The Bedchamber plotting looked to be working and negotiations for the Swedish match moved forward with the gestures of interest from both sides. In acknowledgement of her support, and testament to her perceived influence with the Queen, Erik sent Kat Ashley two sable skins, 'lined with cloth of silver and perfumed'.[22] Encouraged, Kat sent letters to the Swedish chancellor, saying the time was now right for his King to come to England.

On 4 August, Cecil intercepted the letters and ordered an immediate enquiry. Elizabeth reacted furiously at news of the secret correspondence and moved quickly to inform Gyllenstierna that his informants were 'idle cheats' whose tales should not be believed. Elizabeth commanded Kat Ashley 'to keep to her chamber' and committed Dorothy Bradbelt to Cecil's custody.[23] Elizabeth was highly sensitive to any interference in what she termed *arcana imperii* – state secrets – especially by the women closest to her.

News of the scandal at court and the imprisonment of two of Elizabeth's most favoured women spread abroad. A newsletter circulating in Rome and sent from Louvain, the chief haunt of refugee English priests, reported that, 'Of late there have been committed to the Court of London some, as well men as women, that were formerly high in favour with the Queen, among them being Mrs Ashley, who had such influence with the Queen that she seemed, as it were, patroness of all England.'[24] However, within less than a month, to the astonishment of many people both at home and abroad, both women were restored to their former positions. Was this because of their high favour with Elizabeth and her desire to have her long-serving women back in the Bedchamber; or might this have been another example of Elizabeth using her women to serve her political ends? Elizabeth clearly had little intention of going through with the Swedish marriage, but, at a time when the rumours about her relationship with Dudley were engulfing Europe, her apparent encouragement of the match would have served a useful purpose. The fact that Ashley and Bradbelt regained the Queen's favour so quickly suggests the latter. The correspondence was a means by which Elizabeth could test opinion at home and abroad for the match and then blame her women if it did not meet with general approval. Once again Elizabeth was using the women of her Bedchamber to act on her behalf, while protecting her own position and reputation.

10

Smallpox

In the early years of her reign, the riverside palace of Hampton Court was a regular destination for Elizabeth. It was a truly magnificent sight, with its red-painted bricks, three storeys of lattice windows, manicured gardens transformed by Henry VIII in the year of Elizabeth's birth, and its gilded weather vanes, held aloft by golden beasts, high above the pinnacles and cupolas that lined the rooftop.[1] Inside, the eight hundred-room palace was every inch as majestic. Brilliantly coloured tapestries hung from every wall and in each room of the privy lodgings the floors and ceilings were gilded with individual designs.[2]

Privileged visitors came to wonder at the splendour of its most impressive room, the Queen's Presence Chamber – the famous 'Paradise Chamber' – where, seated on a throne covered in brown velvet, embroidered with gold thread and ornamented with diamonds, Elizabeth would give audiences, receive ambassadors and hold public ceremonies. Above the throne hung a canopy of state, embroidered with the royal arms of England, encircled by the garter and studded with huge pearls and a diamond, which had been made for her father. A table stood nearby with a cloth 'embroidered all over with pearls' and on it a jewelled water clock, a looking-glass decorated with pearls and a chess set made of alabaster. Next door was a library which, besides housing a range of books, displayed a number of curiosities including a walking stick 'made from a unicorn's horn', a cup made out of elk's horn which was reputed to break if poison was put into it, and a mother-of-pearl casket. Another room contained the bed which Henry VIII had taken on his expedition to lay siege to Boulogne in the last years of his reign, and the bed in which Jane Seymour gave birth to Edward VI.

The palace was also, one Italian visitor noted, 'replete with every convenience'. Three miles of lead piping brought fresh spring water to the palace for bathing, as well as cooking. Elizabeth had a tile-stove in her bathroom which was fired by sea coal and was likely to have been used to create steamy conditions in the manner of a Turkish bath.[3]

In early October 1562, while at Hampton Court, the Queen began to feel unwell and decided to take such a bath, before going for a bracing walk in her garden. A day or two later she felt feverish, faint and began to shiver. On the fifteenth she was forced to hastily sign off a letter to Mary Queen of Scots, adding, 'the fever under which I am suffering, forbids me to write further'.[4] Dr Burcot, a highly respected German physician, was sent for immediately. His diagnosis was smallpox.[5]

The awful manifestations of the disease had recently been described by Thomas Phaer, a lawyer, translator and physician whose *Regiment of Life* (1544) was one of the most widely read medical treatises of the day:

> [The signs are] itch and fretting of the skin as if it had been rubbed with nettles, pain in the head and back etc: sometimes as it were a dry scab or lepry spreading over all the members, other whiles in pushes, pimples and whayls running with much corruption and matter, and with great pains of the face and throat, dryness of the tongue, hoarseness of the voice and, in some, quiverings of the heart with sownings.[6]

Since the Queen was suffering from few of these symptoms, at first she refused to believe Burcot's diagnosis and demanded that the 'knave' be removed from her sight. Doubtless Elizabeth was extremely frightened. Even if she managed to survive the illness it was probable that she would be left with a badly scarred face, a horrific prospect for one so vain. Several women at court had contracted smallpox in the weeks before the Queen's illness and Margaret St John, the Countess of Bedford, aged twenty-nine, the same age as the Queen, and a mother of seven, had died from it.

The following day Elizabeth's condition worsened. Writing to the Duchess of Parma from the court, de Quadra described how,

> The Queen has been ill of fever at Kingston, and the malady has now turned to smallpox. The eruption cannot come out and she is in great danger. Cecil was hastily summoned from London at midnight. If the Queen dies it will be very soon, within a few days at the latest, and now all talk is who is to be her successor.[7]

Four days passed and still there were no marks on her pale skin, yet her temperature soared and she fell into a coma. Elizabeth was gravely ill; England's fate depended entirely on the outcome of her illness. As news of the Queen's condition spread, the country held its breath. This was the crisis that her councillors had feared since the beginning of the reign. Not expecting her to survive, as she lay in feverish delirium at Hampton Court, they called an urgent meeting to agree upon a successor.[8]

'There was great excitement that day in the palace,' reported de Quadra, 'and if her improvement had not come soon some hidden thoughts would have become manifest.' The Privy Council discussed the succession twice and failed to reach a consensus. Some 'wished King Henry's will to be followed and Lady Katherine declared heiress'; others favoured the Stuart claim of Mary Queen of Scots. Robert Dudley, among others, was said to be 'much against' Katherine Grey and instead supported the Yorkist claim of Henry Hastings, 3rd Earl of Huntingdon, a committed Protestant and descendant of Edward III who was married to Katherine Dudley, Robert Dudley's youngest sister.[9] Discussions went on long into the night, but no decision was reached.

Believing that the end was near, Elizabeth's councillors gathered anxiously around her bed. After about four hours she regained consciousness and in the event of her death asked them to appoint Lord Robert Dudley as Protector of the Realm with an income of £20,000 a year. According to one report, sensing their unease, 'the Queen protested at the time that although she loved and always loved Lord Robert dearly, as God was her witness, nothing improper had ever passed between them'. She also ordered that Tamworth, the groom of Dudley's chamber, have an income of £500 per year.[10] Was Elizabeth rewarding Tamworth for his discretion and for keeping details of the relationship with his master and the Queen secret?

Two men on horseback were urgently sent to bring the physician Dr Burcot back to court. But, still chastened after his earlier encounter with the Queen, he angrily told them, 'By God's pestilence, if she be sick, there let her die! Call me a knave for my good will!' One of the messengers threatened to kill the doctor if he did not come and do all he could to save the Queen. Compelled by the summons, Burcot mounted his horse and galloped back to Hampton Court where he was brought to Elizabeth's bedside. He arrived almost too late. On the night of the 16 October, the 'palace people were all mourning for her as if she was already dead'. Then, soon after midnight, small, reddish spots began to appear on the Queen's hands. Noticing these she apprehensively asked Burcot what they were.

'Tis the pox,' he replied, at which Elizabeth moaned, 'God's pestilence! Which is better? To have the pox in the hand or in the face or in the heart and kill the whole body?'[11]

Adopting, 'the red treatment', an old Japanese remedy practised for centuries and first used in Europe from the twelfth century onwards, which recommended that the patient be wrapped in red cloth as it was thought the red light given out by the cloth prevented scarring, Elizabeth's body, with the exception of her head and one hand, was wrapped in a length of scarlet cloth and laid on a mattress in front of the fire in her room.[12] Burcot then put a bottle to her lips and told her to drink as much as she could. She said it was 'very uncomfortable'. As the hours passed the flat spots of the rash became raised pimples, then blisters and then pustules which dried up and turned into scabs or crusts.

Ambassadors urgently pressed for news from the Bedchamber. Martin Kyernberk, the Swedish envoy, reported to Nils Gyllenstierna:

> Our Queen is now ill with the smallpox, and before this broke out she was in the greatest danger of her life, so that her whole Council was in constant session for three days; on the third day she was somewhat better, but she is yet not free from symptomatic fever, as part of the poison is still between the flesh and skin.[13]

At Elizabeth's bedside sat her loyal attendant Mary Sidney. Following the birth of her fourth child, a daughter, on 27 October 1561, Lady Sidney had returned to court and resumed her service in the Queen's private chambers. Now, as Elizabeth lay dangerously ill, she performed the most selfless service. By attending the Queen at the height of her illness Mary Sidney risked very probable infection herself. Each sufferer would remain infectious from just before the rash appeared until the last scab dropped off about three weeks later. The virus could spread through blankets and bedding or clothes soiled with scabs or pus or most commonly by inhaling contaminated air. After having been in close contact with the Queen, Mary Sidney did contract the disease, and though she survived she was left disfigured and her skin terribly scarred. As Sir Henry Sidney, her husband later wrote,

> When I went to Newhaven [Le Havre] I left her a full fair Lady in mine eye at least the fairest and when I returned I found her as foul a lady as the small pox could make her, which she did take by continual attendance of her Majesty's most precious person sick of

the same disease, the scars of which, to her resolute discomfort ever since hath done and doth remain in her face.[14]

Lady Sidney had contracted an especially virulent dose of the virus and was forced to withdraw from court and recuperate at Penshurst Place. Philip, her eldest son, then almost eight years old, also caught the disease and bore its facial scars for the rest of his life, something he came to resent bitterly. It was small consolation that her baby daughters Elizabeth and Mary, then aged one and two years old, escaped the infection.[15]

Gradually the Queen's condition improved, although only the women of the Bedchamber and Robert Dudley were allowed to be in her presence as she made her recovery. In a letter to the Scottish secretary, William Maitland of Lethington, Dudley alluded to the debate over the succession that the Queen's illness had provoked:

> Thanks be to Almighty God. He has well delivered us for this present, for the Queen's Majesty is now perfectly well out of all danger and the disease is so well worn away as I never saw any in so short [time]. Doubtless, my Lord, the despair of her recovery was once marvellously great, and being so sudden the more perplexed the whole state, considering all things, for this little storm shook the whole tree so far as it proved the strong and weak branches. And some rotten boughs were so shaken as they appeared plainly how soon they had fallen. Well this sharp sickness hath been a good lesson, and as it hath not been anything hurtful to her body, so I doubt not it shall work much good otherwise. For ye known seldom princes be touched in this sort, and such remembrances are necessary in His sight that governeth all . . .[16]

Elizabeth had been extraordinarily lucky: Sybill Penn, a former nurse of Edward VI had died of the disease in November, and thousands of others had been killed in England, as the epidemic spread through Europe. Having attended on the Queen in her gravest hour, Dr Burcot disappeared into obscurity, but as a sign of Elizabeth's gratitude he was rewarded with a grant of land and a pair of golden spurs that had belonged to the Queen's grandfather, Henry VII. Thereafter Elizabeth 'wished never to be reminded of her illness'.[17]

When Elizabeth heard that, during the emergency sessions, Protestants on the Privy Council looked to Henry Hastings, the Earl of Huntingdon, as her successor, she gave Katherine (nee Dudley) Hastings, the Countess of Huntingdon, a 'privy nippe [a sarcastic remark]'.[18] Although the countess would become a close confidante of the Queen's towards the end of the reign, in the early years the earl's royal blood undoubtedly caused 'some jealous conceit' of him and his wife. Whereas Lady Mary Sidney had proved her faithful service during the smallpox outbreak, her sister, the countess, managed to provoke the Queen's resentment. She now felt that the Earl and Countess of Huntingdon had dangerous pretensions to the throne. Elizabeth publicly snubbed the countess at court and was slow to promote the earl to any major office. The relationship did not begin to mend until the early 1570s, when Elizabeth came to appreciate the couple's unswerving loyalty.

In one of the many prayers that Elizabeth wrote she referred to this time of contagion and fear:

> Whether by being heartfully warned or justly punished and, this corrected and amended by grace, Thou has afflicted me in this body with a most dangerous and nearly mortal illness. But Thou hast gravely pierced my soul with many torments; and besides, all the English people, whose peace and safety is grounded in my sound condition as Thy handmaid nearest after Thee, Thou hast strongly disregarded in my danger, and left the people stunned.'[19]

It was believed that divine intervention had saved Elizabeth's life and her complexion, and this was celebrated by the production of gold medals to commemorate Elizabeth's recovery. On the obverse of the medal the face of the Queen appears free of any physical effects of the disease; on the reverse, a hand is shown shaking a snake into the fire. It is an allusion to the biblical account of St Paul being bitten by a snake, an incident that left him similarly unharmed (Acts 28:1-6): 'If God be with us, who can be against us.'[20]

The Queen's recovery from smallpox was hailed as a sign of God's favour, as was her supposedly blemish-free complexion. But it seems that Elizabeth's unmarred face was a necessary fiction. On 27 October, de Quadra sent a report to the Duchess of Parma, explaining the 'Queen is now out of bed and is only attending to the marks on her face to avoid disfigurement', and in his letter to Philip II in February of the following year, the ambassador described how Elizabeth assured her councillors that she did not have wrinkles, but that they were smallpox scars.[21] However, in the years that followed an official narrative of Elizabeth's immaculate beauty and perfect complexion was adopted, embellished in poems, plays and state-controlled portraits. Elizabeth understood how beauty could amplify her power and it was therefore crucial that, regardless of the reality of smallpox scars and the ravages of time, Elizabeth maintain her reputation as a beautiful and beguiling queen. Such a fiction would also protect the Queen from accusations of promiscuity which might have been levelled against her if people confused her smallpox scars with those of the 'great pox', syphilis, which was seen as the product of sexual immorality.

It was perhaps her need to deny her own scarring that led her to regard with hostility other people's pockmarked faces. Rather than show compassion to Mary Sidney, the woman who had nursed her through her illness and been so badly scarred as a result, Elizabeth regarded her with disdain. Later the Queen would also make very clear her distaste for a marriage with the Duke of Alençon, another smallpox sufferer who, like Mary Sidney, had been left disfigured.

———— ⋅ ————

Following the Queen's illness, Christmas and the New Year was a time of particular celebration and thanksgiving. Each year the twelve days of Christmas feasting and festivity would take place at Whitehall. Besides the banquets and special entertainments, one of the traditional high points was the exchange of presents with the Queen on New Year's Day. This year, 1563, Kat Ashley, not long after her transgressions over the Swedish match, gave the Queen twelve handkerchiefs edged with gold and silver. Elizabeth reciprocated with two bowls, a salt cellar, spoon, and pepper box, all in gilt – gifts that showed the Queen's untarnished affection for her. Dorothy Bradbelt, having also earned the Queen's disfavour, gave Elizabeth a pair of cambric sleeves.[22] Katherine Knollys was absent from the New Year festivities and a portrait at this time shows her heavily pregnant.[23] A son, Dudley, the last of Katherine's fourteen children, had been born on 9 May 1562 but died weeks later. Katherine had yet to return to court. Despite her absence and her mourning, she sent the Queen as her New Year offering a fine carpet, fringed with gold and silk.[24]

Gift-giving was a very public occasion and precise orders were laid down regarding the gift to the Queen, according to one's rank and status and gender. A duke, marquis, bishop or earl might give a coloured silk purse containing £20–£30 in gold coins, whilst an archbishop was expected to give £40. In return the Queen would give an appropriate weight of silver gilt plate. The Queen's ladies and lower-ranking servants also gave presents.[25] All the gifts and plate given and received were recorded on great rolls bearing the royal signature, and many of these survive. While the coins would be delivered to one of the senior male household officers, the gifts were handed to the women of the Privy Chamber, as the Queen looked on and nodded in appreciation. Ornate sleeves, which would be attached separately to the wrists, were particularly popular, as were finely bound books, handkerchiefs, ruffs and bags filled with aromatic herbs. Foodstuffs were popular gifts and ginger candy, marzipan structures, a 'pie of quinces', and two 'pots of preserved things' were among the items recorded in the gift rolls. Elizabeth's ladies were able to be more inventive in choosing a gift as they were best placed to judge what the Queen might especially like or need. Some gave particular fabrics or linen, others gave buttons, clasps, jewels or tassels of gold to adorn the Queen's clothing. Elizabeth was inclined to lose or mislay her personal belongings, and her ladies were often sent looking for a missing pair of gloves, a purse, a jewelled feather or fan or some other adornment from the royal gowns. All losses were duly noted in detail by Blanche Parry, Keeper of the Queen's Jewels; one such entry read: 'Lost, from her Majesty's back, the 17th of January. [1568] at Westminster, One Aglet of gold enamelled blue set upon a Gown of (black) purple velvet . . . set all over with Aglets of two sorts the Aglet which is lost being of the bigger sort'.[26]

In early January 1563, the Queen and her court moved to Windsor as the bubonic plague spread through London killing hundreds.[27] Rigorous measures were enforced. No one was permitted to carry wood or other items along the Thames to and from London, upon pain of hanging without judgement, and anyone who received wares out of London into Windsor would be turned out of their homes and their houses shut up.[28] Extra precautions were taken for the Queen's safety. The court instituted a special code of quarantine regulations, primarily to prevent direct access to the Queen's person: foreign ambassadors would not be received by the Queen until forty days after their arrival in the country. An anonymous Tudor chronicler recorded the 'great lamentation made' at the time of the Queen's illness, and poignantly added, 'No man knoweth the certainty for the succession; every man asketh what part shall we take.'[29]

I I

Devouring Lions

As Elizabeth lay in her Bedchamber at the height of her smallpox, three conspirators – Arthur Pole,[1] his brother Edmund and brother-in-law Anthony Fortescue – were apprehended and thrown into the Tower as they tried to flee to France.[2] They were charged with conspiring 'to depose the Queen, change the state of the realm, compass the Queen's death, raise insurrection in the realm and make Mary Queen of Scots Queen of England'.[3] Under interrogation they revealed the involvement of both France and Spain.[4] Elizabeth wrote to Philip asking that his ambassador either be ordered to desist from his interference in English affairs, or be recalled.[5] In the meantime, de Quadra was put under house arrest.

Elizabeth's near fatal smallpox had provoked the plotters into action. Whilst Pole and his accomplices confessed the details of the plot, they denied acting treasonously against the Queen, claiming they did not intend to enter the kingdom with an army until Elizabeth had died. Months earlier they had consulted John Prestall, a notorious Catholic necromancer, occult conjurer and alchemist who lingered on the margins of the court, who had assured the conspirators that Elizabeth would be long dead before their plan was put into effect.[6] They were tried the following February, found guilty of treason and sentenced to be executed.[7] Elizabeth commuted the sentences and they remained imprisoned in the Tower until their deaths in 1570.

Following the massacre of Vassay earlier in the year, civil war had broken out in France. The Huguenots, led by the Prince of Condé and Admiral Coligny, sought English support against the Guise relations of Mary Stuart.[8] Elizabeth had been initially reluctant to intervene but was persuaded by Dudley, who was seeking to re-establish his Protestant credentials after his failed attempt to secure marriage to Elizabeth with Spanish and Catholic backing.[9] The plot of the 'devouring Lions', as Cecil described it, was supported by the Duke of Guise and so served to allay any lingering doubts about supporting the French Protestants against the Guise.[10] An English army of 6,000 troops was assembled and sent to France in October 1562, under the command of Robert Dudley's brother, Ambrose Dudley, the Earl of Warwick. The letter to Mary Queen of Scots which Elizabeth had been in the middle of writing when she was struck down with smallpox had been an attempt to justify English intervention against her cousin's French family. As the Queen recovered, Parliament was summoned in order to raise funds to maintain the army in France and their defence of Newhaven. Its business would also be sure to include the question of the succession and the Queen's marriage in particular.[11]

At 11 o'clock on Tuesday, 12 January, a stately procession made its way from Whitehall to Westminster Abbey.[12] The streets had been swept clean, and fresh sand laid for the horses. Elizabeth, wearing her parliamentary robes, a red velvet mantle lined with white ermine spotted with black, arrived in a coach flanked by her Gentlemen Pensioners, dressed in red. Robert Dudley, Master of the Horse, followed behind, leading the Queen's spare horse, and then came her ladies riding two by two.[13]

At the abbey, Elizabeth listened to the sermon preached by Dr Alexander Nowell, the Dean of St Paul's, who set the tone for the parliamentary business that was to follow. He urged the Queen, for the 'surety of the realm', to marry and produce an heir of her own body: 'When your Majesty was troubled with sickness, then I heard continual voices and lamentations, saying, "Alas! What trouble shall we be in? ... For the succession is so uncertain and such division of religion! Alack! What shall become of us?"'[14]

After the service, the Queen, Lords and Commons left the abbey and moved to the Parliament Chamber where Lord Keeper Nicholas Bacon delivered his opening oration. He emphasised the danger of 'the foreign enemy abroad', particularly the Guise in France, but also enemies 'bred and brought up here amongst ourselves' who had sought to aid the foreign enemy and raise rebellion within the realm.[15] Only if Elizabeth married and secured the succession could the safety of the realm be assured. Cecil wrote to a friend,

> The heads of both houses are fully occupied with the promise of surety to the realm if God should, to our plague, call her Majesty

without leaving of children. The matter is so deep I cannot reach into it ... I think somewhat will be attempted to ascertain the realm of a successor to the crown, but I fear the unwillingness of her Majesty to have such a person known, will stay the matter.[16]

The Queen's recent illness had been a stark reminder of her mortality and the chaos that was likely to ensue in the interregnum if she died without settling the succession. Both houses were now determined to make their voices heard. One draft bill went so far as to propose that in the event of the Queen's death, her Privy Council should exercise all powers until a Protestant successor had been established.[17] Whilst the bill was never passed, the radical nature of the proposal, which would be revived later in the reign, shows the extreme anxieties of the time.

On 28 January, a Commons petition presented by the Speaker to the Queen at Whitehall, called directly on her to marry. Referring to the 'great terror and dreadful warning' brought by her illness with smallpox, and their fears of 'contentious and malicious Papists', the petition made clear the Commons' fears: 'We see nothing to withstand their desire but only your life ... we find how necessary it is for your preservation that there be more set and known between your Majesty's life and their desire.'[18] The Queen was urged to ensure that the succession would fall to the 'most undoubted and best heirs of your crown', by marrying 'whomsoever it be that your Majesty shall choose'. In the meantime, the MPs requested, she should name her successor. In return they assured her that they would 'employ their whole endeavours, wits and powers' to devise the strongest laws for the preservation and surety of her and her issue, 'and the most penal, sharp and terrible statutes to all that shall but once practise ... against your safety'.[19]

Elizabeth responded graciously to the petition and, as the clerk noted, 'thankfully accepted' their words. She assured them that having survived the smallpox epidemic when,

> death possessed almost every joint of me ... I know now as well as I did before that I am mortal. I know also that I must seek to discharge myself of that great burden that God hath laid upon me ... Think not that I, that in other matters have had convenient care of you all, will in this matter, touching the safety of myself and you all, be careless ... I am determined in this so great and weighty a matter to defer mine answer till some other time.[20]

Four days later, the Lords presented their own petition.[21] It fully supported the Commons' position and stressed the practical difficulties following the death of a monarch with no known successor and the fear that the realm would fall into the hands of its enemies. They requested, 'that it would please your Majesty to dispose yourself to marry, where it shall please you, to whom it shall please you, and as soon as it shall please you'. In the meantime Elizabeth was once more urged to name a successor, as without it the Lords could not see 'how the safety of your royal person and the preservation of your imperial crown be or can be sufficiently or certainly provided for'.[22]

She had listened tolerantly to the Commons petition just days before, but now the twenty-nine-year-old Queen lost her patience, angrily telling the Lords, 'that the marks they saw on her face were not wrinkles but pits of smallpox, and that although she might be old, God could send her children as He did to Saint Elizabeth'. She insisted that she was not too old to have a child and that if in the meantime she named a successor, it would 'cost much blood to England'.[23]

As the Lords and Commons waited for the Queen to give a more detailed reply to their petitions, Parliament occupied itself with the business of passing laws to preserve the Queen's safety and enforce the religious settlement. The penalties imposed by the Act of Supremacy of 1559 for those who maintained the authority of the Pope, were stepped up and the obligation to swear the Oath of Supremacy was extended to include anyone who held office in the kingdom. A first refusal to swear the oath would lead to the loss of goods and imprisonment, a second would result in a charge of treason.[24] Whilst Elizabeth did assent to this bill, she was not anxious that it be enforced and, acting on her instructions, Matthew Parker, the Archbishop of Canterbury, ordered the bishops not to tender the act a second time and so put anyone in peril of death without a written mandate.[25]

The plot for 'devouring lions', which had been foiled as Elizabeth lay in her sick bed, had demonstrated the threat to the Queen of sorcery and witchcraft. These offences were no longer covered by common law, that statute having been repealed in 1547, so new legislation was passed.[26] By the terms of the 'Act Against Conjuration, Enchantments and Witchcrafts', any magic which proved to be a cause of death would result in the death penalty for the guilty party.[27] An act was also passed 'against fond and fantastical prophecies' which could be used to condemn those who foretold the death of the Queen by 'casting nativities', as in the Pole conspiracy. Its preamble described the disturbances of the previous few years and ordered that if any person or persons, 'do advisedly and directly advance publish and set forth in writing, printing, singing, or in any other open speech or deed . . . and fond fantastical or false prophecy . . . to the intent thereby to make any rebellion, insurrection, dissension, loss of life or other disturbance within the Queen's realms', they would be imprisoned and fined. The penalty for the first offence was a year's imprisonment and a £10 penalty, for the second offence, imprisonment for life and forfeiture of goods.[28]

On the morning of 10 February, with Parliament still in session, the urgency of the succession issue was highlighted by the news that Katherine Grey had given birth to another baby, a boy, Thomas. Elizabeth was enraged; her twenty-two- year-old Protestant heir now had two sons. The Queen ordered an immediate investigation into the night-time liaisons between Katherine and the Earl of Hertford, which Sir Edward Warner the Lieutenant of the Tower had evidently allowed to take place.[29] Hertford was brought before the Court of Star Chamber where he was found guilty of having compounded his original offence of having 'deflowered a virgin of the blood royal in the Queen's house' by having 'ravished her a second time'. He was fined the ruinous sum of £5,000 for each offence and returned to the Tower.[30]

Meanwhile Katherine remained in custody, trying to care for her newborn child as well as an eighteen-month-old son. In August, with the plague in London, Katherine was relocated to the home of her uncle, Lord John Grey, at Pyrgo in Essex, where she was kept under strict house arrest. Over the next few years she was moved to a number of other residences, and would remain in close custody for the rest of her life, never seeing her husband again. As there was no evidence that a marriage had taken place, her children were pronounced illegitimate, yet as long as debate raged on the succession, Katherine Grey and her two sons would remain significant challengers to Elizabeth's throne.[31]

Mary Stuart, Elizabeth's Catholic heir, also became the subject of court gossip, when a young and infatuated French courtier and poet Pierre de Bocosel, Seigneur de Chastelard, was found hiding under her bed armed with a sword and dagger.[32] When he was discovered by the grooms of the chamber he protested that he had nowhere else to sleep. He was kept in the custody of the Captain of the Guard overnight and Mary, unaware of events in her own Bedchamber, was informed the next morning. When

Chastelard was examined before the council he claimed he had been sent by 'persons of distinguished position' in France, presumably Huguenots, to try and make himself 'so familiar' with Mary and her ladies that he could 'seize an opportunity or obtain some appearance of proof sufficient to sully the honour of the Queen'.[33] Mary ordered him from court, but the Frenchman followed her when she moved to Dunfermline days later, and was again found hidden in her Bedchamber, protesting that he was there to profess his innocence. The news soon reached the English court, provoking the lewd gossip that the young Chastelard did 'privily convey himself behind the hangings of the Queen's chamber, and in the night would have lain with her', had Mary not discovered him.[34] The Frenchman was arrested and then beheaded in St Andrew's marketplace. The episode left Mary terrified and provided a timely warning to Elizabeth as to the importance of scrupulous security surrounding the Bedchamber.

At three o'clock on the afternoon of Saturday 10 April 1563, Elizabeth travelled by royal barge from Whitehall to Westminster for the final session of Parliament, and there took her place in the Parliament Chamber. The Lord Keeper, Sir Nicholas Bacon, read on her behalf the speech that she had written. In it, the Queen thanked the Lords and Commons for their efforts throughout the session and gave her assent to the bills brought before her. She then responded directly to the marriage petitions presented by both houses. It had, she said, saddened her that they had pressed her to name a successor when there was still a good chance that she would marry and produce an heir of her body. Though she had little personal inclination to take a husband, she realised that her duty as Queen might compel her to do so and assured them, 'And if I can bend my liking to your need, I will not resist such a mind.'[35]

Amongst their urgent petitions for the Queen to marry, Parliament had voted the funds Elizabeth needed to support the English expedition in France. Writing to Ambrose Dudley, Earl of Warwick, in command of the English army, she assured him that she would now send reinforcements and do all she could to ensure the troops were well supplied. However her efforts proved futile. The Huguenots had become increasingly suspicious of Elizabeth's intentions and when the warring French factions made peace, they united to drive the English forces out of Le Havre. Then, as the English struggled to mount a defence, plague spread through the town killing countless soldiers. On 28 July the English were forced to surrender and the remnants of the army returned to England.[36] Within weeks London was in the grip of a serious epidemic as the returning soldiers brought the plague with them. Orders were issued for every London householder to lay a fire in his street at seven in the evening to 'consume the corrupt airs'.[37]

By August, deaths from the plague in London were reaching a thousand a week. Among the victims was the Spanish ambassador, Don Alvaro de Quadra, who had done so much to undermine relations between England and Spain.[38] Fears for the Queen's health forced her to leave London in September and move to Windsor, where she remained for the rest of the year. The castle was cold and draughty and Elizabeth, Cecil and other members of the court soon fell ill with an affliction known as 'pooss'. Cecil suffered so badly that he could hardly see and Elizabeth complained of a pain in her nose and eyes. Many people died of similar complaints that winter. Gallows were set up on the edge of the town and anyone suspected of bringing the plague from the capital was hanged. Even passing up and down the Thames through Windsor could be punished by hanging without trial.[39]

12

Ménage à Trois

'I thank God with all my heart, especially since I knew the danger you were in, and how you have escaped so well, that your beautiful face will lose none of its imperfections.' In her letter, written to Elizabeth after her recovery from smallpox, Mary Queen of Scots referred to her own experience of the disease as a child and gave thanks that Elizabeth was now restored to health. Thomas Randolph, the English ambassador in Scotland, had asked Mary on Elizabeth's behalf for the recipe of a potion that would prevent the disease recurring, which Mary had been given years earlier. Unfortunately, the Scottish Queen explained, Fernel, the French King's chief physician who administered it, was now dead and he 'would never tell me the recipe of the lotion that he applied to my face having punctured the pustules with a lancet'.[1]

Mary's warm words of comfort and concern did little to mask the reality of the continued threat to Elizabeth's crown. In January news reached Scotland of a plan to exclude Mary from the succession to the English throne, and it was reported that Mary was 'in great choler' because of it.[2] English intervention in support of the Huguenots against the Guise had further antagonised the Scottish Queen. With little chance of Elizabeth naming her cousin as heir, Mary resolved to seize the initiative and choose a husband for herself, thereby enabling her to secure her dynastic rights in England.

Mary considered the prospect of a Spanish union through a marriage with Don Carlos, Philip of Spain's eldest son. Whilst this would be a hugely significant political match with the heir to the Spanish throne and primary Catholic power in Europe, personally Don Carlos had little to recommend him; he was a sickly youth, hunchbacked and pigeon-breasted, prone to fits of violent insanity, and rumoured to be impotent. Nevertheless Don Carlos remained Mary's most prized suitor and Elizabeth made it clear that she would see such a marriage as a hostile act which would ruin

Mary's chances of inheriting the English throne.[3] Elizabeth needed to keep Scotland Protestant and urged Mary to take 'a person mete whose natural disposition will be to continue and increase the love and concord between both people and countries', and urged her to marry a nobleman of 'this isle'.[4] In the end, the Spanish match came to nothing. Mary's position was further weakened in February 1563 by the assassination of her uncle, the Duke of Guise. As long as he lived there was always the possibility that he could mobilise French military might to assert his niece's ambitions to the English throne. Now Mary's keenest champion was dead.

In March, William Maitland of Lethington, the Scottish secretary, again came to England in the hope of persuading Elizabeth to officially recognise Mary as her heir.[5]

When the subject of Mary's marriage came up, Elizabeth responded with an extraordinary proposal. If Mary wanted to marry 'safely and happily', she would do well to take Lord Robert Dudley as her husband. Maitland was thrown entirely off guard, and replied judiciously that although this was 'great proof of the love she bore to his Queen, as she was willing to give her a thing so deeply prized by herself', he felt 'certain that Mary would not wish to deprive her cousin of 'all the joy and solace she received from his company'. When Elizabeth persisted, Maitland replied,

> The Queen his mistress was very young yet, and what this Queen [Elizabeth] might do for her was to marry Lord Robert herself first and have children by him, which was so important for the welfare of the country, and then when it should please God to call her to himself she could leave the Queen of Scots heiress both to her kingdom and her husband.[6]

The following spring, Thomas Randolph made the formal proposal of Dudley to Mary Queen of Scots, with the assurance that if she agreed to 'content us and this our nation in her marriage', Elizabeth would proceed to the 'inquisition of her right and title to be our next cousin and heir and to further that which shall appear advantageous to her'.[7] Mary's response was swift and to the point. 'Is that to conform to her promise to use me as her sister?' she demanded sharply. 'And do you think it may stand with my honour to marry my sister's subject?' Horribly compromised, Randolph could only mumble that 'there was not a worthier man to be found' than Robert Dudley.[8]

The Scots, Randolph informed London, were in disbelief. Knowing the Queen's deep affection for Dudley and judging Elizabeth and her Master of the Horse to be inseparable, they could only suppose that her offer was merely to give the appearance of goodwill rather than being genuine.[9] Meanwhile, Catherine de Medici and her uncle the Cardinal of Guise were quick to remind Mary that it was not safe to trust Elizabeth's 'counsel in her marriage who meaneth therein only to [deceive] her'.[10]

Whilst pretending to entertain the idea of Dudley as a possible match, Mary secretly hoped to marry another Englishman: the strikingly handsome, six-foot-two, seventeen-year-old Henry Stuart, Lord Darnley.[11] Like Mary Queen of Scots, Darnley was a grandchild of Margaret Tudor, Henry VIII's eldest sister. His mother Margaret, Countess of Lennox, was a staunch Catholic, granddaughter of Henry VII and cousin to Elizabeth, and had been advocating Darnley as a match for Mary since the death of François II. The countess had repeatedly denounced Elizabeth as an illegitimate usurper and claimed she and her heirs were the rightful sovereigns of England. When Mary had returned to Scotland following the death of her husband, the Earl and Countess of Lennox were placed under surveillance at their Yorkshire estates. Shortly afterwards they were arrested and imprisoned for allegedly plotting a marriage between Mary and Darnley. Examination of their servants revealed that the earl and countess had heard Catholic mass and had their jester mock Queen Elizabeth, including in a sketch depicting her love affair with Robert Dudley, who had been portrayed as a pox-ridden traitor.[12] Lennox was imprisoned in the Tower and Darnley left for France. By the summer of 1563, Darnley and his parents were apparently back in favour.[13] On 19 July it was reported that the Earl and Countess of Lennox were at court at Greenwich and 'my Lord Darnley, their son and heir, is also a daily waiter and playeth very often at the lute before the Queen, wherein it should seem she taketh pleasure as indeed he plays very well'.[14]

Whilst Elizabeth had no intention of nominating a successor, she was angered by Parliament's support for Katherine Grey, particularly after the birth of Katherine's second son. She now resolved to promote an alternative candidate. 'Many people think that if the Queen of Scots does marry a person unacceptable to this Queen, the latter will declare her successor the son of Lady Margaret, whom she now keeps in the palace and shows such favour to as to make this appear probable.'[15]

In June, Elizabeth petitioned Mary to restore the Lennox family's hereditary lands, which had been confiscated by Henry VIII. It was undoubtedly a disingenuous move that sought to stir up troubles for Mary at a time when she was courting marriage prospects. At the end of April 1564, Mary granted the passport for the Earl of Lennox and allowed him to return to his ancestral home.

By autumn, relations between Mary and Elizabeth had soured because of the 'jealousies and suspicions' that lay between them. Mary sent to the English court Sir James Melville, an urbane young Scotsman and one of her most trusted agents and diplomats in an attempt to smooth relations between the two queens and defend Mary's dynastic claim to the English throne if Parliament should reassemble. Melville was also instructed to secretly deliver a message to Darnley's mother, the Countess of Lennox, 'to procure liberty for [Darnley] to go to Scotland'.[16]

13

Visitor to the Bedchamber

At eight o'clock on a bright September morning, the twenty-nine-year-old Sir James Melville arrived on horseback at Whitehall Palace. He was shown into the privy garden where the Queen was expecting him. A delicious bouquet of scents emanated from the garden's aromatic herbs and flowers, planted in raised beds, enclosed by low rails painted in the Tudor colours. Sculptures of men, women, children, monsters and other strange figures, rose up from the grassy avenues in high and low relief, and thirty-four tall columns, decorated with carvings and gilded animals and flags bearing the Queen's arms. At the centre of the garden, a sundial blade 'showed the hours in thirty different ways' and a fountain sprayed water up through concealed pipes, soaking anyone who stood nearby.

The palace itself was renowned for its splendid furnishings, tapestries and pictures, and the number and length of galleries. The Hans Holbein mural of Henry VIII dominated the Privy Chamber. 'The King as he stood there,' wrote one visitor, 'majestic in his splendour, was so lifelike that the spectator felt abashed, annihilated in his presence.'[1] Melville spent nine days at court and charmed Elizabeth with his wit and sophisticated manners. The Queen, for her part, was keen to show off her many talents to the Scottish envoy; she knew he would report them in minute detail to Mary. Melville was treated to the most remarkable access to Elizabeth during these days and enjoyed daily audiences, often 'before noon, after noon and after supper', in her privy lodgings and in her Bedchamber.[2]

Late one evening after supper, Elizabeth invited Melville into her Bedchamber. It was a dark and airless place; weak candlelight lit up the gold ceiling and rich tapestries of glistening threads which hung on the walls. Next to the Queen's lavish bed, adorned with sumptuous embroidered quilts, was a table entirely covered with silver and a chair with no actual seat but built up from the floor with cushions. There were 'two little silver cabinets of exquisite work in which the Queen kept her paper and which she used as writing boxes, a silver inkstand and a Latin prayer book that the Queen had written and, in a beautiful preface, had dedicated to her father'.[3] Next door to the Bedchamber was Elizabeth's bathroom containing an exotic bath into which the water poured from 'oyster shells and different kinds of rock'. A room on the east side of the Bedchamber contained the Queen's musical instruments, including a virginal and an organ, and a clock 'which played tunes by striking on bells'. A library close by was filled with Greek, Latin, Italian and French books, bound in red velvet 'with clasps of gold and silver', some with pearls and precious stones set in their bindings. A secret entrance led from the Bedchamber into the garden, where there was a walkway down to the gatehouse on the river, from which the Queen could depart in her royal barge. When she travelled along the Thames, perfumed oils were burned to camouflage the odours from the river.

In the flickering candlelight of her Bedchamber, Elizabeth led Melville to a 'little desk' in which there were several portrait miniatures that she kept wrapped in paper. On each she had written the names of the sitters. She had intended to show him a picture of Mary, which she said she 'delighted often' to look at, but the first she unwrapped was that of Robert Dudley upon which she had written, 'My Lord's picture'. When Melville asked if he might take the picture back to Scotland for Mary, Elizabeth refused saying that she 'had but one of his picture'. Melville quipped that 'she had the original' – Dudley was 'at the farthest part of the chamber, speaking with Secretary Cecil'. Elizabeth then took out the miniature of Mary Queen of Scots and kissed it. Melville responded by kissing Elizabeth's hand, 'for the great love I saw she bore to my mistress'. He suggested that she might send to Mary either the picture of Dudley or a ruby – 'great like a tennis ball' – which she also showed him. If Mary 'would follow her counsel, then she would, in the process of time, get both, and all she had'. In the meantime she agreed to send her cousin a diamond as a token of her intentions.[4]

During his time at Whitehall, Melville often sat next to Dorothy Stafford so that, 'I might be always near her Majesty that she might confer with me'. He knew Lady Stafford and her daughter from their time in exile on the continent, during the reign of Mary I, and spoke of how he made 'their acquaintance when they passed through France'.[5] Dorothy and her husband Sir William, together with two of their children, Elizabeth and Edward Stafford, had taken up residence in Geneva and joined the English Church there soon in October 1556. Another son,

John, was born and baptised in Geneva and became godson to Jean Calvin. Sir William died several months later.[6] Having then travelled to France in the early months of Elizabeth's reign, Lady Dorothy returned to England and joined the Queen's entourage.

Elizabeth was keen to impress Melville with her extensive wardrobe. Each day she wore something different, showing off the styles of France, Italy and England. 'She asked me which of them became her best?' Melville noted, to which he replied, 'the Italian dress'. This, 'pleased her well, for she delighted to show her golden coloured hair, wearing a caul and bonnet as they do in Italy. Her hair was more reddish than yellow, curled in appearance naturally.' When Elizabeth asked, 'What colour of hair was reputed best; and which of the two queens was the fairest?' Melville replied diplomatically, 'I said she was the fairest Queen in England and ours the fairest Queen in Scotland.' Elizabeth pressed Melville who was forced to respond that, 'they were both the fairest ladies of their courts, and that Her Majesty was whiter, but our Queen was very lovely'. Elizabeth then quizzed the Scot as to who was taller. Melville said Mary, but that Elizabeth was neither too high nor too low.

> Then Elizabeth asked what sort of exercises Mary did. I answered that [when] I was despatched out of Scotland, the Queen was lately come from the Highland hunting, that when she had leisure from the affairs of her country, she read good books, the histories of diverse countries, and sometimes would play upon the lute and virginals.

She asked if she played well, to which Melville responded, 'reasonably for a queen'.

One evening, Melville was taken to a 'quiet gallery' and stood outside one of the Queen's rooms to hear her playing the virginals. Elizabeth was an accomplished musician; she sang well and also played the lyre and the lute.[7] After a while, Melville drew aside the tapestry covering the door and seeing that Elizabeth had her back to him, entered. A few moments later the Queen noticed him and rose and, rather than chastise him, explained that she was not used to playing before men but normally played when she was alone to 'shun melancholy'. Melville spoke apologetically of how he was walking with Lord Hunsdon, brother of Katherine Knollys, past her chamber door and having heard 'such a melody as ravished me' was drawn to the chamber. As he spoke, Elizabeth sat down low on a cushion and Melville fell on his knees before her but she passed him a cushion to rest under his knee. He refused the honour at first but she insisted that he take it. She called Dorothy Stafford from the next room to join them and then asked whether she or the Scottish Queen played best. 'In that I gave her the praise,' Melville recorded.

After a few days, the young envoy prepared to return to Scotland, but Elizabeth was reluctant to let him go. 'She said I was weary sooner of her company than she was of mine,' and urged him to stay for another two days so that he might see her dancing, one of her favourite pastimes. Every morning to keep fit, Elizabeth practised the demanding galliard – a court dance involving vigorous leaps and hops; she always loved to dance with her courtiers and visiting ambassadors. After performing, Melville was asked the inevitable question, 'Whether she or my queen danced best.' The Scotsman replied that Mary 'danced not so high and disposedly as she did'.

Elizabeth had repeatedly expressed her desire to meet Mary in person and Melville urged her not to wait for a formal royal meeting but to come with him back to Scotland, disguised as a page. He suggested that the Queen's Bedchamber, 'might be kept in her absence as though she was sick', and that she need only tell Lady Stafford and one of the grooms of her chamber. According to Melville, Elizabeth replied, 'Alas! If I might do it.' The envoy pressed her again: no one else need know; the court could be told she was ill and not to be disturbed. Elizabeth resisted although, as Melville noted, she used 'all the means she could to cause me to persuade the Queen of the great love she did bear unto her, and that she was minded to put away all the jealousies and suspicions, and in times coming to entertain a straighter friendship to stand between them than ever had been of before'.

Melville returned to Scotland with an agreement that the English and Scottish commissioners should meet at Berwick to discuss a possible marriage between Mary and Robert Dudley. In an attempt to make Dudley a more attractive proposition for the Scottish Queen, Elizabeth raised him to the peerage and on 29 September, Melville witnessed Dudley's ennoblement as the Earl of Leicester. It was an act of enormous honour and, as the Spanish ambassador Diego Guzman de Silva reported, a title 'usually given to the second sons of the Kings of England'.[8] Elizabeth also gave Leicester the manor of Kenilworth, along with a number of other grants and offices. He might now be considered of the appropriate status to marry a queen.

At the formal ceremony at Westminster it was still possible to see the intimacy that Dudley and the Queen shared. As Dudley knelt before her and she girded the sword on his neck, Elizabeth could not 'refrain from putting her hand in his neck to tickle him smilingly'. The two were 'inseparable', Melville observed. Elizabeth asked the Scotsman how he liked Dudley and he responded that Leicester was a worthy subject and he was happy she could discern and reward good service. 'Yet,' said Elizabeth, 'you like better of yonder long lad' – pointing to Lord Darnley, who attended the ceremony as Dudley's nearest prince of the blood. Mary's agent again responded carefully:

> My answer was that no woman of spirit would make choice of such a man, that was more like a woman than a man; for he was very lusty, beardless and lady-faced. And I had no will that she should think that I liked him, or had any eye or dealing that way ... Albeit, I had a secret charge to deal with his mother, my Lady Lennox, to procure liberty for him to go to Scotland that he might see the country and convey the earl, his father, back again to England.[9]

Elizabeth had talked of Dudley as 'her brother and best friend', the man 'she would herself have married had she ever minded to have taken a husband'; but now she appeared adamant that she was happy to see him marry Mary Queen of Scots. She had 'determined to end her life in virginity', and therefore wished the Queen, 'her sister', to have him secure in the knowledge that 'being matched with [Dudley], it would best remove out of her mind all fear and suspicion, to be offended by usurpation before her death; being assured that he was so loving and trusty that he would never give his consent nor suffer such thing to be attempted during her time'.[10] Yet as Cecil wrote to a friend, 'I see the Queen's Majesty very desirous to have my Lord of Leicester placed in this high degree to be the Scottish Queen's husband, but when it cometh to the conditions which are demanded, I see her then remiss of her earnestness.'[11] Elizabeth soon began to change the terms in which she imagined the union, and talked of how Mary and Dudley might instead live at her court, in a ménage à trois that would allow Elizabeth to see Dudley daily. She would 'gladly bear the charges of the family' of the couple, 'as shall be mete for one sister to do for another', she said.[12]

Dudley was horrified by Elizabeth's designs.[13] As he and Melville travelled by barge along the Thames, the new Earl of Leicester said that he was not worthy of Mary, not even to 'wipe her shoes', and claimed the plan for them to marry was the invention of 'Mr Cecil, his secret enemy'. As Dudley continued, if he appeared keen on the marriage he would lose the favour of both Mary and Elizabeth. He begged Melville to tell Mary that 'it would please Her Majesty not to impute unto him that clumsy fault, but unto the malice of his enemies'.[14]

On his return to Edinburgh, Mary quizzed her ambassador about his time with her cousin. 'In my judgement,' Melville told her, 'there was neither plain-dealing nor upright meaning, but great dissimulation, emulation and fear that [Mary's] princely qualities should over soon chase her out and displace her from the kingdom.'[15] Meanwhile, Elizabeth wrote to Cecil, who was at home ill in bed. In a scrappy note written in Latin she told him, 'I am in such a labyrinth that I do not know how I shall be able to reply to the Queen of Scots after so long a delay. I am at a loss to know how to satisfy her, and have no idea as to what I now ought to say.'[16]

14

Sour and Noisome

In early December 1564, after a short sojourn at St James's Palace the court returned to Whitehall for Christmas and the New Year. Though only a distance of about a mile, with heavily laden horse and carriages and in bitter winter weather, it was a slow and difficult journey. The River Thames was frozen and people walked on it 'as they did on the streets'.[1] Courtiers indulged in games such as football, bowls and skittles on the ice, as the business of the city ground to a halt.

On 9 December, the Saturday shortly after the court was due to move, Elizabeth fell 'perilously ill' with what her councillors called a 'flux' (gastric flu) or 'diarrhoea'. It was so serious that for the next five days there was a panic that she might die.[2] However by the following Friday she was recovering, 'weakened but in health' as Cecil described in a letter to Sir Thomas Smith and added, 'for the time she made us sore afraid'. He thanked God that they might take 'good warning by her sickness and comfort from her recovery'.[3] Mary Queen of Scots wrote, sending Elizabeth her good wishes, for 'she is every day more dear to me than any other, and I am assured that her life, and that company that I trust to have with her, shall be more worth to me then her whole kingdom with her death, if she were disposed to leave it me'.[4] But the distrust ran deep; Elizabeth discerned something more sinister and believed that Mary 'doth look for her death, and that all this kindness is pretended only to hunt a kingdom!'[5] Cecil was already receiving reports from Scotland that moves were afoot for Henry Stuart, Lord Darnley, to marry Mary.[6]

Christmas was bleak. Though Elizabeth was out of danger, she suffered through the festivities with 'very bad catarrh' and a fever. When Guzman de Silva met with her on Christmas Eve, she 'complained of pains in the stomach and all over the body'. She spent long hours resting in her dark and stuffy Bedchamber, attended to by her women, including Kat Ashley, Blanche, Dorothy Stafford and Katherine Knollys, who now returned to court after the loss of her baby son Dudley. Mary Sidney remained at Penshurst Place after the birth of her fifth child just weeks before.[7]

Particularly when Elizabeth was ill, but also on a regular monthly basis, John Hemingway, the Queen's apothecary, would supply her and her ladies with various pills, lotions and fragrances. Hemingway kept precise records listing various medicines and scents despatched to the royal household. Kat Ashley was, it appears, the 'home doctor' in the Bedchamber and was regularly supplied with chamomile flowers, rose leaves, oil or roses and vinegar. She also had a regular order for lotions, oxicrocin plaster, pectoral powders, Venice turpentine and almond milk in addition to her 'accustomed pills'.

During a six-month period in 1564 for which records survive, John Hemingway provided the Ladies of the Bedchamber with two pounds of orris powder (made from the root of iris flowers) to use in a perfuming pan to scent the room.[8] Elizabeth and her ladies would also hold aromatic pomanders to their noses and burn juniper wood or sweet-smelling herbs in their chambers. Benjamin, rosewater and storax was used to scent the Queen's elaborately embroidered gowns. The Queen was considered to be fastidious about cleanliness and unpleasant smells were a constant problem, particularly given that a number of animals, among them a pet toy spaniel, a monkey, a cat (used for catching the mice that were endemic in the palaces) and a parrot, were also kept in the Queen's rooms.[9] The monkey required a 'chain with a collar' which apparently became worn or broken as a new one was then ordered with a collar specifically 'of iron with joints made full of holes with a hasp' and a longer chain with three swivels.[10] It seems the monkey remained a lively presence as over the next two years a further three steel chains were supplied by the court's locksmith, William Hood.[11]

Whilst Blanche Parry took care of what one warrant describes as 'our musk cat', most likely to have been a ferret or a civet cat known for its musk-like odour, the Queen's parrot, kept in a specially designed cage, was the responsibility of Dorothy Bradbelt. In 1563, John Grene, the Queen's coffer-maker, 'delivered to Dorothy Bradbelt to our use one great Cage of Tynker wire, and plate made strong for a parrot',[12] and with it 'two pots of pewter to put water in the one for our monkey the other for our parrot'. Locksmith William Hood made hinges for the cage[13] and 'six yards of double green sarceonet' were delivered 'to make curtains for a birdcage of needlework'.[14]

With no flushing lavatories in the palaces, the Queen used a 'close stool', a portable wooden toilet which had to be emptied by hand. Even in the

Queen's Bedchamber, where the close stools were disguised in 'cases of satin and velvet', the air was often 'sour and noisome'.[15] Chamber pots used only for urination were available in the Bedchamber and made of porcelain or silver or tin glazed stoneware. The Queen's lidded chamber pot, engraved with the royal initials, was set in a padded box. She would have a number of such close stools and all would be suitably luxurious: four of them, 'covered with black velvet embroidered upon and garnished with ribbon and gilt nails, the seat and laythes covered with scarlet fringed with silk and gold', were delivered to the Bedchamber in 1565, with their 'three pans of pewter with cases of leather-lined with canvas to put them in'. Kat Ashley was the keeper of the close stools, and after her death in 1565 these duties – including helping their mistress in her large, complex gowns – probably fell to whichever Lady of the Bedchamber was on duty at the time.[16] The padded adorned boxes in which the chamber pots were kept allowed for their discreet removal away from the privy lodgings to be emptied. When travelling and on royal progresses, Elizabeth had a dedicated close-stool carriage.

———

Elizabeth spent much of Christmas ill in bed and it was not until 2 January that she emerged from the Bedchamber into the Presence Chamber, where she could be seen by her courtiers. The Queen was 'very thin' and her physicians described her constitution as 'a weak and unhealthy one'. De Silva added gleefully to his dispatch, 'it is true young people can get over anything, but your Majesty should note, that she is not considered likely to have a long life'.[17]

By the New Year the weather had warmed up and the ice on the Thames had melted. The sudden thaw throughout England caused 'great floods and high waters', and the 'deaths of many and the destruction of many houses'. In early February, Elizabeth gave Lord Darnley permission to travel to Scotland, and soon he began his ride north.[18] It proved to be a reckless decision. The Queen had hoped that Darnley would stir up trouble for Mary, and she was also beginning to believe that he might be a better match for the Queen of Scots than Dudley, whom she was so loath to lose. She hoped that Darnley, 'being a handsome lusty youth, should rather prevail, being present, than Leicester who was absent'.[19]

Mary first met Darnley on Saturday 17 February in Edinburgh and was instantly attracted to him, describing him as the 'lustiest and best-proportioned lang [tall] man that she had ever seen'.[20] Before long, ambassadorial dispatches described how Darnley 'had wonderfully awakened' the Scottish court and how many believed that 'the Scottish Queen shall marry him'.[21] In a letter to his friend Sir Henry Sidney, husband of Mary Sidney and Dudley's brother-in-law, Thomas Randolph criticised Dudley for not taking more of an interest in Mary. 'How many countries, realms, cities and towns have been destroyed' to satisfy the lusts of men for such women; and yet Dudley who had been offered a kingdom and the opportunity to lie with Mary 'naked in his arms' had spurned both, resulting in the arrival of Darnley.[22] One of the first letters Darnley wrote after arriving in Scotland was to Robert Dudley himself, thanking him 'assuredly as your own brother'. 'Though I am far from you … I shall not be forgetful of your great goodness and good nature showed sundry ways to me.' It was clear who was behind his journey.[23]

Almost as soon as Darnley left for Scotland, Elizabeth began to worry about the dangers of his union with Mary; their joint claim to the English crown could unite Catholic Europe behind them. As Philip made clear in his letter to his ambassador, de Silva, the marriage would be a favourable one to Spanish interests and 'should be forward and supported to the full extent of our power. You will make Lady Margaret [Lennox] understand that not only shall I be glad for her son to be King of Scotland and will help him thereto, but also to be King of England if this marriage is carried through.'[24]

Elizabeth did 'simply mislike' the proposed marriage and was reluctant for negotiations to proceed any further, now believing that it was 'a matter danger to the common amity that is presently betwixt these our two kingdoms'. Sir Nicholas Throckmorton, having been replaced as ambassador to France, was sent to Scotland with instructions to do all he could to 'break or suspend' the match and to tell Mary that 'excepting the Lord Darnley', Elizabeth 'shall be well content with the choice of any'.[25] Throckmorton had little success and a month later wrote from Edinburgh that the matter was now 'indissoluble'.[26]

15

Untouched and Unimpaired

On 5 March 1565, Dudley hosted a supper for the Queen and her ladies. There was a joust and tourney on horseback and later a comedy in English based on the question of matrimony as discussed between Juno (advocating marriage) and Diana (advocating chastity). After both sides had presented their respective arguments, Jupiter gave a verdict in favour of matrimony, at which the Queen turned to Guzman de Silva and exclaimed, 'This is all against me.'[1] Mary's imminent marriage plans had put Elizabeth under tremendous pressure to wed and settle the succession. In a very revealing conversation with de Silva she explained how marriage,

> is a thing for which I have never had any inclination. My subjects, however, press me so that I cannot help myself, but must marry or take the other course, which is a very difficult one. There is a strong idea in the world that a woman cannot live unless she is married, or at all events that if she refrains from marriage she does so for some bad reason, as they said of me that I did not marry because I was fond of the Earl of Leicester, and that I would not marry him because he had a wife already. Although he has no wife alive now, I still do not marry him ... We cannot cover everybody's mouth, but must content ourselves with doing our duty and trust in God, for the truth will at last be made manifest. He knows my heart, which is very different from what people think, as you will see some day.[2]

It seems it was the prospect of marriage itself to which the Queen was so averse. Nevertheless her enduring affection for Dudley was clear and she continued to court his attention both for her own pleasure and to keep the more unwelcome suits of foreign princes at arm's length. As Dudley himself acknowledged, 'She is so nimble in her dealings and threads in and out of this business in such a way that her most intimate favourites fail to understand her, and her intentions are variously interpreted.'³

———•———

During the spring and summer of 1565, Cecil made moves to revive the long-running negotiations for the Queen's marriage with the Archduke Charles of Austria. He had come to believe that the archduke's Catholicism, which it was hoped he would forsake, was much less of a threat to the realm than Elizabeth's unmarried state.⁴ However, the Emperor Ferdinand, mindful of how Elizabeth had already once rebuffed his son's suit, met Cecil's overtures with suspicion. In June, when Ferdinand died and was succeeded by his eldest son Maximilian, fresh hopes were raised. The new emperor appointed Adam von Zwetkowich, Baron von Mitterburg, his councillor and gentleman of the chamber, to go to London with specific instructions to discuss terms for the match.⁵

First Zwetkowich was to find out whether or not Elizabeth was disposed to marry and then, most importantly, he was to 'with all means endeavour to discover what people say about the morals, virtues, sentiments and reputation of Her Highness'. As his orders continued, 'should he from sure and certain signs and utterances learn that the virtue of Her Highness is untouched and unimpaired', then if asked he might indicate that the emperor would be willing to instigate negotiations if there was a belief that would not be 'vain and futile'. The archduke would not, as on the last occasion, 'suffer himself to be led by the nose'. However, if he 'should learn, not from conjectures, but from sure judgements and from the general opinion, that the integrity of the morals and life of Her Highness is not such as becomes a Princess, he shall be careful not to say one single word about this matter'.⁶

Fearful of the threat to France of an Anglo-Habsburg alliance, Catherine de Medici proffered her son Charles IX, the King of France, as a rival candidate for Elizabeth's hand.⁷ The marriage of the Protestant Queen of England, then thirty, to the fourteen-year-old Catholic King of France, was an unexpected and ambitious proposal. Charles declared himself keen on Elizabeth and Sir Thomas Smith, the English ambassador in France, believed the French King would make a good husband. He assured the Queen that although the young King was 'pale and not greatly timbered', he seemed 'tractable and wise for his years' and gave 'wittier answers than a man would think'. Smith added in his letter to Elizabeth,

'I dare put myself in pledge to your Highness that your Majesty shall like him.'[8]

Elizabeth was not convinced and told Paul de Foix, the French ambassador, that his King was 'both too big and too small'; in other words, France was too powerful a match for England, and Charles, some sixteen years Elizabeth's junior, was too young. Such a marriage would imperil the independence of her realm, put her in the power of a Catholic and make her an elderly wife to a child of fourteen. 'She would not,' she then explained to de Silva, 'make the world laugh by seeing at the church door an old woman and a child.'[9] Zwetkowich, the emperor's envoy now arrived in England, described how,

> the Queen's jester spoke the truth when he said in English . . . she should not take the King of France, for he was but a boy and babe; but she should take the Archduke Charles and then he was sure that she would have a baby boy. I told the Queen that babes and fools speak the truth and so I hoped that she had now heard the truth, but she only laughed.[10]

Many of Elizabeth's councillors shared her reservations. The Earl of Sussex feared that the King was bound to neglect his older wife by going home, 'and in accordance with the French usage live with pretty girls there, and thus all hope of an heir would be rendered nugatory'.[11] But de Foix argued that all the world 'stood amazed at the wrong she did to the grand endowments that God had given her of beauty, wisdom, virtue and exalted station, by refusing to leave fair posterity to succeed her,' and adding that, 'if such marriage could happen, then would commence the most illustrious lineage that had been known for the last thousand years.'[12] For a time Elizabeth pretended to be considering the proposal, partly to secure a rapprochement with France, and partly to conciliate her own Parliament who never wearied in their petitions for her to marry. By the spring, however, negotiations were effectively over: Charles IX's suit had won very little backing in the Privy Council; the way was clear for the suit of the Archduke Charles.

When Zwetkowich arrived in May, the court was reeling from the news that Mary Queen of Scots was to marry Lord Henry Darnley. The council agreed that 'the only thing of most moment and efficacy to remedy all these perils and many others . . . was to obtain that the Queen Majesty would marry and use therein no long delay'.[13] When Zwetkowich had an audience with the Queen on 20 May she indicated her desire for marriage negotiations to begin:[14] whilst she had 'formerly purposed by all means to remain single . . . in consequence of the insistent pressure that was brought to bear upon her by the Estates of the realm, she was now resolved to marry'.[15] However she would not agree to marry anyone that she had not first seen. Might the archduke now visit, incognito, to see if they took a liking to one another?

'I have through several persons made diligent inquiries concerning the maiden honour and integrity of the Queen,' Zwetkowich reported, 'and have found that she has truly and verily been praised and extolled for her royal honour, and that nothing can be said against her, and all the aspersions against her are but the spawn of envy and malice and hatred.' Dudley is a 'virtuous, pious, courteous and highly moral man,' he continued, 'whom the Queen loves as a sister her brother in all maidenly honour, in most chaste and honest love . . . that she desires to marry him or entertains any but the purest affection is quite out of the question.'[16] Elizabeth had assured Zwetkowich that she was 'mindful of her royal and virginal honour' and that she would 'vindicate herself' to the emperor 'against all the slander that had been cast at her', and she hoped that he would find that she had 'all the time acted in all matters with due decorum and attention'.[17] She said she 'had heard of the great love that the late Emperor Ferdinand had had for his wife, and therefore hoped that the same could be expected of his son.' Zwetkowich assured her that Archduke Charles had inherited the virtues of his father and 'would hold his wedded consort dear all his life long'. Zwetkowich concluded, 'The Queen was pleased to hear this and told me that she had a Lady of the Bedchamber who told her everything and who had said that even if her husband was not handsome, she, the Queen, should be content, if he but loved her and was kind to her.'[18] One might confidently assume that the lady to whom Elizabeth referred was Kat Ashley. Kat had been long married to her husband John and as such could offer Elizabeth the benefit of her experience. Since Elizabeth's early infancy she had guided her with counsel and reassurance.

Despite the Queen's apparent enthusiasm, Zwetkowich remained cynical about Elizabeth's motives, and feared 'subterfuge'. He believed, 'she was determined not to marry and therefore found none who pleased her; that if she were to marry she would take none but the Earl of Leicester'. Indeed, as negotiations went on, rumours continued as to Elizabeth and Leicester's latest indiscretions. Shortly before the arrival of the emperor's envoy, the feud between Dudley and his great enemy, Thomas Howard, the 4th Duke of Norfolk, England's leading nobleman and a cousin of the

Queen, had become very public. When Norfolk and Dudley were playing tennis in front of the Queen, Dudley 'being very hot and sweating', took the Queen's napkin out of her hand and wiped his face. It was an action that implied great intimacy and was highly disrespectful. Norfolk was incensed and threatened to hit Dudley, who he believed was 'too saucy', across the face with a racket. Elizabeth naturally took Dudley's side and was 'offended sore with the duke', one observer recalled.[19]

A delegation of noblemen led by Norfolk later approached Dudley and ordered him to stop touching the Queen or visiting her Bedchamber early in the morning before she was up. Norfolk claimed that Dudley often, 'took upon himself the office of her lady-in-waiting, by handing to her a garment which ought never to have been seen in the hands of her Master of the Horse'. He also accused Dudley of 'kissing her Majesty, when he was not invited thereto'.[20] The Duke of Norfolk threatened Dudley if he did not support the archduke's suit, saying, 'Evil could not fail to befall him since all those who wished to see the Queen married, the whole nation in short, blamed him alone for the delay that had taken place.'[21]

16

Greatly Grieved

One afternoon in May 1565, tensions at court, anxieties about Mary Queen of Scots's marriage and pressures to settle the succession finally got the better of Elizabeth and she erupted with a hysterical outburst. Hurling wild reproaches at Dudley, Cecil and Throckmorton, she claimed that all those who pressed her to marry were in reality seeking her ruin. She knew Mary's marriage would only mean louder calls for her to find a husband and produce an heir and the prospect filled her with dread. Cecil reassured her that no one would force her to do anything against her will and that whatever course she chose to follow, her subjects would always remain loyal. However they both knew that such assurances would do nothing to silence the calls for her to wed.[1]

As fears for the unsettled succession continued, so too did malicious talk. In conversation with de Silva, Elizabeth revealed her frustration at the constant rumours about her conduct and behaviour:

> They charge me with a great many things in my own country and elsewhere, and amongst others, that I show more favour to Robert than is fitting; speaking of me as they might speak of an immodest woman. I am not surprised that the occasion for it should have been given by a young woman and young man of good qualities, to whose merits and goodness I have shown favour, although not so much as he deserves, but God knows how great a slander it is, and a time will come when the world will know it. My life is in the open and I have so many witnesses that I cannot understand how so bad a judgement can have formed of me.[2]

These were difficult months for Elizabeth. As she grew weary with the business of government and the pressures upon her, she relied ever more heavily on the comfort and companionship of her Bedchamber women.

When in the early summer Katherine Knollys fell ill, Elizabeth immediately sent her own physician Dr Robert Huick to attend on her. Not only was Elizabeth concerned as to the seriousness of Katherine's condition but she knew that Katherine needed to regain her health quickly. Indeed the timing of her illness could not have been more inauspicious. In just a few weeks, Katherine's eldest son Henry was to marry Margaret Cave, one of the Queen's maids of honour, at Durham House on the Strand. The Queen was to be the guest of honour and with urgent preparations still to be made it was important that Katherine be restored to full health.

Fortunately Huick's visit appears to have served its purpose and Katherine's condition quickly improved so she could enjoy her son's wedding on 16 July.[3] It was a splendid lavish occasion with plentiful food, entertainments and dancing which continued long into the night. After Katherine's period of ill health and Elizabeth's fear and fretting, it was the perfect event to raise the spirits.

———※———

The Queen was at this time at Richmond, a palace famed for its turrets, its bulbous domes surmounted by gold and silver weather vanes which 'sang' on windy days, and for the beauty of its gardens. Elizabeth referred to the palace as her 'warm box'; its covered passages – paved, glazed and painted with badges of gold, roses and portcullises – connected each building to the next and meant it was not necessary to go outside to enter any of its buildings. The great hall measured a huge one hundred by forty feet, and was decorated with the murals of heroic English kings. The privy lodgings were in a large three-storey stone building comprising twelve rooms, and the extra rooms were used by Elizabeth's most favoured women. The palace grounds covered ten acres, with a large orchard producing magnificent peaches, apples and damsons for the royal household. The royal gardens also supplied salads, herbs to the eighteen kitchens in the palace, whilst rosewater and masses of flowers were sent from Richmond to other palaces.

Then, just two days later after the celebrations of the Knollys' wedding, Elizabeth was thrown into a deep and all-consuming grief. On 18 July, her beloved Kat Ashley, the closest thing Elizabeth had had to a mother, died. Kat had fallen ill some months earlier but had then recovered. Her final illness was quick and her condition rapidly deteriorated. The Queen had spent the previous day at her bedside, and the following morning was told that her most devoted woman was dead. The privy lodgings were immediately thrown into a state of mourning and in quiet whispers and with sombre reflection the Queen and her women shared their grief. A sense of shared loss bound them together as over the following weeks and months they struggled to get used to life without the woman upon whom they had all come to rely.

Zwetkowich wrote to the Emperor Maximilian that the death of Kat Ashley 'grieved the Queen so much that she did not command me to appear until the 22nd of July'. However, even in the midst of her mourning Elizabeth realised the need to continue with the business of government and gave her attention to the proposed marriage with the Archduke Charles. 'On this day,' wrote Zwetkowich, 'I apprised her of Your Imperial Majesty's resolve, in order that she might forget her sorrow. She, however, informed me that in such an important matter she must have time for consideration and I left her in a somewhat more joyous mood.'⁴

The news of Kat Ashley's death quickly spread beyond the court and overseas. Her death 'greatly grieved' the Queen, wrote the Spanish ambassador in his dispatch to Madrid. On receiving de Silva's letter Philip added in the margin, 'What a heretic she was'.⁵ Hugh Fitzwilliam, an English agent at the French court lamented that now 'Mistress Ashley is gone he has no friend about her to make his moan to'.⁶ Her absence was a great loss for those ambassadors and agents who had used her for gossip and information.⁷

Blanche Parry, Elizabeth's longest-serving lady, now became Chief Gentlewoman of the Privy Chamber, an unrivalled position close to the Queen. As her nephew Rowland Vaughan described, the court was now 'under the command of Mistress Blanche Parry'.⁸ Since the earliest days of her life, when Blanche had rocked the princess's cradle, Elizabeth and her devoted Welshwoman had a close bond which evolved and deepened as Elizabeth grew up. They shared a love of books and horses, and until Blanche grew too old and blind, they would often ride out together. To Blanche alone was paid an allowance of 'horse-meat' over and above her ordinary wage, a testament to the Queen's gratitude and affection for her.

With Kat Ashley's passing, Elizabeth now relied on a handful of her other women for day-to-day attendance and for the friendship and comfort which she had long enjoyed with Kat. Frances Newton, the daughter of Sir John Newton from Gloucestershire, had served as a Chamberer in the privy lodgings since the beginning of the reign, before marrying William Brooke, Baron Cobham, in February 1560 at Whitehall Palace.⁹ Alongside her service to Elizabeth, Lady Frances Cobham had six children, all of whom feature along with Lady Frances, her husband and sister in *The Cobham Family* portrait dated 1567. In spite of her frequent pregnancies and absences from court, she rose in the Queen's favour and having returned from her second pregnancy at the end of the previous year, by 1565 she was Mistress of the Robes, with responsibility for the Queen's clothes, a position hitherto occupied by Lady Dorothy Stafford.

Following Kat Ashley's death, Elizabeth became increasingly reliant on Lady Frances who, then pregnant, was not given leave to withdraw from court until her delivery drew near.[10] During her period of confinement at the family home in Kent, Lady Frances, a skilled seamstress, and spent the final weeks of her pregnancy working on some needlework as a New Year's gift for the Queen.[11] She had been working on the dress alongside her great friend Bess St Loe (later to be known as Bess of Hardwick). Bess had been appointed as a Gentlewoman of the Queen's Privy Chamber at the beginning of the reign but had lost Elizabeth's favour over her alleged involvement in Katherine Grey's illicit marriage five years before, and had been dismissed from the Queen's service. Whilst in the years that followed her relationship with Elizabeth became amicable once more, she was not restored to her place in the Queen's trusted entourage. Now, in a letter to Bess at her estate at Chatsworth in Derbyshire, Lady Cobham described how she was making the sleeves 'of a wideness that will best suit the Queen . . . they are fine and strange. I have sent you enclosed the braid, and lengths of caulle [netting] for the Queen of the same work, for your to suit with the sleeves . . . The fashion is much altered since you were here. Ten yards is enough for the ruffs of the neck and hands.'[12] Lady Frances's son Henry was born on 22 November 1566 and within weeks Frances was back at court having left her baby in the care of a wet nurse.

In the months of mourning that followed Ashley's death there was also an event of much excitement. In November 1565, Anne Russell, the Earl of Bedford's sixteen-year-old daughter, who had become a maid of honour soon after Elizabeth's accession, married Ambrose Dudley, Earl of Warwick, twenty years her senior and brother of the Queen's favourite, in the chapel royal at Whitehall. The marriage was a great court occasion and represented the coming together of two leading Protestant families at court. Anne, now the Countess of Warwick, was promoted to the position of Gentlewoman of the Privy Chamber and thereafter remained in close attendance on the Queen who came to regard her as a dear friend and confidante. Her niece, Anne Clifford, would later claim that her aunt was 'more beloved and in greater favour with the Queen than any other woman in the Kingdom, and no less in the whole Court and the Queen's dominions'.[13]

<hr />

On 29 July 1565 the court moved to Windsor. Elizabeth tended to stay here only in the summer months as the old castle was particularly cold and damp and difficult to heat. A stone terrace had been added beneath the windows of the Queen's apartments along which she could 'take the air' before supper or briskly walk each morning 'to get up a heat'.[14] In Windsor Great Park she would indulge her passion for riding and hunting. She loved to show off her horsemanship in the chase. As Guzman de Silva described, 'she went so hard that she tired everybody out, and as for the ladies and courtiers who were with her, they were all put to shame. There was more work than pleasure in it for them.'[15] Elizabeth and her ladies would also sometimes shoot game from specially constructed stands north-east of the castle.

At the end of August, Zwetkowich and de Silva came to Windsor to take formal leave of the Queen. Elizabeth had specified the conditions for a marriage and Zwetokowich was now to report back to Vienna.[16] Given that the ambassadors arrived at the palace late in the evening and were to depart the following day, they were allocated just one chamber to share. Elizabeth was shocked when she learned of the arrangements, believing it was disrespectful not to have given them separate lodgings. 'My people shall learn in a way they shall not forget how you are to be treated,' the Queen raged and, turning to the ambassadors said, 'you shall occupy my own chamber and I will give you my key.'[17] Having reassured her that no slight had been felt, the ambassadors went on to their own lodgings whilst Elizabeth remained in hers.

The next morning Dudley took the ambassadors for a tour of Windsor Park. As they made their way back to the palace along the footpath by the riverside, they passed the building which contained the Queen's privy lodgings. Underneath the Queen's Bedchamber windows, Robert Dudley's fool, who walked with them, shouted so loudly that the Queen came to the window only in her nightgown. An hour and a half later, having dressed and been suitably made up, she came downstairs to greet the ambassadors, and no doubt chide Dudley and his fool.[18] On another occasion, later in her reign, Gilbert Talbot, son of the Earl of Shrewsbury, was wandering in the tiltyard at Greenwich at eight o'clock in the morning and caught Elizabeth looking out of the window:

> My eye was full towards her; she showed to be greatly ashamed
> thereof, for that she was unready in her nightstuff. So, when she
> saw me after dinner as she went to walk, she gave me a great fillip
> on the forehead, and told the Lord Chamberlain ... how I had
> seen her that morning, and how much ashamed thereof she was.[19]

———·———

Soon after arriving at Windsor, Elizabeth had received the news that Mary Queen of Scots had secretly married Henry Darnley at Holyrood Palace in Edinburgh on 29 July.[20] The threat to the Queen's throne escalated significantly; the two Catholic claimants to the English succession were now husband and wife.[21] As Thomas Randolph, Elizabeth's envoy, noted wryly, they 'went not to bed, to signify unto the world that it was no lust [that] moved them to marry, but only the necessity of her country, not long to leave it destitute of an heir'.[22]

Relations between Mary and Elizabeth were now in tatters. 'All their sisterly familiarity was ceased, and instead thereof nothing but jealousies, suspicions and hatred.'[23] For the English government, the marriage represented an explicitly aggressive move for the crown of England. Elizabeth refused to acknowledge Darnley as Mary's husband or as King of Scotland. Mary now began to openly display her Catholicism in Edinburgh, giving hope and heart to Catholics both in Scotland and in England.[24] Two years before, the Pope had issued a resolution calling on faithful Catholics to assassinate Queen Elizabeth. A pardon and a 'perpetual annuity' in heaven would be granted 'to any that would assault the Queen, or to any cook, brewer, baker, vintner, physician, grocer, chirurgeon, or of any other calling whatsoever that make her away'.[25] Mary's marriage now heightened fears of all such assassination attempts.[26]

17

Suspicious Mind

Whilst at Windsor, Elizabeth received news of a second unwelcome marriage. One of the Grey sisters, nineteen-year-old Mary – the shortest woman at the court and described by de Silva as 'crook backed and very ugly' – had secretly married the six-foot Thomas Keyes, the Queen's Sergeant Porter, responsible for palace security and expected to be of unimpeachable loyalty. He was a widower and twice her age.[1] They had married at nine o'clock on the evening of 16 July 1565, when Elizabeth had left court to attend the wedding of Henry Knollys at Durham House. In Keyes's room over the Watergate at Whitehall, eleven friends and relations had gathered by candlelight as the couple exchanged vows and he gave his tiny bride a tiny wedding ring. They celebrated with wine 'and banqueting meats' after which Thomas and Mary were left alone and went to bed. When Elizabeth returned to the palace in the early hours of the next morning, the couple had returned to their own chambers and the Queen was none the wiser.

A month later, with Elizabeth still reeling from the news that Mary Queen of Scots had married Darnley, word of Mary Grey's marriage leaked out. 'Here is an unhappy chance and monstrous,' wrote Cecil to a friend; 'the Sergeant Porter, being the biggest gentleman of this court, has secretly married the Lady Mary Grey; the least of all the court . . . the offence is very great.'[2] Elizabeth was furious.[3] Lady Mary was imprisoned at Windsor and Keyes was put in solitary confinement in the Fleet, the notorious London prison, his huge frame painfully squashed into a small cell.[4]

The tensions at court around the marriages of Mary Grey and Mary Queen of Scots, not to mention Elizabeth's grief at the death of Kat

Ashley, impacted on her relationship with Dudley. As Cecil wrote to Sir Thomas Smith, 'The Queen's Majesty is fallen into some misliking with my Lord of Leicester and therewith he is much dismayed. She is sorry for the loss of time and so is every good subject.'[5]

In August, Elizabeth began a flirtation with Sir Thomas Heneage, a good-looking and trusted courtier. As de Silva reported, the Queen 'has begun to smile on a gentleman of the Bedchamber named Heneage which has attracted a good deal of attention'.[6] Even though Heneage was a married man, Dudley still regarded him as a serious threat and jealously resented his rise to favour. When Dudley confronted the Queen directly, 'she was apparently much annoyed at the conversation'. Cecil believed Elizabeth's flirtation with Heneage was 'baseless nonsense' and the Queen 'made a show of it for purposes of her own'.[7] Dudley stormed off to his chamber in 'deep melancholy' where he remained for four days 'showing by his despair he could no longer live'.'[8]

Dudley retaliated by lavishing attention on Lettice Knollys, the twenty-four-year-old daughter of Elizabeth's faithful servant and cousin Katherine Knollys. Although she was named as a Gentlewoman of the Privy Chamber on Elizabeth's accession, Lettice had withdrawn from court after her marriage to Walter Devereux in December 1560. Over the next few years she gave birth to five children in quick succession, although still occasionally attended court. It was during her visit to Windsor in the summer of 1565 when heavily pregnant with her son Robert, that Dudley began paying court to her. When Elizabeth learned of Dudley's flirtation she flew into 'a great temper' and, according to the Spanish ambassador, 'upbraided' Dudley 'with what had taken place ... in very bitter words'. Cecil wrote in his diary that, 'the Queen's Majesty seemed to be much offended with the Earl of Leicester, and so she wrote an obscure sentence in a book at Windsor'.[9] The book survives and Elizabeth's inscription reads:

> No crooked leg, no bleared eye
> > No part deformed out of kind,
> > Nor yet so ugly half can be
> > As is the inward, suspicious mind.
> Your loving mistress, Elizabeth R.[10]

Elizabeth would undoubtedly have been jealous of Dudley's interest in any other woman, but the fact that Lettice was her second cousin and described by the Spanish ambassador as 'one of the best looking ladies of the court' made Dudley's betrayal even more keenly felt.

Philip of Spain read the dispatches from his ambassadors in London with great interest. 'The whole affair and its sequel,' he wrote, 'clearly show that the Queen is in love with Robert, and for this reason, and in case at last she may take him for her husband, it will be very expedient to keep him in hand.'[11] Elizabeth reportedly told Bruener, the imperial envoy, 'I have never said hitherto to anybody that I would not marry the Earl of Leicester, but Lord Robert was married then and there was no possibility of treating such a thing at the time.'[12] At Christmas, de Foix, the French ambassador, reported that Dudley had asked Elizabeth to marry him, to which she had responded that he need only wait until Candlemas in February before she would 'satisfy him'.[13] Then on New Year's night, de Foix told his Spanish counterpart that Elizabeth had slept with Dudley in her Bedchamber at Whitehall. But, as de Silva wrote in his dispatch, 'the author of the rumour was a Frenchman who is strongly against the archduke's marriage'. By now the match with the young French King Charles IX had been abandoned and the French were supporting Dudley's suit.

Both Dudley and Heneage were in attendance on the Queen during the Christmas and New Year festivities and the drama at the English court was closely followed by diplomats abroad. Giacomo Surian, the Venetian ambassador in France, wrote to the Doge and Senate that Sir Thomas Smith, the English envoy in Paris, had described how Heneage was chosen on Twelfth Night as King of the Revels, which allowed him to rule the court for the evening and direct the festivities. In one of the games, Heneage instructed Dudley to ask the Queen, 'which was the most difficult to erase from the mind: an evil opinion created by a wicked informer, or jealousy?' Elizabeth replied that both were difficult, but jealousy was harder. Dudley threatened to chastise Heneage with a stick (rather than a sword as he regarded him as an inferior). The Queen told Dudley that, 'if by her favour he had become insolent, he should soon reform and that she would love him just as she had, at first raised him'. Again Dudley withdrew to his chamber 'in deep melancholy', before the Queen, 'moved by pity', restored him to favour.[14]

—•—

It was to be a short-lived reconciliation. Early the following year, after a series of rows with Elizabeth, Dudley sought her permission to leave court on the pretence of visiting his sister Lady Huntingdon who had fallen ill. 'He thinks that his absence may bring the Queen to her senses,' reported de Silva, 'and even may cause her to take steps regarding her marriage with him; although Leicester thinks that if she forgets to call him back and treats him like she treats everything, he will return to his house for a short time, and thus will not lose his place'.[15] It was the first time in years that he had been away from the Queen's side. Initially Elizabeth seemed glad to let him go and told her cousin Henry Carey, Lord Hunsdon, that 'it hath often been said that you should be my Master of the Horse, but now it is likely to come true'.[16] As Dudley remained absent from court, gossip began to spread. 'Of my Lord of Leicester's absence, and of his return to favour,' Cecil wrote to Sir Thomas Smith in Paris, 'if your man tell you the tales of court or city, they be fond [foolish] and many untrue. Briefly, I affirm that the Queen's Majesty may be by malicious tongues not well reported; but in truth she herself is blameless, and hath no spot of evil intent.'[17]

In mid-March, Elizabeth became ill. De Silva told the Spanish King, 'she is so thin that a doctor who has seen her tells me her bones may be counted, and that a stone is forming in her kidneys. He thinks she is going into consumption, although doctors sometimes make mistakes, especially with young people.'[18] For some days the Queen lay in her Bedchamber overlooking the Thames, weak and lifeless. The Queen's bed once again became the focus of the court, as rumours and prophecies circulated that her death was imminent. This time there was no Mary Sidney on hand. She had left for Ireland with her husband Sir Henry, who had been appointed as Lord Deputy of Ireland. With his sister absent and the Queen's desire for him undiminished, Dudley was advised by a friend to hurry back to court as soon as he could: 'Touching your coming here, I hear diverse opinions; some say tarry, others, come with speed. I say, if you come not hastily, no good will grow, as I find Her Majesty so mislikes your absence that she is not disposed to hear of anything that may do you good.'[19] He returned, only to leave again on bad terms with the Queen a few weeks later.

Elizabeth grew increasingly resentful of Dudley's errant behaviour; she wished him back at her side permanently. Blanche Parry urged him to make a 'hasty repair' on account of 'Her Majesty's unkindness taken with your long absence'.[20] Having tried to assure Elizabeth that he would soon return, Blanche warned Dudley that the Queen 'much marvelled she had not heard from you since last Monday'. Dudley was assured by his agent at court that in the absence of Dorothy Bradbelt, their other ally amongst Elizabeth's ladies, 'our best friend in the Privy Chamber is Mrs Blanche'.[21] When he was away, Dudley relied on Blanche to intervene with Elizabeth on his behalf and to keep him privy to the Queen's desires; no one knew Elizabeth better. By the end of May, Dudley was back by her side.

18

The Elixir of Life

On 7 February 1565, Cornelius de Lannoy, an alchemist from the Netherlands, wrote to Elizabeth offering her an unimaginable gift. He claimed to be able to transmute base metals like lead into gold and distil the elixir of life, a mythical potion that cured all infirmities and brought eternal life.[1] It was all that Elizabeth needed to safeguard her realm. The Philosopher's Stone, the agent that was believed not only to make alchemical gold, but heal disease and bring immortality, had been the elusive dream of alchemists over the centuries. The compound called 'pantaura' which de Lannoy promised to distil, incorporated the virtues of 'the soul of the world' to instantly heal diseases, maintain 'vigour of limbs, clearness of memory' and be the 'best and surest remedy again all kinds of poison'.[2] It held out the prospect of achieving the beauty that Elizabeth's women sought to artificially create each day, preserving her health, and making a reality of Elizabeth's motto *Semper Eadem* – 'Always the Same'.[3]

The Queen received de Lannoy's letter with keen interest and enthusiasm. Her knowledge of 'all parts of Philosophy' and 'favour of science', including alchemy, was known throughout Europe.[4] Alchemists dedicated books to her and on at least one occasion she received an alchemical book as a New Year's gift.[5] She invested in distilling houses at Hampton Court and one Millicent Franckwell also distilled in her Privy Chamber, for a fee of £40 per annum, what was described as 'the Queen's medicine' and 'Queen Elizabeth's potion'. This was thought to be a purgative she used twice a year.[6] As testament to her patronage of alchemy, an emblem was later built into a window at Whitehall Palace describing her as the 'true elixir', the ultimate icon of perfection and immortality.[7]

Whilst alchemy was a felony punishable by death and forfeiture of goods, it was a practice highly prized by the Queen and her court and would-be practitioners were required to obtain a royal dispensation.[8] De Lannoy offered to transmute gold worth £33,000 and precious stones on an annual basis.[9] Faced by an empty treasury and the pressure of war, both Elizabeth and Cecil wanted to believe de Lannoy's claims. He was granted a generous £120 pension per annum, living expenses for his family and servants, and an alchemical laboratory was set up for him in Somerset House in London under the supervision of Cecil's agent Armagil Waad.[10]

Later that year, Thomas Charnock, an alchemist from Somerset, wrote a *Book Dedicated vnto the Queen's Majesty,* in which he too sketched out a scheme to transmute gold for her and discover the Philosopher's Stone.[11] He promised to produce a medicine, 'an elixir', that would 'prolong her grace's most royal life ... heal more diseases than any other medicine of physic, gladden the mind, comfort youth, renew age and will not allow blood to putrefy or phlegm to have domination nor choler to become melancholy and exalted'.[12] Despite having a wife and children, Charnock urged the Queen to commit him to the [White] Tower where he would be cloistered to complete his work. He even offered his own beheading on Tower Hill as guarantee of his scheme.[13] However, Charnock was disappointed to discover that he was too late: de Lannoy was already installed in Somerset House and at work to deliver on his promises of health and riches.[14]

Having promised quick results but with nothing to show after a few months, de Lannoy began complaining about the poor quality of the English laboratory supplies which he claimed were of 'insufficient strength to sustain the force of his great fires' and hindering his process. He informed the Queen that he had sent to Antwerp and Kassel for suitable replacements to ensure his success. Elizabeth and Cecil both readily accepted his explanation for the delay and showed no concern that de Lannoy's evasions masked fraud.[15] They continued to believe de Lannoy's claims and keenly anticipated the fruits of his labours. Indeed it was a growing sense that de Lannoy was being distracted from his task by the presence of a young Swedish princess now living adjacent to Somerset House, rather than doubts about the efficacy of his promises, that led to de Lannoy being placed under careful watch.

———◦———

Princess Cecilia of Sweden, the younger sister of King Erik XIV, arrived in England in September 1565. She had come to visit the Queen, about whom she had heard so much, and to persuade Elizabeth to accept her brother's hand in marriage.[16] The princess was an attractive, learned woman with a keen sense of adventure and a taste for extravagant living.

During the past few years she had been at the centre of a series of scandals at the Swedish court. At the wedding of her eldest sister, Princess Catherine to Edward II of Ostfriesland in 1559, a man had been spotted climbing into her window several nights in a row. When the matter was investigated, the brother of the groom was found in Cecilia's room half-naked. He was thrown into gaol and, according to some sources, castrated.

In 1564, the princess was married to Christopher II, Margrave of Baden-Rodemachern. Immediately after the wedding they travelled to England. After a circuitous journey that took more than a year, they arrived in September 1565 and were warmly received by the Lord and Lady Cobham who accompanied them to London. The arrival of Princess Cecilia, who was by then heavily pregnant, was greeted with great enthusiasm. As de Silva, the Spanish ambassador, wrote:

> On the 11th instant [of September] the King of Sweden's sister entered London at 2 o'clock in the afternoon. She is very far advanced in pregnancy, and was dressed in a black velvet robe with a mantle of black cloth of silver, and wore on her head a golden crown ... she had with her six Ladies dressed in crimson taffeta with mantles of the same.[17]

She was lodged at Bedford House in London, which had been furnished with beds and hangings belonging to the Queen. Four days after her arrival in the city she gave birth to her first child, Edward. His christening took place with great ceremony at Westminster Abbey with the Queen, the Archbishop of Canterbury and the Duke of Norfolk standing as godparents. Thereafter Cecilia and her entourage became regular visitors at Whitehall and were welcomed at court banquets and entertainments.

Cecilia was to remain in England for more than a year, but after several months her extravagant lifestyle caught up with her and she fell heavily into debt. When she announced her intention to return to Sweden, the Queen demanded that she pay her creditors in full and sell whatever she could to raise the funds. Meanwhile her husband, who had already tried to flee the country, was arrested at Rochester.

It was then that the princess, whose lodgings were close to Somerset House, sought out Cornelius de Lannoy. He had formerly served the King of Sweden and his ambitious alchemical claims drew Cecilia to him. Now desperate to pay her creditors, Cecilia petitioned him for help. In mid-January 1566, de Lannoy agreed to lend her £10,000 and a further £13,000 in early March. When Cecil learned of the bond between them he worried that Lannoy was not focussing on his work for the Queen and that the development of the elixir might be impeded. All future correspondence between de Lannoy and Cecilia was intercepted.[18] When Elizabeth was informed as to de Lannoy's agreement with Cecilia she immediately forbade the Dutchman to have any further contact with the princess. Aware that he had aroused the Queen's suspicions, de Lannoy wrote to her swearing 'on the Holy Gospels' that he would 'carry through successfully' his promise to produce the elixir and would 'hold no communication' with Cecilia. But by the end of March, Waad believed that both de Lannoy and Cecilia were plotting to escape to the Netherlands.[19] On discovering their designs de Lannoy and his laboratory were removed to the Tower. Yet still Elizabeth remained confident that the alchemist would fulfil his promises.[20] Indeed Waad claimed that de Lannoy had already created the alchemical elixir and planned to take it with him. However, if de Lannoy could be caught as he made his escape, 'her Majesty shall come by the Art [the method] and the thing itself'.[21]

Finally Princess Cecilia left for Sweden in April 1566, declaring that she was 'glad enough to get out of this country'.[22] De Lannoy remained under close surveillance, with Elizabeth and her councillors waiting anxiously for the elixir he had promised. In July he addressed a letter to the Queen:

> I know how grievous this delay must be to you. I have nothing to offer you in this kingdom but my life, which would be a heavy loss to my innocent wife. As to the business of transmuting metals and precious gems to greater perfection, either the work has been disturbed or some wicked man had been present, or I have erred through syncopation. Pray permit me to write to my friends for help, for I can indubitably perform what I have promised.[23]

De Lannoy's attempts to prove his innocence failed and in July 1566 he was confined to the Tower of London charged with having 'greatly abused her Majesty'.[24] Waad was sent to examine the alchemist and reported that de Lannoy admitted having made mistakes, but only because of the demands of haste from the Queen, Cecil and Dudley.[25] In desperate letters, de Lannoy assured them that if he was allowed to write to his friends for help, he would be able to fulfil his promises within a month and produce a 'medicine' capable of producing over thirty million times its own weight in gold.[26]

After leaving the distressed alchemist to stew for several weeks, Cecil wrote to Waad and Sir Francis Jobson, the Lieutenant of the Tower, ordering them to arrange the immediate resumption of de Lannoy's alchemical operations within the Tower and his furnaces were moved there.[27] But it appears that de Lannoy continued to deceive Cecil and the Queen, and by early 1567, Cecil's patience was exhausted. Again de Lannoy defended his process and promised the Principal Secretary that he would 'transmute lead into gold with only a further two days' work'.[28] It was all too late. In February, Cecil recorded in his diary that Cornelius de Lannoy had been imprisoned for 'abusing the Q[ueen's] Majesty in Somerset House in promising to make the Elixir' and 'to convert any Metal into Gold'.[29]

While Cecil continued to urge the patronage of other alchemists, Elizabeth was reluctant to pursue another alchemical dream; as Cecil explained, she 'will in no wise hear of such offers, which she thinketh are but chargeable without Fruit'.[30]

19

Barren Stock

On New Year's Day 1566 the announcement was made at the Scottish court that Mary Queen of Scots was pregnant.[1] She was in her third month. Whilst Elizabeth had been waiting for de Lannoy to produce his elixir of unlimited riches and eternal life to secure her hold on the English throne, her Scottish rival's pregnancy now promised a more certain outcome. Queen Mary was now twenty-three, married and pregnant. Elizabeth was thirty-two, with no prospect of a match and with her child-bearing years fading fast. The Queen reacted by urgently reviving marriage negotiations with the Archduke Charles, and by sending an envoy to encourage him to visit England.[2] Around the same time, de Silva reported that he had received information so 'strange and fickle', that the Queen had expressed a renewed interest in the French match with Charles IX, King of France.[3]

But as Mary continued in her pregnancy, her relationship with Lord Darnley grew ever more embittered. As Randolph wrote on 13 February, 'I know now for certain that this Queen repenteth her marriage, that she hateth the King and all his kin.'[4] Darnley had proved to be a violent drunkard and he had become convinced that David Rizzio, Mary's Italian secretary with whom Darnley himself 'would lie sometime in one bed together', was the father of Mary's unborn child.[5] On Saturday 9 March, fuelled with alcohol and murderous ambition, Darnley led a group of nobles into Mary's Bedchamber where they found Rizzio and fatally stabbed him with their daggers. A murder had been committed at the very heart of the royal palace.

Elizabeth was shocked by news of the events that had been played out in Mary's private apartments. De Silva described Elizabeth's 'great sorrow' and her 'desire to assist the Queen of Scotland'.[6] She told the ambassador that if she had been Mary and faced with the assault on Rizzio and insult to herself, she 'would have taken her husband's dagger and stabbed him with it' – although she added that she would not want Philip II to think that if her current suitor, the Archduke Charles, were to become her husband she would be ready to stab him.[7]

The murder in Mary Queen of Scots's apartments added to the climate of fear at Elizabeth's court. The locks were changed on the doors of her Privy Chamber and Bedchamber at all her palaces. 'The Queen has ordered all the keys of doors leading to the chambers to be taken away and the only entrance in by one door. Great care has been ordered in the guard of her house,' noted de Silva. 'I do not know whether the Scotch business is the cause of this, or if there have been any signs of disaffection in the city which has made a special guard necessary.'[8]

———•———

In May 1566, Elizabeth fell ill again, this time with a fever. Sir James Melville described how 'no man believed any other but death to be the end of it, all England being the overthrow in a great perplexity'.[9] Elizabeth wrote an embittered letter to Dudley, petitioning him to return to court and he professed his despair at the Queen's unkind manner and harsh treatment towards him: 'If many days service and not a few years proof have made trial of unmovable fidelity enough without notable offences what shall I think of all that past favour which in some unspeakable sort remained towards me.' 'In times past,' he admitted, 'it would have been of great comfort to receive a letter from the Queen,' but the situation had 'so changed as I dare scarce now think what I have been told before to say and write.'

Instead of writing to her in person, Dudley requested that Throckmorton 'give humble thanks' to Elizabeth, 'for the pain taken with her own hands, although I could wish it had been of any other's report or writings; then I might yet have remained in some hope of mistaking'. The contents of the Queen's letter had so upset him, he said, 'it makes me another man, but towards them ever faithful and best wishing, whilst my life shall last'. Dudley added a desperate postscript: 'I see I need not to make so great haste home, when no good opinion is conceived of me; either a cave or in a corner of oblivion, or a sepulchre for perpetual rest, were best homes I could wish to return to.'[10] It was typical of the man: melodramatic and attention-seeking; he knew that the Queen would want him to return. Despite his initial refusal to do so, he did write directly to Elizabeth and signed his letter with a new cipher – a black heart representing his grief. After reading it three times, Elizabeth was reported to have shown 'sundry affections, some merry, some sorrowful, some betwixt both'. Within days her favourite was back at court.[11]

Cecil tried to reconcile himself to the idea that the Queen might yet marry Robert Dudley, although he continued to believe that the marriage had few benefits to England and he favoured a match with the Archduke Charles. He collected his thoughts in a memorandum entitled, '*De Matrimonial Reginae Anglia cum extern Principe*', and in two columns listed, 1. 'Reasons to move the Queen to accept Archduke Charles', and 2. 'Reasons against Earl of Leicester'. In nearly every respect Dudley appeared less desirable: he was of common birth, he would bring nothing to the marriage, his marriage had been childless and he might prove sterile. In the section 'In likelihood to love his wife', Cecil wrote: this would be a 'carnal marriage' and such marriages begin in pleasure and end in sorrow. If the marriage went ahead, 'it will be thought that the slanderous speeches of the Queen with the earl have been true'.[12]

On 19 June, Sir James Melville set out from Edinburgh Castle with the news that Mary Queen of Scots had given birth to a healthy baby boy.[13] On his arrival in London, Melville went straight to Cecil's house to tell him, and Cecil immediately went to the court at Greenwich to tell the Queen. He arrived at the palace just after supper, as Elizabeth was enjoying her ladies' dancing. Suddenly, 'all merriness was laid aside for the night; all present marvelling what might move so sudden a change for the Queen did sit down, with her hand upon her cheek, bursting out to some of her ladies that the Queen of Scots was lighter of a fair son, while she was of barren stock.'[14]

When the following morning Melville came to court for his official audience, Elizabeth hid her true feelings. She welcomed Melville with a 'merry volt', a French dance, doubtless to demonstrate her extreme jollity, health and vigour. She then proceeded to tell him that 'Queen her sister's delivery of a fair son' was 'joyful news' which had 'recovered her out of a heavy sickness which had holden her for fifteen days'. In vivid detail, Melville then recounted to Elizabeth the Scottish Queen's long and traumatic labour. It was 'dear bought with the peril of her life, for I said that she was so sore handled that she wished she had never been married'.[15] This account of the birth was, Melville later admitted, a ploy to put Elizabeth off the idea of marriage and childbirth altogether.

The birth of Prince James, her son and heir, strengthened Mary's cause immeasurably and Elizabeth, now thirty-three, was besieged by demands to marry and finally settle the succession.[16] One petition entitled *The Common Cry of Englishmen made to the most noble lady, Queen Elizabeth, and the High Court of Parliament* made a dramatic case: 'If you O Queen do die ... void of issue and wanting a known successor and ordered succession, as the case now standeth, what good can continue? What evil shall not come? ... This lack is that rack whereon England rubbeth, the same where it sticketh and sinketh daily to destruction.' It continued: 'It is uncertain whether you shall marry. It is uncertain whether you shall have issue in your marriage. It is uncertain whether your issue shall live to succeed you, if you have one.'[17] Dr William Huick, Elizabeth's physician, was accused of having frightened the Queen from marriage by persuading her that childbirth would be hurtful to the constitution and delicate frame of her body, and now he was cursed by certain members of the Commons for being 'a dissuader of marriage'.[18]

On Saturday 12 October, the Privy Council broached the issue of marriage directly with the Queen herself. Thomas Howard, the Duke of Norfolk, as the most senior member of the nobility, reminded her of the petitions that both houses had presented to her in Parliament, and that they were still waiting for a response. They begged her to allow the upcoming session of Parliament to discuss both the marriage and the succession. Elizabeth's response was emphatic: the succession was her business and she had no wish for their counsel. She had no desire to be 'buried alive', as she believed her sister Mary I had been in the dying days of her reign, when people flocked to Elizabeth at Hatfield. As to her marriage, 'they knew quite well that it was not far off'. And with that she left the chamber.[19]

When Parliament met it was suggested that the granting of desperately needed funds would be conditional on Elizabeth either agreeing to marry or settle the succession. Elizabeth was outraged. The Commons, she declared, would never have dared attempt 'such things during the life of her father'. As for the Lords, they had no right to 'impede her affairs' and 'what they asked was nothing less than wishing her to dig her grave before she was dead'.[20] When the Lords and Commons then made a joint appeal to the Queen, Elizabeth lashed out at Norfolk, who presented the petition, calling him a traitor. And when she saw that Dudley was part of the delegation she became distraught, saying she had assumed that even, 'if all the world would have abandoned her he would not have done so'. She now forbade him to appear before her.[21]

Later, Elizabeth complained to de Silva of Dudley's ingratitude, especially 'after she had shown him so much kindness and favour that even her honour had suffered for the sake of honouring him'. She was now glad, she admitted, of having 'so good an opportunity of sending him away'.[22] Her anger with Dudley was, as usual, short-lived; when, with convenient timing, the earl fell ill, Elizabeth softened. By early December she told de Silva that she now believed Dudley had 'acted for the best, and that he was deceived'. As the ambassador subsequently explained, 'she is quite certain that he would sacrifice his life for hers, and that if one of them had to die, he would willingly be the one'.[23]

Finally Elizabeth responded to Parliament's petition and before a deputation of some thirty members of the Lords and Commons she delivered what would become one of her most celebrated speeches:

> As for my own part, I care not for death; for all men are mortal. And though I be a woman, yet I have as good a courage, answerable to my place, as ever my father had. I am your anointed Queen. I will never be by violence constrained to do anything. I thank God I am endowed with such qualities that if I were turned out of the realm in my petticoat, I were able to live in any place in Christendom.

Elizabeth made clear that only she would decide if and whom she should marry and whether she named an heir. Marriage and the succession were her prerogative and she would not be browbeaten by her Parliament. She did, however, give some cause to hope:

> I will never break the word of a Prince, spoken in public place, for my honour's sake. And therefore I say again, I will marry as soon as I can conveniently, if God take not him away with whom I mind to marry, or myself, or else some other great let happen.[24]

Her words seemed to signal that she would be willing to discuss marriage negotiations with the Archduke Charles, and in June the following year, after several months of delay, an embassy led by the Earl of Sussex left for Vienna to commence talks. Once again religion proved to be a stumbling block though for a time a compromise agreement was sought in which the archduke would hear mass in the privacy of his own chamber and accompany Elizabeth to Protestant church services. However, there was little enthusiasm from either side for such an arrangement and when the prospect of the match was discussed in the Privy

Council, the opposition led by Dudley and Sir Francis Knollys left Elizabeth in no doubt that marriage to the archduke would be always vehemently opposed.

By late 1567 the negotiations were ruined and Sussex returned home in the New Year bitter that Dudley and the other opponents of the marriage had used the pretext of religion to cover their own self-interested motives to the detriment of the realm: 'When subjects begin to deny princes titles for private respects, it seems to me good reason and counsel that the Queen's Majesty should look to her own surety and make her self strong against such as be so cold in her marriage.'[25]

In December 1566 the Scottish court celebrated the baptism of Prince James with spectacular festivities at Sterling Castle. The birth held out the promise of a settled future in Scotland and a stronger claim on the English throne. Yet such hopes for the future belied a far bleaker reality.

In the months following Rizzio's assassination, James Hepburn, the Earl of Bothwell, had assumed a position of great favour close to the Queen, and her relationship with Darnley had grown steadily worse. On the night of 9 February 1567, a violent explosion resounded throughout Edinburgh. The house in Kirk o' Field, where Darnley had been sleeping, was blown apart by a huge quantity of gunpowder and razed to the ground. The bodies of Darnley and his servant were found lying nearby in the orchard – not killed by the blast, but strangled. The news quickly spread across the border and throughout the courts of Europe. Suspicions began to be voiced that Mary had been complicit in the murder.

Elizabeth was horrified and wrote immediately to Mary assuring her cousin of her support, 'Madame, My ears have been so deafened and my understanding so grieved and my heart so affrighted to hear the dreadful news of the abominable murder of your husband and my killed cousin that I scarcely have the wits to write about it.' She added, 'I cannot dissemble that I am more sorrowful for you than for him.' Drawing on her own experience of malicious talk in the wake of Amy Robsart's death, she wrote earnestly,

> I exhort you, I counsel you, and I beseech you to take this thing so
> much to heart that you will not fear to touch even him which you
> have nearest to you [Bothwell] if the thing touches him and that

no persuasion will prevent you from making an example out of this
to the world: that you are both a noble princess and a loyal wife.[26]

At this moment of great crisis in Mary's life, Elizabeth offered her
Stuart cousin support and solidarity. 'Every day,' de Silva wrote to Philip
II, 'it becomes clearer that the Queen of Scotland must take steps to prove
that she had no hand in the death of her husband, if she is to prosper in
her claims to the succession here'.[27]

Such advice was not to be heeded. Rather than act against Bothwell,
one of the prime suspects in Darnley's murder, just four months after the
deed, Mary married him. The ceremony took place in the early hours of
the morning on 15 May at the Palace of Holyroodhouse with only a
handful of witnesses in attendance.[28] Her decision to wed spelled disaster
for her rule in Scotland. Suspicions about her involvement in Darnley's
murder united Catholic and Protestant lords in opposition to her and by
July she was forced to abdicate. James became King and a regency council
led by the Earl of Moray, Mary's half-brother, was appointed to rule
during his minority.

Mary, meanwhile, was taken to the island fortress of Lochleven.
Elizabeth was incensed at the action taken by the Scottish lords against
their sovereign Queen, 'a precedent most perilous for any Prince', and
demanded that her cousin be restored to her throne.[29]

20

Wicked Intentions

In January 1568, Katherine Grey fell seriously ill. She had been moved to several different residences since her release from the Tower in 1563, before finally being detained at Cockfield Hall, in Yoxford, Suffolk, home of Sir Owen Hopton. Having been forcibly separated from her husband, she had sunk into a deep melancholy and, hardly eating, her health steadily deteriorated. Elizabeth was finally persuaded to send her own physician, Dr Symondes, to Cockfield Hall where he found Katherine close to death. As she lay dying she petitioned Hopton to deliver messages to the Queen, asking for her forgiveness for marrying without her consent, and begging her to 'be good unto my children and not impute my fault unto them'.[1] She died on 27 January 1568.[2] As de Silva reported, 'The Queen expressed sorrow to me at her death, but it is not believed that she feels it, as she was afraid of her.'[3]

Four months after Katherine Grey's death, Mary Queen of Scots, now Elizabeth's strongest rival for the throne, orchestrated a daring escape from Lochleven Castle, and fled over the Scottish border into England. She crossed the Solway Firth in a fishing boat and eventually landed at Workington in Cumberland. Mary had made her journey to England confident that Elizabeth would show her mercy and restore her by armed force to the Scottish throne.[4] It would prove to be a fateful decision. Elizabeth immediately ordered that Mary should be kept under close guard at Carlisle Castle while she debated with her council over what to do. De Silva summed up the dilemma that Elizabeth now faced: 'If this Queen has her way now, they will be obliged to treat the Queen of Scots as a sovereign . . . If they keep her as if in prison, it will probably scandalise all neighbouring princes, and if she remain free and able to communicate with her friends, great suspicions will be aroused.'[5]

Mary's flight into England marked a turning point in Elizabeth's reign.[6] Her presence at once intensified the succession crisis and sparked off another series of plots and conspiracies; Mary became a focus for disaffected Catholics at home and abroad. Within weeks of her arrival, Sir Henry Norris, Elizabeth's envoy in France, warned of plans fostered by Mary's uncle the Cardinal of Lorraine and her other Guise relatives to rescue her and act against Elizabeth. In July, Norris wrote urging Elizabeth to pay special attention to her safety, 'for there are certain Italians being sent into England by the Cardinal of Lorraine to practise against her'. The cardinal, he reminded Cecil, was 'a most cruel enemy to the Queen and her country', and will leave 'nothing unattempted that may be to her prejudice'.[7]

Norris advised Cecil to employ an Italian soldier named Captain Franchiotto to investigate further. Franchiotto had been working undercover for many years in the service of the French crown, but his Protestant faith had now caused him to defect. He soon uncovered a list of suspected agents and a plot, sponsored by the Guise, which sought to assassinate the Queen by contaminating her Bedchamber with poison. Sir Francis Walsingham hastily sent a report to Cecil based on Franchiotto's intelligence and urged that Elizabeth and her gentlewomen 'exercise great watchfulness over her food, utensils, bedding, and other furniture, lest poison should be administered to her by secret enemies'. He stressed how 'there are at the present time a great number of malcontents in that country, whose greatest desire is to upset and change the existing regime, and who would spare no means to carry out their wicked intentions'.[8]

Elizabeth deliberated over what to do with Mary following her arrival in England. As an anointed sovereign, she was reluctant to take action against her and believed she should be restored to her legitimate throne. However, she knew that this would alienate James Stewart, the Earl of Moray, Regent of Scotland for his young nephew King James VI, which she could ill afford to do. Finally she resolved that a hearing was necessary to adjudicate upon the charges made against Mary in Scotland as to her involvement in the murder of her late husband. Proceedings opened in York at the beginning of October 1568.

At the heart of the case against her was a silver-gilt casket of letters purportedly written in Mary's hand, which was said to provide stark evidence that she had plotted her husband's murder and had had an adulterous affair with the Earl of Bothwell, the chief suspect in Darnley's death. The letters have since been shown to be almost certainly fakes but within three months the tribunal formally recognised the authenticity of the letters and so by implication demonstrated its belief that the deposed Queen was guilty. When Mary refused to answer to the charges before a deputation sent by Elizabeth, judgement was deferred and the trial adjourned indefinitely. Whilst Mary continued to protest that her imprisonment was entirely unlawful, Elizabeth had little choice but to keep her in close custody. Cecil's words of warning to her were unambiguous: 'The Queen of Scots is, and always shall be, a dangerous person to your estate.'[9]

With the trial adjourned and the matter of Mary left unresolved, Elizabeth moved to Hampton Court ahead of the festive season. When the Queen was in residence, and particularly before Christmas, the palace would become a hive of activity. Servants in red liveries carried trays laden with food, or armfuls of firewood from the woodyard to stack by the palace's hearths ready to fuel the great fires that would burn throughout the festivities. Horses could constantly be heard clattering across the cobbles bringing guests to the palace, or conveying the Queen's personal messengers across the country and abroad.

During the preparations, Katherine Knollys, Elizabeth's cousin and trusted woman of the Bedchamber, fell gravely ill. Sir Francis, then custodian of the imprisoned Mary Queen of Scots at Bolton Castle in north Yorkshire, begged to be allowed to return to London and visit his sick wife. 'I would to God I were so dispatched hence that I might only attend and care for your good recovery,' he wrote to Katherine. Yet Elizabeth refused to grant him leave from his post. When Katherine's condition improved a little, she urged the Queen to let her join her husband in the north, but still Elizabeth refused, saying the 'journey might be to her danger or discommodity'. Sir Francis' response to Cecil was curt: as Elizabeth would not let him look after his wife, hopefully 'her Majesty will comfort her with her benign clemency and gracious courtesy'. Cecil assured him that Katherine was 'well amended', but Sir Francis remained desperate to return to London and complained bitterly of Elizabeth's 'ungrateful denial of my coming to the court'.[10]

On New Year's Eve, Sir Francis wrote to his wife from Bolton Castle, pouring out his feelings and frustrations. The Queen had never granted them what they wanted nor rewarded them enough for their service. 'For the outward love that her Majesty bears you, she makes you often weep for unkindness to the great danger of your health.' He wished they could now retire from court to a 'country poor life', adding 'whereunto I thank God I am ready to prepare myself for my part if you shall like thereof'.[11] He would leave the decision to Katherine.

Lady Katherine never responded. Soon after Christmas and still with the Queen at Hampton Court, her condition worsened. Elizabeth ordered that she be nursed in a chamber close by her own and made regular visits to her bedside, but on Saturday 15 January 1569, she died aged forty-six. Elizabeth was overwhelmed with remorse. Only the day before, she had written to Sir Francis but had deliberately made no reference to his wife's illness. Now she hastily sent a messenger north with news of his wife's passing. In the meantime, arrangements were made for Mary Stuart to be brought south to the medieval and semi-derelict Tutbury Castle in Staffordshire and placed in the custody of George Talbot, Earl of Shrewsbury, one of Elizabeth's leading noblemen.

Sir Francis Knollys returned to London on 8 February, 'distracted with sorrow for his great loss'. After nearly thirty years of marriage he was now bewildered as to how to care for his family and manage their large household. Katherine had 'disburdened him' of many cares and had been the bookkeeper of his 'public charges' and his 'private accounts'. Without her, he wrote, 'my children, my servants and all other things are loosely left without good order'.[12] Elizabeth meanwhile retired to her Bedchamber in deep mourning. Katherine Knollys had become a dear friend. She had served the Queen since her accession and remained in close attendance in the Bedchamber despite the needs of her husband and many children.[13] Such was Elizabeth's grief, that 'forgetful of her own health, she took cold, wherewith she was much troubled'.[14] Visiting Hampton Court five days after Katherine's death, Bertrand de Salignac de La Mothe-Fenelon, the French ambassador, found the Queen full of sorrow for the woman whom she had 'loved better than all the women in the world'.[15] Visiting the court around the same time, Nicholas Whyte, one of Cecil's emissaries, found the Queen beset by grief and hardly able to talk of anything other than her beloved servant and kinswoman:

> From this she returned back again to talk of my Lady Knollys. And after many speeches past to and fro of that gentlewoman, I perceiving her to harp much upon her departure, said that the long absence of her husband ... together with the fervency of her fever, did greatly further her end, wanting nothing else that either art of man's help could devise for her recovery, lying in a prince's court

near her person, where every hour her careful ear understood of her estate, and where also she was very often visited by her Majesty's own comfortable presence.

This rather tactless remark was followed by another. 'Although her Grace was not culpable of this accident,' said Fenelon, 'yet she was the cause without which their being asunder had not happened.' Elizabeth replied disconsolately that she was 'very sorry for her death'.[16] Katherine had attended tirelessly and selflessly on the Queen and had been forced to endure long absences from her husband and her children. The years of unrelenting service had, as Elizabeth was forced to acknowledge, doubtless taken its toll.

Elizabeth spent £640 2s. 11d. on a lavish funeral ceremony complete with interment in Westminster Abbey.[17] Katherine's hearse was so elaborate that the Dean of Westminster and the heralds both wanted to keep it. Her tomb, erected by her husband, identified her as 'The Right Honourable Lady Katherine Knollys chief lady of the Queen Majesty Bed Chamber and Wife to Sir Frances Knollys, Knight Treasurer of her Highness' Household'. A printed epitaph extolled her virtues, calling her a 'mirror pure of womanhood' with 'wit and counsel sound, a mind so clean and devoid of guile', she had been 'in favour with our noble queen, above the common sort'.[18]

In the years following Katherine Knollys's death, Elizabeth continued to show care and affection for her children. On 14 March, Katherine's brother wrote to Cecil that he 'was glad to hear of her Majesty's good disposition to his late sister's children'.[19] Her daughter Anne became a paid member of the Queen's chamber and was the recipient of several gifts.[20] The following year Henry Knollys became an Esquire of the Body and his brother William became a Gentleman Pensioner.[21] In a letter of January 1570 to the Earl of Sussex, Lord Chamberlain of the Household, and to Sir Ralph Sadler, the Queen wrote, 'We require you to have consideration of the custody appointed to Henry Knollys, whom you know what reason we have to regard, in respect of his kindred to us by his late mother'.[22]

Secret Enemies

Mary Stuart's arrival in England could not have come at a worse time. Europe was riven with conflict and the Protestant cause was in grave danger. Civil war in France continued, with Huguenots fighting Catholics; the Protestants in the Low Countries, led by William of Orange, faced the might of a huge Spanish army led by the Duke of Alva. Now it seemed only a matter of time before the Catholic powers would turn their attention across the Channel. Sir Henry Norris, the ambassador in Paris, was in no doubt that 'if the Duke of Alva do bring his purpose to desired effect he will forthwith invade England'.[1]

As relations with Spain and France cooled in recent months, England had become increasingly isolated. The French King, Charles IX, and his mother Catherine de Medici were convinced that Elizabeth was sending covert aid to the Huguenots and the Dutch rebels and this, together with growing resentment over English pirates preying on French shipping, left England vulnerable to French hostility. Meanwhile diplomatic relations with Spain had broken down completely after Elizabeth impounded treasure from Spanish ships bound for the Low Countries which had been forced to shelter in English ports. The imprisonment of Mary Stuart in England served only to heighten tensions and raise fears of an imminent Catholic invasion. In December 1568 an English agent in Paris reported that the monarchies of France and Spain were conspiring to undermine English security, 'for the alteration of religion and the advancement of the Queen of Scots to the crown'.[2]

In early 1569, Cecil made a stark assessment of the safety of the realm. 'The perils are many, great and imminent, great in respect of Persons and Matters.' At the top of his list came a 'conspiration of the Pope, King Philip, the French King and sundry potentates of Italy to employ all their forces for the subversion of the professors of the gospel'.[3] Pope Pius V was, he believed, determined to recover the 'tyranny' of his authority and restore England to the Catholic fold and to support Elizabeth's 'eviction' from her throne' and replacement with Mary Stuart. Elizabeth was also under threat from within her realm. Don Gureau de Spes, who had been appointed Spanish ambassador the previous year, wrote to Philip describing Mary Queen of Scots as a 'lady of great spirit', gaining so many friends where she was that 'with little help she would be able to get this kingdom into her hands'.[4] In her own over-optimistic epistle to Philip, Mary claimed that if the King could 'help me, I shall be Queen of England in three months, and mass shall be said all over the country'.[5] By July, de Spes was reporting that 'this Queen sees that all the people in the country are turning their eyes to the Queen of Scotland, and there is now no concealment about it. She is looked upon generally as the successor.'[6]

At the end of 1568 rumours circulated at court that the Duke of Norfolk was about to propose marriage to Mary Queen of Scots. The match had first been suggested by Sir William Maitland of Lethington, Mary's adviser, who believed that a union between Scotland's deposed Queen and England's pre-eminent noble could revive her fortunes and resolve the Anglo-Scottish impasse. Elizabeth had considered Norfolk as a possible consort for Mary four years earlier, as a means to secure the Scottish Queen's loyalty, but now in very different circumstances, she was not consulted.

In response to the gossip, the Queen quizzed Norfolk. Was there any truth to the rumour? The duke strongly denied any such accusation. 'Should I seek to marry her, being so wicked a woman, such a notorious adulteress and murderer? I love to sleep on a safe pillow.'[7] In truth, by early 1569, Norfolk had resolved to press ahead with a marriage to Mary and set about winning support from the leading men at court. By the spring, Dudley, the Earl of Arundel and Sir Nicholas Throckmorton had all declared themselves in favour of the match and were working secretly to bring it to fruition. Having secured Mary's consent, Norfolk made contact with the leading Catholic noblemen in the north, the Earls of Northumberland and Westmoreland, to secure their support. The challenge now was to gain Elizabeth's approval. Would she see the merits of the match as a means to securely bring about Mary's restoration to the Scottish throne and make it safe for her to declare Mary her heir? Or would she regard Norfolk's designs as more the product of his own personal ambition?

No one wanted to broach the subject with the Queen. Finally, on 6 September, Dudley feigned illness, took to his chamber and then summoned Elizabeth to his bedside where he revealed details of Norfolk's proposal. Despite Dudley's assurance that in supporting the plan he believed he was acting in her best interests, the Queen regarded his actions as a betrayal. If Norfolk married Mary, Elizabeth would, she believed, find herself in the Tower within four months of the ceremony. How could he, Dudley, the man she trusted above all others, support a marriage alliance between her greatest rival and her premier nobleman?

Fearing the Queen's reaction, Norfolk now fled to his estates in East Anglia. When Elizabeth summoned him back to court he initially resisted but then set out for the court at Windsor, to submit to her and profess his loyalty. Three days later he was arrested by Sir Francis Knollys and by 10 October he was a prisoner in the Tower of London where he would remain until the following summer. His sister, the Countess of Westmoreland, wrote scornfully of her brother's weak resolve: 'What a simple man the duke is, to begin a matter and not go through with it.'[8]

In the first clear rebellion of her reign, Elizabeth faced a dangerous challenge to her crown as members of her Privy Council and leading Catholic noblemen conspired against her in support of Mary Queen of Scots. It was only Norfolk's lack of resolve and Dudley's belated loyalty that had saved her. But the matter was not yet over. With Norfolk in the Tower, the two northern earls knew they were compromised. They had been plotting for months and their intentions were widely known. The Earl of Northumberland sent a message to de Spes, the Spanish ambassador, that he would now have to rebel, or 'yield my head to the block, or else be forced to flee and forsake the realm, for I know the Queen's Majesty is so highly displeased at me and others that I know we shall not be able to bear it nor answer it'.[9] Elizabeth summoned the earls to court, but instead they rallied over 5,000 rebels to their cause in a spontaneous uprising. On 14 November the earls stormed Durham Cathedral where they ripped apart the Protestant prayer book, overturned the communion table, and celebrated a Catholic mass.[10] Two days later they issued a proclamation declaring:

> Forasmuch as diverse evil-disposed persons about the Queen's Majesty have, by their subtle and crafty dealings to advance themselves, overcome in this Realm the true and Catholic religion towards God, and by the same abused the Queen, disordered the realm and now lastly seek and procure the destruction of the nobility. We, therefore, have gathered ourselves together to resist by force,

and rather by the help of God and you good people, to see redress of these things amiss, with the restoring of all ancient customs and liberties to God's church, and this noble Realm.[11]

Elizabeth had prepared for the worst and quickly mobilised 14,000 men who were sent north, whilst a special reserve guard was put in place for the Queen's own protection.[12] The Aldermen of London ordered that guns be put in readiness and the city gates and portcullises be fixed. Meanwhile, the Earl of Shrewsbury was commanded to move Mary south to the walled city of Coventry.

On 20 December, the conflict came to an end without a shot being fired. As the Queen's forces rode north, Northumberland and Westmoreland fled over the border and the rebels disbanded. Despite the speed of its collapse, the rebellion had represented a major threat to Elizabeth and her government. There had been rumours of promised Spanish assistance, her Catholic nobles had demonstrated their opposition to her and the north of England had responded to their call to arms. Moreover, the Queen's most senior nobleman, the Duke of Norfolk, remained alienated and ambitious and, despite his imprisonment, he continued scheming with Mary Queen of Scots. In the months that followed nearly 800 of the rebels were executed on hastily erected gallows. It was a ruthless and very timely reminder of the price of disloyalty to Elizabeth and her crown.

On 25 February 1570, Pope Pius V issued a bull of excommunication, *Regnans in Excelsis,* in which he formally declared Elizabeth to be a usurper and absolved her subjects from allegiance to her.

> Since that guilty woman of England rules over two such noble kingdoms of Christendom and is the cause of so much injury to the Catholic faith and loss of so many million souls, there is little doubt that whosoever sends her out of the world with the pious intention of doing God's service, not only does not sin but gains merit ... And so, if those English gentlemen decide actually to undertake so glorious a work, your Lordship can assure them they do not commit any sin. We trust in God also that they will escape danger.[13]

In the early hours of the morning of 15 May, John Felton, a wealthy Catholic living in Southwark, nailed a smuggled copy of the bull to the gate of the Bishop of London's palace. Felton was immediately arrested, tried for high treason and within months was hanged, disembowelled, decapitated and quartered. The issuing of the papal bull signalled the start of the long-awaited Catholic crusade against England and the moment when Catholics in England were marked out as traitors to the realm. The Pope had effectively sanctioned Elizabeth's murder and she now became the legitimate target of any wilful Catholic plotter.

22

Want of Posterity

In an audience at Hampton Court on 23 January 1571, Elizabeth told the French ambassador Fenelon that 'she was determined to marry, not for the wish of her own, but for the satisfaction of her subjects'. In a remarkably candid exchange, she explained that marriage would also 'put an end, by the authority of a husband or by the birth of offspring, (if it should please God to give them to her), to the enterprises' which, she felt, 'would perpetually be made against her person and her realm, if she became so old a woman that there was no longer any pretence for taking a husband, or hope that she might have children'. Whilst 'she had formerly assured him that she never meant to marry', she now said that 'she regretted that she had not thought in time about her want of posterity'.[1] It was a dramatic and very personal revelation which appeared to demonstrate a new resolve finally to settle the succession.

Marriage had become a necessity. The lessons of the Norfolk affair and the northern rebellion were plain to the Queen and her government; so long as her death meant the accession of a Catholic queen, her life would always be under threat. The papal bull of excommunication and Spanish intrigues in Ireland, coming after de Spes's involvement with the northern earls, all seemed compelling evidence that an international conspiracy spearheaded by Spain was operating against Protestant England. Cecil held out hope that the Queen was at last sincere in her pledge to marry: 'If I be not much deceived, her Majesty is earnest in this'; if a marriage went ahead, 'the curious and dangerous question of the succession would in the minds of quiet subjects be buried – a happy funeral for all England'.[2]

In this renewed atmosphere of hope, Fenelon took the opportunity to revive the proposal of a match with Charles IX's younger brother, Henri, Duke of Anjou, which had been first mooted two years before. The French King was still keen to use a marriage alliance with Elizabeth to conciliate the French Huguenots, draw Anjou away from the influence of the

Cardinal of Lorraine, the senior member of the Guise family, and form the first stage of a defensive alliance against Spain. Anjou was, as Fenelon enthused, 'the only prince in the world worthy of her'.[3] But it was hardly an ideal pairing. Anjou was eighteen years younger than Elizabeth, 'obstinately papistical' according to the English ambassador, and a blatant transvestite who regularly appeared at court balls in elaborate female dress and was rumoured to be bisexual. As a Venetian envoy described, 'He is completely dominated by voluptuousness, covered with perfumes and essences. He wears a double row of rings and pendants in his ears.'[4] Marriage to Anjou also risked a further decline in relations with Spain, where a 'coldness of amity' had already developed mainly as a result of Spanish action in the Netherlands.

Elizabeth had immediately expressed her doubts about the Anjou match, as had the duke himself, who, encouraged by the Guise faction at the French court, considered Elizabeth a 'heretical bastard'.[5] As Catherine de Medici admitted in her letters to Fenelon, 'so much has he heard against her honour, and seen in the letters of all the ambassadors who have ever been there, that he considers he should be utterly dishonoured and lose all the reputation he has acquired if he was to marry Elizabeth'.[6] Catherine had tried to convince her son by explaining that, 'the greatest harm which evil men can do to noble and royal women, is to spread abroad lies and dishonourable tales of us', and that 'we princes who be women, of all persons, are subject to be slandered wrongfully of them that be our adversaries: other hurt they cannot do us'.[7] Nevertheless, the queen mother was forced to concede that, 'he will never marry her, and in this I cannot win him over, although he is an obedient son.'[8]

Besides her own reservations about taking a teenage boy to bed as a husband, Elizabeth had also received warning from her agents in France that some people were encouraging Anjou for malicious ends. They believed that he would do well to marry 'an old creature who had had for the last year the evil in her leg, which was not yet healed and never could be cured' – a reference to a leg ulcer – 'and that under pretext of a remedy, they could send her a potion from France of such a nature, that he would find himself a widower in the course of five or six months; and then he might please himself by marrying the Queen of Scotland, and remain the undisputed sovereign of the united realms.'[9] Elizabeth was naturally alarmed at the suggestion of murderous plotting against her in France but was also affronted by the reference to her age, apparent infirmity, and the unfavourable comparisons to her Scottish cousin. Especially vain, Elizabeth pointedly informed Fenelon that, 'notwithstanding the evil report that had been made of her leg, she had not neglected to dance on the preceding Sunday at the Marquess of Northampton's wedding; so she hoped that Monsieur would not find himself cheated into marrying a cripple instead of a lady of proper paces'.[10]

Negotiations for a French marriage were revived and by March, Catherine wrote to Fenelon that her son had changed his mind and now 'infinitely desires the match'. King Charles sent his envoy de Foix to England and talks continued through the spring and summer of 1571. However, though Elizabeth was, according to her closest councillors, 'more bent to marry than heretofore she hath been', religion remained the sticking point. Whilst the Queen made it clear that Anjou would have to conform to the laws of the realm, the French were equally uncompromising in their demands that Anjou and his servants should have 'free exercise' of their religion.[11] But as Walsingham wrote, such was the necessity of a marriage that all reservations could be reasoned away: 'When I particularly consider her Majesty's state, both at home and abroad . . . and how she is beset with Foreign peril, the execution whereof stayeth only upon the event of this match, I do not see how she can stand if this matter break off.'[12]

On 9 July the French ambassador was pleased to inform Catherine de Medici that the Queen had told one of her ladies, when they were alone, that she 'had of her own accord commenced talking of Monsieur' and had made clear that, despite her concerns about the age gap and his religion she was 'resolved on the match'. Elizabeth had naturally turned to her Bedchamber women for counsel and reassurance; she feared especially that Anjou might grow to despise her if she was unable to have children. The Queen asked Elizabeth Fiennes de Clinton, the Countess of Lincoln, and Lady Frances Cobham – 'two of the most faithful of her ladies' in whom she placed 'more confidence' than the others – to tell her 'freely their opinions' on the match. Lady Cobham spoke of how 'those marriages were always the happiest when the parties were of the same age, or near about it, but that here there was a great inequality'; she hoped in this case that 'since it had pleased God that she was the oldest' that the duke would be 'contented with her other advantages'. Lady Clinton, who had known Elizabeth since childhood and sensed the need to reassure the Queen, spoke favourably of Anjou, 'whose youth', she said, 'ought not to inspire her with fear, for he was virtuous, and her Majesty was better calculated to please him than any other princess in the world'.[13] Elizabeth said 'she would place all her affection on the prince, and love and honour him as her lord and husband' and hoped that this would be enough for him.

Yet her doubts lingered, and on receiving a portrait of Anjou, Elizabeth again expressed concerns as to the 'disparity of age between herself and the prince'; considering her 'time of life' she should be 'ashamed' to marry one so young.[14] Once more Fenelon sought to assure her of her suitability and persuade Anjou, 'God had so well preserved her Majesty, that time had diminished none of her charms and perfections, and that monsieur looked older than her by years; that the prince had shown an unchangeable desire for their union.' She would find in the duke, 'Everything she could wish for her honour, grandeur, the security and repose of her realm, with the perfect happiness for herself.'[15]

Elizabeth suggested that Anjou might cross the Channel incognito to meet with her, but he refused, and she remained adamant that she would not marry a prince that she had not seen. For all Fenelon's assurances of the duke's enthusiasm for the marriage, by October, Anjou was refusing to marry Elizabeth under any circumstances and was now so 'assottied' in religion that he was hearing mass two or three times a day.[16] After months of talks and false promises, all hope for a match with the flamboyant young Frenchman had vanished.

23

Compass Her Death

In a letter to Henry Bullinger in the summer of 1571, Robert Horne, the Bishop of Winchester, wrote of the 'dangerous and dreadful state of agitation' that had plagued the English government 'for almost the last three years'. Not only had Elizabeth and her councillors been 'shaken abroad by the perfidious attacks of our enemies', but they had been threatened at home by 'internal commotions' which Horne described as the 'brood and offspring of popery'. Pope Pius V was sponsoring 'desperate men' who sought to 'besiege the tender frame of the most noble virgin Elizabeth with almost endless attacks and most studiously endeavour to compass her death both by poison and violence and witchcraft and treason and all other means of that kind which could ever be imagined and which it is horrible even to relate'.[1]

Swift action had to be taken to meet the mounting threats against the Queen. When Parliament met in April, Thomas Norton, the Lord Keeper, was quickly to his feet to remind the house that 'her Majesty was and is the only pillar and stay of all our safety'. He continued, 'the care, prayer and chief endeavour' of Parliament must therefore be for the preservation of her life and estate'.[2] Further measures were enacted to 'regulate' Catholics. One Act forbade anyone to obtain, circulate or make use of papal bulls and prohibited any subject to reconcile others to Rome or to be reconciled.[3] Another Act made it high treason and punishable by death to 'compass, imagine or practise the death or bodily harm of the Queen, to practise against the Crown or to write or signify that Elizabeth was not lawful Queen, or to publish, speak, write, etc. that she was an heretic, schismatic, tyrant, infidel or usurper or to entice a foreign country to invade'.[4] Moreover, anyone who named in print any person as heir to the throne except her own 'natural issue', faced a year's imprisonment. It was also now a capital offence to speculate on how long the Queen might live, 'by setting or erecting of any figure or figures, or by casting of nativities, or by calculation, or by any prophesying, witchcraft, conjurations'.[5] The battle lines had been drawn; Catholics could now be treated as traitors by reason of their faith alone.

On 12 April 1571, Charles Bailly, a young Scotsman working as a courier and servant for John Leslie, the Bishop of Ross, Mary Stuart's agent in London, was seized as he arrived at Dover on a ship from the Low Countries. He was searched and found to be carrying a number of seditious books and incriminating letters addressed to the Bishop of Ross, which pointed to a plot to assassinate the Queen and invade England.[6] Cecil immediately ordered that Bailly be sent to the Marshalsea prison in London and kept under close watch.[7]

Under interrogation and the threat of torture, Bailly confessed the details of a conspiracy masterminded by Roberto di Ridolfi, a Florentine merchant and banker then living in London. Ridolfi had been put under surveillance two years earlier when it was discovered that he was bringing bills of foreign exchange into the country for the Bishop of Ross and for the Duke of Norfolk, Thomas Howard, at the time of the rising of the northern earls. After little more than a month's house arrest at the London home of Sir Francis Walsingham in Aldgate, Ridolfi was released with a warning not to meddle again in affairs of state.[8] Yet it seemed, unbeknown to the English authorities, that Ridolfi had become a secret envoy of the Pope and a key contact between the Spanish government and English Catholics sympathetic to Mary's cause.[9]

In the summer of 1571, as details of Norfolk's involvement in the Ridolfi plot emerged, Elizabeth, then on her summer progress in the Home Counties, visited the Duke of Norfolk at Audley End near Saffron Walden in Essex. Her councillors disapproved of her journey and were anxious about her absence from London, 'upon doubt of some great trouble both inward and beyond the seas'. But the Queen 'would not forbear her Progress'.[10] During her five-night stay at Audley End, Norfolk assured Elizabeth of his innocence and swore his allegiance to her. Given her kinship ties with him – they were cousins through Anne Boleyn's family – and his senior position among the nobility, Elizabeth 'seemed to give favourable ear' to his petitions.

Yet four days after Elizabeth's departure, Norfolk was arrested and sent once more to the Tower. Walsingham had uncovered evidence that the

duke had sent money to Mary's supporters and had been acting in treasonous complicity with her since 1568.[11] In the weeks that followed, the
repeated examinations of Norfolk and his servants confirmed his disloyalty to Elizabeth and his complicity in the Ridolfi conspiracy.

On 16 January 1572, Norfolk was brought to trial in Westminster Hall
in London. Three charges of treason were read out to him, the principal of
which focussed on his designs to marry Mary Queen of Scots, through
which he had conspired to deprive Elizabeth of her crown and life and
thereby 'to alter the whole state of government of this realm'.[12] He was
found guilty, condemned to death and returned to the Tower to await
execution.

Within weeks a plot emerged involving two minor Norfolk gentlemen,
Edmund Mather and Kenelm Berney, fostered by the Spanish ambassador, which sought to liberate the Duke of Norfolk by means of 'a bridge
of canvas', a rope bridge, and to assassinate the Queen and Cecil and place
Mary Stuart on the English throne. Mather had talked about his plans to
William Herle, one of Cecil's agents. Berney and Mather were promptly
arrested and questioned, and subsequently confessed to their conspiracy
and to the involvement of the Spanish ambassador.[13] De Spes was now
ordered to depart the realm for 'his practices to disturb our state, to
corrupt out subjects, to stir up rebellion', and Mather and Berney were
executed on 13 February.[14]

Elizabeth finally signed Thomas Howard, the Duke of Norfolk's death
warrant on Saturday 9 February and the execution was set for the following Monday morning; but late on Sunday night she sent for Cecil and
ordered that the warrant be revoked. The Queen had, Cecil reported,
'entered into a great misliking that the duke should die the next day'. She
wrote to Cecil that the 'hinder part' of her brain would not trust 'the
forwards side of the same'; her emotions, she said, had got the better of
her, and so the duke remained in the Tower.[15]

———————

Whether Ridolfi was indeed a genuine conspirator who had masterminded a plot to deprive Elizabeth of her throne, or a double agent used
by Cecil to expose the danger of Mary Stuart and the Catholic threat
from abroad, remains unclear. The leniency of his treatment after he was
shown to have been supporting Mary Queen of Scots, the Duke of
Norfolk and the northern earls in 1569 suggests perhaps that during his
weeks of house arrest, Ridolfi was 'turned' by Walsingham and thereafter

began working in the service of the Elizabethan government's spy network. Whatever or whoever Ridolfi was, the plot that had taken his name exposed a vast conspiracy against the Queen and her crown, and one which had gained the support of the Pope and Spanish King, implicated the Duke of Norfolk and demonstrated the continuing threat posed by Mary Stuart. As Cecil outlined in a long memorandum, when 'the great part of the people of the realm' saw Elizabeth without a husband or any successor, they could be 'easily induced' to give their support to a Scottish Queen who had a son and who, if she sat on the English throne, could unite England with Scotland, 'a thing these many hundred years wished for'.[16]

Danger was everywhere, at home and abroad. Ports were watched, the guard around the Queen increased and the militia put on a state of alert. Further precautions were introduced into the privy lodgings after Cecil received new warnings that the Queen 'should be careful of her meats and drinks, for some say she shall not reign long'.[17] No one was immune from the gaze of suspicion. The climate of fear even led to action being taken against one of the Queen's most trusted Ladies of the Bedchamber.

In 1572, Lady Frances Cobham, Mistress of the Robes and a woman upon whom Elizabeth increasingly relied for counsel, had lost her place in the Queen's service following her husband's temporary disgrace over the Ridolfi plot. As Lord Warden of the Cinque Ports and Constable of Dover Castle, William Cobham was responsible for gathering intelligence, scrutinising arrivals and searching suspicious diplomatic bags from the continent. However, in April 1571, when he seized letters from Ridolfi, Cobham alleged that 'his ungracious brother Thomas' begged him to keep them from the Privy Council, 'for he said they would otherwise be the undoing of the Duke of Norfolk and of himself'.[18] Cobham was placed under house arrest for his apparent disloyalty and his wife lost her place in the Privy Chamber.

That Lord Cobham was only imprisoned for seven months and later restored to favour suggests perhaps that he had been acting with the approval of his friend Cecil, who had wanted the continental correspondence to reach its intended recipient in order for the Ridolfi plot to be exposed. Certainly Lady Cobham's loss of the Queen's favour was short-lived and by the summer of 1574, she had been restored to her position in the bedchamber with her backpay credited. As Dudley reported on 9 June, 'My La[dy] Cobham I thank God is grown into very good favour and liking again & I think very shortly shall be in her old place as her Majesty hath of late fully promised.'[19]

24

Beside Her Bed

At the end of March 1572, Elizabeth, then at Richmond, succumbed to a short but violent stomach ache. Some believed worry over the Duke of Norfolk's execution warrant had made the Queen ill, but it was most likely the result of food-poisoning, or a failed attempt to poison her. Fenelon described in his dispatch to Paris the 'great twisting (*torcion*)' of the Queen's stomach, 'on account, they say, of her eating some fish' and 'the heavy and vehement pain (*douleur*) that she had suffered'. For three anxious days and nights, Dudley, Cecil and Elizabeth's women had kept a vigil at her bedside.[1]

When her sickness subsided, the Queen emerged from her Bedchamber and in an audience with the French ambassador described the 'extreme pain' which for five days had so 'shortened her breath and so clutched her heart' that she thought she was going to die. She dismissed the idea that the cause was the fish she had eaten, saying that she often ate it without ill effects. Elizabeth believed that her sickness had been brought on by complacency; for the last three or four years she had found herself 'so well' that she had 'disregarded all the strict discipline which her physicians formerly had been accustomed to impose upon her by purging her and drawing a bit of her blood from time to time'.[2]

For Elizabeth's councillors, her ill health raised the spectre of assassination attempts, the unresolved succession and the fragility of the Queen's body. Sir Thomas Smith, Elizabeth's envoy in France, who had received regular updates from the English court on the Queen's health, now thanked Cecil for 'calling to our remembrance and laying before our eyes the trouble, the uncertainty, the disorder, the peril and danger which had been like to follow if at that time God had taken from us that stay of the Commonwealth and hope of our repose'.[3] The English agent John Lee wrote to Cecil from Antwerp on 2 April: 'It has been rumoured by the Italians that the Queen is very sick and in great danger, which causes

Papists in the Low Countries to triumph not a little, and to substitute the Queen of Scots, without contradiction, in the place.'[4]

On 8 May 1572, less than a year after its previous sessions, Parliament assembled again. It was late in the season for a Parliament as summer sessions were generally avoided given the heat and spread of disease, however, as the Lord Keeper Bacon explained in his opening address, 'the cause was so necessary and so weighty as it could not otherwise be'.[5] He then described the 'great treasons and notable conspiracies very perilous to her Majesty's person and to the whole state of the realm'. Two main issues had to be addressed: the fate of Thomas Howard, Duke of Norfolk, and what to do with Mary Queen of Scots.

Within weeks both houses had resolved to act against the Queen of Scots, 'for the better safety and preservation of the Queen's Majesty's Person'. The proposed bill would declare Mary a traitor and so deprive her of her 'pretended claim' to the throne.[6] Predictably, Elizabeth procrastinated. She thanked the house for 'their carefulness' of her safety and preservation, but ruled out 'by any implication or drawing of words' to have Mary Stuart, 'either enabled or disabled to or from any manner of title to the crown of this realm or any other title'.[7] Cecil's sense of weariness and despair were palpable:

> I cannot write patiently: all that we laboured for . . . I mean a law
> to make the Scottish Queen unable and unworthy of succession of
> the crown, was by Her Majesty neither assented to nor rejected, but
> deferred until the feast of All Saints; but what all other wise and
> good men may think thereof you may guess.[8]

Elizabeth had pledged only to move Mary to a harsher state of imprisonment; yet the life of one cousin was bought at the cost of that of another. Finally Elizabeth agreed to sign the Duke of Norfolk's death warrant and a little after seven o'clock on the morning of Monday 2 June, Thomas Howard was beheaded on Tower Hill.[9]

Increasingly, Elizabeth's stance on the succession was met with frustration and disbelief. 'Jesus!' Catherine de Medici told Sir Thomas Smith, 'And doth not your mistress, Queen Elizabeth, see plainly that she will always be in such danger till she marry? If she marry into some good house, who shall dare attempt aught against her?'

'Madame,' replied Smith, 'I think if she were once married, all in England that had traitorous hearts would be discouraged, for one tree alone may soon be cut down, but when there be two or three together, it is longer doing; for if she had a child, all these bold and troublesome titles of the Scottish Queen, or of the others who make such gapings for her death would be clean choked up.'

'I see that your queen might very well have five or six children.'

'I would to God we had one!' Smith replied.[10]

Catherine nonetheless remained determined to construct a defensive alliance against the threatening Spanish presence in the Netherlands (and the threat of the Guise in France) and so after Henri Duke of Anjou's refusal to marry Elizabeth, she had immediately offered her youngest son François Duke of Alençon, believing he 'would make no scruple' in accepting only the right to a private mass.[11]

Once again there was a considerable age gap. Elizabeth aged thirty-eight was far from enamoured with the suit of the sixteen-year-old French prince. She talked of the 'absurdity' of the match given their ages and made clear that she disliked the descriptions of Alençon as short with an extraordinarily large nose and hideous smallpox scars.[12] The Queen had initially rejected the Alençon proposal out of hand, given the 'contrary dealing' of his elder brother. However, Cecil believed the marriage was absolutely necessary and that the survival of England depended on it. Not only had the Ridolfi plot highlighted the threat of Spain and the papacy, but the situation in the Netherlands was deteriorating and Elizabeth and Cecil had reason to fear that the French would seize the opportunity to invade the Netherlands as allies of William of Orange, the leader of the Protestant rebels.

'You shall understand that I see the imminent perils to this state,' Cecil wrote to Walsingham, 'and namely how long so ever Her Majesty shall by course of nature live and reign, the success of this crown, so manifestly uncertain or rather so manifestly pernicious for the state of religion, that I cannot but persist in seeking for marriage for her Majesty.'[13] An alliance with Catholic France was the apparent cost of the preservation of Protestant England.

———•———

By the end of April, as Parliament prepared to meet, Elizabeth modified her stance and Cecil informed Fenelon that the Queen was now ready to hear a formal proposal of marriage.[14] It was a rather gilded interpretation of Elizabeth's position, but it demonstrated a desire to conciliate the French. Charles IX instructed de Foix and François Duke of Montmorency, who were being sent to England to ratify a defensive alliance against Spain, the Treaty of Blois, to commence negotiations. Upon their arrival in June, Elizabeth made clear that she considered marriage to a man twenty-two years younger than herself to be ridiculous but, as discussions continued, she admitted that given England's isolation in Europe and the pressure from her subjects to settle the succession, it was now in her interest to marry. The issue of the duke's religious demands overshadowed discussions. Whilst Alençon was more flexible in religion than his brother had been, he still demanded the right to hear mass. He did, however, agree to a ban on the public exercise of his religion, exclusion of all the Queen's subjects from his chamber when mass was celebrated and his own attendance at English church services.

As the council debated the merits of the match, Walsingham was instructed to discover Alençon's 'inclination to Religion' and report in more detail on his appearance and character. Elizabeth also wanted him to investigate the possibility of the French ceding Calais to her or to any child born of the union – compensation for Alençon's unsuitability.[15] Walsingham's report did little to allay Elizabeth's doubts. Whilst he believed there was every hope that the duke could be easily 'reduced to the knowledge of the truth' and might cease hearing mass after the marriage, the French King and his mother remained committed to their demand for a private mass.

On 23 July, Elizabeth explained that because of Alençon's age and reports of his scarred face, 'we cannot indeed bring our mind to like this offer'.[16] Four days later and under pressure from Cecil and the French ambassador she agreed that the duke might 'come hither in person' before she made up her mind.[17] The French had initially been reluctant to agree to a meeting unless assurances were given beforehand, but on 21 August, Catherine de Medici wrote to Fenelon suggesting a secret meeting on a ship somewhere in the Channel.[18]

———•———

Hopes for a marriage between Elizabeth and Alençon were then thrown by the news from France. On St Bartholomew's Day, 24 August, a number of the Huguenot leaders, who had gathered in Paris for the wedding of Henri of Navarre and Marguerite de Valois, had been murdered on the

King's orders.[19] The next three days saw the indiscriminate slaughter of Huguenots in Paris and then across the country in the weeks that followed. By October, some 10,000 Huguenots lay dead. Reports of the events in France reverberated around Europe. The new Pope, Gregory XIII, celebrated the news with a Te Deum at St Peter's and Philip of Spain congratulated his historic enemies for their decisive rejection of Protestantism.

The Queen was told of events while she was hunting at Woodstock in Oxfordshire.[20] The hunt was abandoned and her court went into mourning. The Privy Council immediately held an emergency session and sent an extra twenty-five of the Queen's men to guard Mary Queen of Scots. Within weeks, coastal counties such as Devon, Sussex, Dorset, Norfolk and Kent had received a call to arms in preparation for a possible invasion.[21] In Cecil's view the massacre demonstrated that the French King had allied himself with the Duke of Guise and 'the faction of the papists', and would now move to extirpate heresy in England and Scotland.[22]

Elizabeth at first refused to give audience to the French ambassador, but after three days agreed to an interview with him. She received Fenelon in her Privy Chamber in the presence of the members of the council and her ladies, all of whom, like her, were dressed in mourning clothes. Fenelon was met by a pointed, solemn silence after which the Queen moved forward and took him to one side. She asked him 'if it were possible that the strange news she had heard of the prince, whom she so much loved, honoured and confided in, could be true?' The ambassador said he had come to 'lament with her over the sad accident that had just occurred', that he, King Charles, had been forced to act for 'security of his life' and that 'what he had done, was as painful to him as if he had cut off one of his arms to preserve the rest of his body'.[23]

In late August, Elizabeth left Woodstock and continued on her progress through Bedfordshire and Buckinghamshire, much to the alarm of many of her councillors and clerics. Edwin Sandys, Bishop of London, wrote to Cecil on 5 September from his house at Fulham, of how 'these evil times trouble all good men's heads, and make their hearts ache, fearing that this barbarous treachery will not cease in France, but will reach over unto us'. He urged Cecil to, 'hasten her Majesty homewards, her safe return to London will comfort many hearts oppressed with fear'. With his letter the bishop sent a paper with suggested measures for the Queen's safety, which included: 'Forthwith to cut off the Scottish Queen's head'.[24]

Sandys's view was shared by many. Cecil urged Elizabeth to follow this advice, telling her 'that it was the only means of preventing her own deposition and murder'.[25] As Walsingham wrote from Paris, having witnessed the Huguenot massacre, 'Can we think that the fire kindled here in France will extend itself no further? . . . Let us not deceive ourselves but assuredly think that the two great monarchs of Europe together with the rest of the Papists do mean shortly to put into execution . . . the resolutions of the Council of Trent.'[26] England was, it was feared, their next target.

Robert Beale, a clerk of the Privy Council and Walsingham's brother-in-law, composed a paper entitled, 'Discourse after the Great Murder in Paris & other places in France'. In it Beale wrote of the 'detestable conspiracy' engineered by the Catholic powers of Europe and the desire by the Queen's enemies to take her life.[27] The House of Guise, the family of Mary Queen of Scots, was in the ascendancy in Paris and the might of Spain was threatening in the Low Countries. It was now time, wrote Beale, 'and more than time',

> that her Majesty were thoroughly resolved to take some right course [for] both her own safety and wealth of this realm . . . The French King is become a man or rather an incarnate devil. The Prince of Condé and Admiral be slain. The Spaniard is placed in the Low Countries. The Prince of Orange's force be like after this to be weakened as he shall never be able to lift up his head again. We are left destitute of friends on every side, amazed and divided at home; and consider not that where there is any such irresolute-ness and security, that estate cannot in policy upon any foreign invasion, (as is intended against this) continue long.

'The chiefest means,' he continued, 'is to be found inwardly, I mean the faction of the Queen of Scots and papists in this realm.' Beale emphasised that there was only one remedy: 'the death of the Jezebel'. He wrote of how 'all wise men generally throughout Europe cannot sufficiently marvel at her Majesty's over-mild dealing with her, in nourishing in her own bosom so pestiferous a viper'.[28] But still Elizabeth refused to consider having Mary executed.

The Queen's health continued to cause panic. In early August she had become unwell having walked late in the cold night air and hunted too much the previous day; and a little more than a week later she was once again suffering from stomach pains which left her bedridden for two days. As Antonio de Guarras reported, 'it is said that she was dangerously ill for one or two nights but is now recovered'.[29] Then, in late September, amid fears and anxiety about threats abroad and Catholic plotting at home, Elizabeth fell ill at Windsor. On 15 October, Sir Thomas Smith told Cecil, 'her Majesty hath been very sick this last night, so that my Lord of Leicester did watch with her all night. This morning, thanks be to God! She is very well. It was but a sodden pang. I pray God to long preserve her. These be shrewd alarms.'[30] Cecil wrote to Walsingham of the 'sudden alarm' the previous night when the Queen 'being suddenly sick in her stomach, and as suddenly relieved by a vomit'.[31]

The sickness was thought to be another bout of smallpox, but given that we now know the disease is non-recurring, it is not clear what it was. One unsigned letter of intelligence, dated 26 October, to the Duke of Alba, described how 'the Queen has been very ill and the malady proved to be smallpox'. As Elizabeth lay in bed ailing, her councillors had once more sought to settle the succession and discussed the prospect, in the event of the Queen's death, of proclaiming one of the sons of Catherine Grey as King.[32]

On her recovery, Elizabeth wrote to the Earl of Shrewsbury, Mary Queen of Scots's gaoler, explaining that she was well and the suspected relapse had left no marks on her face:

> Red spots began to appear in our face, like to be smallpox, but, thanks be to God, and contrary to the expectation of her physicians and others, they vanished away and at this day, we thank God, we are so free from any token or mark of any such disease that none can conjecture any such thing ... My faithful Shrewsbury, let not grief touch your heart for fear of my disease, for I assure you, if my credit were not greater than my show, there is no beholder would believe that I had been touched with such a malady.[33]

A postscript in the Queen's own hand reiterated her point: 'I assure you, if my credit were not greater than my show, there is no beholder would believe that ever I had been touched with such a malady.'[34] It was important for Elizabeth to emphasise that she had not been left scarred. Special prayers of thanksgiving for the preservation of the Queen and the realm from her enemies were now to be used in churches across the country:

> O God, most merciful Father, who in Thy great mercies hast both given unto us a peaceable princess and a gracious Queen, and also hast very often and miraculously saved her from sundry great perils

and dangers, and by her government hast preserved us and the whole realm from manifold mischiefs and dreadful plagues, wherewith nations round about us have been and be most grievously afflicted, have mercy upon them, O Lord . . .[35]

If Elizabeth died, civil war and invasion would surely follow. Prayers of protection, signs of devotion and demonstrations of loyalty were for many people all that they could do to try and guard against this most feared fate.

25

Lewd Fantasy

During the investigations into the Ridolfi plot, stories circulated about Elizabeth's sexual depravity and her relationships with her male favourites, with disaffected Catholics claiming that both Robert Dudley and Sir Christopher Hatton, the Captain of her Guard, were her lovers. On 29 January 1571, when Kenelm Berney was seized for his involvement in a plot to kill Cecil and depose Elizabeth, he claimed under interrogation that his accomplice, Edmund Mather, had told him,

> the Queen desireth nothing but to feed her own lewd fantasy, and to cut off such of her nobility as were not perfumed, and court like, to please her delicate eye, and place such as were for her turn, meaning dancers, and meaning Lord Leicester and Mr Hatton, whom he said had more recourse unto her Majesty in her Privy Chamber, than reason would suffer, if she were so virtuous and well inclined, as some noiseth her![1]

It was a story which many repeated and, it seems, many believed. Matthew Parker, the Archbishop of Canterbury, became so deeply concerned about Elizabeth's reputation and the aura of immorality which surrounded her that he wrote to Cecil to warn him about a man who had been seized at Dover and had uttered 'most shameful words against her'. It was a 'matter so horrible' concerning the Queen and both Dudley and Hatton, said the archbishop, that he could not write down the details but would tell Cecil only in person.[2] Not only had the slanderer made allegations about Elizabeth's conduct, he had predicted that such rumours would cause civil war with 'as many throats cut here in England, as be reported to be in France'. Catholic would rise against Protestant, a Catholic regime would be installed and Elizabeth murdered or executed with her bones then 'openly burned' in Smithfield along with those of her father.

It was a gruesome picture that the St Bartholomew's Day massacre in France had made very real. As Archbishop Parker made clear, a realm and Church with an immoral sovereign at its head in such a threatening climate was a realm and Church in peril. This was the archbishop's most 'fearful opinion' about the impact of Elizabeth's worsening reputation in the eyes of Christendom. He had heard, he warned Cecil, that the Dover slanderer had not been imprisoned, but had been turned loose to make mischief again. 'Sir, if this be true,' Parker ended his letter, 'God defend her Majesty and all her trusty friends.'[3]

Sir Christopher Hatton, an unmarried courtier some seven years younger than the Queen, had first captured her attention by his graceful dancing at a court masque. He was dark and good looking, 'of comely tallness of body and countenance'. Hatton, like Dudley, had risen to power because of Elizabeth's affection for him. He became a Gentlemen Pensioner in 1562 or 1564 and thereafter ascended rapidly in royal favour. Five years later he became a Gentleman of the Privy Chamber and by May 1572 had advanced to the trusted position of Captain of the Guard, thereby giving him very close access to the Queen and responsibility for ensuring her safety.[4] Whilst Elizabeth referred to Robert Dudley as her 'eyes', Hatton was her 'lids'.

A letter written to Hatton on 9 October 1572 by his friend, the poet Edward Dyer, warned of the rumours about his intimacy with the Queen, 'for though in the beginning, when her Majesty sought you (after her good manner) she did bear with rugged dealings of yours, until she had what she fancied; yet now, after satiety and fullness, it will rather hurt than help you'. Dyer advised Hatton that, however familiar he was with Elizabeth, he should not forget who she was. 'Consider with whom you have to deal, and what we be towards her who, though she do descend very much in her sex as a woman, yet we may not forget her place and the nature of it as our sovereign.'[5]

In May 1573, when Hatton lay seriously ill with kidney pain, the Queen visited him almost every day.[6] Weeks later, when Hatton was absent from Elizabeth for two days because of his continued ill health, he wrote passionately to her, expressing his devotion and distress at being away from her side:

> No death, no, not hell, not fear of death shall ever win of me my
> consent so far to wrong myself again as to be absent from you [for]

one day . . . Would God I were with you but for one hour. My wits are overwrought with thoughts. I find myself amazed. Bear with me, my most dear sweet Lady. Passion overcometh me. I can write no more. Love me; for I love you . . . Shall I utter this familiar term (farewell)? Yea, ten thousand thousand farewells . . . [7]

Hatton's supposed influence over Elizabeth led to an assassination attempt in October 1573 by a fanatical Puritan named Peter Burchet. He declared that Hatton was a 'wilful papist' who 'hindereth the glory of God so much as in him lieth'. Yet Burchet mistook his man and seriously wounded another, Sir John Hawkins, near Temple Bar. The would-be assassin was committed to the Tower and subsequently executed. Elizabeth's fury at the attack together with her concern for Hatton's safety, certainly fuelled the gossip.[8] Hatton denied all such accusations. The Queen's godson, Sir John Harington, later stated, the Captain of the Guard 'did swear voluntarily, deeply and with vehement assertion, that he never had any carnal knowledge of her body'.[9]

In May 1573, Gilbert Talbot, the young son of the Earl of Shrewsbury, having recently arrived at court, wrote to his father about what he had observed. Dudley 'is very much with her Majesty, and she shows the same great affection to him that she was wont; of late she has endeavoured to please her more than heretofore'. However, the young Talbot had already noticed Dudley's favour with the women of the court and Elizabeth's resentment of it. His letter continued, 'there are two sisters now in the court that are very far in love with him [Dudley] . . . they (of like striving who shall love him better) are at great wars together, and the Queen thinketh not well of them, and not the better of him; by this means there are spies over him'.[10]

The two sisters were Lady Douglas and Lady Frances, the daughters of Baron William Howard of Effingham, whom Elizabeth had appointed Lord Chamberlain on her accession. Both had become maids of honour at the beginning of the reign, but Douglas Howard – probably named after her godmother Margaret Douglas, Countess of Lennox – had soon left court to marry John Lord Sheffield, a Lincolnshire nobleman, in October 1560. The couple had two surviving children before Lord Sheffield's death on 10 December 1568. Lady Douglas then returned to court as an honorary Gentlewoman of the Privy Chamber.[11] Within a few years of rejoining the Queen's service, Douglas began an affair with Dudley which continued in secret for many years.[12]

It is likely that Dudley initiated the relationship, given his jealousy and resentment at Hatton's growing influence and favour with the Queen. However, as Lady Douglas began to pressurise him to marry, Dudley made clear he wanted nothing more. Having 'thoroughly weighed and considered both your own and mine estate', he said, he did not believe he could 'proceed to some further degree than is possible for me, without mine utter overthrow'.[13] Dudley knew that Elizabeth would never let him marry without bringing about his ruin. His greatest fear was, he once told the Duke of Norfolk, that the Queen's affection might one day turn 'into anger and enmity against him, which cause her, womanlike, to undo him'.

Lady Douglas's urgency to wed was explained by the birth of a son on 7 August 1574. Having little choice, Dudley admitted the child was his and placed him in the custody of his cousin John Dudley, in Stoke Newington. Years later when their son Robert sought a share of his father's inheritance, Lady Douglas claimed that she and Dudley had in fact married in a secret ceremony in 1573.[14] But with little evidence to prove that the marriage had taken place, the case collapsed.

26

Blows and Evil Words

On a cold January day in 1574 Mary Shelton, Elizabeth's twenty-four-year-old second cousin, secretly married John Scudamore, heir to one of the principal families in Herefordshire and now one of the Queen's Gentleman Pensioners.[1] Mary had become a Gentlewoman of the Privy Chamber on 18 November 1568 at the age of eighteen and was promoted to a Chamberer of the Queen's Bedchamber on 1 January 1571.[2] Both of Mary's parents had significant connections to Elizabeth. Her paternal grandfather Sir John Shelton married Anne Boleyn's aunt and was governor of Hatfield when Elizabeth was there as an infant; her uncle, Henry Parker, was later Elizabeth's Chamberlain.[3] The Queen was acutely conscious of the family links and enjoyed giving her relatives positions in the royal household. Following the deaths of Kat Ashley and Katherine Knollys, Mary Shelton's appointment at court was doubtless a great comfort to Elizabeth.

There is no extant record of where the marriage of Mary Shelton and John Scudamore was celebrated, but it may well have taken place away from court, as they knew the Queen would disapprove. When Elizabeth found out Mary Shelton faced the full force of her wrath. Eleanor Brydges, a maid of honour at court wrote how, 'the Queen hath used Mary Shelton very ill for her marriage: she hath dealt liberal both with blows and evil words, and hath not yet granted her consent', and added, 'no one ever bought her husband more dearly'.[4] Some years later, when the story was told to Mary Queen of Scots by 'Bess of Hardwick' (the Countess of Shrewsbury) whose daughter Lady Mary Talbot was a close friend of Mary Shelton's, Elizabeth was said to have broken Mary's finger by hitting her with a hairbrush and then tried to blame the injury on a falling candlestick. Mary Shelton, now Scudamore, was sent away from court though was soon reinstated and by October 1574 had been promoted to a Lady of the Privy Chamber.[5]

Following her marriage, Mary Scudamore moved out of the cramped and uncomfortable quarters at court used by unmarried staff and, when both her and her husband were in attendance on the Queen, was given use of conjugal lodgings. She was now stepmother to five children from her husband's first marriage and mistress of Holme Lacy, the Scudamore family home in Herefordshire, yet she was seldom there as it was hard to obtain leave from the Queen to be away from court.

On 9 October 1576, when Mary was away with her husband, she was hastily summoned back to court, as Lady Dorothy Stafford, the Queen's regular bedfellow, had broken her leg in a riding accident. The Earl of Sussex wrote to Mary at Holme Lacy: 'I fear until you come her Majesty shall not in the night have for the most part so good rest as shall take after your coming.'[6] Mary had become one of Elizabeth's most trusted intimates and favourite sleeping companions. Weeks later, when the Queen fell ill, Mary was at her side preparing warm drinks and possets and providing comfort through the day and night.

Whilst Mary Scudamore was cementing her position in the Queen's favour, Lady Mary Sidney, sister of Robert Dudley, was losing Elizabeth's goodwill and becoming increasingly embittered at what she felt was a lack of regard by the Queen. Despite having nursed Elizabeth through her smallpox, Lady Sidney suffered as a result of the Queen's strained and volatile relationship with her brother, and no matter how selfless and faithful she was, Elizabeth just seemed to be irritated by her. In July 1573, when Mary Sidney appeared at court wearing a gown made from velvet that her husband had sent from Ireland, the Queen immediately demanded that he send some for her. Mary was forced to write a somewhat hysterical letter to her steward, John Cockrame, urging him to procure the material at any cost:

> Her Majesty likes so well of the velvet it my Lord gave me last for a Gown as she hath very earnestly willed me to send her so much of it as will make her a loose gown. I understand my Lord had his at Coopers or Cookes I pray you fail not to inquire certainly for it of whom and what is left of it. If there be 12 yards it is enough. You may not slack the care here of for she will take it ill and it is now in the worst time for my lord for diverse considerations to dislike her for such a trifle. Wherefore I once again earnestly require it.[7]

It remains unclear whether Mary's petition was successful and if Cockrame managed to buy the last twelve yards of the cloth. There is no record of that length a piece of cloth entering the Wardrobe of Robes at this point so perhaps her efforts to keep Elizabeth happy failed.

The Sidneys had grown increasingly impoverished. As an unsalaried member of the Privy Chamber, Mary was dependent upon annual stipends from her husband, Sir Henry Sidney, but he too was sinking further into debt, thanks to the huge sums he had paid out in Ireland and in his Welsh estates. Mary was regularly petitioning the Queen to repay her husband some of the money he had spent in government service. When Sir Henry was offered a barony, the lowest of the aristocratic titles in 1572, he could scarcely afford the expenses that went with it, and his wife therefore begged Cecil that he might be excused from the honour unless it was accompanied by an increase in his estate.[8] As Mary explained, Sir Henry was 'greatly dismayed' with the 'hard choice' he had to make – either to bear the financial burden or 'else in refusing it to incur her Highness' displeasure'.[9] Their loyalty to the Queen and years of service had cost the Sidney family much of their fortune. In August 1573, Mary was forced to beg Cockrame, her own servant, to provide her with £10 to cover expenses incurred since Sir Henry had last departed – mainly for hats, gloves, medical bills and the furthering of clients' suits at court – as, she explained in her letter to him from Greenwich, 'I am already very near moneyless,' and added, 'under ten pounds at this present will not serve my turn ... send it this night though you strain your uttermost credit'.[10]

Having been absent from court because of ill health, Lady Sidney returned to find that her accustomed rooms which, thanks to her brother's intervention, were spacious and comfortable and close to the Queen, had been given to somebody else. The chamber which she had been allocated, formerly a servant's, was too cold and had no easy access to Elizabeth. As Mary wrote angrily, 'I dare say her Majesty would not wish me to be in it. Neither ever will I with my goodwill ... I have lately with an ill lodging taken heavy pain more than I am likely to be rid of this year.'[11] Mary grew more and more aggrieved and by 1574 was refusing to attend on Elizabeth unless she could return to the chamber she had come to regard as hers. She resolved to write to the Lord Chamberlain, her brother-in-law the Earl of Sussex, who was one of the most outspoken opponents of her brother, Dudley, but who was responsible for room allocation at court. 'Her Majesty hath commanded me to come to the court and my chamber is very cold and my own hangings very scant and nothing warm,' she complained. Her health had been irreparably damaged by the smallpox, and her living conditions at court had aggravated her various ailments. She told the Lord Chamberlain that her 'great extremity of sickness' meant that she dare not 'venture to lie in so cold a lodging without some further help'. She was now forced to beg for '3 or 4 lined pieces of hangings' to keep out the draughts. She assured Sussex that as soon as the weather turned warmer, 'they shall be safely delivered again. And I shall think myself most bound unto you if your pleasure be to show me this favour.'[12]

Lady Sidney's pleas fell upon deaf ears. Sussex was keen to prevent Mary from attending court so that she could not influence the Queen in favour of her brother's policies and went as far as accusing her of stealing 'certain things' from the Queen's wardrobe that had been lent to her during the birth of her son, Thomas, five years before. Sidney assured him that a servant of hers had been instructed to return the items but had clearly acted fraudulently. She promised that restitution would be made on her husband's return.[13]

Mary did, however, receive the Queen's full sympathy with the death of her nine-year-old daughter Ambrosia in February the following year. The Sidneys received a touching letter of condolence from the Queen offering to accept their last surviving daughter Mary into her entourage of ladies at court:

> Good Sidney. Right trusty & wellbeloved . . . Yet for as much as we conceiving the grief you yet feel thereby (as in such cases natural parents are accustomed) we would not have you ignorant (to ease your sorrow as much as may be) how we take parts of your grief upon us . . . He [God] hath yet left unto you the comfort of one daughter [Mary] of very good hope, whom if you shall think good to remove from those parts of unpleasant air (if it be so) into better in these parts, & will send her unto us before Easter, or when you shall think good, assure youself that we will have a special care of her, not doubting but as you are well persuaded of our favour towards yourself, so will we make further demonstration thereof in her, if you will send her unto us.[14]

The continued rehabilitation of the Sidneys culminated in July 1575 with their invitation to join the Queen at Kenilworth, Robert Dudley's Warwickshire residence.

27

Kenilworth

At eight o'clock on the warm summer evening of Saturday 9 July, Elizabeth and her entourage approached Kenilworth Castle, some twelve miles north-east of Stratford-upon-Avon. As the Queen's cavalcade came into view, illuminated by 200 horsemen holding thick waxen torches, a round of artillery sounded from the battlements.

Over the large artificial lake which surrounded the castle, Dudley had built a 600-foot bridge with pillars decorated with a cornucopia of fruits and vines, representing bounty and munificence. On the lake itself was a specially erected floating island 'bright blazing with torches' from which the 'Lady of the Lake' addressed Elizabeth with an oration in which she claimed that she had kept the lake since the days of King Arthur but now wished to hand it over to Elizabeth:

> Pass on, Madame, you need no longer stand:
> The Lake, the Lodge, the Lord are yours for to command.[1]

As the Queen entered the castle precinct, musicians on stilts played outsize trumpets, guns were fired and a spectacular fireworks display, which could be seen and heard over twenty miles away, lit up the night sky.

The gold and blue enamelled clock on the turret of the keep had been stopped at the moment of her arrival to suggest that during the royal visit time stood still. The Queen was then led from the inner courtyard to the three-storey tower where Elizabeth, her ladies and her most favoured courtiers would be lodged, and which Dudley had built for her use. It had been designed to face east for the sunrise. Elizabeth's chambers at the top had the biggest windows and the best views and Dudley occupied the floor directly beneath her. Decorated with dazzling plasterwork, hung with rich tapestries and furnished sumptuously, this would have been the height of Elizabethan luxury. Dudley had also ordered a beautiful privy garden to be created for Elizabeth, closed to all but the Queen and her closest companions.

For the next nineteen days, Robert Dudley, Earl of Leicester, was to host Elizabeth in what came to be regarded as the most elaborate festivities of her reign. Although Dudley had previously received Elizabeth at Kenilworth in 1565 and 1572, the festivities and entertainments laid on in 1575 were on an unprecedented scale, with various dramatic interludes designed to promote his matrimonial suit.[2] This was Dudley's most extravagant and, as it turned out final, attempt to demonstrate his suitability as a husband for the Queen and he had recruited the soldier-poet George Gascoigne to write and produce spectacular masques and pageants that he hoped would encourage Elizabeth to marry him.

In hot summer weather, with only a few days of light showers, Elizabeth enjoyed hunting in the park and chase, which had been well stocked with deer and game, and bear-baiting in the courtyard. Thirteen bears were baited by snarling mastiffs as the Queen looked on from a safe distance. According to the Spanish ambassador, de Guaras, whilst the Queen was hunting at Kenilworth 'a traitor shot a crossbow at her. He was immediately arrested, although other people maintained that the man was only shooting at the deer and meant no harm.'[3] Perhaps the ambassador's account was deliberately exaggerated; nevertheless the rumour and the swift action taken demonstrated a heightened climate of fear following the events of the years before.

Out of the heat of the day or to shelter from the rain, Elizabeth and her ladies would withdraw to their chambers to play cards, to read or gossip away from the crowds that filled the castle and the grounds. Each day the Queen would also enjoy the gardens with their long expanses of grass, arbours of fruit trees and fragrant flowers and herbs. An enormous fountain decorated with the stone figures of Neptune and Thetis and scenes from Ovid's *Metamorphoses* stood at the centre of the garden and would 'squirt water over bystanders when they least expected it'. There was also a huge aviary filled with exotic birds from Europe and Africa, 'delightsome in change of tune, and harmony to the ear'.

On the second Sunday of her visit, after attending the local parish church, Elizabeth was entertained in the tiltyard with a folk wedding feast, 'or bride ale', by country people from the surrounding areas. It was a strange sight. The bride was in her thirties and 'ugly, foul and ill-favoured'; the groom was young but was lame from playing football. After morris dancing and a pageant performed in the open air by a company of players from Coventry, the Queen, who had watched 'the great throng and unruliness' from her window, requested that the pageant be performed again two days later.

The finale of each day was a lavish feast. Although typically Elizabeth ate 'smally or nothing', every kind of animal, bird and fish was offered to her, including roast veal, lamb, wild boar, stag, partridge, capon, sliced beef, sirloin steak, mutton and chicken, gammon and venison pies and pasties. And this was just the first course. Elizabeth was then presented with a host of fish and fowl dishes; salmon, turbot, roach, cod, pike, perch, red herring, lobster, shrimp, crayfish and oysters. The range of fowl and game birds was especially impressive: duck, duckling, turkey, quail, gull, goose, crane, heron, peacock, pheasant, swan and the list went on. Later in the evening a vast array of sweets, designed to appeal to Elizabeth's famous sweet tooth – sweetmeats such as candies containing aniseed, caraway or coriander seeds as well as gingerbread, fruit tarts, candied flowers and almond macaroons – were served in the banqueting house in the garden. Special sweets had been prepared including sugar-work bears holding ragged staffs (Dudley's emblem) and a gilded marzipan model of Kenilworth castle. Everything was presented on sugar plates and in sugar glasses which could be smashed or eaten at the end of the meal.

Then, in the illuminated grounds of the castle, the Queen enjoyed spectacular 'interludes' and entertainments, with musicians performing in rowing boats around the lake, fireworks lighting up the night sky, acrobats turning somersaults along the paths and on one evening an Italian contortionist tumbling 'with sundry windings, gyrings and circumflexions'.[4] Such entertainments were open to the public and some three to four thousand visitors came each day.[5]

On the second Monday of her visit, after a morning's hunting and before watching a water pageant in the evening, time was set aside for royal ceremony. Five young men, including William Cecil's son Thomas, were knighted and afterwards Elizabeth received nine men and women afflicted with the 'King's evil' – scrofula – an inflammation of the lymph glands in the neck. It was a condition which anointed monarchs were believed to have the power to heal by laying their hands on the sufferer's afflicted areas.[6] It was a practice Elizabeth carried out often. First she knelt in prayer, then, having washed her hands in the basin held before her, she would press the sores and ulcers of the sufferers, 'boldly and without disgust' and make the sign of the cross. In his *Charisma sive Donum Sanationis*, a tract celebrating the power of English monarchs to cure scrofula, William Tooker, her chaplain, described how he had often seen Elizabeth with her 'very beautiful hands, radiant as whitewashed snow, courageously free from all squeamishness, touching their abscesses not with finger tips, but pressing hard and repeatedly with wholesome results, and how often did I see her handling ulcers as if they were her own'.[7]

Elizabeth took the ceremony very seriously and at times did not feel that she had the inspiration to cure by touching. At Gloucester, when throngs of the afflicted came to Elizabeth for her aid, she had to deny them, telling them, 'Would that I could give you help and succour. God is the best and greatest physician of all – you must pray to him.' It is possible that Elizabeth may have refused to touch because she was menstruating, which would have made her touch 'polluting'. Popular culture in medieval and early modern England believed the touch of a menstruating woman could have disastrous effects on men, on animals such as cows and insects like bees as well as on produce such as milk and wine, even if medical authorities of the time refuted it.[8]

Touching for the 'Queen's evil' became ever more popular over the course of her reign. Both her chaplain, William Tooker,[9] and her surgeon, William Clowes,[10] wrote books about scrofula and Elizabeth's remarkable talent for healing it through touch. Indeed English Protestants discounted the papal bull of excommunication on the grounds that Elizabeth still had the God-given ability of a true monarch to cure by touch.[11] Elizabeth generally held healing ceremonies every Sunday and on holy days and feast days at St Stephen's Chapel in the ancient Palace of Westminster but, as at Kenilworth, she would also touch when on progress in order to demonstrate her royal majesty and power.[12]

———•———

The climax of the entertainments at Kenilworth was the performance of Gascoigne's *Masque of Zabeta*, the tale of one of Diana's 'best-loved Nymphs' who had resisted marriage for 'near seventeen years past'. Gascoigne's commentary was intended to draw direct parallels between the figure of Zabeta and Elizabeth with the 'seventeen years' which Zabeta had remained a virgin – the length of time Elizabeth had then been on the throne. In the masque, commissioned by Dudley, Diana, chaste goddess of hunting, would debate with Juno, wife to the king of the gods, as to which was Zabeta's best destiny: marriage or virginity, with marriage winning the debate and Juno's messenger Iris explaining, 'How necessary were for worthy Queens to wed/That know you well, whose life always in learning hath been led.'

Yet the masque was cancelled. Gascoigne's printed account of the Queen's visit, *The Princely Pleasures at the Court of Kenilworth*, subsequently blamed 'lack of opportunity and [un]seasonable weather'. However, it is most likely that the Queen censored the entertainment given its blunt message.[13] Indeed Elizabeth had declared her dislike for the masque of Juno and Diana presented to her in March 1565, in which 'Jupiter have a verdict in favour of matrimony'.[14]

***

Elizabeth announced her intention to leave Kenilworth the following day. It was a sudden and unexpected departure. The blissful ease of her days in Warwickshire had been shattered by someone daring to tell her what the whole court had been whispering about: Robert Dudley had begun an affair with Lettice Knollys, former Gentlewoman of Elizabeth's Privy Chamber. There had been rumours of a flirtation between Lettice and Dudley ten years before, when Lettice had come to court heavily pregnant with her son Robert. Then it seemed that Dudley was acting out of jealousy of the Queen's relationship with Sir Thomas Heneage, and he stopped courting Lettice as soon as Elizabeth displayed hurt and anger at his betrayal. Now it seemed Dudley had renewed his suit. In the autumn of 1573, after the departure of her husband Walter Devereux, Earl of Essex, for Ireland that July, rumours spread that Lettice and Dudley, who had now tired of Lady Douglas Howard, had grown close once more.

Elizabeth was devastated to learn of the renewal of Dudley's romance with Lettice. She refused to attend supper and with the evening's specially prepared entertainment cancelled she got ready to depart; the scandal robbed Dudley of a last chance to appeal to Elizabeth. He swiftly instructed Gascoigne to write some farewell verses overnight to be delivered before the Queen left.

The following day, as Elizabeth was leaving the castle, Gascoigne, playing the part of Sylvanus, god of the woods, delivered a final farewell song. The Queen was reminded of 'Deep Desire's Loyalty': 'Neither any delay could daunt him, no disgrace could abate his passions, no time could tire him, no water quench his flames, nor death itself could amaze him with terror.' His passion for the Queen had turned him into a holly bush, 'now furnished on every side with sharp pricking leaves, to prove the restless pricks of his Privy thoughts'. Then a familiar voice came from out of the holly bush, speaking of his continuing love for the virgin Zabeta and urging Elizabeth to,

> Stay, stay your hasty steps.
> O Queen without compare . . .
> Live here, good Queen, live here. [15]

Yet it was all too late. Elizabeth knew of Dudley's betrayal with one of her own gentlewomen; worse, her own cousin. How could she ever forgive him?

28

Badness of Belief

From the mid-1570s, Catholic priests trained on the continent in Rome, Rheims and Douai, returned to England to supplement the dwindling number of Marian priests who had remained since the beginning of Elizabeth's reign. It was from Douai in the Netherlands, the seminary, founded by Cardinal William Allen in 1569, that the first missionary priests arrived in 1574. The mission's attempts to reinvigorate the English Catholic community swiftly led to more intense English government surveillance and persecution, raids on suspect recusant homes with priests often forced to assume false identities in order to elude government spies.[1] By 1580 there were some hundred missionary priests in England. Their impact was disproportionate to their number; they hardened Catholic resistance, strengthened leadership and provided a boost to morale.[2] Tougher legislation against Catholics had already been passed in 1571, but it was not until now that the law began to be enforced with full rigour and determination.

On 30 November 1577, Cuthbert Mayne was the first of 200 priests and laypeople to die for their faith during Elizabeth's reign. He had arrived in the country two years before with a copy of Pope Pius V's bull of excommunication and had managed to elude the government agents who were keeping watch on the ports. Thereafter Mayne had worked as a chaplain in the household of a Cornish gentleman named Francis Tregian. When the house at Probus was searched on 8 June, Mayne was arrested, paraded through local villages and imprisoned in chains in Launceston Castle.

During the course of his examination, Mayne admitted that if a foreign prince invaded a realm to restore it to the 'Bishop of Rome' then Catholics were bound to assist to 'the uttermost of their powers'. Mayne's alarming words opened Walsingham's eyes to the enemy within England: Mayne and other missionary priests like him threatened to be the vanguard of a crusade to reclaim England for the Holy See.[3] Mayne was sentenced to be hanged, drawn and quartered. On 30 November he was dragged through the streets of Launceston, fastened to a hurdle and then hanged in the market place. While he was still alive he was cut down, disembowelled, and quartered. His head was placed on the gate of Launceston Castle.

The tide of government policy had now turned against the Catholics and Mayne's execution marked the beginning of a rabid period of persecution against the missionary priests and those harbouring them.

On Friday 11 July 1578, the Queen left Greenwich Palace to begin her summer progress into Norfolk and Suffolk. She was accompanied by a huge entourage of courtiers, chamber officers, privy councillors, all their servants and her ladies, plus an escort of 130 Yeomen of the Guard and their captain, Sir Christopher Hatton. From Greenwich, Elizabeth first travelled to her own palace of Havering in Essex, where she remained for ten days, transacting business and receiving messengers and ambassadors. She left Havering early on Monday 21 July and the progress resumed a familiar pattern of arranged stops along the route including Audley End which she left on 30 July.[4]

Elizabeth now visited parts of East Anglia that she had not been to before. She was hosted by loyal country gentlemen until she reached Melford Hall, the house of Sir William Cordell, Master of the Rolls, where for three days the Queen and the court were extravagantly entertained. On the evening of 5 August, Elizabeth arrived at Bury St Edmunds where she knighted a few local young men and visited the recently rebuilt manor house of Sir William Drury at Hawstead. Sir William was well known to the Queen. He had married Elizabeth Stafford, one of the women of the Bedchamber, who had had a baby early in the year but was probably now travelling with the court. Having left Bury after dinner on Saturday 9 August, Elizabeth arrived a few hours later at Euston Hall, near Newmarket, the home of a young Catholic gentleman, Edward Rookwood. It was a rather unlikely stopping place, and the very public disgrace of Rookwood that followed suggests it had been deliberately planned to be the first show of the Queen's power and authority in East Anglia.

A vivid account of events during the Queen's stay exists in a letter written three weeks later by Richard Topcliffe, honorary Esquire of the Body and the Queen's notorious persecutor of Catholics, to the Earl of Shrewsbury, then custodian of Mary Queen of Scots.[5]

On her arrival all seemed amiable and when Rookwood was first brought into Elizabeth's presence, she gave him her hand to kiss and thanked him for the use of his house. Then Rookwood was called before the Lord Chamberlain, the Earl of Sussex, who knew that Rookwood had been excommunicated for his Catholicism, and berated him for daring to come before the Queen. Sussex ordered him to leave the court – indeed, to remove himself from his own house. But events then intervened and Rookwood was publicly exposed as a practising Catholic. A statue of Our Lady was found hidden in a hayrick and brought before the Queen as she watched some country dancing.[6] On Elizabeth's orders, the statue was burnt in front of a large crowd, 'to her content', as Topcliffe described, and the 'unspeakable joy of everyone but some one or two who had sucked of the idol's poisoned milk'.[7]

Within a few days Edward Rookwood and seven other local Catholic gentlemen, who were also arrested for 'badness of belief', were summoned to appear before the council sitting in Norwich.[8] Rookwood and one Robert Downes of Melton Hall were imprisoned in the city's gaol whilst the others were put under house arrest and required to pay a bond of £200 guaranteeing that they would take daily instruction from a bishop or another cleric until such time as they were willing to conform to the Established Church. It seems probable that the icon was planted in the hayrick as a means to expose and punish papistry and in this, Topcliffe suggests, Elizabeth was complicit: 'Her Majesty hath served God with great zeal and comfortable examples; for by her counsel two notorious Papists, young Rookwood . . . and one Downes, a gentleman, were both committed [to prison] . . . for obstinate Papistry.'[9]

This signalled the Queen's own determination to enforce the anti-Catholic measures, particularly in East Anglia, where loyalty to the Howards was still evident. Thomas Howard's arrest and execution had taken place only six years before. Although the duke had remained loyal to the Elizabethan Church, the Catholic sympathies of his friends and supporters were well known. Elizabeth's action in respect of Rookwood demonstrated her commitment to the reformed faith, as well as being a dramatic assertion of her royal authority.

From Euston Hall the Queen moved to Kenninghall Palace and then on to Norwich, the second largest city in the kingdom. The Queen reached the city boundary on the afternoon of 16 August where a vast crowd of dignitaries, officials and common people had gathered to greet her. Great preparations had been made in advance of the royal visit; roads had been widened and cleared; inhabitants ordered to repair and paint their houses 'towards the streets side', and to see that their privies were emptied and their chimneys swept. The city council had ordered that for the month of August, the city had to be clear of livestock and all butchers' waste carted away and buried. The market cross had been repainted, 'timber colour' and white, and the pillory and cage, which had been there for miscreants, was removed a few days before she arrived. Elaborate pageants and entertainments had also been prepared to welcome the Queen.[10]

Elizabeth arrived in the city on Saturday 16 August and was greeted by the mayor, the officers of the city and other wealthy gentlemen before moving through the city towards the cathedral. Over the next few days the Queen was entertained and hosted with elaborate ceremony, but then four days into her visit she received dramatic news from London. Reports from the commissioners responsible for security in the city described how evidence of witchcraft had been found. Under a dunghill in Islington they had discovered three wax images about twelve inches high, one with 'Elizabeth' etched on its forehead and two dressed like her ministers and pierced with hog's bristles.[11] The images had been deliberately placed so the heat of the decomposing dung would melt the wax and slowly 'kill the Queen'. The Privy Council ordered that the London committee, 'learn by some secret means where any persons are to be found that delighted are thought to be favourers of such magical devices'.[12] According to Don Bernardino de Mendoza, the new Spanish ambassador, 'When it reached the Queen's ears she was disturbed, as it was looked upon as an augury', and heralded a Catholic assassination plot against her.[13]

The Privy Council immediately called upon John Dee, the Queen's 'philosopher', to 'prevent the mischief' that they 'suspected to be intended against her Majesty's person'.[14] Within hours of arriving in Norwich he had performed some 'counter magic' to nullify the enchantment of the images.[15] What Dee had done to neutralise the threat of the malevolent witchcraft is unclear and only Secretary Thomas Wilson found the courage to observe his 'godly' magic and report to Elizabeth.[16] Dee then returned to London to assist with the investigation and hunt down the likely suspects.[17]

On 30 August, a young Catholic named Henry Blower was arrested and committed to the Poultry Compter in London, a small and filthy prison near Cheapside. Ten days later the commissioners moved Blower to the Tower of London to be tortured, whilst at the same time arresting his father, also called Henry Blower.[18] On the rack, the younger Blower accused Thomas Harding, the vicar of Islington, of making the wax images.[19] The previous April, Harding had been accused of conjuring, but then the Privy Council had had insufficient proof to press charges. Now he was arrested and brutally tortured.[20]

The fact that Elizabeth was suffering from excruciating facial pain at the time cast the wax image plot into a particularly sinister light. To her Protestant councillors this proved that the wax images were Catholic magic. Fears were heightened because it was widely believed that the death of Charles IX of France four years earlier had been caused by the same type of witchcraft. One Cosmo Ruggieri, a native of Florence, was accused of a conspiracy to destroy the King by magic. It was alleged that Ruggieri had made a wax figure of the monarch which he had pierced with pins.[21] He was immediately arrested and imprisoned but Charles's death of an unidentified disease, little more than a month later, raised suspicions that he had been fatally enchanted by Protestant sorcerers who had melted wax images of him.[22]

Yet the investigations into the wax image conspiracy soon stalled and the Privy Council now tried to tie in other Catholics who had been previously suspected of treasonous activity. John Prestall was arrested in early October, four years after being released under bonds for good behaviour. He had been indicted and imprisoned in 1571 for a treasonous conspiracy to kill Elizabeth by necromancy. In this highly charged political atmosphere, Prestall's track record of 'magical devices' against Elizabeth meant he was suspected of involvement in the wax image conspiracy and was now rearrested. Both Prestall and Harding were condemned to death for high treason.[23]

***

The Privy Council now began seeing conspiracies everywhere and Dudley used pamphlets and ballads to stir up a national scandal against the Catholics and their 'conjured images'.[24] In January 1579 the council fretted over some witches in Windsor – worryingly close to the court – who used wax images like those used against 'her Majesty's person'.[25] On 3 February there was information before the council of certain persons in the bishopric of London who were 'privy to the secret keeping of certain images which are reserved to some ill purpose of sorcery or idolatry'. The council wrote at the same time to the Bishop of Norwich to report that at Thetford and other places in his diocese, 'there hath been seen, not long since, in some men's houses certain images' of a similarly dubious character.[26]

As the government moved to make a lesson of the wax image suspects, the notorious 'conjuror' Thomas Elkes, confessed that he had created the images 'not to destroy the Queen', but to enable a wealthy young client to obtain a woman's love.[27] The Privy Council were now forced to face the reality that innocent men had been tortured. In April the younger Blower was quietly moved from the Tower and released shortly afterwards,[28] and Harding and Prestall's sentences were commuted to indefinite detention in the Tower. The conspiracy, Catholics gleefully recalled, 'being a little too foolishly handled by the accusers at the beginning, was for very shame in the end, let fall and sink away'. The French lawyer Jean Bodin gave the affair European publicity in his *De la Demonomanie des Sorciers* – 'On the Demon-mania of Sorcerers' – in which he reported the true identity of the wax image caster.[29]

Dudley had been determined to uncover the conspiracy to justify action against his Catholic rivals at court and to demonstrate his personal loyalty to the Queen. However, whilst the wax image investigation was continuing, on the morning of Sunday 21 September, he secretly married Lettice Knollys, the Countess of Essex. Her husband, Walter Devereux, had died in Dublin in September 1576 and some suspicions were raised that he had been poisoned. The covert ceremony was performed by Dudley's chaplain at Wanstead House in Essex, with Lettice being given away by her father, Sir Francis Knollys.[30]

Just two days later, Dudley hosted a magnificent feast for the Queen at Wanstead, to mark the end of her summer progress. The beautiful Lettice doubtless attended on the Queen in her usual role as one of the ladies of the court. The marriage remained a closely guarded secret; no open mention was made of it for some months. At New Year, 'the Countess of Essex' gave the Queen a 'great chain of Amber slightly garnished with gold and small pearls'. This would be the last time Lettice would appear on the New Year's gift rolls.[31]

29

Toothache

Elizabeth was now approaching her forty-fifth birthday and had suffered persistently poor health during her progress. By the time she arrived at Richmond in mid-September she felt distinctly unwell.[1] John Dee was called to Elizabeth's bedside where he described her as suffering from what he called a 'fit' from nine o'clock in the evening until one o'clock the next morning. Only days before, Dr Bayly, her personal physician had talked about 'her Majesty's grievous pang and pains'.[2]

By early October, the Queen was in constant facial pain. In a letter to Sir Christopher Hatton, Walsingham wrote of how Elizabeth had agreed that her physicians should confer with other expert practitioners in London. However, Walsingham, now Principal Secretary, wrote, they could not reach agreement 'touching the disease, nor the remedy'.[3] Once again, the thought of the wax images that had killed King Charles IX of France loomed large in the minds of Elizabeth's ladies and the councillors that thronged the privy lodgings.[4] As had always been the case at her times of most need, Elizabeth called for Dudley. He sat up all night at her bedside giving comfort as her pains persisted, the Queen unaware of his betrayal just a month before.[5]

In early November, with no diagnosis confirmed, Dudley and Walsingham instructed John Dee to go abroad to seek the advice of foreign experts.[6] Dee vividly described the 'very painful and dangerous' 1,500-mile winter journey, which he undertook 'to consult with the learned physicians and philosophers beyond the seas for her Majesty's health-recovering and preserving'.[7] He had been entrusted with a flask of Elizabeth's urine to take to the physician and alchemist Leonhard Thurneysser in Frankfurt on the Oder, who had invented a famous device to diagnose illnesses using urine distillation. This consisted of a square glass bottle divided into twenty-four horizontal bands, each corresponding to a part of the body. When filled with the urine and set in a lukewarm bath, steam settled on the band corresponding to the diseased part.[8] As Elizabeth's pain persisted through November, seventy-one-year-old Blanche Parry, one of Elizabeth's most trusted and long-serving intimates, fell seriously ill. Few expected her to survive and Cecil came to Blanche's bedside to allow her to dictate her will.[9] Blanche clearly retained her intelligence and meticulous attention to detail as she asked that only proved debts be paid and that a discharge certificate for her heirs be obtained. She made provision for a tomb for herself in the family mausoleum at Bacton Church, Herefordshire. However, the indomitable Blanche rallied and recovered and before long resumed her duties in the Queen's chambers.

As Christmas approached, Elizabeth remained in her Bedchamber at Greenwich, tormented by the agonies in her face. John Anthony Fenotus, 'an outlandish physician of some note', was sent for. It was a perilous thing to entrust the sacred person of the sovereign to a foreign practitioner, who might well be a papist. Fenotus was therefore not permitted to see Elizabeth in person but wrote a prescription.[10] Only now had Elizabeth's doctors started to consider that the pain might be caused by her rotting teeth and infected gums. In a long and elaborate letter, Fenotus prescribed numerous remedies: 'If the tooth were hollow, when all was said and done, it was best to have it drawn, though at the cost of some short pain.' However, the physician had heard of Elizabeth's anxieties and added that if her Majesty could 'not bring herself to submit to the use of surgical instruments', he advised, that the juice of *chelidonius major* (fenugreek) might be put into the tooth, and then stopped with wax. This, Fenotus explained, would then loosen the tooth so that in a short time it might be pulled out with the fingers.[11]

With Elizabeth unable to sleep and in extreme discomfort, her physician decided the extraction was necessary, even though he knew she was afraid of pain and perhaps given her vanity did not want to lose a tooth. Elizabeth proved resistant and Sir Christopher Hatton and her councillors tried to convince her that her tooth needed to come out. Finally the aged John Aylmer, Bishop of London, offered that one of his few remaining teeth might be extracted to reassure the Queen and encourage her to submit to a similar procedure.[12] Having watched Aylmer's extraction, Elizabeth finally agreed, and after nine months of agony her doctors were permitted to remove her tooth. This would be the first and only time she would agree to an extraction and thereafter, as her teeth continued to decay, Elizabeth experienced intermittent pain in her face and neck from gum disease.

For the New Year celebrations of 1579, just weeks after her tooth extraction, Elizabeth received her favourite sugary confectionary. John Smythesone, alias Taylor, her master cook, gave a 'fayre marchpane' (flavoured marzipan) and John Dudley, Sergeant of the Pastry, made her a quince pie. Other regular offerings to the Queen included comfits (crystallised lemons, oranges, and other fruit) and boxes of ginger and nutmeg.[13] As Elizabeth grew older she often ate little else but cakes, sweets, custards and puddings, comfits, gingerbread and custard tarts.

Lady Mary Sidney's offering to the Queen for the New Year of 1579 is also recorded in the gift rolls. She gave Elizabeth a 'smock and two pillowbiers [pillowcases] of cambric, fair wrought with black work and edged with a broad bone lace of black silk', doubtless the product of her own handiwork.[14] These Christmas and New Year festivities were to be the last that Lady Mary would spend resident at court and the following summer she retired to her Welsh estates.[15] The pressures of trying to supervise the running of the family home at Penshurst while her husband was away for long periods in Wales or Ireland, as well as attending on the Queen, proved too much for her failing health. The smallpox from which she had suffered fifteen years before, together with the premature death of three of her daughters and the family's ongoing financial troubles had all taken their toll. It had been a constant battle for Mary to protect her position at court and to maintain suitable lodgings for her and her husband. She left the court feeling aggrieved and neglected, and concluded that she was 'ill thought on', despite her years of loyal service. As Sir Henry wrote to her, 'When the worst is known, old Lord Harry and his old Moll will do as well as they can in parting, like good friends the small portion allotted our long service in court; which as little as it is, seems something too much.'[16]

Her departure the following summer prompted no acknowledgement from the Queen and it was left only for Mendoza, the Spanish ambassador, who was clearly unaware of the deterioration of Mary's relationship with her Majesty, to report that 'the sister of the Earl of Leicester, of whom the Queen was very fond and to whom she had given rooms at court, had retired to her own home'.[17]

Just weeks before the Queen and her ladies had mourned the death of Isabella Harington. Isabella had been one of the most favoured and long-serving ladies, who had been imprisoned with the Princess Elizabeth during the years before her accession. She had become one of the Queen's most intimate companions and had served in the Queen's Bedchamber as her bedfellow. She died at her house in London on 20 May 1579 and was buried five days later at the church of St Gregory's in St Paul's Churchyard.[18]

Blanche Parry meanwhile remained in the Queen's service and at the heart of the court, despite having been seriously ill. It was likely to have been Blanche's unexpected recovery that led the Queen to give her a gift of 'two pieces of old sables taken out of a cloak and two pieces of like sables being taken out of a night gown of chequered velvet' on 9 April 1579.[19] The skins of beautiful soft fur were brought into England from Russia by the Muscovy Company. This was the second or third pair of sables that Blanche now had, highly unusual as the sumptuary laws specifically reserved sables for the nobility; Elizabeth treated Blanche as if she were a baroness. Around this time, John Dee, who had returned from his European travels, asked Blanche to be godmother to his son Arthur and when his daughter was born, he asked the same of Mary Scudamore. Clearly Dee saw the benefits of courting the favour of Elizabeth's most trusted women as a means to secure his own advancement.[20]

30

Amorous Potions

The progress of 1578 through East Anglia to Norwich had been dominated by Elizabeth's marriage negotiations. The prospect of a match with
François – formerly the Duke of Alençon, but after his brother's accession
to the throne the Duke of Anjou – had been revived as a means to contain
the threat of him gaining control of the Netherlands by coming to terms
with the States-General.[1] As the progress wound its way through Norfolk
and into Suffolk, Elizabeth's councillors debated the merits of the match.
Would Anjou keep the French out of the Netherlands, or would he draw
them in? Was he sincere in his overtures to renew his suit or was he
merely looking for English aid to finance a new army to shore up his position in the Low Countries and continue to fight against Spain? Was it
necessary for the Queen to marry him? Sir Francis Walsingham remained
firmly opposed to the match believing Anjou was deceiving the Queen.[2]
The Earl of Sussex wrote of the benefits which might 'grow by this
marriage at this time', and about the perils which would follow 'if she
married not at all'.[3]

Whilst Anjou was now a more respectable twenty-three years old, and
Elizabeth forty-five, they still remained an odd couple. Elizabeth had
always felt uneasy about the age difference, considering herself to be an
old woman compared to this 'beardless' youth and her reservations had
begun to be shared by Anjou's mother and brother, Catherine de Medici
and Henri III. Now Anjou was heir presumptive they believed the duke
should not be thinking about marrying a woman in her mid-forties who
was unlikely to deliver a son. The question of Elizabeth's age and fertility
were central to the negotiations: the French needed a fertile bride.
Elizabeth attempted to allay fears by promising to agree to an annulment
if she proved to be barren.

Whilst having for so long petitioned the Queen to marry, many of
Elizabeth's councillors now began to have doubts about whether she was

now too old to contemplate marriage and children. Walsingham believed 'the danger that women of her Majesty's years are most commonly subject unto by bearing of children' was too high. If Elizabeth conceived she ran the risk of dying in childbirth and, if she failed to conceive, her husband might 'seek by treason to be delivered of her' in the hope of having children by another wife.[4] The desire for an heir now had to be considered against the risk that Elizabeth would die in the attempt.[5]

Cecil, typically methodical and judicious, weighed the 'objections' against the 'benefits' of the marriage. In an attempt to discover the truth as to Elizabeth's health and fertility, he questioned her doctors, her laundress, and the Ladies of the Bedchamber about the Queen's general health, menstrual cycle and the likelihood of her conceiving. He recorded his findings in a memorandum in which he concluded that:

> considering the proportion of her body, having no impediment of smallness in stature, of largeness in body, nor no sickness nor lack of natural functions in those things that properly belong to the procreation of children, but contrary wise, by judgement of physicians that know her estate in those things and by the opinion of women, being more acquainted with her Majesty's body in such things as properly appertain, to show probability of her aptness to have children, even at this day. So as for anything that can be gathered from argument, all other things, save the numbering of her years, do manifestly prove her Majesty to be very apt at the procreation of children ... it may be by good reasons maintained that by forbearing from marriage her Majesty's own person shall daily be subject to such dolours and infirmities as all physicians do usually impute to womankind for lack of marriage, and especially to such women as naturally have their bodies apt to conceive and procreate children.[6]

While Cecil admitted that it would have been better if the forty-five-year-old Queen had married when she was younger, he believed that she had five or six fertile years left. He wrote of the Duchess of Savoy, 'a woman of sallow and melancholy complexion, and in all respects far inferior to her Majesty', who had been older than Elizabeth when she gave birth to a baby son. Following the medical theory of the day, Cecil argued that Elizabeth suffered ill-health 'for lack of marriage', in other words sexual intercourse. Cecil attributed the pains in her cheek and face to her spinsterhood. Marriage would, he argued, improve the Queen's general health. A more serious problem, Cecil concluded, lay in 'the mislike of the people to be governed by a foreign prince and especially by the blood of France'.[7]

Robert Dudley stood firmly opposed to the match and he too believed the danger to Elizabeth's health of attempting to conceive an heir was too great. In a revealing letter to Walsingham, he wrote of how 'the more I love her, the more fearful am I to see such dangerous ways taken. God of his mercy help all'[8] – at the same time keeping the secret of his marriage to Lettice Knollys from the Queen and fearing that the arrival of a foreign suitor for Elizabeth might lead to the extent of his betrayal being revealed.

In August, Anjou sent two envoys, 'M[onsieur] de Bacqueville' and 'M[onsieur] de Quissy', to England to reopen the marriage negotiations. They were to reassure Elizabeth that the duke was 'at her Majesty's devotion' and would follow her directions in the Netherlands. Anjou promised that he had no expansionist aims in Flanders and wanted only to help the people of the Netherlands gain 'their liberties by force of armies against the Spanish tyranny'.[9] He was also anxious for Elizabeth to know that his feelings for her had 'nothing to do with avarice or ambition' but were inspired by her beauty and virtue. Yet one later report described how Catherine de Medici had claimed that her son 'was somewhat embarrassed, when as a young man devoted to pleasure, he called to mind the advanced age and repulsive physical nature of the Queen, she being, in addition to other ailments, half-consumptive [a reference to her weight loss] ... but the lust to reign will contend with the lust of the flesh, and we shall see which of these two passions possesses the greater force'.[10]

During their stay Elizabeth showed the ambassadors great favour, spoke of her desire to marry and made light of the age difference; Anjou would be to her a son as well as a husband.[11] She suggested religious disagreements could be overcome, but raised doubts as to the duke's sincerity. She had been let down in the past by the duke and his brother and now insisted that he prove his affection by visiting the court in person.[12] Elizabeth was, it seemed, allowing herself to at last indulge in the prospect of taking a husband; she knew it would be the last chance that she would have.

Yet many fiercely opposed the marriage. When the court was at Norwich during the summer, the playwright Thomas Churchyard had been commissioned by the city's staunchly Protestant lord mayor to put on entertainments which criticised the renewal of the Anjou marriage negotiations, urged Elizabeth to remain single and for the first time publicly celebrated her as the 'Virgin Queen'.[13] In the pageant *Cupid's Fall from Heaven*, Venus and her son Cupid, both 'thrust out of heaven', fall to earth where they meet a philosopher and Dame Chastity who teaches them the error of their ways. Chastity then hands over Cupid's bows and arrows to the Queen with the message that she could do with them 'what she pleased' and 'learn to shoot at whom she pleased' since 'none could wound her highness's heart' and she had chosen the 'best life' of celibacy. The message to Elizabeth in respect of the Anjou negotiations was clear.

<hr />

The Duke of Anjou's courtship of Elizabeth began in earnest the following year with a series of passionate letters promising undying love. In January 1579 his best friend and trusted household servant, Jean de Simier, Baron de Saint-Marc, arrived to woo her with gifts and jewels and to negotiate a marriage treaty.[14] Elizabeth quickly became enamoured with Simier and for the next two months they met for long, intimate meetings, sometimes up to three times a day. She flirted amorously with him in public, calling him her 'ape' – a Latin pun on his name – and entertained him at countless feasts, jousts, masques and dances. She gave him gloves, handkerchiefs and a miniature portrait of herself as love tokens for the duke.[15] When Elizabeth's councillors learned that Simier had, with the Queen's permission, entered her Bedchamber to purloin a handkerchief and nightcap as 'trophies' for his master, they were shocked and condemned Simier's behaviour as 'an unmanlike, unprincelike, French kind of wooing'. Elizabeth had apparently also visited Simier's bedchamber one morning as he was dressing and insisted that he talk with her 'with only his jerkin on'.[16] Mary Queen of Scots would later repeat gossip that Elizabeth had enjoyed sexual relations with Simier.

The French ambassador, Michel de Castelnau, Sieur de Mauvissière, wrote that the wooing made Elizabeth seem younger. 'This discourse rejuvenates the Queen; she has become more beautiful and bonny than she was fifteen years ago. Not a woman or a physician who knows her does not hold that there is no lady in the realm more fit for bearing children than she is.'[17] Simier was cautiously optimistic about the prospects for the match with Anjou, writing, 'will wait to say more till the curtain is drawn, the candle out and Monsieur in bed'.[18] To Elizabeth, Catherine de Medici expressed similar sentiments: she would not be content until she saw her son and Elizabeth in bed together.[19]

On the first Sunday of Lent, Elizabeth was delivered a sermon which prophesied that the marriage would bring about the destruction of the kingdom. The preacher said 'that marriages with foreigners would only result in ruin to the country' and then invoked the memory of how Queen Mary had 'married a foreigner, and caused the martyrdom of so many persons, who were burnt all over the country'. Before the sermon ended, Elizabeth stormed out.[20] So many sermons were 'speaking so violently against the marriage', that according to George Talbot, son of the Earl of Shrewsbury, Elizabeth prohibited ministers from preaching on any text that might be seen as related to the issue.[21]

In the spring of 1579 the debate raged in the Privy Council. There were now mounting suspicions that Philip of Spain was planning to assert his claim to the Portuguese throne. Its recently crowned King, an elderly Catholic cardinal, was likely to die soon without issue. This raised the threatening prospect of Philip inheriting the Atlantic state and the overseas empire of Portugal, which would give him the resources he needed to reconquer the Netherlands and launch an invasion of England.[22] Cecil believed the marriage to Anjou was the only realistic way to see off the foreign threats mounting against the realm. Without it, he claimed, 'her Majesty shall stand alone, without aid of any mighty prince . . . and weakened at home'. The danger as he saw it came from the 'joining of the Kings of Spain & France together with the Pope, the Emperor & others'. Together they made up a formidable Catholic threat which, he argued, was conspiring to stir up rebellion in England and Ireland, aid the Marian faction in Scotland, and attempt a 'common war by their own joint forces' against England. By marrying Anjou, Elizabeth would forge an alliance with France that would cause a split in the Catholic coalition, strengthen the Huguenots and 'compel the King of Spain to agree with his subjects [in the Low Countries] upon reasonable conditions'.[23]

Yet Walsingham believed that the danger from France had been exaggerated, that Anjou's abortive campaign in the Low Countries had demonstrated he was hardly a dangerous enemy and the power of the King and the Guises in France was being held in check by the Huguenots who were gaining strength under Henri of Navarre. Similarly the peril from Philip II could be contained as long as the forces of the States-General in the Low Countries continued to pin down Spanish forces. Indeed, Walsingham argued the international Catholic threat was less serious than it had been before. He said that Elizabeth should lend the Huguenots money and give military assistance to the Duch rebels. The marriage he believed would only make matters worse and would alienate

James VI of Scotland by threatening to end his hopes of inheriting the English crown.[24]

＊

On 17 July, as the Queen, accompanied by Simier, was travelling along the Thames by barge from Greenwich to Deptford, a passing boatman named Thomas Appletree shot at them. One of the shots passed within six feet of the Queen, hitting her bargeman and forcing him 'to cry and screech out piteously, supposing himself to be slain'. Ever since the Ridolfi plot many had feared such an event. Appletree was caught, condemned to death and four days later brought to the gallows; but, choosing to believe it was an accident and not a failed assassination attempt, 'when the hangman had put the rope about his neck, he was, by the Queen's most gracious pardon, delivered from execution'.[25] Even so, Elizabeth took the precaution of declaring, by public proclamation, that the French envoys and their servants were now under her royal protection, and forbade any persons from molesting them, on peril of severe punishment.

Dudley tried to undermine Jean de Simier's efforts to woo the Queen by spreading rumours at court that the Frenchman had used 'amorous potions and unlawful arts' and had 'crept into the Queen's mind and insisted her to the love of [Monsieur]'.[26] It was also rumoured that Dudley was behind attempts to murder the envoy, that he tried to have Simier poisoned and, when that plan failed, employed a man called Robin Tider to lie in wait and shoot him as he came out of a garden gate at Greenwich. However, Tider baulked when he saw how well guarded Simier was.[27] Thereafter Simier took the precaution of wearing a privy doublet beneath the shirt.[28]

Realising that Dudley was a key obstacle to the match, as soon as Simier learnt of Dudley's secret marriage to Lettice Knollys he told the Queen. Elizabeth was furious and deeply shaken. Dudley had been by her side throughout her reign. She had come to depend on his devotion, but now after twenty years their relationship was ruptured. For nearly a year, since the autumn of 1578, Dudley had been deceiving her and whilst concealing the fact of his own marriage, had done all he could to hinder Elizabeth from taking a consort. At first she threatened to send him to the Tower, but she was persuaded to modify her punishment. He was confined at Greenwich and then banished to his own house at Wanstead. Lettice was exiled from court. The Queen would take her hostility towards her to her grave.[29]

Elizabeth now agreed to grant the Duke of Anjou safe conduct to visit England.[30] She added an important caveat: the duke's visit was to be kept secret and he was to travel into England in disguise and with only a small retinue.

31

Froggie Went A-Courtin'

François, Duke of Anjou, arrived at Greenwich early in the morning of 17 August 1579. He was shown to the house in the grounds of the palace, where Simier was staying. He immediately woke his envoy and demanded to be taken to Elizabeth. Simier cautioned his master to bide his time, telling him the Queen did not like rising early and that it would be better not to take her by surprise.

Though Elizabeth sought to keep the duke's visit a secret, even before his arrival the news had leaked, forcing her to ban all such discussion among her courtiers and to take drastic measures to ensure Anjou's safety. On 26 July a proclamation was issued 'against the common use of Dagges, Handguns, Harquebuses, Callivers and Coats of defence': no one was to carry a firearm in the vicinity of the court.[1] There had already been two attempts on Simier's life and at least one was believed to have been instigated by a murderously possessive Robert Dudley.[2]

Anjou spent the next ten days being lavishly entertained with balls, parties and banquets and enjoying hours of flirtatious conversation with the Queen. She had always longed to be wooed in person by one of her illustrious suitors and for once seemed to be genuine in her affections and interest in the marriage. The Queen appeared won over by Anjou's charm and to have put aside her fears about his ugliness and the scarring of his pox-marked skin. At dusk most evenings Elizabeth would slip out of the palace with one of her ladies, most probably the wise and discreet Dorothy Stafford, to dine at the pavilion where the duke and Simier were staying. Perhaps because of his complexion, or his deep gravelly voice or bandy legs, Elizabeth gave him the nickname 'Frog'.[3] At court, frog jewellery became popular gifts for the Queen.[4] The ballad 'Froggie Went A-Courtin'', which survives as a traditional folksong, was originally circulated in 1580 as a mocking account of Elizabeth's courtship with François of Anjou.

Pamphlets and popular ballads bitterly opposing the marriage began to pour forth from printing presses throughout England. In August, a long and subversive tract written by John Stubbs, a Lincoln's Inn lawyer, was secretly printed in London and widely distributed. *The Discoverie of a Gaping Gulf whereinto England is like to be swallowed by an other French marriage, if the Lord forbid not the banes, by lettering her Majestie to see the sin and punishment thereof*' was inspired by a combination of religious fervour and patriotic zeal.[5] Stubbs wrote as one who was, 'her Majesty's loving true servant', but who dreaded the prospect of Elizabeth being 'led blindfold as a poor lamb to the slaughter' in a shameful marriage with a French Catholic prince. Using vivid allusions to penetration and invasion, Stubbs described how 'the old serpent in shape of a man' would 'seduce our Eve' so that she may 'lose this English paradise'.[6] Syphilis (the 'French disease') might contaminate the Queen's body and childbirth could destroy it. He argued that Elizabeth was putting the satisfaction of her personal desires before her duty to protect 'the welfare of her body politic or commonweal body, which is her body of majesty'.[7] He also believed that Anjou could never possibly be in love with a woman twenty years his senior. 'Not one in a thousand of those younger men that seek their elder matches but doth it in side respects,' he announced, 'it is quite contrary to his young appetites, which will otherwise have their desire.'[8]

Elizabeth was appalled by Stubbs's tract and on 27 September issued a proclamation banning the 'lewd desitious book' and ordering the Lord Mayor of London to collect and burn all copies. Preachers were instructed to speak out against the 'seditious libeller'.[9] Stubbs was swiftly arrested and condemned to the barbarous punishment of losing his right hand.[10] It did little to silence opposition to her marriage; according to the Spanish ambassador, the proclamation which Elizabeth issued, 'instead of mitigating the public indignation against the French, has irritated it and fanned the flame'. A letter from England to the Venetian ambassador in France on 29 November claimed that defamatory libels against Anjou were still appearing every day and that Dudley's chaplain had presented the Queen with a petition against the marriage.[11] Philip Sidney, the son of Mary Sidney, who had recently retired, also wrote against the marriage. 'A Letter to Queen Elizabeth', which was circulated widely at court, sought, through a combination of flattery and counsel, to describe the dangers to the realm if the marriage went ahead, and petitioned Elizabeth, 'there can almost happen no worldly thing of more evident danger to your state royal'.[12]

On 28 August, the Duke of Anjou left for France. Simier subsequently gave the Queen an account of the duke's last evening in England. Unable to sleep, Anjou had spent the night sighing, lamenting, waking Simier again and again to speak of the Queen's 'divine beauties and his extreme regret at being separated from your Majesty [Elizabeth], the gaoler of his heart and mistress of his liberty'.[13]

Elizabeth was unsure as to what course to follow. At the beginning of October she ordered her council to discuss the question of the Anjou match and give their opinion of it. Meeting after meeting was held, but all 'without proceeding to any full resolution'. Their final decision was that the Queen should 'do what best shall please her'. Elizabeth had not wanted her councillors to leave the decision to her; she had wanted them to override her doubts and persuade her that it would be right to marry Anjou. Now she 'uttered many speeches and not that without shedding of many tears', as Cecil recorded, in her disappointment that her councillors should have shown 'any disposition to make it doubtful whether there could be any more surety for her and her realm than to have her marry and have a child of her own body to inherit, and so continue the line of Henry VIII'. The Spanish ambassador reported that she 'remained extremely sad', and 'was so cross and melancholy that it was noticed by everyone who approached her'. She told Walsingham, the arch opponent of the match, to get out of her sight, vowing that 'the only thing he was good for was a protector of heretics'.[14]

Finally, despite the chorus of protest, on 20 November, Elizabeth instructed a small group of privy councillors to draw up a draft marriage treaty and within weeks Simier left England to take it to France.[15] There was still one major obstacle, however. Elizabeth had promised to sign the treaty on condition that she secured her people's consent over the next two months.[16] If not, as Simier was forced to agree, the marriage articles would be null and void.

After the envoy's departure, the heady romance of the Anjou courtship began to fade. Sensing the Queen's growing uncertainty, Simier wrote in January that he could tell her change of heart had been brought about by those wishing to prevent the marriage. In a deliberate reference to Dudley, whose coat of arms contained the bear and ragged staff, he begged Elizabeth to 'protect her monkey [Simier] from the paw of the bear'. He tried to play on her pride and mused, 'who would have thought that a queen of the heavens and the earth, a princess of all virtue in the world, could be mistaken in her knowledge of certain people who feel neither love than affection otherwise than ambition for power impels them'. Yet without the attentive presence of either Simier or Anjou, the Queen was drawn back to Dudley for affection and companionship.[17]

At the end of January, Elizabeth regrettably informed Anjou that, although there was no prince in the world to whom she would rather give herself than him, her subjects' objections to the match had not been overcome and they would not tolerate a king-consort who openly celebrated his Catholic faith. Whilst refusing to make any such concession over religion, Anjou remained committed to the match and urged Elizabeth to think again.[18] For the rest of the year, Elizabeth's position in respect of the negotiations with the duke remained in a deliberately managed state of limbo as she sought to maintain an alliance with France.

With each passing month the international Catholic threat appeared to become ever more serious. In January 1580, the new Pope, Gregory XIII, reissued his predecessor's bull of excommunication against Elizabeth and was known to be plotting a new enterprise against her in Ireland. The Spanish were also consolidating their position. The assertion of Spanish control in the Netherlands continued unrelentingly and following the death of the King of Portugal, Philip II began to prepare a military offensive to assert his claim to the throne. In August, Spanish troops crossed the Portuguese border and captured Lisbon, and in September, Spanish troops landed in the west of Ireland and occupied Smerwick. Despite her incarceration, Mary Stuart had embarked upon a fresh round of plots against Elizabeth, in league with the Spanish ambassador Mendoza. At the same time the young King James VI of Scotland was falling under the influence of the 'very Catholic' Esmé Stuart d'Aubigny, whom James had created Earl of Lennox and had also become involved with his mother's Guise relations, raising fears that he might 'be conveyed into France and so governed and directed by the Guisians'.[19]

Sir Christopher Hatton wrote to Walsingham in April 1580, telling him that England was entirely isolated and living in fear of a Catholic invasion, 'beset on all sides with so great and apparent dangers'.[20] To offset the threat, Elizabeth had entered into an alliance with the French, but France was now a much weakened power. The latest outbreak of wars of religion had left the country riven with internal dissent and no effective ally against the might of Spain. Dudley and Walsingham led calls for Elizabeth to send direct military intervention to the Netherlands, but the Queen was reluctant to make such an explicit commitment of troops and instead looked to give Anjou hope for a future alliance and cultivate good relations with the French King, Henri III. When in late June, the

States-General seemed set to offer Anjou sovereignty of the Netherlands, Elizabeth hastily sent Sir Edward Stafford to France to express her renewed commitment to the French match. Anjou immediately agreed to the dispatch of French commissioners to England to conclude the marriage treaty.[21]

In April 1581, a huge French embassy of some five hundred people arrived in England to agree terms. So fearful was the Queen of disturbances in London that before the French commissioners arrived, she issued a proclamation commanding that due honour be shown to the ambassadors on pain of death.[22] During their six-week stay, the commissioners were magnificently entertained with feasts and tournaments. A vast banqueting hall decorated with greenery and a ceiling painted with stars and sunbeams had been specially built on the south-west side of Whitehall Palace. It was a spectacular stage on which to host the large number of French nobility who had come to the English court for a marriage – as would become clear – a marriage that would never take place.

On the 15 May, the play *The Four Foster Children of Desire* was enacted for the visitors in the adjoining tiltyard. In a chivalrous spectacle, 'Desire' and his 'foster children' endeavoured to storm the 'Fortress of Perfect Beauty', using 'pretty scaling ladders' and 'flowers and such fancies'. They addressed the Queen, pleading with her to render up her beauty to the forces of desire, but were driven back by Virtue, leaving the maiden fortress intact. The challengers were rebuked by an angel who proclaimed, 'If in besieging the Sun you understand what you had undertaken, you would destroy a common blessing for a private profit.'[23]

Anjou was now vainly pursuing the Queen of England who had resolved that a strategic alliance not a marriage was what she sought with the French. Considering the 'growing greatness of Spain' it seemed necessary that 'some straighter league should be made between the two countries whatsoever became of the marriage'. At an audience with the French commissioners on 28 April, Elizabeth warned that she might not be able to marry Anjou because the earlier obstacles to the match remained and others had intensified with the passing of time: childbirth would be undoubtedly more dangerous to Elizabeth, now aged forty-eight. The arrival of missionary priests to England heightened the difficulties posed by Anjou's Catholicism and the duke's activities in the Netherlands threatened war against Spain.[24]

The French ambassador responded by telling Elizabeth that the most important reason to marry Anjou was to save her honour, a reason 'of more importance than any namely that it was said that [Anjou] had slept with her'. Elizabeth responded that she could disregard such a rumour. Hardly so, said the ambassador, she might well do so in her own country, but not elsewhere, where it had been publicly stated. Elizabeth angrily insisted that a clear and innocent conscience feared nothing.[25] Nevertheless, she now expressed her reluctance to pursue the marriage citing the age gap and in May 1581 wrote to the French envoy that, 'I am afraid that I am too much advanced in years to please the duke, on which subject I have written him a long letter.'[26]

Yet Anjou still remained committed to the marriage as a means to secure aid for his military campaign in the Low Countries. He continued to write Elizabeth love letters, which became increasingly explicit, and in which he expressed his desire to be 'kissing and rekissing all that Your beautiful Majesty can think of', as well as to be 'in bed between the sheets in your beautiful arms'.[27] He had no doubt that their passion would soon engender a son, 'made and forged by the little Frenchman who is and will be eternally your humble and very loving slave'. In October 1581, Anjou returned to England, intending to stay for three months. 'The principal object of his visit is to ask for money,' the Spanish ambassador Mendoza boldly warned the Queen. Yet once again Elizabeth seemed enthralled and enraptured by Anjou's presence.

This time his visit was made public and when he arrived in London on 1 November he was placed in a house near the palace of Richmond, where the court was then located. Mendoza noted that 'the Queen doth not attend to other matters but only to be together with the duke in the chamber from morning till noon, and afterwards till two or three hours after sunset. I cannot tell what the devil they do.'[28] It was said that every morning, as Anjou lay in bed, Elizabeth visited him with a cup of broth, and that 'when the Queen and Anjou were alone together, she pledges herself to him to his heart's content, and as much as any woman could do to a man, but she will not have anything said publicly'.[29] Yet the French delegation became increasingly disillusioned as to whether the match would actually take place and their resentful mutterings even began to cast doubt on the prospect of any alliance between the two countries. Elizabeth promptly took action to show her suitor just how in earnest she was.

At eleven o'clock on 22 November Elizabeth walked with Anjou in her gallery at Whitehall, where the court was assembled to watch the Accession Day festivities. When the French ambassador approached and told her that Henri III had ordered him to 'hear from the Queen's own lips her intentions with regard to marrying his brother', Elizabeth responded decisively: 'You may write this to the King: that the Duke of Anjou shall be my husband.' She turned to the astonished duke, kissed him full on the lips and drew a ring from her finger which she gave to him 'as a pledge'.[30] It was a moment of high drama. When the Queen summoned her ladies and gentlemen and repeated what she had said, many of the women burst into tears. A messenger was immediately despatched to carry the news to the French court. King Henri III announced that his brother would be King of England and would soon be 'a nasty thorn' in the leg of the Spanish King.[31]

Yet whilst Mendoza claimed that 'people in London consider the marriage as good as accomplished, and the French are of the same opinion', in his view the Queen's display 'is only artful and conditional'. The art lay in her ability to make Anjou believe she was in earnest; the condition was whether or not her people would accept her decision. Elizabeth could remain comfortably certain that Parliament and her councillors would demonstrate their implacable resistance to the marriage. As Mendoza put it, 'by personally pledging herself in this way, she binds him to her', and added, 'she rather prefers to let it appear that the failure of the negotiations is owing to the country and not to herself, as it is important for her to keep him attached to her, in order to counterbalance his brother [Henri III] and prevent anything being arranged to her prejudice'.[32]

The Privy Council responded with predictable hostility. Sir Christopher Hatton sobbed that she might be deposed if she insisted on marrying against the will of the people. Dudley, unnerved by Elizabeth's display of affection to Anjou and her pledge to him, went as far as to ask her directly whether she were 'a maid or a woman'.[33] It was an incredibly audacious question to ask of the Queen. Yet despite Dudley's insolence, Elizabeth responded calmly that she was still a maiden; perhaps she was flattered to be asked the question at her age, and perhaps it was an opportunity to demonstrate her credentials as the Virgin Queen.

The night after Elizabeth made her announcement, her Bedchamber was a place of great torment. Elizabeth lay with Dorothy Stafford, Mary Scudamore and Blanche Parry, who 'wailed and laid terrors before her, and did so vex her mind with argument' that the Queen could not sleep. They entreated her 'not to share her power and glory with a foreign spouse, or to sully her fair fame as a Protestant queen, by vowing obedience to a Catholic husband'.[34] Elizabeth barely slept and in the morning sent for Anjou. He found her pale and in tears. 'Two more nights such as the last,' she told him, 'would bring her to the grave.' She explained that 'although her affection for him was undiminished, she had, after an agonising struggle, determined to sacrifice her own happiness to the welfare of her people'.[35] According to one account, she told him that it would be unfair to marry him as he needed a wife who could bear him children and continue the Valois line. However, she promised to be 'very much more attached to him as a friend even than if he were her husband'.[36]

When Anjou left England for the Netherlands in early February 1582, he departed as a protégé of the Queen. Elizabeth made much of being grief-stricken at the loss of her lover, saying she could no longer stay at Whitehall, 'because the place gives cause of remembrance to her of him, with whom she so unwillingly parted'. After he had gone she professed a sense of grief as to what she had lost. She cried that she would give a million to have her Frog swimming in the Thames again, instead of the stagnant waters of the Netherlands, though Mendoza claimed that in truth, Elizabeth danced for joy in the privacy of her Bedchamber at the prospect of being rid of the Frenchman. [37]

Anjou's departure from England signalled the end of Elizabeth's courting days, and she knew it. Now that he was gone so too was the chance of any marriage, or children. In her poem 'On Monsieur's Departure', which she penned after Anjou left for France, Elizabeth revealed her conflicted feelings; her resistance to marriage but, perhaps also her loneliness and yearning for love:

> I grieve, and dare not show my discontent;
> I love, and yet am forced to seem to hate;
> I dote, yet dare not say I ever meant;
> I seem stark mute, yet inwardly do prate.
> I am and am not – freeze and yet I burn
> Since from myself my other self I turn.
> My care is like my shadow in the Sun–
> Follows me flying, flies when I pursue it . . .[38]

The Queen and the duke continued to exchange ardent letters and the marriage was talked about long after it had become impossible. Anjou's campaign in the Low Countries had proved a failure and in the summer of 1584 he died of fever. Elizabeth went into mourning and wrote to Catherine de Medici,

... your sorrow, I am sure cannot be greater than my own. For in as much as you are his mother, so it is that there remain to you several other children. But for me, I find no consolation except death, which I hope will soon reunite us. Madame, if you were able to see an image of my heart you would see the portrait of a body without a soul. But I will trouble you no longer with my plaints, since you have too many of your own.[39]

Whilst the negotiations for a French match were finally at an end, rumours persisted as to what had happened between Elizabeth and Anjou during his time in England. On 17 November 1583, Sir Edward Stafford, now the English ambassador in Paris, reported with alarm that lewd pictures of Elizabeth and Anjou had been publicly exhibited across the city. Writing to Walsingham, the Queen's Principal Secretary, Stafford described how a 'foul picture' of the Queen's Majesty had been put up, 'she being on horseback her left hand holding the bridle of the horse, with her right hand pulling up her clothes showing her hindpart ('Sir reverence') ... under it was a picture of Monsieur, very well drawn, in his best apparel, having upon his fist a hawk which continually baited and would never make her sit still.' As Stafford reported, 'I am afraid some of our good English men here have a part in it for I think there are not many naughty people in the world as some of them be.'[40] The pictures were displayed on the Place de Grève, one of the main public spaces on the Right Bank, directly in front of the Hôtel de Ville, and on the Left Bank, on the corner of the Augustins and outside College Montaigu. The timing and positioning was very deliberate as these sites would have been heavily frequented both by exiles and locals.

Although the primary intent of such cartoons was to stir up anti-Elizabethan sentiment in Paris, Stafford wrote that 'in my opinion it toucheth more Monsieur's honour then the Qu[een's] if every body interpret it as I do'. Seemingly Anjou was also being mocked and degraded for his unsuccessful attempts to woo the ageing and immoral Elizabeth. The focus of the attack was again the person of the Queen whose regal authority was undermined by the exposure of her lower body and Stafford's exclamation – 'Sir reverence' – is a euphemistic allusion to defecation.[41]

Less than a month later, Stafford discovered that this was part of a larger campaign. Visual and written media were being employed to link Elizabeth's heresy and 'sexual depravity' and to portray the cruelty and injustice practised by Elizabeth's government on its Catholic subjects.[42] Stafford obtained drafts of Richard Verstegan's broadsheets in late 1583 which referred to Elizabeth as the 'She-wolf,' a classic symbol of lewdness. Stafford pushed for a raid on the printing house and finally Verstegan, an English exile and publisher, and his associates were arrested.[43] It was but a temporary reprieve; time and again in the years that would follow, the Catholic League would use images of the English Queen's corrupt body to challenge the legitimacy of her rule.

32

Semper Eadem

Elizabeth was almost fifty now; with no hope of having a child of her own, it was clear that she would be the last of the Tudor line. Concern over her fertility, the pressure to marry and produce an heir, had dominated her health and politics since the beginning of her reign. Now she began to be celebrated as the Virgin Queen who had selflessly sacrificed the desires of her natural body for that of the inviolable sovereign body politic. A series of seven portraits, painted at the time of the Anjou negotiations, all depict Elizabeth holding a sieve. The sieve was a symbol of virginity by virtue of its reference to the Roman Vestal Virgin, Tuccia. When accused of breaking her vestal vows, Tuccia proved her virginity by filling a sieve with water from the River Tiber and carrying it back to the Temple of Vesta without spilling a drop.[1] This imagery was designed to show that Elizabeth's virginity was her strength, providing her with the ability to make the sieve, which here represented the state, impenetrable.

Whilst Elizabeth's virginity was now being championed as a great political asset, it was also important that she was not seen to age or be regarded as the post-menopausal woman that she now was. Instead, as the years passed and she continued to refuse to name her successor, it became ever more necessary for the Queen to always appear radiant and youthful to reassure her subjects as to her good health and longevity. In 1586, Elizabeth revealed something of this pressure to maintain a suitable public image when, in the Presence Chamber at Richmond Palace, she addressed a delegation of representatives of the Lords and Commons: 'We princes, I tell you, are set on stages in the sight and view of all the world duly observed; the eyes of many behold our actions; a spot is soon spied in our garments; a blemish quickly noted in our doings.'[2]

As Elizabeth's facial imperfections inevitably multiplied, the Ladies of her Bedchamber laboured to perfect a 'mask of youth'. Smallpox scars, wrinkles, tooth decay and changes in the colour of her complexion increasingly demanded attention and the women of Elizabeth's intimate entourage patiently ministered to the Queen's withering face. The marks left by her smallpox, which despite her protestations were definitely there, together with the lines and wrinkles around her eyes and mouth, were skilfully hidden with layers of caustic cosmetics. Besides the pungent white lead and vinegar, which created Elizabeth's famous pale skin, egg white was increasingly used to glaze her face, to help hide her wrinkles and to smooth out her complexion, though making it rather difficult for the Queen to smile. The use of lead over time ate into her skin, making it grey and wrinkled, and so she would have to wear the lead base even more thickly. As Elizabeth aged, more vivid colours were used on her cheeks and lips. Besides using cochineal, she now wore a garish vermilion, also known as cinnabar, which gave an intense red colour.[3] However, vermilion was mercuric sulphide and so every time Elizabeth licked her lips she ingested this toxic substance and may have begun to experience symptoms of mercury poisoning, including lack of coordination, sensory impairment, memory loss, irritability, slurred speech, abominable pain and depression. By painting Elizabeth's face with these noxious substances, the Queen's ladies were slowly, unwittingly administering cosmetic poisoning which only accelerated the process of ageing.

The use of cosmetics had other unfavourable associations: make-up was regarded by some as synonymous with moral impurity and wayward sexuality; courtesans and prostitutes were notorious users of make-up. Pamphleteer Philip Stubbes noted that, 'the women of England colour their faces with certain oils, liquors, unguents and waters made to that end . . . their souls are thereby deformed and they brought deeper into the displeasure and indignation of the Almighty'.[4] In a court sermon delivered before the Queen and her ladies at Windsor more than ten years earlier, Bishop Thomas Drant had rebuked female vanity and been at pains to stress that face paint, bracelets, jewels and earrings counted for nothing in the contest against death.

> God made apparel, and God make the back; and he will destroy both the one and the other; yea, those heads that are now to be seen for their tall and bushy plumes – and that other sex, that have fine fresh golden caules so sheen and glossing – give me but a hundred years, nay, half a hundred years, and the earth will cover all these heads before me, and mine own to.[5]

And just to drive home his message Drant added,

Rich men are rich dust, wise men wise dust, worshipful men worshipful dust, honourable men honourable dust, majesty's dust, excellent majesty's excellent dust . . .[6]

Though Elizabeth is now well known for her extravagant use of cosmetics, contemporaries were notably silent on her use of them, the issue seeming to have been something of a taboo at court and the subject of censorship. There are no references to cosmetics on the New Year's gifts rolls; more likely, creams, paints or dyes for the Queen's face were not regarded as appropriate presents. The one contemporary mention of Elizabeth's face-painting that does survive, describing her make-up as being 'in some places near half an inch thick', was reported by a Jesuit priest. The same hardly unbiased source also said, 'her face showeth some decay, which to conceal when she cometh in public, she putteth many fine cloths into her mouth to bear out her cheeks.'[7]

Besides being sure to always appear in her 'mask of youth', it was also important for an idealised face of the Queen to be captured in portraits as a means to promote her authority. As Nicholas Hilliard, who entered Elizabeth's service as her principal portraitist, quickly realised, it was less about a need for an accurate portrayal of the Queen but rather an ideal image of delicately drawn and youthful features. Hilliard began painting miniatures for Elizabeth in 1572, but it was two full-size oil portraits, the *Pelican* and *Phoenix* portraits that began a transformation of the royal image.

Elizabeth's face in both portraits appears as smooth and emotionless as a mask and other than her delicate hand which holds her glove across her stomach, her body is encased in an overlarge, heavily embroidered gown.[8] At a time when Elizabeth, then in her forties, was beyond the age of fertility, it is no longer her natural body that attention is drawn to, but the body politic. The use of symbols and objects cast Elizabeth as an icon of virginity. The jewels suspended from the necklaces in each picture are motifs of piety, celibacy, self-denial and eternal youth; the phoenix is a symbol of resurrection and the triumph of immortality over death, an image particularly prescient after the papal excommunication and the Ridolfi plot to assassinate her.

Whilst Hilliard's miniatures and full-size paintings had moved towards the creation of his standard face for images of the Queen, it was very likely an Italian Frederigo Zuccaro, who had come to England at Elizabeth's request in 1576, that provided the master pattern that was to be adopted as the officially sanctioned image. In Zuccaro's 'Darnley' portrait, Elizabeth's face is unreal, like a mannequin's, and she is pictured wearing a simple gown of white and gold brocade with fine, lace ruff sleeves and a pearl necklace which is looped to form an oval across her right breast. In her right hand she holds a multi-coloured ostrich feather fan close to her body, and in her left a half-concealed small box. On the table to her left is a sceptre and crown, emphasising her status as queen and her identification with the body politic. Here the placement of the necklace and the fan on her breast and in front of her groin, draw attention to the Queen's natural, indeed sexual, body, whilst at the same time the prominent use of pearls symbolises her virginity and her triumph over lusts of the flesh and sexual appetite. Here then is a representation of the Queen's two bodies: the natural, physical and sexual body of a woman and the royal body politic represented by the royal regalia positioned next to her.

Zuccaro's blanched, mask-like face pattern was thereafter inserted on portraits of every size throughout the 1580s and early 1590s. The first of the so-called 'sieve portraits' adopted the Darnley face. No other face pattern of the Queen was to be so widely disseminated and this is testament to the government's ability to control the royal image during this period. For the women of the Bedchamber, who daily ministered the mask of youth to the Queen's face, and for the artists who captured it on canvas, Elizabeth's motto '*Semper Eadem*' – 'Always the Same', became a necessary instruction.

33

The Die is Cast

In Easter week of 1580, a mighty earthquake shook southern England. The earth heaved with a 'wondrous violent motion' and in London stones fell from buildings on to people in the streets below. It was feared that this was a portent of terrible things to come and new prayers were introduced into the litany for God's protection.[1] Within the next few months, Jesuit priests, direct from Rome, began to appear in England, raising fears that they were the vanguard of a Catholic crusade.

In June, Edmund Campion and Robert Persons crossed the Channel from France to Dover. Both were Oxford graduates who had fled to Rome to become Jesuit priests and they now returned to England in disguise, so as to elude capture by the port authorities. Campion and Persons then disappeared into the Catholic community of London and in the months that followed moved around the country, preaching, saying mass and hearing confessions.[2] Shortly after arriving in England, Campion set out an account of the Jesuit mission and his own personal calling in a letter which became known as 'Campion's Brag'.

'My charge,' he wrote, is 'to preach the Gospel, to minister the Sacraments, to instruct the simple, to reform sinners, to refute errors, and, in brief, to cry spiritual against foul vice and proud ignorance, wherewith my poor countrymen are abused.' He made clear that his Jesuit superiors had strictly forbidden him 'to deal in any respect with matters of state or policy of this realm, as those things that appertain not to my vocation. The enterprise is begun, it is of God, it cannot be withstood.'[3] Whilst this was written as a letter for the Privy Council, to be read in the event of his capture, copies quickly began to circulate among English Catholics. By October, Persons and a printer called Stephen Brinkley had set up a secret printing press in London, thereby ensuring Catholics could be fed with other inspiring texts, printed books and sermons.

Together the activities of Persons and Campion strengthened the resolve of the Catholic community and as rumours circulated of preparations for a papal-sponsored invasion of England, the perceived threat of the Jesuits intensified. The danger to the Queen and her realm came not only from an invasion supported by Spain and the Pope but also from priests arriving from Rome and Rheims. They were agents of foreign powers sent to stir sedition and rebellion and remove Elizabeth from her throne. On 10 January 1581, a royal proclamation ordered the return of all English students from foreign seminaries, and the arrest of all Jesuits in England. The intent and purpose of the seminaries it stated, was to turn the Queen's subjects in matters of religion and 'from the acknowledgement of their natural duties unto Her Majesty'. Young English Catholics had been made 'instruments in some wicked practices tending to the disquiet of this realm . . . yea to the moving of rebellion'.[4]

Parliament convened against this background of national anxiety. The opening speech, delivered by Sir Walter Mildmay, Chancellor of the Exchequer, spoke of anxieties about Jesuit infiltration which, he claimed, sought not only to 'corrupt the realm with false doctrine', but also, under that pretence, to 'stir sedition'.[5] The Pope had already emboldened 'many undutiful subjects to stand firm in their disobedience to her Majesty and to her laws' but now, Mildmay argued, he had 'sent hither a sort of hypocrites naming themselves Jesuits, a rabble of vagrant friars newly sprung up and coming through the world to trouble the Church of God'. Growing ever more impassioned as he continued, Mildmay claimed their 'principal errand is, by creeping into the houses and familiarities of men of behaviour and reputation, not only to corrupt the realm with false doctrine, but also, under that pretence, to stir up sedition to the peril of her Majesty and her good subjects'. Harsher laws were needed to meet the threat and to ensure the preservation and security of the Queen.[6]

The 1581 'Act to Retain the Queen's Majesty's Subject in Due Obedience' heralded the start of a period of severe persecution of the Catholics. It was now treason for a priest to absolve Elizabeth's subjects from their 'natural obedience' to her or to convert them 'for that intent to the Romish religion'.[7] This was directly targeted at the Jesuits and seminary priests and their converts.[8] Such was the climate of fear that conversion to Catholicism now became synonymous with treason. The Act also stiffened the penalties for saying mass or for not attending church. Any priest who celebrated mass now faced a year's imprisonment and a fine of 200 marks and the penalty for non-attendance was raised to a ruinous £20 a month.

The statute 'against seditious words and rumours uttered against the Queen's most excellent Majesty' was aimed especially at those who 'not only wished her Majesty's death' but by 'prophesying, calculation or other lawful act', tried to determine how long the Queen would live or who would succeed her.[9] Prophesying the Queen's death was also now a treasonable offence.

Despite intense searches for the Catholic priests, Campion and Persons had managed to elude capture by regularly changing disguises and staying constantly on the move. But then, on Sunday 16 July, Campion was found at Lyford Grange in Berkshire, the home of Francis Yates, a prisoner in Reading gaol, who had asked Campion to visit his family. Having become suspicious of the activity at the house, royal officials arrived with a warrant 'to take and apprehend, not any one man, but all priests, Jesuits and such like seditious persons' that they found. When they broke through a hollow wall the priests were discovered and promptly arrested. Campion, three fellow priests and eight others were then taken under armed guard to the Tower of London where they were imprisoned and interrogated.[10]

Campion was examined directly about his loyalty to Queen Elizabeth and asked whether he believed her to be 'a true and lawful queen, or a pretended queen and deprived, and in possession of her crown only de facto'. Campion refused to answer, saying only that 'he meddleth neither to nor fro, and will not further answer, but requireth that they may answer'. Under questioning he revealed details of his time in England, including the Catholic families with whom he had stayed, where he had preached and left books and details of the secret printing press which had been moved from London to Stonor Park, near Henley-on-Thames in Oxfordshire. This was now promptly destroyed. After agonising torture on the rack and formal disputation with theologians of the English church in St Peter ad Vincula, the parish church of the Tower of London, the trial of Campion and the other priests took place in November at Westminster Hall. Edmund Campion with twelve priests and laymen, including William Allen and Robert Persons in their absence, were charged with plotting to kill the Queen, to change the government and 'to incite, procure and induce diverse strangers and aliens . . . to invade the realm and raise, carry on and make war against the Queen'.[11] All were found guilty of treason.

On Friday 1 December, Campion was tied to a wicker hurdle and dragged by horse through the streets of London to the place of execution at Tyburn; the inscription hung around his head read, 'Edmund Campion, the seditious Jesuit'. He was hanged, as were the other priests, until he was almost dead, cut down from the gallows and then whilst still alive cut open and his bowels and genitals burned before him.[12]

Campion's execution did little to lessen anxiety over the threat of the Jesuits to the realm and to the 'safety of the Queen's person'. Priests were now regularly captured and interrogated, Catholic families placed under surveillance, letters intercepted, seditious books burned and ports watched for Catholics coming in and out of England. Sir Francis Walsingham used his powerful network of spies across Europe to uncover Catholic plots, most of which sought to place Mary Stuart on the throne, and to preserve the Queen from harm. He planted agents in harbours across Europe, intercepted correspondence and brutally interrogated those who were believed to conspire against Elizabeth's life and the security of the realm.

On 31 October 1581, while Edmund Campion was being held and interrogated in the Tower, John Payne, a Catholic priest who had returned from Douai with Cuthbert Mayne four years before, was being tortured on the rack after being accused of being involved in a conspiracy to murder Elizabeth and her leading councillors.[13]

The plot had been revealed to Robert Dudley by George Eliot, an 'ordinary Yeoman of Her Majesty's Chamber', as he described himself, and one of the royal officials who had captured Campion at Lyford Grange. Eliot, who had recently recanted his Catholic faith, claimed that Payne, whom he had known during his time spent in Catholic gentry homes in Essex and Kent, had masterminded the conspiracy, which also involved the rebel Earl of Westmoreland and leading exile Cardinal William Allen. This 'horrible treason' was, Eliot now claimed, 'shortly to happen'.

The plan, sponsored by the Pope, was for fifty armed men to assassinate Elizabeth while she was on a royal progress. Three other groups would target Dudley, Cecil and Walsingham 'and diverse others whose names he doth not well remember'. Eliot claimed that when he had asked Payne about 'how they could find in their hearts to attempt an act of so great cruelty', the priest responded by saying 'that the killing [of] her Majesty was no offence to God, nor the uttermost cruelty they could use to her, not [to] any that took her part; but that they might lawfully do it to a brute beast'. Having heard Eliot's statement, Dudley passed on the intelligence to Cecil who ordered that the priest be brought in and 'examined'.[14]

On 20 March 1582, John Payne left the Tower and was delivered to the Sheriff of Essex in order to be conducted to his trial in Chelmsford.[15] Despite his assertion of innocence and his claim that 'his feet never did tread, his hands never did write, nor his wit ever invent any treason against her Majesty', he was found guilty of treason and condemned to death. On Monday 2 April he was hanged, drawn and quartered. By the end of the reign some 200 priests and laypeople would share a similar traitor's fate.

When a comet appeared over London that summer, fears were reignited that it boded the death of 'some great person'.[16] Elizabeth, then at her palace in Richmond, was urged by her women not to look out of her window, but 'with a courage answering to the greatness of her state', she ignored their petition and, looking towards the light, declared, '*Jacta est alea*' – the die is cast.[17]

34

The Enemy Sleeps Not

In the autumn of 1583, John Somerville, a wealthy and well-born Catholic from Edstone, Warwickshire, began to engage in regular and intense conversation with what appeared to be a gardener on the estate of his father-in-law, Edward Arden, High Sheriff of Warwickshire. The gardener was in fact Hugh Hall, a Catholic priest whom Arden was secretly harbouring. According to the subsequent trial reports, Hall had talked to Somerville about the plight of Catholics in England, of Mary Queen of Scots being the rightful heir, and the moral corruption of the excommunicated Elizabeth, Henry VIII's bastard daughter.

On 24 October, Somerville left his wife and two young daughters and set out for London. After about four miles he stopped for the night at a tavern in Ayno-on-the-hill, where he announced his plan to shoot the Queen with his pistol and 'see her head set on a pole, for that she was a serpent and a viper'.[1] Somerville had already been under surveillance as a Catholic and known sympathiser of Mary Stuart. He was immediately arrested and a few days later found himself under interrogation in the Tower of London. After examination it was apparent he was a man 'of weak mind', and had been several times 'affected with frantic humour', yet such was the fever of the times that he and his father-in-law Edward Arden, his wife, sister and mother-in law together with Hugh Hall, their chaplain, were all arrested. Somerville was convicted of high treason, and he and his father-in-law were condemned to death. However, on the night before the sentence was to be carried out, Somerville hanged himself in his cell. This did not prevent the authorities from cutting off his head and placing it on a spike on London Bridge where the heads of all those who suffered the fate of traitors were displayed as a warning to others.[2]

Two weeks later, Francis Throckmorton, a young Catholic gentleman, was arrested at his house at Paul's Wharf by the Thames in London. He had long been under surveillance having been suspected 'upon secret intelligence given to the Queen's majesty, that he was a privy [secret] conveyor and receiver of letters to and from the Scottish Queen'. Now, following the anxiety caused by the arrest of John Somerville, the government decided to act. Whilst Throckmorton was taken into custody, his house was searched and a number of incriminating papers discovered that had been copied out in his own hand. These included a list of safe harbours 'for landing of foreign forces', the names of prominent Catholics who could be relied on to support an invasion, pedigrees detailing Mary's claim to the throne and a number of 'infamous pamphlets against her Majesty printed beyond the seas'. Indeed he was 'taken short at the time of his apprehension' in composing a letter in cypher to Mary Queen of Scots.[3]

Throckmorton had been working as a secret courier, carrying letters between Mary and the French ambassador in London, Michel de Castelnau. Walsingham knew that Throckmorton was a regular visitor at Castelnau's residence at Salisbury Court, just off Fleet Street, as the embassy was subject to his monitoring. Through the French ambassador, Throckmorton had become acquainted with three powerful members of the English Catholic nobility: Lord Henry Howard, the brother of Thomas, the 4th Duke of Norfolk, who had been executed as a traitor in 1572; Henry Percy, 8th Earl of Northumberland, whose brother Thomas, the 7th Earl had also been executed for treason in 1572; and Lord Thomas Paget, brother of Charles Paget, English émigré and known agent for the Guise.

On Friday 15 November, as Throckmorton was taken to the Tower, William Herle, Cecil's long-serving intelligencer in London, wrote to his master of a great international plot that he had discovered that involved the Duke of Guise, cousin of Mary Queen of Scots, Francis Throckmorton and Lord Henry Howard. As Herle revealed in his letter to Cecil:

> The chief mark that is shot at is her Majesty's person, whom God doth and will preserve, according to the confident trust in him. The Duke of Guise is the director of the action, and the Pope is to confer the Kingdom by his gift, upon such a one as is to marry with the Scottish Queen.

Throckmorton was, as Herle described him, 'a party very busy and an enemy to the present state'. His letter the following day added, 'the world is full of mischief, for the enemy sleeps not'.[4]

Under interrogation Throckmorton denied his involvement in the plot and any knowledge of treason. He claimed the papers found at his house were not his but belonged to one of his household servants. Having refused to talk, Throckmorton was 'somewhat pinched' on the rack in the Tower on at least two occasions, before making his confession. He had been recruited to carry letters to and from the Spanish ambassador in London by Sir Francis Englefield, a leading Catholic exile at the Spanish court, who was long considered a significant threat to English interests. Throckmorton then proceeded to reveal the details of the conspiracy: a popular uprising in the north of England would coincide with an invasion led by the Duke of Guise and financially supported by Philip of Spain.[5]

Francis Throckmorton was tried and condemned for treason at the Guildhall in London on 21 May 1584.[6] He threw himself on the Queen's mercy, asking her to forgive the 'inconsiderate rashness of unbridled youth', but was executed on 10 July at Tyburn. It was just one more traitor put to death; many more would go the same way. As Elizabeth wrote in a letter to the French ambassador, 'There are more than two hundred men of all ages who, at the instigation of the Jesuits, conspire to kill me.'[7] Throckmorton had not been the only Catholic noble under surveillance during the previous year. In November, William Herle had reported to Cecil that he had seen Charles Arundell, another Catholic gentleman, buying gloves and perfume from a new perfumier in Abchurch Street. Arundell was, Herle deduced, intending to 'use them to poison the Queen, she having her sense of smelling so perfect, and delighted with good savours'.[8]

With Throckmorton's 'confession' and the examination of the other nobles, Walsingham and the Privy Council believed that they had uncovered a major invasion plot, masterminded by the Duke of Guise and involving both the French and Spanish ambassadors, Michel de Castelnau, and Don Bernardino de Mendoza, together with senior noblemen in England and English Catholic émigrés. Although the Duke of Guise had been the 'director' of the plot, the unravelling of the conspiracy led to a significant rupture in Anglo-Spanish relations. Throckmorton had specifically identified Mendoza as the source for the duke's invasion plans. Long despised by the Elizabethan government, Mendoza was dismissed.[9] He was not replaced and thereafter would become a key ally of the Duke of Guise.[10]

Weeks later, as Mendoza prepared to depart England, he reported that 'a soldier returned from Terceira [a Portuguese-owned island in the Azores] had come to the court to give a letter to the Earl of Bedford and to see the Queen'. Mendoza described how the soldier 'proceeded with such boldness' that he entered the palace and found his way to 'the place where the Queen was with two other ladies'. Elizabeth 'cried out angrily for him to be seized', and he was taken to Dudley's chamber where he was asked whether Mendoza had sent him to 'kill the Queen'. Later the soldier said his entrance was to irritate the people against the Spanish ambassador and make them think that it was by his intervention that the mariner wanted to kill the Queen.[11] Dudley believed that any Catholic had become a danger to the Queen's own safety. 'There is no right papist in England that wisheth Queen Elizabeth to live long,' he wrote, 'and to suffer any such in her court cannot be but dangerous.'[12]

35

In Defence of the Queen's Body

On 10 July 1584, William of Orange, the Protestant leader in the Netherlands, was shot dead by a fanatical Spanish Catholic – a murder many believed was sponsored by Philip II of Spain. At once Elizabeth's own demise seemed to draw far closer. As Edward Stafford, son of Lady Dorothy, reported, similar atrocities were being planned, including an attack on the Queen: 'There is no doubt that she is a chief mark they shoot at and seeing there were many who would kill William of Orange anything could be done.'[1]

The assassination threat was now at its highest since the start of Elizabeth's reign. Throughout the year evidence of foiled plots and conspiracies filled diplomatic bags and personal correspondence. One intelligence report detailed how 'the life of our glorious sovereign lady Queen Elizabeth hath been most traitorously and devilishly sought', and might even have been taken 'if almighty God, her perpetual defender, of his mercy had not revealed and withstood the same'.[2] In March, Giordano Bruno, in a letter addressed from Paris and sent personally to Elizabeth, described how he had been visited by a Spaniard called Zubiaur, an agent for Mendoza, who had confessed 'the most ignoble things'. Zubiaur claimed that he had been charged by the Spanish ambassador, to procure Elizabeth's death, 'very shortly by arms, by poisons, bouquets, under-clothes, smells, waters or by any other means; that it will be the greatest St Bartholomew's Day there has ever been; and that neither God nor Devil will stand in the way of their doing it'.[3]

Later in the year, an undated and unsigned sheet of paper was given to Walsingham entitled, 'The Speeches of a Friar in Dunkirk', and outlined another conspiracy against Elizabeth. If, said the friar, that wicked woman were 'dispatched and gone', all Christendom would be in 'peace and quiet-ness'. The friar had shown Walsingham's informant a picture depicting the murder of William of Orange. 'Behold and see well this picture,' the friar told him. 'Look how this Burgundian did kill this prince. In such manner and sort, there will not want such another Burgundian to kill that wicked woman and that before it be long, for the common wealth of all Christendom.'[4]

The Privy Council believed Elizabeth and Protestant England to be in real and imminent danger. Dramatic and unprecedented measures were now taken as Cecil and Walsingham drew up, 'The Instrument of an Association for the Preservation of Her Majesty's Royal Person' (or 'the Bond of Association'), which bound signatories to defend the Queen's life and avenge any assassination attempt against her. It obligated all signatories 'to the uttermost of their power, at all times, to withstand, pursue and suppress all manner of persons that shall by any means intend and attempt any thing dangerous or harmful to the honours, estates or persons of their sovereign'. All those who signed the bond pledged 'never to accept, avow, or favour any such pretended successor, by whom or for whom any such detestable act shall be committed or attempted'. Members of the association were 'to prosecute such person or persons to the death ... and to take the uttermost revenge on them ... by any possible means ... for their utter overthrow and extirpation'.[5] The intention was clear. Should an attempt be made on Elizabeth's life, Mary Queen of Scots would be killed, whether she was a direct party to the plot or not. A sacred oath sealed the bond.[6]

From October to November 1584, while elections were held for a new Parliament, copies of the bond were circulated throughout the realm, acquiring thousands of signatures and seals.[7] Whilst the government claimed that this demonstrated a spontaneous outpouring of loyalty for Elizabeth, it took significant steps to ensure certain individuals swore the oath and signed the bond. In a letter drafted by Cecil for circulation to the lord lieutenants in the counties, Walsingham added the words:

> Your lordship shall not need to take knowledge that you received the copy from me, but rather from some other friend of yours in these parts; for that her Majesty would have the matter carried in such sort as this course held for her [safety] may seem to [come more] from the particular cause of her well affected subjects than to grow from any public direction.[8]

The Privy Council's correspondence over the next few months included reports from all parts of England on the progress of the Bond of

Association, with local officials devising signing ceremonies fit for the solemnity and significance of the undertaking.[9]

When the new Parliament met on 23 November, Elizabeth expressed her gratitude for the displays of popular loyalty:

> I am not unmindful of your Oath made in the Association manifesting your great goodwills and affections ... done (I protest to God) before I heard of it or ever thought that such a matter, until a great number of hands were showed me at Hampton Court, signed and subscribed with the names and seals of the greatest of this land. Which I do acknowledge as a perfect argument of your true hearts and great zeal for my safety, so shall my bond be stronger tied to greater care for your good.[10]

In a long and impassioned opening speech, Sir Walter Mildmay identified the Pope as their 'most mortal and capital enemy', who had sponsored sedition in the realm.[11] He described the 'malicious and secret practices' which were dependent on the Pope and emphasised that Edmund Campion and other Jesuits had met their deaths not simply for the 'superstitious ceremonies of Rome, but for most high and capital offences and conspiracies', including 'the deposing of our most gracious Queen, advancing of another in her place,' and the 'alteration and subversion of this whole state and government'. He called on members to consider if these 'priests, rebels, fugitives and papists' were set at 'the helm of the Church and Commonwealth', and painted a terrifying picture of the 'ruin, subversion and conquest of this noble realm'. Strong laws were needed to provide for the queen's safety 'against all such malicious enemies' and, as Mildmay deliberately added, 'straight laws also against troublers of this state under pretence of titles, either present or future, thereby to cut off their expectation if they or any of them dare to lift up their hands or hearts to endanger the person or state of our gracious Queen'.[12] After a day of strong words and rallying rhetoric, Mildmay set out their task: to provide the highest penalty to avert three types of danger: invasion, rebellion and violence to the Queen. The stage was now set for what would become the principal measure of the Parliament, the 'Act for the Queen's Safety'.

This sweeping new law 'for Provision to be Made for the Surety of the Queen's Majesty's most Royal Person and the Continuance of the Realm in Peace' was justified as a direct response to the 'sundry wicked plots of late devised and laid, as well in foreign parts beyond the seas as also within the realm'.[13] Inspired by the Bond of Association, it gave the Queen's subjects the right to pursue to death anyone involved in an invasion, rebellion, attempt on Elizabeth's life or anything at all that 'compassed or imagined, tending to the hurt of her Majesty's royal person'. With Mary Queen of Scots again clearly in mind, the act decreed that any pretender to the English throne could also be pursued to death for any conspiracy organised in their name.

In fierce debates, MPs questioned how, if the Queen was killed and all royal authority lapsed, effective action could be taken against the culprits of her murder. Fears were raised of a kind of vigilante justice and an orgy of 'mutual slaughter' between rival claimants. To counter this danger the call was made for statutory provision during an interregnum. Royal authority would reside with a 'Great Council' formed of the 'great officers of the realm', and the privy councillors would execute royal justice, take action against those responsible for the Queen's death and choose a successor who appeared 'to have best right . . . in blood by the royal laws of the Realm', at which point the interregnum would end.[14] During this period, the union of the natural body of the monarch with the body politic of the realm would be broken until it was reunited in the appointed heir on their accession.[15] Ultimately this proposal was rejected and never presented to the Queen as her councillors knew she would oppose it.

On 18 December, Sir Christopher Hatton informed members that the Queen thankfully accepted their care for her, which, 'her Majesty said (but he might not say), was more than her merit'. She expressed approval for the bill but added that her confidence 'was in God only for her safety'. She also said she 'would not consent that anyone should be punished for the fault of another'. In other words if Mary Stuart was implicated in a treasonous conspiracy, she did not wish the penalties to extend 'to the issue of the offender', James VI, except if 'the issue was also found faulty'. The bill was then put aside for the Christmas recess.

The second bill of the session also addressed the issue of the Queen's safety by seeking 'to bar the coming in of Jesuits and seminary priests, the only disturbers of the peace of the realm and the very instruments to work her Majesty's destruction'.[16] All Jesuits and priests that remained within the kingdom forty days after the passing of the law were to be regarded as traitors to the realm.[17] It also became treason for any person to 'willingly and wittingly receive, relieve, comfort or maintain' any Jesuits or other priests. This was the harshest legislation of the period and was testament to the growing numbers of missionary priests now in England and their perceived threat as agents of sedition.

The bill was brought to the Commons for a first reading on 12 December and then three days later was given its second reading along with the bill for the Queen's safety. It seemed that all in the house was in agreement. After one final reading, they would be ready to pass to the Lords and then receive royal assent.

With Parliament apparently united behind the bills for the Queen's safety and against the Jesuits and seminary priests, an entirely unexpected voice of opposition was raised. Dr William Parry, a member who was sitting in his first Parliament as MP for the tiny borough of Queenborough in Kent, rose to his feet and affirmed that he 'favoured not the Jesuits or seminaries but was to speak for English subjects'. He 'spoke directly against the whole bill', he said, which sought to banish the Jesuit and seminary priests. He denounced it as savouring treasons, 'full of blood, danger, despair and terror to the English subjects of this realm'; full also 'of confiscations – but into whom?' Parry asked. 'Not, said he to her Majesty (which he wished they were),' but to others. Whilst he was sure that bill would be carried by both houses, 'he hoped when it should come into her Highness's most merciful hands, that it would stay and rest there, until which time,' he said, 'he would reserve his reasons of his negative voice against the bill, then to be discovered by him only unto her Majesty'.

The MPs listened in stunned silence, clearly grieved by Parry's questioning of the house's motives and his suggestion that they were acting 'not so much for the Queen's safety . . . as for the satisfying of their own greedy desires'. They were also angered that he would not give an explanation for his words, 'a thing contrary to the orders of the house'. Parry was immediately removed from the Commons into the Sergeant's custody, brought before the Privy Council and the Speaker of the Commons before returning to the house the following day to apologise for his hasty actions. He said he meant no offence to the Queen or the house, but repeated that he would reserve his reasons for the Queen herself.[18] The question in many minds was: what had caused a member of the Commons to behave so rashly?

36

Agent Provocateur?

Seven years earlier, Dr Parry had left England for the continent with mounting debts and disaffected with a lack of favour and patronage from Elizabeth. In 1582 he was received into the Catholic Church in Paris and became involved in the politics of Catholic exiles in France. In May the following year he wrote to Cecil, from whom he continued to seek patronage, 'If I were well warranted and allowed, I would either prevent and discover all Roman and Spanish practices against our state, or lose my life in testimony of my loyalty to the Queen's majesty,' while at the same time pledging to others 'to employ all my strength and industry in the service of the Catholic Church'.[1] It is difficult to determine whether he was a traitor or, as he later claimed, a freelance English spy.

In 1583, Parry made his first traitorous step, writing to Cardinal Campeggio, the Pope's nuncio in Paris, offering to help the Catholic cause. Later that year, Parry met Thomas Morgan, Mary Queen of Scots's chief intelligence gatherer, in Paris. Morgan encouraged him to act and Parry agreed to kill 'the greatest subject in England', Queen Elizabeth, on condition that it would be sanctioned by the Pope who would absolve him of his sins.

On his return to England, Parry, having acquired a doctorate of law in Paris, played the part of agent provocateur and 'very privately discovered to her Majesty' the assassination plot that he himself had engineered. It was a dangerous game, and unfortunately for Parry he was unable to convince Elizabeth of the veracity of the plot (she 'took it doubtfully'). Parry soon feared he had fatally incriminated himself. He wrote to Thomas Morgan in Paris, renouncing the mission and resolving instead to lie low at court and continue in the Queen's service. Yet as long as Parry remained in debt, and unsure about his future, he proved susceptible to Catholic persuasion.

Parry received a letter from Cardinal di Como informing him of the Pope's commendation of him and the granting of a plenary indulgence in his Holiness's name for the sin and punishment for all his errors. Parry resolved to go ahead with his murderous mission.[2] He recruited a fellow conspirator, Edmund Neville, a disaffected gentleman from the north of England, to join him in carrying out the assassination. They discussed the best means to kill Elizabeth. First they planned to target her as she rode in her carriage on progress; they would approach her from each side and lunge their daggers at her. They then considered an even more daring plan. Parry suggested he attack the Queen at Whitehall as she 'took the air' in her privy garden. Having committed the deed, he could escape over the palace wall to one of the landing stairs nearby and flee by boat along the Thames. Having committed to carry out the plan, Parry hid in waiting near the gardens, but when Elizabeth appeared he claimed he 'was so daunted with the majesty of her presence, in which he saw the image of her father, King Henry VIII, that his heart would not suffer his hand to execute that which he had resolved'.[3] The conspirators made no further move, though Parry's feelings of injustice and resentment continued to fester.

After his outburst in Parliament and subsequent rebuff, it seems that Dr Parry revived his treasonous plan. On the evening of Saturday 6 February 1585, he visited Edmund Neville at Whitefriars, ready to act. However Neville had begun to have doubts and told Parry that he had decided 'to lay open this his most traitorous and abominable intention against her Majesty'.

Two days later Neville surrendered to the authorities and confessed to his involvement in Parry's plot.[4] According to a court observer, 'the Queen, when she heard about this doctor [Parry], went into the garden, wept aloud, and said she would like to know why so many persons sought her life. She tore open her garment, exposing her breasts, exclaiming that she had no weapon to defend herself, but she was only a weak female.'[5]

Parry was arrested and taken to the Tower. Walsingham gave him the opportunity to reveal anything he knew of the plots against Elizabeth, and specifically whether he 'himself had let fall any speech unto any person (though with an intent only to discover his disposition) that might draw him into suspicion, as though he himself had any such wicked intent'.[6] If Parry was a self-styled agent provocateur then this was his moment to reveal himself. Instead Parry vacillated and by the time he confessed it was too late. Under torture, Parry named Thomas Morgan and Cardinal di Como as having persuaded him to kill Elizabeth in order to place Mary Queen of Scots on the throne.

On 25 February, Parry was tried in Westminster Hall. He appealed to Cecil and Dudley that his case was quite unique: 'My case is rare and strange, and, for anything I can remember, singular: a natural subject solemnly to vow the death of his natural Queen ... for the relief of the afflicted Catholics and restitution of religion'.[7] He also wrote to Elizabeth that he hoped 'most graciously (beyond all common expectation) to be pardoned',[8] but he was executed in Westminster Palace Yard the following week. On the scaffold he maintained his innocence, denying that he had ever thought of murdering the Queen and claimed his plot had intended to trap others: 'I die a true servant to Queen Elizabeth; from any evil thought that ever I had to harm her, it never came into my mind; she knoweth it and her conscience can tell her so ... I die guiltless and free in mind from ever thinking hurt to her Majesty.'[9]

Parry's performance at his trial had been confident and compelling. Cecil realised that the government needed to take steps to control the account of events and ensure accurate reporting of what they called 'the truth' of Dr Parry's treason. The official account was ruthless in its description of Parry's treachery denouncing him as a 'vile and traitorous wretch', testament to the depth and horror of his perceived betrayal.[10]

Whatever Parry's real purpose, his plotting fed the already widespread deep Protestant anxiety. Following his execution, a special service of public worship was published, 'An Order of Prayer and Thanksgiving for the Preservation of the Queen's Majesty's Life and Safety':

> Thy divine providence from time to time hath many ways mightily and miraculously preserved and kept her from the crafty cruel and traitorous devices of her bloody adversaries and the deadly enemies of Thy Gospel, which with barbarous cruelty have sought to distinguish the light thereof by shedding her Majesty's most innocent blood.
>
> But this Thy gracious goodness and mighty providence never so apparently showed itself at any other time as within these few days when a traitorous subject ... had of long time retained a wicked and devilish purpose and have often sought occasion and opportunity to lay violent hands upon her royal person and to have murdered her. But still the vigilant eye of Thy blessed providence did either prevent him by sudden interruption of his endeavour or, by the majesty of her person and princely behaviour toward him,

didst strike him so abashed that he could not perform his conceived
bloody purpose . . .'[11]

Preachers were also instructed to read from the pulpit Dr Parry's
confession, which declared that the Pope had authorised him to assassinate the Queen and had granted absolution for the murder. The Parry
plot, according to official propaganda, showed that the Catholic powers
would readily sponsor Elizabeth's assassination as a means to bring about
the return of Catholicism in England.[12]

Given the fears for her safety, Elizabeth chose to remain close to
London that summer, cancelling any long progresses and often staying at
her own royal houses or making only isolated visits into nearby counties.
In June 1585, Sir Thomas Pullyson, the Lord Mayor of London, was so
worried about the level of threat against the Queen that, in a letter to
Walsingham, he offered to guard her in person as she travelled to
Greenwich. As he noted, 'considering the present perilous times and
continual malice and mischievious purposes of the papistical faction', he
was logical and prudent in his concern for the Queen's wellbeing.[13]

For the next few years, Elizabeth shunned Whitehall, feeling too that
her personal security could better be provided in some more compact and
less accessible palace. Yet Elizabeth impatiently refused Dudley's suggestion that courtiers with Catholic leanings should be forbidden access to
court, and the proposal of an armed bodyguard. She remained determined
to show herself to her people and said she would sooner be dead than 'in
custody.'

37

Unseemly Familiarities

'My very good Lord,' Sir Francis Walsingham wrote to Robert Dudley on 29 September 1584. 'Yesterday I received from the Lord Mayor enclosed with a letter, a printed libel against your Lordship, the most malicious written thing that was ever penned since the beginning of the world.'[1]

The book had come from a secret press in Paris or Antwerp; entitled *The Copy of a Letter Written by a Master of Art of Cambridge*, it was known almost immediately as *Leicester's Commonwealth*. When the work first appeared, written in English, in Paris in August 1584, it proved an overnight sensation and after being smuggled across the Channel it was avidly read at the English court.[2] The book took the form of a conversation between a London gentleman, a Catholic lawyer and a Cambridge academic. The Earl of Leicester was attacked for his power at court and his influence over the Queen, 'his diligent besieging of the prince's person', and his 'taking up the ways and passages about her'. He was also accused of preventing the Queen from marrying by his 'preoccupation of her Majesty's person' and his impudent behaviour in 'giving out everywhere that he (forsooth!) was assured to her Majesty and that all other princes must give over their suits to him'.[3]

The tract included lurid allegations, centring on Dudley's relationships with various women and his supposedly voracious sexual appetite. It was said that there were not two single noblewomen who attended upon the Queen 'whom he hath not solicited';[4] he was even accused of paying £300 for sex with one of them. *Leicester's Commonwealth* described the extreme lengths to which Dudley had gone to cover up his relationship with Lettice Knollys, hiding her from the Queen, sending her 'up and down the house, by privy ways, thereby to avoid the sight and knowledge of the Queen's Majesty'. Lettice was accused of falling pregnant with Dudley's child before her husband Walter Devereux had died and she and Dudley were held responsible for his 'murder'. The death of their son, Lord

Denbigh, in July, was seen as a sign of God's vengeance on Dudley: 'the children of adulterers shall be consumed and the seed of a wicked bed shall be rooted out'.[5] He was also accused of having conspired in his wife Amy Robsart's death and having attempted to assassinate the French envoy Simier.[6]

The tract belonged to a swathe of Jesuit propaganda that was being distributed to highlight the threat of the Protestant Earls of Leicester and Huntingdon to Mary Stuart's succession. For some, *Leicester's Commonwealth* was seen as preparing the ground for the Catholic-sponsored murder of the Queen, which could then be blamed on Dudley.[7] The piece also suggested that Dudley would try to foist one of his many illegitimate children on the throne by pretending that the child was Elizabeth's. The Earl of Leicester had 'contracted to her Majesty' that 'he might have entitled any one of his own brood (whereof he hath store in many places, as is known) to the lawful succession of the crown ... pretending the same to be by her Majesty' and that he was behind the decision to put 'words of natural issue' into the statute of the succession for the crown; 'against all order and custom of our realm ... whereby he might be able after the death of her Majesty to make legitimate to the crown any one bastard of his own by any of so many hackneys he keepeth, affirming it to be the natural issue of her Majesty by himself'.[8]

Elizabeth went out of her way to defend Dudley and issued a proclamation ordering that all copies of the publication be surrendered:

> [In] their most shameful, infamous and detestable libels they go about to reproach, dishonour and touch with abominable lies ... many of her most trusty and faithful councillors ... greatly touching thereby her Highness' self in her regal and kingly office, as making choice of men of want both of justice, care and other sufficiency to serve her Highness and the Commonwealth. And further, in the said books and libels they use all the means, drifts, and false persuasions they can devise or imagine to advance such pretended titles as consequently must be most dangerous and prejudicial to the safety of her Highness's person and state.[9]

An amnesty was offered to anyone who instantly submitted their copies to the authorities; thereafter the penalty for retaining a copy was imprisonment.[10] It made little difference, and in June, Elizabeth was forced to issue another proclamation in a further attempt to suppress the work. She blamed the 'great negligence and remissness' of the authorities in London 'where it was likely these books would be chiefly cast abroad', for not doing enough to enact her initial proclamation:

> The very same and diverse other such like most slanderous, shameful and devilish books and libels have continually spread abroad and kept by disobedient persons, to the manifest contempt of her Majesty's regal and sovereign authority, and namely, among the rest, one most infamous containing slanderous and hateful matter against our very good Lord the Earl of Leicester, one of her principal noblemen and Chief Counsellor of State, of which most malicious and wicked imputations, her Majesty in her own clear knowledge doth declare and testify his innocence to all the world.

She added that, before God, she knew in her conscience, 'in assured certainty, the libels and books against the said Earl, to be most malicious, false and slanderous, and such as none but the devil himself could deem to be true'.[11]

Dudley quickly came to the view that Mary Queen of Scots was behind the libel and Walsingham suggested Thomas Morgan, Mary's agent in France, as its author.[12] However, Charles Arundell, a known Catholic conspirator who was implicated in the Throckmorton plot, had fled to Paris in December 1583 and had always been hostile to Dudley, emerged as the likely writer. He was the cousin of Lady Douglas Howard, who was formerly the lover and, as she maintained, the wife, of Robert Dudley. She was now married to Sir Edward Stafford, the English ambassador in France. When Arundell fled to France, Walsingham had warned the Staffords not to get involved with him, but the couple ignored the request and entertained Arundell on a number of occasions.

Leicester's Commonwealth talked in lurid detail about Dudley's affair with Lady Douglas. Such was Douglas's embarrassment at the revelations that Stafford reported it made his wife ill; her 'sickness', he later recalled, 'was so long and almost of life, as in truth I was a good while greatly afraid of'.[13] He was worried about the impact of the forthcoming French edition. It seems that Lady Douglas may have considered returning to England, but Stafford persuaded her to 'pluck up a good heart' and stay with him.[14] Stafford had been assured by the compilers, to whom he must have been sufficiently close, that while Lady Douglas was identified by name in the first edition she would not be in the second. When in the spring of 1585, the French translation of *Leicester's Commonwealth* appeared (*Discours de la vie abominable . . . le my Lorde of Leicestre – A Discourse on the abominable*

214

lifes, plots, treasons, murders, falsehoods, poisonings, lusts, incitements and evil stratagems employed by Lord Leicester), Lady Douglas's name was indeed missing. However the book now included a salacious addition, which claimed that the Earl of Leicester had seduced a lady at Elizabeth's court with an aphrodisiac containing his own semen. Whilst the lady was not identified, the fact that she was said to be still living made Lady Douglas the obvious candidate.

On 30 March, Stafford wrote to Walsingham recommending that he not be ordered to attempt to suppress the tract, since his 'nearest have a touch in it' and so he might be suspected of personal motives. His greatest fear was that he would be blamed or believed to have been implicated and that this would incur Dudley's anger. 'If you command me I will send you [one] of them, for else I will not, for I cannot tell how it will be taken.' He had, he explained, not written to inform the Earl of Leicester, for he 'would be loth to do anything subject to bad interpretation'.[15]

The extent to which Sir Edward and his mother Lady Douglas were involved with the compilers of *Leicester's Commonwealth* remains rather puzzling. There is no reason to think that Lady Douglas would have wanted details of *her* affair with Dudley exposed in such sensational fashion. However, the Staffords were close to Charles Arundell and it is unclear how else he would have got so much of the detail that was contained in the tract. Certainly Walsingham believed Lady Douglas was the source of the incriminating information about Dudley and both she and Sir Edward would have wanted to damage or destroy the earl's reputation. In late 1585, Walsingham detained and examined William Lilly, Stafford's servant. He wrote to Sir Edward Stafford informing him that he thought Lilly was involved in the affair, and berating the ambassador's inadequate efforts to stop the distribution of the book. In his response of 20 January 1586, Stafford sought to excuse himself by saying that he had not thought it fitting for a public official to deal with a private man's cause, even though he had had orders to the contrary. He also protested that he had still burned what copies he could find (thirty-five of them) until he could no longer keep up with the numbers being printed.[16]

Despite Edward Stafford's protestations of innocence, the Queen was plainly not convinced. In a letter to Cecil on 11 August, Sir Edward wrote how he had,

> received from my mother [Lady Dorothy Stafford] to my extreme grief, how much her Majesty is still offended with me (the cause God knoweth, for I do not) and withal her advice to write to her Majesty

about it, I have done so and sent my mother the letter, to present it to her when she shall see the best opportunity. But I have told her to show it to you first, and unless you like it, not to present it at all.[17]

Lady Dorothy's importance, both as a means to represent her son's interests and as one of the Queen's closest intimates is clear.

———•———

The year 1585 also saw the publication of another tract, *The Letter of Estate*, which vilified Dudley and reiterated the accusations made in *Leicester's Commonwealth*.[18] In it, Dudley's arrogance and desire to rule England is mirrored by that of his rapacious wife Lettice Knollys. They are both united in their determination to overthrow the Queen. 'But now who but his Lordship in the court, and as pride and ambition he passed, so in like manner wedded he in every degree with a countess fitting her husband's humour, for more liker princess than a subject . . .'[19] According to *The Letter*, Lettice,

> who seeing her Lord to be the master over all the nobility and conceiving well that they durst do nothing and that, as it were, they had him at a beck, thought in like sort all this were nothing if she in like sort had not all the other good countesses in the court at the like stay, and therefore in all that ever she might, practised and devised to effect the same, in so [sic] as if ever once her Majesty were disposed for the entertainment of some strange prince or ambassador to have any new gown made her she will be sure with [sic] one fortnight after, or at the least afore the departure of the ambassador, to have an other of the same sort and fashion suitable in every degree with her Majesty's and in every respect as costly as her Majesty's, if not more costly and sumptuous then hers.[20]

Lettice is described as publicly competing with Elizabeth at important state occasions:

> [her] intolerable pride her Majesty noting, after some admonitions for it and the same slightly regarded, told her as one son lightened the earth, so in like sort she would have but one Queen in England, and for her presumption, taking her a wherret on the ear in plain terms strictly forbade her the court.[21]

However, as the tract described, while Lettice has been banned from court, her husband continues 'insinuating with her Majesty, that upon him [as the] chiefest pillar in the land she wholly relies'.[22] Ultimately Dudley is able to satisfy his lust for power by becoming the Queen's favourite; by monopolising her natural body, he monopolises England's body politic.

As the gossip circulated at court, Dudley kept a low profile. Writing to a friend he said, 'In these dangerous days, who can escape lewd or lying tongues? For my part I trust the Lord will give me His grace to live in His fear, and to behave myself faithfully to my sovereign and honestly to the world. And so I shall pass over such calumniations.'[23]

———————

Around 1584, Mary Queen of Scots sent a scandalous letter to Elizabeth with information which she had apparently been given by Bess of Hardwick, the Countess of Shrewsbury.[24] It is very likely that Elizabeth did not see the letter and that Cecil intercepted it. Bess had previously served as one of Elizabeth's Ladies of the Bedchamber, alongside Kat Ashley, Blanche Parry and Dorothy Stafford, but she had lost the Queen's favour over her role in the secret marriage of Katherine Grey. She married her fourth husband, George Talbot, the Earl of Shrewsbury, in 1568, the nobleman becoming Mary Queen of Scots's gaoler the following year. Bess was forty-one when Mary was moved to Tutbury Castle; Mary was twenty-six. They spent a good deal of the day together, embroidering and gossiping, but had fallen out over Bess's suspicions over the relationship between Mary and her husband, George Talbot. Mary reported that Bess had been disloyal about Elizabeth and then proceeded to reveal gossip that Bess had told her about her time at the English court.

Mary prefaced the letter to her cousin,

> I declare to you now, with regret that such things should be brought into question but very sincerely and without any anger, which I call my God to witness, that the Countess of Shrewsbury said to me about you . . . to the greater part of which I protest I answered, rebutting the said lady for believing or speaking so licentiously of you as a thing which I did not at all believe.

Bess had allegedly told Mary that Elizabeth had, in front of one of her ladies-in-waiting, made Dudley a promise of marriage, 'and that she had slept with him an infinite number of times with all the familiarity and licence as between man and wife'. The letter claimed that Elizabeth had also seduced other men, including Sir Christopher Hatton, the Captain of her Guard, whom she had then taken as her lover. She had kissed the French envoy Simier and had taken 'various unseemly familiarities with him' and betrayed to him the secrets of the realm. She had also 'disported' herself with the 'same dissoluteness' with the Duke of Anjou, 'who had been to find you one night at the door of your chamber where you had met him with only your nightdress and dressing gown on and that afterwards you let him enter and that he remained with you nearly three hours'.

In this remarkable letter, Mary alluded to rumours that Elizabeth had some kind of physical defect that would prohibit regular sexual relations and thus make conception impossible: 'You were not like other women . . . and you would never lose your liberty to make love and always have your pleasure with new lovers.'[25]

Bess of Hardwick denied making any such slanderous accusations and the Privy Council eventually accepted her innocence; the letter, however, demonstrates the dangers of rumours emanating from the Queen's Bedchamber and how intimate details about the Queen's body continued to have huge political significance, even when Elizabeth was beyond her childbearing years. Whilst assassins conspired against Elizabeth's life, Mary Queen of Scots, like other Catholic polemicists, looked to target the Queen's honour by undermining her claims to be the 'Virgin Queen' – which had become so central to her political identity.[26]

38

Especial Favour

During 1584–85, a German noble named Lupold von Wedel journeyed through England and Scotland, observing the countries, its people and visiting a number of royal palaces. On 27 December 1584 he travelled down the Thames to Greenwich where the court was assembled for Christmas and New Year.[1] Elizabeth was still formally in mourning for the deaths of her last suitor, the Catholic Duke of Anjou, and for her leading Protestant ally in Europe, the Prince of Orange, and was dressed in black velvet with silver and pearls. Over the top of her gown was draped a piece of diaphanous silver lace. In private her clothing was said to be simple, almost austere, but her public self was always scrupulously luxuriant.

While Elizabeth attended chapel, von Wedel watched as preparations were made for the Queen to dine. A long table was set in the Presence Chamber beneath her canopy of state. Normally, he noted, the Queen ate in private, in her Privy Chamber, and it was only on festival days when she might eat so 'strangers may see her dine'. After Elizabeth emerged from the chapel with her ladies, forty silver gilt dishes, some large and some small, were placed on the table as she sat down 'quite alone by herself'. As the musicians played, she was served by a young gentleman in black who carved her meat, whilst another young man dressed in green, handed her a cup and knelt while she drank watered-down wine. To the right of her table stood a small number of her senior courtiers, including the Earl of Hertford, who, von Wedel wrote, had recovered his favour having 'deflowered one of the Queen's ladies' (a reference to his marriage with Katherine Grey); the Lord Treasurer William Cecil; the Master of the Queen's Horse Robert Dudley; and Sir Christopher Hatton. Each of the men carried white wands which marked them out as officers of state. Having been in England for some months, von Wedel had heard the gossip about Elizabeth's relationship with her favourites, and in his subsequent account wrote that 'the Queen for a long time had illicit intercourse' with Leicester, and Hatton whom 'the Queen is said to have loved after Le[ice]ster'.

As Elizabeth dined she would call individual gentlemen to her, who would kneel before her until she ordered them to rise. Von Wedel was evidently struck by the ceremonious reverence of it all and described how when the gentlemen left the Queen, each would 'have to bow down deeply, and when they have reached the middle of the room they must bow down a second time'. When the food was brought in, the officers of state marched before the gentlemen who bore the dishes. Finally, once all the dishes had been presented, and the Queen had picked at what was before her, she rose from the table and a large silver gilt basin was brought to her in which she washed her hands.

After dinner Elizabeth took a cushion and sat on the floor as the dancing began. First only the senior courtiers danced but then 'the young people took off their swords and mantles, and in hoses and jackets invited the ladies to the galliard with them'. As Elizabeth sat watching, she summoned whom she pleased among the courtiers to talk with her and joked and laughed with them. Von Wedel noted that with one of them, whom he identified as 'Ral', the familiarity extended to particular tenderness and intimacy. When Elizabeth pointed to a spot of dirt on his face and moved to wipe it away with her handkerchief, he shrugged it off, rebuffed the Queen's hand, and removed the mark himself.[2]

'Ral' was Walter Ralegh, then around thirty years of age, the son of a Devon gentleman and a nephew of Elizabeth's favoured intimate, the late Kat Ashley. It was likely that Kat secured his position at court and therefore Elizabeth directly connected him with her affection for Kat Ashley, 'for the especial care that we have to do him good, in respect of his kindred that have served us, some of them (as you know) near about our person'.[3] Ralegh was strikingly attractive, six foot tall with a trimmed beard and piercing blue eyes and a love of extravagant clothes, jewels and pearls. His boldness, blatant ambition, vanity, and self-confidence all greatly appealed to the Queen. He had first come to court in 1581 and thereafter experienced a rapid rise in his wealth and status as a result of the Queens' favour.

In 1583, Elizabeth granted him one of her favourite palaces, the handsome London dwelling Durham Place on the Strand. Elizabeth's pet name for Ralegh was 'Water', given his ties to the sea and his West Country pronunciation of his name. Ralegh wooed her with poetry and after the departure of Anjou, Elizabeth and Ralegh spent increasing amounts of time together, talking, playing cards and riding out. He was frequently in the Privy Chamber by day and night, and would often be at the door of the bedchamber, waiting for Elizabeth to emerge in the morning. A letter from the courtier Maurice Brown reported, 'Mr Water Rawley is in very high favour with her Majesty, neither my Lord of Leicester nor Mr Vice-Chamberlain [Hatton] in so short time ever was in the like, which especial favour hath been but this half-year. But the greatest of all hath been within this two months.'[4]

Having observed Elizabeth and Ralegh together, von Wedel concluded 'that she loved this gentleman now in preference to all others; and that may be well believed, for two years ago he was scarcely able to keep a single servant, and now she has bestowed so much upon him that he is able to keep five hundred servants'.[5] Ralegh was knighted on 6 January 1585. In May, one of Mendoza's spies reported that Ralegh and Dudley were, unsurprisingly, on bad terms, as they both vied to dominate the Queen's affections.

Following William of Orange's assassination and the Duke of Parma's military advance, a Spanish victory in the Low Countries looked a near certainty. Now, with the Catholic League in France allied to Philip II, Elizabeth faced the possibility of Spanish domination of both France and the Low Countries, leaving England dangerously exposed to invasion. A Catholic enterprise against England seemed imminent. In the Treaty of Nonsuch in August 1585, Elizabeth agreed to send money and troops to support the Protestant rebels in the Netherlands and resolved to appoint Dudley Captain-General to lead the expeditionary force. But as the date of his departure loomed nearer Elizabeth began to have doubts about letting him ago. After spending the night of 27 September with the Queen, Dudley sent Walsingham what is perhaps his most revealing description of their relationship:

> Mr Secretary, I find her Majesty very desirous to stay me, she makes the cause only the doubtfulness of her own self, by reason of her oft disease taking her of late & this last night worst of all. She used very pitiful words to me of her fear she shall not live & would not have me from her. You can consider what manner of persuasion this must be to me from her.[6]

But by the end of the year, Dudley had entered the Netherlands as head of the English army. He was hailed as the Prince of Orange's successor and shortly afterwards took the fateful decision to accept an appointment as Governor-General of the Netherlands without consulting Elizabeth. In her letter to him she did little to disguise her fury:

> How contemptuously we conceive ourselves to be used by you ... We could never have imagined (had we not seen it fall out in experience) that a man raised up by ourselves and extraordinarily favoured by us, above any other subject of this land, would have in so contemptible a sort broken our commandment in a cause that so greatly toucheth us in honour ... And therefore our express pleasure and commandment is that, all delays and excuses laid apart, you do presently of your allegiance obey and fulfil whatever the bearer hereof shall direct you to do in our name. Whereof fail you not, as you will answer the contrary to your utmost peril.

Whilst many of the Queen's councillors supported Dudley's position, believing that a show of strength in the Low Countries was necessary, Elizabeth 'would not endure to hear speech in defence' of him. Cecil thought her attitude, as he said on several occasions, to be 'both perilous and absurd'.[7]

Thomas Heneage, once Dudley's rival for the Queen's affection, was now sent as Elizabeth's emissary to tell the earl that he must, at once, relinquish his office. When Heneage at first objected to the task, Elizabeth upbraided him, 'Jesu! What availeth wit when it fails the owner at greatest need? Do that you are bidden and leave your considerations to your own affairs ... I am assured of your dutiful thought but I am utterly at squares with this childish dealing.' Heneage was dispatched with the order for Dudley to resign. But when the States-General protested, Elizabeth was persuaded to allow the earl to keep his title and, in time, grudgingly accepted that he 'had no other meaning and intent then to advance our service [and] to think of some way how the point concerning the absolute title may be qualified, in such sort as the authority may, notwithstanding, remain'.[8]

Elizabeth's initial rage at Dudley's actions was doubtless also provoked by gossip that Lettice was planning to join her husband, 'with such a train of ladies and gentlewomen, and such rich coaches, litters and side saddles as her Majesty had none such, and that there should be a court of ladies as should far pass her Majesty's court here'. Elizabeth was furious: she 'would have no more courts under her obeisance than her own'.[9] In fact, Lettice was most likely innocent of this ambition and was 'greatly troubled with the tempestuous news she received from the court'.[10]

39

The Deed shall be Done

In the summer of 1585, an English Catholic exile and mercenary soldier in Rheims named John Savage plotted to assassinate Elizabeth. The conspiracy's architect was once again Thomas Morgan, Mary Queen of Scot's chief agent in Paris. In England, Savage had met up with Gilbert Gifford, a young man from a family of Staffordshire Catholics who had been working as a courier carrying letters between Mary and Guillaume de l'Aubépine, Baron de Châteauneuf, the new French ambassador in London. Unbeknown to Morgan, Mary and the other Catholics, Gifford was a double agent working for Walsingham. He had defected from Catholicism and having become known and trusted among Catholic exiles, was drawn close in to the conspiracy.

In August 1585, Savage travelled to England to murder the Queen as planned, but apparently lost his nerve and made no attempt to do so. The following year he was introduced by John Ballard, an exiled Catholic priest, to a number of other disaffected young Catholics. The group included Anthony Babington, a twenty-five-year-old nobleman from Derbyshire who was developing another conspiracy to free Mary Queen of Scots and assassinate 'the usurper' Elizabeth, in advance of what they hoped would be a Catholic invasion sponsored by France and Spain.[1]

On 11 August, Mendoza, at the Spanish embassy in Paris, reported to Philip that he had been 'advised from England by four persons of account, who have entry to the Queen's court, that they have plotted her assassination for more than three months'. Mendoza's dispatch continued:

> at last they have all four unanimously agreed and sworn to do it. [They] also [say] that they will inform me as soon as possible, whether it is to be done with poison or the sword, and at what time, in order that I may write to his Majesty about it, and beg him to succour them, when the deed shall be done. They will not tell

any other person but myself, to whom they are much obliged, and in whose secrecy they confide.[2]

Such was Babington's confidence in their plan and his vainglorious vanity, that he had the conspirators' portraits painted as a group to celebrate their forthcoming mission.

Babington and his accomplices had no idea that Walsingham had infiltrated the plot and had successfully planted two of his agents at the very heart of the conspiracy. Meanwhile his network intercepted Mary Queen of Scots's secret correspondence, which was smuggled in ale barrels and sealed in a leather pouch. Each of the letters was opened, decyphered and then resealed. Elizabeth was kept closely briefed about the plot as it unravelled and was shown the conspirators' portraits. In Richmond Park one day she spotted one of the men, an Irishman called Robert Barnwell, watching her. Elizabeth asked her Captain of the Guard, Hatton, 'Am I not fairly guarded, that have not a man in my company with a sword about him?' But she said nothing to suggest she had recognised Barnwell, choosing to bide her time and let the conspiracy run its course.[3] There seemed to be threat and danger everywhere, even within Elizabeth's own lodgings. At the end of June, the Spanish ambassador described how, 'when the Queen was going to chapel the other day, as usual in full magnificence, she was suddenly overcome with a shock of fear, which affected her to such an extent that she at once returned to her apartment, greatly to the wonder of those present'.[4]

In early July, Babington wrote to Mary to fully apprise her of the plotters' plans. He had been approached by John Ballard, who had informed him of the great preparations by the Catholic princes of Europe 'for the deliverance of our country from the extreme and miserable state wherein it hath too long remained'. England would be invaded, Mary freed and Queen Elizabeth, the 'usurping competitor', would be killed. Babington proceeded to explain how Elizabeth would be murdered by his men: for 'the dispatch of the usurper, from the obedience of whom we are by excommunication of her made free, there will be six noble gentlemen, all my private friends, who for the zeal they bear to the Catholic cause and your Majesty's service will undertake that tragical execution.'[5]

Ten days later, Mary responded. She took care to ensure that no evidence was left in her own handwriting and so dictated the letter to one of her secretaries who wrote it in cypher. She acknowledged Babington's 'zeal and affection' to Catholicism and to her cause, and commended his efforts to prevent the 'designments of our enemies for the extirpation of our religion out of this realm with ruin of us all'. She urged him to consider carefully what he had proposed and to confer with Mendoza, Philip's ambassador in Paris. Only once in the letter did she directly refer to the conspiracy: 'By what means do the six gentlemen deliberate to proceed?' She instructed Babington 'fail not to burn this present quickly' once he had read it.[6]

The letter was quickly intercepted and within twenty-four hours, Thomas Phelippes, Walsingham's agent, had decyphered it and notified his master: 'It may please your honour. You have now this queen's answer to Babington which I received yesterday.' He was confident that this would now be enough to condemn Mary and he hoped that God would inspire Elizabeth, 'with that heroic courage that were meet for avenge of God's cause and the security of her self and this state'.[7]

On Thursday 28 July, Phelippes met with Walsingham in person at Greenwich to show him the original letter. They discussed whether it was sufficient proof against Mary and decided that in order to provide definitive evidence against her they would doctor the letter. Mary's letter was carefully reopened and a postscript added in the same cypher that she had used, asking for the names of the accomplices:

> I w[ould] be glad to know the names and qualities of the six gentlemen which are to accomplish the designment, for that it may be I shall be able, upon knowledge of the parties, to give you further advice necessary to be followed therein; and as also from time to time particularly how you proceed, and as soon as you may for the same purpose who be, already, and how far every one privy hereunto.[8]

The faked postscript was intended to prove beyond doubt Mary's connection with Babington's treasonous conspiracy. It was a risky business; if the fabrication was discovered the whole plot to ensnare Mary would fail. In the event, on receipt of the doctored letter, Babington grew suspicious and promptly burned it.

Meanwhile, Walsingham watched and waited. John Scudamore, the stepson of the Queen's bedfellow Mary Scudamore, was employed as a confidential secretary to Walsingham, and was sent to watch Babington. Believing Scudamore was sympathetic to the plot, Babington invited him to dinner at a local tavern. As they ate, a note arrived for Scudamore. Babington managed to get a surreptitious look at it and saw enough to see that it was an order for Scudamore to arrest him. He stood up, walked to the counter as if to 'pay the reckoning' and then, once out of John Scudamore's sight, he fled, leaving his cape and sword on the back of the chair. [9]

Walsingham now swung into action. A proclamation was issued on 2 August ordering the arrest of the Babington conspirators, including Chidiock Tichborne, John Ballard and Babington himself, whose pictures were to be displayed around London and other parts of the realm. No one was allowed to leave the country until they were captured:

> whereas certain persons, natural born subjects of their realm, whereof A.B [Anthony Babington]., C.T. [Chidiock Tichborne] etc. are principal parties, finding their consciences charged with guilt of matter by them practiced tending both to the peril of her Majesty's person and to the disturbing of and altering of the present quiet state of this realm by way of force and arms, have lately withdrawn themselves from their ordinary houses and lodging, and by removing from place to place keep themselves hidden and remain lurking in corners, sometimes within the city and suburbs of the sane and sometimes in other places not far distant from the city, as of late hath been discovered . . .[10]

The conspirators' families and servants were interrogated, watchmen patrolled the villages and towns near London and houses throughout the city were searched.

John Savage, priest and conspirator, was arrested on Thursday 4 August; Babington and his accomplices remained free. Savage was brought before Walsingham and Sir Christopher Hatton to be interrogated.[11] It was reported that Savage had confessed 'that the Queen of Scots was made acquainted with the designs as well of invasion as attempt against her Majesty's person by the letters of Babington and that there came an answer from her touching her assent and advice but what it was the contents particularly knew he not'. He also admitted that 'by means of Gilbert Gifford' they had intelligence with the French ambassador.[12]

After ten days on the run, on 14 August, Babington and two other conspirators were arrested. They had been in hiding in St John's Wood, to the north of London, having disguised themselves by cutting their hair and staining their complexions with green walnut shells. Across the city, bonfires were lit and bells rang out as Babington and the others were paraded through the streets and taken to the Tower for questioning.[13]

A most Joyful song made in the behalf of all her Majesty's faithful and Loving subjects of the great joy which was made in London at the taking of the late traiterous conspirators was published in 1586, illustrated with images of heads of the 'traitorous conspirators', and described the many thousands who ran to see the captured felons, crying after them, 'there go ye traitors false of faith' and 'there go the enemies of England'.[14] wrote to the Lord Mayor of London asking that her letter be read aloud at the Guildhall on 22 August. In it she informed her people that she did not so much rejoice at her escape from death, but at the happiness manifested by her subjects at the capture of the conspirators.[15]

Babington and his men were tried in two groups between 13 and 15 September. John Savage was arraigned before the judges first since he was said to have plotted the assassination of the Queen before becoming involved with Babington. All the conspirators were charged with assenting to a plan to assassinate Elizabeth, attempting to stir up a rising of English forces with the help of foreign powers, and of plotting to release Mary Queen of Scots and put her on the English throne.[16] So angered was Elizabeth by their treason that she did not believe that the usual punishment was enough. She wrote to Cecil the day before the trial ordering him to tell the judge to deliver the expected sentence but to add that 'considering the manner of horrible treason against her Majesty's own person which had not been heard of in this kingdom, it is reason that the manner of their death, for more terror, be referred to her Majesty and the Council'.[17] Cecil responded that the customary punishment – hanging, drawing and quartering – was 'cruel enough', although the victim was more often than not dead before the disembowelling and emasculation took place. 'I told her Majesty,' he informed Hatton, that the normal way of proceeding but 'prolonging' the pain of the traitors in front of the London crowd 'would be as terrible as any new device could be'. Nevertheless Elizabeth insisted that the judge and the privy councillors understand her royal will. She wanted the conspirators' bodies to be torn to pieces.[18]

Gallows were set up near St Giles in the Fields and the condemned were bound to hurdles at the Tower of London and dragged through the streets of the city to the scaffold. Father John Ballard and Babington were executed first on 20 September with a brutality that shocked even the hundreds of onlookers who were baying for their blood. Ballard died first. He was left to swing briefly by the neck and then, whilst still alive and conscious, was cut down and made to watch as the executioner hacked off his genitals and then cut out his guts and finally his heart. His innards were then cast into a fire, as his body was dismembered. Having stood to watch Ballard's agonising death, not kneeling down to pray as was customary, but standing with his hat on his head 'as if he were a beholder of the execution' and displaying a 'sign of his former pride', Anthony Babington readied himself for his fate. Having been hung and then pulled down from the gallows to face the executioner's knife, he cried out again and again *Parce mihi Domine Iesu!* – 'Spare me Lord Jesus'. His cries were ignored as his body was hacked apart.[19] When Elizabeth heard of the butchery of the executions and the crowd's disgust she ordered that the next batch of conspirators should be killed by hanging alone.

In the summer of 1586, the Queen did not go on progress at all but stayed in her royal residences in the Thames Valley and in the tense autumn of that year, resided at Windsor. It was from here, on 6 October, that Elizabeth wrote a letter to Mary Stuart. She had been 'given to understand' that she had conspired against her in a 'most horrible and unnatural attempt on her life'.[20] Mary would now be tried according to the Act for the Queen's Surety.

Five days after Elizabeth's letter, commissioners were sent to Fotheringhay Castle in Northamptonshire to 'examine all things compassed and imagined tending to the hurt of our royal person' and then to pass sentence or judgement.[21] Mary immediately questioned the legitimacy of the hearing and its jurisdiction over her as a foreign prince and demanded the right to be heard in full Parliament or before the Queen and Privy Council. She denied all knowledge of Babington or any letter from him and rejected the charge that she had written to him. When Elizabeth ordered Cecil not to allow a sentence to be given on Mary's guilt, the commission was recalled to London and ten days later resumed proceedings in the Star Chamber at Westminster Palace where, in Mary's absence, all the evidence was reviewed in full. Finally the commissioners passed sentence:

> By their joint assent and consent, they do pronounce and deliver their sentence and judgement ... diverse matters have been compassed and imagined within the realm of England, by Anthony Babington and others ... with the privity of the said Mary, pretending title to the crown of this realm of England, tending to the hurt, death and destruction of the royal person of our said lady the Queen.[22]

Young Elizabeth at thirteen or fourteen years old, standing in front of a bed with the curtains open behind her. It was shortly after this that she got caught up in scandalous rumours as to her relationship with her stepfather, the Lord Admiral Thomas Seymour.

Katherine 'Kat' Ashley, Elizabeth's former governess, Chief Gentlewoman of the Privy Chamber and trusted confidant.

Blanche Parry was one of the Queen's longest-serving women. She attended the infant princess and remained in Elizabeth's service until her death at the age of eighty-two.

Lady Katherine Knollys, Elizabeth's cousin and confidant. She was appointed a Lady of the Bedchamber from the beginning of the reign and her death in 1569 left the Queen grief-stricken. Here Katherine appears during one of her sixteen pregnancies.

Robert Dudley, Earl of Leicester, Master of the Horse and Elizabeth's great favourite. His relationship with the Queen was the source of much scandalous rumour.

Lady Frances Cobham pictured with her husband, their six young children and her sister (*left*). Lady Frances had to balance childbirth and the demands of family life with service to the Queen, to whom she became a loyal friend and Lady of the Bedchamber.

A copy of a now-lost portrait of Elizabeth in her coronation robes, her long hair flowing as a symbol of her virginity.

Miniature of Elizabeth I at thirty-eight by Nicholas Hilliard, 1572.

*The Rainbow Portrait, c.*1600. Elizabeth is in her late sixties but in this highly symbolic portrait appears much younger.

164   Cap. 13.   *A thankfull Remembrance*

to be payd out of the King of Spaines Coffers, to poyson Queene Elizabeth, and these were the goodly Wares of Doctor Lopez, precious and of high esteeme in the eye of the Spanyard, as Manoel Lowys expounded that mysticall Letter written in a Merchants stile. This practice of poysoning, it was one of the sinnes of the Canaanites, it was brought into the Church by Popes, and reckoned among the sinnes of the Antichristian Synagogue, and taught for Doctrine by the Romish Rabbies.

Fter this great tempest from *Spaine* was past, the Sunne did shine as pleasantly on *England*, as before. By all the *Spanish* preparations there was not a man called from his husbandry in

'Lopez compunding to poyson the queene.'
A woodcut illustration depicting Dr Roderigo Lopez, physician to Elizabeth, who was accused of conspiring to poison her.

Medal commemorating Elizabeth's recovery from smallpox, 1562.

The Priests seditious Books against the Queene brings on Somervils furious attempt to kill her. They move with the Ladies of Honor to doe it. The Queenes mildnes and wonderfull mercy towards this vermine. Mendoza the Spanish Ambassador, for practising against the Queene, is thrust out of England. Throgmortons confession, and condemnation for treason.

An engraving depicting John Somerville's attempt to kill the Queen.

Sir Christopher Hatton, gentleman pensioner, Captain of the Guard and later Lord Chancellor. Hatton was one of the Queen's most favoured male courtiers. The Queen gave him, as with other intimates, special names: he was her 'lids'.

Francis, Duke of Anjou. He was twenty-one years younger than Elizabeth but was a suitor for the Queen's hand in marriage during the 1570s.

Robert Devereux, Earl of Essex, who became one of the Queen's great favourites but ended up being executed for treason in 1601.

Lady Mary Sidney, sister of Lord Robert Dudley and Elizabeth's long-suffering attendant.

Lady Mary Scudamore incurred the Queen's wrath on her marriage but thereafter became a favoured lady who slept with the Queen in her bedchamber.

Blanche Parry's memorial at Bacton Church in Herefordshire. Blanche is depicted on the left kneeling before the Queen.

This image by Isaac Oliver, *c*.1592, is one of the few in which Elizabeth is depicted as a significantly older woman.

Lettice Knollys, whom Elizabeth referred to as the 'she wolf' after she married Robert Dudley, Earl of Leicester.

Anne Dudley, Countess of Warwick, who was, according to her niece, one of Elizabeth's favourite ladies, 'more beloved and in greater favour … than any other woman in the kingdom'.

Elizabeth's funeral procession. These drawings, by an anonymous artist, are the first ever pictorial records of the funeral procession of an English monarch.

The effigy of Elizabeth I from her tomb in Westminster Abbey.

When Parliament reassembled on 29 October, the Queen was urgently petitioned to carry out the sentence and have Mary executed.[23] Elizabeth was warned that if the Scottish Queen escaped punishment, she would be 'exposed to many more plots', and more 'secret and dangerous conspiracies than before'.[24] demanded instead that action should be taken against her cousin according to the Bond of Association and that she be killed by some 'private means'. Cecil insisted Elizabeth must sign a warrant for a public execution and fostered rumours that Spanish troops had landed in Wales and that another assassination plot to kill Elizabeth had been 'discovered'. The formal warrant for Mary's death was drawn up and now only awaited the Queen's signature.[25]

40

Blow up the Bed

In the winter of 1586, as Elizabeth finally decided to act against Mary, William Stafford, the second son of the Queen's bedfellow Dorothy Stafford – 'a lewd, young miscontented person' – became involved in a plot to kill Elizabeth.[1] The chief plotter was Michael Moody, a former servant of Sir Edward Stafford who was being held in Newgate gaol as a recusant debtor, and was soon to be released. Moody planned to gain access to the court, lay a trail of gunpowder to Elizabeth's Bedchamber and under the Queen's bed, and blow her to pieces.[2]

Having been apparently won over to the plot, William Stafford drew in Chateauneuf, the French ambassador and his secretary Leonard des Trappes. He told the ambassador of his 'intention of killing the Queen on religious grounds and in order that the Queen of Scotland might ascend the throne'. When the French ambassador pointed out that the plan to kill Elizabeth in her Bedchamber would also involve blowing up Stafford's own mother, 'as she and the Queen both slept in one room', Stafford agreed instead that it would be better to kill the Queen by stabbing.[3]

With the revised plan in place, early in the New Year, William Stafford reported the whole affair to Walsingham describing how a 'graceless' man has gone to kill the Queen, and 'her Majesty should take good heed to herself as to who comes near her'.[4] William Stafford, Moody and des Trappes were swiftly arrested and confined in the Tower and Chateauneuf placed under house arrest. The guard around the Queen was now doubled. Under examination by a committee of the council, the French ambassador confirmed that William Stafford had come to him with a hare-brained scheme, but Chateauneuf maintained that he had rejected it. He could not, however, avoid the charge of having concealed knowledge of a conspiracy. It is possible that Stafford was one of Walsingham's agent provocateurs. Two years earlier, in June 1585, he had acknowledged some kind of deep obligation to Walsingham, writing, 'I am as ever at your command and there is no man living to whom I am so beholden. If I should live to see my blood shed in your cause I should think it but some recompense for the great good I have received at your hands.'[5] Moody was also known to Walsingham, the spy master had paid him to carry letters between London and Paris in 1580–84.

Writing to Philip of Spain from Paris on 7 February 1587, Mendoza described how William Waad had been sent by Elizabeth to inform the French King of the reasons for the arrests.

> A brother [William Stafford] of the English ambassador here [Edward Stafford] and a son of the Queen's Mistress of the Robes [Dorothy Stafford] (neither of whom however have spoken to him for years owing to his bad contact) pretended to be Catholic and frequented the house of the French ambassador with whom he was on close terms of intimacy.

He had disclosed his intention to kill Elizabeth by placing 'barrels of gunpowder in his mother's apartment, which is underneath the Queen's bedroom and she could thus be blown up'.[6]

Following the investigation, Moody was sent back to gaol for another three years. Chateauneuf was kept under close surveillance and forbidden to communicate with the French court. He knew it was a trap. The plot was intended to put pressure on Elizabeth and also effectively neutralised the French ambassador at a crucial time. The secretary des Trappes was later quietly released from the Tower and after two months, when the danger was passed, the government declared that it had all been a terrible misunderstanding and sought to smooth Anglo-French relations. The whole episode was, as Walsingham later told the ambassador, merely an attempt by Stafford to exhort money.[7]

In January, Elizabeth sent a letter to Sir Edward Stafford through Waad that 'although she does not doubt his loyalty and innocence in the matter yet, as the delinquent is his brother, she thinks better that the communication respecting it should be undertaken by another envoy, who would give him a full account if it'. The Queen also referred to the effect of the revelations on Dorothy Stafford: 'Your mother, whose sorrow being so near as she is unto us, cannot but add some affection to ours, as for your own person, occupying the place you hold.'[8] Such was Lady Stafford's own 'inward grief' and distress at her son's 'odious dealing' in a plot against her beloved queen that she stopped petitioning the Queen for certain family properties which had fallen into the Queen's hands by attainder.[9]

Whilst Lady Dorothy remained selflessly devoted to Elizabeth, clearly her sons exasperated her both as a mother and as a loyal servant to the Queen.

The 'Stafford plot' was more than likely a Walsingham creation, a ruse to convince the Queen of the extreme danger that Mary Queen of Scots posed. However, given the distress caused to Lady Stafford, which one would imagine Elizabeth would want to prevent, it is likely that Elizabeth was not told the origins of the plot until much later. The uncovering of the conspiracy also enabled the government to place Chateauneuf under house arrest and sever his links with France at the time that action was being taken against the deposed Scottish Queen. When Elizabeth received the French ambassador back into her favour in May, she joked with him about the matter, behaving as if there had been no substance to the plot.[10] If all this is true, William Stafford emerges not as the traitor that Elizabeth had initially perhaps feared, but as a crucial member of Walsingham's spy network. Ultimately no charges were brought against William Stafford but, for reasons unknown, he remained in the Tower for at least eighteen months.[11]

William's brother, Edward Stafford, was also accused of dabbling in treasonous activity in support of Mary Queen of Scots. His appointment as ambassador in France in 1583 was not least because of the influence of his mother. Once in post and writing his first dispatch to the English court, Edward requested that Cecil, 'seal up this in another paper and to deliver it to my mother, sealed, as all copies that hereafter I shall send you'.[12] Lady Stafford was therefore privy to significant foreign affairs and although Cecil may not always have complied with Edward Stafford's request, Dorothy undoubtedly became her son's most informed and important advocate with the Queen. This was much to the annoyance of Walsingham, who demanded that he be kept at the centre of the diplomatic and intelligence networks. He instructed his 'searchers' at the port of Rye to intercept and open all Stafford's letters.[13] Edward Stafford complained to Cecil, 'I have been served but very evil touches since I came here . . . I know that by his [Walsingham's] means the Queen . . . has been incensed that news of importance should come from others; but some have come from me and he has kept them a day and delivered his first.'[14]

Desperate to prove his worth and demonstrate his independence, Sir Edward began to use increasingly rash methods. In November 1583 he proposed to include some deliberately false information in his consular dispatches in case some of them were being intercepted. He warned the Queen that such passages would be indicated by a special mark in his letters so that she would know they were 'written for a purpose and not for a truth'.[15] As Stafford wrote defensively, 'I never heard of any ambassador being blamed for seeking intelligence any way he could.'[16] He undertook more and more risks to gather intelligence. In the spring of 1584, Sir Edward became involved with the Catholic conspirator Charles Arundell and in October, Michael Moody, one of his servants at the English court, was detained at Walsingham's command on the grounds that he was conveying letters to and from Catholics. The following autumn Walsingham detained William Lilly, another of Stafford's servants on the grounds that he had read *Leicester's Commonwealth*.[17]

Walsingham persisted in his attempts to get the ambassador recalled and looked to exploit Sir Edward's reputation as a notorious gambler. As Stafford fell into greater debt, he became compromised and accepted an advance of 6,000 crowns from the Duke of Guise in return for sharing the contents of his diplomatic bag, thereby betraying his English informants and selling the country's secrets to the enemy at a time of great national danger.[18] Stafford was also accused of acting in the interests of Spain by repeatedly denying the existence of any hostile intention by Philip II, and by passing on English intelligence to Madrid. Writing from Paris in July 1587, Mendoza, the former Spanish ambassador in England who had himself been implicated in more than one plot to assassinate the Queen, told his master that Sir Edward had sent Charles Arundell to see him, 'to ascertain from your Majesty in what way he might serve you'. Stafford was known to be 'much pressed for money', Mendoza added; 'even if he [Stafford] had not made such an offer as this, his poverty is reason enough to expect from him any service, if he saw it was to be remunerated'. Shortly afterwards, Charles Arundell arrived with news from Sir Edward that an English fleet was about to sail against Portugal:

> The ambassador told Arundell to advise your Majesty of this instantly, which, he said, would serve as a sample and handsel [token] of his goodwill; and within a fortnight or three weeks he would report whether the despatch of the fleet was being persisted in, together with the exact number of ships, men, stores and all other details of the project.[19]

In a letter dated 28 February, Mendoza described how he had authorised the payment of 2,000 crowns to his valuable 'new correspondent'.[20] For the next eighteen months, Mendoza's dispatches were full of detailed information on English policy from his 'new friend'. The evidence points to this being the English ambassador, though Sir Edward later claimed he was acting as a double agent, deliberately providing false information to the Spanish with the full knowledge of the Elizabethan government. Stafford also began to supply information, in December 1586, on Sir Francis Drake's preparations for his raid on Cadiz (to 'singe the King of Spain's beard') and warned the Spanish in advance of the English attack.[21] That Walsingham had sought to give Stafford false information about Drake's plans suggests that he suspected the ambassador of treason. The quality of intelligence Stafford passed back to the English court was low and he exaggerated the hostility of French Catholics in order to make out that they, rather than the Spanish, were Elizabeth's principal enemy. As the Spanish threat grew, Sir Edward's activities threatened to fatally undermine national security.

41

Nightmares

The sentence of Mary Queen of Scots' guilt had been proclaimed on 4 December 1586, but Elizabeth continued to resist signing the warrant for its enforcement.[1] She remained deeply ambivalent about the execution of one who had been an anointed monarch. Elizabeth still hoped that Mary could be killed in private, by an assassin, at Fotheringhay, rather than by public execution, but Sir Amyas Paulet, Mary's gaoler, professed himself shocked at the suggestion. But, as Elizabeth insisted, had the signatories of the Bond of Association not pledged to pursue to their death any that sought her harm? Finally in late December, the Queen authorised Cecil to draw up the warrant for Mary's execution. It was charged to William Davison, the recently appointed Secretary to the Privy Council, to secure Elizabeth's signature.

It was a time of great tension, with fears of disturbances, plots to rescue Mary, and conspiracies against the Queen's life. At the end of January 1587, great alarm spread across the country, as Walsingham described,

> False bruits were spread abroad that the Queen of Scots was broken out of prison; that the City of London was fired; that many thousand Spaniards were landed in Wales; that certain noblemen were fled; and such like ... The stir and confusion was great; such as I think happened not in England these hundred years past, for precepts and hue and cries ran from place to place, even from out of the north into these parts, and over all the west as far as Cornwall.[2]

William Davison had kept the warrant in his possession for five or six weeks, hoping that Elizabeth might be ready to sign it. On 1 February, the Queen sent for him. Alarmed by the rumours that were spreading through the country, she declared that she was now fully resolved to proceed with Mary's execution and signed. Later that day, as Elizabeth had instructed,

Davison gave the warrant to the Lord Chancellor Sir Thomas Bromley to attach the great seal.

However, the next morning, as the Queen was speaking with Sir Walter Ralegh in the Privy Chamber at Greenwich, Elizabeth called secretary Davison to her and described to him a distressing dream she had had the night before in which her Scottish cousin had been executed without Elizabeth's consent. She told Davison that the sealing of the warrant must be delayed. It had already passed, he replied. According to Davison, Elizabeth said nothing further.[3]

Now unsure of whether to act on Elizabeth's signed warrant or not, Davison sought out Hatton and Cecil who called a Privy Council meeting for the following day. It was agreed that they would proceed without further consultation, it being 'neither fit nor convenient to trouble her Majesty any further'.[4] Robert Beale, the clerk of the council, was sent immediately to Fotheringhay, accompanied by two executioners. A covering letter signed by the councillors and by Walsingham, who was ill in bed, to the Earls of Shrewsbury and Kent, appointed to preside over the execution, justified this subterfuge, as 'for [the Queen's] special service tending to the safety of her royal person and universal quietness of her whole realm'.[5]

At eight o'clock on the morning of Wednesday 8 February, Mary, dressed in black and clutching an ivory crucifix in her hand, was led out to the scaffold which had been erected in the great hall at Fotheringhay. She laid her head on the block to await the fall of the axe. The first blow missed her neck and sliced into the side of her skull. As the second blow severed her head, Richard Fletcher, the Dean of Peterborough, cried out, 'So let Queen Elizabeth's Enemies perish!'[6]

The following evening it fell to Cecil to break the news to Elizabeth that her cousin, the Scottish Queen, was dead.[7] Elizabeth immediately took 'to bed owing to the great grief she suffered through this untoward event'.[8]

By the morning her feelings had turned to incandescent rage. She summoned Sir Christopher Hatton and berated him for his part in what she saw as 'a thing she never commanded or intended'.[9] She threatened to throw all her councillors in the Tower for such blatant defiance of her orders, and in the meantime 'commanded them out of her sight'.[10] Davison bore the brunt of the Queen's wrath; she believed he had abused her trust by allowing the signed warrant to leave his possession. He was stripped of his office, interrogated by Star Chamber and sent to the Tower. By the end of the month Elizabeth was threatening to have him summarily executed, but in the event he was fined £10,000, a sum far beyond his means, and was to stay in prison for 'as long as her Majesty decreed'. Though his fine was remitted, he remained in the Tower for twenty months and was never allowed back into the Queen's service. [11]

Cecil, after years of loyal service, was banished from the Queen's presence and remained out of favour for several months, during which time Elizabeth referred to him as that 'traitor, false dissembler and wicked wretch'. Normally proud and pragmatic, the sixty-six-year-old Cecil was now reduced to writing despairing epistles in which he pleaded just to even be allowed just to lie at Elizabeth's feet, in the hope 'that some drops of your mercy [might] quench my sorrowful panting heart'. [12] His friend, Lady Cobham, one of Elizabeth's most trusted women, assured him, 'If you will write I will deliver it. I do desire to be commanded by you.' [13] She proceeded not only to speak favourably of him to the Queen, but to keep him informed of everything that happened at court during his absence. Finally, in March, Cecil was admitted back into the Queen's presence.

In the days after learning of Mary's execution, Elizabeth neither ate nor slept. A joint letter from her senior councillors of 12 February urged her 'to give yourself to your natural food and sleep, to maintain your health'. [14] On the Sunday after Mary's death, Richard Fletcher, one of Elizabeth's most favoured preachers, faced the daunting task of delivering a sermon before the Queen in the small chapel royal at Greenwich. [15] As Dean of Peterborough, Fletcher had served as chaplain during Mary's trial and execution, and now condemned the Scottish Queen for her traitorous Catholicism. Elizabeth sat in an elevated gallery, her courtiers in the chapel stalls below. Fletcher hailed Mary's execution as an act of God's deliverance and urged Elizabeth to rise above her grief and pursue her enemies and those who sought her life. [16]

Soon after receiving the news from Fotheringhay, Elizabeth wrote to James VI, denying that she had authorised his mother's execution:

> My dear Brother, I would you knew (though not felt) the extreme
> dolor that overwhelms my mind, for that miserable accident which
> (far contrary to my meaning) hath befallen ... I beseech you that
> as God and many more know, how innocent I am in this case ... I
> am not so base-minded that fear of any living creature or Prince
> should make me afraid to do that were just; or done, to deny the

same. I am not of so base a lineage, nor carry so vile a mind ... Thus assuring yourself of me, that as I know this was deserved, yet if I had meant it I would never lay it on others' shoulders; no more will I not damnify myself that thought it not ... for your part, think you have not in the world a more loving kinswoman, nor a more dear friend than myself; nor any that will watch more carefully to preserve you and your estate ... your most assured loving sister and cousin Elizabeth R.[17]

Robert Carey, youngest son of Lord Hunsdon and now a trusted courtier, was charged with delivering the letter to James, who took the news of his mother's death 'very heavily'. On the streets of Edinburgh, violence erupted against the English Queen. An agent in the Scottish capital reported to Walsingham a libellous epigram that addressed Elizabeth as 'Jezebel, that English whore'.[18]

In Catholic Europe too there was outrage.[19] From Paris, Sir Edward Stafford reported, 'Truly I find all men here in a fury, and all that love not her Majesty in a great hope to build some great harm to her upon it.' He added that Henri III, the French King and Mary's former brother-in-law, 'took it very evil' when he heard the news and immediately severed diplomatic ties with England.[20] For several months the King refused to receive Walsingham as Elizabeth's envoy, who had requested an audience to explain the execution. The French immediately called for vengeance and such was the strength of feeling that the French King felt obliged to send a message to Stafford imploring him, for sake of his personal safety, not to leave the embassy in Paris.

Parisian preachers and polemicists denounced the execution. A propaganda war of images broke out: Catholics displayed hideous portraits of Elizabeth, while Huguenots set up pictures of the English Queen in all her magnificence, accompanied by laudatory verses.[21] In April 1587, Walsingham wrote to Stafford to say that he was editing his dispatches so that Elizabeth would not know how enraged the French were over the execution; he feared the news would only increase her anger towards members of the Privy Council.[22]

English and Scottish Catholic exiles in France denounced Elizabeth in print and made great play of the nightmares and fitful sleep that she was rumoured to have had on the night after she signed Mary's death warrant.[23] Adam Blackwood's *Martyre de la royne d'Escosse*, written shortly after Mary's death, claimed that Sir Walter Mildmay had gone to Dudley while he was in bed at court and warned him of 'the evident danger and ruin of his

Majesty', if with 'inexcusable cruelty', Mary was executed 'without all pretence of law, right or reason, or any apparent show of justice'. Blackwood then described how Dudley immediately got out of bed and in his nightgown went straight to Elizabeth's Bedchamber – 'whether often he was wont to go for less necessary business' – to warn her of the consequences if the execution went ahead'. Dorothy Stafford 'being in her bed' had cried out in a 'terrible voice' that awakened the Queen and then began to weep. She told Elizabeth that she had had a nightmare in which the Queen of Scotland was beheaded and immediately after that Elizabeth's head was also cut off. Elizabeth declared that the 'same vision had appeared to her in her sleep leaving her greatly terrified' and as a result she had changed her mind about putting Mary to death.[24] Another version of Blackwood's account describes how, having given orders to go ahead with the execution, Elizabeth – 'the harpy' – did not sleep the entire night 'having another demoness within her soul who tormented her strangely and vengefully about the execution of her cousin, to such an extent that she repented of having ordered it'.[25]

Blackwood's propagandist tract, in which Elizabeth was once more condemned for her innate depravity, was printed in France and distributed throughout Catholic Europe.[26] Attacks on Elizabeth could always fall back on the lurid details of her conception – choice material for any opponents of the Elizabethan regime. Blackwood referred to her illegitimate and incestuous birth, alleging that the Queen was 'not only a bastard' but also born 'of triple incest and had no right to the throne of England'.[27] She owed her sexually corrupt body to the unrestrained sexual immorality of her mother, Anne Boleyn, the 'hacquenee [mare] d'Angleterre'.[28]

Other attacks used similar imagery. In 1587, *De Jezebelis Anglae*, a collection of French and Latin poems reviling Elizabeth was printed. The 'de Jezebelis' poem was posted at the door of Notre Dame and described how Anne Boleyn had slept both with her own brother and with Henry VIII and that it was unclear who Elizabeth's father was.[29] The *Vers Funebres* attributed to Cardinal du Perron developed the theme of Elizabeth as a 'monster, conceived in adultery and incest, her fangs bared for murder, who befouls and despoils the sacred right of sceptres and vomits her choler and gall at heaven'.[30] Other poems claimed that Elizabeth had illegitimate children who were the fruit of her promiscuous conduct with members of the Privy Chamber, especially the Earl of Leicester, and that Elizabeth deliberately avoided marriage because she wanted to be free to enjoy these licentious pleasures.[31]

While with Mary's death, English Catholics lost the figurehead and focus for their plots, the threat of Spain came into sharper relief. Mary had made Philip II of Spain a written promise that she would bequeath him her right to the English succession. In the event she never did so, but her death left him the leading Catholic candidate for the succession. As a descendent of John of Gaunt and Edward III, he had English royal blood and had the military might to enforce his claim. The English Jesuits, William Allen and Robert Persons, now back on the continent, pressed Philip to take action against Elizabeth, and Philip was urged by his confessor to attack England, 'to avenge the wrongs done to God and to the world by that woman, above all in the execution of the Queen of Scotland'.[32]

42

Secret Son?

In June 1587 a young Englishman found shipwrecked off the northern coast of Spain was arrested and taken for questioning, suspected of being a spy. He was sent to Madrid, to the house of Sir Francis Englefield, formerly Catholic councillor to Elizabeth's half-sister, Mary I, and now Philip II's English secretary. The details of the interrogation were recorded by Englefield in four letters he subsequently wrote to Philip.[1]

The Englishman, who was thought to be about twenty-five, proceeded to reveal an incredible story. His name, he told Englefield, was Arthur Dudley. He had been raised by Robert Southern, whose wife had been a servant to Queen Elizabeth's most senior Bedchamber woman, 'the heretic' Kat Ashley. Her husband, John, a Gentleman of the Chamber and Master of the Jewel House, had given Southern the post of Keeper of one of the Queen's houses in Enfield; and it was to here, each summer, or if there was any plague or sickness in London, that Arthur from the age of eight would be taken and schooled in Latin, Italian, French, music, arms and dancing.

When he was about fifteen, Arthur told Ashley and Southern that he wanted to seek adventure and go abroad. When they refused to let him go he stole a purse of coins and fled to the port of Milford Haven in Wales, where he planned to board a ship for Spain. Before he could do so he was arrested by order of the Privy Council and returned to London. He was taken to Pickering Place, the home of Sir Edward Wotton, where, in the presence of Sir Thomas Heneage, he was reunited with John Ashley.

Finally, four years later, Arthur was granted permission to go abroad as a soldier in the service of the French Colonel de la Noue in the Netherlands, and was accompanied there by a servant of Robert Dudley's. When de la Noue was subsequently captured, Arthur fled to France but was called back to England by news that Robert Southern was gravely ill. He found Southern in a tavern in Evesham, where he had been working as an innkeeper. On his deathbed, Southern revealed to him the true circumstances of Arthur's birth. One night in 1561, Southern had been sent for by Kat Ashley who instructed him to go to Hampton Court. There he met 'Lady Harington', probably Isabella Harington, one of the Queen's ladies and the mother of the Queen's godson, John, who handed him a newborn baby boy. He was told that the child belonged to a lady at court, 'who had been so careless of her honour' that if it became known, it would 'bring great shame on all the company and would highly displease the Queen if she knew of it'. The boy was called Arthur and Southern and his wife were ordered to take him home and bring him up with their own children, in place of their son who had died in infancy.

The dying man refused to tell Arthur any more, but under pressure, and saying he wished to clear his conscience before his death, Southern then confessed that the true identities of the boy's parents were Queen Elizabeth and the Earl of Leicester. Arthur then travelled to London to confront John Ashley with the information. Ashley told him to repeat what he had been told to no one and to remain near court, but fearing he might be in danger, Arthur left London and headed for France. There, he explained to Englefield, he learned of the Duke of Guise's plans for a league against England and so warned Ashley and Sir Edward Stafford of the threat. It was soon after this, at Greenwich Palace, that he was first introduced to Robert Dudley, who took him to his chamber and confirmed that he was his father. Dudley showed 'by tears, words and other demonstrations' so much affection for him that Arthur recognised Southern's deathbed confession to be true. Walsingham, who had been notified of Arthur's arrival, was suspicious of the mysterious youth and began asking questions. Arthur fled the court and joined a ship carrying English soldiers to the Netherlands.

In Englefield's report to Philip, he described how the Englishman claimed to be a Catholic and to have become involved in various plots to forward the Catholic cause: he had opened up a dialogue with the Elector of Cologne and the Pope, and had undertaken a pilgrimage to the shrine of Our Lady of Montserrat in Catalonia. In early 1587 after hearing of Mary Queen of Scots's execution he decided to head for Spain. During this voyage he was shipwrecked on the Biscay coast and taken to Madrid for questioning by Englefield. He told Englefield that he believed Robert Dudley had plotted against Mary Stuart and this had led to her being condemned to death. He was now worried, he said, that agents of Queen Elizabeth would seek him out and arrange to have him murdered so that the secret of his birth would never be known. He promised the King's secretary that if Philip would protect him, he would write an account of his birth and life which the Spanish could use as they wished. [2]

Arthur's account, written in English, filled three sheets of paper and was translated by Englefield for Philip. Thereafter Arthur was sent to the Castle of La Alameda and spent the next year under interrogation. Hieronimo Lippomano, the Venetian ambassador in Spain, reported to the Doge and Senate that the young man 'gives himself out as the son of the Queen of England, but is in disgrace with her because he is a Catholic, has been arrested'.[3] In another despatch he described Arthur as being 'spirited', with 'the air of a noble', and able to speak Italian and Spanish, though 'he is thought to be a spy'.[4] Arthur's claims caught the interest of the Spanish government, his revelations coming at the time when Philip II was preparing to claim the crown of England for himself and for his daughter the Infanta Isabella. 'It will certainly be safest,' Philip wrote in the margins of Englefield's report, 'to make sure of his person until we know more about the matter.' Neither he nor Englefield was willing to take any chances.

A letter to Cecil, dated 28 May 1588, from an English agent known only as 'BC' recounted Arthur Dudley's claim to be have been 'begotten between our Queen and the Earl of Leicester'. It has been suggested that 'BC' was Anthony Standen alias Pompeio Pellegrini, one of Walsingham's chief intelligence-gatherers in Spain.[5] The letter reported that Arthur, identified as being 'around twenty-seven years old', was still in Spanish hands 'very solemnly warded and served', at a cost to the King of six crowns a day, and 'taketh upon him' [behaves] like the man he pretendeth to be'. Another letter, written in September, mentioned that 'the varlet that called himself her Majesty's son is in Madrid, and is allowed two crowns a day for his table, but cannot go anywhere without his keepers, and has a house for a prison'. The spy explained that Arthur bore more than a passing resemblance to the man he claimed was his father, though this was not something that Philip's secretary, Sir Francis Englefield, who was aged and virtually blind, would have been able to confirm.[6]

Two years later, a report sent to England on 'the State of Spain' spoke of Alcantara, 'where an Englishman of good quality and comely personage was imprisoned who avowed himself Leicester's son by no small personage'.[7] Thereafter Arthur Dudley disappears from the record. Perhaps he remained there until his death, or perhaps he escaped and simply discarded his elaborate claim.

Sir Francis Englefield clearly did not know what to make of the tale he had been told by the young Englishman, but he suspected that Elizabeth and her councillors 'may be making use of him for their iniquitous ends'. Perhaps it was a plot intended to dupe the Spanish into acknowledging Arthur as the Queen's son so that he could be offered as a possible heir to the throne, thereby cutting James VI of Scotland out of the succession. Or perhaps he was a spy who was being used by the English government to learn of Spain's preparation for the invasion of England. During the spring of 1587, Walsingham certainly drew up detailed plans of how to gather information on the Queen's foreign enemies and determined that agents should be sent into Spain to pose as disaffected Englishmen. One of his memos specifically noted the need to get a spy into the very heart of the Spanish court.[8]

Ultimately Englefield came to the conclusion that there was a good chance that Arthur was telling the truth and was unaware of how he was being used:

> I think it very probable that the revelations that this lad is making everywhere may originate with the Queen of England and her Council, and possibly with an object that Arthur does himself not yet understand. Perhaps, if they have determined to do away with the Scottish throne, they may encourage the lad to profess Catholicism and claim to be the Queen's son, in order to discover the minds of other princes, as to his pretensions, and the Queen may thereupon acknowledge him, or give him such other position as to neighbouring princes may appear favourable. Or perhaps in some other ways they may be making use of him for their iniquitous ends.

Englefield continued:

> It is also manifest that he [Arthur] has had much conference with the Earl of Leicester, upon whom he mainly depends for the fulfilment of his hopes. This and other things convince me that the Queen of England is not ignorant of his pretensions, although, perhaps, she would be unwilling that they should be thus published to the world, for which reason she may wish to keep him [Arthur] in his low and obscure position as a matter of policy, and also in order that her personal immorality might not be known (the bastards of princes not usually being acknowledged in the lifetime of their parents) and

she has always considered that it would be dangerous to her for her heir to be nominated in her lifetime, although he alleges that she has provided for the Earl of Leicester and his faction to be able to elevate him (Arthur Dudley) to the throne when she dies, and perhaps marry him to Arbella (Stuart) . . . For this and other reasons I am of opinion that he should not be allowed to get away, but should be kept very secure to prevent his escape . . . it cannot be doubted that France and the English heretics, or some other party, might turn it to their own advantage, or at least make it a pretext for obstructing the reformation of religion in England (for I look upon him as a very feigned Catholic) and the inheritance of the crown by its legitimate master; especially as during the Queen's time they have passed an Act in England, excluding all but heirs of the Queen's body.

If Englefield was right and Arthur Dudley was an English agent, or an English stooge, it would explain why the Spanish kept him close and did not make capital out of his claims, even at a time when it might have been used to decisively prove Elizabeth's immorality. Rather it seems that Elizabeth, and her advisers, had skilfully played on the rumours that had for so many years emanated from the Bedchamber, and used them for their own ends, as a means of infiltrating the Spanish court.

43

Satan's Instruments

Astrologers and prophets were predicting disaster for 1588. Raphael Holinshed, the contemporary chronicler, described an ancient prophecy which was 'now so rife in every man's mouth' that this year would see great change or final dissolution. Holinshed's chronicle ended with a prayer asking God 'to bless the realm of England; and the precious jewel of the same – good Queen Elizabeth – to save her, as the apple of His eye', from all the 'pernicious practices of Satan's instruments . . . We beseech God . . . that the gospel . . . may be glorified in the Commonwealth of England: a corner of the world, O Lord, which Thou hast singled out for the magnifying of thy Majesty'.[1]

Since the execution of Mary Queen of Scots in February 1587, the main focus of Catholic exiles abroad, led by Cardinal William Allen and the Jesuit priest Robert Persons, had become 'the Enterprise of England', an invasion of Elizabeth's realms by the combined forces of Spain and papal Rome. Allen and Persons petitioned Philip of Spain to take action and assured him that they would support his claim to the throne through his descent from the royal house of Lancaster.[2] Philip had already made the strategic decision to support the Enterprise and preparations for an invasion were underway. Detailed proposals for the plan of attack were being considered, the fleet readied, munitions procured, and men recruited. In July 1587, Pope Sixtus V promised money to support the venture and granted the right for Philip to be nominated as a suitable Catholic successor for the English throne.

In 1588, William Allen wrote an *Admonition to the Nobility and People of England and Ireland concerning the Present Warres*.[3] It was a tract calling on English Catholics to overthrow Elizabeth, whom Allen denounced in familiar terms as 'an incestuous bastard, begotten and born in sin' to Henry VIII and his 'Protestant whore' Anne Boleyn, and a sacrilegious heretic guilty of ruining the Commonwealth.[4] Elizabeth's sexual depravity was its central theme. He wrote that with Robert Dudley, 'and diverse others, she hath abused her body, against God's laws, to the disgrace of princely majesty and the whole nations reproach, by unspeakable and incredible variety of lust'.[5] Allen accused Elizabeth of having 'made her Court as a trap, by this damnable and detestable art, to inta[n]gle in sin and overthrow the younger sort of nobility and gentlemen of the land'.[6] According to Allen, Elizabeth was not simply unfit to rule because of her governance, but because of her illegitimacy and debauchery.

Allen's pamphlet was printed and copies were prepared to be shipped over to England once the Armada had made a successful landing. Cecil immediately ordered that the *Admonition* be suppressed as treasonous. A royal proclamation was issued on 1 July 1588, subjecting to martial law 'the importation, transcription, distribution and possession' of,

> false, slanderous and traitorous libels, books and pamphlets ... in covert and secret manner dispersed through this realm, wherein they do not only go about with most false and abominable lies to slander and dishonour her Majesty ... but also by subtle and pestilent persuasions to withdraw her highness's subjects from their due obedience, and to excite and stir the people to take arms against God and their sovereign and to join with foreign enemies ...[7]

Throughout the spring and early summer, as fears were raised that a Spanish invasion was imminent, England's defences were strengthened. In June a letter from the Queen to the Marquis of Winchester and the Earl of Sussex, Lieutenants of the County of Southampton, informed them of the 'great preparations of foreign forces, made with full intent to invade this our realm and other our dominions'. Elizabeth ordered them to ensure that her subjects within their lieutenancies, be 'in readiness for defence of any attempt, that might be made against us and our realm'. Watches were to be set in all towns at night and all suspicious persons to be detained. The hunt for priests and those that concealed them was intensified. To block the passage of enemy ships up the Thames, a makeshift barrier of huge, heavy chains and ship's cables was locked together and stretched across the river from Gravesend to Tilbury, held in place by a cordon of small boats anchored in the river and by the masts of over a hundred tall ships laid end to end.[8]

Whilst Lord Hunsdon was to command the army to defend the Queen, Lord Thomas Howard was to lead the fleet and Robert Dudley, now in his fifties, was given command of the troops at Tilbury that were being mustered to engage the enemy.[9] It marked a return to favour for the Earl of Leicester, who, ever since his ignominious return from the Netherlands had experienced Elizabeth's aloofness.[10]

As preparations for England's defence were made at home, the Queen's ambassador in France, Sir Edward Stafford, continued to deceive his government by repeatedly sending assurances that the Spanish Armada was being disbanded and the threat to England had abated. A copy of one letter, in January 1588, was forwarded to Admiral Thomas Howard, in command of the English fleet. He greeted Stafford's words with incredulity:

> I cannot tell what to think of my brother[-in-law] Stafford's adver-
> tisement; for if it be true that the King of Spain's forces be dissolved,
> I would not wish the Queen's Majesty to be at this charge that she
> is; but if it be a device, knowing that a little thing makes us too
> careless, then I know not what may come of it.[11]

If Stafford had made a mark in the margin to indicate this was deliber-ately false, then the government had forgotten its significance; otherwise to advise his government that Spain no longer intended to launch an invasion at a time when every effort was being made to get the Armada to sea, clearly amounted to treason.

On 3 May 1588, Stafford suggested the Armada was intended for Algiers. When, the following day, he finally reported that he had seen a letter in the study of Mendoza, the Spanish ambassador in Paris, mention-ing an enterprise against England, he speculated that it had been left out deliberately to deceive him and so was further evidence that the Armada was intended for some other place and purpose. His subsequent dispatches back to the English court reported similar spurious intelligence, designed again to mislead. On 16 June he told Walsingham that he thought the Armada was bound for the Indies; on 8 July he claimed that an outbreak of plague had driven it back to Spain and on 13 July he asserted that bets of six to one were being made in Paris against it ever reaching the Channel.[12] Clearly the Elizabethan government did not rely on Sir Edward's information alone and received other, more accurate, intelli-gence; however, the fact that no action was taken against the ambassador is striking. Perhaps the close position of favour that Lady Dorothy Stafford, Edward's mother, enjoyed in the Bedchamber accounted for the Queen's lenient treatment of him.

On Friday 19 July, after months of rumour and false alarms, the Armada was sighted in the Channel off the Isles of Scilly. All along the English coast, beacons were lit to spread word of imminent invasion. The next day English and Spanish ships engaged in skirmishes along the Channel. On the night of the twenty-eighth, with the Spanish fleet anchored just off Calais, English fireships were sent downwind, forcing the Spanish fleet to scatter.[13] The Queen's forces, however, were far from ready and would not be fully mobilised for several weeks.

On 8 August, putting aside concerns for her own safety, Elizabeth sailed out on the tide from St James's Palace to rally Dudley's forces, the royal barge surrounded by a flotilla of boats carrying her Gentlemen Pensioners and Yeoman of the Guard. At Tilbury, Elizabeth was met with a fanfare of trumpets. Riding a huge white horse, she inspected the ranks of her infantry, accompanied by Dudley and the marshal of the camp, Lord Grey. Eight footmen rode with her, the Queen's ladies behind them, and a troop of guardsmen bringing up the rear. Every man fell to his knees as the Queen passed and called on God to preserve her.[14]

In a speech which has come to define her, Elizabeth reconciled the contradiction of her womanly sex and her masculine courage:

> Although I have the body of a weak and feeble woman, I have the heart and stomach of a King, and a King of England too – and take foul scorn that Parma [the Duke of Parma, who was to invade from the Netherlands] or any other Prince of Europe dare to invade the borders of my realm.[15]

Here Elizabeth identified her virginal, impenetrable female body with her inviolable island realm. As her natural body was pure and unpenetrated so too would the body politic withstand any invading force. Elizabeth stayed at Tilbury until 10 August, when she returned to St James's Palace.

Ultimately, Philip II's Armada would be defeated by a combination of the English weather – storms and ill winds – and the skill of naval officers under the command of Elizabeth's Lord Admiral, Baron Howard. The Spanish fleet had been forced out of formation by the attack of the fire-ships and at dawn the following day was attacked by the English off Gravelines in a decisive battle. What was left of the Armada was forced to retreat north to Scotland where, battered by storms and for want of supplies, it sailed hard back to Spain.

At the end of August, the Dean of St Paul's officially announced the defeat of the Armada, although weeks of uncertainty followed and with it the fear that the Spanish fleet would return. As Marco Antonio Micea, a Genoese resident in London, described, 'We are in such alarm and terror here that there is no sign of rejoicing amongst the Councillors at the victories they have gained. They rather look like men who have a heavy burden to bear.'[16] Even Elizabeth was persuaded by her council to stay away from the service of thanks at St Paul's, 'for fear that a harquebus might be fired at her'.[17]

Before the year was out, the Queen's Sergeant Painter, George Gower, was commissioned to paint a huge portrait fanfaring the English victory over the Armada.[18] Elizabeth is pictured in the centre between two scenes, one depicting English fireships being sent to wreak havoc on the Spanish fleet, the other showing the remnants of the Spanish vessels as they limp home. The Queen's body, which is less a representative image and more an icon of sovereignty, fills the whole canvas: she is almost entirely encased in a magnificent gown, with huge, pearl-encrusted billowing sleeves, and velvet skirts. A large ruff and jewelled headdress dwarf Elizabeth's ageless, smooth-skinned face. In her left hand she holds a feather; her right rests on a globe with her tapering white fingers pointing to America. By 1588 the Colony of Virginia had been founded, thereby establishing an empire in the New World. An imperial crown is pictured by her right elbow. Elizabeth is shown as the sun conquering the forces of darkness. A lace ribbon with a large bow is placed where a codpiece for a male monarch would otherwise be, and from it hangs a large teardrop pearl pendant. The pearl symbolises her virginity and is linked with the inviolable boundaries of the body politic. Elizabeth's slight, feminine frame is subsumed within this exaggerated spectacle of her body representing the state. A direct link is made between Elizabeth's virtuous chastity and the English nation's emerging power; the strength and integrity of the English body politic depending on the strength and inviolability of the Queen's natural body.[19]

44

Barricaded from Within

On 26 August 1588, Robert Devereux, the young 2nd Earl of Essex, staged a triumphant military review at Whitehall to celebrate the Armada victory. The Queen watched seated alongside Robert Dudley, Essex's stepfather, from a window at the palace. Dudley was now restored to favour and regularly dined with Elizabeth in her Privy Chamber.[1] Days later Dudley left court for Kenilworth and then on to the medicinal springs at Buxton, in the hope that taking the waters would restore his failing health. On the morning of Thursday 29 August, he wrote to Elizabeth from Rycote in Oxfordshire:

> I most humbly beseech Your Majesty to pardon your poor old serv-
> ant to be thus bold in sending to know how my gracious lady doth,
> and what ease of her late pain she finds, being the chiefest thing in
> the world I do pray for, for her to have good health and long life.
> For my own poor case, I continue still your medicine, and it amends
> much better than any other thing that hath been given me. Thus
> hoping to find perfect cure at the bath, with the continuance of my
> wonted prayer for Your Majesty's most happy preservation I
> humbly kiss your foot.[2]

But just a few miles later, Dudley grew sicker and was forced to take refuge in the hunting lodge in Cornbury House in the forest of Wychwood in Oxfordshire. He was suffering with a 'continual burning fever' and 'sore pains in his stomach'. He died at four o'clock in the morning of 4 September, probably from a malarial infection, aged fifty-six. His wife, Lettice, was with him when he died, though Dudley's death would do little to ease Elizabeth's hostility towards her.

Whilst the court celebrated the defeat of the Spanish Armada, Elizabeth confined herself to her Bedchamber at St James's Palace, locking the door and ordering her ladies away so that she might grieve alone. She had lost her greatest love, the man whom she had grown up with, had become infatuated with and adored. According to the report of a Spanish agent, the Queen remained in her Bedchamber refusing to speak to anyone 'for some days', as her anxious women and councillors gathered outside.[3] Walsingham described how he was unable to conduct any state business with the Queen, by 'reason that she will not suffer anybody to access unto her, being very much grieved with the death of the Lord Steward'.[4] Finally, as concern for the Queen's state of mind grew, Cecil ordered that the doors of her Bedchamber be broken down. Elizabeth now accepted that it was time to return to her duties; she rose from her bed, signalled that her ladies be admitted and prepared to have her public face re-applied.

In response to a letter from the Earl of Shrewsbury congratulating her on the Armada victory and offering his condolences for the Earl of Leicester's death, Elizabeth made clear her distress and that she never wished to discuss the loss of her favourite again,

> We desire rather to forebear the remembrance thereof as a thing whereof we can admit no comfort, otherwise by submitting our will to God's inevitable appointment. Who notwithstanding His goodness by the former prosperous news hath nevertheless been pleased to keep us in exercise by the loss of a personage so dear unto us.[5]

Marco Antonio Micea reported to Philip of Spain that, 'the Queen is much aged and spent and is very melancholy. Her intimates say that this is caused by the death of the Earl of Leicester', but Marco Antonio thought it was more likely brought on by the 'fear she underwent [of a revenge attack by Spain] and the burden she has upon her'.[6]

Elizabeth always rejected the idea that she had ever been in love, or at least allowed herself the time to love.

> I am too much burdened with cares to turn my attention to marriage, for Love is usually the offspring of leisure, and as I am so beset by duties, I have not been able to think of Love. As therefore, nothing has yet urged me to marry, I have not been able to mediate on this man or that man.

Yet, after Elizabeth's own death, a small silver-gilt casket was discovered next to her bed. Inside, folded and bound in silk ribbon was Dudley's final note from Rycote, and on which she had written, 'his last letter'.[7]

The gossip about Elizabeth and Dudley continued long after his death. One anonymous pornographic satire, 'News from Heaven and Hell', circulated weeks later, purported to be an account of his 'futile attempt to enter heaven and his subsequent reception in hell'. In it Dudley is portrayed as having insatiable sexual appetites and political ambitions. Appropriating the Queen's nickname for him, 'Robin', this manuscript imagines, 'his Robinship's entertainment' in hell to be a future spent gazing into the vagina of a 'naked fiend' disguised as one of his former mistresses. As such, Dudley's penis, 'the member wherewith he had most offended', will become the instrument of his eternal punishment.

> Now there was no doubt made but that this pleasant sight ... would ... give him such an edge that he could not forbear, especially having been all his life a valiant cavalier in arms, to give a charge with his lance of lust against the centre of her target of proof, and run his ingredience up to the hard hilts into the unsearchable bottom of her gaping gulf. And if he should not be disposed thereunto of his own accord, it was ordained that every small touch of the chain should drown the member of his virility in the bottomless barrel of her virginity, through which runneth a field of unquenchable fire, which, at every joining together did so hiss his humanity, that he was in continual danger to lose the top of his standard of steel ...[8]

Given the satire's derisive allusion to the Pope, the author of the piece was probably not a Catholic; given the critique of Dudley's abuse of patronage it was perhaps someone at court.

There were continued rumours of supposed children of the Queen and her favourite. Two years after Dudley's death a widow named Dionisia Deryck claimed that Elizabeth 'hath already had as many children as I, and that two of them were yet alive, one a man child and the other a maiden child, and the others were burned'. Deryck claimed the father of the Queen's children was the Earl of Leicester, and that he had 'wrapped them up in the embers in the chamber where they were born'. In the same year, 1590, Robert Garner told a similar story: Dudley 'had four children by the Queen's Majesty, whereof three were daughters alive, and the fourth a son that was burnt'. Both Deryck and Garner stood in the pillory for their indiscretions.[9]

Now fifty-five years old, Elizabeth spent the Christmas and New Year festivities at Richmond. Rain and sleet battered the palace as fires blazed high, and the court was entertained with plays, feasting, dancing and the usual exchange of gifts. It was Elizabeth's first Christmas without Dudley and now she showed especial favour to his twenty-one-year-old stepson, Robert Devereux, with whom she had grown particularly close over the last year.[10] Tall, strikingly attractive with dark eyes and auburn hair, the 2nd Earl of Essex was intelligent, witty and flirtatious. Dudley had introduced him at court four years before and, having served under his stepfather's command in the Low Countries, Essex returned to England where he established himself at court. Elizabeth would grow increasingly captivated by the russet-haired young man whose youth enlivened her and gave her new energy.

Essex was charming and confident whilst at the same time being stubborn, egotistical, fiercely ambitious and, like the Queen, short-tempered. Elizabeth and Essex spent a great deal of time together and despite the thirty-year age gap, many people began to speculate on the nature of their relationship. At court entertainments he would either sit next to Elizabeth, or adjacent to her; she was often reported to whisper to him or touch him fondly. All through the summer of 1587, Essex had ridden or walked with the Queen and played cards long into the night. Antony Bagot, one of Essex's servants, boasted that 'even at night my lord is at cards or one game or another with her, that he cometh not to his own lodging till the birds sing in the morning'. Bagot wrote excitedly to his father in Shropshire about the attention the Queen was paying their master: 'He [Essex] told me with his own mouth that he looked to be Master of Horse within these ten days.'[11] Indeed, Elizabeth bestowed the position on the young earl on 18 June 1587, the role his stepfather, Robert Dudley, had exchanged for that of Lord Steward.

Elizabeth's relationship with the earl was impassioned and volatile. In July 1587, the year before Robert Dudley's death, whilst the court then on progress approached North Hall, Hertfordshire, the home of the Earl of Warwick, Essex quarrelled with Elizabeth over her slighting of his sister, Dorothy, who had incurred the Queen's wrath by marrying without permission a few years earlier. When Essex told Elizabeth that his sister was already at North Hall, the Queen ordered that Dorothy be detained in her chamber. Essex was furious, accusing Elizabeth of acting to disgrace him and his family honour 'only to please that knave Ralegh'. He proceeded to pour out his pent-up jealousy of Sir Walter Ralegh who, he believed, dared to compete for the affection of the Queen. Elizabeth soon lost her temper with Essex and began to berate him about the behaviour of his mother Lettice. The earl realised he had gone too far and in the middle of the night ordered his servants to prepare his and Dorothy's belongings for their departure from North Hall. Essex subsequently reported the encounter in a letter to a friend,

> It seemed she could not well endure anything to be spoken against him [Ralegh]; and taking hold of one word 'disdain', she said there was no such cause why I should disdain him. This speech troubled me so much that as near as I could I described unto her what he had been, and what he was, and then I did let her see whether I had cause to disdain his competition of love, or whether I could have comfort to give myself over to the service of a mistress that was in awe of such a man. I spake, what grief and choler, as much against him as I could, and I think he standing at the door might well have heard the worse that I spoke of himself. In the end I saw she was resolved to defend him, and to cross me. For myself, I told her, I had no joy to be in any place but loath to be near about her when I knew my affection so much thrown down, and such a wretch as Ralegh highly esteemed of her . . .[12]

Essex resolved to leave England for the Low Countries: 'If I return, I will be welcomed home; if not *una bella morire* is better than a disquiet life.'[13] However, as he rode towards Sandwich in Kent to embark on his voyage, he was overtaken by Robert Carey with a message from the Queen commanding him to return to court. All was forgiven, at least for now. The following year, when Dudley retired from court, Elizabeth asked Essex to move into his stepfather's lodgings in the palace.

———·———

With Dudley's death, Elizabeth's reliance on Essex increased; but having spent Christmas and the New Year by the Queen's side, as she mourned the loss of his stepfather, the young earl began to grow restless. In the spring of 1589 he ignored Elizabeth's orders to remain at court and slipped away to join Sir Francis Drake and Sir John Norris's voyage to Portugal. Their expedition sought to destroy what remained of the Armada and free Portugal from Spanish domination by securing Dom Antonio on the throne, before going on to the Azores to capture the Spanish treasure fleet. When Elizabeth learned of the planned departure, she immediately sent orders for the earl's return.

> Essex: your sudden and undutiful departure from our presence and your place of attendance [as Master of the Horse] you may easily conceive how offensive it is, and ought to be, unto us. Our great favour bestowed on you without deserts hath drawn you this to neglect and forget your duty; for other constructions we cannot make of those your strange actions . . . We do therefore charge and command you forthwith, upon receipt of those our letters, all excuses and delays set apart, to make your present and immediate repair unto us, to understand our further pleasure. Whereof see you fail not, as you will be loath to incur our indignation and will answer for the contrary at your uttermost peril.[14]

He did not obey, however. The expedition proved a failure on all fronts and Essex was back in England by the end of June to face the Queen's wrath.

As Elizabeth became increasingly demanding and irascible, Essex turned his attention to the ladies who surrounded her, particularly Frances Sidney, the widow of Sir Philip Sidney who had died in the Netherlands expedition, and daughter of spymaster Sir Francis Walsingham. As Sir Philip lay dying, Essex had reportedly promised to look after his wife. In the spring of 1590, true to his word, he secretly married Frances and soon afterwards she fell pregnant.[15] The precise date of the marriage is uncertain but it might well have taken place shortly after Walsingham's death on 6 April, and perhaps he had given them his blessing as he lay dying at his home in Seething Lane in London. He was buried in St Paul's Cathedral the following evening in the tomb where his son-in-law Sir Philip Sidney had been placed just weeks before.

Essex was all too aware of the Queen's explosive reaction when, a decade earlier, she had discovered his mother's marriage to Robert Dudley. The young earl now feared a similar fate. As Frances's belly swelled through the summer, Essex found excuses to keep her away from court.

When later that year the Queen found out about the marriage she was furious, but after only a fortnight Essex was welcomed back at her side. His relationship with the Queen was very different from that which Elizabeth had shared with Dudley. There had been – on both sides – genuine love and perhaps unrequited ambition for a marriage; whereas Essex's relationship with her was a flirtation which made the ageing Queen feel young and attractive again.[16] Nevertheless, Elizabeth forbade Frances to return to court, causing Essex long periods of separation from his wife.

Months later, Essex convinced Elizabeth to place him in command of an army being sent into France to help the Protestant King Henri IV against his French and Spanish enemies. In August 1591 he landed in Dieppe and from there wrote to the Queen assuring her of his love and loyalty:

> The two windows of your Privy Chamber shall be the poles of my sphere, where, as long as your Majesty will please to have me, I am fixed and unmovable. When your Majesty thinks that heaven too good for me, I will not fall like a star but be consumed like a vapour by the sun that draws me up to such a height. While your Majesty gives me leave to say I love you, my fortune is as my affection, unmatchable. If ever you deny me that liberty, you may end my life, but never shake my constancy, for were the sweetness of your nature turned into the greatest bitterness that could be, it is not in your power, as great a queen as you are, to make me love you less.[17]

He returned from France at the beginning of 1592, aged twenty-four, and in January, Frances gave birth to their second son. Only weeks before, Mistress Elizabeth Southwell, one of the Queen's maids of honour with whom Essex had been conducting a secret affair, also gave birth to a son, named Walter Devereux. The illegitimate child's existence was hushed up and the infant was passed into the care of Essex's mother Lettice, the Countess of Leicester, and raised at Drayton Basset. Southwell had put her absences from court during the later stages of pregnancy down to a 'lameness in her leg'. When it emerged that she had been pregnant and given birth, her lover was named as 'Mr Vavisor'[18] – Thomas Vavasour, a Gentleman Pensioner – who was then banished from court for misconduct and imprisoned. The ruse held for a further four years; only then did the Queen discover that the father of Walter Devereux was not Thomas Vavasour but Robert Devereux, the Earl of Essex. Elizabeth Southwell had by then left court in disgrace and remained banished until her death in 1602.[19]

A few months later, another scandal broke; another secret marriage from among the maids of honour and the birth of another illegitimate child.

Sir Walter Ralegh had, like Essex, been unfaithful to the Queen's affection and favour and in April 1592 his secret marriage to Elizabeth Throckmorton was exposed by the birth of their first child.

'Bess' Throckmorton had entered the Queen's service as a Gentlewoman of the Privy Chamber in 1584. Aged nineteen, this was a prestigious position for one so young. She was attractive, passionate, strong-minded and determined. By 1590 she had caught the eye of Sir Walter Ralegh, a dashing courtier and adventurer whose job it was to protect the Queen and her ladies, and before long the two began meeting clandestinely. In July 1591, Bess discovered she was pregnant and begged Ralegh, then in his late thirties, to marry her. He agreed, though he dreaded the Queen's reaction. They married in secret on 19 November.[20] Meanwhile Bess remained in the Queen's service, disguising her growing belly as best she could, and Sir Walter continued with his preparations for his next military expedition to Panama. At the end of February, in her final month of pregnancy, Bess left court and went to her brother's house at Mile End to prepare for the birth. She had remained at court until the very last moment knowing that, if she could be away for less than a fortnight, she would not need a licence to authorise her absence.

After her sudden departure rumours began to circulate about Bess's relationship with Ralegh. Robert Cecil, the twenty-seven-year-old son of William Cecil, and now a privy councillor, became suspicious and started questioning Ralegh. Sir Walter explicitly denied any relationship with Bess, and swore that there had been no marriage, there would be no marriage and that he was entirely devoted to Queen Elizabeth:

> I mean not to come away, as they say I will, for fear of a marriage and I know not what. If any such thing where I would have imparted it unto yourself before any man living. And therefore I pray believe it not, and I beseech you to suppress what you can any such malicious report. For I protest before God, there is none on the face of the earth that I would be fastened unto.[21]

Ralegh was unaware that Robert Cecil had already found out about the marriage and therefore knew that he was being lied to. Bess meanwhile was left to endure childbirth alone and on 29 March was safely delivered of a son, who was later baptised Damerei. A messenger was immediately despatched to Ralegh who sent his wife £50, and then continued with the preparations for his voyage. He was keen to get as far away from the court as possible before the Queen found out about Bess and the child.

Four weeks later Bess was back in the Queen's service as if nothing had happened, leaving Damerei in the care of a wet nurse in Enfield. Sir Walter meanwhile embarked on the first leg of his voyage. He was back in Plymouth by mid-May, when the scandal broke. The Queen, then at Nonsuch at the start of her summer progress, immediately ordered the arrest and detainment of her Gentlewoman and the Captain of the Guard, Ralegh at Durham House, Bess in the custody of the Vice-Chamberlain, Sir Thomas Heneage. On 7 August, both husband and wife were moved to the Tower.[22] Ralegh sent urgent messages and poems to the Queen, assuring her of his love, bemoaning his misery and trying to win back her favour. Bess, however, remained unrepentant, signing her letters from the Tower, 'Elizabeth Ralegh'.

In mid-September, Ralegh was released to travel to Dartmouth to greet the Portuguese carrack, the *Madre de Dios*, which his fleet had captured in the Azores and had returned laden with treasure; but Bess remained in the Tower. It was a sweltering late summer and plague was rife throughout the capital. She was freed shortly before Christmas, only to learn that their infant son Damerei had died, most likely in the plague. Bess retired to her husband's estate at Sherborne in Dorset and by the following spring she was pregnant again. In November she bore another son, named Walter.

For the time being both Ralegh and his wife remained exiled from court. Bess continued to petition her friends to help her regain the Queen's favour but Elizabeth proved unforgiving and would never welcome Bess back to court. At the end of the reign, Lord Henry Howard, an enemy of the Raleghs, wrote gloatingly that although 'much hath been offered on all sides to bring her [Bess] into the Privy Chamber of her old place', Elizabeth refused to receive her. Sir Walter Ralegh finally returned to court in 1597 and resumed his duties as Captain of the Guard.

Every scandal involving Elizabeth's women of the Bedchamber and maids of honour soon became the stuff of alehouse gossip and malicious rumour. Even Anne Clifford, the Countess of Warwick's young niece, reported that, 'there was much talk of a Mask which the Queen had at Winchester, & how all the Ladies about the Court had gotten such ill names that it was grown a scandalous place & the Queen herself was much fallen from her former greatness and reputation she had in the world'.[23]

45
Suspected and Discontented Persons

After the defeat of the Armada, Elizabeth resumed her summer progresses beyond London and the Home Counties, where she had remained for most of the 1580s. Now, despite reports of the gradual build up of a new Spanish fleet, Elizabeth refused to be cowed by fears for her safety and ventured further afield. In an attempt to inspire loyalty across the confessional divide and to seek out signs of disloyalty or discontent, she visited many houses that were owned by open or suspected Catholics.

The route of Elizabeth's progress in 1591 was carefully planned through Surrey, Sussex and Hampshire with visits to the homes of five Catholic gentlemen. Many of Elizabeth's councillors regarded such stops as being unnecessarily dangerous and there was real anxiety for the Queen's safety. One courtier, Richard Cavendish, sought to dissuade her from going to what he believed was a 'tickle [dangerous] country and places fraught with suspected and discontented persons'.[1]

In August, Elizabeth spent six days at Cowdray in Sussex, the seat of Anthony Browne, 1st Viscount Montague, a leading Catholic nobleman.[2] Having been employed on a number of embassies at the beginning of the reign and appointed to the lord lieutenancy of Sussex, Montague lost his position in 1585 and had thereafter become increasingly marginalised from Elizabethan political life as actions against Catholics intensified. His household included active supporters of both the Jesuits and the Spanish invasion and he was the owner of a number of houses where missionary priests were thought to have received help and support. Montague had also been implicated in the plot to have Mary Queen of Scots marry Thomas Howard, Duke of Norfolk. Whilst he had acted to defend Elizabeth as the Armada threatened, Montague might well have feared that an example would now be made of him, as it had been with Edward Rookwood of Euston Hall in 1578, during the East Anglian progress. However this time, as the government looked to combat accusations of the cruel persecution of Catholics at home, a demonstration of loyalty to the Queen by a prominent Catholic nobleman suited better their purpose.

Montague was keen to prove his devotion to her Majesty and laid on lavish entertainments at Cowdray Park in August to emphasise his position as the leader of a loyal local gentry. The country dances performed by local people and joined by Montague and his wife pointed to a 'beautiful relation' among all classes; speeches by the characters the 'Pilgrim' and 'Wild Man' extended the notion of order and loyalty to the entire county, whilst claiming that the world outside was one of treachery and instability. Montague sought to dismiss claims that Roman Catholicism amounted to treason and threatened the peace of the realm and the life of the Queen. He, like many other Catholics, instead pointed to Protestantism as the main source of 'rebellion and civil disobedience', with Protestants being 'men that are full of affection and passions and that look to wax almighty, and of power, by the confiscation, spoil and ruin of the houses of noble and ancient men'.[3]

The uproar in London caused by William Hacket, a fanatical Protestant, little more than a fortnight earlier appeared to be evidence of just the kind of disorder that Montague described. In July, Hacket claimed to be the Messiah and on the streets of London he and his two followers preached the overthrow of the government and the usurpation of the Queen.[4] Having declared the Day of Judgement to be near at hand, he then took an 'iron instrument' to a picture of the Queen hanging in his lodgings and 'villainously and treacherously' defaced it, especially that part of the picture which represented Elizabeth's heart, and railed 'most traitorously against her Majesty's person'.[5] By one o'clock on 26 July 1591, the three men had been arrested.[6] Hacket was found guilty of high treason, and was executed two days later at the Cross at Cheapside.[7]

Whilst other Protestants were anxious to disassociate themselves from Hacket and regarded him as a madman, the Attorney General at Hacket's trial dismissed arguments about the defendant's 'frantic humours' and instead stated that he had led a carefully constructed plot to overthrow the state. Even though Hacket was a fanatical puritan, Elizabeth's government was quick to cast him as a Catholic. As the Jesuit priest Robert Southwell wrote in a letter to Rome, 'the puritan Hacket had been posted over to us as a papist and is named to the vulgar sort'.[8]

In the face of such disorder, Montague represented his estate at Cowdray as a bastion of stability and loyalty. Yet his show of loyalty to the Queen did not serve its purpose, for on 18 October, Elizabeth issued a new anti-Catholic proclamation which further criminalised anyone found harbouring Catholic priests.[9] The proclamation, which may have been drafted by privy councillors whilst they were being hosted by Montague, referred to Catholic activity as 'treasons in the bowels of our Realm'.[10] Sir John Harington observed that as the laws against Catholics became more and more harsh, 'their practices grew fouler and fouler', yet he wondered which came first: whether Catholics' 'sinister practices drew on these rigorous laws, or whether the rigour of these laws moved them to these unnatural practices?'[11]

The following year there were reports of another major plot abroad. Thomas Phillipes, an agent working for the Earl of Essex and formerly used by Walsingham, had acquired intelligence from Flanders about a plot to kill Elizabeth and hasten a foreign invasion supported by the Pope and the Duke of Parma and led by recusant officer Sir William Stanley.

When fighting under Robert Dudley in the Low Countries, Stanley had spectacularly defected to the Spaniards, handing over the town of Deventer which he was then occupying. He remained in post as governor of Deventer for a year, during which time he became involved with the English Catholic exile community in Flanders and came into contact with Cardinal Allen. Stanley would become one of the Elizabethan government's most implacable enemies among the exiles abroad and he and his disaffected regiment were perceived to be plotting tirelessly against the Queen and her realm.

In the general confusion that would follow Elizabeth's assassination, when 'the people will be together by the ears about the succession', it was anticipated that Stanley would give support to James VI. Phillipes explained that this plot had been brewing 'since the Great Enterprise was disappointed'. The Pope was said to have 'revoked the assassin from the camp of the French King [Henri IV], whom he was to have killed, to attempt the like on the Queen'.[12]

Stanley and his conspirators aimed to target Elizabeth during her progress into Wiltshire that summer, which would give them the 'means and opportunity fit for this practice'.[13] In 1592, Phillipes reported that, 'Sir William Stanley's force has long been preparing, and it is fully expected that the desperate Italian that is to come over [to kill the Queen] will do the deed.' The plot was foiled because of Phillipes's intelligence, as was another conspiracy the following year, also sponsored by Stanley and other English exiles, which saw Father Persons and Gilbert Laton debating how best to kill the Queen and 'show how it might be performed – her Majesty being in the progress – and to be executed with a wire made with jemos or with a poignard'.[14] Over the next few months and on into the new year, the activities of Jesuit priests, factions at the English court, disaffected soldiers and impressionable young men seduced by the promise of a fortune, combined to produce a deluge of assassination plots, most of which seemed to have Sir William Stanley at their heart.

In 1594 it was reported that a number of former soldiers from Stanley's regiment came secretly to England with the aim of murdering Elizabeth. In February, an Irish soldier called Patrick O'Collun was captured and imprisoned in the Tower. It was alleged that he had been sent to England by Stanley and the Jesuit priest Nicholas Owen to carry out the deed.[15] Two witnesses testified to O'Collun's mission, one of whom was William Polwhele. Polwhele was also a soldier in Stanley's regiment who had been arrested and had admitted to having been sent by Stanley to assassinate Elizabeth. He described how that summer, Captain 'Jacques', Stanley's deputy in the regiment, had urged him to go to England and kill the Queen, saying that 'no action could be more glorious than cutting off so wicked a member, who is likely to overthrow all Christendom'. Polwhele was instructed to go to England, gain William Cecil's trust and then ingratiate himself at court. The plan was to be put into action 'when the Queen went for a walk or to the sermon: that she might be shot or stabbed', for, they claimed, 'she takes no care'.[16]

Around the same time, Hugh Cahill, another Irish soldier from Stanley's regiment, was examined at William Cecil's House in Westminster, where he revealed that, like O'Collun and Polwhele, he had been approached by the Jesuit priests Fathers Holt, Archer and Walpole at Stanley's behest to assassinate the Queen.[17] The plan was that he should go to England, enter the service of a courtier, 'and then manage to waylay her (the Queen) in some progress, and kill her with a sword or a dagger at a gate or narrow passage, or, as she walked in one of her galleries'. Cahill approved the scheme and a fee was agreed. However, upon arriving in England, Cahill divulged the plot to William Cecil.[18] It was claimed that John Scudamore, stepson of Elizabeth's long-standing Lady of the Bedchamber Mary Scudamore, was party to the plot. Scudamore was arrested and questioned, but released soon afterwards, presumably having proved his innocence or perhaps because of a timely intervention from his stepmother, and then returned to Rome, where he had become a priest.[19]

All of the prisoners denied any serious intent to kill the Queen. Beyond their confessions there is no proof as to what had been planned, though it seems likely that there had been an intention by some to assassinate Elizabeth. Hugh Owen protested that, 'neither he, Owen, nor Sir William Stanley, had any more to do with killing the Queen than the man in the moon'. He said that John Annais, another accused solider, 'is a sorry fellow, who can make a white powder, but would not kill a cat if she looked him on the face'. He denied ever seeing Cullen and protested that he barely knew Cahill or Polwhele.[20]

In February 1594, Henry Walpole, the Jesuit whom Cahill had accused, was arrested on landing near Flamborough Head in Yorkshire. The Queen's priest-hunter–interrogator Richard Topcliffe was sent to York to question Walpole, who was subjected to long and painful torture. Again and again Walpole insisted that his mission was a purely religious one: to administer the sacraments and urge English Catholics to remain faithful to their queen. He rejected with horror the suggestion that he had encouraged the assassination of Elizabeth. His pleas were rejected and on 7 April he was hanged, drawn and quartered. There was no evidence beyond Cahill's claims, but the fact that he was a Jesuit seemed sufficient to condemn him.

William Cecil now introduced new defensive measures to protect the Queen and tighten access to court. He advised barring unnecessary people and limiting the numbers of servants. The ushers and clerks of the household would inspect all petitioners seeking an audience with the Queen. By proclamation, it was declared that 'her Majesty forbiddeth all persons that are not servitors upon the council or upon other lords and ladies or gentlemen attending on her Majesty, to forbear to come to the court or near to the court'.[21] No one should use the back doors at palaces, except for the designated servants who should keep them locked. Most importantly, the Knight Harbinger and Knight Marshal should prevent crowds from lodging within two miles of the court when on progress: 'If any are found not allowed they shall be examined, and if they cannot give just cause be committed to prison.'[22]

On 17 February the council sent officers to every English port to search, interrogate and, if needed, detain anyone entering the country.[23] Special precautions were to be taken against Irishmen in London and near Elizabeth's court, and particularly those who had served in Sir William Stanley's rebel regiment. A royal proclamation was issued announcing that some men had come secretly into the kingdom, 'with full purpose, by procurement of the Devil and His Ministers, her Majesty's enemies, and rebels on the other side of the sea, to endanger her Majesty's noble person'. The proclamation ordered the arrest of vagabonds and deportation of Irishmen: 'No manner of person born in the realm of Ireland without proper purpose or residence shall remain in this realm.'[24]

Whilst the proclamation attempted to restrain suspect persons from approaching the Queen, particularly when she went on progress, opportunities to do her harm abounded.[25] Elizabeth and her advisers knew that royal progresses especially exposed her to attack, but she refused to limit contact with her subjects and declared she would rather be dead than 'in custody'.[26] As it was, suspicions of a second suspected invasion in 1593 kept her close to London and she spent most of the late summer and early autumn at Windsor.

The following year, Edmund Yorke, formerly a captain in Stanley's regiment, gave himself up to the Privy Council. Under harsh interrogation, Yorke confessed to having plotted with Sir William Stanley, Father William Holt and Charles Paget, a ruthless English émigré, to kill Elizabeth. Detailed plans had been laid including what weapons Yorke and his accomplice Richard Williams would use. Whilst some of the group thought using a small steel crossbow with poison arrows would be most effective, Yorke ultimately agreed to shoot the Queen with a small pistol while Williams would carry a rapier tipped with a 'poison' made from bacon, garlic juice and juniper.[27] By February 1595, both Captain Yorke and Richard Williams had been sent to the gallows.

These were times of heightened fear for the Elizabethan government. The Queen had come close, sometimes very close, to having been killed, and it was only the ruthless investigations of Cecil and Essex to unearth the threats, and so prove their own devotion to her, that had saved her from harm. The factional politics of the court, the anxieties wrought by the succession issue and the ambitions of disaffected English exiles abroad, all conspired to produce an atmosphere of intense fright and panic in the kingdom.

46

Age and Decay

'There is a rumour in London that the Queen is dead and hath been carried away to Greenwich, but it is being kept very secret in Court.'[1] The gossip was traced to William Hancock, a tailor and servant to a musician at court, who vigorously denied spreading the story. He said he had heard from John Rogers, a chandler in Whitechapel, that the Queen was ill and that her sickness had caused her removal from Hampton Court to Greenwich.[2] He was not discussing her death, he said; he was expressing concern for her recovery.

Soon all discussion of the Queen's health and the succession was banned. Anyone who ignored the ruling risked charges of sedition and libel. When in February 1593 the puritan MP Peter Wentworth petitioned Elizabeth to name a successor he was promptly arrested and imprisoned in the Tower. John Harington, the Queen's godson, later recalled how, from his cell, Wentworth wrote, 'to tell [the Queen] that if she named not her heir in her life her body should lie unburied after her death'.[3] Wentworth remained in the Tower for four years until his death, though he refused to keep silent on the succession.[4]

In early 1596, Dr Matthew Hutton, Archbishop of York, expressed similar sentiments in a bold sermon delivered before the Queen and the Lords in the chapel royal at Whitehall. After a brief survey of English history and a tribute to the blessings of the current reign, Hutton spoke of the duty Elizabeth owed, both to God and her people, to unequivocally appoint a successor. The uncertainty of the succession gave hope to foreigners to attempt invasion and bred fears in her subjects of a new conquest; 'the only way to quiet these fears, was to establish the succession'. Sir John Harington subsequently recalled how after Hutton had finished the sermon everyone assumed the Queen would be highly offended and 'imagined such a speech was as welcome as salt to the eyes', or in Elizabeth's own words, 'to pin up a winding-sheet before her face, so

266

as to point out her successor, and urge her to declare him'. But she responded magnanimously. She,

> supposed many of them were of his opinion, and some of them might have persuaded him to this motion; finally, she ascribed so much to his years, place and learning, that when she opened the window of her closet we found ourselves all deceived, for very kindly and calmly, without show of offence, as if she had but waked out of some sleep, she gave him thanks for his very learned sermon.

But that was not to be her last word. Having 'better considered the matter, and recollected herself in private', she sent Hutton a 'sharp message' which left the archbishop scarcely knowing whether 'he were a prisoner or a free man'.[5]

The political pressures caused by war, poverty, disease and the torrent of conspiracies against the Queen, were all exacerbated by creeping signs of Elizabeth's physical deterioration, her body the living symbol of an exhausted government. As Elizabeth approached her sixties, this prompted urgent and increasingly desperate attempts to recreate her former youthful appearance and reassure her subjects of her health and vigour. John Clapham, a servant of William Cecil, was in attendance at court in the early 1590s and in his 'Certain Observations' described what he saw:

> In the latter time, when she showed herself in public, she was always magnificent in apparel, supposing happily thereby, that the eyes of her people, being dazzled with the glittering aspect of those accidental ornaments would not so easily discern the marks of age and decay of natural beauty. But she began to show herself less often so as to make her presence the more grateful and applauded by the multitude, to whom things rarely seen are in manner as new.[6]

With age came a greater need to control images of the Queen, to overcome the discrepancy between her weakening body, revealed only to the ladies of her Bedchamber, and her public image of strength and fortitude.[7] In 1592 the artist Isaac Oliver produced one of the few images ever painted from life of Elizabeth as an older woman. Oliver had been granted a rare sitting with the Queen and, contrary to her own preference, he positioned her next to a window so a natural revealing light shone on her face. The painting was intended to be a pattern, kept in his studio for future repetition and so the details of her dress and jewels were left unfinished. Instead the focus is on Elizabeth's pale and rather sallow face with tightly drawn lips and lively eyes. It was undoubtedly the most revealing, realistic portrait ever produced of the ageing Elizabeth; as far as the Queen was concerned it was therefore not a success. Elizabeth let her Privy Council know that portraits based on this model were unacceptable and her councillors swiftly issued instructions that 'all likenesses of the Queen that depicted her as being in any way old and hence subject to mortality' were to her 'great offence' and should be sought out and destroyed.[8] Oliver was to be left in no doubt as to his mistake. He received no further patronage from the Queen, who looked elsewhere for a more flattering portrait painter.

Around the same time that Oliver was granted a sitting with Elizabeth, Marcus Gheeraerts the younger, the future brother-in-law to Oliver, was also admitted to the Queen's presence. He had been commissioned by Sir Henry Lee to paint a full-length picture of the Queen to commemorate her visit to his home at Ditchley Park in Oxfordshire. The picture is huge; nearly eight feet high, the largest painted of Elizabeth and very deliberately intended to make a visual statement identifying her as the embodiment of the nation. She stands at the top of a globe, her feet positioned on England adjacent to Ditchley in Oxfordshire, her body encased in a richly embroidered and bejewelled white dress that sweeps across the country. She appears, Goddess-like, her face framed by a lace ruff and jewelled veil. Her body spans heaven and earth and is captured between two sky scenes; one dark and stormy on the left, another calm and serene on the right. Elizabeth is presented as having calmed tempestuous heavens and the sunshine after storms. As Sir John Harington later said of his godmother, 'When she smiled, it was a pure sunshine, that everyone did choose to bask in, if they could; but anon came a storm from a sudden gathering of clouds, and the thunder fell in wondrous manner on all alike.'[9]

The 'Ditchley portrait' established the pattern of portraying the Queen in her later years. In future versions the face was rejuvenated somewhat and its features softened in order to conform to the obligatory 'mask of youth' pattern which was soon to be imposed by the government. From the mid-1590s, Elizabeth's face ceased to be painted from life.[10] With no heirs to the throne, all signs of ageing and infertility were removed in order to present a reassuring image of longevity and continuity.

Many of Elizabeth's longest-serving ladies, who had been with her since her youth, were approaching their final years. In March 1589, Elizabeth lost her cousin, Lady Elizabeth Fiennes de Clinton, who had been at the heart of the court for more than thirty years. Lady Elizabeth Fitzgerald, as she was then known, had joined the household of her young cousins Mary and Elizabeth in the 1530s, before entering the Princess Elizabeth's service in June 1539. One contemporary described her as a woman in whom Elizabeth 'trusted more than all others' and they spent many hours in one another's company. Lady Clinton's favour was widely acknowledged and she was besieged by petitioners who urged her to present their suits to the Queen.[11] When 'Fair Geraldine', as the poet Henry Howard, Earl of Surrey, described Lady Clinton, died, Elizabeth was heartbroken. Another link with her childhood had gone. The Queen ordered a magnificent funeral to be conducted at Windsor where her cousin's body was interred next to that of her second husband, Edward Fiennes de Clinton, the Lord High Admiral.[12]

Less than a year later, Elizabeth was in deep mourning again. On 12 February 1590, Blanche Parry died, after fifty-seven years of loyal service. She was eighty-two and up until the final few weeks of her life remained in attendance on the Queen. Three years earlier, because of her failing eyesight, Blanche had been forced give up her responsibility for the Queen's jewels to Mary Radcliffe, a former maid of honour, who was then promoted to become a Gentlewoman of the Privy Chamber. In July 1587, 'a book of such jewels and other parcels delivered to the charge and custody of Mrs Radcliffe, one of the Gentlewomen of the Queen's Majesty's Privy Chamber, as were parcel of the jewels as were in the charge of Mrs Blanche Parry' was drawn up.[13] Radcliffe, like Blanche, never married and would go on to serve Elizabeth to the end of the reign.

Despite her advanced years, Blanche's death shook the Queen. One letter from court described the 'great sorrow' of the Queen and her ladies.[14] For the first time in her life, Elizabeth had no one left who had been with her since infancy, and after the death of Kat Ashley, Blanche had been the closest thing to a mother that Elizabeth had. The news of Mistress Parry's passing soon spread from the court. On 17 February, the Earl of Shrewsbury received a letter from Thomas Markham at Westminster informing him that 'on Thursday last Mrs [sic] Blanche Parry departed; blind she was here on earth, but I hope the joys in heaven she shall see'. [15]

Blanche's funeral took place in the late evening of Friday 27 February at the church of St Margaret's chapel, directly in front of Westminster Abbey. Blanche had left £300 towards the cost of her burial but Elizabeth paid all the expenses for a ceremony befitting a baroness.[16] Monarchs were not expected to attend funerals and so the chief mourner for Blanche's obsequies was her great-niece, Frances Lady Burgh. Blanche was interred in St Margaret's near her nephew John Vaughan, as she had requested in her final will. Five years later, a beautifully carved and richly decorated marble and alabaster monument was erected, with a painted effigy of Parry kneeling on a cushion placed beneath an arched recess. The effigy, which survives in the chapel, is dressed soberly in a black gown with a modest neck ruff and a black, French hood. Her face is full of character, unlike the usual rather bland countenance of Elizabethan tombs, so it is likely that the effigy was sculpted by someone who knew Blanche. She has high cheekbones, pursed lips, slightly slanting eyebrows and piercing eyes. Underneath Parry's kneeling figure is a plaque with the following inscription:

> Hereunder is entombed Blanche Parry, daughter of Henry Parry of New Court in the County of Hereford, Esquier, Gentlewoman of Queen Elizabeth's most honourable Bedchamber and keeper of her Majesty's jewels whom she faithfully served from her Highness' birth. Beneficial to her kinsfolk and countrymen, charitable to the poor, insomuch that she gave to the poor of Bacton and Newton in Herefordshire seven score bushels of wheat and rye yearly for ever with divers sums of money to Westminster and other places for good uses. She died a maid in the eighty-two years of her age the twelfth of February, 1589.[17]

Cecil helped Blanche draw up her will in 1589, which she had signed in a shaky hand.[18] She was clearly a wealthy woman when she died and she bequeathed more than six diamonds, eight pieces of plate, some weighing as much as sixty ounces, one set of wall hangings, three carpets, approximately £2,000, nine pieces of jewellery that did not contain diamonds including 'one chain of gold and girdle which the Queen gave me', twelve napkins, one towel, over six annual annuities from rents of various people and some clothing.[19] The first item in Blanche's will was the bequest of her 'best diamond' to Elizabeth. She also bequeathed to the Queen 'a pair of sables garnished with 8 chains of gold', possibly those that Elizabeth had given Blanche after she recovered from serious illness many years before. Blanche also made generous bequests to her relatives and to friends at court, including William Cecil, Sir Christopher Hatton, Lady Dorothy Stafford, and to her 'very good friend the Lady Cobham, one gold ring'.[20]

Blanche left provision for a magnificent tomb to be erected in her home church of Bacton, Herefordshire. She had originally intended to be buried there, in the Parry family mausoleum, but by 1589 she had changed her mind and instead decided to be buried in St Margaret's. The epitaph on the Bacton tomb which again depicts her kneeling before the figure of the Queen was composed by Blanche herself and attests to the personal sacrifice that her service to Elizabeth entailed and the pride which she derived from it:

> ... I lived always as handmaid to a queen
> In chamber chief my time did overpass
> ... Not doubting want whilst that my mistress lived
> In woman's state whose cradle saw I rocked.
> Her servant then as when she her crown attached
> And so remained till death my door had knocked ...
> So that my time I thus did pass away
> A maid in Court and never no man's wife
> Sworn of the Queen Elizabeth's Bedchamber always
> With maiden queen a maiden did end my life.[21]

As her ladies faded and passed away, Elizabeth's own infirmity seemed to become more pronounced. Her eyes had become severely strained from short-sightedness which increasingly caused her headaches. Although still partial to sweets and candied fruits, she remained frugal in her diet and now ate even less and took care to mix a greater proportion of water to her wine, so 'her faculties might remain unclouded'.[22] Her women nursed her through illnesses and looked after her minor complaints, but there was a growing sense that the ravages of old age could not be held at bay for much longer. One apothecary bill submitted by Mary Scudamore to the Treasurer of the Household, in 1588 contains the entry, '*Thragea regal cum rhabarbaro incisso, ex mandate Regina pro Domina Scudamore, xvi d*'. Rhubarb was frequently prescribed at that time as both a general tonic and as a cathartic. Purges were also popular as a form of preventative medicine intended to cleanse the system of the 'evil humours' that could cause disease. One recipe notes, 'This was made use of by Queen Elizabeth twice a year.' The concoction contained cypress nuts, senna, rhubarb, dried fruit and seeds, which would be boiled together in water and administered in quarter-pint doses. The recipe claimed to, 'purgeth Choler, and melancholy, helpeth much the consumption of the Lungs, Cureth the Liver, and strengthenth the Back. Also it Cleareth the Kidneys, and breaketh the wind Colic, purgeth ill humours'.[23] At least, so was the intention. Clearly Elizabeth was doing all she could to sustain her health and vigour, in spite of her age.

With the death of Blanche and Lady Elizabeth Clinton a year earlier, the Queen relied even more on her remaining long-serving intimates. Anne Dudley, Countess of Warwick, the eldest daughter of the Earl of Bedford, had served her continuously throughout the 1570s and 1580s, and she and her husband, the Lord High Admiral, lived either at court or at North Hall, his house at Northaw, Hertfordshire.[24] When Anne, Countess of Warwick, heard she was being ignored by the Queen over an important suit, her husband had written an angry letter to Walsingham, insisting she should be better treated, 'considering she hath spent the chief part of her years both painfully, faithfully and serviceably, yea after such sort as without any dishonour to her Majesty any kind of wage nor yet any blemish to her poor self'.[25]

Little over a week after Blanche's death, the Earl of Warwick died and Anne was left distraught. They appear to have enjoyed a genuinely loving and companionable marriage; when Sir Edward Stafford had visited the dying earl he found Anne, 'sitting by the fire so full of tears that she could not speak'.[26] The countess remained an honorary Gentlewoman of the Privy Chamber until Elizabeth's death and, according to her thirteen-year-old niece Anne Clifford, was 'more beloved and in greater favour with the Queen than any other woman in the kingdom'.[27] No longer with a husband to care for, the countess could devote herself entirely to the service of the Queen. Lady Warwick received more requests for favour than any other of the Queen's ladies.[28] By virtue of her marriage and then her relationship with the Queen, she had a wide range of allies in England and abroad and was kept abreast of international affairs through her contacts with English ambassadors. When George, Lord Hunsdon was appointed ambassador to Hesse in 1596 he sent Anne secret reports on the Langrave of Hesse.[29] Following her husband's death, when Anne fell ill, her sickness was reported as far afield as Venice.[30]

Other trusted women like Mary Scudamore rarely got time away from the Queen and Elizabeth would only agree to very short absences. When the court was at Oatlands Palace in June 1590, Mary and her husband left for a short visit to see John Dee at his home Mortlake in Surrey. They were old friends and Mary had been one of the sponsors at the christening of Dee's daughter Katherine in June 1581. In his diary Dee records the visit by Mr and Mrs Scudamore. Accompanying the party, he noted, was the Queen's jester, a dwarf called Mistress Tomasin – also known as Tomasina – an Italian woman who had been at court since the 1570s and was greatly favoured by Elizabeth. She wore clothes adapted from those in the Queen's wardrobe and regularly received gifts from Elizabeth including gilt rings, Spanish gloves, taffeta aprons, table napkins and towels and several ivory combs, a 'penner' (pen case) and 'Inkhorne' (vessel for holding writing ink).[31]

The Scudamores spent the night at Mortlake and next day rejoined the Queen and the court. Although Mary Scudamore appears from the surviving accounts to have remained officially a Chamberer in 1589, she had undoubtedly become a close intimate of the Queen and, as an earlier letter reveals, was one of Elizabeth's regular bedfellows.

47

Abused her Body

In September 1591, Thomas Pormant, a Catholic priest who had returned to England from the English seminary in Rome, was apprehended and interrogated by Richard Topcliffe. Topcliffe had designed his own torture rack which he was authorised to keep at his house at Westminster to 'examine' priests.[1] The rack consisted of an open iron framework with wooden rollers at each end. The victim was stripped off and laid on his back in the centre of the frame whilst his hands and feet were tied with ropes to the rollers. The rollers were then turned and when the ropes were drawn to full tension, interrogation would begin. The prisoner would be in terrible pain as tendons were ripped, joints separated and bones fractured. Refusal to answer questions or an unsatisfactory reply would induce another click of the ratchet mechanism, gradually stretching the limbs until 'the bones started from their joints'. Topcliffe also claimed to have invented the use of 'manacles' as a torture instrument whereby the prisoner's wrists would be placed into iron gauntlets and then he would be hung up on an iron bar for hours on end. All the body weight would be put on the wrists resulting in excruciating pain to the victim.

Topcliffe quickly got a reputation for the ferocity of his examinations and many were horrified by his excesses. For twenty-five years Topcliffe zealously hunted and examined recusants, Jesuits and seminary priests. Thomas Pormant was one such seminary priest that he arrested and brought to his house to be interrogated for information about Catholic designs on England.

Later that year, Richard Verstegan, an exiled English Catholic polemicist, printer and engraver, sent a letter from Flanders to Robert Persons, the Jesuit priest who was then resident in Madrid. With his letter, Verstegan enclosed a document headed, 'A copy of certain notes written by Mr Pormant Priest and Martyr, of certain speeches used by Top[cliffe] unto him while he was prisoner in the house and custody of the said

Topcliffe . . .' In it Pormant claimed that during the course of his interrogation, Richard Topcliffe, an honorary Esquire of the Body in the
Queen's household, told him of his favour and intimacy with Elizabeth.
According to Pormant, Topcliffe declared that 'he himself was so familiar
with her Majesty that he hath very secret dealings with her', having not
only seen her legs and knees but 'feeleth them with his hands above her
knees, he had also felt her belly, saying to her that it was the softest belly
of any womankind'. She said to him, 'Be not these the arms, legs and body
of King Henry?' to which he answered, 'Yea'.

So, great and 'familiar' with the Queen was Topcliffe, that 'he many
times putteth [his hands] between her breasts and paps, and in her neck'.
The intimacy they shared was demonstrated, Topcliffe had told him, by
the fact that the Queen bestowed on him not the conventional glove or
handkerchief but rather 'a white linen hose wrought with white silk'.[2]
According to Pormant, Topcliffe boasted that if he wanted Elizabeth, he
could take her away from any company, although he added that she did
not save her favours for him alone and, she is 'as pleasant with every one
that she doth love'.

According to the independent account of another Catholic priest
named James Younge, Pormant had made these charges openly at his trial,
where he suggested that Topcliffe had hoped to persuade him to recant by
suggesting he might then come to preferment through Topcliffe, because
of his 'great favour' with the Queen. The rhetorical question that Elizabeth
was said to have asked, 'Be not these the arms, legs and body of King
Henry?' would have extra resonance as the Privy Chamber at Whitehall
was dominated by Holbein's imposing image of Henry VIII. The implication is therefore that the alleged intimacies took place there within the
privy lodgings.

Both at Pormant's trial and later at his execution, Topcliffe strongly
denied the priest's allegations, but by then the damage had been done.
Even if the reported salacious exchange did not take place, the account
was spoken in court and the recorded notes read by the Privy Council
were highly significant and hugely embarrassing; the Queen's body had
been discussed in a highly sexualised and erotic way and the alleged intimacies that she had had were being discussed in open court. When
Pormant was executed for treason on 21 February 1592, he was forced to
stand outside only in his shirt for almost two hours while Topcliffe pressed
him to deny his story, but he refused and finally went to his death.[3]

Pormant's account was printed and circulated by Verstegan as one of
the many printed defamations and attempts by Catholics abroad to

undermine Elizabeth's authority by focussing on her body and her sexual conduct. However, rather than Pormant having irreverently discussed the Queen sexual proclivities, Catholics could claim that Pormant had remained loyal to the crown and was simply repeating the lewd accusations that Topcliffe had made.

During the 1590s, anxieties about the succession and the anger felt towards the Elizabethan government refocused on the Queen's gender. A number of English poems drew on explicit sexual imagery and referred to her in sexually compromising contexts.

In 1589, *The Arte of English Poesie*, published anonymously but attributable to George Puttenham, depicted the Queen's two bodies and the improper accessibility of both. Access to the monarch is characterised in the form of sexual availability and particular attention is paid to her mouth and breasts, areas of the body that suggest privileged sexual contact. The breasts, depicted as the very source of Elizabeth's authority, from which issue the rays 'of her justice, bounty and might', are described in bawdy detail:

> Her bosom sleak as Paris plaster,
> Held up two balls of alabaster,
> Each byas was a little cherry
> Or else I think a strawberry.[4]

The Queen's breast, the emblem of royal beneficence, is here transformed, in the tasting or biting of the succulent royal nipples, into an erotic image. The intimacy suggested draws on contemporary accounts of Elizabeth's habit of revealing her bosom as she grew older, as a means to suggest her youth and virginity.[5]

Edmund Spenser's *The Faerie Queene* (1590) also drew on the image of the Queen's two bodies: 'the one of a most royal Queen or Empress', Gloriana; the other a 'most virtuous and beautiful lady' whom Spenser identifies as the virgin huntress, Belphobe.[6] Whilst Puttenham chose the Queen's mouth and breasts as symbols of royal authority, Spenser's focus is on Belphobe's genitalia, with her vulva styled as the focus of royal power. Ultimately Belphobe is open to sexual misinterpretation. Braggadocio, a knight, misunderstands the nature of their relationship, interpreting her body as an invitation to sexual rather than political intimacy, a misreading that culminates in attempted rape.[7] Here Spenser draws attention to the problems inherent in a political rhetoric that aims to celebrate a commitment to virgin authority.

From around the 1590s until the end of Elizabeth's reign, satirists would often refer to the vulva in terms of a metaphorical space, describing it in sensual detail as smooth, soft, and moist and a place of delicious, intoxicating tastes. Such sexually explicit descriptions of the Queen's genitalia in some late Elizabethan verse suggest a rejection of the Queen's self-styled cult of virginity, perhaps in reaction to what many saw as the hypocrisy of her own court and Bedchamber. In Thomas Lodge's *Scillaes Metamorphosis* (1589) – dedicated to 'the Gentlemen of the Inns of Court and Chancery' – Glaucus, the amorous sea-god, blazes his mistress's body in sexually explicit terms:

> But why alas should I that Marble hide
> That doth done the one and other flank,
> From whence a mount of quickened snow doth glide;
> Or else the vale that bounds this milkwhite bank.
> Where Venus and her sisters hide the fount,
> Whose lovely Nectar doth all sweete surmount.

In its suggestion of cunnilingus and its explicit sexualisation of the female body, the poem describes a means by which aspiring men might gain favour.[8] In Shakespeare's *Venus and Adonis,* (1599) which became an instant commercial success, Venus is the sexual aggressor and it is she who dominates her lover, Adonis, and is consumed with sexual excitement. Rather than the traditional form of an aspiring youth courting his queen, Shakespeare creates a fantasy in which an older, sexually voracious Queen/Empress is forced to plead for the attentions of her younger male lover.[9]

48

The Physician's Poison

Elizabeth celebrated Twelfth Night at the beginning of 1594 at Whitehall. As she sat watching the entertainments with Essex at her side, she was observed caressing him in a 'sweet and favourable manner'.[1] The earl flirted and laughed with the Queen, and they danced as the court looked on. The courtier and former spy Anthony Standen wrote, she 'was so beautiful to my old sight as ever I saw her'.[2] Elizabeth was in her element, dancing, displaying to all her health and vigour, with a handsome young knight, despite having now passed her sixtieth birthday. Yet the carefree scene belied a shocking truth. Essex had just uncovered a plot against Elizabeth and the principal offender, someone very close to her, had just been arrested.

Dr Roderigo Lopez, a Portuguese Jew, had come to London in the winter of 1558 when he was in his mid-thirties. In 1581 he had become personal physician to the Queen, having formerly attended on high-ranking courtiers including Robert Dudley, Walsingham and until recently the Earl of Essex himself. As the Queen's physician, Lopez had a dual task: the preservation of the body of the Queen and with it the survival of the Elizabethan state. He was one of a few men who would have had permission to attend on the Queen in her Bedchamber. Elizabeth liked and trusted him and granted him a valuable perquisite: a monopoly for importing aniseed and other herbs essential to the London apothecaries. Yet it appeared that Lopez used his position to mask treason; he had been leading a double life as a physician and a spy, a servant of the Queen of England and an agent of the King of Spain. On 28 January 1594, Essex placed his discovery in a simple written statement: 'I have discovered a most dangerous and desperate treason. The point of conspiracy was her Majesty's death. The executioner should have been Doctor Lopez. The manner by poison. This I have so followed that I will make it appear as clear as the noon day.'

Lopez had recently incurred Essex's anger by revealing that he had treated the earl for syphilis.[3] Besides seeking revenge for this awkward indiscretion, Essex was also keen to demonstrate his loyalty to the Queen and usurp the dominance of the Cecils.[4] Since the death of Walsingham, Essex had been hugely active at the centre of an intelligence-gathering network. He had employed two of Walsingham's former counter-intelligence agents as agent provocateurs to infiltrate the Portuguese-Jewish community in London. At first his agents intended to 'plant' evidence of a plot, so that Essex could rush to Elizabeth and claim credit for 'discovering' it. However, his agents had uncovered a ring of real Portuguese-Jewish spies who were found to be working for Philip of Spain.

Unbeknown to Essex, William Cecil had already infiltrated the group and was using a Portuguese-Jewish double agent called Manuel de Andrada, with the Queen's physician, Dr Lopez, acting as mediator.[5] Moreover, for the last three years Cecil had been encouraging Lopez as a double agent and using him to penetrate the Spanish spy network in England. However, what William Cecil did not know was that Andrada had encouraged the Spanish King to use Dr Lopez as a spy.

Essex's agents discovered a number of incriminating letters, including one which Andrada had sent to William Cecil in 1591, claiming that, 'The King of Spain had gotten three Portuguese to kill her Majesty and three more to kill the King of France.'[6] Now that a clandestine correspondence with Spain had been unearthed, Essex moved to unmask Andrada's three unnamed Portuguese assassins. They were found to be Manuel Luis Tinoco, Esteban Ferreira da Gama and Dr Roderigo Lopez. Tinoco revealed to Essex, under interrogation, that the Jesuits in Spain had sent him to England to help de Gama persuade Lopez to work for Philip. When asked whether Lopez would have been willing to poison the Queen, he confirmed that he would have been.

On 21 January, at Essex's instigation, Roderigo Lopez was arrested on suspicion of conspiracy to murder.[7] He was confined to Essex House, the earl's home on the Strand, while his own house was searched. Nothing incriminating was found. He was then examined by William Cecil, Robert Cecil and Essex and gave convincing answers. After the first day of examination, both Cecils went to Hampton Court to tell the Queen that they were certain Lopez was innocent and the whole episode had been blown out of proportion by Essex in an attempt to whip up popular support for a new offensive against Spain. The Queen sided with the Cecils; she accused Essex of being a 'rash and temerarious youth' and said she knew Lopez's innocence 'well enough'. Angered by Essex's impudence, Elizabeth sent him away, forbidding 'access to her except only of four persons, besides the council and the ladies of nearest attendance'.[8]

Essex left court bent on proving Lopez's guilt. His efforts reaped almost immediate rewards. Little over a week later, Lopez was committed to the Tower. Early the following morning, the doctor was examined before Essex and William Cecil and confessed, as Anthony Standen put it, 'more than enough'. Under torture, or the threat of it, other suspects were also interrogated and insisted that Lopez was at the heart of the plot and that he had agreed to poison the Queen for 50,000 crowns paid by Philip II. This was the evidence Essex had been looking for. Worn down by relentless interrogation, Lopez agreed to all manner of improbable plots, signed his confession and so sealed his fate.

By the end of February, Essex had gathered enough evidence to have Lopez tried for high treason. Special commissioners were immediately appointed for his trial, and he was indicted at the Guildhall two days later. Tinoco and da Gama were also tried for treason. Sir Edward Coke, the Attorney-General, opened the trial by claiming that Lopez, like so many other conspirators, has been seduced by Jesuit priests with great rewards to kill the Queen, 'being persuaded that it is glorious and meritorious, and that if they die in the action, they will inherit heaven and be canonised as saints'. As Coke continued, 'This Lopez, a perjuring murdering traitor and Jewish doctor, more than Judas himself, undertook the poisoning, which was a plot more wicked, dangerous and detestable than all the former.'[9] Even graver was Lopez's sin as, he was 'her Majesty's sworn servant, graced and advanced with many princely favours, used in special places of credit, permitted often access to her person, and so not suspected, especially by her who never feareth her enemies nor suspecteth her servants'.[10]

Lopez denied any intention to poison the Queen and claimed he had only confessed to save himself from torture. Now Lopez's defence was premised on the very intimacy with Elizabeth which his accusers claimed he had abused. He had promised de Gama, his fellow conspirator, that he would 'minister the poison in a syrup', which, as Lopez explained during his interrogation, he had said 'because I knew her Majesty never doth use to take any syrup'. Lopez was aware, as were the Queen's ladies, that Elizabeth was wary of attempts to poison her and never took medication in the dilute form, because the thick, sugary liquid of syrup might hide the bitter taste of toxins; a last defence against her enemies. By saying he would poison her syrup, Lopez was saying he would never kill her.

Ultimately Lopez was found guilty of leaking secret intelligence to the King of Spain and his ministers, of attempting to stir up rebellion within the realm, and of conspiring to poison the Queen. He was sentenced to be hanged, drawn and quartered at Tyburn, as were the two Portuguese agents, his alleged intermediaries. However, the Queen remained doubtful of her doctor's guilt and delayed giving the approval needed to carry out the death sentences. This provoked what government officials described as 'the general discontent of the people, who much expected this execution'.[11] Lopez was the Queen's prisoner while he was in the Tower and her permission was needed for either release or execution. Doubtless Elizabeth intended to play a waiting game, perhaps until the affair had blown over and then Lopez could be released and go into exile, as he desired.

Such was her delay that the jurisdiction of the commission appointed to deal with the Lopez case collapsed and its members discharged. Elizabeth had resolved neither to release Lopez nor sanction his execution. However, six weeks later, and unbeknown to Elizabeth, new writs were issued out of the Court of Queen's Bench, the senior criminal court in England. Sir Michael Blount, Lieutenant of the Tower, was ordered to bring Lopez, da Gama and Tinoco to the Court of the Queen's Bench at Westminster Hall on the following Friday. The prisoners were then sentenced again before being delivered to the custody of the Marshal at the Queen's Bench prison in Southwark. Lopez and the others were now beyond Elizabeth's protection: the warrant for their execution could no longer be blocked on grounds of the Queen's special reprieve. Lopez and his accomplices were executed, without Elizabeth ever having signed a death warrant. William Cecil wanted to ensure that Lopez was executed to protect himself from a possible investigation and intelligence coup by Essex into his links with the Portuguese double agent Andrada. From Cecil's point of view Lopez knew too much and therefore had to be silenced.

On 7 June, Lopez and his accomplices were hanged, drawn and quartered on Tyburn Hill; when Lopez announced that he loved the Queen as he loved Christ, the assembled crowd hooted with derision.[12] Elizabeth allowed his widow Sarah to retain the whole of her late husband's estate and to carry on living with her family in Mountjoy's Inn in Holborn, a sign of her continued affection for, and perhaps belief in, her Portuguese physician.

The government quickly published an official account of the plot, *A True Report of Sundry Horrible Conspiracies of Late Time Detected to have (by barbarous murders) taken away the life of the Queen's most excellent Majesty,* stressed that the King of Spain had attempted to take away Elizabeth's life not only by arms or other warlike actions but by secret murder. Once again, 'Almighty God, the just avenger of such horrible wickedness' and 'rewarded of piety and innocency' had preserved the life of the Queen.[13]

49

Love and Self-Love

Early in November 1595, Rowland Whyte wrote to his master Sir Robert Sidney, son of the late Mary Sidney, from court: 'My Lord of Essex, as I wrote unto you in my last, was infinitely troubled with a printed book the Queen showed him ... yet doth he keep his chamber.' The book which had been smuggled into England from Antwerp, was titled, *A Conference about the next Succession to the Throne of England*, and was dedicated to Essex. The preface was signed with the pseudonym 'R. Doleman ... from my chamber in Amsterdam', but was soon recognised to be the work of Robert Persons, leader of the English Jesuits.[1]

The *Conference* discussed the claims of fourteen potential successors for the English crown. 'Doleman' disingenuously styled himself as an impartial commentator on the debate and declared that in seeking a successor to Elizabeth 'the first respect of all others ought to be God and religion'.[2] As such, the book rejected the Tudors' right to sit on the throne and dismissed all claimants descended from them, including King James of Scotland and his cousin Arbella Stuart. The ideal successor to Elizabeth was held to be Philip II's daughter, the Infanta Isabella Clara Eugenia,[3] who could claim English descent through her father's line back to Edward III. As 'a princess of rare parts both for beauty, wisdom and piety', who came from a rich kingdom, Isabella was less likely to 'pill and poll' her English subjects than the King of Scotland, it declared.[4] 'Doleman' also considered the benefits that would be brought if Thomas Seymour, the youngest son of Lady Katherine Grey, then married the infanta in return for the throne, thereby both satisfying the religious conditions and creating a good match, 'for making of compositions of peace and union with the opposite parties'.

The book was not the first to be published abroad on the subject of the English succession, but Elizabeth's government and James VI viewed it more seriously than the others. The English authorities interrogated captured priests closely about the work and anyone who was found to possess a copy of it came under suspicion of treason.[5] In response to the *Conference*, Elizabeth showed a new wariness towards the Seymours. In July 1595 she ordered the book, which recounted the legal process that had been taken against the 'pretended matrimony' of Katherine Grey to the Earl of Hertford, to be placed on record in the Tower and forbade its removal without her express permission. A few months later she ordered Hertford's imprisonment for the offence of trying to prove his son's legitimacy.[6]

The *Conference* had speculated on a subject which Elizabeth had forbidden to be discussed. The 1571 Treason Act had imposed severe penalties on publication of any claims to the royal succession, other than that 'established and affirmed' by Parliament.[7] Anyone who debated it publicly was put in the Tower. Yet here was a book that blew the subject wide open, dedicated to Robert Devereux, the Earl of Essex, because 'no man is more high and eminent in place or dignity at this day in our realm than your self'. The dedication to the earl was deliberately mischievous; he was Spain's leading enemy at the English court. But at the same time it was very calculated; Essex had a large Catholic following and, as the book claimed, 'no man like to have a greater part or sway in deciding this great affair'.

When Elizabeth was shown the work she summoned Essex to see her. Afterwards he was reported to have looked 'wan and pale, being exceedingly troubled at this great Piece of Villainy done unto him'.[8] He had already incurred the Queen's displeasure when in May it had been revealed that he was the father of a son by Mistress Southwell.[9] But having raged at Essex at his involvement in the book, after a few days the Queen accepted his word that he knew nothing about it.

———•———

The annual Accession Day tilt at Whitehall Palace was one of the highlights of the court calendar, marking the return of the court to London after its absence during the summer progress. Shortly before 17 November, as the city bells rang and people rode out to meet her, the Queen made her state entry into London in advance of the tournament. From being an informal joust arranged by the gentlemen of the court in the Queen's honour in the early 1570s, the tilt was now deliberately staged as an opportunity for young male nobles to pay homage to the Queen. With Sir Henry Lee, the organiser and principal promoter of the tilt, now retired, Essex resolved to use the tilt of 1595 as a means to regain royal favour.

In the months leading up to the tilt, each knight would work on his disguise, from which would emerge the symbolic colours for his liveried servants and lance-bearers, the emblem for his shield, the props and costumes. Appearing at the tilt was expensive. Honour came through strength and skill, but also in spectacular, ingenious pageantry. Elaborate outfits were designed for the young men and their servants, and painted shields inscribed with pithy mottos, *impresas*, tended to the glorification of the Virgin Queen. Tiltyard speeches, often witty or romantic in sentiment, were expected to be delivered before the Queen during the festivities.

The event was much anticipated by the court and public alike; Londoners would come clutching their 12d entry fee, eager for a spectacular day out. The Tiltyard, near to where Horse Guards Parade is today, could accommodate over 10,000 spectators. At one end was the tilt gallery or 'long room' in which Elizabeth sat with her ladies. Bordering the tiltyard were scaffolds and stands from where those who paid for admittance would watch the knights shattering their lances against one another.

After the day's jousting was done and the supper enjoyed, Essex laid on an entertainment for Elizabeth entitled 'Erophilus' ('Love'). The earl's squire (representing Essex) called upon the Queen to observe how his master was 'tormented with the importunity' of the three representatives of Philautia (Self-Love): a Hermit, a Soldier and a Statesman. Each urges Erophilus (Essex), to abandon his love for his mistress and instead look to his own desires and fulfilment through either study (as the Hermit), martial glory (the Soldier), or political power (the Statesman). However, Essex's squire dismisses these 'enchantments' of Philautia and reaffirms his master's undying devotion to the Queen.

Despite Essex's best efforts, Elizabeth was far from pleased by the performance; it was not the display of loyalty and glorification that she expected on Accession Day. Although seemingly a celebration of love and devotion to her Majesty, Elizabeth thought the entertainment was too much about Essex himself and complained, 'If she had thought there had been so much said of her, she would not have been there that night, and so went to bed.'[10]

The earl's bid to re-establish his position at court and in the Queen's affection had failed, and instead of returning to his favoured position by the Queen's side in the approach to Christmas, Essex was sent north. Henry Hastings, the Earl of Huntingdon and Lord President of the

Council in the North since 1572, had fallen ill and the Queen needed to ensure order there, 'till a trusty President can be found, if God should call him away'. By sending Essex away she could ensure that royal authority was upheld, though it meant that the earl was away from court for the festive season. She would not be happy but it would prove a point.

As the Earl of Huntingdon's health continued to deteriorate, Elizabeth ordered that the news be kept from his wife, Katherine, Countess of Huntingdon, for fear of worrying her unnecessarily. Katherine spent long periods of time at their estate in Ashby-de-la Zouch in Leicestershire and also made regular visits to the court. By the early 1590s, Lady Katherine was in almost permanent attendance on Elizabeth and was sufficiently rehabilitated for her husband to thank the Queen, for being 'so gracious to my poor wife, which I can no ways in any sort do anything to deserve'.[11] Such was her favour with the Queen that in September, Rowland Whyte, Robert Sidney's agent at court, urged his master, 'I pray you write to my Lady Huntingdon by every passage, for tis looked for, and desire her favour to obtain your leave to return to see her, which will much advance it; for the Queen is willing to given any such contentment that may comfort her.'[12]

When a messenger arrived on 14 December 1595 with the news that the Earl of Huntingdon had died, the court was away from London. Elizabeth set off at once for the capital determined to tell the countess herself. 'The Queen is come to Whitehall on such a sudden that it makes the world wonder when it is but to break it unto her herself,' observed Rowland Whyte.[13] On learning of her husband's death, Katherine was distraught. 'I am not able to deliver unto you the passions she fell into and which yet she continues in,' Whyte told his master. Elizabeth was so concerned about Katherine that she returned again the following day to console her. 'The Queen was with my Lady Huntingdon very private upon Saturday,' said Whyte, 'which much comforted her.'[14]

Overcome by her loss, Katherine fell seriously ill and it was feared her death was imminent. On 3 January it was reported that 'my lady of Huntingdon continues so ill of grief that many doubt she cannot live. She is so much weakened by sorrow that no officers of hers dare go to her sign to know her pleasure, either in her own private fortune or to know what shall be done with the dead body of my Lord.'[15] The countess, with no children of her own, was now desperate to see her nephew, Sir Robert Sidney, who was away serving in the Netherlands. The Queen's concern for Lady Huntingdon was such that she recalled Sir Robert so that her dear friend had all the comfort she required. Lady Katherine's condition improved and for the next few years she lived at Chelsea, made regular visits to court and remained close to Elizabeth until the Queen's death. The countess also devoted herself to advancing the career of her nephew Sir Robert Sidney, and delighted in having his young children in her care during his embassies abroad. Robert Sidney now had the influential favour of both his aunts, the Countess of Huntingdon and Lady Anne, the Countess of Warwick who would also further his suits at court.

Essex returned from the north early in 1596. Whilst he remained the Queen's favourite, the honeymoon period between them was clearly over. When Elizabeth seemed reluctant to admit the earl to his favoured place at her side, Essex retired to his chamber and feigned illness in order to regain the Queen's attentions. On 19 February, Rowland Whyte reported, 'My Lord of Essex keeps his Chamber still'. Three days later: 'My Lord of Essex kept his Bed the most Part of all Yesterday, yet did one of his Chamber tell me, he could not weep for it, for he knew his Lord was not sick.' Elizabeth was taken in by this charade. 'Not a Day passes,' Whyte told Sir Robert Sidney, 'that the Queen sends not often to see him, and himself every Day goeth privately unto her.' On 25 February, Whyte wrote, 'My Lord of Essex comes out of his Chamber in his Gown and Night Cap ... Full 14 Days, his Lordship kept in; her Majesty ... resolved to break him of his Will, and to pull down his great Heart ... but all is well again, and no Doubt he will grow a mighty Man in our state.'[16]

For now, Essex was restored to favour, as Elizabeth continued to entertain his petulance.

<hr/>

The daring raid on the Spanish port of Cadiz in the summer of 1596 was the Earl of Essex's finest hour. Throughout the previous year he had grown frustrated as Elizabeth ignored his intelligence that Spain was preparing a fresh invasion. However, after a Spanish naval squadron attacked the west coast of Cornwall, and the Irish rebels led by the Earl of Tyrone became increasingly militant, Elizabeth ordered that her own forces be made ready. In the first days of April, while the fleet awaited Elizabeth's permission to sail, a Spanish army from the Netherlands had marched on Calais, taken the town and laid siege to the garrison. Spain now had a foothold just across the Channel. Finally in June, the English fleet set sail for Cadiz, a major port on the Andalusian coast some forty miles from Seville and raided in an audacious attack by Sir Francis Drake ten years before. Three weeks later the fleet rounded the cape into the Bay of Biscay and began demolishing the Spanish navy. Essex led the troops ashore and stormed Cadiz in a dramatic coup, plundering the city's vast riches.

In August, Essex returned to England and was given a hero's welcome when his ship dropped anchor at Plymouth. However, when he went to court, he did not receive the reception he had anticipated: Elizabeth was furious. She had heard reports of the great booty brought back from Cadiz which everyone had seemed to benefit from bar her. After an investigation led by the Cecils into Essex's conduct of the campaign, the earl was cleared of incompetence. Nevertheless, the relationship between Queen and Essex had undoubtedly soured.

It was not only Elizabeth who gave Essex a frosty reception on his return from Cadiz. In December he received a furious letter from Lady Anne Bacon, the mother of his close friends, Anthony and Francis Bacon. She rebuked Essex for the 'lust of concupiscence' and charged him with 'inflaming a noble man's wife and so near about her Majesty'. Lady Anne warned the earl that in doing so he courted 'God's severe displeasure', and risked provoking violence from the woman's husband; 'if a desperate rage, as commonly followeth, he will revenge his provoked jealousy and most intolerable injury'.[17] Essex refuted Lady Bacon's claims and denied any improper dealings with 'the lady you mean'. Nevertheless, his response was not entirely reassuring. He claimed that 'since my departure from England towards Spain, I have been free from taxation of incontinency with any woman that lives', suggesting he may have been guilty of philandering before he left for Cadiz.[18]

The woman to whom Lady Anne Bacon referred was Elizabeth Stanley, the granddaughter of William Cecil, who, with the Queen's encouragement, had married the Earl of Derby in January 1595. Just five months later rumours circulated about the Earl of Essex and the 'new crowned countess', although these claims were energetically denied by the earl. Essex's enemies maintained however that 'he lay with my Lady of Derby before he went [to the Azores]'.[19] The Earl of Derby had been prepared to overlook his wife's indiscretions with Essex at the time because he needed her help with a family financial dispute. But when Essex returned from his expedition later in the year, gossip about the earl and the countess revived. The news, Cecil wrote of his rival, left Essex 'in no great grace' with the Queen;[20] the affair clearly demonstrated that the earl was 'to fleshly wantonness . . . much inclined'.[21]

50

Privy Matters

Elizabeth's late bedfellow, the greatly mourned Katherine Knollys, had nine children. One son in particular, William, cousin to the Queen, profited from his mother's favour and secured a career at court. Elizabeth had promised to take care of Katherine's children in the event of her death and in 1560, Sir William became a Gentleman Pensioner and under his father, Sir Francis, responsible for guarding Mary Queen of Scots at Bolton Castle in Yorkshire. Sir William later spent time as a captain under the command of his brother-in-law Robert Dudley, and eventually became Comptroller of the Royal Household in 1596, a position formerly occupied by his father.

When Mary Fitton, the fifteen-year-old daughter of Sir Edward Fitton, a Cheshire knight, came to court as a maid of honour in 1595, Sir William Knollys, then in his fifties, earnestly promised Mary's father that he would play 'the good shepherd and will to my power defend the innocent lamb from the wolvish cruelty and fox-like subtlety of the tame beasts of this place, which when they seem to take bread at a man's hand will bite before they bark'. He assured Fitton that he would 'be as careful of her well doing as if I were her true father'.[1] But instead, Sir William's behaviour towards Mary turned lecherous.

The maids of honour slept together, dormitory-style, in the Coffer Chamber, which was right next door to Sir William's room. He protested that their 'frisking and heying about' kept him awake. One night, having grown particularly frustrated, he walked in on the maids wearing only his spectacles and nightshirt and carrying a copy of a book by Aretino.[2] He then began pacing around their chamber reading aloud the obscene sonnets of the Italian author, which had been written to accompany a series of engravings depicting sexual positions, by Marcantonio Raimondi in *I Modi* or *The Sixteen Pleasures* published in 1524, for which the artist was imprisoned by the Pope.

In the months that followed, Knollys became infatuated with the young Mary Fitton. When she spurned his advances, he wrote a series of letters to her sister, Anne Newdigate, in which he confided the pains of his unrequited love. Sir William was already married to the dowager Lady Chandos and in flowery parables he wrote to Mary's sister of how 'my looking for any fruit of my garden is in vain, unless the old tree be cut down and a new graft of a good kind planted'. If his wife died he could freely press his suit for Mary Fitton; 'hope is the only food I live by & patience is my pillow to rest upon'.[3] In another letter he described himself as 'cloyed with too much and yet ready to starve for hunger' and expressed the frustrations of sleeping next door to Mary's chamber: 'My eyes see what I cannot attain to, my ears hear what I do scant believe, and my thoughts are carried with contrary conceits. My hopes are mixed with despair and my desires starved with expectation; but were my enjoying assured, I could willingly endure purgatory for a season to purchase my heaven at the last.' He closed his letter explaining that he could write no more being so distempered with toothache and 'your sister's going to bed without bidding me goodnight'.[4]

John, the son of another of Elizabeth's bedfellows, the late Isabella Harington and Sir John Harington, also proved to be a dubious influence on the maids of honour and risqué in his choice of literature. As Elizabeth's first godson, John was regarded with obvious affection by the Queen. She appreciated his intelligence and enquiring mind. When he was studying at Cambridge, aged fifteen, he received a letter from the Queen containing a copy of a recent speech she had made to Parliament in which she defended her right not to marry. 'Boy Jack', she affectionately addressed him,

> I have made a clerk write fair my poor words for thine use, as it cannot be such striplings have entrance into Parliament Assemblies as yet. Ponder them in thy hours of leisure and play with them till they enter thine understanding, so shalt thou hereafter perchance find some good fruits hereof when thy godmother is out of remembrance, and I do this because thy father was ready to serve us in trouble and thrall.[5]

Following his father's death in July 1582, John Harington returned to the family home of Kelston in Somerset and there began to translate into English the Italian poet Ludovico Ariosto's epic romance *Orlando Furioso* ('The Frenzy of Orlando'). It was a herculean task and it took, Harington described, 'some years, & months, & weeks, and days'.[6]

The twenty-eighth sonnet contained the racy tale of Giacondo.[7] It tells of the adventures of Jocundo and Astolfo who, having discovered that both their wives had been unfaithful, begin a journey across Europe to see if a faithful woman can be found. Having tried many ladies and even been 'beguiled' in their own bed by their maid, they conclude that 'fidelity was no part of woman's nature', and there is not a woman in the world whose favours could not be won by wooing or by money.

In February 1591, having completed the translation of this piece, Harington circulated his manuscript among the Queen's maids of honour, whom he felt needed relief from the daily routine of needlework. When Elizabeth discovered what her maids were reading, she reprimanded them, believing it was an improper 'bawdy' text for the young ladies in her charge. When she discovered that her godson was responsible, she summoned him and 'severely censured him for endangering the manners of her ladies with such an indelicate tale'.[8] As a punishment, she told Harington to stay away from court until he had translated Ariosto's entire poem – some 33,000 lines of verse. Harington took her at her word and by the end of 1592 had completed the full translation. When Elizabeth visited him at his home near Bath, he presented her with a splendidly bound copy of it with a frontispiece displaying a portrait of himself and his beloved dog Bungay.[9]

Harington's next offering was *A New Discourse upon a Stale Subject*, subtitled *The Metamorphosis of Ajax*, which he presented to the Queen in 1596[10] (Ajax being a play on 'a *jakes*', the Elizabethan word for a privy). In the book Harington unveiled his new invention, a 'flushing close stool'. He claimed the idea came to him during a conversation with a group of men, including Henry Wriothesley, Earl of Southampton, while at Wardour Castle in Wiltshire, the home of Sir Matthew Arundell. Although Harington wrote the *New Discourse* under the pseudonym 'Misacmos', he dropped many clues to his identity throughout, and would soon become known as Sir Ajax Harington.

Whilst Harington's main purpose in his *New Discourse* was to popular-ise his invention, he also used the privy as a metaphor to criticise court corruption and urge moral and spiritual reform. 'May not I, as a sorry writer among the rest, in a merry manner, and in a harmless manner, professing purposely of vaults and privies ... draw the reader by some pretty draught to sink into a deep and necessary consideration, how to mend some of their privy faults?'[11] The book is divided into three sections. The first consists of two letters exchanged between Misacmos and his cousin Philostilpnos (a lover of cleanliness) in which Philostilpnos exhorts

Misacmos to make his invention public. Philostilpnos, who can be identified as John's cousin, Sir Edward Sheldon, encourages Misacmos to use
'homely' words in his descriptions by christening the new device in 'plain
English, a shitting place'.

The book then goes on to present, 'An Anatomy of the Metamorphosed
Ajax' – or 'A Plain Plot of a Privy in Perfection'. Written and illustrated by
Harington's servant Thomas Combe, it is a practical guide to the construction and workings of the privy and includes details of where the parts can
be obtained and at what price. When a handle in the seat is pulled, releasing a valve, water was drawn from a cistern (pictured in the book with fish
swimming in it) into the pan of the bowl, and flushed into a cesspool
beneath.

Throughout the text, Harington is particularly concerned with the bad
odours emanating from privies. It is the 'breath' of Ajax that makes those
using a privy 'glad to stop their noses'. Miasmic theory attributed disease
to 'corruption of air' and given the poor sanitation of the palaces, the court
could never stay long in one place before the pungent smells forced the
Queen to move on. Harington describes how the removal of excrement
had long been a problem and cites Deuteronomy 23: 12–14, in which the
Israelites leave camp to relieve themselves by digging a hole for the excrement, which they then cover. He notes that the problem of dealing with
excrement extends to everyone, 'even in the goodliest & stateliest palaces
of this realm, notwithstanding all our provisions of vaults, of sluices, of
grates, of pains of poor folks in sweeping and scouring, yet still this same
whoreson saucy stink'. He extols his readers to better themselves by cleaning their household privy latrines and correcting their personal shortcom-
ings: 'To keep your houses sweet, cleanse privy vaults/To keep your souls
as sweet, mend privy faults.'

Harington rightly saw the 'standing close stool' as a radical improvement in sanitation.

> I think I might also lay pride to their charge, for I have seen them
> in sugared cases of satin and velvet – which is flat against the
> Statute of Apparel – but for sweetness or cleanliness I never knew
> yet any of them guilty of it; but that if they had but waited on a lady
> in her chamber a day or a night, they would have made a man, at
> his next entrance into the chamber, have said 'So, good speed ye.'[12]

One of his epigrams, which he addressed, 'To the Ladies of the Queen's
Privy Chamber at the Making of their Perfumed Privy at Richmond', is

evidence that one of Harington's water closets was installed at Richmond Palace and was working well.

> Fair Dames, if any took in scorn and spite,
> Me, that Misacmos Muse in mirth did write,
> To satisfy the sin, lo, here in chains
> For aye to hand, my master he ordains.
> Yet deem the deed to him no degradation,
> But doom to this device new commendation
> Sith here you see, feel, smell that his conveyance
> Hath freed this noisome place from all annoyance.
> Now judge you, that the work mock, envy, taunt,
> Whose service in this place may make most vaunt:
> If us, or you, to praise it, were most meet,
> You, that made sour, or us that made it sweet?[13]

The *New Discourse* ends with a lengthy 'Apology', in which during a dream of a trial for slander, Harington answers charges which he says have been brought against the book and apologises for his subject matter. Certainly Elizabeth did not outwardly encourage her godson's book, particularly as she believed it contained a ribald reference to the late Robert Dudley – 'the great Bear that carried eight dogs on him when Monsieur [the Duke of Alençon] was here'.[14] When Elizabeth refused to grant Harington a licence to publish it he defied her and it enjoyed considerable, if short-lived popularity. Four editions were printed in 1596, and whilst Harington avoided an appearance before Star Chamber, he was for a time banished from the court. However, as his cousin Robert Markham was soon able to report,

> Your book is almost forgiven and I may say forgotten; but not for its lack of wit or satire. Those whom you feared most are now bosoming themselves in the Queen's grace; and tho' her Highness signified displeasure in outward sort, yet did she like the marrow of your book ... The Queen is minded to take you to her favour, but she sweareth that she believes you will make epigrams and write *misacmos* again on her and all the court; she hath been heard to say, 'that merry poet, her godson, must not come to Greenwich, till he hath grown sober, and leaveth the ladies sports and frolics'. She did conceive much disquiet on being told you had aimed a shaft at Leicester. I wish you knew

the author of that ill deed: I would not be in his jerkin for a thousand marks.

Markham reassured Harington that, 'You yet stand well in her Highness's love.'[15] Harington maintained that his aim in writing the pamphlet had been to 'give some occasion to have me thought of and talked of', and in this he undoubtedly succeeded.[16]

51

Foolish and Old

During Lent 1596, Dr Anthony Rudd, Bishop of St David's, preached a tactless sermon before the Queen and the court at Richmond. Taking as his text from Psalm 90:12, 'Lord, teach us how to number our days, that we may incline our hearts unto wisdom', Rudd spoke of the infirmities of old age and the necessity that Elizabeth prepare her soul for death.

> Let me now come to the most revered age of my most dear and dread Sovereign, who hath (I doubt not) learned to number her years, that she may apply her heart unto wisdom.

Not only did Rudd draw attention to the Queen's exact age, sixty-three, but by the prayer he imagines her saying, he puts morbid words into her mouth:

> I conceive in mind, that in her *soliloquia* or private meditations, she frameth her speech in this way: 'O Lord, I am now entered a good way into the Climacterical year of mine age, which mine enemies wish & hope to be fatal unto me ... I have now put foot within the doors of that age, in the which the Almond tree flourisheth: wherein men begin to carry a Calendar in their bones ... I have outlived almost all the Nobles of this Realm whom I found possessed of Dukedom, Marquises, Earldoms & Baronies at mine entering into the Kingdom: and likewise all the Judges of the land, and all the Bishops set up by me after my coming to the Crown'.[1]

Here Bishop Rudd publicly discussed the unmentionable: the Queen's preparations for her impending death. Considering the extreme lengths Elizabeth and her ladies went to to ensure that she always appeared with a 'youthful radiance', the Queen was not surprisingly appalled at his observation that time had 'furrowed her face and besprinkled her hair with meal'.[2] In the prayer that Rudd imagines the Queen intoning, Elizabeth begs that she will not die until she has 'met with dangers present, or imminent, and established the state for the time to come'.[3]

As the Queen listened to the bishop's words her anger soared. Eventually she called out loudly that he should 'keep his arithmetic for himself' and she was 'so able a sovereign that she required no advice and was quite competent to manage her own affairs'. At the end of the sermon she made her feelings known, observing, 'that the greatest Clerks are not the wisest men'.[4] Rudd was put under house arrest and all printed copies of his sermon were suppressed. It was a short punishment and the bishop was soon released and forgiven. He had, he apologised, been 'deceived in supposing her limbs ... were of a similar nature of decay than his own ... and thanked God that neither her stomach nor her strength ... nor sight nor wit decayed'.[5]

Yet the signs of the Queen's decrepitude were hard to ignore, as were the outlandish attempts to try and maintain her former appearance. As she aged, she imagined, observed Sir Francis Bacon, 'that the people, who are more influenced, by externals, would be diverted, by the glitter of her jewels, from noticing the decay of her personal attractions'.[6] Despite her failing health and desire to retreat within her private chambers, John Clapham wrote that, not long before her death, the Queen, 'would often show herself abroad at public spectacles, even against her own liking, to no other end but that the people might the better perceive her ability of body and good disposition, which otherwise in respect of her years they might perhaps have doubted; so jealous was she to have her natural defects discovered for diminishing her reputation.'[7] The concealing of her 'natural defects', the smallpox scars, wrinkled skin, sagging face and rotting teeth, to protect her reputation, was increasingly an art form, perfected by the women of the Bedchamber.

The Queen's considerable vanity and her political insecurity meant she found her ageing appearance hard to accept. According to one source, if she saw her reflection by accident in a looking glass she would be 'strangely transported and offended' because it did not show what she had once been. Her ladies would often hide their mirrors and 'sometimes for haste broke them'.[8]

On a cold December afternoon in 1597, André Hurault, Monsieur de Maisse, ambassador to Henri IV of France, disembarked from the royal barge at the privy stairs of Whitehall Palace. He had come to talk with Elizabeth on the subject of war with Spain. The extraordinary detail with which he described his subsequent audiences has left a vivid pen portrait of the Queen at sixty-four. Here we see the Queen's bejewelled extravagance, her clothes, her undiminished wit, her love of music and dancing, and we glimpse a new vulnerability that has come with age.

On arriving at the palace, de Maisse was led along corridors, past huge stone chimneypieces gaudy with heraldry, through the Guard's Chamber and into the Presence Chamber, where he sat down upon a cushion to await the Queen. On the walls hung huge tapestries in bright blue, reds and burnished golds; there were thick Persian and Indian carpets draped over every table, and soft rugs on the floors.[9] Displayed about the room were various oddities including ostrich eggs, coconut cups and earthenware objets d'art that had been given to the Queen by foreign visitors and dignitaries.

After a while the Lord Chamberlain came and led the Frenchman along a dark passage into the Privy Chamber where he saw a number of lords and ladies and, seated on a low chair, the Queen herself. As de Maisse entered, Elizabeth rose and came forward to embrace him. She apologised for not granting him an audience sooner, but explained that 'the day before she had been very ill with a gathering on the right side of her face', and that 'she did not remember ever to have been so ill before'. De Maisse described how the Queen was splendidly yet strangely dressed in a nightgown, albeit one of 'silver cloth, white and crimson'. Perhaps having noticed the ambassador's reaction, Elizabeth turned to her councillors and, gesturing to de Maisse and those that accompanied him, said, 'What will these gentlemen say to see me so attired? I am much disturbed that they should see me in this state.'

As Elizabeth sat back down on her chair and gestured for a stool to be brought, de Maisse delivered the French King's good wishes and desire to, 'learn the news of her wellbeing and health'. With the Queen sitting before him, the ambassador described how Elizabeth, 'kept the front of her gown open', so that he could see 'the whole of her bosom' which he described as 'somewhat wrinkled', although he added, 'lower down her flesh is exceeding white and delicate, so far as one could see'. She was heavily bejewelled, with a string of pearls around her neck, and on her head a red wig with 'a great number of spangles of gold and silver', worn to signify virginity.[10] As for her face, 'it is and appears to be very aged', wrote the ambassador. 'It is long and thin, and her teeth are yellow and unequal, compared with what they were formerly, so they say, on the left side less than on the right. Many of them are missing so that one cannot understand her easily when she speaks quickly.'

When de Maisse tried to raise the subject of peace-making with France, he was struck by the Queen's restlessness and the fact that she never seemed to sit still. At first she had sat in her chair, twisting and untwisting her fingers around the fringe of her gown. Then she got up and began pacing around the room, trembling with a nervous energy, all the while opening and shutting her gown. The fire was too hot, she complained, it was hurting her eyes. She called for her servants to put it out, and de Maisse then had to wait while buckets of water were poured over the sizzling logs. As de Maisse prepared to leave, Elizabeth once again expressed her distress that all the gentlemen whom the ambassador had brought should see her in that condition. She called them to her and 'embraced them all with great charm and smiling countenance'.

A week later, when de Maisse was to meet with the Queen a second time, she again displayed vulnerability about her appearance. De Maisse recounted how, just as Elizabeth was about to send a coach to bring him to the palace, she cancelled, having looked into a mirror and announced that she was 'too ill' and was 'unwilling for anyone to see her in that state'. The following day, they met, and de Maisse noticed that 'she looked in better health than before'. She was wearing a beautiful black taffeta dress, a petticoat of white damask, girdled and open at the front, as was her chemise. The ambassador was again struck by how often she opened her dress and described how 'one could see all her belly, and even to her navel'.[11] It is a bizarre, youthful and provocative image; Elizabeth perhaps seeking to demonstrate to de Maisse and to herself, her continued attractiveness and allure with such provocation. The claim that Elizabeth exposed her breasts was repeated by a number of foreign dignitaries at court.

The ambassador described how the Queen greeted him with 'very good cheer' and sat on her chair of state and called for a stool to be brought for him. She referred to herself as 'foolish and old', lamenting that 'after having seen so many wise men and great princes', the ambassador should come to see 'a poor woman and foolish'.[12] De Maisse responded with suitable flattery, 'telling her the blessings, virtues and perfections that I had heard of her from stranger Princes, but that was nothing compared with what I saw', which clearly pleased the Queen. De Maisse noted how she always responded contentedly when anyone commended her for 'her judgement and prudence, and she is very glad to speak slightingly of her intelligence and sway of mind, so that they may give occasion to commend her'. However, of her looks, 'she says she was never beautiful, although she had that reputation thirty years ago'; yet De Maisse noted, 'she speaks of her beauty as often as she can'. Elizabeth, always proud of her long, slim fingers, then removed her glove to show de Maisse her hand. As he later commented in his journal, 'it was formerly very beautiful, but is now very thin, although the skin is still most fair'.

Elizabeth was, as de Maisse presented her, an ageing sinewy woman in her sixties, not the majestic, eternally youthful beauty of the state portraits. Yet there was also clearly something about Elizabeth that remained striking, even beautiful. She was 'tall and graceful' and 'as far as may be she keeps her dignity, yet humbly and graciously withal'. As to her 'natural form and proportion', the envoy wrote, 'she is very beautiful'. He added, 'save for her face, which looks old, and her teeth, it is not possible to see a woman of so fine and vigorous disposition both in mind and body'.[13]

—·—

Integral to the construction of the Queen's image was her wardrobe. As Elizabeth aged her clothes became more elaborate and a means of diverting attention away from her flesh. De Maisse had been amazed to learn that she had over 3,000 dresses, all housed in the Great Wardrobe in the Palace of Westminster. These included some 102 'French gowns', 100 'loose gowns', and 67 'round gowns', 99 robes, 127 cloaks, 85 doublets, 125 petticoats, 126 kirtles.[14] Her clothes were made from extravagant fabrics and were richly embroidered with roses, suns, moons and planets, pomegranates, (another symbol of virginity), serpents (representing wisdom), and hawthorns (a symbol of purity and prudence). As such, the Queen's gowns were an important mode of communicating certain messages or celebrating her virtues. Her ostentatious clothes, like her portraits, were a means by which the growing tension between the Queen's two bodies could be smoothed.

In 1593, when John Aylmer, Bishop of London, had preached on 'the vanity of decking the body too finely', he had incurred Elizabeth's 'great displeasure'. She told her ladies that, 'if the Bishop held more discourse on such matters she would fit him for Heaven, but he should walk thither without a staff and leave his mantle behind him; perchance the Bishop hath never seen her Highness wardrobe, or he would have chosen another text.'[15] Indeed, as Sir John Harington observed, if the bishop had first enquired as to the extent of her Majesty's wardrobe, he would have chosen to preach on a different topic.[16] De Maisse's final audience with the Queen was on Christmas Eve 1597. He arrived in Elizabeth's chamber as she was having the spinet played to her. When she looked round he 'feigned' surprise and apologised for disturbing her. She told him 'that she loved music greatly and that she was having a pavane played', to which he answered that she was a 'very good judge and had a reputation of being a mistress in the art'. He described how Elizabeth took great pleasure in music and watching her ladies dance and how, 'although she was extremely tired', she 'smiled at the ladies' who would often go before her and 'make their obeisance' before falling back into the dance.[17] As de Maisse prepared to depart, he asked Elizabeth what he should say to King Henri on her behalf. Drawing close to him, she told him to say that there was,

> no creature on earth ... who bore him such affection or so greatly desired his good and prosperity as she, but that she begged him to consider the position in which she was placed; that she was a woman, old and capable of nothing by herself; she had to deal with nobles of diverse humours, and peoples, who, although they made great demonstration of love towards her, nevertheless were fickle and inconstant, and she had to fear everything.

Whilst the English people still professed love for her, the sentiments of the nobility were such that 'the English would never again submit to the rule of a woman'.[18] She then talked of 'the attempts that had been made against her life as against her state' and explained how she found it 'marvellous strange that the King of Spain should treat her in a fashion that she would never have believed to proceed from the will of a prince; yet he had caused fifteen persons to be sent to that end, who had all confessed'.

Elizabeth was beginning to fear for the future. She spoke of how she stood 'on the edge of the grave'. It was a moment of genuine candour and realising what she had said to a visiting ambassador, she quickly checked herself and added, 'I think not to die so soon, Master Ambassador, and am not so old as they think.'[19]

52

Mask of Youth

The thwarting of the plots against Elizabeth and defeat of the Armada gave further impetus to the fashion among courtiers and nobles for wearing some token of loyalty and love for the Queen, and she in turn gave miniatures of herself as demonstrations of her affection. However, as the demand grew, so too did the need to control the images reproduced, to ensure that the reality of Elizabeth's advanced years was never depicted. In art, as in all other propaganda, her features were transformed into those of a much younger woman. Elizabeth's government had been concerned to regulate the production and dissemination of the royal image from the earliest years of her reign. In 1563 a draft proclamation was drawn up by William Cecil which addressed the grievous and offensive 'errors and deformities' in widely available representations of the Queen:

> Forasmuch as through the natural desires that all sorts of subjects and people, both noble and mean, hope to procure the portrait and picture of the Queen's majesty's most noble and loving person and royal majesty, all manner of painters have already and do daily attempt to make in short manner portraiture of her Majesty in painting, graving and painting, wherein is evidently seen that hitherto none hath sufficiently expressed the natural representations of her Majesty's person, favour or grace, but that most have so far erred therein as thereof daily are heard complaints amongst her loving subjects.

It was proposed that until such time as a specially commissioned painter might be permitted to have a sitting with the Queen, and 'to take the natural representation' of her, then no other persons might 'draw, paint, grave or portray her Majesty's personage or visage'.[1] The 1563 proclamation almost certainly remained in draft but nevertheless it demonstrates that the 'natural representation' of the Queen was the primary goal of early state portraiture.

Now, more than thirty years later, the government had again become concerned about representations of the Queen's image and the 1596 proclamation, which was issued, delivered a strong and urgent message. Any 'unseemly and improper' portraits of the Queen would be destroyed.[2] Not only were painters who were unable to produce a true likeness of the Queen merely errant, as the 1563 proclamation implied, but they were also considered to be abusive. Now it was no longer the Queen's subjects but the Queen herself who took 'great offence' by the presentation of such images.

The purpose of the royal portrait, and with it the definition of what was considered acceptable, had changed. Artists were no longer merely required to achieve 'the natural representation of her Majesty's person, favour or grace', but in representing 'her Majesty's person and visage' were obliged fully to convey 'that beautiful and magnanimous Majesty where-with God hath blessed her'. All images produced would be vetted by the Sergeant Painter, George Gower, to ensure they conformed to the officially approved face pattern.[3]

Nicholas Hilliard was called upon to evolve this formalised timeless mask of the Queen's face which would then be used in subsequent images. Each time a new portrait of Elizabeth was created, this new face pattern would be inserted into different arrangements of hair, dress and jewellery.[4] It is very unlikely that Elizabeth ever sat for another painting and Hilliard's face pattern became the official public statement of the Queen's appearance in the final years of the reign. Elizabeth's face appears radiant and moon-shaped, in stark contrast to the contemporary accounts of her long, thin, wrinkled face in the last decade of her life.

The 'Rainbow' portrait of around 1600–03, attributed to Marcus Gheeraerts the younger, for example, conforms to Hilliard's pattern and portrays an improbably radiant and youthful queen. She wears a golden cloak painted with eyes and ears and bordered with pearls. The motto inscribed on the rainbow grasped by the Queen reads, '*Non Sine Sole Iris*' – 'No Rainbow without the Sun'. Elizabeth stands against a dark background, her bare cleavage, smooth, plump skin and unbound hair suggesting improbable youth.[5] The painting is rich in symbolism. The ruby heart jewel in the mouth of the serpent embroidered on Elizabeth's left sleeve signifies wise counsel which is also represented by the symbols of eyes, ears and mouths which cover the golden mantle. We know from the

Queen's inventory that she owned a gown like that depicted in the Rainbow portrait, embroidered with eyes and ears.[6] Whilst the face of the Queen is a timeless mask, clearly her clothes are painted from life and likely to have been modelled by Elizabeth's ladies.

53

The Poisoned Pommel

In 1598, Edward Squires, a middle-aged married man from Greenwich who described himself as a 'scrivener', appeared before the Privy Council. He was accused of plotting to kill the Queen by smearing poison on the pommel of her riding saddle, and to kill Robert Devereux, the Earl of Essex, by applying poison to the arms of his dining chair.

Edward Squires was employed in the Queen's stables at Greenwich Palace, but 'being of wit above his vocation, disliked that condition of life', and being ambitious for better things, in August 1595, accompanied Sir Francis Drake on his voyage to the West Indies. However the ship, the *Frances*, on which he sailed became separated from the main fleet off Guadeloupe, and Squires was captured with his companion Richard Rolls and taken to Seville. During his imprisonment he was visited by leading English Jesuits, including Father Richard Walpole, with whom, it was later claimed, he plotted to assassinate Elizabeth and Essex.[1] Squires would use his contacts at the Queen's stable to gain access and then place poison on the pommel of the Queen's saddle. When she mounted her horse, went for a ride and gripped the pommel, the poison would transfer to her hand and then, transmitted to her 'face, mouth and nostrils', whereupon the fatal administration of the dose would be accomplished.

Squires returned to England in June 1597 and later that month is said to have gone to the stables as the Queen's horse was being prepared, pricked holes in the bladder, which Father Walpole had supplied him, and applied the poison to the Queen's velvet saddle.[2] The Queen went riding, and returned safely, the poison having had no effect. According to the official account of the plot, the Queen's life was saved by 'God's power and doing', particularly as in the heat of a July day her 'pores and veins' would be open to receive any malign vapour or tincture.

A week or so later, partly to escape detection and partly to make an attempt on the Earl of Essex's life, Squires went to sea again this time on the earl's ill-fated voyage to the Azores. Between Fayal and St Michael's he is said to have rubbed some poison on Essex's chair on his ship. Essex returned to England feeling unwell, but alive.

Squires quietly resumed his work in the Queen's stables and settled back into life with his wife and children. Yet, over a year later, on 7 September 1598, he was arrested at Greenwich, following the apparent testimony of John Stanley, a captured soldier and adventurer who had converted to Catholicism and returned to England for interrogation. In an attempt to ingratiate himself with the English government, Stanley proceeded to reveal alleged Jesuit plots and the activities of Catholic exiles, and in doing so named Squires, among others. It is very likely that Squires's subsequent arrest was as much a product of the government's own paranoid plottings as Stanley's unadulterated confession.[3]

Squires quietly resumed his work in the Queen's stables and settled back into life with his wife and children. Yet, over a year later, on 7 September 1598, he was arrested at Greenwich. Fears of assassination had been heightened by rumours of new Spanish and Scottish schemes to kill the Queen that had been circulating since the spring. On 4 May, John Chamberlain, the prolific London-based letter writer and gossip-gatherer, mentioned certain men 'apprehended for a conspiracy against the Queen's person and my Lord of Essex, whereof one should be a Scottishman or somewhat that way; much buzzing hath been about it, but either the matter is not ripe or there is somewhat else in it, for it is kept very secret'.[4] The conspirator was Valentine Thomas, and he claimed that he had been commissioned by James VI to assassinate Elizabeth. James was furious and feared that Thomas's accusation would damage his claim to the English throne. Eventually Thomas was exposed as the fraud he was, and Elizabeth assured the Scottish King that she was not 'of so viperous a nature to suppose or have thereof a thought'. Nevertheless in the climate of the times, any talk of rumoured conspiracies against the Queen naturally raised fears for her safety.[5]

After his arrest, Squires was held in the Counter, a gaol in Wood Street, before being transferred to the Tower around 18 October.[6] At first he denied all that the investigators put to him. However, after being tortured he broke down and confessed to having returned from his imprisonment in Spain as a 'resolute papist' and having plotted with Father Walpole to kill the Queen by means of a poison-covered pommel and the earl by a poisonous chair.[7] In the days that followed, Squires made a number of confessions in which he gave varying accounts of what happened. In one he claimed Walpole had written out a prescription for a 'poisonous confection' which would remain potent for some time after being spread out; its constituents were opium, white mercury, and two powders, 'one yellowish, and the other brownish, and called by Latin or Greek names'. Squires had been instructed to get someone else to buy the ingredients, each one at a different place 'for fear of suspicion'. He was then to beat the powders and opium together, steep them in the mercury water and place them in an earthen pot to stand in the sun for a month. Squires went on to describe how he had purchased the ingredients and then experimented with the concoction on 'a whelp of one Edwardes of Greenwich'.

When Squires was examined the next day, he completely changed his story and claimed that Walpole had already prepared the poison and gave it to him, 'in a double bladder, wrapped about with many parchment wrappers'. He then described the assassination attempt against the Earl of Essex on 9 October 1597. During the voyage, 'I carried the poison to sea in the Earl's ship, in a little earthen pot closely corked,' he explained, and applied it to the Earl of Essex's chair. 'I did this of an evening a little before suppertime, when the Earl was at sea between Fayal and St Michael. The confection was so clammy that it would stick to the pommel of the chair, and I rubbed it on with parchment; and soon after, the Earl sat in the chair all supper time.'

At his trial on 7 November in the great hall at Westminster, Squires was charged with plotting in Seville to poison the Queen and Earl of Essex. Squires denied all that he had previously confessed, but then had an apparent change of heart and was induced to write and sign a full admission of guilt: 'I confess my sin and acknowledge mine own wicked-ness.'[8] On 13 November, Edward Squires was hanged, disembowelled and quartered at Tyburn for high treason. An official account of the plot was soon published. It took the form of a letter written to an Englishman residing in Padua. It included 'An Order for Prayer and Thanksgiving' and was most likely to have been written by Sir Francis Bacon.[9] Bacon had been present when Squires was interrogated and maintained that Father Walpole had converted Squires to Catholicism and then used him to carry out his plot against the Queen.

Although Squires was very likely not guilty of all the charges laid against him, the trial served to reinvigorate loyalty to the Queen and whip up popular indignation against Spain. To Protestants, Edward Squires was a despicable traitor whose activities served to expose the perfidy of English Jesuits overseas. To Catholics, he was an unfortunate creature who, under torture, allowed himself to become the tool of an unscrupu-lous government in discrediting and calumniating the Catholic cause. In a letter to his fellow Jesuit Henry Garnet, dated 30 January 1599, Robert Persons denounced the 'whole fable of poison' as a fiction intended to discredit Spain and the Jesuits: 'It seemeth to be one of the most notorious fables and tragical comedies that hath been exhibited in all this time.'[10]

54

Crooked Carcass

Following the disappointing reception from the Queen after his failed Azores expedition in November 1597, the Earl of Essex had withdrawn to his estate at Wanstead, believing Elizabeth had unjustly favoured and rewarded his rivals with important offices. When, in December 1597 the Queen appointed him Earl Marshal, Essex returned to court and resumed his efforts to influence foreign policy. Whilst Essex remained committed to waging an aggressive war against Spain and continued to urge her to pay heed to the continued threat of Spain, Elizabeth was now looking for peace. By 1598 the Queen let it be known that Essex 'hath played long enough upon her, and that she meant to play awhile upon him'.[1]

At the end of June, the earl's frustrations erupted during a meeting of the Privy Council over the appointment of a new Lord Deputy in Ireland. Elizabeth suggested Essex's uncle Sir William Knollys, but Essex wanted to keep his ally at court and so nominated Robert Cecil's friend Sir George Carew. Elizabeth was livid at the earl's insolence and responded by striking Essex across the head.[2] When Essex impetuously reached for his sword, the Lord Admiral, Nottingham, threw himself between the earl and the Queen. Essex hastily beat a retreat but as he left the room was unwise enough to shout that, 'he neither could nor would put up [with] so great an affront and indignity, neither would he have taken it at King Henry the Eighth's hands'.[3] Another source claims he told the Queen that 'she was as crooked in her disposition as in her carcass'.[4]

The earl, back on his estate in Wanstead, was petitioned by his friends to make peace with Elizabeth. The Lord Keeper, Sir Thomas Egerton, urged him to conquer his false pride and show the obedience to the Queen owed by all her subjects. Yet Essex remained defiant and in his reply to Egerton wrote, 'the Queen is obdurate, and I cannot be senseless. I see the end of my fortunes and have to set an end to my desires ... Princes may err and subjects receive wrong, as I have done, but I will show constancy in suffering'.[5] The impasse continued for several weeks. In August, one observer wrote that, Essex 'is still from Court, and vows not to come till sent for; but none is over-hasty to entreat him, so it stands whose stomach comes down first'.[6]

———————

On 9 August, William Cecil, Lord Burghley, died. He had spent his last few months being carried from room to room in a chair and passed away a few weeks short of his seventy-eighth birthday. Elizabeth sat by his bedside during his final illness, tending to him 'as a careful nurse', and feeding him broth with a spoon. Cecil had continually feared an international Catholic conspiracy to depose Elizabeth and destroy the 'true faith'. He referred to this in the epitaph he composed for his tomb in his hometown of Stamford, Lincolnshire. His life's achievement, he declared, had been to safeguard the Queen and the Protestant state.

Having come to London to attend Cecil's funeral on 29 August, Essex returned to Wanstead. Relations with the Queen remained fractured, but when Essex fell ill with a fever on 7 September, Elizabeth sent her own physicians and showed some concern for his recovery. Soon Essex admitted his error and, as Rowland Whyte described, 'My Lord is reinstated into the Queen's favour; he was lately afflicted with a double disease, one in deed and another upon design; but as if one had depended upon the other, he is recovered of the former by the cure of the latter.'[7]

However, as Essex was being restored to the Queen's side, gossip spread about his relationship with another of Elizabeth's maids: the earl 'is again fallen in love with his fairest B', Whyte explained.[8] The 'fairest B' was likely to have been Mistress Elizabeth Brydges, one of the two maids of honour who had been in trouble with the Queen the previous year for flirting with Essex. The Queen was then said to have exchanged 'words and blows of anger' and Mistress Brydges and Mrs Russell, 'were put out of the Coffer Chamber', and had to spend three nights lodging with Lady Dorothy Stafford. They had been reprimanded for secretly going through the privy galleries to watch Essex and other male courtiers playing sport, and were only allowed to return to the Queen's service when they promised not to repeat the offence.[9]

Gossip had already revived on Essex's return from Azores as to his continuing relationship with the Countess of Derby. It was only a matter of time before Elizabeth now found out about Essex's involvement with

Mistress Brydges. As Rowland Whyte continued in his letter, it could not but 'come to the Queen's ears' and then he is 'undone, and all they that depend upon his favour. I pray God that it may not turn to his harm'.[10] In continuing to court the Queen's ladies, whilst trying to win back the favour of Elizabeth herself, Robert Devereux was playing a very dangerous game.

On 6 September, Paul Hentzner, a German traveller, came to Greenwich Palace having procured an order from the Lord Chamberlain that he be admitted to see the royal apartments. He arrived at court on a Sunday, when there was usually the greatest attendance of nobles, and was taken into the Presence Chamber. The room was full of the Queen's councillors, bishops, officers of state and other gentlemen, all of whom were waiting for the Queen to emerge from her Privy Chamber and pass through on her way to the chapel.

The Sunday and holy day procession to and from the chapel royal were major ceremonial events, but the Queen's appearances in public were becoming rarer making the processions more significant. As the Queen emerged in the late morning, Hentzner described how her guard formed an aisle in the midst of the crowd through which she could pass. The procession through the privy apartments followed a strict order of precedence: 'First went the Gentlemen, Barons, Earls, Knights of the Garter all ... bareheaded.' Immediately before the Queen walked the Lord Chancellor or Keeper of the Great Seal, who was flanked by two earls, one bearing the sceptre, the other the sword of state. Elizabeth moved slowly through the Presence Chamber, followed by her ladies mostly dressed in white, guarded on each side by the fifty Gentleman Pensioners carrying gilt battleaxes.

Hentzner describes the Queen, now aged sixty-four, as being of striking appearance, a 'very majestic' and 'stately' figure. Her face is 'fair but wrinkled, her eyes small, yet black and pleasant, her nose a little hooked; her lips narrow and her teeth black'. She wore two pearls with 'very rich drops' in her ears; on her head red false hair and a small crown; around her neck a string of 'exceeding fine jewels'. Once again Elizabeth's dress was low-cut, to show her bare cleavage which, as Hentzner explained, 'all the English ladies have it till they marry'. She was dressed in a white silk gown, bordered with large pearls 'of the size of beans' and a mantle of black silk, shot through with silver threads. A marchioness bore the end of the Queen's very long train. As she went along in all this 'state and magnificence, she spoke very graciously, first to one, then to another, whether foreign minister or those who attended for different reasons, in English, French and Italian . . . whenever she turned her face as she was going along, everybody fell on their knees'. [11]

But beneath the pomp and reverence, there was a feeling of langour at court. After the recent loss of William Cecil, and the deaths of Robert Dudley, Walsingham and Hatton (in 1591) it was as though an era was coming to an end. John Harington later described how, at the beginning of 1598, the universities of Oxford and Cambridge did 'light on one question that bewailed a kind of weariness of this time, *mundus senescit*, that the world waxed old'. And added, 'Which question I know not how well it was meant, but I know how ill it was taken.' Alongside the mood of the court, Elizabeth was very aware of the passage of time and of her own mortality.

55
Lèse Majesté

During the Twelfth Night festivities at Whitehall in 1599 all eyes were fixed on the Queen. Elizabeth stepped down from her chair, took the Earl of Essex's hand and danced with him, 'very richly and freshly attired'. It was a sign that Robert Devereux had returned to the Queen's favour, but not that he was to remain at her side. Elizabeth was to give him one more opportunity to prove his worth as a military commander.

The massacre of English forces at Yellow Ford, County Armagh, in August meant Elizabeth faced a total defeat in the Irish provinces. She needed Essex to lead the English army, to put down the rebellion led by Hugh O'Neill, Earl of Tyrone. Essex knew that this would be his final chance to distinguish himself and secure the rewards of favour that he sought. On 27 March 1599, Elizabeth bade him a tender farewell as he and his army set out from London, along streets thronged with well-wishers crying out, 'God preserve your Honour', and 'God bless your Lordship'.[1]

On his arrival in Dublin a month later, Essex faced an alarming situation. His army, despite being the largest yet sent to Ireland, was significantly outnumbered. A Spanish invasion to support the 20,000 Irishmen up in arms under Tyrone was also expected any day. Essex grew increasingly suspicious of Robert Cecil's activities back in London and believed that he was encouraging Elizabeth to refuse his request for more money, men and horses. 'Is it now known,' he wrote to Elizabeth, 'that from England I receive nothing but discomforts and soul wounds.'[2] He believed that his position at court was being undermined in his absence: it was said he aspired to make himself King of Ireland, even to have the crown of England, and of plotting to bring over an Irish army to dethrone the Queen. In the face of such accusations, Essex resolved to return to London and plead his case. In September, having long ignored direct orders to engage the main body of the rebel army, he negotiated a truce with Tyrone, against Elizabeth's orders, before setting sail for England.

———•———

During the summer of 1599 there were growing fears that another Spanish fleet was being prepared and that King James VI of Scotland was ready to invade and support a Catholic uprising. England was put on a state of high alert, and letters were sent to bishops and noblemen ordering them to 'prepare horses and all other furniture as if an enemy was expected within fifteen days'. By royal command on Sunday 5 August in London, 'chains were drawn across the streets and lanes of the city, and lanterns with lights, of candles (eight in the pound) hanged out at every man's door, there to burn all the night, and so from night to night, upon pain of death, and great watches kept in the streets.'[3] There was speculation that the Queen 'was dangerously sick' and at the beginning of September, Elizabeth moved quietly from Whitehall to Hampton Court, where she was seen at the windows of the palace, 'none being with her but my Lady of Warwick'.[4]

———•———

Given the fears for her safety and rumour of a Spanish invasion, Elizabeth did not go on a long progress but travelled between her royal residences outside London. From Hampton Court she moved to Nonsuch in Surrey. It was something of a fairy tale palace, famed for its novel octagonal towers and its extensive deer park. It was built in the 1530s by Henry VIII in emulation of the great French palaces of the Loire. The walls were of white stucco with a deep relief pattern picked out in gold and there was a vast array of classical statuary in the picturesque grounds. There were two quadrangles surrounded by beautiful gardens. When the court was in residence the meadow outside the palace would be full of tents, where many of those attending on the court had to stay, as Nonsuch stood outside any village or township where extra accommodation would otherwise be provided.

On Sunday 26 September, Thomas Platter, a Swiss-born traveller arrived at Nonsuch for an official tour of the palace. In the Presence Chamber around midday, he watched as men with white staffs entered, after them some lords and then the Queen. Elizabeth sat on a red damask-covered chair with cushions embroidered in gold thread. The chair was so low that the cushions almost lay on the ground, and there was a canopy above, fixed ornately to the ceiling. Having sat down, Platter describes how a lady-in-waiting, 'splendidly arrayed', entered the room and while Elizabeth's secretary stood on her right and her others officers with their white staffs stood on the left Elizabeth 'was handed some books'. Anyone who approached her did so on their knees; 'I am told they even play cards with the Queen in kneeling posture', Platter noted. Elizabeth read the books for a while and then a preacher delivered a sermon standing before her. After a time, since it was very 'warm and late', the Queen called one of her gentlemen to her and commanded him to sign to the preacher to draw to a close. When the prayer ended she withdrew to the Privy Chamber.

Platter remained in the Presence Chamber to observe the Queen's luncheon being served. Her guardsmen, wearing red tabards with the royal arms embroidered in gold, carried two tables into the room and set them down where the Queen had been sitting. Then another two guardsmen entered each bearing a mace, 'and bowed three times, first at their entrance, then in the centre of the room and lastly in front of her table'. Two more guards then appeared with plates and goblets and two more carrying carving knives, bread and salt, all bowing before the table. A 'gentleman bearing a mace' entered, together with one of the Queen's ladies who, having bowed before the empty table, stood before it as guardsmen brought in covered dishes of food. Platter describes how, when the guardsman had removed the cover and handed over the food, the Queen's lady carved a large piece off which she gave to a guard to taste. Wine and beer were also poured out and tasted. Once the table had been fully laid out and served 'with the same obeisance and honours performed as if the Queen herself had sat there', Platter watched as each of the dishes, including large joints of beef and all kinds of game, pasties and tarts were taken to the Queen in her chamber for her 'to eat of what she fancied privily', as, 'she very seldom partakes before strangers'. Finally, once the food had been served, 'the Queen's musicians appeared in the Privy Chamber with trumpets and shawms, and after they had performed their music, everyone withdrew bowing before the table and the tables were cleared away'.

Elizabeth was, as Platter adds, 'most gorgeously apparelled, and although she was already seventy [sixty-] four, was very youthful still in appearance, seeming no more than twenty years of age. She had a dignified and regal bearing.' Referring to the Lopez and Squires plots, Platter added, 'although her life has often been threatened by poison and many ill designs, God has preserved her wonderfully at all times'.[5] Yet, as

Nottingham, the Lord Admiral told Platter, her Majesty was now taking greater care of her safety, as 'a short time before, an attempt had been made to poison the Queen by smearing powder on the chair she was accustomed to sit and hold her hands on'. Now she 'refused to allow anyone in her apartments without my Lord Admiral's command'.[6]

Two days after Platter's visit, one unannounced visitor would not only fail to seek permission to enter the Queen's apartments, but would do what no man had done before; he would cross the threshold into the Queen's Bedchamber and glimpse Elizabeth far from 'gorgeously apparelled' and with a 'dignified bearing', but newly up, half-undressed, wigless and without her make-up.

⸻

Essex arrived at Nonsuch on Friday 28 September, little more than three days after his departure from Dublin. The manner of his arrival at the palace was unexpected and unorthodox and left Essex's plans to consolidate his position at court and in the Queen's favour in tatters. Without stopping at Essex House to change his spoiled, mud-splattered clothes, the earl hastily crossed the Thames at Westminster by the horse-ferry, and rode on to Nonsuch Palace. Rowland Whyte was at court that day and described what happened.

On arriving, Essex 'made all haste up to the Presence [Chamber] and so to the Privy Chamber and stayed not till he came to the Queen's Bedchamber, where he found the Queen newly up, the hair about her face'. Elizabeth had just a simple robe over her nightdress, her wrinkled skin was free of cosmetics and without her wig Essex saw her bald head with just wisps of thinning grey hair 'hanging about her ears'. This was the unadorned reality of the Queen's natural body that no one, except her trusted ladies, should ever have seen. 'Tis much wondered at,' Whyte wrote with considerable understatement, 'that he went so boldly into her Majesty's presence, she but being unready, and he so full of dirt and mire, that his very face was full of it.'[7]

As the Queen stood speechless at the sight of the unheralded intruder, Essex flung himself, repentant and subdued, at her feet. Kneeling before her, he 'kissed her hands and her fair neck, and had some private speech with her, which seemed to give him great contentment'. Although no man had ever entered her Bedchamber uninvited, the Queen remained calm, not knowing whether or not she was in danger, and, as Whyte reported, 'her usage very gracious towards him'.

Later that evening, however, the Queen's mood had changed and she 'began to call him to question for his return, and was not satisfied in the manner of his coming away'. She now ordered that Essex should keep to his chamber.[8] This was the last time that she would ever see him.

———•———

The following day Essex was summoned before the Privy Council and Robert Cecil read out a list of the six charges. Among them was, 'His rash Manner of coming away from Ireland: His overbold going Yesterday to her Majesty's Presence to her Bedchamber: His making of so many idle Knights.'[9] He was placed under house arrest in the custody of Lord Keeper Egerton at his official residence, York House. His wife, Frances, Countess of Essex, was heavily pregnant and when the baby was born the next day, Essex was kept from them.

There was rising public discontent at the earl's unexplained house arrest. He petitioned Elizabeth with letters explaining how he was 'wonderfully grieved at her Majesty's displeasure towards him', and drew up a detailed explanation of what had happened in Ireland and the arrangements he had put in place when he left.[10] By December, Essex's health was deteriorating and his wife was finally given access to him. The Queen once more sent her physicians to report on his illness. The prognosis was poor: the earl was suffering from dysentery and was unlikely to live. When Elizabeth heard the news, she 'was very pensive and grieved, and sent Doctor James unto him with some Broth. Her Message was, that he should Comfort himself and that she would, if she might with her Honour, go to visit him; and it was noted, that she had Water in her Eyes when she spoke it.'[11]

Essex did begin to recover and resumed his attempts to regain the Queen's favour. He sent a New Year's gift to her at Richmond, which was 'neither received nor rejected', but remained in the hands of Sir William Knollys, the Comptroller of the Royal Household.[12] Lady Penelope Rich, the earl's sister, who had formerly been one of the Queen's maids of honour, presented Elizabeth with a strongly worded letter. In it she defended her brother, denounced his enemies and complained that Essex had not been allowed into the Queen's presence to answer his critics. Elizabeth was outraged at Lady Penelope's 'stomach and presumption', and never fully forgave her for it.[13]

By the end of January, Essex's mother, Lettice Knollys, the Countess of Leicester, had left her country estate to come to London to petition for her son's release.[14] The following month she sent a gown for Elizabeth that was presented by Mary Scudamore, one of the Queen's favoured women, who was sympathetic to Lettice's cause and had known her from her time in the Queen's service.[15]

> Her Majesty liked it well, but did not accept it, nor refuse it, only answered, that Things standing as they did, it was not fit for her to desire what she did; which was to come to her Majesty's Presence, to kiss her Hands ... and her Majesty's Displeasure nothing lessened towards him, nor any Hope of his Liberty.[16]

Lady Warwick also tried to promote Essex's case and sent him a message assuring him that if he came to Greenwich, where the court was then in residence, she would contrive an opportunity to let him into the palace gardens, when the Queen was in a good mood, so that he could plead forgiveness in person.[17] In March, Essex was allowed to return to Essex House, but still under conditions of house arrest, 'by her Majesty's express commandment', with his wife and friends all removed from there.

On 5 June, the earl was taken to York House to appear before a special commission of enquiry which was to hear the charges against him. He was found guilty of disobedience and dereliction of duty, although cleared of the most serious charge of disloyalty. In an act of humility, Essex knelt for much of the twelve-hour-long hearing, but he refused to admit insubordination. He acknowledged he had 'grievously offended' her Majesty, but pitifully urged that it was 'with no malicious intent'. He was stripped of his offices and was to remain a prisoner at his house at the Queen's pleasure.[18]

Essex continued to plead his case with the Queen. Philadelphia Carey, Lady Scrope, daughter of the late Katherine Knollys, wrote to tell him how favourably Elizabeth had received his letters: 'She seemed exceedingly pleased with it yet her answer was only to will me to give you thanks for your great care to know of her health.' Lady Scrope continued, 'I told her that now the time drew near of your whole year's punishment and therefore I hoped her Majesty would restore her favour to one that with so much true sorrow did desire it but she would answer me never a word but sighed and said indeed it was so.' She added, 'I do not doubt but shortly to see your Lordship at the court.'[19]

———•———

On the night of 2 October, Essex returned to the deserted Essex House where, 'he lives private, his gate shut day and night'. His petitions to the

Queen were now desperate. Sir John Harington met with the earl and warned him that he was an example of how 'ambition thwarted in his career doth speedily lead on to madness'. Essex now 'shifteth from sorrow and repentance to rage and rebellion so suddenly as well proveth him devoid of good reason or of right mind'.[20]

Essex believed that his path back to the Queen's favour was only blocked by the evil counsel of his enemies at court. By the end of the year he was gathering around him other 'discontented persons', deployed soldiers, persecuted Catholics, failed courtiers and bankrupt nobles. Essex House was becoming something of an anti-court. 'These things are brought to the Queen's ears,' it was reported, 'and alienate her affection from him more and more, and especially one speech inflameth her most of all, for he said that being now an old woman, she is no less crooked and distorted in mind than she is in body.'[21] Elizabeth might have begun to fear the dangerous plottings of her former favourite, but she was, and would remain, always acutely sensitive to comments that slighted her royal majesty.

56

Dangerous and Malicious Ends

In early February 1601, 'a concourse of people and great resort of Lords and others' gathered at Essex House.[1] Fearing disorder, the Privy Council met in urgent session on Saturday 7 February and summoned Essex to appear before them to explain himself and to reprimand him for holding unlawful assemblies.

The earl ignored the first summons, and the second, pleading ill health. He had been in disgrace for more than a year, was heavily in debt and was convinced that a plot had been laid by his enemies to entice him from his home and then 'bring about his death'.[2] Throughout the night, as Essex fortified his house and more nobles assembled with their followers, the council moved to secure the court by erecting a barricade of coaches between Whitehall and Charing Cross.[3]

At ten the following morning, a delegation from the court was sent to Essex House. The four commissioners, who included the earl's uncle, Sir William Knollys, came to offer the chance for Essex to have his grievances heard on condition that the gathering at his house disperse. Fearing another attempt to lure him to his death, Essex rejected the commissioners' overtures. He placed the delegation under armed guard in his library and then set off with a group of two hundred friends and followers, carrying firearms, for the city, to take control of the Tower and force their way to the Queen.[4] Essex urged the people of London to join with him against the forces that threatened the Queen and the country.[5] He claimed that his enemies were going to murder him and that 'the crown of England was offered to be sold to the Infanta [Isabella of Spain]'.

The Queen received the news that Essex had entered the city while at dinner at Whitehall. She responded calmly, 'only said [that] He that had placed her on that seat would preserve her in it; and so she continued at her dinner, not showing any sign of fear, or distraction of mind, nor omitting anything that she had been accustomed to do at other times'.[6] The

Queen's Guard were immediately deployed and when Essex's band moved to Ludgate Hill they were met by a company of soldiers.[7] As Essex's followers scattered, several men were killed, including the earl's page, Henry Tracy, and Essex himself was shot twice in the hat. The remaining fifty or so men were forced to withdraw and at Queenhithe, taking as many boats as they could, they rowed furiously back to Essex House.

As dusk fell, Essex returned to find his house surrounded by the Queen's forces. By nine that evening he surrendered and was rowed across the river to spend the night a prisoner in Lambeth Palace. The next day he was taken to the Tower. A proclamation was issued announcing his arrest and ordering people to remain vigilant 'to the speeches of any that shall give out slanderous and undutiful words or rumours'.[8]

On Thursday 12 February, Captain Thomas Lee, one of Essex's Irish captains, was discovered and arrested outside the door of the Queen's Privy Chamber at Whitehall.[9] He admitted he was going to break in that evening, at supper time when, he said, Elizabeth 'is attended with a few Ladies, & such as that are known in court and have credit might easily come to the Privy Chamber door without suspicion'. He planned to take the Queen captive and force her to sign a warrant for the earl's delivery from the Tower.[10] Lee had demonstrated that the Queen's privy lodging could be penetrated. Although the Irishman swore that he 'would not have hurt her Royal person', he was tried at Newgate two days later and, as Robert Cecil wrote from court, 'he received the due reward of a Traitor at Tyburn', two days later.[11]

On 19 February the Earl of Essex was brought up river from the Tower to Westminster Hall to be tried. Essex and the other conspirators were accused of plotting to deprive the Queen of her crown and life as well as imprisoning councillors of the realm and inciting Londoners to rebel. The Attorney General Sir Edward Coke was determined to prove that Essex had intended to take 'not a town, but a city, not a city alone, but London the chief city; not only London, but the Tower of London; not only the Tower of London, but the royal palace and person of the prince, and to take away her life'. Essex protested that 'he never wished harm to his sovereign more than to his soul'.[12] The coup, it was claimed, was merely intended to secure access for Essex to the Queen.[13] He believed that if he was able to gain an audience with Elizabeth, and she heard his grievances, he would be restored to her favour. Despite his protestations, he was sentenced to be hanged, drawn and quartered.

On the day after his trial, Elizabeth signed Essex's death warrant.[14] She had made up her mind that no mercy could be shown to a man who had threatened to take up arms against her.[15] In the Tower, after his trial, Essex broke down claiming he had been pressured by his followers and his sister, Lady Penelope Rich, to take seditious action.[16] Lady Penelope denied her brother's claim and argued that she had been drawn into the conspiracy against her will. After a brief period of confinement, and examination by the Privy Council, she was released.[17]

In the early morning of 25 February, Ash Wednesday, Robert Devereux, 2nd Earl of Essex, attended by three priests, sixteen guards and the Lieutenant of the Tower, walked to his execution. Elizabeth had granted him one final favour: in deference to his rank, his beheading would take place in private, within the grounds of the Tower of London. As he knelt before the scaffold the earl made a long and emotional speech of confession in which he acknowledged that his 'courses', if successful, might have imperilled the Queen, with 'more dangerous and malicious ends for the disturbance of her Estate'.[18] His head was severed in three blows. Elizabeth was playing the virginals in the Privy Chamber when a messenger brought confirmation of Essex's death. She received it in silence. No one else spoke. After a time she began to play again.

———•———

The first Sunday after the execution, William Barlow, the royal chaplain, delivered the sermon from the pulpit at St Paul's Cross on what he called a 'matter of state rather than divinity'. Sir Robert Cecil had drawn up specific guidelines on what the chaplain could say about Essex's plot. Barlow described how the Jesuit Robert Persons had corrupted the late earl, persuading him 'that it is lawful for the subject to rise against his sovereign'.[19] He emphasised the danger to the Queen, dismissed the earl's claim that he meant her no harm and said it was the most dangerous plot that had ever been hatched within the land.[20]

Shortly afterwards, orders were sent out to preachers across the country to disseminate the official version of events and copies of William Barlow's sermon. Francis Bacon's *Declaration of the Practices and Treasons Attempted and Committed by Robert, Late Earl of Essex . . .* was also published.[21] This authorised account described how a serious threat to the crown had been narrowly defeated; that the earl had planned to overthrow Elizabeth and then either take the crown for himself or King James VI of Scotland. In the weeks following the rebellion, defences in London were increased and on 5 April a proclamation described how a number of 'traitorous and slanderous' libels had lately been discovered 'tending to the slander of our royal person and state, and stirring up rebellion and sedition within this our realm'. A reward of £100 was offered for anyone who named the 'authors, writers or dispersers of such libels'.[22]

The Queen was visibly broken by Essex's death and slipped into a deep melancholy. Many were surprised that she had been able to have the sentence carried out at all. Beaumont, the French ambassador, described her great grief and how, with her eyes full of tears, she had told the envoy how she had warned Essex that 'he should beware of touching my sceptre'. She later said, 'when the welfare of my state was concerned, I dared not indulge my own inclination'.[23]

57

No Season to Fool

In the months following Essex's death, Elizabeth's health deteriorated and she suffered bouts of depression that drove her to seek sanctuary, away from the public glare of the court, among her women in the Privy Chamber. Dorothy Stafford and Mary Scudamore remained in loyal service and were ready to comfort the Queen by day and in the royal bed at night. Elizabeth had also grown particularly close to the widowed Katherine Hastings, Countess of Huntingdon.[1] It was noted that 'she governs the Queen, many hours together very private'.[2] Catherine Howard, Countess of Nottingham, was also now at the heart of the court; she was one of the few bedchamber women who had known Elizabeth before she had become Queen. Although Catherine Howard had five children, she had always returned to court soon after each birth. The Earl of Nottingham had played a key role in securing Essex's surrender and conviction and now his wife gave support to Elizabeth following the earl's execution.

Whilst it was among these women that Elizabeth now sought solace, her relationship with another of her long-serving ladies and confidantes, Anne Dudley, Lady Warwick, the sister-in-law of the Countess of Nottingham, was strained. Lady Warwick had supported Essex and now appealed in desperation to his old adversary, Sir Robert Cecil to secure a return to the Queen's favour. 'Your help is sought for and found,' she wrote, 'now let it be obtained for one that hath lived long in court with desert sufficient, being coupled with others.' The countess insisted that she did not by nature have 'much of the fox's craft or subtlety and as little of the lion's help; having lost friends almost all, not face to crave, no desire to feign'.[3] Perhaps Cecil did speak for the countess or maybe Elizabeth simply missed her old friend, as Lady Warwick was soon restored to favour.

When Sir John Harington arrived at court in early October he was shocked by what he saw. His letter to his friend, Sir Hugh Portman, paints a vivid picture of Elizabeth's lonely, diminished state and how much the Essex affair had taken its toll on her. 'So disordered is all order,' that she had not changed her clothes for many days, she was 'quite disfavoured, and unattired, and these troubles waste her much.' She ate little but 'manchet' and 'succory pottage' (wheaten bread and chicory soup) and 'disregardeth every costly cover that cometh to the table'. The 'evil plots and designs' which had been focussed against her in the previous few years had left her suspicious and anxious and had 'overcome all her Highness's sweet temper'. She 'swears much at those that cause her griefs in such ways, to the small discomfiture of all about her'. She now kept a sword close by her and, as Harington described, 'constantly paced the Privy Chamber, stamping her feet at bad news and thrusting her rusty sword at times into the arras in great rage'. Every new message 'from the city doth disturb her' and she 'frowns on all her ladies', clearly taking out her fears and frustrations on those closest to her. Even Harington himself, her favourite godson, received a sharp message from her to 'get home' as it 'is no season to fool it here'.[4]

Shortly after Harington's departure, Sir Robert Sidney was able to write and tell him that the Queen had been 'very pleased' with his presents – some verses, prose and sweets: 'The Queen hath tasted your dainties and saith, you have marvellous skill in cooking of good fruits.' But, he added, 'she doth wax weaker since the late troubles, and Burghley's death often draws tears from her goodly cheeks. She walketh out but little, meditates much alone and sometimes writes in private to her best friends.'

Shortly afterwards, Elizabeth visited Sidney's house at Baynard's Castle, near Blackfriars. She came finely dressed in a 'marvellous suit of velvet borne by four ladies' and sat on an improvised throne to watch the entertainments. She ate and drank a little, 'two morsels of rich comfit cake' and a 'small cordial from a gold cup' and 'smiled with pleasure' as she watched her ladies dance and then went on a tour of the house.[5] She tired quickly and on 'going upstairs she called for a staff and, much wearied in walking about the house', said that she would instead come another day.[6]

On 27 October, Elizabeth opened what was to be her final Parliament. Its primary purpose was to raise funds to repeal the Spanish invasion that, just weeks before, had landed in Ireland to support Tyrone's rebellion against the English. At the opening ceremony her frailty was evident: the ceremonial robes of velvet and ermine had proved too heavy for her and on the steps of the throne she had become unsteady on her feet and would have fallen, 'if some gentleman had not suddenly cast themselves under that side that tottered and supported her'.[7]

Yet despite her weak and ageing body, her mind remained powerful and Elizabeth, nearly seventy, could still rise magnificently to the occasion. On the afternoon of 30 November, a delegation of some 150 members of the House of Commons entered Whitehall Palace for an audience with the Queen. As the assembly kneeled before her and after the Speaker of the Commons addressed her, Elizabeth replied with one of the most celebrated speeches of her reign. She thanked members of the house for their loyalty and love and pledged her continued commitment to their welfare. 'There will never [be a] queen sit in my seat,' she told them, 'with more zeal to my country, care for my subjects, and that will sooner with willingness venture her life for your good and safety, than myself. For it is my desire to live nor reign no longer than my life and reign shall be for your good.' Elizabeth spoke with the courage and conviction of her younger self at Tilbury, boasting that God had given her 'a heart that yet never feared any foreign or home enemy'. She told them, 'thou God has raised me high, yet this I count the glory of my Crown that I have reigned with your loves ... I do not so much rejoice that God hath made me to be a Queen as to be a Queen over so thankful a people.' As Sir John Harington remarked, 'We loved her, for she said she did love us.'

But the realities belied such declarations of mutual love. When Parliament was dissolved in December, Elizabeth spoke of the many 'strange devices, practices and stratagems' that had been attempted against her and the realm.[8] In October, customs officials had intercepted a chest bound for France. It contained a small box in which was found, 'her Majesty's picture in metal, and a kind of mercury sublimate which had eaten the metal'. The owner of the chest was identified as one Thomas Harrison who was promptly questioned as to why an image of the Queen was contained in such poison.[9] Once again it seemed that image magic had sought to bring harm to the Queen.[10] Harrison claimed that he was merely concerned with the substance from which the image was made and that it was alchemy not witchcraft that he was interested in. However, he had close ties with Catholic clerics in France and the image of Elizabeth was made for the second Great Seal of the reign. The seal was the ultimate symbol of royal authority, and so raised suspicions as to Harrison's motives and left him open to charges of treason and sacrilege.[11]

As Elizabeth concluded her speech in Parliament, she said that ultimately only God had delivered the state from 'danger' and herself from 'dishonour'.[12] Elizabeth once again identified threats to the body of the state with threats to her honour. Her virginity was not simply a personal preference, but an act of self-sacrifice made for the defence of the realm.

More and more Elizabeth was tormented by, 'the questions of the succession every day rudely sounding in her ears'. Bishop Godfrey Goodman recalled that 'the court was very much neglected and in effect the people were very generally weary of an old woman's government'.[13] Increasingly ministers looked north of the border. The topic that the Queen had long refused to discuss could be ignored no longer: hope and expectation were now directed at her heir, not at her.

Robert Cecil had begun a covert correspondence in cypher with the Scottish King. Cecil told James that all knowledge of their communication should be kept from the Queen because, 'that language, which would be tunable in other princes' ears would jar in hers, whose creature I am'. Whilst knowing that Elizabeth would thoroughly disapprove of their contact, he said it was justifiable for the good of the state: 'I know it holdeth ... even with strictest loyalty and soundest reason for faithful ministers to conceal sometimes both thoughts and actions from princes when they are persuaded it is for their greater service.' The two men agreed a secret code for their correspondence: Cecil was '10', Elizabeth '24' and James '30'. An element of concealment was in the Queen's own interest, Sir Robert explained, 'if her Majesty had known all I did ... her age and orbity joined to the jealousy of her sex, might have moved her to think ill of that which helped to preserve her'.[14] The subject of the succession was so 'perilous to touch among us', Cecil continued, 'as it setteth a mark upon his head for ever that hatched such a bird; next, on the faith I owe to God, that there is never a prince or state in Europe with whom either mediate or immediate her Majesty hath entered into speech these xii years of that subject'.[15] James accepted Cecil's advice to 'enjoy the fruits of my pleasure, in the time of their greatest maturity' rather than 'hazard my honour, state and person, in entering the Kingdom by violence as a usurper'.[16]

The Pope, meanwhile, issued a secret brief to his nuncio in Flanders ordering all English Catholics to oppose any Protestant successor to Elizabeth, 'whenever that wretched woman should depart this life'. Led by William Allen and Robert Persons, many English Catholics who were implacably opposed to James's succession after he had shown himself to be sympathetic to the Puritan cause, championed the claim of Isabella, the Spanish Infanta.

There was also another potential claimant to the throne whose actions were causing Elizabeth some unease. Arbella Stuart was of royal blood and, some believed, was better placed than her cousin King James to inherit Elizabeth's crown as she had been born on English soil. Arbella was also favoured by Catholic nobles with Spanish sympathies, after James had strengthened his ties with France. Arbella had been linked to a whole host of suitors in the late 1590s and it was even rumoured that Sir Robert Cecil sought the throne for himself by marrying her.[17] Her grandmother Bess of Hardwick had always been determined to secure Arbella's place in the succession and when she had visited court in 1592, she was confident that Elizabeth would use the opportunity to name her as her heir, but Elizabeth stopped short of doing so.[18] During the years that followed, Lady Arbella was kept in strict custody by her grandmother first at Chatsworth and then at Hardwick Hall. The tight control forced Lady Arbella to the edge of a reckless insanity, which made her an uncertain and potentially dangerous threat to the Queen and to a peaceful succession.

So 'thus you see,' wrote the privy councillor Thomas Wilson, 'the crown is not likely to fall to the ground for want of heads that can wear it'.[19]

58

Age Itself is a Sickness

As Elizabeth approached her seventieth birthday, Bishop Anthony Rudd – undaunted by his blundering sermon years before – now delivered another. The diary entry of John Manningham, a London student at the Middle Temple, records that, 'Dr Rudd made a sermon before the Queen upon the text, "I said yee are Gods, but you shall all die like men", wherein he made such a discourse of death that her Majesty, when his sermon was ended, said unto him, "Mr Rudd you have made a good funeral sermon, I may die when I will."'[1]

Elizabeth, always reluctant to admit to any frailty or illness, invariably withdrew to her Bedchamber when she felt unwell or was in pain, 'retiring herself from all access for three or four hours together'.[2] That spring she began complaining of an ache in one of her arms. She had summoned a 'cunning bonesetter', a surgeon, who told her that a 'cold rheumatic humour' (rheumatism) had settled there which might be removed by rubbing and applying ointments.[3] Elizabeth was indignant, her blood and constitution was of its very nature very hot and so she could not be suffering from a 'cold humour'. According to Father Anthony Rivers, a Jesuit priest who was in London during these years reporting on events at court, Elizabeth banished the bonesetter from her presence and was 'most impatient to hear of any decay in herself, and thereupon will admit no help of physic or surgery'.[4] But her pain persisted,[5] and it was soon reported that 'the ache in the Queen's arm is fallen into her side'. Rivers described how she remained, 'thanks to God, frolic and merry', 'only her face showing some decay, yet sometimes she felt so hot that she would take off her petticoat while at other times she would shake with cold'.[6] In June, Elizabeth told the French ambassador, the Comte de Beaumont, 'that she was a-weary of life'.[7]

That summer Elizabeth made a short two-week progress in the vicinity of London through Buckinghamshire, Middlesex and Surrey.[8] It was a desperate attempt to maintain her yearly routine. By August, Elizabeth's pains had moved to her hip, but, defiantly, she continued to hunt every two or three days. Writing to Lord Cobham on 6 August, the Earl of Northumberland described how on, 'Wednesday night, the Queen was not well, but would not be known of it, for the next day she walked abroad in the park, lest any should take notice of it . . . the day of her remove, Her Majesty rode on horseback all the way, which was ten miles, and also hunted, and whether she was weary or not I leave to your censure'.[9] Elizabeth was determined to regain her health and vigour lest her courtiers think she was too exhausted by her activities. Rivers reported that a countrywoman who saw the Queen on her progress had commented that her Majesty looked very old and ill. A guard terrified the woman by warning that 'she should be hanged for those words'.[10]

Yet when it was necessary, Elizabeth could still rise to the occasion. Early in 1602, she had entertained the Duke of Bracciano, 'very graciously; and, to show she is not so old as some would have her, danced both measures and galliards in his presence.' In April, during the visit of the Duke of Nevers, John Chamberlain noted in his diary, how 'the Queen graced him very much, and did him the favour to dance with him', with a 'disposition admirable for her age' as the French ambassador noted.[11] Normally the Queen no longer danced but watched others instead. The ambassador de Maisse sat next to her on one of these occasions and reported that 'when her Maids dance she follows the cadence with her head, hand and foot. She rebukes them if they do not dance to her pleasure, and without doubt she is an expert.'[12]

Sometimes Elizabeth still could not resist dancing, when she thought she was alone. In 1599 was seen by the Scottish ambassador doing a 'Spanish panic', a dance with single and double steps and leaps to the music of a whistle and tabor, in her privy lodgings. Elizabeth retained her instinct for political opportunism and on one occasion when Sir Roger Aston, the ambassador from the King of Scotland, came for his audience she kept him waiting in a place behind a deliberately turned-back tapestry, from where he could see her dancing in her Privy Chamber to the sound of a small fiddle, performing *corantos* (a French dance) and other feats of dancing. He might then report to his sovereign how vigorous and sprightly she was, and that James's inheritance would be long in coming.[13]

When the Queen was at Oatlands, celebrating her sixty-ninth birthday, she was visited by the Duke of Stettin-Pomeramia who observed her walking in the grounds as briskly as though she were eighteen years old.

He was told she had been 'never so gallant many years, nor so set upon jollity'.[14] Shortly afterwards, the courtier Fulke Greville was able to inform Lady Shrewsbury, 'The best news I can yet write your ladyship is of the Queen's health and disposition of body, which I assure you is excellent good, and I have not seen her every way better disposed these many years.'[15]

However, there were now signs that Elizabeth's memory was fading and this, together with her failing eyesight, meant she found it increasingly difficult to concentrate on state business. Robert Cecil warned the clerk of the Privy Council that he must now read out letters to her. On 8 October at Greenwich, some courtiers arrived to pay their respects to her; although she could remember their names she had to be reminded of the offices that she herself had bestowed upon them. Gradually Elizabeth was becoming weaker and at times now struggled to maintain the dignity of her royal office. Her councillors increasingly played host to Elizabeth at their own houses, to keep her in London and to avoid her travelling. In early October, Robert Cecil entertained the Queen at his new house on the Strand and found her 'marvellously contented', but on her departure, refusing any help to enter the royal barge, she fell and 'strained her foot'.[16] Weeks later when the Queen was expected to move from Whitehall to Richmond with 'great pomp', Father Rivers reported how she was 'taken with some sudden distemper by the way, and so went in her closed barge, whereby our Lord Mayor and citizens, that rode out to meet her, lost their labour. She is not yet perfectly well.'[17]

In early December, Sir John Harington arrived at Whitehall in advance of the Christmas celebrations. He had just completed his *Tract on the Succession to the Crown*, although this was not something he shared with Elizabeth.[18] The work was dedicated to King James of Scotland and asserted James's right to succeed to the English throne on Elizabeth's death. Harington intended to send the tract to the Scottish King with a New Year's gift, by way of currying favour. Knowing the Queen's determination not to have the question of her succession discussed, Harington dared not have the work made public during the Queen's lifetime.

Harington was granted an audience with the Queen and was escorted into the Presence Chamber and then down the corridor into the Privy Chamber where, seated on a raised platform, his godmother awaited him. His letter to his wife, Mary Rogers, who was at home in Kelston, Somerset caring for their nine children, presents a vivid image of Elizabeth in decline:

> Sweet Mall, I herewith send thee what I would God none did know, some ill bodings of the realm and its welfare. Our dear Queen, my royal godmother, and this state's natural mother, doth now bear signs of human infirmity, too fast for that evil which we will get by her death, and too slow for that good which she shall get by her releasement from pains and misery . . .[19]

Elizabeth was troubled not only by illness but by 'choler and grief' prompted by thoughts of the Irish rebel the Earl of Tyrone and of the Earl of Essex. As she talked of Essex and his execution, Harington describes how she 'dropped a tear, and smote her bosom'. Towards the end of the audience, the Queen rallied a little and asked her godson to come back at seven that evening with some of his witty verses. The poetry cheered her a little but after a time she told him, 'When thou dost find creeping time at thy gate, these fooleries will please thee less; I am past my relish for such matters. Thou see my bodily meat doth not suit me well; I have eaten but one ill-tasted cake since yesternight.'[20] The following day when Harington saw the Queen again, he described how her memory was playing tricks on her. She had sent for a number of men but when they arrived she angrily dismissed them for arriving without an appointment. Yet, as Harington wrote to his wife, 'Who shall say that your Highness hath forgotten?'[21] No one dared to point out the Queen's mistake or openly voice their concerns as to the seriousness of her condition.

Much attention at court had turned to life beyond Elizabeth, with some courtiers, as Harington described, 'less mindful of what they are soon to lose than of what they may perchance hereafter get'.[22] Such apparent disregard for the Queen prompted Harington to reflect on his own relationship with her and the kindness she had shown him throughout his life:

> I cannot blot from my memory's table, the goodness of our Sovereign Lady to me, even (I will say) before [I was] born; her affection to my mother who waited in her Privy Chamber, her bettering the state of my father's fortune, (which I have, alas! so much worsted), her watching over my youth, her liking to my free speech, and admiration of my little learning and poetry, which I did so much cultivate on her command, have rooted such love, such

dutiful remembrance of her princely virtues, that to turn *askante* from her condition with tearless eyes, would stain and foul the spring and fount of gratitude.[23]

Nevertheless, as Harington admitted, he now looked forward to the accession of a king instead of, 'a lady shut up in a chamber from her subjects and most of her servants, and seen seld[om] but on holy-days'.[24] He talked of the unpopularity of Elizabeth's government, and contrasted the growing weakness and infirmity of the aged Queen with the youth of James VI. 'Age itself is a sickness,' he wrote.[25]

In a letter to Dudley Carleton, John Chamberlain wrote that, having heard the Queen was unwell in December; he was expecting 'no show of any great doings at court this Christmas'. Yet he was pleasantly surprised to find that the court 'flourished more than ordinary'. There was, he said, 'much dancing, bear-baiting and many plays', as well as a great deal of gambling which the Queen continued to enjoy.[26] But by the end of the year, Elizabeth succumbed again to depression, described by Chamberlain as 'a settled and unremovable melancholy'. She spent more and more of her time in her privy lodgings, surrounded by her friends, among them Catherine Howard, the Countess of Nottingham, the Countess of Warwick, Mary Scudamore and Dorothy Stafford.[27]

59

All are in a Dump at Court

On 21 January, Elizabeth left Whitehall and made the ten-mile journey to Richmond Palace, her 'warm winter box'. Despite the 'very foul and wet weather', the Queen refused to put on her furs and instead wore 'summer-like garments', much to her courtiers' exasperation.[1] Thomas, Lord Burghley, warned his brother Robert Cecil that, 'Her Majesty should accept that she is old and have more care of herself, and that there is no contentment to a young mind in an old body.'[2]

The Queen's physical wellbeing evidently continued to impress visitors to her court although as De Beaumont, the French ambassador wryly noted, the 'Queen's confidence respecting her age' is an illusion 'promoted by the whole court, with so much art, that I cannot sufficiently wonder at it'.[3] Shortly after arriving at Richmond, she was reported to have begun to 'grow sickly' but continued her official duties through February, attending to the final negotiations for the Earl of Tyrone's surrender in Ireland and on the nineteenth, entertaining the Venetian ambassador, Giovanni Carlo Scaramelli.[4] When Scaramelli arrived at Richmond he was escorted by the Lord Chamberlain to the Presence Chamber where Elizabeth waited to receive him. She sat on a chair on a raised platform surrounded by members of the Privy Council and many ladies and gentlemen, all being entertained by musicians. After many hours of preparation by her ladies, Elizabeth appeared resplendent, possessing the confidence of a much younger woman. The Venetian ambassador described her as dressed in silver and white taffeta trimmed with gold, her dress 'somewhat open' in the front which showed a throat encircled with gems and rubies down to her breast. Her hair was of 'light colour never made by nature', and she wore great pearls 'like pears' round her forehead. She had 'a coif arched round her head and an Imperial crown, and displayed a vast quantity of gems and pearls upon her person; even under her stomacher she was covered with golden jewelled girdles and single gems, carbuncles, balas-rubies, diamonds; round her wrists in place of bracelets she wore double rows of pearls of more than medium size'.[5] It was an ostentatious and, to some, an absurd sight.

As the Queen rose to greet Scaramelli, he knelt down to kiss her robe but she raised him up with 'both hands' and offered him her right hand to kiss. The envoy then delivered his prepared speech on behalf of the Republic and congratulated the Queen on 'the excellent health' in which he found her.[6] Elizabeth greeted him in Italian, welcoming him to England, and then rebuked the Doge for not having sent an envoy to her before. It was 'high time', she said, 'that the Republic sent to visit a queen who has always honoured it on every possible occasion.' Scaramelli described Elizabeth as 'almost always smiling' and that she remained standing throughout his audience.[7]

It was the first visit of an Italian envoy since the beginning of her reign, when the Doge and Senate had refused diplomatic ties with Elizabeth on the grounds that she was a heretic. Now, as English piracy threatened Venetian trade in the Mediterranean, Scaramelli had been sent in an effort to broker peaceful relations, and to see that Elizabeth's government brought the pirates under control. As the ambassador handed Elizabeth a letter from the Senate, she responded gravely, 'I cannot help feeling that the Republic of Venice, during the forty-four years of my reign, has never made herself heard by me except to ask for something.' However she now assured him that, 'as the question touches my subjects ... I will appoint commissioners who shall confer with you and report to me, and I will do all that in my lies to give satisfaction to the Serene Republic, for I would not be discourteous.'[8]

Scaramelli later reported that the Queen was 'in perfect possession of all senses', and added, 'as she neither eats nor sleeps except at the call of nature, everyone hopes and believes that her life is much further from its close than is reported elsewhere'. He added, 'the safety of her Realm is on secure foundation'.[9]

In fact it was the Queen's age and 'her Majesty's bodily troubles' that were becoming the matter of most intense interest, anxiety and speculation.[10] Shortly after Scaramelli's audience, Elizabeth had to have her coronation ring, worn on her wedding ring finger, filed off because 'it was so grown into the flesh'. It was an event that her courtiers read as 'a sad presage, as if it portended that the marriage with her kingdom, contracted by the ring, would be dissolved'.[11]

On 20 February, Catherine Howard, the Countess of Nottingham, died. She was the Queen's cousin, the longest-serving Lady of the Bedchamber and one of her closest friends. The courtier Philip Gawdy wrote to his brother that the Queen had taken the death 'much more heavily' than had the countess' husband, the Lord Admiral, Charles Howard.[12] De Beaumont reported that the Queen was so overwhelmed by her grief for the countess, 'for whom she has shed many tears, and manifested great affliction', that she refused his request for an audience.[13] Elizabeth remained secluded within her privy lodgings, while the whispers of concern for her health grew louder.

By March, Elizabeth's symptoms had become more alarming. On the ninth, Robert Cecil wrote to George Nicholson, the Queen's agent in Edinburgh, that Elizabeth 'hath good appetite, and neither cough nor fever, yet she is troubled with a heat in her breasts and dryness in her mouth and tongue, which keeps her from sleep, greatly to her disquiet'. Cecil then assured Nicholson that despite this, Elizabeth 'never kept her bed, but was within these three days in the garden'.[14] Cecil proceeded to write a fuller report to Sir John Herbert, one of the secretaries of state.

> It is very true that her Majesty hath of late for eight or nine days been much deprived of sleep, which you know was ever wont to moisten her body, and whenever she lacked it, she was ever apt to be impatient. This continuance for nine or ten days decays her appetite somewhat, and drieth her body much, wherein, though she be free from sickness in stomach or head, and in the day catcheth sleep, yet I cannot but affirm unto you that if this should continue many months, it promiseth no other than a falling into some great weakness of consumption which would hardly be recovered in old age.[15]

Another letter from court by Father Anthony Rivers to a Venetian correspondent claimed that Elizabeth, 'rests ill at nights, forbears to use the air in the day, and abstains more than usual from her meat, resisting physic and is suspicious of some about her as ill-affected'.[16] Rivers also wrote to Giocomo Creleto in Venice.

> [The Queen now] complaineth much of many infirmities wherewith she seemeth suddenly to be overtaken; as imposthumation in her head, aches in her bones and a continual cold in her legs, besides a notable decay of judgement and memory, insomuch as

she cannot abide discourses of government and state, but delighteth to hear old Canterbury tales, to which she is very attentive; at other times impatience and testy so as none of her Council, but [her] Secretary dare to come into her presence.[17]

De Beaumont reported that the Queen,

> Has not had any sleep during this time, and eats much less than usual. Though she has no actual fears, she suffers much from incessant restlessness, and from so great a heat of the mouth and stomach that she is obliged to cool herself every instant, in order that the burning phlegm, with which she is oppressed may not stifle her ... she has been obstinate in refusing everything prescribed by her physicians during her sickness.[18]

The ninth of March was the second anniversary of the execution of the Earl of Essex and this added to the Queen's 'melancholic humour'. On the same day an anonymous correspondent described Elizabeth as 'infinitely discontented'. Her courtiers found the Queen's low mood contagious, and Anthony Rivers reported that 'all are in a dump at court'.[19] Elizabeth believed that since Essex's death, 'the people's affection towards her wax more cold than had been accustomed'.[20] Lady Arbella Stuart had taken the opportunity of the anniversary to call for those who had loved Essex to act in *her* defence, claiming that her life was being threatened by the same faction that ended his.[21] As Scaramelli wrote, 'it is well known that this unexpected event has greatly disturbed the Queen, for she has suddenly withdrawn into herself, she who was want to live so gaily – specially in these last years of her life'. He added, 'so anxious is she that rumours of this beginning of troubles should not spread beyond the Kingdom, that she forbade either persons or letters to leave any of the ports although when realising it was too late, she abandoned this'.[22] Another letter sent to Venice describes how 'every man's head is full of proclamations as to what shall become of us afterwards'.[23]

Elizabeth then appeared to improve. On 12 March, Roger Manners, the Earl of Rutland, reported to his brother, 'it has been a troublesome and heavy time here owing to the Queen's dangerous sickness; but now we rest in better hope, because yesterday she found herself somewhat better'.[24] Three days later William Camden noted that the 'excessive sleepless indisposition of her Majesty is now ceased, which being joined with an inflammation from the breast upward, and her mind altogether averted from physic in this her climacterical year, did more than terrify us all'.[25] The Venetian ambassador to France, Marin Cavali, described how,

> The Queen of England's illness is inflammation and a swelling in the throat, contracted by sitting late at court. On retiring she felt the beginning of the mischief, which at once caused the entire loss of appetite the first day, and the second deprived her of sleep; and for two days she went without nourishment, but would never submit to take medicine. She saw some rose water on her table and some currants, and she took a fancy for some. After her forehead was bathed she fell asleep. When she woke the gathering in her throat burst, and the attendants were alarmed lest the blood should suffocate her, or cause her to break a blood vessel.[26]

De Beaumont's dispatch, written on 14 March, detailed how,

> The Queen was given up three days ago; she had lain long in a cold sweat, and had not spoken. A short time previously she said, 'I wish not to live any longer, but desire to die.' Yesterday and the day before she began to rest and found herself better after having been greatly relieved by the bursting of a small swelling in the throat. She takes no medicine whatever, and has only kept her bed two days; before this she would on no account suffer it, for fear (as some suppose) of a prophecy that she should die in her bed. She is more-over said to be no longer in her right senses: this, however, is a mistake; she has only had some slight wanderings at intervals.[27]

Elizabeth's condition was monitored closely and reported across Europe. On 15 March, Sir Noel de Caron, the Dutch ambassador, wrote to the deputy of the States in Paris with details of the 'defluxion' in her throat which left the Queen 'like a dead person'.[28] But de Caron assured the deputy that although Elizabeth had been ill for a fortnight and not slept for '10 or 12 days' she was beginning to recover: 'for the last three or four nights she has slept four or five hours, and also she begins to eat and drink something'.[29] When Robert Cecil and John Whitgift, the Archbishop of Canterbury, knelt down on their knees to beg Elizabeth to eat and take her medicine, the ambassador reported, 'she was angry with them for it, and said, that she knew her own strength and constitution better than they; and that she was not in such danger as they imagin'd'.[30]

But within days her condition deteriorated alarmingly. By 18 March, Cecil's secretary wrote: 'She began to be very ill: whereupon the [lords] of the counsel were sent for to Richmond.'[31] The Queen's musicians were also summoned because, de Beaumont speculated, 'she means to die as cheerfully as she lived'. He described her condition in vivid detail:

> The Queen is already quite exhausted, and sometimes, for two or three days together, does not speak a word. For the last two days she has her finger almost always in her mouth, and sits upon cushions, without rising or lying down, her eyes open and fixed on the ground. Her long wakefulness and want of food have exhausted her already weak and emaciated frame, and have produced heat in the stomach, and also the drying up of all the juices, for the last ten or twelve days.[32]

As the symptoms worsened, Elizabeth's councillors began to make preparations for her death and to take steps to avoid a much feared civil war over the succession. John Stow reported that as the Queen grew 'dangerously sick' in March, 'straight watches were kept in the City of London, with warding at the gates, lanterns with lights hanged out to burn all the night'.[33] On 12 March, Chief Justice Popham urged Robert Cecil to fortify London because 'the most dissolute and dangerous people of England are there, and upon the least occasion will repair thither'.[34] Three days later warrants were issued to local government officials to assist the Countess of Shrewsbury 'in suppressing some disorderly attempts and riots intended by certain ill-affected persons' who wanted Arbella Stuart, in the countess's custody, to be placed on the throne.[35] The following day the Earl of Shrewsbury was ordered by the Privy Council to 'suppress all uncertain and evil rumours concerning the state of the Queen's health ... and also to prevent all unlawful assemblies and disorderly attempts, which such rumours may breed in the country about [him]'.[36]

The Earl of Northumberland wrote to James VI to tell him about the steps being taken to maintain order: 'all such rogues as might be apt to stir ... are sent unto the Low Countries', and, as John Clapham noted, 'all wandering and suspected persons ... in most parts of the realm' are gaoled.[37] On 17 March, Scaramelli reported that 'five hundred vagrants were seized in the taverns and elsewhere, under pretext of sending them to serve the Dutch, and are still kept as a precaution under lock and key on that pretence'.[38] Three weeks later he described how 'foreigners to the number of five hundred were shipped over to Holland, and a like number of Catholics were imprisoned'.[39] Theatres in London, Middlesex and Surrey were shut to prevent public gatherings and ports closed to secure England against rebellion or invasion and to control the flow of information to the continent. The guards at Richmond were doubled and the Queen's jewels and silver were locked in the Tower with the crown jewels.

On Saturday 19 March, Robert Carey arrived at Richmond. It was likely to have been his sister Lady Philadelphia Scrope that had warned him that the Queen was dying. Carey had ready access to the privy lodgings in the final weeks of her life and witnessed her decline.[40] When he was admitted on the Saturday night, he found Elizabeth in one of her 'withdrawing chambers sitting low upon her cushions'. She called him to her and he kissed her hand. It was his 'chiefest happiness to see her in safety and in health', he told her, which he hoped might 'long continue'. Elizabeth then took him by the hand and, wringing it hard, said, 'No, Robin I am not well', and then with long and heavy sighs, proceeded to tell him about her ill health and how her heart had been 'sad and heavy for ten or twelve days'. Carey was distressed at seeing her 'plight' and remarked that 'for all my lifetime before I never knew her fetch a sigh but when the Queen of Scots was beheaded'. Despite his best efforts to cheer Elizabeth, he found her 'melancholy humour' to be 'deep-rooted in her heart'. He described how she had 'come to look upon herself as a miserable forlorn woman', and talked of how she no longer had anyone she could trust and believed that her authority among the people is now 'sensibly decayed'.[41]

The following morning Carey returned to see the Queen at Richmond. He had expected to see her in the chapel for the morning service and gathered with the rest of the congregation in the long narrow room with pews either side. But 'after eleven o'clock one of the Grooms [of the Chambers] came out, and bade make ready for the Private Closet.' The Private Closet was a room just off the passage way between the Presence Chamber and the Privy Chamber where the Queen's chaplain held private religious services. But Elizabeth did not appear there either. Instead 'she had cushions laid for her in the Privy Chamber, hard by the Closet door; and there she heard service'. As Carey wrote, 'From that day forward she grew worse and worse.'[42]

Councillors, courtiers, ambassadors and other visitors at court now waited for news from within the Queen's privy lodging. John Clapham was among those watching every move of the privy councillors who 'were seen to pass to and fro, sometimes with heavy countenances, as betraying their fears, and sometimes again more cheerful'.[43] The Dutch ambassador Noel de Caron observed those who had access to the Queen, 'being between the Coffer Chamber and [the Queen's] Bedchamber, he saw great weeping and lamentation among the lords and ladies', and 'perceived that there was no hope that Her Majesty could escape'.[44] The capital held its breath. Father William Weston, who was then confined in the Tower of London, described how, 'a strange silence descended on the whole city, as if it were under interdict and divine worship suspended. Not a bell rang out, not a bugle sounded – though ordinarily they were often heard.'[45]

As 'variable rumours' of the Queen's death swept across London, those who lived outside the city walls brought their plate and jewels to the city where 'continual strong watches' were kept.[46] People went to churches 'to be assured whether the Queen was living or dead' and to pray for her.[47]

By mid-March, Elizabeth had stopped eating and bathing, and was refusing to be undressed or put to bed. As John Chamberlain reported, she 'had a persuasion that if she once lay down she should never rise' and so the Queen 'could not be gotten to her bed in a whole week'. Determined not to go to her deathbed, Elizabeth 'sat up for whole days, supported by pillows mostly awake and speaking not at all'.[48] The once iconic beauty, heralded for her magnificence and splendour, now spent her days lying on cushions on the floor, fully dressed, her women kneeling down and tending to her.

60

Deathbed

As Elizabeth grew weaker, her physicians and privy councillors sent for the Earl of Nottingham, her Lord Admiral.[1] When he told Elizabeth to have courage and that she should retire to her Bedchamber, she is said to have responded, 'If you were in the habit of seeing such things in your bed as I do when in mine, you would not persuade me to go there.' But finally, 'by fair means' and 'by force', her frail body was carried and placed in her high wooden bed, with its carved beasts and satin headboard, topped with ostrich plumes and spangles of gold.[2]

The Queen's life was drawing to an end, and, according to de Beaumont, 'had been given up by all the physicians'. Once she was in bed she seemed to feel better and asked for meat broth, 'which gave some fresh hopes'. However soon after, her voice began to fail; she ate nothing more, and lay motionless on one side 'without speaking or looking at anybody'.[3] Young Elizabeth Southwell, who cared for Elizabeth in her final days, later described the Queen's torment as she lay dying.[4] The Queen requested a 'true looking glass' and when she caught sight of her reflection exclaimed that it was the first time in twenty years that she had truly seen herself. 'All those who had commended and flattered her 'she now banished from her chamber'.[5] This incident also appears in the memoirs of John Clapham: 'It is credibly reported that not long before her death, she had a great apprehension of her own age and declination by seeing her face, then lean and full of wrinkles, truly represented to her in a glass; which she a good while very earnest beheld, perceiving thereby how often she had been abused by flatterers.'[6]

On 23 March, the law student John Manningham went to the court at Richmond Palace to hear Dr Henry Parry preach, and 'to be assured whether the Queen were living or dead'.[7] Later the same day, he dined with Parry in the Privy Chamber and heard reports of the Queen's condition from him and her other chaplains. They described how Elizabeth 'took great delight in hearing prayers' and would 'often at the name of Jesus lift up her hands and eyes to heaven'. By now Elizabeth had lost the ability to speak and so 'made signs' to summon her prelates. She would not hear the archbishop speak of hope of a longer life, but when he 'prayed or spoke of heaven' she would hug his hand.[8]

That same afternoon, Elizabeth responded to the Privy Council's request to see her and motioned that they come before her. When asked whether she agreed that King James of Scotland should be her successor, Robert Carey described that she lifted up her hand to her head, as a sign that James should be king.[9] At six o'clock in the evening, the Queen motioned for Archbishop Whitgift and her other chaplains to come and pray with her. 'I went with them,' Carey recalled, 'full of tears to see the heavy sight' as her chaplains surrounded her bed. Elizabeth was lying on her back with one arm hanging out of the bed. The archbishop told her that although she had been a great queen, she now had to yield an account of 'her stewardship to the King of Kings'. For the next few hours Whitgift knelt quietly praying at her bedside. When he finally rose to leave, Elizabeth 'made a sign with her hand' for him to stay on his knees. Carey's sister, Lady Scrope, knowing her Majesty's meaning, told the bishop the Queen desired that he continue to pray.[10]

Finally all but the Queen's women that were in attendance on her, remained in the Bedchamber, and it was in their company that she breathed her last.[11] Elizabeth died between two and three in the morning on Thursday 24 March. 'Her Majesty departed this life, mildly, like a lamb, easily like a ripe apple from the tree,' reported Parry, her chaplain.[12]

———•———

The Privy Council immediately moved from Richmond to Whitehall, where they re-convened. By ten o'clock in the morning the proclamation of the accession of King James I of England was made at the palace gates. Over the next few hours it was read at locations across the city and in the days that followed across the whole country.[13]

As soon as the Queen was dead, a message was sent to Robert Carey who immediately went to the Coffer Chamber where he found 'all the ladies weeping bitterly'.[14] There his sister, Lady Philadelphia Scrope, passed him a sapphire ring, which had been given to her by King James VI to be used as a sign of the Queen's death.[15] Carey set off for Scotland in haste and reached Edinburgh less than three days later, arriving at Holyrood Palace at six o'clock on the night of 26 March with news of James's accession.

As the Queen's passing was made known, John Manningham wrote of the sense of bewilderment and suspense in London. There was a great fear of 'garboiles' (disturbances) and uncanny quiet across the capital, as news spread that James was now King of England:

> The proclamation was heard with great expectation, and silent joy, no great shouting: I think the sorrow for her Majesty's departure was so deep in many hearts. They could not so suddenly show any great joy, though it could not be less then exceedingly great for the succession of so worthy a King.

By evening, the streets of London were lit up by bonfires, and bells rang across the city. There was no disorder, 'no tumult, no contradiction, no disorder in the city; every man went about his business as readily as peaceably, as securely, as though there had been no change, nor any news ever heard of competitors'.[16] As one court official wrote, 'Such is the condition of great princes more unhappy in this respect than their own subjects, in that, while they live, they are followed by all men, and at their death lamented of none.'[17]

61

Regina Intacta

In the hours immediately following the Queen's death, as her councillors left Richmond for Whitehall, Elizabeth's ladies remained, watching over her body, 'with charge [for it] not to be opened, such being her desire'.

Given the time taken to make the necessary preparations for a suitably lavish funeral, it was common practice for the bodies of monarchs to be disembowelled and embalmed upon their death. The bodies of Henry VIII, Mary I and Mary Queen of Scots had all been prepared in this way. The process, usually performed by surgeons, involved slicing the corpse open from the sternum to the pelvis and taking out the organs and other viscera. The chest and abdominal cavity would then be washed and filled with preservatives, herbs and spices, or sawdust, to prevent further decay. The body was then closed, wrapped in searcloth, and soldered shut into a lead casket, before being placed in a wooden coffin.

Yet Elizabeth, her body having long been a subject of prurient interest, slanderous gossip and speculation, had left specific instructions that her body should not be disembowelled or examined. Early modern anatomists believed changes in the size and shape of a woman's uterus proved whether or not she had borne children,[1] and Elizabeth may well have been anxious about what the surgeons might have found and the impact of rumours that an examination of her body might have spawned. Any finding that indicated she had been sexually active, physically malformed or had at some stage given birth would have rewarded her enemies, undermined the Tudor legacy, the religious settlement, and the late Queen's claim to have lived and died a virgin.

Stories that Elizabeth was physically incapable of having sex had been commonplace for years. Ben Jonson and others had claimed that the Queen had 'a membrane on her which made her incapable of man, though for delight she tried many'.[2] Sir John Harington had repeated the rumours in his *Tract for the Succession* and, drawing on the testimony of his mother Isabella Harington, declared that the Queen's virginity was a 'secret of state', yet one about which he had intimate knowledge:

> To make the world think she should have children of her own, she entertained till she was fifty years of age, notions of marriage; and though in mind she hath ever had an aversion and (as many think) in body some indisposition to the act of marriage, yet hath she ever made show of affection to some men which in Court were her favourites, to hide that debility, enduring rather to run into some oblique among strangers of a fault that she could not commit, then to be suspected to want anything that belongs to the perfection of a fair lady . . .
>
> Sir Christopher Hatton . . . did swear voluntarily, deeply and with vehement assertion, that he never had any carnal knowledge of her body, and this was also my mother's opinion, who was until the XXth year of her Majesty's reign of her Privy Chamber, and had been sometime her bedfellow.[3]

For Harington, both the Queen's formal marriage negotiations and her courtly dalliances constituted an elaborate and extended charade: Elizabeth exposed herself to the defamatory gossip to mask her physical 'indisposition'. Here the son of her former bedfellow reveals the Queen's ultimate 'secret of state' by claiming intimate knowledge of the Queen's intact condition.[4] An intimate examination of the Queen's body would have revealed the truth as to these rumours and speculations.

Most sources agree that the Queen's wishes not to have her body opened or 'embowelled', though most unusual, were obeyed. The Venetian ambassador described how Elizabeth's body was carefully guarded by her ladies and, 'meantime the body of the late Queen by her own orders has neither been opened, nor, indeed, seen by any living soul save by three of her ladies' – the Countess of Warwick, Helena Marchioness of Northampton and Elizabeth Southwell.[5] John Chamberlain similarly described how the body 'was not opened but wrapped in sear cloths and other preservatives'.[6] Surviving financial records from 1603 also point to the fact that Elizabeth's body was embalmed, wrapped in sear cloth, sealed in a leaden shroud and then placed in a wooden coffin which was 'sumptuously lined with purple velvet, and finished with gilt nails'.[7] Abraham Greene, 'a plumber', was paid for 'Lead solder' and for 'the entombing of the corpse of her late Majesty at Richmond'.[8]

Whilst John Manningham's account also insists that there was no disembowelling of Elizabeth's body, he suggests that those responsible for preparing her corpse might not have done their job properly: 'It is certain the Queen was not embowelled, but wrapped in sear cloth, and that very ill to, through the covetousness of them that defrauded her of the allowance of cloth was given them for that purpose.'⁹ Sear cloth – linen coated with wax – was extremely costly, and several yards of it would have been required to wrap a corpse properly.

However, there is one exception to the narrative that the Queen's body was not opened that should not be readily dismissed. Elizabeth Southwell, in attendance upon the Queen's body at the time, described how, as the Queen's councillors left the Bedchamber to proclaim James King of England, Robert Cecil gave a secret warrant for a surgeon to open the Queen's body.¹⁰ Elizabeth Southwell was about eighteen or nineteen years old in March 1603, granddaughter of the Earl and Countess of Nottingham and one of the Queen's godchildren. Four years after Elizabeth's death, Southwell converted to Catholicism and, having been in contact with Jesuits including Father Robert Persons, she wrote or dictated her account of Elizabeth's death. No other account corroborates Southwell's claim that the Queen's body was opened, nor do any of the Privy Council records mention a warrant, secret or otherwise.¹¹

By refusing to allow the Queen's corpse to be opened and embalmed, the Ladies of the Bedchamber were very likely acting to suppress questions about Elizabeth's virginity. In so doing they, and her councillors, may have been performing a final act of loyalty to their Virgin Queen by allowing her to remain *regina intacta*. Her councillors would also have been keen to avoid uncertainties over the succession by avoiding any difficult questions that an inspection of her body might have raised about possible illegitimate heirs.

On the night of Saturday 26 March, two days after Elizabeth's death, a torchlit procession of black-draped barges carried the Queen's coffin along the Thames to Whitehall. Elizabeth was accompanied for one final time by her ladies, her Gentlemen Pensioners and household officers, together with a number of privy councillors.¹² Upon reaching the palace, the coffin was carried to her Bedchamber which had been hung with yards of black cloth covering the walls, ceiling and floor. The coffin was laid upon her bed, which had been covered in black velvet trimmed with taffeta, and surmounted by huge new bunches of ostrich plumes.[13]

During the days and nights that followed, the Queen's body was never left alone; her ladies were in constant attendance as it lay in state.[14] Elizabeth Southwell claimed that as she attended the body, she heard a crack; kneeling down before the coffin she realised that the decomposing corpse had burst, splitting the 'bord coffin' and releasing the 'breath' of the corpse.[15] It is not impossible that this had happened. The body had been soldered into a lead casket which could trap gases produced by decomposing tissues and cause the splitting of the body, lead, and wood. It is also true that if Elizabeth's orders had been obeyed and her corpse had not been opened, then decomposition would have processed more quickly than in a disembowelled and embalmed corpse. Yet, no other account corroborates Southwell's claims, and one would have expected such a spectacular incident to have been widely reported.

Southwell afterwards maintained that 'no man durst speak it publicly' for fear of Robert Cecil, who dominated the court during the days before and after Elizabeth's death and who oversaw the succession of James I. Fear of 'displeasing Secretary Cecil' might have silenced other witnesses to the story. However, there may have been rumours of it suggested by John Chamberlain's letter on 30 March to Dudley Carelton, who wrote that 'even here the papists do tell strange stories, as utterly void of truth, as if all civil honesty or humanity'. It is also possible that the indecency of an exploding corpse, with its association with moral corruption, might explain why other accounts do not mention it. It is however more likely that the account of the exploding corpse was deliberately fabricated by Southwell after she became a Catholic. Such a story provided Rome with the final verification of Elizabeth's innate depravity and moral corruption.*

In 1608, Robert Persons wrote *The Judgement of a Catholic Englishman, Living in Banishment for His Religion*. The tract was written against the Oath of Allegiance that the new King of England, James I, insisted his subjects take.[16] Persons argued that James had been misled by bad councillors to enforce the oath which would require Catholics to deny the supremacy of the Pope. The supporters of the oath had portrayed Elizabeth

---

* A similar story that the coffin of Henry VIII had cracked open had been circulated buy hostile observers after the King's death.

as a godly monarch who had ruled with clemency and God's favour and had only executed Catholics for treason, not for religion.[17] Persons believed James was being wrongly encouraged to follow his predecessor's example and so proceeded to enlighten him about Elizabeth's character and the details of her reign. She was, he claims, a godless tyrant who persecuted loyal Catholics for their religion, and, to prove his point, he focused on the circumstances of Elizabeth's death.

At the time, an individual's death was believed to indicate whether or not they had lived a good life and had achieved salvation. Robert Persons therefore attacked Elizabeth's virtue with his knowledge about her 'lamentable end' which he had received from 'a person of much credit that was present at all her last sickness, combats and death and related all that passed as eyewitness'.[18] This was clearly a reference to Elizabeth Southwell. Persons then went on to talk of the Queen's dishonourable birth to a woman who 'was never King Henry's lawful wife' and Elizabeth's role in the Thomas Seymour affair. All these events, Persons claimed, connected her sexual immorality with political illegitimacy. It was the charge that Catholic propaganda had been making for years, but now, it seemed, there was actual corroboration that Elizabeth's body was corrupt.

Following a rebuttal of Persons's account by William Barlow, Bishop of Lincoln, the Queen's chaplain who had been present at her death, Persons wrote a longer and more detailed tract.[19] *A Discussion of the Answer of Mr William Barlow* included the majority of Elizabeth Southwell's account of the Queen's last days, culminating in her death, including the opening of her body against her wishes and the explosion of her corpse. In both of Persons's accounts, Elizabeth's natural, corrupt body is connected to the illegitimate and corrupt body politic. Although he does not identify any of the people he mentioned, in his retelling of Southwell's account, he constantly refers to the women who were physically or emotionally close to the Queen to verify his version of events. Just as ambassadors at the beginning of Elizabeth's reign needed her Privy Chamber women for information about the health, fertility and virginity of her natural body, now Robert Persons, a Catholic Jesuit, was invoking the women to authenticate his account. As such the Queen's closest women and their knowledge of the Queen's body could be used to attack or defend her monarchical authority.

62

The Queen's Effigy

Immediately after Elizabeth's death, instructions were issued for the construction of a life-like waxwork and wooden effigy of the Queen. This was a medieval custom which was used to maintain continuity and sustain the fiction of the Queen's 'two bodies' during the period before the funeral. As the natural body would begin to decay and the political body was threatened by disorder and usurpation, the effigy sought to preserve an 'immortal dignity' for the deceased monarch.[1] The face of the effigy which, as Scaramelli described, was 'carved in wood and coloured so faithfully that she seems alive', representing Elizabeth's forever youthful face, and completed with a flaming red wig, would therefore become the focus of attention and grief.[2] The Venetian ambassador reported with some surprise that at Whitehall:

> The council waits on [the Queen] continually with the same cere-
> mony, the same expenditure, down to her very household and table
> serve, as though she were not wrapped in many a fold of sear cloth,
> and hid in such a heap of lead, of coffin, of pall, but was walking as
> she used to do at this season, about the alleys of her gardens. And
> so, in accordance with ancient custom will it continue till the King
> gives orders for her funeral.[3]

The effigy was placed on the coffin during her lying-in state and remained there until the burial.[4] No monarch was officially dead until that day when he or she would be de-robed of majesty and buried and the great officers of state would break their white wands of office and hurl them into the grave. Until that point the court went on as before; it was now just an effigy of Elizabeth clothed in her parliamentary robes, wearing the crown and carrying the orb and sceptre that was the focus of attention rather than Elizabeth herself.[5] The effigy sustained the image of

349

the Queen's natural body in the period between death and burial: James could not officially assume the throne until Elizabeth was buried because, theoretically, there could not be two 'natural bodies' inhabiting the political body.[6] It was at the royal funeral that the body politic, created by the investing rituals of coronation, would be finally separated from the corpse of the dead monarch.

After James had been notified of Elizabeth's death he 'settled the Kingdom of Scotland in good and peaceable order'[7] and began his progress south to London. He reached Berwick on 14 April and from there gave orders that Queen Elizabeth's funeral be observed, 'with all due rites of honour according to the ancient custom' at Westminster Abbey.[8] As was customary for a monarch James would not attend.

Preparations in London immediately began in earnest. The funeral procession and ceremony was planned by the College of Arms with the help and advice of the Privy Council. Twelve thousand yards of black cloth were ordered to make mourning clothes.[9] All members of the court were mentioned in the Wardrobe accounts individually by name, with the amount of material allotted to each for the making of dresses, suits, cloaks and veils.[10] Arrangements were made for the procession through London and the ceremony itself and Arbella Stuart, as the lady of highest rank related to the Queen, was named as chief mourner. She declined the honour, however, saying that 'sith her access to the Queen in her lifetime might not be permitted, she would not after her death be brought upon this stage for a public spectacle'.[11] Instead Helena Parr, the Lady Marchioness of Northampton, was appointed chief mourner, because of her rank and gender rather than her relationship with the Queen.

On Thursday 28 April, a month after Elizabeth's death, a procession of more than a thousand people made its way from Whitehall to Westminster Abbey with 'great pomp and magnificence'.[12] Led by bell-ringers and knight marshals, who cleared the way with their gold staves, the funeral cortege stretched for miles. First came 260 poor women 'four in a rank, apparelled in black, with linen kerchiefs over their heads'. Then came the lower ranking servants of the royal household and the servants of the nobles and courtiers. Two of the Queen's horses, riderless and covered in black cloth, led the bearers of the hereditary standards of the Dragon, the Greyhound and the Lion and the supporters of the arms of England. More members of the Queen's household and government followed, from apothecaries and musicians, to a large number of clerks, the gentlemen and children of the Chapel in copes and surplices, singing 'in a mournful tone'. Following them came the Mayor and Aldermen of London.

The focal point of the procession was the royal chariot carrying the Queen's hearse, draped in purple velvet and pulled by four horses trimmed with black. On top of the coffin was the life-size effigy of Elizabeth, a crown upon its head, dressed in parliamentary robes of red velvet and clasping the ball and sceptre. The coffin was covered by a canopy, held aloft by six earls, of twelve embroidered banners that traced the Queen's ancestry.[13] Following behind the chariot was a riderless horse led by the Queen's Master of the Horse, the Gentlemen Ushers of the Privy Chamber and the Garter King of Arms and then the chief mourner, Helena Parr. She was supported on either side by two officers of state, the Lord Treasurer, Lord Buckhurst and the recently widowed Lord Admiral, the Earl of Nottingham. Fourteen countesses followed, then the 'Ladies of Honour.'[14] Next came the remaining countesses, earls' daughters and baronesses. The parade of mourners ended with the 'Maids of Honour of the Privy Chamber'.[15] Sir Walter Ralegh and the Guard walking five abreast, brought up the rear, their halberds held downwards as a sign of sorrow.

'Multitudes of all sorts of people' watched the final procession from all available vantage points; 'streets, houses, windows, leads and gutters'.[16] Even the rooftops were crowded with those who hoped for a glimpse of the spectacle. When the royal chariot went by bearing the effigy of Queen Elizabeth, a 'sighing, groaning and weeping went up as the like hath not been seen or known in the memory of man'.[17]

———⋅———

At Westminster Abbey, the coffin was 'placed under a sumptuous hearse' and the ceremony commenced, conducted by the Bishop of Chichester 'according to the usual manner'.[18] The courtier Philip Gawdy claimed that the ceremony 'held some six hours with the sermon'.[19] However, the Venetian ambassador's source told him that 'at the actual funeral service little else was done except the chanting of two psalms in English and the delivery of the funeral oration'.[20]

After Elizabeth's coffin was placed in its temporary grave, the Queen's officers broke their white rods over their heads and threw the broken pieces onto the coffin to signify their duties had ended. It was customary to display the hearse and the coffin in the church for at least a month, but by 15 May, James had ordered the coffin to be buried 'without the usual delay' and two weeks later the Queen's effigy was also removed.[21] However, it seems that these early attempts to remove Elizabeth from the hearts and minds of her subjects, failed. Scaramelli reported, 'The glory of that Queen, which they pretended to have buried along with her body, having gone the great length of removing her effigy, now becomes, in such circumstances as these, greater than ever.'[22] Elizabeth's final resting place was the crypt beneath the altar in the sepulchre of her grandfather, Henry VII.[23]

Of those of Elizabeth's women present at her funeral it was ironic that the only person to have been at her coronation forty-four years earlier was the woman whom Elizabeth had come to loathe: her cousin Lettice Knollys, Countess of Leicester, and daughter of Katherine Knollys, her much-loved Lady of the Bedchamber. Of Elizabeth's other long-serving women, Mary Scudamore was too ill to attend and died just a few months later on 15 August and was buried at Holme Lacy in Herefordshire. Dorothy Stafford also did not attend Elizabeth's funeral, possibly because of ill health, and died in September 1604. She was buried in St Margaret's, Westminster, close to the tomb of Blanche Parry. Her funeral monument records that 'she served Elizabeth for forty years, lying in her Bedchamber'.

EPILOGUE:
Secret Histories

Three years after Elizabeth's death and burial, on the instruction of King James I, her body was moved from its original resting place in the central tomb of Henry VII in Westminster Abbey, to the north aisle and re-buried with her sister and rival, Mary Tudor.[1] At the same time James ordered a tomb to be erected on the south side for his mother, Mary Stuart, whose body was then moved from Peterborough Cathedral.[2] Mary's tomb was placed behind that of Lady Margaret Beaufort, Henry VII's mother, and in front of the monument to Lady Margaret Douglas, Countess of Lennox, daughter of Henry VII and James's paternal grandmother. As such, James was emphasising his mother's claim to the English crown and establishing her dynasty as a means of legitimising his own right to the throne.[3] Elizabeth, now buried with her sister Mary, both childless Tudor queens, was isolated from the line of inherited power.

During her lifetime, Elizabeth and her councillors were meticulous curators of her public persona, but upon her death, control of her image was lost.[4] Whilst James commissioned a grand monument to Elizabeth, celebrating her achievements, this was deliberately smaller and less costly than the monument he erected for his mother, Elizabeth's great rival. The figure of the Queen on Elizabeth's tomb was carved in marble with the face most likely copied from her funeral effigy.[5] The 'mask of youth' that Elizabeth had sought to maintain was now removed and the Queen was shown as the elderly woman she had become. Representations of Elizabeth, her body and her memory, now became public property free to be used, and abused, to suit new political realities.

In the days and weeks that followed Elizabeth's death, poems and pamphlets, verses and eulogies were available for sale to 'feed plebeian eyes', praising the Queen and her triumphs, but also depicting her as a decaying corpse or as a now penetrable virgin with death cast as her lover. In his *Atropoion Delion* (1603), Thomas Newton questioned the Queen's attendants: 'Why let ye death approach her Privy Chamber?' as if death were an unwanted suitor.[6] Newton's elegiac verses vividly describe Elizabeth's grave as her 'palace' with 'greedy worms' as her courtiers penetrating her 'body bare.'[7] Portraits too, now free from strict Elizabethan censorship, also began to show a very different image of Gloriana. Marcus Gheeraerts's portrait of 1620, deliberately parodied the 1588 Armada portrait, and showed Elizabeth no longer triumphant and powerful, but old, tired and dying, slumped over in a chair with the two figures, Time and Death, waiting in the darkness. The painting showed its increasingly nostalgic Jacobean audience, that the age of Elizabeth was now past.

Long after the Queen's death, rumour-mongering about illegitimate children, illicit liaisons and physical deformities continued. In 1609 a Catholic book in Latin entitled *Purit-Anus* was smuggled into England and claimed that Elizabeth had prostituted herself with men of various nationalities, 'even with blackamoors', and had given birth to illegitimate children.[8] In 1658, Francis Osborne, in his influential *Traditional Memoirs on the Reign of Queen Elizabeth*, heralded the Queen for her political accomplishments and pragmatic moderation, but also repeated the gossip about Elizabeth's promiscuity, though dismissing it as 'strange tales . . . fit for romance'. Yet he suggested it might be true that 'the Ladies of her Bedchamber denied to her Body the Ceremony of Searching and Embalming, due to dead monarchs', to protect her sexual honour or perhaps, a physical abnormality.[9]

In 1680, speculation about Elizabeth's private life exploded into the widest readership yet with the appearance of *The Secret History of the Most Renowned Queen Elizabeth and the Earl of Essex*.[10] This book was translated from the original French text *Comte D'Essex, Historie Angloise* and thereafter widely reprinted and rehashed during the next century. This and *The Secret History of the Duke of Alancon and Queen Elizabeth*, which appeared eleven years later, inaugurated a tradition of writing about the Queen's love life and claiming that her reign could only be understood in terms of secret compulsions and desires. From then on stories about Elizabeth's innermost passions were marketed at London bookstalls in cheap editions and dramatised on the London stage, appealing to the growing public appetite for scandal in high places. John Banks's play *The Unhappy Favourite*, which was performed in 1682, was an adaptation of *The Secret History of Elizabeth and Essex*. Banks centred his drama on the conflict between the Queen's private and public self, thereby reworking the concept of the Queen's two bodies. Elizabeth was championed here as a vulnerable queen, notable for the personal cost of the public sacrifices she was compelled to make.[11] Questioning Elizabeth's virginity was no longer confined to hostile Catholic discourse and there was a growing sense that Elizabeth's private feelings compromised the integrity of her rule and her status as a national icon.

Fostered by the rise of popular biographies of queens and their courtiers, Elizabeth was now increasingly regarded with a mixture of admiration and contempt for her vanity, jealousy, vindictiveness and secret passions. In 1825 the antiquary and writer Hugh Campbell described her as 'wanton and licentious', consumed by lust and repeated long-held suspicions that she was a virgin only because of 'some obstructions from nature'. In the mid-nineteenth century a public debate over Elizabeth's 'morals' was even played out in popular print. *Fraser's Magazine* ran a two-part article in 1853 evaluating the claims of Elizabeth's 'wantonness' and ultimately concluding that whilst the historical evidence was 'doubtful, at the best', in such a case when 'the character of a lady is at issue, to doubt is to condemn'.[12] The scandal of Elizabeth's assumed conduct was in sharp contrast with the much-celebrated wifely and maternal instincts of the reigning queen, Victoria.

Increasingly attention focussed on Elizabeth's postmenopausal body, and paintings depicted the ageing Queen in her private apartments. In Augustus Leopold Egg's *Queen Elizabeth Discovers She Is No Longer Young*, which appeared at the Royal Academy in 1848, Elizabeth is pictured in her Bedchamber as an old woman amid her ladies who force her to face up to her mortality in the mirror that is held before her. Critics heralded the picture as an unmasking of the real Gloriana. Similar depictions followed of Elizabeth as an old harridan. So obsessed did mid-Victorian culture become with the figure of the elderly Queen that one contemporary commentator observed ruefully that 'it is much nowadays to find anyone who believes that Queen Elizabeth was ever young, or who does not talk of her as if she was born about seventy years of age covered with rouge and wrinkles'.[13]

Whilst early twentieth-century academic biographies, led by John Neale's *Queen Elizabeth I* (1934), focused on strictly political motives rather than on Elizabeth's sexual self, historical novels, plays and operas continued to cast Elizabeth as a queen with a private life.[14] The old charges that Elizabeth was malformed or infertile were revived with some going so far as to claim that Elizabeth was in fact a man,[15] or at least a hermaphrodite.[16] Others dealt with Elizabeth's sexuality in more subtle, psychological ways, underpinned by a sense that her chastity was distinctly odd if not perverse. Lytton Strachey's *Elizabeth and Essex* (1928) read the

Queen's life in a post-Freudian fashion, with her sexual desires and dysfunction traceable to her childhood and adolescence.[17] Many reviewers criticised Strachey's portrayal of Elizabeth as tawdry and salacious and a similar critique was levelled at Benjamin Britten's opera *Gloriana* (1953) which was based on Strachey's book. The opera's central theme was the clash between public responsibility and private desires, and contrasted the public persona of the Queen with the reality of a tragic, vain old woman. For the young, newly crowned Queen Elizabeth II, in whose honour the production had been staged, and for most of the audience, the opera was not well received. The scene in the Bedchamber where the elderly Queen 'removed her wig from her head and was revealed as almost bald' was regarded as being in particular 'bad taste'.[18]

Meanwhile Elizabeth was increasingly becoming the focus of Hollywood attention and from Bette Davis's portrayal of her in the *Private Lives of Elizabeth and Essex* (1939) and *The Virgin Queen* (1955), to that of Glenda Jackson (*Elizabeth R,* 1971), Judy Dench, (*Shakespeare in Love*, 1998), Helen Mirren in *Elizabeth I* (2007) and Cate Blanchett in Shekar Kapur's *Elizabeth* (1998) and *Elizabeth, The Golden* Age (2010), the quest for the true woman behind the crown continued. Each film, in the tradition of the 'secret histories', portrayed Elizabeth's sexuality in different ways. Whilst Kapur's *Elizabeth* shows the Queen having a sexual relationship with Dudley, by the end of the film she makes the ultimate sacrifice, renouncing her sexual self, thereby becoming the 'Virgin Queen' complete with the dramatic cropped hair and white, leaded face. In the BBC drama *The Virgin Queen*, Elizabeth, played by Anne-Marie Duff, also appears in bed making love with Dudley but then wakes up screaming in dread; it was only a dream. Elizabeth's unconscious desire for intimacy conflicted with her primal fear of it.

The opening scene of Helen Mirren's much-celebrated portrayal shows Elizabeth, in her forties, as she is being undressed by her ladies, slowly, piece by piece, laces untied, sleeves removed until she remains only in her white embroidered chemise. She lies back on her bed, a sheet is draped over her legs and a doctor appears at her side holding a speculum. This is the ultimate exposure, her body bared for the sake of the country. She shows no emotion as the doctor pronounces, 'All is as it should be, ma'am' and then, illustrating the political nature of such private affairs, immediately reports his findings to Cecil and Walsingham, who are waiting in the corridor outside: the Queen is still *virgo intacta* and is capable of having children.

Such dramatic portrayals, together with historical novels such as those by Jean Plaidy and more recently Philippa Gregory, feed a perennial appetite for new interpretations of the 'life and loves' of the Virgin Queen.[19] The questions that the 'secret histories' raised at the end of the seventeenth century continue to intrigue popular audiences today. In life Elizabeth and the ladies of the Bedchamber had tenaciously defended the chastity of her body to protect her reputation and defend her crown. In death, it is the very questioning and searching for the true story of the Virgin Queen, and the possibility that she was not chaste, that continues to fascinate and has ensured her enduring popularity and appeal.

Notes

Abbreviations used in the Notes and Bibliography

AGS	Archivo General de Simancas
APC	*Acts of the Privy Council of England*, ed. J. R. Dasent, 46 vols, (London, 1890–1964)
BIHR	*Bulletin of the Institute of Historical Research*
BL	British Library, London
BLO	Bodleian Library, Oxford
CKS	Centre for Kentish Studies
CP	Cecil Papers, Hatfield House, Hertfordshire
CSP Dom	*Calendar of State Papers, Domestic Series, of the reigns of Edward VI, Mary and Elizabeth, 1547–1625*, ed. C. S. Knighton, 12 vols (London, 1856–72)
CSP Foreign	*Calendar of State Papers, Foreign Series, of the reigns of Elizabeth, 1558–89*, ed. J. Stevenson et al., 23 vols (London, 1863–1950)
CSP Rome	*Calendar of State Papers Relating to English Affairs in the Vatican Archives, vol. 1, 1558–1571*, ed. J. M. Rigg (London, 1916)
CSP Scot	*Calendar of State Papers, Scotland, 1547–1603*, ed. J. Bain et al., 12 vols (Edinburgh, 1898–1969)
CSP Span	*Calendar of State Papers, Spanish*, ed. G. A. Bergenroth at al., 13 vols (London, 1862–1954)
CSP Ven	*Calendar of State Papers, Venetian*, ed. H. F. Brown, 3 vols (London, 1864–1947)
Dudley Papers	Dudley Papers at Longleat House
HMC Rutland	*HMC, Twelfth report, appendix, part iv–v. fourteenth, part I, The Manuscripts of His Grace the Duke of Rutland*, GDC, preserved at Belvoir Castle, 4 vols (London, 1888–95)
HMC Salisbury	HMC, *A calendar of the manuscripts of the Most Hon. The Marquis of Salisbury, K.G., & c, preserved at Hatfield House, Hertfordshire*, 24 vols (London, 1883–1976)
HMC Bath	HMC, *Report on the Manuscripts of the Most Honourable the Marquess of Bath* (London, 1968)

LP	*Letters and Papers, Foreign and Domestic, of the Reign of Henry VIII, 1509–1547*, ed. J. S. Brewer et al., 21 vols and addenda (London, 1862–1932)
LPL	Lambeth Palace Library, London
NLS	National Library Scotland
ODNB	*Oxford Dictionary of National Biography*, ed. H. C. G. Matthew and Brian Harrison, 60 vols (Oxford, 2004)
Paget Papers	Paget Papers, Keele University
SP	State Papers, National Archives, London
Statutes	*Statutes of the Realm*, ed. A. Luders et al.
TNA	The National Archives, Kew, London
TRHS	*Transactions of the Royal Historical Society*
TRP	*Tudor Royal Proclamations*

Epigraphs

1 'Elizabeth's Address to Parliament', 12 November 1586, in Leah S. Marcus, Janel Mueller and Mary Beth Rose, eds, *Elizabeth I, Collected Works* (London, 2002), p. 194.
2 Sir John Harington, *A Tract on the Succession to the Crown, AD 1602* (London, 1880), pp. 40–1.
3 BL Cotton MS Caligula B 10 fol. 350v.

Prologue: Shameful Slanders

1 Janet Arnold, 'The Picture of Elizabeth I When Princess', in *The Burlington Magazine*, 113, No. 938 (1981), pp. 303–4.
2 Maria Perry, *Elizabeth I: The Word of a Prince: A Life from Contemporary Documents* (London, 1990), pp. 31–5. See David Starkey, *Elizabeth: Apprenticeship* (London, 2001), pp. 42–9.
3 *A Chronicle during the Reigns of the Tudors from 1485–1559 by Charles Wriothesley, Windsor Herald*, ed. W. D. Hamilton, 2 vols, Camden Society NS 11 and 20, 2 vols (London, 1875–77), vol. I, p. 182.
4 Samuel Haynes, *A Collection of State Papers . . . Left by William Cecil Lord Burghley and Now Remaining at Hatfield House* (London, 1740), p. 99.
5 Ibid.
6 Ibid.
7 Haynes, *Burghley State Papers*, p. 96; *Elizabeth I: Collected Works*, pp. 17–18.
8 J. Stevenson, ed., *The Life of Jane Dormer, Duchess of Feria by Henry Clifford* (London, 1887), pp. 86–7.
9 Mary Seymour disappears from the historical record after 1550 and it seems likely that she died by the age of two.
10 *APC* (1547–50), pp. 236–8. See G. W. Bernard, 'The Downfall of Sir Thomas Seymour' in his edited collection, *The Tudor Nobility* (Manchester, 1992), pp. 212–40.
11 Haynes, *Burghley State Papers*, pp. 89–90.
12 TNA SP 10/6, fol. 57.
13 Haynes, *Burghley State Papers*, p. 96.
14 Ibid., pp. 99–101.
15 Ibid., p. 102.

16 *CSP Dom*, 1547–53, p. 82; *APC* (1547–50), p. 240.
17 Haynes, *Burghley State Papers*, p. 70.
18 Ibid., p. 107.
19 Ibid., pp. 108–9.
20 BL Lansdowne MS 1236 fol. 35; Henry Ellis (ed.), *Original Letters Illustrative of English History*, 11 vols (London, 1824–46), third series, II, pp. 153–5.
21 See Sheila Cavanagh, 'The Bad Seed: Princess Elizabeth and the Seymour Incident', in Julia M. Walker, ed., *Dissing Elizabeth: Negative Representations of Gloriana* (London, 1998), pp. 9–29. See Janel Mueller, 'Elizabeth Tudor. Maidenhood in Crisis', in *Elizabeth I and the 'Sovereign Arts', Essays in Literature, History and Culture*, Donald Stump and Linda Shenk, eds, (Arizona, 2011), pp. 15–28.
22 Marc Shell, *Elizabeth's Glass* (Lincoln, Nebraska, 1993). See J. Dewhurst, 'The Alleged Miscarriages of Catherine of Aragon and Anne Boleyn', *Medical History*, 28 (1984), pp. 49–56.
23 J. L. Vives, *De Institutione Feminae Christianae*, C. Fantazzi and C. Matheeussen eds, 2 vols (Leiden, 1996), pp. 63, 65, 71.
24 Ibid., pp. 40–1.
25 Ibid., pp. 41, 51–3.
26 See Frank A. Mumby, *The Girlhood of Queen Elizabeth: A Narrative in Contemporary Letters* (London, 1909), pp. 69–72.

Chapter 1: The Queen's Two Bodies

1 See Vincent Joseph Nardizzi, Stephen Guy-Bray, Will Stockton, eds, *Queer Renaissance Historiography, Backward Gaze* (Farnham, 2009). Alan Bray's seminal study of male friendship showed how habits of touching, eating and sleeping were shared between men outside of a sexual context. See A. Bray, *The Friend* (Chicago, 2003). It is more difficult to chart this for women given the greater political invisibility of women's friendship.
2 See Judith M. Richards, 'To Promote a Woman to Beare Rule: Talking of Queens in Mid-Tudor England', *The Sixteenth-Century Journal*, 28. 1 (1997), pp. 101–21; Constance Jordan, 'Women's Rule in Sixteenth-Century British Political Thought', *Renaissance Quarterly*, 40 (1987), pp. 421–51; Paula Louise Scalingi, 'The Scepter or the Distaff: The Question of Female Sovereignty, 1515–1607', *The Historian*, 42 (November, 1978), pp. 59–75. See Margaret R. Somerville, *Sex and Subjection: Attitudes to Women in Early Modern Society* (London, 1995); Jacqueline Eales, *Women in Early Modern England: 1500–1700* (London, 1998); P. Crawford, 'Sexual Knowledge in England, 1500–1700' in R. Porter and M. Teich, eds, *Sexual Knowledge, Sexual Science: The History of Attitudes to Sexuality* (Cambridge, 1994), pp. 82–106. See also Lawrence Stone, *The Family, Sex and Marriage in England, 1500–1800* (New York, 1977).
3 See, for example, *LP*, 1536, pp. 47–54. Elizabeth is here referred to by Chapuys, the imperial ambassador, as 'the Little Bastard', p. 51.
4 Elizabeth had been included in the third Succession Act (1544) and Henry VIII's will two years later, but was declared illegitimate in 1536. The Act was never repealed. This opened the way for Mary Stuart's claim, even though Henry VIII had always tried to block it. Henry believed that by his will he

could determine the order of the succession and eliminate the Stuart claim. His settlement set aside the strict rules of hereditary descent. If his children died without heirs, then the throne was to pass to the offspring of the Duchess of Suffolk. For details of succession see Mortimer Levine, *Tudor Dynastic Problems, 1460–1571* (London, 1973) and his *The Early Elizabethan Succession Question, 1558–68* (Stamford, 1996).

5 A. N. McLaren, 'The Quest for a King: Gender, Marriage and Succession in Elizabethan England', *Journal of British Studies*, 41 (July, 2002), pp. 259–90.

6 Susan Dunn-Hensley, 'Whore Queens: The Sexualised Female Body and the State', in Carole Levin, Jo Eldridge Carney and Debra Barrett-Graves, eds, *High and Mighty Queens of Early Modern England: Realities and Representations* (Basingstoke, 2003), pp. 101–16.

7 William Allen, *An Admonition to the Nobility and People of England and Ireland . . .* (Antwerp, 1558), p. xviii.

8 Francis Osborne, *Historical Memoires on the Reigns of Queen Elizabeth and King James* (London, 1658), p. 61.

9 BL Cotton MS Galba C IX fol. 128.

10 Edmund Bohun, *The Character of Queen Elizabeth; or a full and clear account of her policies* (London, 1693), p. 73. These also included Edward Courtenay, Philip of Spain, Eric of Sweden, the two French dukes, the Duke of Norfolk, the Earl of Arundel, Sir William Pickering, Robert Dudley.

Chapter 2: The Queen is Dead, Long Live the Queen

1 Stevenson, ed., *Life of Jane Dormer*, p. 69.

2 BL Harleian MS 6949 is a transcript of the will.

3 *CSP Span*, 1554–8, p. 438.

4 Stevenson, ed., *Life of Jane Dormer*, p. 72; *CSP Span*, 1554–8, p. 438.

5 J. G. Nichols, ed., *The Diary of Henry Machyn, Citizen, and Merchant Taylor of London, 1550–63*, Camden Society, 43 (London, 1848), p. 178.

6 R. Naunton, *Fragmenta Regalia, or Observations on the Late Queen Elizabeth, her Times and Favourites*, 1641, ed. E. Arber (London, 1879), p. 15.

7 TNA SP 12/1/ fol. 12.

8 Marie Axton, *The Queen's Two Bodies: Drama and the Elizabethan Succession* (London, 1977), p. 12; see also Ernst Kantorowicz, *The King's Two Bodies* (Princeton, 1957) and Albert Rolls, *The Theory of the King's Two Bodies in the Age of Shakespeare, Studies in Renaissance Literature*, 19 (Lewiston, Queenston and Lampeter, 2000). For the purposes of law it was found necessary by 1561 to endow the Queen with two bodies: a body natural and a body politic. See Edmund Plowden, 'The Treatise of the Two Bodies of the King', BL Cotton MS Caligula B IV, fols 1–94. See also Marie Axton, 'The Influence of Edmund Plowden's Succession Treatise', *Huntington Library Quarterly* 37 (3) (1974), pp. 209–26.

9 TNA SP 12/1 fol. 3v.

10 *CSP Span*, 1558–67, p. 7.

11 TNA SP 70/5 fol. 31r–v; William Murdin, *A Collection of State Papers Relating to Affairs in the Reign of Queen Elizabeth left by Lord Burghley, from the year 1571 to 1596* (London, 1759), pp. 748–9.

12 *CSP Span*, 1558–67, p. 45.

13 Ibid.

14 Ibid., p. 122.

15 *HMC Salisbury*, I, p. 158.

16 TNA PC 2/8 fol.198; *APC*, 1558–70, pp. 6–7; John Strype, *Annals of the Reformation . . .* 4 vols (Oxford, 1820–40), I, p. 7.

17 *APC*, 1558–70, p. 22; however, there was no legislation against conjuring, and so the culprits were sent for 'severe punishment' under ecclesiastical law to Edmund Bonner, Bishop of London. *APC*, 1558–70, p. 22; *CSP Span*, 1558–67, pp. 17–18.

18 Francis Coxe, *A Short Treatise Declaring the Detestable Wickednesse of Magicall Sciences as Necromancie, Coniurations of Spirites, Curiouse Astrologie and Such Lyke* (London, 1561), sigs. A4v–A5v.

19 *The Diary of Henry Machyn*, p. 185. For English responses to Nostradamus see, for example, William Fulke, *Antiprognosticon, that is to saye, an invective against the vayne and unprofitable predictions of the astrologians as Nostradame etc* (London, December 1560), sig. A8r–v. See also V. Larkey, 'Astrology and Politics in the First Years of Elizabeth's Reign', *Bulletin of the History of Medicine*, III (1935), pp. 171–86.

20 'The Compendious Rehearsal of John Dee', in T. Hearne, ed., *Joannis, confratis & monachi Glastoniensis, chronica sive historia de rebus Glastoniensibus*, 2 vols (Oxford, 1726), II, pp. 509, 521.

21 As recorded by Richard Mulcaster in his *The passage of our most drad Soveraigne Lady Quene Elyzabeth through the citie of London to Westminster the daye before her coronacion* (London, 1558).

22 1 Eliz.c.2., *Statutes* IV, pp. 358–9.

23 See W. P. Haugaard, 'Elizabeth Tudor's Book of Devotions: A neglected clue to the Queen's life and character', *The Sixteenth-Century Journal* 12:2 (1981), pp. 79–106, at p. 93.

24 J. E. Neale, *Elizabeth I and her Parliaments, 1584–1601*, 3 vols (London, 1957), I, p. 128.

25 *CSP Ven*, 1558–80, pp. 22–3.

26 1 Eliz I, c.1, 'The Act of Supremacy' and 1 Eliz I, c.2, 'The Act of Uniformity', printed in *Statutes* IV, pp. 355–8.

Chapter 3: *Familia Reginae*

1 *CSP Ven*, 1558–80, p. 12.

2 J. R. Planché, *Regal Records, or a Chronicle of the Coronations of the Queen Regnants of England* (London, 1838), p. 35.

3 See Mary Hill Cole, *The Portable Queen: Elizabeth I and the Politics of Ceremony* (Amherst, 1999); Julian Munby, 'Queen Elizabeth's Coaches: The Wardrobe on Wheels', *Antiquaries Journal*, 83 (2003), pp. 311–67.

4 TNA SP 12/6/36 fol. 78.

5 Pam Wright, 'A change in direction: the ramifications of a female household, 1558–1603', in D. Starkey et al., eds, *The English Court: from the Wars of the Roses to the Civil War* (London, 1987), pp. 147–72; C. Merton, 'The Women Who Served Queen Mary and Queen Elizabeth: Ladies, Gentlewomen and Maids of the Privy Chamber, 1553–1603', (PhD thesis, Cambridge, 1992). See also K. Bundesen, 'Circling the crown: political

power and female agency in sixteenth-century England', in J. Jordan, ed., *Desperate Housewives: Politics, Propriety and Pornography, Three Centuries of Women in England* (Cambridge, 2009), pp. 3–28 and William Tighe, 'Familia Reginae: The Privy Court', in Susan Doran and Norman Jones, eds, *The Elizabethan World* (Oxford, 2011), pp. 76–91.

6 TNA LC 2/4/3 fol. 62r.

7 TNA LC 2/4/3 fols 53v–54r. Subsequent documents do not identify the women in these groups, suggesting the boundaries were in practice rather fluid.

8 See A. Hoskins, 'Mary Boleyn's Carey Children and offspring of Henry VIII', *Genealogists Magazine*, 25 (1997), pp. 345–52.

9 See N. M. Sutherland, 'The Marian Exiles and the Establishment of the Elizabethan Regime', *Archive for Reformation History* 78 (1987), pp. 253–84; G. Peck, 'John Hales and the Puritans during the Marian Exile', *Church History* 10 (1941), pp. 159–177 at p. 174.

10 BL Lansdowne MS 94, fol. 21 printed in G. B. Harrison, *The Letters of Queen Elizabeth* (London, 1935), p. 19.

11 BL Lansdowne MS 3, fol. 193 lists Lettice Knollys as a 'gentlewoman of our Privy Chamber'.

12 See S. Varlow, 'Sir Francis Knolly's Latin dictionary: new evidence for Katherine Carey', *BIHR*, 80 (2007), pp. 315–23.

13 She is listed in the Coronation Account Book, TNA LC 2/4/3 fol. 53v; although it does not say 'Gentlewoman of the Privy Chamber', her name is listed under 'the Bedchamber' and listed above the category of 'Chamberers'. Therefore in the Coronation Account Book, she was a Gentlewoman of the Bedchamber, and not a Lady of the Bedchamber as her social rank was only that of a Gentlewoman, denoted with a 'Mrs' before her name as opposed to 'Lady'.

14 He served as Master of the Jewel House until his death in 1596 and was also one of only two men to hold the position of Gentleman of the Privy Chamber under Elizabeth. The other was Christopher Hatton who served from 1572 to 1591. Kat's husband John was made Master and Treasurer of Her Majesty's Jewels and Plate. According to the inscription on his monument at Maidstone he also became 'prime Gentleman of the Privy Chamber'. See A. F. Collins, ed., *Jewels and Plate of Queen Elizabeth I: The Inventory of 1574* (London, 1955), p. 210.

15 See J. Graves, *A Brief Memoir of the Lady Elizabeth Fitzgerald, Known as the Fair Geraldine* (Dublin, 1874).

16 Henry Stafford had re-converted to Catholicism during Mary's reign.

17 See C. H. Garrett, *The Marian Exiles: a Study in the Origins of Elizabethan Puritanism* (Cambridge, 1938); G. Peck, 'John Hales and the Puritans during the Marian Exile', pp. 159–77.

18 BL Lansdowne MS 59, no. 22, fol. 43; TNA LC 2/4/4 fols 45v–46.

19 J. G. Nichols (ed.), *The Progresses and Public Processions of Queen Elizabeth*, 3 vols (London, 1823), I, p. 38; TNA LC 2/4/3 is the account book for Elizabeth I's coronation.

20 See *CSP Dom*, 1547–80, p. 648.

21 BL Additional [hereafter Add.] MS 48161, Robert Beale, 'A Treatise of the Office of ... Principall Secretarie', printed in C. Read, *Mr Secretary*

Walsingham and the Policy of Queen Elizabeth, 3 vols (Cambridge, Mass, 1925), vol. I, pp. 423–43.

Chapter 4: Not a Morning Person

1 BL Add. MS 35185, fol. 23v.
2 Simon Thurley, *Whitehall Palace: an Architectural History of the Royal Apartments 1240–1698* (New Haven and London, 1999), pp. 65–74. There starts in the reign of Elizabeth a series of accounts of foreign travellers who visited Whitehall. They were generally shown not only the outer chambers but, when the Queen was away, her privy lodgings too. 'Journey through England and Scotland made by Lupold von Wedel in the Years 1584 and 1585', trans. Gottfried von Bulow, *TRHS*, new series, vol. 9 (London, 1895), pp. 223–70 at pp. 234–7; *The Diary of Baron Waldstein: A Traveller in Elizabethan England*, trans. and ed. G. W. Groos (London, 1981), pp. 43–59; 'Diary of the Journey of Philip Julius Duke of Stettin-Pomerania, through England in the year 1602', *TRHS*, n.s. vol. 6 (London, 1892), pp. 1–67 at pp. 23–5; *Thomas Platter's Travels in England, 1599,* trans. Clare Williams (London, 1937), pp. 163–6.
3 'Diary of the Journey of the Duke of Stettin-Pomerania', p. 25; 'Journey of von Wedel', p. 325.
4 *HMC Bath*, vol. IV, p. 186.
5 Manchet or fine white bread came from wheat grown at Heston as it was accounted the purest. See John Norden, *Speculum Brittanie: Description of Middlesex and Hertfordshire* (London, 1723).
6 John Harington, *Nugae Antiquae*, ed. Henry Harington, 3 vols (London, 1779), II, p. 135.
7 R. R. Tighe and J. C. Davis, *Annals of Windsor*, 2 vols (London, 1858), I, p. 641.
8 See N. Williams, *Powder and Paint: a History of the Englishwoman's Toilet* (London, 1957), p. 14.
9 See Sir Hugh Platt, *Delight for Ladies* (London, 1594).
10 For example, 'By Mrs Twiste, six towthclothes wrought with blake silke, and edged with golde', New Years Gift Roll 1579, in Nichols (ed.), *Progresses of Queen Elizabeth*, vol. II, p. 260.
11 See Thomas Cogan, *The Haven of Health: Chiefly Made for the Comfort of Students and Consquently all Those That Have a Care of Their Health* (London, 1565) and William Vaughan, author of *Fifteen Directions to Preserve Health* (London, 1602) – 'Vaughan's water' for the cleaning of teeth was made by boiling together half a glass of vinegar and half a glass of mastic resin with an ounce each of rosemary, myrrh, ammoniac, dragon's herb and rock alum, half an ounce of cinnamon and three glasses of water. Half a pound of honey was added and the mixture was left to cook for a quarter of an hour. The solution was then poured into clean bottles. He also gave four rules for keeping clean, healthy teeth: rinse your mouth after every meal, 'sleep with your mouth somewhat open', expectorate every morning and rub all round the teeth and gums with a linen cloth 'to take away the fumosity of the meat and yellowness of teeth'.
12 Platt, *Delight for Ladies*; G. Hartmann, *The True Preserver* (London, 1682).
13 Williams, *Powder and Paint*, pp. 27–8.
14 *The Queen's Closet Opened* (London, 1696), p. 239.

15 In 1578 Lady Mary Sidney gave 'a pair of perfumed gloves with twenty four small buttons of gold in every of them a small diamond'. New Year Gift roll, 1578. Society of Antiquaries MS 537 printed in Nichols, *Progresses of Queen Elizabeth*, II, p. 72.

16 For the dressing routine of an aristocratic woman of the time see Thomas Tomkis, *Lingua, or The Combat of the Tongues* (London, 1607).

17 It might be that Elizabeth had something akin to drawers later in the reign – there are references to 'six pairs of double linen hose of fine holland cloth' made for her in 1587 but it is not clear if they are drawers or linen hose with a seam up the back of the leg. See Ninya Mikhaila and Jane Malcolm-Davies, *The Tudor Tailor: Reconstructing 16th-century dress* (London, 2006), p. 24 and C. Willett and Phillis Cunnington, *The History of Underclothes* (London, 1951), p. 48.

18 BL Egerton MS 2806, fol. 210.

19 See Nichols (ed.), *Progresses of Queen Elizabeth*, II, p. xlii.

20 TNA LC 5/33 fol. 15; Janet Arnold, 'Sweet England's Jewels', in Anna Somers Cocks (ed.), *Princely Magnificence: Court Jewels of the Renaissance 1500–1630* (London, 1980), pp. 31–40.

21 TNA LC 5/33 fol. 194. Warrant dated 10 February 1566/7 for three 'Burnished' shoe horns.

22 TNA LC 5/33 fol. 144; TNA LC 5/34 fols 81, 169, 308.

23 TNA LC 5/37 fol. 73.

24 John Clapham, *Elizabeth of England*, eds Evelyn Plummer Read and Conyers Read (Philadelphia, 1951), p. 89.

25 *Paul Hentzner's Travels in England during the Reign of Queen Elizabeth*, trans. Richard Bentley, ed. Horace Walpole (London, 1797), pp. 36–7; *Thomas Platter's Travels in England, 1599*, pp. 193–5.

26 John Clapham, *Elizabeth of England*, p. 89.

27 See Janet Arnold, *Queen Elizabeth's Wardrobe Unlock'd* (Leeds, 1988), pp. 139–40.

28 See for example BL Stowe inventory, fols 31/15 and Folger Inventory fol. 6 [21] printed in Arnold, *Queen Elizabeth's Wardrobe Unlock'd*, pp. 263, 340.

29 W. Bailey, *A Briefe Treatise Touching the Preservation of the Eie-sight* (London, 1626), p. 9. See also L. G. H. Horton Smith, *Dr Walter Bailey 1529–1592: Physician to Queen Elizabeth* (St Albans, 1952); William Bullein, *Bulwarke of defence against all Sicknes, Sornes and Woundes* (London, 1562) and *A newe boke of phisicke* (London, 1599). Andrew Boorde, *A Compendious Regiment or a Dyetary of healthe made in Mountpyllier* (London, 1542) and advises similar. See K. H. Dannenfeldt, 'Sleep: Theory and Practice in the Late Renaissance', *The Journal of the History of Medicine and Allied Sciences*, 41, (1986), pp. 415–41.

30 See, for example, Cogan, *The Haven of Health*, pp. 231–9. See also A. R. Ekirch, 'Sleep We Have Lost: Pre-industrial Slumber in the British Isles' in *The American Historical Review* (2001), pp. 343–86 at p. 352.

31 Andrew Boorde, *A Compendious Regiment*, fol. ci, v.

32 BL Harleian MS 6850 fol. 91.

Chapter 5: Womanish Infirmity

1 *CSP Span*, 1558–67, pp. 18, 38.

2 R. A. Vertot and C. Villaret, *Ambassades de Messieurs de Noailles en Angleterre*,

5 vols (Leyden, 1763), III, pp. 86–7.

3 See BL Harleian MS 6986, Art. 12 and F. Chamberlin, *The Private Character of Queen Elizabeth* (London, 1922), pp. 41–9.

4 22 June 1554, Dr Owen to Bedingfeld papers cited in Chamberlin, *Private Character of Queen Elizabeth*, p. 47.

5 See P. Crawford, 'Attitudes to Menstruation in Seventeenth-Century England', *Past and Present*, 91 (1981), pp. 47–73.

6 See Sara Mendleson and Patricia Crawford, *Women in Early Modern England 1550–1720* (Oxford, 1998), pp. 20–5.

7 William Camden, *Annales: The True and Royall History of the famous Empresse Elizabeth* ... (London, 1625), p. 9.

8 Cited in Elizabeth Jenkins, *Elizabeth the Great* (London, 1958), p. 77.

9 *CSP Span*, 1558–67, p. 63.

10 *CSP Ven*, 1558–80, p. 105; R. Bakan, 'Queen Elizabeth I: a case of testicular feminisation?', *Medical Hypotheses*, July 17.3 (1985), pp. 277–84.

11 Chamberlin, *Private Character of Queen Elizabeth*, p. 67.

12 J. M. B. C. Kervyn de Lettenhove, *Relations Politiques des Pays-Bas et de L'Angleterre sous le Regne de Philippe II* (Brussels, 1882–90), I, p. 295, trans. in *CSP Span*, 1558–67, p. 3.

13 Victor Von Klarwill, *Queen Elizabeth and Some Foreigners* (London, 1928), p. 94.

14 William Camden, *Annales*, p. 26.

15 T. E. Hartley (ed.), *Proceedings in the Parliaments of the Reign of Elizabeth I*, 3 vols (Leicester, 1981), I, pp. 44–5.

16 Lettenhove, *Relations Politiques*, I, pp. 398–401, translated in *CSP Span*, 1558–67, pp. 22–3.

17 Quoted in C. Martin and G. Parker, *The Spanish Armada* (London, 1988), p. 281.

18 *CSP Span*, 1558–67, pp. 35, 40.

19 BL Add. MS 48047, fols 97–135 printed in J. Strype, *The Life of the Learned Sir Thomas Smith*, Appendix (Oxford, 1820), pp. 184–259.

20 See Von Klarwill, *Queen Elizabeth*, pp. 52, 53–4, 57, 88, 113.

21 *CSP Span*, 1558–67, pp. 64–78.

22 S. Adams and M. J. Rodriguez-Salgado, 'The Count of Feria's Dispatch to Philip II of 14 November 1558', *Camden Miscellany*, 28, Camden Society, 4th series, vol. 29 (London, 1984), p. 331. For Arundel see BL Royal MS 17 A 19 printed as 'The Life of Henrye Fitzallen', ed. J. G. Nichols, *Gentleman's Magazine*, 103 (1833), pp. 11, 118, 210, 490. This is an anonymous biography written shortly after Arundel's death in 1580.

23 *CSP Span*, 1558–67, p. 19.

24 AGS E 8340/233 fol. 20v. Lettenhove, *Relations Politiques*, I, pp. 273, 279, 566.

Chapter 6: Disreputable Rumours

1 The position was third in rank of major Household officers after Lord Steward and Lord Chamberlain. See M. M. Reese, *The Royal Office of the Master of the Horse* (London, 1976).

2 Bibliothèque Nationale de France, Fonds Français MS 15970, fol. 14.

3 W. K. Jordan (ed.), *Chronicle of Edward VI* (London, 1966), pp. 32–3.

4 BL Cotton Caligula MS E V, fol. 56r; TNA SP 12/1/5.

5 John Bruce, *Correspondence of Robert Dudley, Earl of Leycester: during his Government of the Low Countries, in the years 1585 and 1586* (London, 1844), p. 176.

6 *CSP Span*, 1558–67, pp. 57–8.

7 *CSP Ven*, 1558–80, p. 85.

8 Von Klarwill, *Queen Elizabeth*, pp. 67–71; *CSP Span*, 1558–67, pp. 70–1. See S. Doran, 'Religion and Politics at the Court of Elizabeth I: The Habsburg Marriage Negotiations of 1559–1567', *The English Historical Review* 104 (1989), pp. 908–26.

9 Von Klarwill, *Queen Elizabeth*, p. 78.

10 Ibid., p. 99.

11 'Inquiries to be made by Mundt', 2 June 1559, *CSP Foreign*, 1558–9, pp. 298, 299–300.

12 *CSP Span*, 1558–67, pp. 95–6.

13 *Colección de Documentos Inéditos para la Historia de España*, ed. M. F. Navarete (Madrid, 1842–95), xcviii, p. 89.

14 Von Klarwill, *Queen Elizabeth*, p. 115.

15 Ibid., pp. 113–15.

16 Haynes, *Burghley State Papers*, p. 95.

17 Von Klarwill, *Queen Elizabeth*, pp. 113–15.

18 Ibid., p. 120.

19 Ibid., pp. 120–1.

20 Ibid.

21 TNA SP 31/3/24 fol. 111r.

22 TNA SP 12/6/23 fol. 39r.

23 *CSP Span*, 1558–67, p. 77.

24 See Michael G. Brennan, Noel J. Kinnamon and Margaret P. Hannay, 'Robert Sidney, the Dudleys and Queen Elizabeth', in Carole Levin, Jo Eldridge Carney and Debra Barrett-Graves, eds, *Elizabeth I: Always Her Own Free Woman* (Aldershot, 2003), pp. 20–42.

25 For Mary Sidney's appointment to the Privy Chamber see TNA LC 2/3/4 fol. 53r; TNA LC 2/4/3/104.

26 *CSP Span*, 1558–67, pp. 95–6; BL Add. MS 48023, fol. 352; TNA SP 12/1/1 fol. 5.

27 *CSP Span*, 1558–67, pp. 95–6.

28 Ibid., p. 96.

29 Lettenhove, *Relations Politiques*, II, pp. 9–10, 13, 19–22, 28–9; AGS E 812 fol. 105; *CSP Span*, 1558–67, pp. 95–6; Von Klarwill, *Queen Elizabeth*, pp. 123–6.

30 Von Klarwill, *Queen Elizabeth*, p. 125.

31 *CSP Span*, 1558–67, p. 104.

32 Ibid.

33 Ibid., pp. 101–2.

34 Von Klarwill, *Queen Elizabeth*, p. 151.

35 *CSP Span*, 1558–67, p. 111.

36 Ibid., pp. 104, 115.

37 Ibid., p. 114; Von Klarwill, *Queen Elizabeth*, p. 161.

38 Von Klarwill, *Queen Elizabeth*, p. 161.

39 There is no other identification of Lady Cobham as Mistress of the Robes. *CSP Span*, 1558–67, p. 475.

40 *CSP Span*, 1558–67, p. 115.

41 *Household Accounts and Disbursement Books of Robert Dudley, Earl of Leicester, 1558–1561, 1584–1586*, ed. S. Adams, Camden Society, 5th series, vol. 6 (Cambridge, 1995), p. 151.

42 Von Klarwill, *Queen Elizabeth*, p. 157.

43 *CSP Span*, 1558–67, p. 119.

44 *An anonymous mid-Tudor chronicle*, BL Add. MS 48023, fol. 352. Lettenhove, *Relations Politiques*, II, pp. 123–4.

Chapter 7: Ruin of the Realm

1 P. Forbes (ed.), *A Full View of the Public Transactions in the Reign of Queen Elizabeth* (London, 1740), p. 152.

2 CP 152/94 printed in Haynes, *Burghley State Papers*, p. 233; see Malcolm R. Thorp, 'Catholic Conspiracy in Early Elizabethan Foreign Policy', *The Sixteenth-Century Journal*, vol. 15, no. 4 (1984), pp. 431–48.

3 BL Cotton MS Caligula B X fols 89r–92 as cited in P. Forbes (ed.), *Public Transactions*, p. 391.

4 *CSP Foreign*, 1559–60, pp. 581–2.

5 Haynes, *Burghley State Papers*, I, p. 368.

6 C. C. Jones, *Court Fragments*, 2 vols (London, 1828), vol. II, p. 43.

7 *CSP Span*, 1558–67, pp. 75–6, 83. See Stephen Alford, *The Early Elizabethan Polity: William Cecil and the British Succession Crisis, 1558–1569* (Cambridge, 1998), pp. 53–5; Jane E. A. Dawson, 'William Cecil and the British Dimension of Early Elizabethan Foreign Policy', *History*, 74 (1989), pp. 196–216.

8 BL Cotton MS Titus B II, fol. 419r; *CSP Span*, 1558–67, p. 133.

9 CP 152/127 printed in *HMC Salisbury*, I, p. 257.

10 TNA SP 12/13 fol. 21.

11 TNA SP 12/12/51 fol. 107.

12 *CSP Span*, 1558–67, p. 174.

13 L. Howard (ed.), *A Collection of Letters: from the original manuscripts of many princes, great personages and statesmen* (London, 1753), pp. 210–11; S. Adams (ed.), *Household Accounts of Robert Dudley*, pp. 141–2; TNA SP 70/19 fol. 360.

14 *The Registers of Christenings, Marriages and Burials in the parish of Allhallows, London Wall, Within the City of London, from the year of our Lord 1559 to 1675*, eds Basil Jupp and Robert Hovenden (London, 1878), p. 5.

15 See D. H. Craig, *Sir John Harington* (Boston, 1985); Jason Scott Warren, *Sir John Harington and the Book As Gift* (Oxford, 2001); Ian Grimble, *The Harington Family* (London, 1957), pp. 116–17.

16 For reference to 'boyjacke' see Henry Harington, *Nugae Autiquae: being a miscellaneous collection of papers, written during the reign of Henry VIII, Edward VI, Queen Mary, Elizabeth and King James by Sir John Harington*, 2 vols (London, 1804), II, p. 178.

17 John Harington, *A Tract on the Succession to the Crown*, pp. 40–1.
18 Thomas Wright (ed.), *Queen Elizabeth I and her Times: A Series of Original Letters*, 2 vols (London, 1838), I, pp. 30–2.
19 AGS E814 fol. 24 calendared in *CSP Span*, 1558–67, pp. 174–6, printed in Lettenhove, *Relations Politiques*, II, pp. 529–33.
20 *CSP Span*, 1558–67, p. 175.
21 *CSP Foreign*, 1560–1, p. 385.
22 *CSP Span*, 1558–67, p. 175.
23 AGS E814 fol. 24 printed in Lettenhove, *Relations Politiques*, II, pp. 529–33, and partly calendared in *CSP Span*, 1558–67, pp. 174–6.
24 For a recent discussion of this see Chris Skidmore, *Death and the Virgin. Elizabeth, Dudley and the Mysterious Fate of Amy Robsart* (London, 2010).
25 See *CSP Span*, 1558–67, p. 176.
26 TNA SP 70/22 fol. 43; TNA SP 70/19 fol. 39r.
27 BL Add. MS 48023 printed in 'A Journal of Matters of State Happened from Time to Tme as Well Within and Without the Realme from and Before the Death of King Edw. the 6th Untill the Yere 1562' printed in Ian W. Archer, Simon Adams, G. W. Bernard, Paul E. J. Hammer, Mark Greengrass and Fiona Kisby (eds), *Religion, Politics and Society in Sixteenth Century England* (Cambridge, 2003), pp. 35–112.
28 BL Add. MS 48023, fol. 353v; 'A Journal of Matters of State'.
29 TNA SP 63/2 fol. 82r.
30 See William Vaughan, *Naturall and Artificial Directions for Health* (London 1626), p. 64.
31 See T. Laquer, 'Orgasm, Generation and the Politics of Reproductive Biology', *Representations*, 14 (1986), pp. 1–41. See P. Crawford, 'Sexual Knowledge in England, 1500–1750' in Roy Porter and M. Teich (eds), *Sexual Knowledge, Sexual Science: The History of Attitudes to Sexuality* (Cambridge, 1994), p. 91. On general medical beliefs about the female body in the early modern period, see Ian Maclean, *The Renaissance Notion of Woman* (Cambridge, 1980). See also Peter Stallybrass, 'Patriarchal Territories: The Body Enclosed', in Margaret Ferguson, Maureen Quilligan and Nancy Vickers, eds, *Rewriting the Renaissance: The Discourses of Sexual Difference in Early Modern Europe* (Chicago, 1986), pp. 123–42.
32 See Cogan, *The Haven of Health*, pp. 247–8.
33 F. Chamberlin, *Elizabeth and Leycester* (New York, 1939), p. 93.
34 Philip Yorke, Earl of Hardwicke (ed.), *Miscellaneous State Papers*, from 1501 to 1726, 2 vols (London, 1778), vol. I, pp. 121–3.
35 See David Gaimster, 'London's Tudor Palaces Revisited', *London Archaeologist*, 8, no. 5 (1997), pp. 122–6.
36 BL Add. MS 35830, fol. 66 in P. Forbes, *Public Transactions*, pp. 482–8.
37 Hardwicke (ed.), *Miscellaneous State Papers*, vol. I, p. 167; BL Add. MS 35830, fol. 66.
38 TNA SP 70/21 fol. 137v; *CSP Foreign*, 1560–1, p. 475.
39 BL Cotton MS Nero B III, fol. 155r; *CSP Foreign*, 1560–1, p. 450.
40 *CSP Foreign*, 1560–1, pp. 509–10.
41 *CSP Foreign*, 1561–2, pp. 244, 303–4, 309, 311, 329, 344, 356, 361.

Chapter 8: Carnal Copulation

1 *CSP Span*, 1558–67, p. 313.
2 CP 154/85 printed in Haynes, *Burghley State Papers*, I, p. 420.
3 *CSP Span*, 1558–67, pp. 178–80, and *Colección de Documentos*, vol. 87, pp. 312–16.
4 See Kenneth Bartlett, 'Papal Policy and the English Crown 1563–1565: The Bertano Correspondence', *The Sixteenth Century Journal* 23 (1992), pp. 643–59.
5 *CSP Span*, 1558–67, pp. 178–9.
6 Ibid., p. 194.
7 *An anonymous mid-Tudor chronicle*; BL Add. MS 48023, fol. 353.
8 TNA SP 12/16 fols. 49–50, 59–68.
9 Lettenhove, *Relations Politiques*, II, p. 557. Norman L. Jones, 'Defining Superstitions: Treasonous Catholics and the Act against Witchcraft of 1563', in Charles Carlton et al., eds, *State, Sovereigns and Society in Early Modern England: Essays in Honour of A. J. Slavin* (New York, 1998), pp. 187–203.
10 *CSP Dom Addenda*, 1547–65, pp. 509–10.
11 TNA SP 70/26 fols 61–3.
12 *CSP Foreign*, 1561–2, pp. 93–5, 103–5.
13 AGS E 815 fol. 86 trans. in *CSP Span*, 1558–67, pp. 208–9.
14 *CSP Foreign*, 1561–2, pp. 418–19.
15 *CSP Foreign*, 1560–1, p. 10.
16 W. L. Rutton, 'Lady Katherine Grey and Edward Seymour, Earl of Hertford', *English Historical Review*, vol. 13 (April 1898), pp. 302–7. See also Leanda de Lisle, *The Sisters who would be Queen: The Tragedy of Mary, Katherine and Lady Jane Grey* (London, 2008).
17 BL Add. MS 37749, fols 50–9; BL Add. MS 14291, fol. 157.
18 BL Harleian MS 6286, pp. 35, 53, 70, 77, 81, 89; BL Add. MS 37749, fols 40, 57, 73, 76.
19 BL Add. MS 37749, fol. 59.
20 BL Harleian MS 6286, fol. 37.
21 Lettenhove, *Relations Politiques*, vol. II, p. 608; Wright (ed.), *Queen Elizabeth and her Times*, I, pp. 68–9.
22 Haynes, *Burghley State Papers*, I, pp. 369–70.
23 *CSP Span*, 1558–67, p. 214.
24 François had been succeeded by his brother Charles and his mother Catherine de Medici, the dominating personality in government, now had no interest in the promotion of her widowed daughter-in-law's claims. S. Adams, 'The Lauderdale Papers 1561–70: the Maitland of Lethington State Papers and the Leicester Correspondence', *Scottish Historical Review* 67 (1988), pp. 28–55.
25 *CSP Scot*, 1547–63, p. 559.
26 Ibid., p. 566.
27 *CSP Span*, 1558–67, p. 214.
28 See S. Adams, 'The Lauderdale Papers 1561–1570', pp. 28–55.
29 J. H. Pollen, (ed.) 'Lethington's Account of Negotiations with Elizabeth in September and October 1565', *Scottish History Society*, vol. 43 (1904), pp. 38–45.

30 Pollen (ed.), 'Lethington's Account of Negotiations with Elizabeth', p. 39.
31 *CSP Scot*, 1547–63, p. 559.
32 *Diary of Henry Machyn*, pp. 267–8.
33 Elizabeth drafted letters patent calling for an investigation into the marriage, see TNA SP 12/21/76–7.
34 *CSP Foreign*, 1561–2, p. 330.
35 Ibid., pp. 360–1.
36 *CSP Span*, 1558–67, p. 220.
37 Ibid.

Chapter 9: *Arcana Imperii*

1 Greg Walker, *The Politics of Performance in Early Renaissance Drama* (New York, 1998), p. 203.
2 See Thomas Norton and Thomas Sackville, *Gorboduc or The Tragedy of Ferrex and Porrex* (Menston, 1968); Nichols (ed.), *The Diary of Henry Machyn*, p. 275; see N. Jones and P. W. White, 'Gorboduc and Royal Marriages', in *English Literary Renaissance*, vol. 26 (1971), pp. 3–16. See Henry James and Greg Walker, 'The Politics of Gorboduc', *The English Historical Review* 110 (February, 1995), pp. 109–21.
3 Haynes, *Burghley State Papers*, p. 368.
4 *CSP Foreign*, 1561–2, pp. 122, 129.
5 *Anglia Legaten N. Gyldenstenstiernas Bref. Till Kongl. Maj.* 1561–2, p. 18, cited in Chamberlin, *Private Character of Queen Elizabeth*, p. 264.
6 BL Add. MS 48018, fol. 284v; BL Add. MS 35830, fol. 14v; Haynes, *Burghley State Papers*, pp. 3, 70–2; *CSP Foreign*, 1561–2, pp. 159, 293, 300, 327, and *CSP Span*, 1558–67, pp. 211–215.
7 TNA SP 70/32 fol. 62; TNA SP 70/33 fol. 7v; BL Add. MS 48023, fols 357v–8. BL Add. MS 48018, fol. 284v; BL Add. MS 35830, fol. 14v; *CSP Foreign*, 1561–2, pp. 158–91, 292–3; and *CSP Span*, 1558–67, pp. 211–12, 212–15.
8 BL Add. MS 48023, fol. 258.
9 Ibid., fol. 359v.
10 A. Teulet, *Relations Politiques de la France et de l'Espagne avec l'Ecosse au XVIie Siècle*, 3 vols (Paris, 1862), ii, pp. 175–6; AGS 815, fol. 132, partially trans. in *CSP Span*, 1558–67, p. 233.
11 TNA SP 70/27 fol. 66; *CSP Foreign*, 1561–2, p. 424.
12 *CSP Span*, 1558–67, p. 225.
13 AGS E 815, fols 160, 222, translated in *CSP Span*, 1558–67, p. 241.
14 *CSP Foreign*, 1562, pp. 68, 83 and *CSP Span*, 1558–67, p. 244.
15 *CSP Foreign*, 1562, pp. 68–9.
16 *CSP Span*, 1558–67, p. 244.
17 AGS E 815, fols 183, 218, 224, trans. in *CSP Span*, 1558–67, pp. 234, 241–2, 244–5, 247–9.
18 *CSP Span*, 1558–67, pp. 111–15.
19 *CSP Rome*, 1558–71, p. 105.
20 TNA SP 70/39 fol. 119; *CSP Foreign*, 1562, p. 173; *CSP Span*, 1558–67, pp. 217–24.
21 TNA SP 70/39 fols 118r–119, 175–6; BL Add MS 48023, fol. 366r; *CSP Foreign*, 1562, pp. 216–17.

22 *CSP Foreign*, 1562, pp. 214–17.

23 *APC*, 1558–70, p. 123; Lettenhove, *Relations Politiques*, III, p. 108. The men involved were interrogated, TNA SP 70/40 fols 62–88, fol. 124.

24 *CSP Rome*, 1558–71, p. 105.

Chapter 10: Smallpox

1 See Simon Thurley, *Hampton Court, A Social and Architectural History* (London, 2003).

2 'Diary of the Journey of the Duke of Stettin-Pomerania', pp. 1–67; *Paul Hentzner's Travels in England*, pp. 56–7.

3 *The Diary of Baron Waldstein*, p. 152.

4 *CSP Scot*, 1547–63, pp. 659–60.

5 F. E. Halliday, 'Queen Elizabeth I and Doctor Burcot', *History Today*, 5 (1955), pp. 542–5.

6 *The regiment of life: wherunto is added a treatise of the pestilence, with the boke of children / newly corrected and enlarged by T. Phayre*, ed. and trans. by Jehan Goeurot (London, 1550).

7 *CSP Span*, 1558–67, p. 262.

8 Ibid.

9 Ibid., p. 263.

10 *CSP Span*, 1558–67, p. 263.

11 Ibid., p. 262.

12 The physician John of Gaddesden, author of the earliest English treatise on medicine, the *Rosa Anglica*, had described this treatment in the early fourteenth century. This was to 'let a red cloth be taken, and the patient be wrapped in it completely, as I did with the son of the most noble King of England [Edward II] when he suffered those diseases. I made everything about his bed red, and it is a good cure, and I cured him in the end without marks of smallpox.' John of Gaddesden, *Rosa Anglica*, ed. and trans. Winifred Wulff (London, 1929).

13 Chamberlin, *The Private Character of Queen Elizabeth*, p. 52.

14 TNA SP 12/159 fol. 1, printed in 'Sir Henry Sidney's "Memoir" to Sir Francis Walsingham, 1 March 1583', *Ulster Journal of Archaeology*, 3 (1855), pp. 33–52.

15 See M. Brennan, *The Sidneys of Penshurst and the Monarchy, 1500–1700* (Aldershot, 2006).

16 Quoted in Simon Adams, 'Queen Elizabeth's eyes at Court: the Earl of Leicester', in *Leicester and the Court: Essays on Elizabethan Politics* (Manchester, 2002), p. 137.

17 See Halliday, 'Queen Elizabeth I and Doctor Burcot', p. 545.

18 BL Harleian MS 787, fol. 16.

19 *Elizabeth I: Collected Works*, pp. 139–41.

20 See Edward Hawkins, Augustus W. Franks and Herbert A. Grueber, *Medallic Illustrations of the History of Great Britain and Ireland to the death of George II*, 2 vols (London, 1885), vol. I, p. 116, no. 48. Hawkins dates the medal to 1572. Starkey and Doran in the catalogue date it as 1562, after Elizabeth's first and most significant bout of smallpox, which seems most likely. See Susan Doran (ed.), *Elizabeth: The Exhibition at the National*

Maritime Museum (London, 2003), p. 85; W. K. Clay (ed.), *Liturgies and Occasional Forms of Prayer set forth in the Reign of Queen Elizabeth* (Cambridge, 1847), pp. 516–18.

21 *CSP Span*, 1558–67, pp. 262–3; F. Chamberlin, *The Sayings of Elizabeth* (New York, 1923), pp. 52, 54.

22 TNA C 47/3/38.

23 P. Croft and K. Hearn, 'Only Matrimony maketh children to be certain ... Two Elizabethan pregnancy portraits', *British Art Journal* 3 (2002), pp. 18–24.

24 TNA C 47/3/38.

25 See E. K. Chambers, *The Elizabethan Stage*, 4 vols (Oxford, 1923), vol. I, p. 19.

26 Janet Arnold, *Lost from Her Majesties Back*, Costume Society Extra Series 7 (Wisbech, 1980), p. 36; John Stowe, *Three fifteenth-century chronicles: with historical memoranda by John Stowe, the antiquary, and contemporary notes of occurrences written by him in the reign of Queen Elizabeth*, ed. James Gairdner, Camden Society, third series, (London, 1880), pp. 123–5.

27 Stowe, *Three fifteenth-century chronicles*, p. 127.

28 BL Add. MS 48023, fol. 369.

29 Stowe, *Three fifteenth-century chronicles*, pp. 123–5.

Chapter 11: Devouring Lions

1 Pole had been in the Fleet in April 1561 for being connected to Sir Edward Waldegrave and Sir Thomas Wharton and Hastings. He had not remained in the Fleet for very long and soon began plotting again.

2 Arthur Pole had a claim to the throne as a direct descendant of Edward IV's brother the Duke of Guise. Fortescue was a distant relative of the Queen through her mother's side. Whilst initially the men had plotted to promote Arthur's claim to the throne, their plan changed to support Mary Stuart. TNA KB 8/40; *CSP Span*, 1558–62, p. 262.

3 'Special oyer and terminal roll and file Principal Defendants and Charges: Arthur Pole and others, high treason, conspiring to depose the Queen and to proclaim Mary Queen of Scots,' TNA KB 8/40, BL Hardwicke papers 35831, fol. 87.

4 F. Chamberlin, *The Private Character of Queen Elizabeth*, p. 51; Kristen Post Walton, 'The Plot of the Devouring Lions: The "Divelish Conspiracy" of Arthur Pole and the Parliament of 1563' (unpublished essay); TNA KB 8/40; *CSP Span*, 1558–62, pp. 292–3.

5 *CSP Foreign*, 1563, p. 32.

6 F. Chamberlin, *The Private Character of Queen Elizabeth*, p. 51; TNA KB 8/40; *CSP Span*, 1558–67, pp. 259–60.

7 TNA KB 8/40.

8 J. H. M. Salmon, *Society in Crisis: France in the Sixteenth Century* (New York, 1975); Nicola M. Sutherland, *The Massacre of St Bartholomew and the European Conflict, 1559–1572* (London, 1973); Nicola M. Sutherland, *The Huguenot Struggle for Recognition* (New Haven, Conn., 1980).

9 W. T. MacCaffrey, 'The Newhaven expedition, 1562–1563', *Historical Journal*, 40 (1997), pp. 1–2.

10 Wright (ed.), *Queen Elizabeth and her Times*, vol. I, p. 127.

11 AGS E 816, fol. 43, trans. in *CSP Span*, 1558–67, p. 269.

12 BL Cotton MS Titus F I, fol. 59.

13 Ibid., fols 59–60v, 65–75v.

14 Ibid., fols 61–4, printed in G. E. Corrie (ed.), *A Catechism by Alexander Nowell*, Parker Society (Cambridge, 1853), pp. 223–9.

15 BL Harleian MS 5176, fols 89–92; Hartley (ed.), *Proceedings in the Parliaments*, vol. I, p. 84. See J. E. Neale, 'Parliament and the Succession Question in 1562/3 and 1566', *English Historical Review*, Jan–Oct (1921), pp. 497–519, and Mortimer Levine, 'A "Letter" on the Elizabethan Succession Question, 1566', *The Huntington Library Quarterly*, 19 (1995), pp. 13–38.

16 Wright (ed.), *Queen Elizabeth and her Times*, I, p. 121.

17 TNA SP 12/28 fols 68r–69v. *CSP Span*, 1558–67, pp. 316–17.

18 *Nugae Antiquae*, III, pp. 186–7.

19 TNA SP 12/27/35; Hartley (ed.), *Proceedings in the Parliaments*, I, pp. 90–3.

20 TNA SP 12/27/36; Hartley (ed.), *Proceedings in the Parliaments*, I, pp. 94–5.

21 TNA SP 12/27/85 for clerk's copy with marginal notes by Cecil. See also BL Add. MS 32379.

22 BL Add. MS 32379, fols 17–20.

23 *CSP Span*, 1558–67, pp. 295–8.

24 5 Eliz I c.1 *Statutes* IV, pp. 402–5.

25 *CSP Span*, 1558–67, p. 322; John Bruce and T. T. Perowne, eds, *Correspondence of Matthew Parker, Archbishop of Canterbury 1535–1575*, Parker Society (Cambridge, 1853), pp. 173–5.

26 See Kristen Post Walton, *Catholic Queen, Protestant Patriarchy. Mary Queen of Scots and the Politics of Gender and Religion* (Basingstoke, 2007), p. 51; 'Sir William Cecil to Sir Thomas Smith, 27 February 1563', in Wright (ed.), *Queen Elizabeth and her Times*, vol. 1, p. 127; TNA KB8/40; Kristen Post Walton, 'The Plot of the Devouring Lions'.

27 5 Eliz I c.16 in *Statutes* IV, pp. 446–7.

28 5 Eliz I c.15 in *Statutes* IV, pp. 445–6.

29 Nichols (ed.), *Diary of Henry Machyn*, p. 300.

30 J. H. Baker (ed.), *Reports from the Lost Notebooks of Sir James Dyer*, 2 vols (London, 1994), vol. I, pp. 81–2; BLO Tanner MS 84, fols 191, 196v.

31 *CSP Rome*, 1558–71, p. 51; BL Add. MS 35830, fol. 185; Levine, *The Early Elizabethan Succession Question*, p. 14; TNA SP 12/21 fols 76–7.

32 *CSP Scot*, 1547–63, p. 684.

33 *CSP Span*, 1558–67, p. 314.

34 *CSP Foreign*, 1563, p. 154. *CSP Scot*, 1547–63, pp. 684–6.

35 BL Harleian MS 5176 fol. 97; Neale, *Elizabeth I and her Parliaments*, I, pp. 126–7.

36 *CSP Foreign*, 1563, pp. 439, 443, 453, 473; BL Add. MS 35831, fols 145v–146; TNA SP 70/59/846 fol. 48v.

37 Stowe, *Three fifteenth-century chronicles*, p. 122; Nichols (ed.), *The Diary of Henry Machyn*, p. 310.

38 *CSP Span*, 1558–67, p. 346.

39 Stowe, *Three fifteenth-century chronicles*, p. 127.

Chapter 12: Ménage à Trois

1 *CSP Scot*, 1547–1563, p. 666.
2 BL Lansdowne MS 102, fol. 18r; TNA SP 52/8 nos. 3, 6, 7, 9, 10.
3 *CSP Span*, 1558–67, p. 338.
4 BL Cotton MS Julius F VI, fol. 125 and *CSP Foreign*, 1563, p. 510.
5 *CSP Scot*, 1563–9, pp. 27, 31–3.
6 *CSP Span*, 1558–67, p. 313.
7 *CSP Scot*, 1563–9, pp. 56–7; pp. 19–20.
8 Ibid., pp. 43–4, 56–7.
9 Ibid., p. 44.
10 BL Cotton Ms Julius F VI, fol. 126.
11 See Kimberly Schutte, *A Biography of Margaret Douglas, Countess of Lennox* (New York, 2002); Caroline Bingham, *Darnley: a life of Henry Stuart, Lord Darnley, Consort of Mary Queen of Scots* (London, 1995).
12 *CSP Foreign*, 1562, pp. 14, 23.
13 *CSP Span*, 1558–67, p.176; *CSP Foreign*, 1562, pp. 12–15; see Simon Adams, 'The Release of Lord Darnley and the Failure of the Amity', in *Mary Stewart: Queen in Three Kingdoms*, ed. Michael Lynch (Oxford, 1988), pp. 123–53.
14 *CSP Foreign*, 1563, pp. 463–4.
15 *CSP Span*, 1558–67, p. 339.
16 G. Donaldson (ed.), *The Memoirs of Sir James Melville of Halhill* (London, 1969), p. 36.

Chapter 13: Visitor to the Bedchamber

1 Quoted in Roy C. Strong, *Holbein and Henry VIII* (London, 1967), p. 35.
2 *Memoirs of Melville*, p. 36.
3 'Diary of the Journey of the Duke of Stettin-Pomerania', p. 25; Von Klarwill, *Queen Elizabeth*, p. 320.
4 *Memoirs of Melville*, p. 37.
5 Ibid.
6 See Garrett, *The Marian Exiles: A study in the origins of Elizabethan Puritanism* (Cambridge, 1938), pp. 295–6.
7 André Hurault, Sieur de Maisse, *A Journal of All that was Accomplished by Monsieur de Maisse, Ambassador in England from King Henri IV to Queen Elizabeth Anno Domini 1597*, trans. and ed. G. B. Harrison and R. A. Jones (London, 1931), p. 95; Von Klarwill, *Queen Elizabeth*, pp. 228, 96.
8 *CSP Span*, 1558–67, p. 382.
9 *Memoirs of Melville*, p. 36.
10 *CSP Span*, 1558–67, p. 313; *Memoirs of Melville*, p. 35.
11 BL Lansdowne MS 102, fols 107r–109r.
12 *CSP Scot*, 1563–9, p. 81.
13 *CSP Span*, 1558–67, p. 424.
14 *Memoirs of Melville*, p. 40.
15 Ibid., p. 42.
16 TNA SP 52/9 no. 48.

Chapter 14: Sour and Noisome

1 *CSP Span*, 1558–67, p. 401; Ian Dunlop, *Palaces & Progresses of Elizabeth I* (London, 1962).
2 *CSP Span*, 1558–67, p. 398.
3 BL Lansdowne MS 102, fol. 105r; Wright (ed.), *Queen Elizabeth and her Times*, I, p. 181.
4 *CSP Scot*, 1563–9, p. 110.
5 Ibid., p. 111.
6 BL Lansdowne MS 102, fols 107r–109r.
7 See Brennan, *The Sidneys of Penshurst and the Monarchy*, p. 43.
8 See Leslie Gerard Matthews, *The Royal Apothecaries* (London, 1967), p. 71.
9 TNA LC 5/33 fols 15, 50, 51, 71, 91 and 118.
10 Ibid., fols 71, 91.
11 Ibid., fols 15, 71, 108.
12 Ibid., fol. 50.
13 Ibid., fol. 51.
14 BL Egerton MS 2806, fol. 74 v.
15 John Harington, *Epigrams*, I, p. 44.
16 TNA E351/451 fol.38; TNA LC 5/33 fol. 128.
17 *CSP Span*, 1558–67, p. 401.
18 Stowe, *Three fifteenth-century chronicles*, pp. 131–2.
19 *Memoirs of Melville*, p. 42.
20 Ibid., p. 45.
21 *CSP Foreign*, 1564–5, p. 331.
22 NLS Advocates MS 1.2.2.
23 BL Add. MS 19401 fol. 101.
24 *CSP Span*, 1558–67, p. 432.
25 TNA SP 56/1 fols 95r–101r.
26 TNA SP 52/10 fol. 128r.

Chapter 15: Untouched and Unimpaired

1 *CSP Span*, 1558–67, p. 404; see Susan Doran, 'Juno versus Diana: The Treatment of Elizabeth I's marriage in plays and entertainments', *The Historical Journal*, 28 (1995), pp. 257–74.
2 *CSP Span*, 1558–67, pp. 409–10.
3 Ibid., p. 514.
4 Lettenhove, *Relations Politiques*, ii, p. 55.
5 Haynes, *Burghley State Papers*, p. 430; AGS E 653 fol. 23; Von Klarwill, *Queen Elizabeth*, pp. 203–4.
6 Von Klarwill, *Queen Elizabeth*, pp. 206–7.
7 'Report of the French envoy in England to Catherine de Medici', December 1564, HMC *Third Report*, pp. 262–3; Catherine also proposed that Mary marry Charles's brother and heir, Henry, Duke of Anjou.
8 TNA SP 70/77/915 fols 128v–129.
9 TNA SP 31/3/26 fol. 32.
10 Von Klarwill, *Queen Elizabeth*, p. 233.
11 *CSP Foreign*, 1564–5, p. 321; TNA 31/3/26 fol. 1; Von Klarwill, *Queen Elizabeth*, p. 224.

12 Bertrand de Salignac, Seigneur de La Mothe Fénélon, *Correspondance Diplomatique*, ed. A. Teulet, 7 vols (Paris, 1838–40), vol. II, pp. 117–19.

13 'Summary of the advice given by the Privy Council', 4 June 1565, TNA SP 52/10 fols 148–51.

14 Von Klarwill, *Queen Elizabeth*, pp. 208–9.

15 Ibid., pp. 208–10, 225.

16 Ibid.

17 Ibid., p. 217.

18 Ibid., p. 229.

19 *CSP Scot*, 1563–9, p. 140; TNA SP 52/10 fol. 68r.

20 Fénélon, *Correspondance Diplomatique* II, p. 120.

21 *CSP Span*, 1558–67, p. 518.

Chapter 16: Greatly Grieved

1 TNA SP 31/3/25 fols 200–1.

2 *CSP Span*, 1558–67, pp. 386–7.

3 Ibid., p. 446; Adams (ed.), *Dudley Household Accounts*, p. 478.

4 Von Klarwill, *Queen Elizabeth*, p. 247

5 *CSP Span*, 1558–67, p. 455.

6 *CSP Foreign*, 1566–8, p. 130.

7 TNA 70/39/110; BL Add. MS 48,023, fols 352, 353v, 366.

8 Rowland Vaughan, *His Booke – Most Approved and Long experienced water workes containing the manner of winter and summer drowning of Meadow and Pasture . . .* (London, 1610).

9 TNA LC/4/4/3 fol. 53v; BL Lansdowne MS 4, no. 88, fol. 191.

10 She was first to go to Dover to greet Princess Cecilia of Sweden, TNA SP 12/37, no. 28, fols 58–59v.

11 Folger Library, Talbot MS X.d. 428 (16).

12 Ibid.

13 G. C. Williamson, *Lady Anne Clifford, Countess of Dorset, Pembroke and Montgomery, 1590–1676: Her Life, Letters and Work* (Wakefield, 1967), p. 37.

14 Tighe and Davis, *Annals of Windsor*, p. 639. In 1577 the wall was heightened 'to prevent persons in the dean's orchard seeing into the Queen's walk', *Annals of Windsor*, I, p. 641.

15 *CSP Span*, 1558–67, p. 466.

16 Von Klarwill, *Queen Elizabeth*, pp. 218, 255; J. H. Pollen, 'Papal Negotiations with Mary Queen of Scots during her reign in Scotland 1561–1567', *Scottish Historical Society*, 37 (1901), p. 469. See Wright (ed.), *Queen Elizabeth and her Times*, I, p. 207.

17 *CSP Span*, 1558–67, p. 465.

18 Ibid.

19 Edmund Lodge, *Illustrations of British history, biography and manners, in the reign of Henry VIII, Edward VI, Mary, Elizabeth and James I*, 3 vols (London 1838), II, p. 98.

20 TNA SP 52/19 fol. 180r.

21 *CSP Span*, 1558–67, p. 492; Mortimer Levine, *The Elizabethan Succession Question*, p. 165.

22 TNA SP 52/1 no. 26.
23 'Carte's History of England, books xviii–xx, 1558–1612', BLO Carte MS 188, 385.
24 TNA SP 52/10 fol. 150v.
25 Frank A. Mumby, *Elizabeth and Mary Stuart* (London, 1914), p. 264, n2; Wright (ed.), *Queen Elizabeth and her Times*, I, p. 126.
26 *CSP Foreign*, 1563, pp. 384–7; BL Cotton MS Caligula B X, fols 299–308.

Chapter 17: Suspicious Mind

1 Ellis (ed.), *Original Letters*, vol. II, p. 299.
2 Ibid.
3 *CSP Span*, 1558–67, p. 468.
4 *CSP Dom* 1547–80, p. 277.
5 Wright (ed.), *Queen Elizabeth and her Times*, I, pp. 206–7.
6 *CSP Span*, 1558–67, p. 454.
7 Ibid., p. 505.
8 Ibid., p. 470.
9 CP 140/1; printed in Murdin, *Burghley's State Papers* (London, 1759), p. 760.
10 Printed in *Elizabeth: Collected Works*, p. 132; *CSP Span*, 1558–67, p. 472.
11 *CSP Span*, 1558–67, p. 492.
12 Ibid., pp. 436–7.
13 TNA SP 31/3/26 fol. 102.
14 *CSP Ven*, 1558–80, pp. 374–5.
15 *CSP Span*, 1558–67, p. 530.
16 Quoted in Milton Waldman, *Elizabeth and Leicester* (London, 1944), p. 130.
17 Wright (ed.), *Queen Elizabeth and her Times*, I, p. 225.
18 *CSP Span*, 1558–67, p. 529.
19 *CSP Dom Addenda*, 1566–79, XIII, p.8.
20 Ibid.
21 Ibid., p. 3.

Chapter 18: The Elixir of Life

1 TNA SP 12/36 fol. 24r. He had written to Cecil offering to make alchemical gold in December 1564, TNA SP 70/78 fols 188r–189r. *CSP Dom*, 1547–80, pp. 249, 256, 273, 275–7, 289, 292; *CSP Dom Addenda*, 1566–79, p. 10; *CSP Foreign*, 1564–5, p. 267.
2 *CSP Foreign*, 1564–5, p. 267; TNA SP 12/36/13.
3 Margaret Morison, 'A Narrative of the Journey of Cecilia, Princess of Sweden, to the Court of Queen Elizabeth', *TRHS*, n.s., 12 (1898), pp. 181–224, at pp. 213–14; CP 154/136 printed in *HMC Salisbury*, I, p. 331; CP154/146 printed in *HMC Salisbury*, I, p. 332.
4 TNA SP 15/20/89; Peter Razell, ed., *The Journals of Two Travellers in Elizabethan and Early Stuart England, Thomas Platter and Horatio Busino* (London, 1995), p. 25.

5 Jane A. Lawson, 'This Remembrance of the New Year: Books Given to Queen Elizabeth as New Year's Gifts', in Peter Beal and Grace Ippolo, eds, *Elizabeth I and the Culture of Writing* (London, 2007), pp. 133–72, pp. 151–2.

6 TNA C66/973; TNA C66/970; TNA C54/1763; BLO Ashmole MS 1447, pt VII, p. 30; BLO Ashmole 1402, pt II, fols 1–18.

7 Jayne Archer, '"Rudenesse itselfe she doth refine": Queen Elizabeth as Lady Alchymia', in A. Connolly and L. Hopkins, eds, *Goddesses and Queens: The Iconography of Queen Elizabeth I* (Manchester, 2008), pp. 45–66, 51.

8 See Deborah E. Harkness, *The Jewel House: Elizabethan London and the Scientific Revolution* (New Haven, Conn.,2007); Frank Sherwood Taylor, *The Alchemists* (St Albans, 1976).

9 TNA SP 12/36 fols 24r–24v.

10 TNA SP 12/37 fol. 6r.

11 BL Lansdowne MS 703, fols 48r–49v. Alan Pritchard, 'Thomas Charnock's Book Dedicated to Queen Elizabeth', *Ambix*, 26 (1979), pp. 56–73.

12 BL Lansdowne MS 703, fols 6v–11v. See Jonathan Hughes, 'The Humanity of Thomas Carnock, an Elizabethan Alchemist' in Stanton J. Linden (ed.), *Mystical Metal of Gold: Essays on Alchemy and Renaissance Culture* (New York, 2007), pp. 3–34.

13 BL Lansdowne MS 703, fols 8r, 9v, 39r.

14 TNA SP 70/80/123 fols 11, 52.

15 TNA SP 12/37 fols 6r–6v.

16 'A Narrative of the Journey of Cecilia, Princess of Sweden, to the Court of Queen Elizabeth', pp. 181–214; CP 154/105; CP 154/129; J. Bell, *Queen Elizabeth and a Swedish Princess Being an Account of the Visit of Princess Cecilia of Sweden to England in 1565* (London, 1926), pp. 15–23.

17 *CSP Span*, 1558–67, p. 475.

18 Nathan Martin, 'Princess Cecilia's Visitation to England, 1565–1566' in Charles Beem (ed.), *The Foreign Relations of Elizabeth I* (Basingstoke, 2011), pp. 27–44.

19 CP 154/146 printed in *HMC Salisbury*, I, pp. 332–3.

20 CP 154/112 printed in *HMC Salisbury*, I, p. 327.

21 TNA SP 12/39/39.

22 *CSP Span*, 1558–67, I, p. 546.

23 TNA SP 12/39/88.

24 TNA SP 12/37/3A; TNA SP 12/39/39. Lannoy's treatises and copies of letters to Elizabeth appear in contemporary alchemical collections, such as BL Sloane 3654, fols 4r–6v; 1744, fols 4r–8v;

25 TNA SP 12/40/32.

26 TNA SP 15/13, fols 36r–37v; TNA SP 12/40/321. BL Lansdowne MS 9, fols 191r–192v, TNA SP 12/42/30.

27 TNA SP 12/40/53.

28 TNA SP 12/42/30.

29 Murdin, *Burghley's State Papers*, p. 763. De Lannoy was kept in the Tower at least until 1571. Longleat House MS DU/I, fol. 209r, Petition of Barbara de Lannoy after February 1571. Last reference to Lannoy in state

papers relates to a command to report to court, TNA SP 12/42/70 (28 May 1567).

30 *Cabala, Sive Scrinia Sacra* (London, 1691), p. 139.

Chapter 19: Barren Stock

1 *CSP Span*, 1558–67, p. 512.
2 Ibid., pp. 516, 518–20.
3 Ibid., p. 526.
4 Patrick Fraser Tytler, *History of Scotland*, 9 vols (Edinburgh, 1828–43), VII, p. 23.
5 See John Guy, *'My Heart is my Own': The Life of Mary Queen of Scots* (London, 2004), p. 11.
6 *CSP Span*, 1558–67, p. 534.
7 Ibid., p. 540.
8 Ibid., p. 621.
9 *Memoir of Melville*, p. 54.
10 TNA SP 15/13/73; *CSP Dom Addenda*, 1566–79, pp. 28–9.
11 Milton Waldman, *Elizabeth and Leicester* (London, 1947), p. 123.
12 CP 148/12 printed in *HMC Salisbury*, II, p. 240.
13 TNA SP 63/18 fol. 62 r–v.
14 *Memoir of Melville*, p. 56.
15 Ibid.
16 Neale, *Elizabeth I and her Parliaments*, vol. I, pp. 129–64.
17 TNA SP 12/40 fol. 195.
18 See William Camden, *Annales*, p. 129.
19 Neale, *Elizabeth I and her Parliaments*, vol. I, p. 136.
20 *Elizabeth I: Collected Works*, p. 95; Simonds D'Ewes, *The journals of all the parliaments during the reign of Queen Elizabeth both of the House of Lords and House of Commons* (London, 1682), p. 12.
21 *CSP Span*, 1558–67, pp. 591–2.
22 Ibid., p. 592.
23 Ibid., p. 599.
24 TNA SP 12/41/5 fragment of queen's draft printed in Hartley (ed.), *Proceedings in the Parliaments*, p. 147.
25 TNA SP 70/95 fol. 161.
26 *Elizabeth I: Collected Works*, p. 116.
27 *CSP Span*, 1558–67, p. 623.
28 *CSP Foreign*, 1566–8, p. 232.
29 TNA SP 52/14.

Chapter 20: Wicked Intentions

1 BL Cotton MS Titus, no. 107, fols 124, 131.
2 TNA SP 12/46 fols 1, 28.
3 *CSP Span*, 1558–67, p. 4; W. M. Schutte, 'Thomas Churchyard's "Doleful Discourse" and the Death of Lady Katherine Grey', *Sixteenth-Century Journal* 15 (1984), pp. 471–87.
4 *CSP Scot*, 1563–9, pp. 416–17.
5 *CSP Span*, 1568–79, p. 36.

6 See P. J. Holmes, 'Mary Stewart in England', pp. 195–218.
7 TNA SP 70/133 fol. 185.
8 Ibid.
9 Frederich von Raumer, *Contributions to Modern History from the British Museum and the State Paper Office* (London, 1836), p. 178.
10 'Papers relating to Mary Queen of Scots, mostly addressed to or written by Sir Francis Knollys', *Philobiblon Society Miscellanies*, 14 (1872), pp. 14–69.
11 Ibid.
12 *CSP Scot*, 1563–9, pp. 606, 612. Sally Varlow, 'Sir Francis Knollys's Latin dictionary: new evidence for Catherine Carey', *BIHR* 80, 209 (2007), p. 322.
13 'Papers relating to Mary Queen of Scots', p. 65; her memorial plaque credits her with sixteen children, eight male and eight female, and this may be because of two stillbirths or cot deaths that are otherwise not recorded.
14 Haynes, *Burghley State Papers*, p. 509.
15 Fénélon, *Correspondance Diplomatique*, vol. I, p. 124.
16 Ibid., and Wright, ed., *Queen Elizabeth and her Times*, I, p. 308.
17 CP 198/124.
18 Thomas Newton, 'An epitaph upon the worthy and honourable lady, the Lady Knowles' (1569); Haynes, *Burghley State Papers*, pp. 509–10.
19 CP 4/9 printed in *HMC Salisbury*, I, p. 402.
20 TNA C/115/L2/6697 in Janet Arnold, *'Lost from Her Majesties Back'*, pp. 40, 41, 58, 104.
21 *The House of Commons, 1558–1603*, ed. P. Hasler, 3 vols (London, 1981), vol. II, pp. 416, 417.
22 *CSP Dom Addenda*, 1566–79, XVII, 198.

Chapter 21: Secret Enemies

1 TNA SP 70/102 fol. 30v.
2 TNA SP 12/8/61 fol. 165r.
3 Strype, *Annals of the Reformation*, I, pp. 580–1.
4 *CSP Span*, 1568–79, pp. 96–7.
5 Ibid., p. 97.
6 Ibid., p. 180.
7 Murdin, *Burghley's State Papers*, p. 180.
8 TNA SP 12/81/57.
9 CP 159/46 in *HMC Salisbury*, II, p. 25.
10 TNA SP 15/15 no. 29 (i). See K. J. Kesselring, *The Northern Rebellion of 1569: Faith, Politics and Protest in Elizabethan England* (Basingstoke, 2007); R. Pollitt, 'The Defeat of the Northern Rebellion and the Shaping of Anglo–Scottish Relations', *Scottish Historical Review*, 64 (1985), pp. 1–21.
11 TNA SP 15/15, no. 29(i).
12 TNA SP 12/59, no. 65.
13 Printed in *The Tudor Constitution*, ed. G. R. Elton (Cambridge, 1982); see P. McGrath, *Papists and Puritans under Elizabeth I* (London, 1967), p. 68.

Chapter 22: Want of Posterity

1 Fénélon, *Correspondance Diplomatique*, III, p. 454.
2 *The Egerton Papers*, ed. J. Payne Collier (London, 1840), p. 52.

3   Fénélon, *Correspondance Diplomatique*, III, p. 418.
4   See Katherine B. Crawford, 'Love, Sodomy and Scandal: Controlling the Sexual Reputation of Henry III', *Journal of the History of Sexuality*, 12 (2003), pp. 513–42.
5   *Lettres de Catherine de Médicis*, eds Hector de la Ferrière-Percy and Comte Baugyenault de Puchesse, 10 vols (Paris, 1880–1909), IV, pp. 26–7.
6   Fénélon, *Correspondance Diplomatique*, II, pp. 178, 179.
7   Sir Dudley Digges, *The Compleat Ambassador* (London, 1655), p. 195.
8   Fénélon, *Correspondance Diplomatique*, VII, p. 180.
9   Fénélon, *Correspondance Diplomatique*, IV, pp. 64, 85.
10 Ibid., p. 21.
11 Digges, *Compleat Ambassador*, pp. 43, 70–1.
12 Ibid., p. 96.
13 Secret memorial of M. de Vassal in Fénélon, *Correspondance Diplomatique*, III, pp. 462–9.
14 Fénélon, *Correspondance Diplomatique*, IV, pp. 186, 187.
15 Ibid.
16 *CSP Foreign*, 1572–4, pp. 3, 8–9.

Chapter 23: Compass her Death

1   *The Zurich Letters*, ed. Robinson, 2 vols (Cambridge, 1847), I, pp. 245–54.
2   M. A. R. Graves, 'Thomas Norton, the Parliament Man', *Historical Journal* 23, 1 (1980), pp. 17–35.
3   13 Eliz c.1, *Statutes* IV, pp. 526–21.
4   13 Eliz c.1 and 2, *Statutes* IV, pp. 526–31; Patrick McGrath, *Papists and Puritans*, pp. 174–5; Neale, *Elizabeth I and her Parliaments*, I, pp. 218–34.
5   23 Eliz c.2, *Statutes* IV, pp. 659–60.
6   See Geoffrey Parker, 'The Place of Tudor England in the Messianic Vision of Philip II of Spain', *TRHS*, sixth series 12 (2002), pp. 167–221.
7   TNA SP 12/84 fols 35v–36r.
8   TNA SP 12/84 fol. 35r.
9   Robyn Adams, 'The Service I am Here For: William Herle in the Marshalsea Prison, 1571', *Huntington Library Quarterly* 72 (2009), 217–38. On Spanish involvement in the Ridolfi plot see Francis Edwards, *Plots and Plotters in the Reign of Elizabeth I* (Dublin, 2002), pp. 29–73 and Geoffrey Parker, *The Grand Strategy of Philip II* (London, 2000), pp. 160–4.
10 See Conyers Read, *Lord Burghley and Queen Elizabeth* (London, 1960), p. 40.
11 TNA SP 12/80/117; Read, *Lord Burghley and Queen Elizabeth*, pp. 38–41.
12 T. B. Howell, *A Complete Collection of State Trials and Proceedings for High Treason*, 21 vols (London, 1816–26), I, p. 968.
13 TNA SP 70/122 fol. 153r.
14 CP 7/7 in Murdin, *Burghley's State Papers*, II, p. 185.
15 Digges, *Compleat Ambassador*, pp. 165–6.
16 BL Cotton MS Caligula C 2, fols 86r–v.
17 TNA SP 15/20 fol. 155v.
18 Lettenhove, *Relations Politiques*, vol. VI, p. 189.
19 Paget Papers, X, art. 10. Some rumours lingered. In 1575 Lady Cobham was

accused by Thomas Cockyn, a stationer, implicated in the Ridolfi plot, as a 'favourer' of the Scottish queen. TNA SP 53/10/11, 45, 61. The extent of any involvement with Mary is unclear. There seems to have been an examination of the accusation made by Cockyn against Lady Cobham, but nothing more seems to have been revealed, and Elizabeth continued to trust her and give her lavish New Year gifts. See David McKeen, *A Memory of Honour: The Life of William Brooke, Lord Cobham*, 2 vols (1986), I, pp. 318–22.

Chapter 24: Beside her Bed

1 Fénélon, *Correspondance Diplomatique*, IV, pp. 410–11.
2 Digges, *Compleat Ambassador*, p. 198; Fénélon, *Correspondance Diplomatique*, IV, pp. 411, 412.
3 John Strype, *The Life of the Learned Sir Thomas Smith*, p. 114.
4 TNA SP 15/21 fol. 58.
5 Neale, *Elizabeth I and her Parliaments*, I, p. 244.
6 Ibid., pp. 262–90.
7 Ibid., pp. 310–11.
8 Digges, *Compleat Ambassador*, p. 219.
9 See Neville Williams, *A Tudor Tragedy: Thomas Howard, Fourth Duke of Norfolk* (London, 1964).
10 Digges, *Compleat Ambassador*, p. 167.
11 *CSP Foreign*, 1572–4, p. 12; TNA SP 70/122 fols 37–41, 50, 211. See Digges, *Compleat Ambassador*, p. 195.
12 Digges, *Compleat Ambassador*, pp. 226–8.
13 BL Cotton Vespasian F 6, fol. 7r.
14 Fénélon, *Correspondance Diplomatique*, IV, pp. 438–9.
15 'Instructions for Walsingham', 20 July 1572; TNA SP 70/124 fol. 99.
16 Digges, *Compleat Ambassador*, pp. 226–8.
17 Ibid., pp. 226–30; BL Harleian MS 260, fols 277–8.
18 *Lettrès de Catherine de Medicis*, IV, p. 111–2.
19 See A. G. Dickens, 'The Elizabethans and St Bartholomew', in A. Soman (ed.), *The Massacre of St Bartholomew: reappraisals and documents* (The Hague, 1974), pp. 52–70.
20 Nichols (ed.), *Progresses of Queen Elizabeth*, I, p. 321; *CSP Span*, 1568–79, p. 410.
21 *CSP Dom*, 1547–80, pp. 450–3. *CSP Span*, 1568–79, pp. 411–12.
22 Lodge (ed.), *Illustrations of British History*, I, p. 547.
23 Fénélon, *Correspondance Diplomatique*, V, pp. 123–8.
24 Wright (ed.), *Queen Elizabeth and her Times*, I, pp. 438–9.
25 Ellis (ed.), *Original Letters*, III, p. 25.
26 C. Read, *Mr Secretary Walsingham and Queen Elizabeth*, 3 vols (London, 1955), I, p. 239.
27 BL Add. MS 48049, fols 340r–357v, draft copy, and BL Cotton MS Titus F III, fols 302r–308v is Beale's fair copy.
28 BL Cotton MS Titus F, III, fols 302r–308v.
29 *CSP Span*, 1568–79, p. 408.
30 Wright (ed.), *Queen Elizabeth and her Times*, I, p. 444–55.
31 Lodge (ed.), *Illustrations of British History*, I, pp. 550–1.

32 *CSP Span*, 1568–79, p. 429.
33 TNA SP 12/89 fol. 1572.
34 LPL MS 3197 fols 41–3, printed in *Elizabeth I, Collected Works*, pp. 212–14.
35 *A fourme of common prayer to be vsed, and so commaunded by auctoritie of the Queenes Maiestie, and necessarie for the present tyme and state* (London, 1572), B2v–B3v.

Chapter 25: Lewd Fantasy

1 CP 5/90. CP 5/62 printed in Haynes, *Burghley State Papers*, pp. 203–4, 208.
2 BL Lansdowne MS XV art. 43 in *Correspondence of Matthew Parker*, pp. 400–1.
3 *Correspondence of Matthew Parker*, p. 401.
4 See Eric St John Brooks, *Sir Christopher Hatton: Queen Elizabeth's Favourite* (London, 1946).
5 BL Harleian MS 787, fol. 88.
6 Sir Harris Nicolas, *Memoirs of the Life and Times of Sir Christopher Hatton* (London, 1847), pp. 23–4.
7 Ibid., pp. 25–6.
8 Ibid., pp. 26, 155.
9 Ibid., p. 17.
10 LPL, MS 3197, fol. 79.
11 Gervase Holles, 'Memorials of the Holles Family, 1493–1663', ed. A. C. Wood, Camden Society, 3rd series, 55 (London, 1937), p. 70.
12 LPL, MS 3197, fol. 79.
13 'A letter from Robert, Earl of Leicester, to a lady', ed. C. Read, *Huntington Library Bulletin*, 9 (1936), pp. 23–5.
14 CKS, U, 1475/L 2/3 items 12–13.

Chapter 26: Blows and Evil Words

1 TNA C115/M15/7341. BL Lansdowne MS 59, no. 22, fol. 43; see W. J. Tighe, 'Country into Court, Court into Country: John Scudamore of Holme Lacy (*c*. 1542–1623) and His Circles', in Dale Hoak (ed.), *Tudor Political Culture* (Cambridge, 1995), pp. 157–78.
2 TNA E351/1795. She was now granted an improved annuity of £33 6s. 8d. She became the only lady of Elizabeth's Privy Chamber to have left more than a few bits of correspondence, due largely to the survival of the great collection of Scudamore letters and papers in the National Archives.
3 Queen Elizabeth and Mary Shelton were both great-granddaughters of Sir William Boleyn of Blickling, Norfolk, which made them second cousins.
4 BL Egerton MS 2806, fol. 49. Warrant 28 September 1572; *HMC Rutland*, I, p. 107; BL Add. MS 11049, fol. 2. Brydges says the court is 'full of malice and spite'.
5 TNA C 115/L2/6697, p. 47.
6 TNA C 115/M19/7543. This is 9 October 1576.
7 CKS, document dated July 1573.
8 *CSP Dom*, 1547–80, p. 442.
9 *CSP Ireland*, 1509–85, p. 160. TNA SP 63/36 art. 14.
10 BL Add. MS 15914, fol. 12.

11 BL Cotton MS Titus B, ii, fol. 302.
12 In 1561 Sussex had sought the Lord Presidency of Wales for himself and the appointment of Sir Henry Sidney, partly through Leicester's influence, very much still rankled. BL Cotton MS Vespasian F, xii, fol. 179a.
13 BL Cotton MS Vespasian F, xii, fols 179–81; TNA SP 70/19.360; BL Cotton MS Titus B, ii, 152.
14 TNA SP 12, Warrant book, I; 83; TNA SP 40/1/83.

Chapter 27: Kenilworth

1 George Gascoigne, *Princely Pleasures at Kenilworth Castle* (London, 1576) printed in Nichols (ed.), *Progresses of Queen Elizabeth*, I, p. 492.
2 Ibid., pp. 426–522.
3 *CSP Span*, 1568–79, p. 498.
4 *Robert Laneham's Letter: Describing a Part of the Entertainment unto Queen Elizabeth at the Castle of Kenilworth in 1575*, ed. F. J. Furnivall (New York, 1907).
5 Gascoigne, *Princely Pleasures at Kenilworth Castle*, pp. 426–522.
6 Carole Levin, "'Would I Could Give You Help and Succour': Elizabeth I and the Politics of Touch', *Albion* 21 (1989), pp. 191–205; Marc Bloch, *The Royal Touch: Sacred Monarchy and Scrofula in England and France*, trans. J. E. Anderson (London, 1973); Raymond Crawfurd, *The King's Evil* (Oxford, 1911). The practice had been adopted by kings in England and France since the medieval period. Edward the Confessor was said to have been the first English king to heal scrofula by touch. See Reginald Scot, *The Discoverie of Witchcraft* (London, 1584), pp. 303–4.
7 William Tooker, *Charisma sive Donum Sanationis* (London, 1597), pp. 99–100.
8 See Janice Delaney, Mary Jane Lupton and Emily Toth, *The Curse: A Cultural History of Menstruation* (Chicago, 1988), p. 42 and Audrey Eccles, *Obstetrics and Gynaecology in Tudor and Stuart England* (London, 1982), pp. 49–51.
9 J. Andreas Löwe, 'Tooker, William (1553/4–1621)', *ODNB*, 2004.
10 *A Right Fruitful and Approved Treatise for the Artificial Cure of that Malady Called in Latin Stuma* (London, 1602). See F. N. L. Poynter (ed.), *Selected Writings of William Clowes* (London, 1948), pp. 9–38.
11 Tooker, *Charisma*, pp. 90–2.
12 *CSP Ven*, 1592–1603, p. 238; Tooker, *Charisma*, pp. 94, 100.
13 See Susan Frye, *Elizabeth I: The Competition for Representation* (Oxford, 1993), pp. 70–2.
14 *CSP Span*, 1558–67, pp. 404–5.
15 See Nichols (ed.), *Progresses of Queen Elizabeth*, vol. I, pp. 521–2.

Chapter 28: Badness of Belief

1 John Bossy, *The English Catholic Community 1570–1850* (London, 1975); Patrick McGrath, 'Elizabethan Catholicism: A Reconsideration', *Journal of Ecclesiastical History*, 35 (1984), pp. 414–28. Peter Lake and Michael Questier, 'Prisons, Priests and People in Post-Reformation England', in Nicholas Tyacke (ed.), *England's Long Reformation 1500–1800* (London, 1998), pp. 195–223.

2 C. Haigh, 'The continuity of Catholicism in the English reformation', in C. Haigh (ed.), *The English Reformation Revised* (Cambridge, 1987), pp. 178–208; P. McGrath and J. Rowe, 'The Marian priests under Elizabeth I', *Recusant History*, 17 (1984), pp. 103–120.

3 TNA SP 12/118 fol. 105.

4 Zillah Dovey, *An Elizabethan Progress: The Queen's Journey into East Anglia, 1578* (Stroud, 1996), pp. 27–38. See Nichols (ed.) *Progresses of Queen Elizabeth*, II, pp. 5–15.

5 Lodge (ed.), *Illustrations of British History*, II, p. 187–91; Dovey, *An Elizabethan Progress*, pp. 53–6.

6 Lodge (ed.) *Illustrations of British History*, II, p. 187; P. Collinson, 'Pulling the Strings: Religion and Politics in the Progress of 1578', in Jayne Elizabeth Archer, Elizabeth Goldring and Sarah Knight, eds, *The Progresses, Pageants and Entertainments of Queen Elizabeth* (Oxford, 2007), pp. 122–41.

7 Ibid.

8 Nichols (ed.), *Progresses of Queen Elizabeth*, II, pp. 215–19.

9 Lodge (ed.), *Illustrations of British History*, II, pp. 187–91.

10 Dovey, *An Elizabethan Progress*, pp. 63–87.

11 *CSP Span*, 1568–79, p. 611, n. 524; G. L. Kittredge, *Witchcraft in Old and New England* (Harvard, 1929), pp. 87–8; C. F. Smith, *John Dee* (London, 1909), pp. 19–20; *APC*, 1577–8, p. 309. The sensational scandal featured in numerous contemporary publications, including Jean Bodin's *De la demonomanie des sorciers* (Paris, 1587), sigs. i2r, Kk1v–2r.

12 *APC*, 1577–8, p. 309.

13 *CSP Span*, 1568–79, p. 611; *APC*, X, p. 309.

14 'The Compendious Rehearsal of John Dee', pp. 521–2.

15 *APC*, 1578–80, p. 22; BL Cotton MS Vitellius C, VIII, fol. 7v.

16 *CSP Span*, 1568–79, p. 611; 'The Compendious Rehearsal of John Dee', pp. 521–2; see e.g. BL Sloane MS 3846, fols 95r, 98r for spells defending against witchcraft. *APC*, 1578–80, p. 22; BL Cotton MS Vitellius C, VII, fol. 7v.

17 *APC*, 1577–8, pp. 308–9.

18 TNA SP 12/140 fol. 78v. Collinson, 'Pulling the Strings', p. 141.

19 TNA SP 12/131 fol. 144; Richard Verstegan, *The Copy of a Letter Sent from an English Gentleman, lately Become a Catholike beyond the Seas, to His Protestant Friend in England* (Antwerp, 1589), p. 7. TNA SP 12/131/43.

20 *APC*, 1577–8, p. 328.

21 *CSP Ven*, 1558–80, pp. 509–10. *CSP Foreign*, 1572–4, p. 493.

22 TNA SP 12/126/7; BL Lansdowne MS 25, fols 146r–147r; TNA SP 12/178/74; TNA SP 12/195/32.

23 Verstegan, *The Copy of a Letter*, p. 7; *A Transcript of the Registers of the Company of Stationers of London, 1554–1640 A.D.*, ed. Edward Arber, 5 vols (London, 1875–94), II, pp. 339–40.

24 *APC*, 1578–80, p. 22.

25 Ibid., pp. 36–7.

26 TNA SP 12/276/102; TNA SP 23/186/91, 92. Verstegan, *The Copy of a Letter*, p. 7.

27 TNA SP 12/131 fol. 144r; *APC*, 1578–80, pp. 102–3, p. 212.

28 Verstegan, *The Copy of a Letter*, p. 7; TNA SP 12/276/102, misdated 1600 in the *CSP Domestic* but clearly connected to 1578; J. A. Bossy, 'English Catholics and the French Marriage, 1577–81', *Recusant History* 5 (1959), pp. 2–16; and Thomas M. McCoog, 'The English Jesuit Mission and the French Match, 1579–81', *The Catholic Historical Review*, 87 (2007), pp. 185–213; TNA SP 12/186/91, 92.

29 Jean Bodin, *De la Demonomanie des Sorciers* (Anvers, 1580), sigs. E4v, Gg1r.

30 Longleat House, Dudley MS 3, fol. 61 r.

31 Nichols (ed.), *Progresses of Queen Elizabeth*, II. p. 252.

Chapter 29: Toothache

1 *Memoirs of Sir Christopher Hatton*, pp. 91–4. TNA SP 12/126/10.

2 Edward Fenton (ed.), *The Diaries of John Dee* (Oxford, 1988), pp. 4, 17; 'The Compendious Rehearsal of John Dee', p. 578.

3 *Memoirs of Sir Christopher Hatton*, pp. 93–4.

4 *CSP Span*, 1572–4, p. 493.

5 TNA SP 12/126/10.

6 Fenton (ed.), *Diaries of John Dee*, pp. 4, 18.

7 'The Compendious Rehearsal of John Dee', ii, p. 522.

8 BLO Ashmole MS 487; BL Cotton MS Vitellius C. VII, fol. 7v; *CSP Foreign*, 1572–4, p. 493; BL Lansdowne MS 27, fols 90r–91v, Dr Antonio Fenot's advice; BLO Ashmole MS 1447, pt. VII, p. 48.

9 BL Lansdowne MS 102, no. 94.

10 John Strype, *Historical Collections of the Life and Acts of the right Reverend Father in God John Aylmer, Lord Bishop of London* (Oxford, 1821), pp. 192–3.

11 Ibid., p. 193.

12 Ibid.

13 Nichols (ed.), *Progresses of Queen Elizabeth*, vol. II, p. 262.

14 Ibid., p. 255.

15 BL Cotton MS Vespasian F xii, fol. 179; *CSP Span*, 1568–79, pp. 681–2.

16 Collins (ed.), *Letters and Memorials of State*, I, p. 272; De l'Isle MS U1475 c7/7.

17 *CSP Span*, 1568–79, II, p. 682.

18 BL Lansdowne MS 29, fol. 161.

19 See Arnold, '*Lost from Her Majesties Back*', p. 63.

20 'The Compendious Rehearsal of John Dee', pp. 508, 510, 515, 522–3.

Chapter 30: Amorous Potions

1 *Lettrès de Catherine de Medicis*, VI, p. 14.

2 Lettenhove, *Relations Politiques*, X, pp. 662–3.

3 Ibid., pp. 774–5.

4 CP 148/12

5 BL Harleian MS, 1582, fols 46–52.

6 CP 148/25 printed in *HMC Salisbury*, II, p. 238.

7 *Elizabeth I: Collected Works*, p.157; CP 148/32.

8 TNA SP 83/7/73.

9 Lettenhove, *Relations Politiques*, X, pp. 536–5; IX, pp. 304–5.

10 *CSP Ven*, 1558–80, p. 628.

11 TNA 31/3/27 fols 217–19.

12 Lettenhove, *Relations Politiques*, X, pp. 799–801.

13 Thomas Churchyard, *A discourse of the queens maiesties entertainment in Suffolk and Norfolk* (London, 1578), quoted in Nichols (ed.), *Progresses of Queen Elizabeth*, II, pp. 222–3. David M. Bergeron, 'The "I" of the Beholder: Thomas Churchyard and the 1578 Norwich Pageant', in Jayne Elizabeth Archer, Elizabeth Goldring and Sarah Knight (eds), *The Progresses, Pageants and Entertainment of Queen Elizabeth I*, pp. 142–62.

14 *CSP Span*, 1568–79, p. 627.

15 TNA 31/3/27 fols 259–60, 282; *CSP Span*, 1568–79, p. 655; Lodge (ed.), *Illustrations of British History*, II, p. 141.

16 William Camden, *Annales*, p. 1579; see D. C. Peck (ed.), *Leicester's Commonwealth: The copy of a letter written by a Master of Arts of Cambridge (1584) and related documents* (Ohio, 1985), p. 18.

17 Letter from Mauvissiere dated 7 September 1579, quoted in Read, *Mr Secretary Walsingham*, II, p. 19; TNA Baschet Transcripts.

18 *CSP Foreign*, 1578–9, p. 487.

19 *Lettrès de Catherine de Medicis*, VI, p. 112.

20 See *Colección de Documentos*, p. 359, trans. in *CSP Span*, 1568–79, pp. 658–9.

21 Lodge (ed.), *Illustrations of British History*, II, pp. 149–50.

22 *CSP Span*, 1568–79, p. 629.

23 CP 148/27; see *HMC Salisbury*, II, pp. 238–245, 250–2.

24 See S. Doran, *Monarchy and Matrimony*, p. 160.

25 Victor von Klarwill, *The Fugger News Letters* (London, 1926), p. 28; Nichols (ed.), *Progresses of Queen Elizabeth*, II, pp. 285–6. The ballad was written celebrating both Elizabeth's courage in the face of danger and her mercy in pardoning the barge man. *The Harleian Miscellany*, eds Thomas Park and William Oldys (London, 1808–13), X, pp. 272–3.

26 *CSP Span*, 1568–79, p. 681.

27 D. C. Peck (ed.), *Leicester's Commonwealth*, p. 92.

28 TNA SP 12/151/48, articles 6 and 7.

29 *CSP Span*, 1568–79, pp. 681–2.

30 A. Labanoff, *Lettrès, Instructions et Mémoires de Marie Stuart, Reine d'Ecosse*, 5 vols (Paris, 1844–54), V, pp. 94–5.

Chapter 31: Froggie Went A-Courtin'

1 J. M. B. C. Kervyn de Lettenhove, *Les Huguenots et Les Gueux*, 6 vols (Bruges, 1883–5), V, pp. 390–1; *TRP* III, pp. 141–2.

2 *CSP Foreign*, 1579–80, pp. 45, 48; *CSP Span*, 1568–79, p. 688; I. Cloulas, *Correspondance du Nonce en France, Anselmo Dandino (1578–1581)*, Acta Nuntiaturae Gallicae, vol. VIII (Paris, 1970), pp. 465, 469, 472; G. Canestrini and A. Desjardins, *Négociations Diplomatiques de la France avec la Toscane*, 5 vols (Paris, 1865–75), IV, pp. 260, 261, 265; *CSP Ven*, 1558–80, pp. 667–8.

3 *Elizabeth I: The Collected Works*, pp. 243–4.

4 See Arnold, *Queen Elizabeth's Wardrobe Unlock'd*, pp. 75–6.

5 TNA 31/3/27 fol. 397; John Stubbs, *The discoverie of a gaping gulf whereinto England is like to be swallowed by an other French marriage* (London, 1579), sigs D8v–E6v, printed in Lloyd E. Berry (ed.), *John Stubbs's 'Gaping Gulf' with*

Letters and other Relevant Documents (Charlottesville, Virginia, 1968). See Ilona Bell, '"Soueraigne Lord of lordly Lady of this land": Elizabeth, Stubbs and the Gaping Gulf' in Julia M. Walker (ed.), *Dissing Elizabeth. Negative Representations of Gloriana* (Durham, NJ and London, 1998), pp. 99–117.

6 Berry (ed.), *Gaping Gulf*, p. 3.

7 Ibid., p. 68.

8 Ibid., p. 72.

9 *TRP* II pp. 445–9; Berry (ed.), *Gaping Gulf*, pp. 3–97. See also Natalie Mears, 'Counsel, Public Debate and Queenship; John Stubbs's *The Discoverie of a Gaping Gulf*, 1579', *The Historical Journal*, 44, 3 (2001), pp. 629–50.

10 See K. Barnes, 'John Stubbs, 1579: The French Ambassador's Account', *BIHR* 64 (1991), pp. 421–6.

11 *CSP Ven*, 1558–80, p. 623.

12 The letter is printed in Katherine Duncan-Jones and Jan van Dorsten (eds), *Miscellaneous Prose of Sir Philip Sidney* (Oxford, 1973), pp. 33–7. In a letter to Hubert Languet on 22 October 1580, Sidney explained that he had been carrying out the intentions of others in writing the piece. S. A. Pears (ed.), *The Correspondence of Sir Philip Sidney and Hubert Languet* (London, 1845), p. 187.

13 CP 149/47 printed in *HMC Salisbury*, II, p. 265.

14 *CSP Ven*, 1558–80, p. 621.

15 TNA SP 78/3 fols 133–6.

16 Ibid., fol. 145.

17 Dudley Papers, III, fol. 43052.

18 *Lettrès de Catherine de Medicis*, VII, p. 261.

19 Wright (ed.), *Queen Elizabeth and her Times*, II, pp. 107–9.

20 Ibid., pp. 106–9.

21 Bibliothèque Nationale de Paris, Fonds Français MS 3307, fol. 16.

22 Frederick A. Youngs, *The Proclamations of the Tudor Queens* (Cambridge, 1976), p. 208.

23 *A Briefe Declaration of the Shews, Devices, Speeches and Inventions, Done & Performed before the Queenes Majestie & the French Ambassadours, at the Most Valiaunt and Worthye Triumph, Attempted and Executed on the Munday and Tuesday in Whitson Weeke Last, Anno 1581 Collected, Gathered, Penned & Published by Henry Goldwel, Gen* (London, 1581).

24 TNA SP 78/5, no. 62.

25 *CSP Span*, 1580–6, p. 348.

26 Raumer, *Contributions to Modern History*, pp. 226–7.

27 M. A. S. Hume, *The Courtships of Queen Elizabeth* (London, 1904), pp. 211–12.

28 From a letter from Francis Anthony of Sousa to Diego Botelho in Antwerp in *CSP Foreign*, 1581–2, pp. 473–4.

29 *CSP Span*, 1568–79, p. 226–7. The Venetian ambassador in France repeated information provided by a servant of Anjou, 14 December 1581, Bibliothèque Nationale Italien MS 1732, fol. 230.

30 Ibid.

31 Canestrini and Desjardins, *Négociations Diplomatiques*, IV, p. 412.

32 Colección de Documentos, xcii, pp. 193–4, trans. in *CSP Span*, 1580–6, p. 229.

33 BL Harleian MS 6992, fol. 114r.

34 William Camden, *Annales*, III, p. 12.
35 Bibliothèque Nationale Italien MS 1732, fols 231–2.
36 Ibid.
37 See J. A. Froude, *History of England from the fall of Wolsey to the defeat of the Spanish Armada*, 12 vols (London, 1893), vol. II, p. 476.
38 See Nichols (ed.), *Progresses of Queen Elizabeth*, II, p. 346.
39 BL Cotton MS Galba E VI, fol. 155, printed in *Elizabeth I: Collected Works*, pp. 260–1.
40 TNA SP 78/10/79; see also *CSP Foreign*, 1583–4, pp. 218, 344.
41 See the OED 'Sir-reverence', sense 2, 'Human excrement'. The earliest printed occurrence cited in OED is from Robert Greene, Ned Browne (1592); 'His face ... and his Necke, were all besmeared with the soft sirreverence, so as he stunck.'
42 *CSP Foreign*, 1583–4, p. 344.
43 See *The Letters and Despatches of Richard Verstegan (c. 1550–1640)*, ed. A. G. Petti (London, 1959).

Chapter 32: *Semper Eadem*

1 Roy Strong, *Gloriana: The Portraits of Queen Elizabeth I* (London, 1987), pp. 98–9; see Susan Doran, 'Virginity, Divinity and Power: The Portraits of Elizabeth I' in Susan Doran and Thomas Freeman (eds), *The Myth of Elizabeth* (Basingstoke, 2003), pp. 171–199; A. and C. Belsey, 'Icons of Divinity: Portraits of Elizabeth I' in *Renaissance Bodies: The human figure in English culture c.1540–1600*, ed. Lucy Gent and Nigel Llewellyn (London, 1990), pp. 15–16; John N. King, 'Queen Elizabeth I: Representations of the Virgin Queen', *Renaissance Quarterly* 43 (1990), pp. 30–74. See also Roy Strong, *The English Icon: Elizabethan and Jacobean Portraiture* (London, 1969); Roy Strong, *Portraits of Queen Elizabeth I* (Oxford, 1963).
2 Printed in *Elizabeth I: Collected Works*, p. 194.
3 See *The Secretes of the Reverende Maister Alexis of Piemount* (London, 1558) for examples of popular Renaissance cosmetic recipes and ingredients.
4 Philip Stubbes, *The Anatomies of Abuses* (London, 1583), p. 37. See also Laurie A. Finke, 'Painting Women: Images of Femininity in Jacobean Tragedy', *Theatre Journal*, 36 (1984), pp. 357–70.
5 Thomas Drant, *Two Sermons preached ... the other at the Court of Windsor the Sonday after twelfth day being the viij of January, before in the yeare 1569* (London, 1570), sig. 15v.
6 Drant, *Sermons*, sig. 12v.
7 Father Rivers, 'Letter of 13 January 1601', in Henry Foley, *Records of the English Province of the Society of Jesus: historic facts illustrative of the labours and sufferings of its members in the sixteenth and seventeenth centuries*, 7 vols (London, 1877), vol. I, pp. 8, 24.
8 See Arnold, *Queen Elizabeth's Wardrobe Unlock'd*, p. 23; Strong, *Gloriana*, p. 80.

Chapter 33: The Die is Cast

1 See Alan Haynes, 'The English Earthquake of 1580', *History Today* (1979), pp. 542–4.

2 P. Lake and M. Questier, 'Puritans, Papists and the "public sphere" in early modern England: the Campion affair in context', *Journal of Modern History*, lxxii (2000), pp. 587–627.

3 *The great bragge and challenge of M. Champion a Jesuite, commonlye called Edmunde Campion, lately arrived in Englande, contayninge nyne articles here severallye laide downe, directed by him to the Lordes of the Counsail* (London, 1581).

4 *TRP* II: 481–4.

5 Neale, *Elizabeth and her Parliaments*, I, pp. 383–4.

6 Printed in Hartley (ed.), *Proceedings in the Parliaments*, I, p. 504. BL Sloane MS 326, fols 19–29.

7 23 Eliz. c.1, *Statutes* IV, 657–8.

8 TNA SP 83/29; 148/10.

9 23 Eliz c.2, *Statutes* IV, 659.

10 George Eliot, *A very true report of the apprehension and taking of that Arche Papist Edmund Campion the Pope his right hand, with three other lewd Jesuite priests, and divers other Laie people, most seditious persons of like sort* (London, 1581).

11 *APC*, 1581–2, pp. 144–5; Christopher Barker, *A particular declaration or testimony, of the undutiful and traitorous affection borne against her Majestie by Edmond Campion Jesuite, and other condemned Priestes, witnessed by their owne confessions* (London, 1582), sigs, B1r-b4v. See also Brian Harrison (ed.), *A Tudor Journal: the Diary of a Priest in the Tower 1580–1585* (London, 2000); Howell, *State trials*, I, pp. 1049–72; William Allen, *A Briefe Historie of the Glorious Matyrdom of XII Reverent Priests* (Rheims, 1582).

12 Thomas Alfield, *A true reporte of the death & martyrdome of M. Campion Jesuite and preiste, & M. Sherwin, & M. Bryan preistes, at Tiborne the first of December 1581* (1582).

13 Harrison (ed.), *A Tudor Journal*, pp. 208–9. For George Eliot's submission to the Earl of Leicester see BL Lansdowne MS 33, fols 145r–149r.

14 George Eliot, *A very true report of the apprehension and taking of that Arche Papist, Edmund Campion, the Pope his right hand with three other Jesuit priests and divers other Laie people, most seditious persons of like sort* (London, 1581).

15 *APC*, 1581–2, p. 407.

16 Thomas Day, *Wonderfvll Strange Sightes* (London, 1583), sig. A2r.

17 H. Howard, *A Defensative against the Poison of Supposed Prophecies* (London, 1583).

Chapter 34: The Enemy Sleeps Not

1 TNA SP 12/163/23.

2 *CSP Span*, 1580–6, p. 512, 651–2. For Somerville and his plot: TNA SP 12/163/21–22, TNA SP 12/163/26, TNA SP 12/163/28 and TNA SP/163/4. BL Harleian MS 6035, fols 32–5. *CSP Dom*, 1581–90, pp. 128–30, 182. A foreign visitor to London in 1592 counted thirty-four of them, another in 1598 more than thirty.

3 *A Discoverie of the Treasons Practised and Attempted against the Queene's Majestie and the Realme by Francis Throckmorton* (London, 1584), reprinted in *The Harleian Miscellany* (London, 1808–13), III, pp. 190–200.

4 BL Lansdowne MS 39, fol. 193r.

5 'A Discoverie of the Treasons Practised and Attempted' in *The Harleian*

Miscellany, pp. 190–200; John Bossy, *Under the Molehill: An Elizabethan Spy Story* (New Haven and London, 2001), pp. 31–3, 84–6.

6 BL Stowe MS 1083, fol. 17.

7 Raumer, *Contributions*, pp. 256–7.

8 BL Cotton MS Caligula C viii, fols 204–6. No address or endorsement but identified as William Herle by John Bossy, *Giordano Bruno and the Embassy Affair* (New Haven and London, 1991), p. 206.

9 *CSP Span*, 1580–6, p. 514; see D. L. Jensen, *Diplomacy and Dogmatism: Bernardino de Mendoza and the French Catholic League* (London, 1964), pp. 59–64.

10 *CSP Span*, 1580–6, p. 513; Mendoza informed Philip on 26 January 1584 of Elizabeth's desire that he leave the country. See *CSP Span*, 1580–6, pp. 515–16.

11 *CSP Foreign*, 1583–4, pp. 652–3.

12 *CSP Foreign*, 1577–8, pp. 140–1.

Chapter 35: In Defence of the Queen's Body

1 *HMC Salisbury*, III, pp. 44–5.

2 TNA SP 12/173/81–3.

3 BL Harleian MS 1582, fol. 390–1; trans. in Bossy, *Bruno Affair*, pp. 217–18.

4 TNA SP 12/173/104.

5 TNA SP 12/174/10.

6 See David Cressy, 'Binding the Nation: The Bonds of Association, 1584 and 1596', in D. J. Guth and J. W. McKenna (eds), *Tudor Rule and Revolution* (Cambridge, 1982), pp. 217–34; Patrick Collinson, 'The Elizabethan Exclusion Crisis and the Elizabethan Polity', *Proceedings of the British Academy*, 84 (1994), pp. 51–92; and 'The Monarchical Republic of Queen Elizabeth I' in *Elizabethan Essays* (London, 1994).

7 TNA SP 12/174, no. 10. See Cressy, 'Binding the Nation', pp. 217–26.

8 TNA SP 12/173/88.

9 See Cressy, 'Binding the Nation', pp. 217–34.

10 *Elizabeth I: Collected works*, p. 195.

11 BL Lansdowne MS 41, fol. 45.

12 BL Sloane MS 326, fol. 71.

13 27 Eliz I, c.1, *Statutes* IV, pp. 704–5.

14 See Collinson, *Elizabethan Essays*, pp. 48–55 and Collinson, 'The Elizabethan Exclusion Crisis and the Elizabethan Polity', pp. 51–92.

15 BL, Lansdowne MS 39, fol. 128r.

16 27 Eliz I c.2, *Statutes* IV, pp. 706–8.

17 See Neale, *Elizabeth I and her Parliaments*, II, pp. 13–101.

18 Hartley (ed.), *Proceedings in Parliament*, II, pp. 158–60.

Chapter 36: Agent Provocateur?

1 BL Lansdowne MS 39, fol. 128r–129r.

2 BL Lansdowne MS 96, fol. 48r, which is printed in Christopher Barker, *A True and plaine declaration of the horrible Treasons practised by William Parry the Traitor against the Queenes Majestie. The manner of his Arraignment, Conviction and execution, together with the copies of sundry letters of his and others, tending to divers purposes, for the proofes of his Treasons* (London, 1585), sigs D2r-v.

3 TNA SP 12/176/154–60; Clapham, *Elizabeth of England*, p. 88.
4 TNA SP 12/176/47; TNA SP 12/176/48; TNA SP 12/176/52.
5 'Journey of Von Wedel', pp. 223–270 at p. 267.
6 TNA SP 12/177/1; TNA SP 12/177/4.
7 Barker, *A True and plaine declaration of the horrible Treasons practised by William Parry*, sig. Eiv.
8 BL Lansdowne MS 43, fols 117*v*–118*r*.
9 Barker, *A True and plaine declaration of the horrible Treasons practised by William Parry*, sig. Eiv.
10 TNA SP 12/177/1.
11 *An order of Praier and Thankes-giving, for the preseruation of the Queenes Majesties life and safetie . . . With a short extract of William Parries voluntarie confession, written with his own hand* (London, 1585).
12 See Leo Hicks, 'The Strange Case of Dr William Parry', *Studies* (1948), pp. 343–62. Hicks argues that the plot lacked papal approval and was actually a government plot to discredit the Catholics and justify renewed persecution.
13 TNA SP 12/179/26.

Chapter 37: Unseemly Familiarities

1 BL Cotton MS Titus B VII, fol. 10.
2 *CSP Foreign*, 1584–5, p. 716; Peck (ed.), *Leicester's Commonwealth*, pp. 5–13.
3 Ibid., p. 125.
4 Peck (ed.), *Leicester's Commonwealth*. See also Frank J. Burgoyne (ed.), *History of Queen Elizabeth, Amy Robsart and the Earl of Leicester* (London, 1904), p. 49.
5 Peck (ed.), *Leicester's Commonwealth*, p. 86.
6 Ibid., pp. 85, 92. See D. C. Peck, 'Government suppression of Elizabethan Catholic books: the case of *Leicester's Commonwealth*', *Huntington Library Quarterly*, xlvii (1997), pp. 163–77.
7 P. Holmes, *Resistance and Compromise: the Political Thought of the Elizabethan Catholics* (Cambridge, 1982); P. Holmes, 'The authorship of *Leicester's Commonwealth*', *Journal of Ecclesiastical History*, xxxiii (1982), pp. 424–30; P. Lake, 'From Leicester his Commonwealth to Sejanus his fall: Ben Jonson and the politics of Roman (Catholic) virtue', in Ethan Shagan, *Catholics and the 'Protestant Nation': Religious Politics and Identity in Early Modern England* (Manchester, 2005), pp. 128–61.
8 Ibid.
9 *TRP*, II, pp. 506–8.
10 Harington, *A Tract on the Succession to the Crown*, p. 44.
11 G. Adlard, *Amye Robsart and the Earl of Leycester* (London, 1870), pp. 56–7; Dudley Papers, III, fol. 209.
12 Murdin (ed.), *Burghley's State Papers*, pp. 436–7.
13 TNA SP 78/13/86.
14 *CSP Foreign*, 1584–5, p. 400.
15 TNA SP 78/13/86.
16 TNA SP 78/15/2.
17 *CSP Foreign*, 1584–5, p. 19.
18 Peck (ed.), 'The Letter of Estate', p. 23.

19 Ibid., p. 20.
20 Ibid., pp. 29–30.
21 Ibid., p. 30.
22 Ibid.
23 Dudley Papers, III, fol. 209.
24 CP 133/68 printed in Murdin (ed.), *Burghley's State Papers*, p. 559.
25 It has been suggested that the congenital defect to which contemporaries referred was 'testicular feminisation syndrome' which made her sterile. See R. Bakan, 'Queen Elizabeth I: A case of testicular feminisation', *Medical Hypotheses* 1985, July 17(3), pp. 277–84.
26 CP 133/68.

Chapter 38: Especial Favour

1 'Journey of Von Wedel', pp. 262–5.
2 Ibid.
3 *Calendar of the Carew manuscripts preserved in the Archepiscopal Library at Lambeth*, 6 vols (London, 1867–73), II, pp. 235–7.
4 Longleat House, Thynne Papers, vol. V, 1574–1603, fol. 254.
5 'Journey of Von Wedel', pp. 262–5.
6 TNA SP 12/182/41.
7 Haynes, *Burghley State Papers*, p. x.
8 M. Waldman, *Elizabeth and Leicester* (London, 1946), p. 185.
9 *CSP Dom*, I, viii, p. 403.
10 Bruce, *Correspondence of Robert Dudley*, pp. 112, 144.

Chapter 39: The Deed shall be Done

1 For Savage's oath see in T. B. Howell, *State Trials*, 1, pp. 129–31. Read, *Mr Secretary Walsingham*, III, pp. 18–22.
2 Alexandre Teulet, *Relations Politiques de la France et de l'Espagne avec l'Ecosse au XVIe siècle*, vols 1–3 (Paris, 1862), p. 348; *CSP Span*, 1580–6, pp. 603–8.
3 Howell, *State Trials*, vol. I, pp. 1, 139.
4 *CSP Span*, 1580–6, p. 588; Thomas Morgan writing from Paris a week later (9 July) described something similar: 'That Queen (Elizabeth) going of late to her Churche, was in the Way sodanelye stricken with some great Fear, that she returned to her Chamber, to the Admiration of all that were present,' Murdin, *Burghley's State Papers*, p. 529.
5 TNA SP 53/19/12; CP 15/59, list of papers relevant to Babington's conspiracy.
6 Printed in Pollen, 'Papal Negotiations with Mary Queen of Scots', pp. 38–45.
7 TNA SP 53/18/61.
8 TNA SP 53/18/55.
9 TNA SP 12/250/61.
10 *TRP* II, 525–6.
11 TNA SP 53/19/38.
12 TNA SP 53/19/24.
13 See Pollen, 'Papal Negotiations with Mary Queen of Scots', pp. clxx-clxxiii.

14 Thomas Deloney, *A Most Joyfull Songe Made in the Behalfe Of All Her Maiesties Faithfull and Loving Subiects Of the Great Joy Which Was Made in London At the Taking Of the Late Trayterous Conspirators* (London, 1586).

15 *The True Copie of a Letter from the Queenes Maiestie, to the Lord Maior of London, and His Brethren Conteyning a Most Gracious Acceptation of the Great Joy Which Her Subiectes Tooke Upon the Apprehension of Divers Persons, Detected of Most Wicked Conspiracies, Read Openly in a Great Assemblie of the Commons in the Guidhall of that Citie, the 22 day of August 1586* (London, 1586), sig. Aii.

16 See BL Add. MS 48027, fols 296r–313r. Pollen, 'Papal Negotiations with Mary Queen of Scots', pp. 49–97.

17 BL Egerton MS 2124, fol. 28r-v. Conyers Read, *The Bardon Papers: Documents relating to the imprisonment and trial of Mary Queen of Scots* (London, 1909), p. 45.

18 BL Egerton MS 2124, fol. 28r-v.

19 BL Add. MS 48027, fols 263r–271v and BL Harley 290, fols 170r–173v.

20 BL Harleian MS 290, fol. 187r.

21 BL Add. MS 48027, fol. 569r, printed in Howell, *State Trials*, I, pp. 1166–9.

22 BL Add. MS 48027, fol. 569v.

23 Simonds D'Ewes, *The journals of all the parliaments during the reign of Queen Elizabeth both of the House of Lords and House of Commons* (London, 1682), pp. 97–8.

24 Quoted in Neale, *Elizabeth I and her Parliaments*, II, p. 113.

25 Ibid., p. 194; *Elizabeth I: Collected Works*, p. 189.

Chapter 40: Blow up the Bed

1 TNA SP 12/197 fols 15, 42, 24, 41, 40, 46, 48, 50; TNA SP 15/30 fol. 17. CP 14/44 printed in *HMC Salisbury*, III, p. 214.

2 CP 15/77 printed in *HMC Salisbury*, III, p. 233; *CSP Dom*, 1581–90, pp. 379–80; *CSP Dom Addenda*, 1580–1625, pp. 199–202 and *CSP Span*, 1587–1603, pp. 13, 14, 82.

3 BL Kings MS 119, fol. 50; TNA SP 12/197 fols 9, 41. BL Cotton MS Galba E VI, fol. 333. *CSP Dom*, 1581–90, pp. 379–80; *CSP Dom Addenda*, 1580–1625, pp. 199–202; *CSP Span*, 1587–1603, pp. 13, 14, 82.

4 CP 15/78 in *HMC Salisbury*, III, p. 216.

5 Read, *Mr Secretary Walsingham*, III, p. 60.

6 *CSP Span*, 1587–1603, p. 149.

7 BL Kings MS 119, fol. 50.

8 *CSP Foreign*, 1583–4, p. 190; *CSP Span*, 1587–1603, pp. 13–15.

9 CP 14/43 in *HMC Salisbury*, III, p. 214.

10 *CSP Span*, 1587–1603, p. 82.

11 *CSP Dom*, 1581–90, p. 531.

12 Murdin, *Burghley's State Papers*, p. 380. See Mitchell Leimon and Geoffrey Parker, 'Treason and Plot in Elizabethan Diplomacy: The Fame of Sir Edward Stafford Reconsidered', *The English Historical Review* 111 (1996), pp. 1134–58.

13 *CSP Foreign*, 1583–4, pp. 259, 272.

14 Ibid., pp. 457, 459.
15 BL Cotton MS Galba E VI, fol. 171v.
16 *CSP Foreign*, 1583–4, p. 474.
17 *CSP Foreign*, 1584–5, pp. 266–7, 312; *CSP Foreign*, 1585–6, pp. 222, 306–7.
18 *CSP Foreign*, 1586–8, pp. 34–5.
19 *CSP Span*, 1587–1603, pp. 189, 218.
20 Ibid.
21 See J. S. Corbett, *Papers Relating to the Navy in the Spanish War, 1585–1587* (London, 1898).

Chapter 41: Nightmares

1 *TRP*, II, pp. 528–32.
2 *CSP Foreign*, 1586–8, p. 241.
3 *CSP Scot*, 1587–8, pp. 287–95.
4 Ibid., p. 294.
5 *CSP Scot*, IV, pp. 291, 294.
6 Nichols (ed.), *Progresses of Queen Elizabeth*, vol. II, pp. 495–507.
7 BL Lansdowne MS 102 fol. 10r; Wright (ed.), *Elizabeth and her Times*, vol. II, p. 332.
8 *CSP Ven*, VIII, p. 256.
9 BL Lansdowne MS 1236, fol. 32.
10 William Camden, *Annales*, p. 115.
11 See R. B. Wernham, 'The disgrace of William Davison', *English Historical Review*, 46 (1931), pp. 632–6.
12 Strype, *Annales*, II, ii, p. 407.
13 TNA SP 12/200/20.
14 *HMC Salisbury* III, ii, p. 220.
15 St John's College Cambridge MS I.30, fols 60v–61r..
16 Ibid., and see Peter E. MacCullough, 'Out of Egypt: Richard Fletcher's sermon before Elizabeth' in Julia M. Walker (ed.), *Dissing Elizabeth*, pp. 118–52; see also Margaret Christian, 'Elizabeth's Preachers and the Government of Women: Defining and Correcting a Queen', *The Sixteenth Century Journal* 24.3 (1993), pp. 561– 76; MacCullough, *Sermons at court*, p. 87.
17 Harrison (ed.), *Letters of Queen Elizabeth*, p. 188.
18 *CSP Scot*, 1586–8, pp. 330–1.
19 *CSP Ven*, 1581–91, pp. 259–61.
20 Alexander S. Wilkinson, *Mary Queen of Scots and French Public Opinion, 1542–1600* (Basingstoke, 2004); *CSP Foreign*, 1586–8, p. 227.
21 J. Hooper Grew, *Elisabeth d'Angleterre dans la littérature française* (Paris, 1932), pp. 38–9; see also Strong, *Gloriana*, p. 34.
22 See John Scott, *A Bibliography of works relating to Mary Queen of Scots 1544–1700* (Edinburgh, 1896), pp. 54–5.
23 J. E. Phillips, *Images of a Queen: Mary Stuart in Sixteenth-century Literature* (Berkeley, 1964), pp. 143–170.
24 Adam Blackwood, *Martyre de la royne d'Escosse* (Paris, 1587), pp. 345–9.
25 Ibid.
26 In his second tract *La Mort de La Royne d'Escosse Doubairere de France* (Paris,

1588), Blackwood calls on decades of Catholic attacks upon the bastard Elizabeth and her bastard religion to argue for the destruction of the tyrant Elizabeth.

27 See J. E. Phillips, *Images of a Queen*; Adam Blackwood, *Martyre de la Royne d'Escosse*.

28 Blackwood, *Marytre de la Royne D'Escosse*, A4v–A5r.

29 'Aliud eiusdem argumenti' in *De Iezabelis Anglæ parricido varii generis poemata Latina et Gallica* (France, 1590).

30 Printed in Georges Ascoli, *La Grande-Bretagne devant l'opinion française au XVIIe siècle* (Paris, 1927), p. 294, who attributes it to Perron. Jacques Davy, Cardinal du Perron, was lecteur to Henry III and a spokesman for Catholicism.

31 Printed in Georges Ascoli, *La Grande-Bretagne*, pp. 296–7. See Phillips, *Images of a Queen*, pp. 85–116, 143–70.

32 *CSP Ven*, 1581–91, p. 264.

Chapter 42: Secret Son?

1 See Ettwell A. B. Barnard, *Evesham and a Reputed Son of Queen Elizabeth* (Evesham, 1926); *CSP Span*, 1587–1603, pp. 101–12.

2 *CSP Span*, 1587–1603, pp. 101–12.

3 *CSP Ven*, 1581–91, p. 267.

4 Ibid., p. 288.

5 See Robert Hutchinson, *Elizabeth's Spy Master: Francis Walsingham and the Secret War that Saved England* (London, 2007).

6 Ellis (ed.), *Original Letters*, III, pp. 134–7.

7 *List and Analysis of State Papers, Foreign Series, Elizabeth I*, vol. II, July 1590–1, no. 697.

8 See John Cooper, *The Queen's Agent: Francis Walsingham at the Court of Elizabeth I* (London, 2011).

Chapter 43: Satan's Instruments

1 *Holinshed's Chronicles of England, Scotland and Ireland*, 6 vols (London, 1807–8), III, pp. 1356–7, 1592.

2 AGS E949, fol. 28 cited in M. J. Rodriguez-Salgado and Simon Adams, eds, *England, Spain and the Gran Armada, 1585–1604: Essays from the Anglo-Spanish conferences, London and Madrid 1988* (Edinburgh, 1991).

3 William Allen, *An Admonition to the nobility and people of England and Ireland* (Antwerp, 1588).

4 G. Mattingly, 'William Allen and Catholic propaganda in England', in *Travaux d'Humanisme et Renaissance* (Geneva), 28 (1957), pp. 325–39.

5 William Allen, 'An Admonition to the Nobility, 1588' in D. M. Rogers (ed.), *English Recusant Literature 1558–1640* (Menston, 1979), p. xix.

6 See Valerie Traub, *The Renaissance of Lesbianism in Early Modern England* (Cambridge, 2002), p. 130.

7 *TRP*, III, 13–17; TNA SP 12/215 fol. 144; *The Execution of Justice in England by William Cecil and A True, Sincere and Modest Defense of English Catholics by William Allen*, ed. Robert M. Kingdon (Ithaca, NY, 1965), pp. xxxvi–xxxvii.

8 *CSP Dom*, 1581–91, p. 507.
9 Wright (ed.), *Queen Elizabeth and her Times*, vol. II, pp. 374–6; see John S. Nolan, 'The Militarization of Elizabethan England', *Journal of Military History*, 58 (3) (1994), pp. 391–420; and Neil Younger, 'If the Armada Had Landed: A Reappraisal of England's Defences in 1588', *History*, 93 (2008), pp. 328–54.
10 *CSP Dom*, 1581–91, p. 515.
11 J. K. Laughton, *State Papers Concerning the Defeat of the Spanish Armada* (London, 1898), vol. I, p. 46. Stafford's original letter has not survived.
12 *CSP Foreign*, 1586–8, pp. 597, 641, 652; *CSP Foreign*, 1588, p. 5.
13 Rodriguez-Salgado and Adams (eds), *England, Spain and the Gran Armada 1585–1604*; Colin Martin and Geoffrey Parker, *The Spanish Armada* (London, 1999); James McDermott, *England and the Spanish Armada: The Necessary Quarrel* (New Haven and London, 2005).
14 BL Add. MS 44839; TNA SP 12/213/80; SP 12/214/86.
15 BL Harleian MS 6798, art. 18. *Cabala, Mysteries of State and Government: in Letters of Illustrious Persons and Great Ministers of State* (London, 1663), p. 373; see Janet M. Green, 'I My Self: Queen Elizabeth I's Oration at Tilbury Camp', *Sixteenth Century Journal* 28 (1997), pp. 421–45, and Susan Frye, 'The Myth of Elizabeth at Tilbury', *Sixteenth Century Journal* 23 (1992), pp. 95–114; Miller Christy, 'Queen Elizabeth's Visit to Tilbury in 1588', *English Historical Review*, xxxiv (1919), p. 46; A. J. Collins, 'The Progress of Queen Elizabeth to the Camp at Tilbury, 1588', *British Museum Quarterly* 10 (1936), pp. 164–7.
16 *CSP Span*, 1587–1603, p. 481.
17 Ibid.
18 A. and C. Belsey, 'Icons of Divinity: Portraits of Elizabeth I', in *Renaissance Bodies*, pp. 15–16.
19 Roy Strong, *Gloriana*.

Chapter 44: Barricaded from Within

1 *CSP Span*, 1587–1603, pp. 419–20.
2 BL Cotton MS Caligula D I, fol. 338.
3 *CSP Span*, 1587–1603, p. 481.
4 BL Cotton MS Caligula D I, fol. 333r.
5 *HMC Bath*, V, p. 94.
6 *CSP Span*, 1587–1603, p. 481.
7 TNA SP 12/215/65.
8 BL Sloane MS 1926, fols 35–43v, reproduced in D. C. Peck, '"News from Heaven and Hell": A Defamatory Narrative of the Earl of Leicester', *English Literary Renaissance* 8 (1978), pp. 141–58.
9 See F. G. Emmison, *Elizabethan Life. Vol. 1: Disorder* (Chelmsford, 1971), p. 42; Joel Samaha, 'Gleanings from Local Criminal-Court Records: Sedition amongst the Inarticulate in Elizabethan Essex', *The Journal of Social History* 8 (1975), p. 69.
10 Paul E. J. Hammer, *The Polarisation of Elizabethan Politics: The Political Career of Robert Devereux, 2nd Earl of Essex, 1585–1597* (Cambridge, 1999).
11 Folger Shakespeare Library, L.a.39.

12 BL Tanner MS 76, fol. 29.
13 Devereux, *Lives and Letters of the Devereux*, I, pp. 187–9.
14 Harrison (ed.), *Letters of Elizabeth*, p. 195.
15 LPL MS 3199, p. 116; LPL MS 3201, fol. 208r. The date of the marriage remains uncertain.
16 Lodge, *Illustrations of British History*, vol. II, p. 422.
17 Cited in J. E. Neale, *Queen Elizabeth* (London, 1979), p. 328.
18 CP 168/55, 20/65 printed in *HMC Salisbury*, IV, p. 153.
19 Mistress Southwell did not marry until 1600, by which time she was aged thirty. Her husband, Sir Barantyne Molyns, was notoriously ugly and almost blinded by war wounds, TNA, SP 14/89, fol. 4r. She died in June 1606, having borne a son in 1602, TNA C 142/391/66.
20 See A. L. Rowse, *Ralegh and the Thockmortons* (London, 1962), p. 160.
21 *The works of Sir Walter Ralegh, kt : now first collected : to which are prefixed the lives of the author*, by William Oldys and Thomas Birch, vol. 8, *Miscellaneous works* (Oxford, 1829), p. 659.
22 Ralegh may have married Elizabeth Throckmorton as early as February 1588; see P. Lefranc, 'La date du mariage de Sir Walter Ralegh: un document indit', *Etudes Anglaises* 9 (1956), pp. 192–211. It seems more likely, however, that the wedding occurred in November 1591, after Throckmorton had become pregnant.
23 D. J. H. Clifford (ed.), *The Diaries of Lady Anne Clifford* (Stroud, 1992), p. 27; see Johanna Rickman, *Love, Lust and License in Early Modern England: Illicit Sex and the Nobility* (Aldershot, 1998), pp. 27–68.

Chapter 45: Suspected and Discontented Persons

1 Sir Robert Cecil to Lord Chancellor Hatton, 8 August 1591, printed in *Religion, Politics and Society in Sixteenth Century England*, ed. Ian Archer et al., pp. 228–30 at p. 291.
2 Michael Questier, 'Loyal to a Fault: Viscount Montague Explains Himself', *Historical Research* 77 (2004), pp. 225–53; Curtis Charles Breight, 'Caressing the Great: Viscount Montague's Entertainment of Elizabeth at Cowdray, 1591', *Sussex Archaeological Collections*, 127 (1989), pp. 147–66; Michael Leslie, 'Something nasty in the wilderness: Entertaining Queen Elizabeth on her Progresses', *Medical and Renaissance Drama in England*, 10 (1998), pp. 47–72.
3 See John Strype, *Annals*, I, pp. 442, 445, 446. See also for example the comments of Allen in *Execution of Justice*, ed. Kingdon, pp. 140–1.
4 Curtis Charles Breight in 'Duelling Ceremonies: The Strange Case of William Hacket, Elizabethan Messiah', *Journal of Medieval and Renaissance Studies* 191 (1989), pp. 35–67.
5 'Memorandum of the arraignment at Newgate of William Hacket, of Northamptonshire, for high treason', 26 July 1591, printed in *HMC Fourteenth Report, Appendix, Part IV. The Manuscripts of Lord Kenyon*, p. 607. See Alexandra Walsham, 'Frantick Hacket: Prophecy, Sorcery, Insanity and the Elizabethan Puritan Movement', *Historical Journal* 41 (1998), pp. 27–66.
6 G. B. Harrison, *Elizabethan Journal*, 1591–1594, pp. 41–2.
7 Ibid., pp. 45–6.

8 Quoted in C. Devlin, *The Life of Robert Southwell* (London, 1956), p. 243.

9 *TRP*, III, pp. 86–93.

10 Ibid.

11 Sir John Harington, *A Tract on the Succession to the Crown*, ed. C. R. Markham (London, 1880), p. 104.

12 *CSP Dom*, 1591–4, p. 302.

13 TNA SP 12/113/173; SP 12/247/61.

14 TNA SP 12/244/112.

15 TNA SP 12/247/79; Nicholas Owen has been wrongly identified as Hugh Owen.

16 Harrison, *Elizabethan Journal*, vol. I, p. 283. See TNA SP 12/247/33; TNA SP 12/247/35; SP 12/247/39; SP 12/247/60; SP 12/247/62.

17 TNA SP 12/247/78; Harrison, *Elizabethan Journal*, p. 289.

18 TNA SP 12/247/78.

19 Warren Skidmore, 'Lady Mary Scudamore (*c.*1550–1603)', occasional papers, no. 29.

20 Francis Edwards, *Plots and Plotters in the Reign of Elizabeth I* (Dublin, 2002).

21 *TRP*, III, pp. 134–6.

22 TNA SP 12/247/98.

23 TNA SP 12/247/66.

24 *TRP*, III, pp. 134–6; Harrison, *Elizabethan Journal*, vol. I, p. 286.

25 *TRP*, III, pp. 134–6.

26 Francis Bacon, *A Collection of Apophthegms. New and Old* (London, 1671), p. 225.

27 TNA SP 12/249/68; SP 12/249/91.

Chapter 46: Age and Decay

1 Harrison, *Elizabethan Journal*, vol. I, p. 286.

2 TNA SP 12/247, fol. 79.

3 Harington, *A Tract on the Succession to the Crown*, p. 43.

4 Peter Wentworth, *A pithie exhortation to her Maiestie for establishing her successor to the crowne* (Edinburgh, 1598).

5 Harington, *Nugae Antiquae*, II, p. 248.

6 Clapham, *Elizabeth of England*, p. 86.

7 S. P. Cerasano and M. Wynne-Davies, 'From Myself, My Other Self I Turned', in S. P. Cerasano and M. Wynne-Davies, eds, *Gloriana's Face: Women, Public and Private in the English Renaissance* (Hemel Hempstead, 1992), pp. 1–24.

8 See Strong, *Gloriana*, p. 147.

9 Harington, *Nugae Antiquae*, II, pp. 140–1.

10 See N. Salomon, 'Positioning Women in Visual Convention: the case of Elizabeth I', in B. S. Travitsky and A. F. Seeff, eds, *Attending to Women in Early Modern England* (London, 1994), pp. 64–95; see also R. Strong, *The Cult of Elizabeth: Elizabethan Portraiture and Pageantry* (London, 1977).

11 BL Add. MS 12506, fols 47, 73; BL Add. MS 12507, fol. 131.

12 Graves, *Brief Memoir*, p. 14.

13 BL Royal, Appendix 68.

14 CP 37/105 in *HMC Salisbury*, VII, pp. 41–2.

15 LPL MS 3198, fol. 552.
16 CP 37/105 in *HMC Salisbury*, VII, pp. 41–2.
17 The tomb was dated according to the old calendar. Parry died in 1590 according to the new calendar.
18 BL Lansdowne MS 62, no. 51, fol. 123.
19 BL Add. MS 70038/104/1r–2r.
20 BL Add. MS 70093; Will of Blanche Parry, BL Lansdowne MS 62, no. 51, fol. 123.
21 Tomb inscription in Bacton Church. See C. A. Bradford, *Blanche Parry. Queen Elizabeth's Gentlewoman* (London, 1935).
22 Clapham, *Elizabeth of England*, p. 89.
23 BLO Ashmole MS 1402, II, fol. 4a.
24 Cornwallis described Mary as 'brazen faced'. Rowland Vaughan, *Most Approved and Long Experienced Waterworkes* (1610); I. J. Atherton, *Ambition and failure in Stuart England: the career of John, first Viscount Scudamore* (Manchester, 1999), p. 28.
25 TNA SP 12/181, no 77, fol. 238.
26 CKS, U 1475/L2/4, item 3, m. 80.
27 *Lives of Lady Anne Clifford and of her Parents*, ed. J. P. Gilson (London, 1916), pp. 24–5.
28 TNA SP 46/125, fol. 236. Also BL Add. MS 27401, fol. 21; BL Add. MS 12406, fols 41, 80; BL Lansdowne MS 128, fol. 12; CP 21/33 in *HMC Salisbury*, IV, p. 199; CP 29/87 in *HMC Salisbury*, V, 53; CP 36/46 in *HMC Salisbury*, V, p. 481; CP 45/16 in *HMC Salisbury*, VI, p. 402; CP 58/108 in *HMC Salisbury*, IX, p. 21; CP 78/14 in *HMC Salisbury*, X, p. 86.
29 Nichols (ed.), *Progresses of Queen Elizabeth*, III, p. 394.
30 TNA SP 12/271, no. 106, fol. 171–v.
31 *The Private Diary of Dr John Dee*, ed. J. O. Halliwell (London, 1842), p. 7. For more on Tomasina see John Southworth, *Fools and Jesters at the English Court* (Stroud, 1998) and Janet Arnold, *Queen Elizabeth's Wardrobe Unlock'd*, pp. 107–8, 146–7, 187, 214, 223.

Chapter 47: Abused her Body

1 *The Letters and Despatches of Richard Verstegan*, ed. Petti, pp. 57–60; BL, Lansdowne MS 72, fol. 48.
2 The letter is undated but is endorsed 1592 by its recipient, Father Persons; it is printed in *Letters and Despatches of Richard Verstegan*, pp. 97–98.
3 In John Hungerford Pollen, *Acts of English Martyrs, Hitherto Unpublished* (London, 1891), pp. 118–20.
4 George Puttenham, *The Arte of English Poesie*, eds G. D. Willcock and Alice Walker (Cambridge, 1936). See also Rosemary Kegl, 'Those Terrible Approaches: Sexuality, Social Mobility and Resisting the Courtliness of Puttenham's *The Arte of English Poesie*', *English Literary Renaissance* 20 (1990), pp. 179–208.
5 The accounts of this phenomenon occur in the diary of the French ambassador, André Hurault, Sieur de Maisse, *A Journal of All that was Accomplished by Monsieur de Maisse*, pp. 25, 36–7. Paul Hentzner's description of the Queen in 1598 also refers to her exposed bosom, specifically associating it

with virginity: 'her bosom was uncovered, as all the English ladies have it till they marry'. *Paul Hentzner's Travels in England*, p. 34.

6 Edmund Spenser, *The Faerie Queene*, in *Spenser: Poetical Works*, ed. J. C. Smith and E. De Selincourt (Oxford, 1970).

7 See Hannah Betts, '"The Image of this Queene so quaynt": The Pornographic Blazon 1588–1603' in Julia M. Walker (ed.), *Dissing Elizabeth*, p. 161.

8 Scillaes Metamorphosis, in *The Complete Works of Thomas Lodge*, ed. Edmund W. Goose, 4 vols (1883, New York), I, p. 33.

9 Shakespeare, *Venus and Adonis* in *The Riverside Shakespeare*, ed. G. Blakemore Evans (Boston, 1974). See also Katherine Duncan-Jones, 'Much Ado with Red and White: The Earliest Readers of Shakespeare's Venus and Adonis (1593)', *Review of English Studies*, n.s., 44.176 (1993), pp. 479–504.

Chapter 48: The Physician's Poison

1 Thomas Birch, *Memoirs of the Reign of Queen Elizabeth*, 2 vols (London, 1754), I, p. 150.

2 See Paul E. J. Hammer, 'An Elizabethan Spy Who Came in from the Cold: The Return of Anthony Stranden to England in 1593', *BIHR* 65 (1992), pp. 277–9; L. Strachey, *Elizabeth and Essex: A Tragic History* (London, 1928), p. 27.

3 See Dominic Green, *The Double Life of Doctor Lopez. Spies, Shakespeare and the Plot to Poison Elizabeth I* (London, 2003).

4 Godfrey Goodman, *The Court of King James the First*, ed. John S. Brewer, 2 vols (London, 1839), I, pp. 152–3.

5 TNA SP 12/239/142; SP 12/239/150; SP 12/240/4; SP 12/240/5.

6 *CSP Foreign*, 1591–2, pp. 322–3.

7 Birch, *Memoirs of the Reign of Queen Elizabeth*, p. 152; TNA SP 12/247/103. See also BL Add. MS 48027, fols 147r–184v.

8 Harrison, *Elizabethan Journal*, p. 281.

9 *CSP Dom*, 1591–4, p. 446.

10 Harrison, *Elizabethan Journal*, vol. I, p. 289.

11 *HMC Salisbury*, IV, p. 512.

12 Edgar Samuel, 'Dr Rodrigo Lopes' last speech from the scaffold at Tyburn', in *Jewish Historical Studies*, 30 (1987–8), pp. 51–3.

13 [Anon] *A True Report of Sundry Horrible Conspiracies of Late Time Detected to Have (by Barbarous Murders) Taken Away the Life of the Queenes Most Excellent Maiestie Whom Almighty God Hath Miraculously Conserved Aaginst the Treacheries of Her Rebelles, and the Violence of Her Most Puissant Enemies* (London 1594).

Chapter 49: Love and Self-Love

1 L. Hicks, 'Father Robert Persons and the Book of Succession', *Recusant History*, vol. 4, no. 3 (1957), p. 104.

2 R. Doleman, *A Conference about the Next Succession to the Crown of England* (Amsterdam, 1593, reprinted 1681, London), p. 183.

3 For her claims see Susan Doran, 'Three late-Elizabethan succession tracts', in *The Struggle for the Succession in Late Elizabethan England: Politics, Polemics and Cultural Representations*, ed. Jean-Christophe Mayer (Montpellier, 2004), p. 93.

4 Doleman, *Conference about the Next Succession*, p. 196.
5 Doran, 'Three late-Elizabethan succession tracts', p. 95; Peter Holmes, 'The Authorship and Early Reception of A Conference About the Next Succession to the Crown of England', *Historical Journal*, 23 (1980), pp. 415–29.
6 Susan Doran, 'Revenge her Foul and most Unnatural murder? The impact of Mary Stewart's execution on Anglo-Scottish relations', *History* 85 (2000), pp. 589–612.
7 13 Eliz I, c.1 printed in *Statutes* IV: 526–8.
8 Collins (ed.), *Letters and Memorials of State*, I, p. 357.
9 LPL, MS 651, fol. 122r; *Letters and Despatches of Richard Verstegan*, p. 242.
10 Collins (ed.), *Letters and Memorials of State*, I, p. 362. See Roy Strong, *The Cult of Elizabeth*, p. 209 and Alan Young, *Tudor and Jacobean Tournaments* (London, 1987), p. 204; Paul E. J. Hammer, 'Upstaging the Queen: The Earl of Essex, Francis Bacon and the Accession Day celebrations of 1595', in David Bevington and Peter Holbrook (eds), *The Politics of the Stuart Court Masque* (Cambridge, 1998), pp. 41–66; R. McCoy, *The Rites of Knighthood: the Literature and Politics of Elizabethan Chivalry* (California, 1989), chapter 1.
11 CP 36/51 in *HMC Salisbury*, V, p. 484.
12 Collins (ed.), *Letters and Memorials of State*, I, p. 379; HMC De L'Isle and Dudley Papers II, p. 163.
13 Ibid., pp. 201–2.
14 Ibid., pp. 203–5.
15 Harrison, *Elizabethan Journal*, p. 70.
16 Collins (ed.), *Letters and Memorials of State*, II, pp. 17–19, 21.
17 LPL, MS 660, fol. 149r–v.
18 LPL, MS 660, fol. 281r, fol. 151r.
19 CP 55/45, printed in *HMC Salisbury*, VII, p. 391.
20 CP 55/45.
21 BL Add. MS 22925; TNA E 351/542, M59, fol. 42r.

Chapter 50: Privy Matters

1 *Gossip from a muniment-room: being passages in the lives of Anne and Mary Fytton, 1574–1618* (London, 1897), ed. Lady Newdigate-Newdegate, pp. 9–11.
2 Ibid., pp. 34–5.
3 Ibid., pp. 12–13.
4 Ibid., pp. 13–15.
5 Harington, *Nugae Antiquae*, II, p. 154.
6 Harington, *Letters and Epigrams*, p. 176.
7 L. Ariosto, *Orlando Furioso*, trans. G. Waldman (Oxford, 1974); Simon Cauchi, 'The "Setting Forth" of Harington's Ariosto', *Studies in Bibliography* 36 (1983), pp. 137–68; Miranda Johnson-Haddad, 'Englishing Ariosto: Orlando Furioso at the Court of Elizabeth I', *Comparative Literature Studies*, 31 (1994), pp. 323–50.
8 Harrison, *Elizabethan Journal*, I, pp. 14–15; Richard Townsend, *Harington and Ariosto: A Study in Elizabethan Verse Translation* (New Haven, 1940).

9 John Harington, *Orlando Furioso* in *English Heroical Verse* (London, 1591). The anecdote is recorded in *Nugae Antiquae*, p. x.

10 John Harington, *A New Discourse of a Stale Subject, Called the Metamorphosis of Ajax* (1596), ed. Elizabeth Story Donno (London, 1962); Jonathan Kinghorn, 'A Privvie in Perfection: Sir John Harington's Water-Closet', *Bath History*, 1 (1986), pp. 173–88. See also Alan Stewart, 'The Early Modern Closet Discovered', *Representations*, 50 (1995), pp. 76–100.

11 *The Metamorphosis of Ajax*, ed. Donno, p. 183.

12 Ibid., p. 186.

13 John Harington, *The Letters and Epigrams of Sir John Harington Together with* The Prayse of Private Life, ed. Norman Egbert McClure (Philadelphia, 1930), p. 165.

14 Harington, *The Metamorphosis of Ajax*, p. 171.

15 Harington, *Nugae Antiquae*, I, pp. 239–41.

16 Ibid., II, p. 287.

Chapter 51: Foolish and Old

1 Anthony Rudd, *A sermon preached at Richmond before Queene Elizabeth of Famous memorie, vpon the 28 of March, 1596* (London, 1603), pp. 49–54.

2 Nichols (ed.), *Progresses of Queen Elizabeth*, III, p. 8.

3 Rudd, *Sermon preached at Richmond*, pp. 54, 56.

4 *The Letters of John Chamberlain*, ed. Norman Egbert McClure, 2 vols (Philadelphia, 1939), II, p. 470.

5 John Harington, *A Briefe Viewe of the State of the Church of England* (London, 1653), p. 162.

6 Ellis (ed.), *Original Letters*, vol. II, p. 53.

7 Clapham, *Elizabeth of England*, p. 90.

8 Edmund Bohun, *The Character of Queen Elizabeth* (London, 1693), pp. 301–2.

9 *A journal of all that was accomplished by Monsieur de Maisse*, pp. 25–6.

10 Ibid., pp. 25–6, 36–7.

11 Ibid., pp. 36–7.

12 Ibid.

13 Ibid., pp. 25–6.

14 These were all recorded in an inventory of July 1600. BL Stowe MS 555/7; Arnold, *Queen Elizabeth's Wardrobe Unlock'd*, pp. 251–334.

15 Harington, *Nugae Antiquae*, II, p. 215.

16 Arnold, *Queen Elizabeth's Wardrobe Unlock'd*, pp. 4–5.

17 Collins (ed.), *Letters and Memorials of State*, II, p. 155.

18 *A journal of all that was accomplished by Monsieur de Maisse*, p. 12.

19 Ibid., p. 82.

Chapter 52: Mask of Youth

1 *TRP*, II, pp. 240–1.

2 *APC* 1596–7, p. 69. See Roy Strong, *Gloriana*, p. 20.

3 *APC* 1596–7, p. 69.

4 Marie Axton, *The Queen's Two Bodies: Drama and the Elizabethan Succession* (London, 1977), p. 12.

5 Nanette Salomon, 'Positioning women in visual convention', pp. 64–95; David Howarth, *Images of Rule: Art and Politics in the English Renaissance, 1485–1649* (Basingstoke, 1997), p. 101.
6 Arnold, *Queen Elizabeth's Wardrobe Unlock'd*, pp. 82, 85.

Chapter 53: The Poisoned Pommel

1 Richard Walpole's younger brother Henry Walpole was the celebrated Jesuit martyr who was executed at Tyburn for illegally entering England and accused of plotting to assassinate Elizabeth.
2 Francis Bacon, *A Letter Written out of England . . . containing a True Report of a Strange Conspiracy* (London, 1599); M[artin] A[rray], *The Discovery and Confutation of a Tragical Fiction* (Rome, 1599).
3 See Francis Edwards, 'Sir Robert Cecil, Edward Squier and the Poisoned Pommel' in *Recusant History*, 25.3 (2001), pp. 377–414.
4 *The Letters of John Chamberlain*, I, p. 34.
5 TNA SP 52/62/39; TNA SP 52/62/43; TNA SP 52/62/46.
6 *APC*, 1598–9, p. 506. See also Francis Edwards (ed. and trans.), *The Elizabethan Jesuits: Historia missionis Anglicanae Societatis Jesu (1660) of Henry More* (London, 1981), p. 279.
7 TNA SP 12/83, 86, 89, 91; TNA KB/8/55; Francis Bacon, *A Letter Written out of England* which may confidently be ascribed to Francis Bacon and which is based on Squires' own statements; Walpole's testimony is echoed by Martin Array in a pamphlet giving the Jesuit side of the case, *The Discovery and Confutation of a Tragical Fiction*, but it seems Array based his narrative only on Walpole's own statement.
8 TNA MS KB 8/55.
9 *Liturgies and Occasional Forms of Prayer*, pp. 679–82.
10 TNA SP 12/224/112; TNA SP 12/247/61; TNA SP 12/268/144–5. See also Edwards, 'Sir Robert Cecil, Edward Squier', pp. 377–414.

Chapter 54: Crooked Carcass

1 See James Shapiro, *1599. A Year in the Life of William Shakespeare* (London, 2005), p. 57.
2 Harrison, *Elizabethan Journal*, p. 287.
3 Camden, *Annales*, pp. 771–2.
4 Harrison, *Elizabethan Journal*, p. 132.
5 TNA SP 12/268/45; Birch, *Memoirs of the reign of Queen Elizabeth*, II, p. 387.
6 TNA SP 12/268/18.
7 Collins (ed.), *Letters and Memorials of State*, II, pp. 166–7.
8 *The Letters of Philip Gawdy of West Harling, Norfolk and London: 1579–1616*, ed. Isaac Herbert Jeayes (London, 1906), p. 137.
9 HMC, De L'Isle, II, pp. 265, 322.
10 *Letters of Philip Gawdy*, p. 137.
11 *Paul Hentzner's Travels in England*, pp. 33–4. See Louis Montrose, '"Shaping Fantasies": Figurations of Gender and Power in Elizabethan culture', *Representations* I, no. 2 (1983), pp. 61–94.

Chapter 55: *Lèse Majesté*

1 Harrison (ed.), *Letters of Queen Elizabeth*, p. x.
2 Devereux, *Lives and Letters*, II, pp. 40–1.
3 John Stow and Edmund Howes, *The Annales, or Generall Chronicle of England* (London, 1615), p. 788.
4 Chamberlin, *Private Character of Queen Elizabeth*, p. 110.
5 *Thomas Platter's Travels in England*, p. 192.
6 Ibid., p. x.
7 Collins (ed.), *Letters and Memorials of State*, II, p. 127.
8 Ibid., p. 196.
9 Ibid., p. 129.
10 Ibid., p. 132.
11 Ibid., p. 151.
12 Ibid., pp. 158–9.
13 *HMC Salisbury*, VII, pp. 167–8.
14 Collins (ed.), *Letters and Memorials of State*, II, p. 164.
15 Ibid., p. 172.
16 Ibid., p. 174.
17 Birch (ed.), *Memoirs of the Reign of Queen Elizabeth*, II, p. 218.
18 TNA SP 12/50.
19 CP 81/88 in *HMC Salisbury*, X, p. 330.
20 Harington, *Nugae Antiquae*, I, p. 179.
21 G. B. Harrison, *A Last Elizabethan Journal: Being a Record of Those Things Most Talked of During the Years 1599–1603* (London, 1933), p. 132; Birch, *Memoirs of the Reign of Queen Elizabeth*, II, p. 463.

Chapter 56: Dangerous and Malicious Ends

1 BL Cotton MS Julius F VI, fols 45or, 445r–452r; TNA SP 12/278/73 fol. 124r; M. James, 'At a Crossroads of the Political Culture: The Essex Revolt, 1601' in M. James, *Society, Politics and Culture: Studies in Early Modern England* (Cambridge, 1986), pp. 416–65.
2 TNA SP 12/278/72, fol. 122r.
3 *CSP Dom*, 1598–1601, pp. 351, 550; *APC*, 1600–1, pp. 147–8.
4 TNA SP 12/278/97, fols 155r–158v. A. Wall, 'An Account of the Essex Revolt, February 1601', *BIHR* 54 (1981), pp. 131–3; P. E. J. Hammer, 'The Smiling Crocodile: the Earl of Essex and Late Elizabethan Popularity', in Peter Lake, Stephen Pincus, eds, *The Politics of the Public Sphere in Early Modern England* (Manchester, 2007), pp. 95–115; TNA SP 12/278/72; *CSP Dom*, p. 550.
5 TNA SP 12/278/51.
6 Clapham, *Elizabeth of England*, p. 88.
7 CP 83/64 in *HMC Salisbury*, XI, p. 59.
8 *TRP*, III, pp. 230–2.
9 LPL MS 604, fol. 70v. Howell, *State Trials*, I, pp. 1405–6.
10 TNA SP 12/278, no. 61, fol. 102; Howell, *State Trials*, I, pp. 1403, 1407; LPL MS 604 fol. 70v.
11 TNA SP 12/278/61, fols 104r–106v; Howell, *State Trials*, I, pp. 1403–15; LPL MS 604, fol. 70v.
12 TNA SP 12/278/101, fol. 168r–v.

13 *CSP Dom*, 1598–1601, p. 577. See Paul E. J. Hammer, 'The Earl of Essex's Apprehension, Arraignment and Execution, February 1601', from Jayne Archer, Elizabeth Clarke, Elizabeth Goldring (eds), *Court and Culture in the Reign of Queen Elizabeth I: A New Critical Edition of John Nichols's 'The Progresses of Queen Elizabeth I'*, 4 vols (London, 2008); Howell, *State Trials*, I, p. 1346.

14 Francis Bacon, *A Declaration of the Practises & Treasons Attempted and Committed by Robert Late Earle of Essex and his Complices, against Her Majestie and Her Kingdoms and of The Proceedings as Well at the Arraignments & Convictions of the Said Late Earle, and His Adherents, as After: Together with the Very Confessions and Other Parts of the Evidences Themselves, Word for Word Taken out of the Originals* (London, 1601).

15 A. Hunt, 'Tuning the Pulpits: The Religious Context of the Essex Revolt', in L. A. Ferrell and P. McCullough (eds), *The English Sermon Revised: Religion, Literature and History, 1500–1700* (Manchester, 2000), pp. 86–114; Peter McCullough, *Sermons at Court: Politics and Religion in Elizabethan and Jacobean Preaching* (Cambridge, 1997); M. James, 'At a Crossroads of the Political Culture: The Essex Revolt 1601' in James, *Society, Politics and Culture*, pp. 416–65.

16 TNA SP 12/278/104, fol. 207r, 'An abstract out of the Erle of Essex confession'.

17 BLO Tanner MS 114, fol. 139, printed in Goodman, *Court of King James I*, pp. 18–19.

18 TNA SP 12/278/104, fol. 207r. The earl's 'confession' was published in Bacon's 'A declaration of the practices and treasons . . . of the late Earle of Essex', the official printed account of the rising.

19 W. Barlow, *A Sermon Preached at Paules Crosse, on the First Sunday in Lent . . . 1600 with a Short Discourse of the Late Earle of Essex His Confession and Penitence, Before and At the Time of His Death* (1601), sig. B5v. For Cecil's orchestration of the sermon following Essex's rebellion see *CSP Dom*, 1598–1601, pp. 598–9.

20 Barlow, *A Sermon Preached at Paules Crosse*, sig. E1.

21 TNA SP 12 278/63; Barlow, *A Sermon Preached at Paules Crosse*; Francis Bacon, *A Declaration of the Practises & Treasons Attempted and Committed by Robert Late Earle of Essex*.

22 *TRP*, III, pp. 233–4.

23 Von Raumer, *Contributions*, pp. 451–2.

Chapter 57: No Season to Fool

1 Collins (ed.), *Letters and Memorials of State*, II, pp. 84, 87; I, p. 206.

2 *HMC De L'Isle* and Dudley Papers, p. 472; Collins (ed.), *Letters and Memorials of State*, II, pp, 84, 87; I, p. 236.

3 CP 58/108 in *HMC Salisbury*, IX, p. 21.

4 McClure (ed.), *Letters and Epigrams*, p. 90.

5 Harington, *Nugae Antiquae*, p. 315.

6 TNA SP 12/278 fol. 151; TNA SP 12/278 fol. 246; see Harington, *Letters and Epigrams*, p. 389.

7 J. E. Neale, *Elizabeth I and her Parliaments, 1584–1601* (London, 1957),

p. 375; Chamberlain, *Private Character of Queen Elizabeth*, p. 73; David Dalrymple (ed.), *The Secret Correspondence of Sir Robert Cecil with James VI, King of Scotland* (Edinburgh, 1766), p. 26.

8 *The Journal of Sir Roger Wilbraham for the years 1593–1616*, ed. Harold Spencer Scott (London, 1902), vol. 10, p. 45.

9 CP 88/89 in *HMC Salisbury*, XI, p. 405; Helen Hackett, *Virgin Mother, Maiden Queen: Elizabeth I and the Cult of the Virgin Mary* (London, 1995), pp. 211–13.

10 CP 88/89.

11 *The Journal of Sir Roger Wilbraham*, p. 45; BL Cotton MS Titus C VI, fols 410–11.

12 *CSP Dom*, 1580–1625 *Addenda*, p. 407.

13 Godfrey Goodman, *The Court of King James the First*, I, p. 97.

14 Collins (ed.), *Letters and Memorials of State*, II, p. 362.

15 John Bruce, *Correspondence of King James VI of Scotland* (London, 1861), p. 13.

16 *The Secret correspondence of Sir Robert Cecil with James VI*, p. 62; Joel Hurstfield, 'The Succession Struggle in late Elizabethan England' in S. T. Bindoff, Joel Hurtsfield and C. H. Williams, *Elizabethan Government and Society* (Cambridge, 1961), pp. 369–96.

17 CP 169/102; *CSP Dom*, 1601–2, p. 37.

18 See David Durant, *Arbella Stuart: a rival to the Queen* (London, 1978).

19 Thomas Wilson, *The State of England Anno Dom. 1600*, ed. E. J. Fisher (London, 1936), p. 5.

Chapter 58: Age Itself is a Sickness

1 John Manningham, *The Diary of John Manningham of the Middle Temple 1602–1603* (Hanover, New Hampshire, 1976), p. 194.

2 H. Foley, *Records of the English Province of the Society of Jesus*, 7 vols (London, 1875–83), vol. I, p. 24.

3 H. Foley, *Records of the English Province*, I, pp. 21–2.

4 Ibid.

5 Ibid., p. 21.

6 Ibid., p. 24.

7 Raumer, *Contributions*, p. 451.

8 See Nichols (ed.), *Progresses of Queen Elizabeth*, II, p. 578.

9 *CSP Dom*, 1601–2, p. 232.

10 H. Foley, *Records of the English Province*, I, pp. 47, 50. It has been suggested that the spy 'Rivers' was William Sterrell, Secretary to the Earl of Worcester, which would have placed him at the heart of Elizabeth's court.

11 Nichols (ed.), *Progresses of Queen Elizabeth*, III, p. 577. *The Letters of John Chamberlain*, I, pp. 115, 139. Raumer, *Contributions*, p. 450. See TNA Baschet MS, Bundle 33, p. 260.

12 De Maisse, *A Journal of All that was Accomplished by Monsieur de Maisse*, p. 95.

13 Cited in Strickland, *Elizabeth*, IV, p. 762.

14 'Diary of the Journey of the Duke of Stettin-Pomerania', pp. 1–67.

15 Lodge (ed.), *Illustrations of British History*, II, p. 577.

16 *Manningham's diary*, p. 150. H. Foley, *Records of the English Province*, I, p. 52.

17 H. Foley, *Records of the English Province*, I, p. 52.

18 Harington, *A Tract on the Succession to the Crown.*
19 Harington, *Nugae Antiquae*, II, p. 76.
20 Ibid., pp. 77–9.
21 Ibid., I, pp. 322–3.
22 Ibid., I, p. 321.
23 Ibid., I, pp. 320–4.
24 Harington, *A Tract on the Succession to the Crown*, p. 51.
25 Ibid.
26 See *The Letters of John Chamberlain*, pp. 179–80.
27 Ibid., p. 188.

Chapter 59: All are in a Dump at Court

1 *The Letters of John Chamberlain*, p. 182.
2 *HMC Salisbury*, XII, p. 670.
3 Raumer, *Contributions*, p. 454.
4 *The Diary of Lady Anne Clifford*, ed. Vita Sackville West (London, 1923), p. 3; *CSP Ven*, 1592–1603, pp. 529, 531–2.
5 *CSP Ven*, 1592–1603, pp. 531–2.
6 Ibid., p. 532.
7 Ibid., p. 533; Katherine Duncan-Jones, '"Almost Always Smiling": Elizabeth's last two years' in *Resurrecting Elizabeth I in Seventeenth Century England*, ed. Elizabeth H. Hageman and Katherine Conway (Madison and Teaneck, 2007), pp. 31–47.
8 *CSP Ven*, 1592–1603, p. 533.
9 Ibid., p. 529.
10 CP 92/80.
11 William Camden, *Annales*, p. 26.
12 *The Letters of Philip Gawdy*, p. 126.
13 Raumer, *Contributions*, p. 455.
14 CP 92/18 printed in *HMC Salisbury*, XII, p. 667.
15 CP 183/148 printed in *HMC Salisbury*, XII, p. 668.
16 *CSP Dom*, 1601–3, p. 301.
17 Ibid., p. 298.
18 Raumer, *Contributions*, p. 456.
19 *CSP Dom*, 1601–3, p. 298.
20 John Clapham, *Elizabeth of England*, p. 96.
21 *The Letters of Lady Arbella Stuart*, ed. Sara Jayne Steen (Oxford, 1994), pp. 158–75.
22 *CSP Ven*, 1592–1603, p. 554.
23 *CSP Foreign*, 1601–3, p. 302.
24 *HMC Rutland*, p. 387.
25 Wright, *Queen Elizabeth and her Times*, II, p. 494.
26 *CSP Ven*, 1592–1603, p. 563.
27 Raumer, *Contributions*, pp. 456–7.
28 *CSP Dom*, 1601–3, p. 302.
29 Ibid.
30 Birch, *Memoirs of the Reign of Queen Elizabeth*, vol. II, p. 507.
31 'The Death of Queene Elizabeth', in BL Cotton MS Titus C vii 57, fol. 1.

32 Raumer, *Contributions*, p. 457.
33 John Stow, *A Summarie of the Chronicles of England* (London, 1604), p. 439.
34 CP 92/22.
35 *HMC Rutland*, p. 388.
36 Ibid.
37 Bruce, *Correspondence of King James VI of Scotland* (London, 1861), p. 73; Clapham, *Elizabeth of England*, p. 104.
38 *CSP Ven*, 1592–1603, p. 558.
39 *CSP Ven*, 1601–3, p. 7.
40 *The Memoirs of Robert Carey*, ed. F. H. Mares (Oxford, 1972), p. 58.
41 Ibid.
42 Ibid.
43 Clapham, *Elizabeth of England*, pp. 99–100.
44 *CSP Dom*, 1601–3, p. 303.
45 William Weston, *The Autobiography of an Elizabethan*, ed. and trans. Philip Caraman (London, 1955), p. 222.
46 Clapham, *Elizabeth of England*, p. 99.
47 *The Diary of John Manningham*, p. 205.
48 *The Letters of John Chamberlain*, p. 189; Raumer, *Contributions*, p. 458.

Chapter 60: Deathbed

1 *The Memoirs of Robert Carey*, p. 59.
2 Ibid.
3 Raumer, *Contributions*, pp. 457–8.
4 Elizabeth Southwell, 'A True Relation ...' Stonyhurst Manuscript Ang, iii, Archivum Britannicum Societatis Iesu (London, 1607) printed in Catherine Loomis, 'Elizabeth Southwell's Manuscript Account of the death of Queen Elizabeth', *English Literary Renaissance* 26.3 (1996), p. 485.
5 Ibid., pp. 482–509.
6 Clapham, *Elizabeth of England*, p. 96.
7 *The Diary of John Manningham*, p. 207.
8 Ibid.; *The Memoirs of Robert Carey*, pp. 59–60.
9 *The Memoirs of Robert Carey*, p. 99; all the English accounts carefully record this scene in which Elizabeth verbally or by gesture named James as her successor, whereas ambassadors' reports have conflicting versions, some claiming that Elizabeth made no declaration as to her heir. BL Cotton MS Titus C vii 57, a note of some public proceedings and death of Elizabeth. De Beaumont's account says that she put her hand to her head, Birch, *Memoirs of Reign of Elizabeth*, II, p. 508.
10 *The Memoirs of Robert Carey*, p. 60.
11 Ibid., pp. 59–61.
12 *The Diary of John Manningham*, p. 208.
13 James F. Larkin and Paul L. Hughes, eds, *Stuart Royal Proclamations*, 2 vols (Oxford, 1973), I, pp. 1–2. Nichols (ed.), *The Progresses, Processions and Magnificent Festivities of King James the First*, 4 vols (London, 1828), vol. I, pp. 25–31.
14 Robert Carey, *The True Narration of the Entertainment of his Royall Majestie ...* (London, 1603), p. 61.

15 *The Memoirs of Robert Carey*, p. 9.
16 *The Diary of John Manningham*, pp. 208–9.
17 Clapham, *Elizabeth of England*, p. 99.

Chapter 61: *Regina Intacta*

1 James V. Ricci, *The Genealogy of Gynaecology* (Philadelphia, 1950), p. 230.
2 Ben Jonson, 'Conversations with William Drummond of Hawthornden', in *The Complete Poems*, ed. George Parfitt (London, 1975), pp. 459–80 (at p. 470). The rumour about Elizabeth's imperforate hymen was reported to the Queen by Mary Queen of Scots. See Murdin, *Burghley's State Papers*, pp. 558–60.
3 Harington, *A Tract on the Succession to the Crown*, pp. 39–41.
4 Ibid.
5 *CSP Ven*, 1603–7, p. 3.
6 Clapham, *Elizabeth of England*, p. 190.
7 TNA E351/3145 fols 22ff, 25; TNA LC 2/4/4/2r.
8 TNA E531/3145 fol. 25.
9 *The Diary of John Manningham*, p. 223.
10 Catherine Loomis, 'Elizabeth Southwell's Manuscript Account', p. 485; K. A. Cregan, 'Early modern anatomy and the Queen's body natural: The sovereign subject' in *Body & Society* 13.2 (2007), pp. 47–66; K. A. Cregan, *The Theatre of the Body. Staging Death and Embodying Life in Early Modern England* (Turnhort, Belgium, 2009).
11 It is possible that Elizabeth's body was opened but this was not mentioned in any of the other sources, as her councillors wanted it to appear that they had obeyed her orders.
12 Clapham, *Elizabeth of England*, p. 110.
13 Ibid., p. 111; TNA E351/3145 fols 22ff, 25; TNA LC 2/4/4/2r.
14 *The Diary of Lady Anne Clifford*, p. 4.
15 Catherine Loomis, 'Elizabeth Southwell's Manuscript Account', p. 485.
16 Robert Persons, *The Judgment of a Catholicke English-man, Living in Banishment for His Religion* (St Omer, 1608).
17 Ibid., pp. 26–43.
18 Ibid., pp. 31–2.
19 Robert Persons, *A Discussion of the Answere of M. William Barlow* (St Omer, 1612), pp. 220–8.

Chapter 62: The Queen's Effigy

1 Nigel Llewellyn, 'The Royal Body: Monuments to the Dead, For the Living', in *Renaissance Bodies*, Gent and Llewellyn (eds), pp. 218–240. See R. E. Giesey, *The Royal Funeral Ceremony in Renaissance France* (Geneva, 1960), pp. 19, 145.
2 *CSP Ven*, 1603–7, p. 22. See W. St J. Hope, 'On the Funeral Effigies of the Kings and Queens of England', in *Archaeologist*, LX (1907), pp. 517–70. John Colte was paid £10 'for ye Image representing hir late Majestie with diverse other thinges, viz one paire of straite bodies, a paire of drawers, bumbastm iiij screwing irons & other Irons, a payre of lastes, lace & pointes & also a Chest to cary ye same'. TNA LC2/4 (4) fol. 20. Walter

Ripin was paid £15 'for one new Chariott with wheeles, carriages, boxes, hoopes and one new Cradle to the same, wherein the Corpes & representation was carried'. LC2/4(4) fol. 11. It seems likely that the crimson satin robe listed among the funeral expenses was used to cover the wooden effigy before it was dressed in the royal robes: 'Paied to the said William Jones her late Majesties tayler for making the said Robe of Satten crymsin for the Royall Representacion aforesaid xiijs iiijd (ibid., fol. 11v). See also Anthony Harvey and Richard Mortimer, *The Funeral Effigies of Westminster Abbey* (Woodbridge, 1994).

3 *CSP Ven*, 1603–7, p. 3.

4 Jennifer Woodward, *The Theatre of Death: The Ritual Management of Royal Funerals in Renaissance England, 1570–1625* (Woodbridge, 1997), p. 129.

5 W. Rye, *England as seen by Foreigners* (London, 1865), p. 164. Clare Gittings, *Death, Burial and the Individual in Early Modern England* (London, 1984), p. 223. For Elizabeth's effigy, a crimson satin robe was sewn, lined with white fustian, with batons and a coif of cloth of gold, while £6.13s.4d was spent on 'the crown sceptre and ball, being all gilt with fine gold burnished, the crown set with stones'.

6 See D. R. Woolf, 'Two Elizabeths? James I and the Late Queen's Famous Memory', *Canadian Journal of History*, 20 (1985), pp. 167–91.

7 Stow, *The Annales*, p. 813.

8 Clapham, *Elizabeth of England*, p. 110; *CSP Dom*, 1603–16, p. 9.

9 *CSP Ven*, 1603–7, p. 23.

10 TNA LC 5/37; TNA LC 2/4/4 fol. 19.

11 Clapham, *Elizabeth of England*, p. 144.

12 Ibid., p. 111; for the funeral see TNA LC 2/4/4; E 351/3145; BL Add. MS 35324, fols 26–39; BL Cotton MS Faustina E I printed in Nichols (ed.), *Progresses of Queen Elizabeth*, III, pp. 620–6.

13 Ibid.

14 Henry Cheetle, *Englands Mourning Garment* (London, 1603), sig. F2r.

15 Ibid., sig. F2r.

16 Stow, *The Annales*, p. 815.

17 Thomas Dekker, *The Wonderful Year*, 1603, edited by George B. Harrison (New York, 1924).

18 Clapham, *Elizabeth of England*, pp. 114–15.

19 *The Letters of Philip Gawdy*, p. 128.

20 *CSP Ven*, 1603–7, p. 22.

21 Ibid., pp. 22, 24, 41; Henry Cheetle, *The Order and Proceedings at the Funeral of Elizabeth* (1603).

22 *CSP Ven*, 1601–3, p. 41.

23 Thomas Millington, *The True Narration of the Entertainment of his Majesty from his departure from Edinburgh till his receiving at London*, in *Stuart Tracts 1603–1693*, ed. C. H. Frith (New York, 1964), p. 15.

Epilogue: Secret Histories

1 An entry in the abbey account books for 1606 records: 'for removing of Queene Elizabeth's Body ... 46 shillings 4 pence', Westminster Abbey archives.

2 Letter dated 20 September 1613 – James to Dean of Peterborough, BLO, Ashmole MS 836 fol. 277.

3 See Julia M. Walker, *The Elizabeth Icon, 1603–2003* (*New York, 2004*).

4 See Richard Burt, 'Doing the Queen: Gender, Sexuality and Censorship of Elizabeth I's Royal Image from Renaissance Portraiture to Twentieth-Century Mass Media', in Andrew Hadfield (ed.), *Literature and Censorship in Renaissance England* (London, 2001), p. 207.

5 Julia M. Walker, 'Reading the Tombs of Elizabeth I', *English Literary Renaissance*, 26:3 (1996), pp. 510–30; 'Bones of Contention: Posthumous Images of Elizabeth and Stuart Politics', in Julia M. Walker (ed.), *Dissing Elizabeth*.

6 Thomas Newton, *Atropoion Delion* (London, 1603), sig. A3r.

7 Ibid., sig. B4v.

8 *Purit-Anus* (1609).

9 Francis Osbourne, *Traditional Memoirs on the Reign of Queen Elizabeth and King James* (London, 1658).

10 *The Secret History of the Most Renowned Queen Elizabeth and the Earl of Essex* (London, 1680).

11 John Banks, *The Unhappy Favourite*, ed. Thomas Marshall Howe Blair (New York, 1939).

12 *Fraser's Magazine for Town and Country*, 48 (Oct. 1853), p. 376.

13 Charles Kingsley, 'Sir Walter Raleigh and His Time', in *Plays and Puritans and Other Historical Essays* (London, 1873), p. 123.

14 John Neale, *Queen Elizabeth I* (London, 1934).

15 W. C. Sellar and R. J. Yeatman, *1066 and All That* (London, 1930), p. 59.

16 See for example S. Cunliffe-Owen, *The Phoenix and the Dove* (London, 1930).

17 Lytton Strachey, *Elizabeth and Essex: A Tragic History* (London, 1928).

18 Philip Reed (ed.), *Letters from a Life: The Selected Letters of Benjamin Britton, volume four, 1952–57* (Woodbridge, 2008), p. 150.

19 Jean Plaidy, *Queen of this Realm: The Story of Elizabeth I* (London, 1983); Philippa Gregory, *The Virgin's Lover* (London, 2010).

Bibliography

UNPUBLISHED SOURCES

Manuscripts
Archivo General de Simancas, Spain
Estado 814, 812, 815, 949, 8340

Bibliothèque Nationale, Paris
Fonds Français MSS 15970, Fonds Italien MS 1732

Bodleian Library, Oxford
Ashmole MS, Rawlinson MS, Tanner MS

British Library, London
Additional MSS 12506, 12507, 15914, 19401, 26056, 27401, 30078, 32379, 35183, 35324, 35830, 35831, 37749, 44839, 48018, 48023, 48027, 48049, 70093; Egerton 2124, 2806, 2836; Cotton Caligula C II; Cotton Caligula C IX; Cotton Caligula B X; Cotton Caligula D I; Cotton Caligula E V; Cotton Julius F VI; Cotton Nero B III; Cotton Faustina E I; Cotton Vespasian F XII; Cotton Vitellius C VII; Cotton Titus B II; Cotton Titus F I; Cotton Titus F III; Cotton Vitellius C VII; Cotton Galba E VI; Royal App 68; Stowe MS 143, 145, 147, 167, 555, 557; Tanner 76; Harleian MS 260, 290, 787, 1582, 5176, 6035, 6286, 6850, 6949; Lansdowne MS 29, 30, 33, 39, 41, 43, 62, 72, 102, 128, 703, 982, 1236; Sloane MS 326, 3846

Hatfield House, Herts
Cecil Papers

Keele University Library, Staffordshire
Paget Papers

Lambeth Palace Library, London
MS 604, 651, 664, 3197, 3199, 3201

Longleat House
Dudley Papers

The National Archives, London
C 66, 115; SP 10, 12, 15, 27, 31, 46, 52, 53, 56, 63, 70, 78, 83; E 351/3145; LC 2, 4, 3, 5; KB 8/40, KB 8/55, 31/3

National Library of Scotland, Edinburgh
Advocates MS 1.2

St John's College, Cambridge
MS I.30

PhD Theses
Brogan, Stephen, 'The Royal Touch in Early Modern England: its Changing Rationale and Practice', Birkbeck, University of London, 2011
Bundesen, Kristin, 'No Other Faction but My Own: Dynastic Politics and Elizabeth I's Carey Cousins', University of Nottingham, 2008
Goldsmith, H., 'All the Queen's Women: the Changing Place and Perception of Aristocratic Women in Elizabethan England, 1558–1620', Northwestern University, 1987
Merton, Charlotte, 'The Women who Served Queen Mary and Queen Elizabeth: Ladies, Gentlewomen and Maids of the Privy Chamber, 1553–1603', Cambridge University, 1992

PUBLISHED SOURCES

Primary
Acts of the Privy Council, ed. J. R. Dasent (London, 1890–1907)
Adams, S., 'The Lauderdale Papers 1561–1570: the Maitland of Lethington State Papers and Leicester Correspondence', *Scottish Historical Review*, 67 (1988), pp. 28–55
Allen, William, *An Admonition to the Nobility* (London, 1588)
Anon., *Cabala, Sive Scrinia Sacra: Mysteries of State and Government in Letters* (London, 1691)
———'Dudley and the Catholic Conspirators of 1561, An Anonymous History from Edward VI to December 1562', British Library MS Additional 48023, ff. 350–369v, 1563, in *Religion, Politics, and Society in Sixteenth-century England*, eds Ian W. Archer, Simon Adams, and George Bernard, Camden Society, 5th series, vol. 22 (Cambridge, 2003)
Arnold, Janet, *Lost from Her Majesties Back: Items of clothing and jewels lost or given away by Queen Elizabeth I between 1561 and 1585, entered in one of the day books kept for the records of the Wardrobe of the Robes* (Wisbech, 1980)
Bacon, Francis, 'Apophthegms', in *The Works of Francis Bacon*, ed. Basil Montague (London, 1823)
———*A Letter Written out of England . . . containing a True Report of a Strange Conspiracy* (London, 1599)

Baker, J. H., ed. *Reports from the Lost Notebooks of Sir James Dyer*, 2 vols (London, 1994)

Beale, Robert, *A Treatise of the Office of a Councellor and Principall Secretarie to the Majestie, 1592*, in Conyers Read, *Mr Secretary Walsingham and the Policy of Queen Elizabeth*, vol. 1 (Hamden, 1967)

'Ben Jonson's Conversations with William Drummond of Hawthornden', in *Ben Jonson*, eds C. H. Herford, P. Simpson, and E. Simpson (Oxford, 1925–52)

Berry, Lloyd E., *John Stubbs's 'Gaping Gulf' with Letters and other Relevant Documents* (Charlottesville, Virginia, 1968)

Birch, Thomas, *Memoirs of the Reign of Queen Elizabeth, from the year 1581 till Death*, 2 vols (London, 1754)

Blackwood, Adam, *Martyre de la royne d'Escosse* (Edinburgh, 1588)

Bodin, Jean, *De la Demonomanie des Sorciers* (Anvers, 1580)

Bohun, Edmund, *The Character of Queen Elizabeth* (London, 1693)

Boorde, Andrew, *The Breuiary of Helthe, for all maner of syckenesses and diseases the which may be in man, or woman doth folowe* (London, 1547)

——*The Fyrst Boke of the Introduction of Knowledge* (London, 1547)

Brenchley Rye, William, *England as Seen By Foreigners in the Days of Elizabeth and James the First* (London, 1865)

Bruce, John, 'Annals of the First Four Years of the Reign of Queen Elizabeth by Sir John Hayward', Camden Society (Cambridge, 1840)

——*Letters of Queen Elizabeth and James VI of Scotland* (London, 1849)

——*Correspondence of King James VI of Scotland* (London, 1861)

Bullein, William, *A newe boke of phisicke* (London, 1599)

——*Bulwarke of defence againste all Sicknes, Sornes and Woundes* (London, 1562)

Calendar of Letters, Despatches and State Papers Relating to the Negotiations between England and Spain, Preserved in the Archives at Simancas and Elsewhere, ed. Royall Tyler, 13 vols (London, 1862–1954)

Calendar of the Manuscripts of His Grace the Duke of Rutland, 4 vols (London, 1888)

Calendar of the Manuscripts of Lord De L'Isle and Dudley, Preserved at Penshurst Place, 6 vols (London, 1933)

Calendar of Manuscripts of the Marquess of Bath at Longleat, Wilts, 3 vols (London, HMSO, 1908)

Calendar of the Manuscripts of the Most Hon. the Marquis of Salisbury, K.G, &c, Preserved at Hatfield House, Hertfordshire, 24 vols (London, 1883–1976)

Calendar of State Papers, Domestic Series, Addenda, 1566–1579, ed. M. A. Green (London, 1871)

Calendar of State Papers, Domestic Series of the Reigns of Edward VI, Mary, Elizabeth, 1547–1625, eds Robert Lemon and Mary Anne Everett Green, 12 vols (London, 1856–72)

Calendar of State Papers, Foreign Series, of the Reign of Elizabeth, eds Joseph Stevenson et al. (London, 1863–1950)

Calendar of State Papers and Manuscripts Relating to English Affairs, Existing in the Archives and Collections of Venice and Other Libraries of Northern Italy, eds Rawdon Brown and G. Cavendish Bentinck, 38 vols (London, 1864–1947)

Calendar of State Papers Relating to English Affairs, Preserved Principally in the Archives of Simancas, Elizabeth, eds M. A. S. Hume et al. (London, 1892–9)

Calendar of State Papers Relating to English Affairs, Preserved Principally at Rome at the Vatican Archives and Library, ed. J. M. Rigg (London, 1916–26)

Calendar of State Papers Relating to Scotland and Mary Queen of Scots, eds Joseph Bain et al., 5 vols (Edinburgh, 1898–1952)

Camden, William, *Annales: The True and Royall History of the Famous Empresse Elizabeth* . . . (London, 1625)

Canestrini, G. and Desjardins, A., *Negociations Diplomatiques de la France avec la Toscane*, 5 vols (Paris, 1865–75)

Carey, Robert, *The Memoirs of Robert Carey*, ed. F. H. Mares (Oxford, 1972)

Carleton, Dudley, 'Dudley Carleton to John Chamberlain 1603–1624', in *Jacobean Letters*, ed. Maurice Lee Jr (New Brunswick, 1972)

Castelnau, Michel de, *Memoires*, ed. Jacques Castelnau (Paris, c.1621)

Catherine de Medicis, *Lettres de Catherine de Medicis*, ed. H. de la Ferrière-Percy (Paris, 1880)

Cecil, William, *The Execution of Justice in England for Maintenance of Publique and Christian Peace* (London, 1583)

Chamberlain, J., *The Letters of John Chamberlain*, ed. N. E. McClure (Philadelphia, 1939)

Chettle, Henry, *England's Mourning Garment* (London, 1603)

————*The History of the Most Renowned and Victorious Princess Elizabeth, Late Queen of England* . . . (London, 1630)

Churchyard, R., *The Firste Parte of Churchyardes Chippes, Containing Twelve Severall Labours* (London, 1575)

Clapham, J., *Elizabeth of England: Certain Observations Concerning the Life and Reign of Queen Elizabeth*, eds E. P. Read and C. Read (Oxford, 1951)

Clay, W. K., ed. *Liturgies and Occasional Forms of Prayer Set Forth in the Reign of Queen Elizabeth* (Cambridge, 1847)

Clifford, Arthur, *The State Papers and Letters of Sir Ralph Sadler*, 2 vols (London, 1809)

Clowes, William, *A Briefe and Necessarie Treatise Touching the Cure of the Disease Called Morbus Gallicus* (London, 1585)

————*A Right Fruitful and Approved Treatise for the Artificial Cure of that Malady Called in Latin Struma* (London, 1602)

Colección de Documentos Inéditos para la Historia de España (Codoin), eds M. F. Navarete et al. (Madrid, 1842–95)

Collection of State Papers, Relating to Affairs in the Reigns of King Henry VIII, King Edward VI, Queen Mary and Queen Elizabeth, from the Year 1542 to 1570, ed. Samuel Haynes (London, 1740)

Collins, A. F., ed. *Jewels and Plate of Queen Elizabeth I: the Inventory of 1574, from MS 1650 and Stowe MS 555 in the British Museum* (London, 1955)

A Conference about the Next Succession to the Crowne of Ingland (Antwerp, 1594)

'The Count of Feria's Dispatch of 14 November 1558', eds M. J. Rodriguez-Salgado and S. Adams, *Camden Miscellany*, 27 (1984), pp. 302–44

Coxe, Francis, *A Short Treatise Declaring the Destestable Wickednesse of Magicall Sciences, as Necromancie, Coniurations of Spirites, Curiouse Astrologie and Such Lyke* (London, 1561)

Dalrymple, David, ed. *The Secret Correspondence of Sir Robert Cecil with James VI* (Edinburgh, 1766)

Dee, John, 'The Compendious Rehearsal of John Dee', in *Hoannis, confratis & monachi Glastoniensis, chronica sive historia de rebus Glastoniensibus*, ed. T. Hearne, 2 vols (Oxford, 1726)

D'Ewes, Simonds, *The Journals of all the Parliaments in the Reign of Queen Elizabeth* (London, 1682)

Devereux, W. B., *Lives and Letters of the Devereux, Earls of Essex*, 2 vols (London, 1853)

Digges, Sir Dudley, *The Compleat Ambassador…* (London, 1655)

Donaldson, G., ed. *The Memoirs of Sir James Melville of Halhill* (London, 1969 edn)

Dudley, Robert, Earl of Leicester, *Correspondence of Robert Dudley, Earl of Leycester, during His Government in the Low Countries, in the Years 1585 and 1586*, ed. John Bruce, Camden Society 27 (London 1844)

Duncan-Jones, K. and Van Dorsten, J., *Miscellaneous Prose of Sir Philip Sidney* (Oxford, 1973)

Eliot, George, *A very true report of the apprehension and taking of that Arche Papist Edmund Campion the Pope his right hand, with three other lewd Jesuite priests, and divers other Laie people, most seditious persons of like sort* (London, 1581)

Elizabeth I, Collected Works, eds Leah S. Marcus, Janel Mueller and Mary Beth Rose (London, 2000)

————*Letters of Queen Elizabeth*, ed. G. B. Harrison (New York, 1968)

Elizabeth I and James VI of Scotland, Letters of Queen Elizabeth and King James VI of Scotland, ed. John Bruce (London, 1849)

Ellis, Henry, ed. *Original Letters Illustrative of English History*, series 1–3 (London, 1824–46)

Elton, G. R., ed. *The Tudor Constitution: Documents and Commentary* (Cambridge, 1972)

Fénélon, Bertrand de Salignac, Seigneur de La Mothe, *Correspondance Diplomatique*, ed. A. Teulet, 7 vols (Paris, 1838–40)

Fisher, F. J., ed. 'The State of England Anno Dom. 1600 by Thomas Wilson', *Camden Miscellany* 16:52 (1936), pp. 1–43

Forbes, P., *A Full View of the Public Transactions in the Reign of Queen Elizabeth*, 2 vols (London, 1740)

Fulke, William, *Antiprognosticon, that is to saye, an invective against the vayne and unprofitable predictions of the astrologians as Nostradame* (London, 1560)

Gachard, M., *Correspondance de Philippe II sur les affaires des Pays-Bas* (Brussels, 1851)

Gossip from a Muniment Room: Being Passages in the Lives of Anne and Mary Fitton, 1574–1618, ed. [A. E] Newdigate-Newdegate (London, 1897)

The Great Bragge and challenge of M. Champion a Jesuite, commonlye called Edmunde Campion, lately arrived in Englande, contayninge nyne articles here severallye laide downe, directed by him to the Lordes of the Counsail (London, 1581)

Halliwell, James, ed. *The Private Diary of Dr John Dee* (London, 1842)

Harington, Sir John, *A New Discourse of a Stale Subject Called the Metamorphosis of Ajax* (London, 1586)

————*Nugae Antiquae: Being a miscellaneous collection of original papers . . . by Sir John Harington, Knt*, ed. T. Park, 2 vols (London, 1804)

————*A Tract on the Succession of the* Crown (1602), ed. C. R. Markham (London, 1880)

————*Letters and Epigrams*, ed. N. E. McClure (Oxford, 1930)

Harrison, Brian A., ed. *A Tudor Journal: The Diary of a Priest in the Tower, 1580–1585* (London, 2000)

Harrison, G. B., *The Letters of Queen Elizabeth* (London, 1935)

Hayward, J., *Annals of the First Four Years of the Reign of Queen Elizabeth* (London, 1840)

Hentzner, P., *A Journey into England in 1598* (Edinburgh, 1881–2)

Historical Manuscripts Commission, *Third Report of the Royal Commission on Historical Manuscripts, Appendix*, London, 1872

Holinshed, Raphael, *Holinshed's 'Chronicles of England, Scotland and Ireland'*, ed. Henry Ellis, 6 vols (London 1807–8)

Howell, T. B., *A Complete Collection of State Trials and Proceedings for High Treason*, 21 vols (London, 1816–26)

'A Journal of Matters of State happened from time to time as well within and without the realme from and before the death of King Edw. the 6th until the yere 1562', in *Religion, Politics and Society in Sixteenth-century England*, eds I. W. Archer, S. Adams and G. W. Bernard, Camden Society, 5th series, vol. 22 (2003)

Klarwill, Victor von, ed. *Queen Elizabeth and Some Foreigners, being a series of hitherto unpublished letters from the archives of the Habsburg family* (London, 1928)

Labanoff, A., *Lettres, Instructions et Memoires de Marie Stuart, Reine d'Ecosse*, vols 1–5 (Paris, 1844–54)

Lefevre, Joseph, *Correspondance de Philippe II sur les Affaires des Pays-Bas*, 2 vols (Brussels, 1940–56)

Leicester's Commonwealth: The Copy of a Letter Written by a Master of Art Cambridge (1584) and other Related Documents, ed. D. C. Peck (Athens, 1985)

Le Laboureur, J., *Nouvelles Additions aux Memoires de Michel de Castelnau, Seigneur de la Mauvissiere*, 3 vols (Brussels, 1731)

Lettenhove, J. M. B. C. Kervyn de, *Relations politiques des Pays-Bas et de l'Angleterre, sous le règne de Philippe II*, 11 vols (Brussels, 1882–1900)

The Letters and Despatches of Richard Verstegan, c.1550–1640, vol. 52, ed. A. G. Petti (London, 1959)

Lodge, E., *Illustrations of English History, Biography and Manners...*2nd edn, 2 vols (London, 1938)

McClure, Norman Egbert, ed. *Letters of John Chamberlain*, 2 vols (Philadelphia, 1939)

Machyn, Henry, *The Diary of Henry Machyn*, ed. John Gough Nichols, Camden Society, 42 (London, 1848)

Maisse, André Hurault, Sieur de, *A Journal of All that Was Accomplished by Monsieur de Maisse, Ambassador in England from King Henry IV to Queen Elizabeth, Anno Domini 1597*, edited and translated by G. B. Harrison and R. A. Jones (London, 1931)

The Manuscripts of His Grace the Duke of Rutland, K.G., Preserved at Belvoir Castle, 4 vols (London, 1888–1905)

Melville, Sir James, *Memoirs of Sir James Melville of Halhill*, ed. Gordon Donaldson (London, 1969)

Millington, Thomas, *The True Narration of the Entertainment of his Majesty from his Departure from Edinburgh till his Receiving at London*, in *Stuart Tracts 1603–1693*, ed. C. H. Frith (New York, 1964)

Mulcaster, Richard, *The Passage of Our Most Drad Soveraigne Lady Quene Elizabeth through the Citie of London to Westminster, the Daye before Her Coronacion* (London, 1559)

Munday, Anthony, *A Breede Discourse of the Taking of Edmund Campion, the Seditious Jesuit, and Divers other Papistes, in Barkeshire* (London, 1581)

——*A breefe Answer made unto two seditious Pamphlets, the one printed in French, and the other in English. Contayning a defence of Edmund Campion and his complices, their moste horrible and unnaturall Treasons, against her Majestie and the Realme* (London, 1581)

——*A Discoverie of Edmund Campion, and his Confederates, their Most Horrible and Traitorous Practises, against her Majesties Most Royall Person, and the Realme* (London, 1582)

Murdin, W., *A Collection of State Papers Relating to affairs in the reign of Elizabeth I from 1542 to 1560 left by William Cecil: Lord Burghley* (London, 1759)

Naunton, Sir Robert, *Elizabeth: Fragmenta Regalia* (London, 1641)

Newton, T., *An Epitaphe Upon the Worthy and Honourable Lady, the Lady Knowles* (London, 1569)

Nichols, J. G., *The Progresses and Public Processions of Queen Elizabeth*, 3 vols (London, 1823)

Nicolas, Sir (Nicolas) Harris, *Memoirs of the Life and Times of Sir Christopher Hatton* (London, 1847)

Norton, Thomas and Sackville, Thomas, *Gorboduc or Ferrex and Porrex*, ed. I. B. Cauthen Jr (London, 1970)

Nowell, Alexander, *A Catechism Written in Latin by Alexander Nowell, Dean of St Paul's . . . Together with the Same Catechism Translated into English by Thomas Norton, Appended is a Sermon Preached by Dean Nowell Before Queen Elizabeth . . . January 11, 1563*, ed. G. E. Corrie (Cambridge, 1853)

An Order of Praier and Thankes-giving, for the preservation of the Queenes Majesties life and safetie . . . With a short extract of William Parries voluntarie confession, written in his own hand (London, 1585)

Osborne, Francis, *Traditional Memoirs on the Reign of Queen Elizabeth, In the Miscellaneous Works of that Eminent Statesman, Francis Osborne, Esq*, 2 vols (London, 1722)

'Papers Relating to Mary Queen of Scots, Mostly Addressed to or Written by Sir Francis Knollys', *Philobiblon Society Miscellanies*, 14 (1872), pp. 14–69

Parker, Matthew, *Correspondence of Matthew Parker*, eds John Bruce and T. T. Perowne (Cambridge, 1913)

Peck, D. C. (ed.), 'News from Heaven and Hell: A Defamatory Narrative of the Earl of Leicester', *English Literary Renaissance*, 8 (1978), pp. 141–58

——ed., 'The Letter of Estate: An Elizabethan Libel', *Notes and Queries*, n.s.28 (February, 1981), pp. 21–35

——ed., *Leicester's Commonwealth: The Copy of a Letter written by a Master of the Art of Cambridge (1584) and Related Documents* (Ohio, 1985)

Persons, Robert, *The Judgement of a Catholicke English-man, Living in Banishment For His Religion* (Saint Omer, 1608)

———*A Discussion of the Answere of M. William Barlowe* (Saint Omer, 1612)

Planché, J. R., *Regal Records, or a Chronicle of the Coronations of Queens Regnant of England* (London, 1838)

Platt, Hugh, *Delightes for Ladies, to adorn their Persons, Tables, closets and distillatories with Beauties, banguets, presumes and Waters* (London, 1608)

Platter, Thomas, *Thomas Platters' Travels in England*, ed. Clare Williams (London, 1937)

Pollen, J. H., *Papal Negotiations with Mary, Queen of Scots during her Reign in Scotland 1561–1567* (Edinburgh, 1901)

——— 'Queen Mary's Letter to the Duke of Guise January 1562', *Scottish Historical Society*, 43 (1904)

———'Memoirs of Robert Persons, SJ', *Catholic Record Society*, 2 (1905) and 4 (1907)

———ed. and trans., 'Lethington's Account of Negotiations with Elizabeth Edinburgh in September and October 1565', *Scottish History Society*, vol. XLIII (Jan, 1904), pp. 38–45, p. 39

Poullet, E. and Piot, Charles, *Correspondance du Cardinal Granvelle*, vols 1–9 (Brussels, 1878–96)

Proceedings in the Parliaments of Elizabeth I, 1558–1581, ed. T. E. Harley, 3 vols (London, 1981–95)

Puttenham, George, *The Arte of English Poesie* (Kent, OH, 1970)

Ralegh, Sir Walter, *The Letters of Sir Walter Ralegh*, eds Agnes Latham and Joyce Youngs (Exeter, 1999)

Read, Conyers, ed. *The Bardon Papers: Documents Relating to the Imprisonment & Trial of Mary Queen of Scots*, Camden Society, third series, 17 (London, 1909)

———ed., 'The Proposal to Assassinate Mary Queen of Scots at Fotheringhay', *English Historical Review*, 40 (1925), pp. 234–5

Robinson, H., *The Zurich Letters*, 2 vols, Parker Society (Cambridge, 1842–5)

Sanders, Nicholas, *Historia ecclesiastica del scisma del regno de Ingleterra . . . hasta la muerte de la reyne de Escocia* (Madrid, 1588)

Scot, Reginald, *The Discoverie of Witchcraft* (London, 1584)

Secret History of the Most Renowned Q. Elizabeth and the E. of Essex by a Person of Quality (Cologne, 1680)

Sidney, Sir Henry, *Letters and Memorials of State in the Reigns of Queen Mary, Queen Elizabeth, King James, King Charles the First . . . Written and Collected by Sir Henry Sidney*, ed. Arthur Collins, 2 vols (London, 1746)

Sidney, Sir Philip, *The Correspondence of Sir Philip Sidney and Hubert Languet*, ed. Steuart A. Pears (London, 1845)

Smith, Sir Thomas, 'Sir Thomas Smith's Orations for and against the Queen's Marriage', in *The Life of the Learned Sir Thomas Smith*, John Strype, Appendix III (Oxford, 1820)

Southwell, Robert, *An Humble Supplication to her Majestie* (London, 1600)

Spenser, Edmund, *The Faerie Queene* (London, 1590)

Statutes of the Realm, eds A. Luders et al., 11 vols (London, 1810–28)

Stowe, John, *Chronicles of England* (London, 1580)

————*Three Fifteenth-century Chronicles: with Historical Memoranda, by John Stowe, the Antiquary, and Contempory Notes of Occurances Written by him in the Reign of Queen Elizabeth*, ed. James Gairdner (London 1880)

Strype, John, *Annals of the Reformation and Establishment of Religion and other Various Occurrences in the Church of England During Queen Elizabeth's Happy Reign* (Oxford, 1728) (repr. 1820–40)

————*Ecclesiastical Memorials...* (Oxford, 1820–40)

————*The Life of the Learned Sir Thomas Smith* (Oxford, 1820)

Stubbes, Philip, *The Anatomie of Abuses* (London, 1583)

Stubbs, John, *The Discoverie of a Gaping Gulf Whereinto England is like to be Swallowed by another French marriage, if the Lord forbids not the bans...* (London, 1579)

Teulet, *Relations Politiques de la France et de L'Espagne avec L'Ecosse au XVIe siècle*, 3 vols (Paris, 1826)

Throckmorton, Francis, *A Discoverie of Treasons Practised and Attempted against the Queenes Majestie and the Realme* (London, 1584)

Tooker, William, *Charisma Sive Donum Sanationis* ('*The Royal Gift of Healing*') (London, 1597)

A Transcript of the Registers of the Company of Stationers of London, 1554–1640 AD, ed. Edward Arber, 5 vols (London, 1875–94)

A True and Plaine Declaration of the horrible Treasons, practised by William Parry, the Traitor, against the Queenes Majestie. The maner of his Arraignment, Conviction, and execution, together with the copies of sundry letters of his and others, tending to divers purposes, for the proofes of his Treasons (London, 1585)

Tudor Royal Proclamations, eds Paul L. Hughes and James F. Larkin, 3 vols (New Haven, 1964–9)

Vertot, R. A. and Villaret, C., *Ambassades de Messieurs de Noailles en Angleterre*, 5 vols (Leyden, 1763)

Vives, J. L., *On Education*, trans. F. Watson (Cambridge, 1913)

————*De Institutione Feminae Christianae*, 2 vols, eds C. Fantazzi and C. Matheussen (Leiden, 1996)

Von Klarwill, Victor, *The Fugger News-Letter*, 2nd series (London, 1926)

————*Queen Elizabeth and Some Foreigners; Being a Series of Hitherto Unpublished Letters from the Archives of the Habsburg family*, trans. T. H. Nash (London, 1928)

Walsingham, Francis, 'Journal of Sir Francis Walsingham from December 1570 to April 1583', *Camden Miscellany* VI, Camden Society, Original series 106 (London, 1871)

Watson, F., ed., *Vives and the Renascence Education of Women* (London, 1912)

Weiss, Charles, *Papiers d'Etat du Cardinal Granvelle*, 9 vols (Paris, 1841–52)

Wilson, Thomas, 'A Treatise of England's Perils, 1578', ed. A. J. Schmidt, *Archiv für Reformations Geschichte*, 46 (1955), pp. 243–9

Wright, T., *Queen Elizabeth and her Times: a Series of Original letters, Selected from the Inedited Private Correspondence of the Lord Treasurer Burghley, the Earl of Leicester, the Secretaries Walsingham and Smith, Sir Christopher Hatton, and most of the distinguished persons of the period*, 2 vols (London, 1838)

Wriothesley, Charles, *A Chronicle of England*, ed. W. D. Hamilton, Camden Society, NS 20 (London, 1877)

Yorke, Philip, 2nd Earl of Hardwicke, ed. *Miscellaneous State Papers, from 1501 to 1726*, 2 vols (London, 1778)

Secondary

Adams, Robyn, 'A Spy on the Payroll? William Herle and the Mid-Elizabethan Polity', *BIHR*, 82 (2009), pp. 1–15

Adams, Simon, 'Eliza Enthroned? The Court and Its Politics', in *The Reign of Elizabeth I*, ed. C. Haigh (London, 1984), pp. 55–77

————'The Release of Lord Darnley and the failure of the amity', in *Mary Stewart: Queen in Three Kingdoms*, ed. M. Lynch (Oxford, 1988)

———— 'Favourites and Factions at the Elizabethan Court', in *Princes, Patronage and the Nobility: The Court at the Beginning of the Modern Age*, eds Ronald G. Asch and Adolf M. Burke (Oxford, 1991), pp. 265–87

————*Leicester and the Court: Essays on Elizabethan Politics*, especially 'Queen Elizabeth's Eyes at Court: The Earl of Leicester', pp. 130–50 (Manchester, 2002)

————*ODNB* entries for: 'Brooke, Frances, Lady Cobham (*b*. after 1530, *d.* 1592)'; 'Dudley, Amy, Lady Dudley (1532–1560)'; 'Dudley, Anne, Countess of Warwick (1548/9–1604)'; 'Dudley, Robert, Earl of Leicester (1532/3–1588)'; 'Howard, Katherine, Countess of Nottingham (1545/50–1603)'; 'Radcliffe, Mary (*c.*1550–1617/18)'; 'Scudamore, Mary, Lady Scudamore (*c.*1550–1603)'; 'Sheffield, Douglas, Lady Sheffield (1542/3–1608)'; 'Sidney, Mary, Lady Sidney (1530/35–1586)'; 'Stafford, Dorothy, Lady Stafford (1526–1604)'; 'Sutton, Edward, 4th Baron Dudley (*c.*1515–1586)' (Oxford, 2004 and online edn. 2007–11)

Adler, Doris, 'Imaginary Toads in Real Gardens', *English Literary Renaissance*, 11 (1981), pp. 235–60

Alford, S., *The Early Elizabethan Polity: William Cecil and the British Succession Crisis, 1558–1569* (Cambridge, 1998)

————*Burghley: William Cecil at the Court of Elizabeth I* (New Haven, 2008)

————*The Watchers: A Secret History of the Reign of Elizabeth I* (London, 2012)

Allinson, R., 'These latter days of the world: the correspondence of Elizabeth I and James VI, 1590–1603', *Early Modern Literary Studies*, XVI (2007), pp. 1–27

Alvarez-Recio, Leticia, 'Contemporary visions of Mary Stuart's execution: saintliness and vilification', in *The Rituals and Rhetoric of Queenship: Medieval to Early Modern*, eds Liz Oakley-Brown and Louise J. Wilkinson (Dublin, 2009), pp. 209–21

Anstruther, Godfrey, *The Seminary Priests: Elizabethan 1558–1603* (Ware and Durham, 1969)

Archer, Jayne, 'Rudenesse itself She Doth Refine: Queen Elizabeth I as Lady Alchymia', in *Goddesses and Queens: The Iconography of Queen Elizabeth I*, eds A. Connolly and L. Hopkins (Manchester, 2008)

———— Goldring, Elizabeth and Knight, Sarah, *The Progresses, Pageants, and Entertainments of Queen Elizabeth I* (Oxford, 2007)

Arnold, Janet, 'The "Coronation" Portrait of Queen Elizabeth I', *Burlington Magazine*, 120 (November, 1978), pp. 727–41

———— 'Sweet England's Jewels', in *Princely Magnificence: Court Jewels of the*

Renaissance 1500–1630, ed. Anna Somers Cocks (London, 1980), pp. 31–40
———— 'The Picture of Elizabeth I when Princess', *Burlington Magazine*, 123 (1981), pp. 303–4
————*Queen Elizabeth's Wardrobe Unlock'd* (Leeds, 1988)
Asch, Ronald G., 'A Difficult Legacy: Elizabeth I's Bequest to the Early Stuarts', in *Queen Elizabeth I: Past and Present*, ed. Christa Jansohn (Munster, 2004), pp. 29–44
Ashelford, J., *A Visual History of Costume: The Sixteenth Century* (London, 1983)
————*Dress in the Age of Elizabeth I* (Avon, 1988)
Auerbach, Erna, *Tudor Artists* (London, 1954)
————*Nicholas Hilliard* (London, 1961)
Axton, Marie, 'The Influence of Edmund Plowden's Succession Treatise', *Huntington Library Quarterly*, 37 (3) 1974, pp. 209–26
———— *The Queen's Two Bodies: Drama and the Elizabethan Succession* (London, 1977)
Bakan, R., 'Queen Elizabeth I: a Case of Testicular Feminisation?', *Medical Hypotheses*, 17.3 (1985), pp. 277–84
Barnes, K., 'John Stubbs, 1579: The French Ambassador's Account', *Historical Research*, 64 (1991), pp. 421–6
Barrett-Graves, Debra, 'Highly touched in honour: Elizabeth I and the Alençon controversy', in *Elizabeth I: Always Her Own Free Woman*, eds Carole Levin et al. (Aldershot, 2003), pp. 43–62
Bartlett, Kenneth, 'Papal Policy and the English Crown 1563–1565: The Bertano Correspondence', *Sixteenth-century Journal*, 23 (1992), pp. 643–59
Barton, A., 'Harking Back to Elizabeth: Ben Jonson and Caroline Nostalgia', *English Literary History*, XLVIII (1981), pp. 706–31
Bassnett, Susan, *Elizabeth I: A Feminist Perspective* (Oxford, 1988)
Bates, Catherine, *The Rhetoric of Courtship in Elizabethan Language and Literature* (Cambridge, 1992)
Bayne, C. G., *Anglo-Roman Relations 1558–1565* (Oxford, 1913)
Beem, Charles, *The Lioness Roared: The Problems of Female Rule in English History* (New York, 2006)
Beer, Anna, *Bess, The Life of Lady Ralegh, Wife to Sir Walter* (London, 2004)
Bell, Iona, 'Souereaigne Lord of Lordly Lady of this Land: Elizabeth, Stubbs and the Gaping Gulf', in *Dissing Elizabeth: Negative Representations of Gloriana*, ed. Julia M. Walker (Durham, NC, 1998), pp. 99–117
————'Elizabeth and the Politics of Elizabethan Courtship', in *Elizabeth I: Always Her Own Free Woman*, eds Carole Levin et al. (Aldershot, 2003), pp. 179–91
Bellamy, John, *The Tudor Law of Treason* (London, 1979)
Belsey, A. and Belsey, C., 'Icons of Divinity: Portraits of Elizabeth I', in *Renaissance Bodies: The Human Figure in English Culture, c.1540–1660*, eds Lucy Gent and Nigel Llewellyn (London, 1990), pp. 11–35
Bergeron, David M., *English Civic Pageantry 1558–1642* (Columbia, 1971)
Bernard, G. W., 'The Downfall of Sir Thomas Seymour', in *The Tudor Nobility*, ed. G. W. Bernard (Manchester, 1992), pp. 212–40
Berry, Philippa, *Of Chastity and Power: Elizabethan Literature and the Unmarried Queen* (London, 1989)
Bertelli, Sergio, *The King's Body: Sacred Rituals of Power in Mediaeval and Early*

Modern Europe, trans. R. Burr Litchfield (Pennsylvania, 2001)

Betts, Hannah, '"The Image of this Queene so quaynt": The Pornographic Blazon 1588–1603', in *Dissing Elizabeth: Negative Representations of Gloriana*, ed. Julia M. Walker (Durham, NC, 1998), pp. 153–84

Bevington, David, 'Lyly's *Endymion* and *Midas*: The Catholic Question in England', *Comparative Drama*, 32 (1998), pp. 26–46

Bindoff, S. T., Hurtsfield, J. and Williams, C. H., eds, *Elizabethan Government and Society: Essays Presented to Sir John Neale* (London, 1961)

Bingham, Caroline, *Darnley: a Life of Henry Stuart, Lord Darnley, Consort of Mary Queen of Scots* (London, 1995)

Bloch, Marc, *The Royal Touch: Sacred Monarchy and Scrofula in England and France*, trans. J. E. Anderson (London, 1973)

Bossy, John, 'English Catholics and the French Marriage, 1577–81', *Recusant History*, 5 (1959), pp. 2–16

————'The Character of Elizabethan Catholicism', *Past and Present*, 21 (1962), pp. 39–59

————'Rome and the Elizabethan Catholics: A Question of Geography', *Historical Journal*, 7 (1964), pp. 135–49

————*Giordano Bruno and the Embassy Affair* (New Haven and London, 1991)

Bowler, Gerard, 'An Axe or an Act: the Parliament of 1572 and Resistance Theory in Early Elizabethan England', *Canadian Journal of History*, 19.3 (1984), pp. 349–59

Bowman, Mary R., 'She There as Princess Rained: Spenser's Figure of Elizabeth', *Renaissance Quarterly*, 43 (1990), pp. 509–28

Boyle, Andrew, 'Cultural Life and the Exercise of Power at the Residences of Henry Fitzalan, Earl of Arundel, 1512–1580', in *The Court as a Stage: England and the Low Countries in the Later Middle Ages*, eds S. Gunn and A. Janse (Woodbridge, 2006), pp. 169–82

Bradford, Charles Angell, *Blanche Parry: Queen Elizabeth's Gentlewoman* (London, 1935)

————*Helena Marchioness of Northampton* (London, 1936)

Bradford, Hugh Morgan, *Queen Elizabeth's Apothecary* (London, 1991)

Bray, Alan, *The Friend* (Chicago, 2003)

Breight, Curtis Charles, 'Caressing the Great: Viscount Montague's Entertainment of Elizabeth at Cowdray, 1591', *Sussex Archaeological Collections*, 127 (1989), pp. 147–66

Brennan, Michael G., *The Sidneys of Penshurst and the Monarchy, 1500–1700* (Aldershot, 2006)

————Kinnamon, Noel J. and Hannay, Margaret P., 'Robert Sidney, the Dudleys and Queen Elizabeth', in *Elizabeth I: Always Her Own Free Woman*, eds Carole Levin et al. (Aldershot, 2003), pp. 20–42

Brown, Elizabeth A., 'Companion Me with My Mistress: Cleopatra, Elizabeth I and their Waiting Women', in *Maids and Mistresses: Cousins and Queens: Women's Alliances in Early Modern England*, eds Susan Frye and Karen Robertson (Oxford, 1999), pp. 131–45

Brownlow, F. W., 'Performance and Reality at the Court of Elizabeth I', in *The Mysteries of Elizabeth I*, eds Kirby Farrell and Kathleen Swaim (Amherst, 2003), pp. 3–20

Bundesen, K., 'Circling the Crown: Political Power and Female Agency in Sixteenth-century England', in *Desperate Housewives: Politics, Propriety and Pornography: Three Centuries of Women in England*, ed. J. Jordan (Cambridge, 2009), pp. 3–28

———'Lousy with cousins: Elizabeth I's family at court', in *The Rituals and Rhetoric of Queenship: Medieval to Early Modern*, eds Liz Oakley-Brown and Louise J. Wilkinson (Dublin, 2009), pp. 74–89

Burt, Richard, 'Doing the Queen: Gender, Sexuality and Censorship of Elizabeth I's Royal Image from Renaissance Portraiture to Twentieth-Century Mass Media', in *Literature and Censorship in Renaissance England*, ed. Andrew Hadfield (London, 2001), pp. 207–28

Butler, E. C. and Pollen, J. H., 'Dr William Gifford in 1586', *The Month*, 103 (1902), pp. 243–58; pp. 349–65

Canny, Nicholas, *The Elizabethan Conquest of Ireland: A Pattern Established* (Hansocks, 1976)

Carlton, Charles, Woods, Robert L., Robertson, Mary L. and Block, Joseph S., eds *State, Sovereigns and Society in Early Modern England: Essays in Honour of A.J. Slavin* (New York, 1998)

Carrafello, M. K., 'English Catholicism and the Jesuit Mission of 1580–1581', *Historical Journal* 37, pp. 761–74

Carroll, Stuart, *Martyrs and Murderers: The Guise Family and the Making of Europe* (Oxford, 2009)

Cavanagh, Shelia R., *Wanton Eyes and Chaste Desires: Female Sexuality in 'The Faerie Queen'* (Bloomington, 1994)

———'The Bad Seed: Princess Elizabeth and the Seymour Incident', in *Dissing Elizabeth: Negative Representations of Gloriana*, ed. Julia M. Walker (Durham, NC, 1998), pp. 9–29

Cerasano, S. P. and Wynne-Davies, Marion, eds *Gloriana's Face: Women, Public and Private, in the English Renaissance* (London, 1992)

Chamberlin, Frederick, *The Private Character of Queen Elizabeth* (New York, 1922)

———*The Sayings of Elizabeth* (London, 1923)

———*Elizabeth and Leycester* (London, 1939)

Chambers, E. K., *The Elizabethan Stage*, 4 vols (Oxford, 1923)

Christy, Miller, 'Queen Elizabeth's Visit to Tilbury in 1588', *English Historical Review*, 34 (1919), pp. 43–61

Clifford, Henry, *The Life of Jane Dormer, Duchess of Feria*, ed. H. Stevenson (London, 1887)

Coch, Christine, 'Mother of My Contreye: Elizabeth I and Tudor Constructions of Motherhood', *English Literary Renaissance*, 26 (1996), pp. 423–50

Cole, Mary Hill, *The Portable Queen: Elizabeth I and the Politics of Ceremony* (Amherst, 1999)

Collinson, Patrick, *Elizabethan Essays* (London, 1994)

———'The Elizabethan Exclusion Crisis and the Elizabethan Polity', *Proceedings of the British Academy*, 84 (1994), pp. 51–92

———'The Politics of Religion and the Religion of Politics in Elizabethan England', *BIHR* 82 (2009), pp. 74–92

Colvin, H. M., *The History of the King's Works*, vols III–IV, 1485–1660 (London, 1975–82)

Content, Rob, 'Faire is Fowle; Interpreting Anti-Elizabethan Composite Portraiture', in *Dissing Elizabeth: Negative Representations of Gloriana*, ed. Julia N. Walker (Durham, NC, 1998), pp. 229–51

Cooper, J., *The Queen's Agent: Francis Walsingham at the Court of Elizabeth I* (London, 2011)

Copeman, W. S. C., *Doctors and Disease in Tudor Times* (London, 1960)

Crawford, Katherine, 'Cathérine de Médicis and the Performance of Political Motherhood', *Sixteenth-century Journal*, 31:3 (2000), pp. 643–73

Crawford, P. and Gowing, L., *Women's Worlds in Seventeenth-century England* (London, 2000)

Crawfurd, Raymond, *The King's Evil* (Oxford, 1911)

———*Bonfires and Bells: National Memory and the Protestant Calendar in Elizabethan and Stuart England* (London, 1989)

Cressy, David, 'Binding the Nation: the Bonds of Association 1584 and 1696', in *Tudor Rule and Revolution: Essays for G .R. Elton from his American Friends*, eds Delloyd J. Guff and John W. McKenna (Cambridge, 1982), pp. 217–34

Croly, Christopher P., *Religion and English Foreign Policy, 1558–64* (Cambridge, 2000)

Crooper, Elizabeth, 'The Beauty of Women: Problems in the Rhetoric of Renaissance Portraiture', in *Rewriting the Renaissance: The Discourses of Sexual Difference in Early Modern Europe*, eds Margaret W. Ferguson, Maureen Quilligan and Nancy J. Vickers (Chicago, 1986), pp. 175–90

Cunnington, Cecil W. and Cunnington, Phillis, *A Handbook of English Costume in the Sixteenth Century* (London, 1962)

Dannenfeldt, K. H., 'Sleep: Theory and Practice in the Late Renaissance', *Journal of the History of Medicine and Allied Sciences*, 41 (1986), pp. 415–41

Dawson, Jane E. A., 'Mary Queen of Scots, Lord Darnley and Anglo-Scottish Relations in 1565', *International History Review*, 8 (1986), pp. 1–24

———'Sir William Cecil and the British Dimension of Early Elizabethan Foreign Policy', *History*, 74 (1989), pp. 908–26

Daybell, James, ed. *Woman and Politics in Early Modern England, 1450–1700* (Aldershot, 2004)

De Lisle, Leanda, *After Elizabeth: How James King of Scots Won the Crown of England in 1603* (London, 2005)

———*The Sisters Who Would be Queen: the tragedy of Mary, Katherine and Lady Jane Grey* (London, 2009)

Dewar, Mary, *Sir Thomas Smith* (London, 1964)

Dewhurst, J., 'The Alleged Miscarriages of Catherine of Aragon and Anne Boleyn', *Medical History*, 28 (1984), pp. 49–56

Dickens, A. G., 'The Elizabethans and St Bartholomew', in *The Massacre of St Bartholomew: Reappraisals and Documents*, ed. Alfred Soman (The Hague, 1974), pp. 52–70

Diefendorf, Barbara B., *Beneath the Cross: Catholics and Huguenots in Sixteenth-century Paris* (New York and Oxford, 1991)

Dillon, A., *The Construction of Martyrdom in the English Catholic Community, 1535–1603* (Aldershot, 2002)

Dimock, Arthur, 'The Conspiracy of Dr Lopez', *English Historical Review*, 9 (1894), pp. 440–72

Dolan, F. E., 'Taking the Pencil out of God's Hand: Art, Nature, and the Face-Painting Debate in Early Modern England', *PMLA*, CIII (1993), pp. 224–39

Doran, Susan, 'Why Did Elizabeth Not Marry', in *Dissing Elizabeth: Negative Representations of Gloriana*, ed. Julia M. Walker (London, 1988), pp. 30–59

———'Religion and Politics at the Court of Elizabeth I: The Hapsburg Marriage Negotiations of 1559–67', *English Historical Review*, 104 (1989), pp. 908–26

———'Juno versus Diana: The Treatment of Elizabeth I's Marriages in Plays and Entertainments 1561–81', *Historical Journal*, 38 (1995), pp. 257–74

———*Monarchy and Matrimony: The Courtships of Elizabeth I* (London, 1996)

———ed., *Elizabeth: The Exhibition at the National Maritime Museum* (London, 2003)

———and Freeman, T. S., eds *The Myth of Elizabeth* (Basingstoke, 2003)

———and Jones, Norman, eds *The Elizabethan World* (Oxford, 2011)

Douglas, Mary, *Purity and Danger* (London: Routledge and Kegan Paul, 1966; reprint: 1996)

Dovey, Zillah, *An Elizabethan Progress: The Queen's Journey into East Anglia, 1578* (Teaneck, NJ, 1996)

Dunlop, Ian, *Palaces and Progresses of Elizabeth I* (New Haven, 1993)

Dunn, Jane, *Elizabeth and Mary: Cousins, Rivals, Queens* (New York, 2004)

Dunn-Hensley, Susan, 'Whore Queens: The Sexualised Female Body and the State', in *'High and Mighty Queens of Early Modern England: Realities and Representations*, eds Carole Levin, Jo Eldridge Carney and Debra Barrett-Graves (Basingstoke, 2003), pp. 101–16

Eccles, A., *Obstetrics and Gynaecology in Tudor and Stuart England* (London, 1982)

Edwards, Francis, *The Marvellous Chance: Thomas Howard, Fourth Duke of Norfolk, and the Ridolphi Plot, 1570–1572* (London, 1968)

———*Robert Persons: The Biography of an Elizabethan Jesuit 1545–1610* (St Louis, 1995)

———*Plots and Plotters in the Reign of Elizabeth I*, (Dublin, 2002)

Ekirch, R., 'Sleep We Have Lost: Pre-Industrial Slumber in the British Isles', *American Historical Review*, 106:2 (2001), pp. 343–86

Erikson, Carolly, *The First Elizabeth* (New York, 1983)

Finsten, Jill, *Isaac Oliver: Art at the Courts of Elizabeth I and James I* (New York, 1981)

Fischlin, Daniel, 'Political Allegory, Absolutist Ideology and the "Rainbow Portrait" of Queen Elizabeth I', *Renaissance Quarterly*, 50 (1997), pp. 175–206

Freeman, Arthur, *Elizabeth's Misfits. Brief Lives of English Eccentrics, Exploiters, Rogues and Failures, 1580–1660* (London, 1978)

Frye, Susan, 'The Myth of Elizabeth at Tilbury', *Sixteenth-century Journal*, 23 (1992), pp. 95–114

———*Elizabeth I: The Competition for Representation* (Oxford, 1993)

———'Sewing Connections: Elizabeth Tudor, Mary Stuart, Elizabeth Talbot and Seventeenth-century Anonymous Needleworkers', in Susan Frye and

Karen Robertson, eds *Maids and Mistresses, Cousins and Queens: Women's Alliances in Early Modern England* (Oxford, 1999), pp. 165–82

————'Elizabeth When a Princess: Early Self-Representations in a Portrait and a Letter', in *The Body of the Queen. Gender and Rule in the Courtly World*, ed. Regina Schulte (New York, 2006), pp. 43–60

Furdell, Elizabeth Lane, *The Royal Doctors 1485–1714: Medical Personnel at the Tudor and Stuart Courts* (New York, 2001)

————'Boorde, Andrew (*c.*1490–1549)', *ODNB*

Garrett, C. H., *The Marian Exiles: a Study in the Origins of Elizabethan Puritanism* (Cambridge, 1938)

————*English Catholic Exiles in Late Sixteenth-century Paris* (Woodbridge, 2011)

Gibbons, K., 'No home in exile? Elizabethan Catholics in Paris', *Reformation*, XV (2010), pp. 115–31

Girouard, Mark, *Elizabethan Architecture: Its Rise and Fall, 1540–1640* (London, 2009)

Giry-Deloison, C., 'France and Elizabethan England', *Transactions of the Royal Historical Society*, XIV (2004), pp. 223–42

Gowing, Laura, *Common Bodies: Women, Touch and Power in Seventeenth-century England* (New Haven, 2003)

————'The Politics of Women's Friendship in Early Modern England', in *Love, Friendship and Faith in Europe, 1300–1800*, eds Laura Gowing, Michael Hunter and Miri Rubin (New York, 2005), pp. 131–49

Graves, J., *A Brief Memoir of the Lady Elizabeth Fitzgerald, Known as the Fair Geraldine* (Dublin, 1874)

Graves, M. A. R., 'Thomas Norton, the Parliament Man', *Historical Journal*, 23:1 (1980), pp. 17–35

Green, Dominic, *The Double Life of Doctor Lopez* (London, 2003)

Green, Janet M., 'I My Self: Queen Elizabeth I's Oration at Tilbury Camp', *Sixteenth-century Journal*, 28 (1997), pp. 421–5

Greenblatt, Stephen J., *Sir Walter Ralegh, The Renaissance Man and His Roles* (New York, 1973)

Gristwood, Sarah, *Arbella: England's Lost Queen* (London, 2003)

————*Elizabeth and Leicester: Power, Passion, Politics* (London, 2007)

Guilday, Peter, *Catholic Refugees on the Continent, 1558–1795: vol. I: The English Colleges and Convents in the Catholic Low Countries, 1558–1795* (London and New York, 1914)

Gunn, Fenja, *The Artificial Face: A History of Cosmetics* (New York, 1975)

Guth, Delloyd J., and McKenna, John W., eds *Tudor Rule and Revolution* (Cambridge, 1982)

Guy, John, '*My Heart is My Own': The Life of Mary Queen of Scots* (London, 2004)

————ed., *The Reign of Elizabeth I: Court and Culture in the Last Decade* (Cambridge, 1995)

Hackett, Helen, *Virgin Mother, Maiden Queen: Elizabeth I and the Cult of the Virgin Queen* (London, 1995)

————'The Rhetoric of (In)fertility: Shifting Responses to Elizabeth I's Childlessness', in *Rhetoric, Women and Politics in Early Modern England*, eds Jennifer Richards and Alison Thorne (London, 2007), pp. 149–71

Haigh, C. A., *The Reign of Elizabeth I* (London, 1984)
————*Elizabeth I: Profile in Power* (London, 1988)
————*Elizabeth I* (London, 2001)
Hammer, Paul E. J., 'Patronage at Court, Faction and the Earl of Essex', in *The Reign of Elizabeth I*, ed. John Guy (Cambridge, 1995), pp. 65–86
————'Upstaging the Queen: the Earl of Essex, Francis Bacon and the Accession Day Celebrations of 1595', in *The Politics of the Stuart Court Masque*, eds David Bevington and Peter Holbrook (Cambridge, 1998), pp. 41–66
————*The Polarisation of Elizabethan Politics: The Political Career of Robert Devereux, 2nd Earl of Essex, 1585–1597* (Cambridge, 1999)
———— 'Sex and the Virgin Queen: Aristocratic Concupiscence and the Court of Elizabeth I', *Sixteenth-century Journal*, 31:1 (2000), pp. 77–97
Hansen, Elizabeth, 'Torture and Truth in Renaissance England', *Representations*, 34 (1991), pp. 53–84
Harkness, Deborah, *John Dee's Conversations with Angels* (Cambridge, 1999)
————*The Jewel House: Elizabethan London and the Scientific Revolution* (New Haven, 2007)
Harrison, G. B., *An Elizabethan Journal*, 3 vols (London, 1928)
Haugaard, W. P., 'Elizabeth Tudor's Book of Devotions; A Neglected Clue to the Queen's Life and Character', *Sixteenth-century Journal*, 12:2 (1981), pp. 79–106
Hawkins, Edward, Franks, Augustus W. and Grueber, Herbert A., *Medallic Illustrations of the History of Great Britain and Ireland to the Death of George II* (London, 1885)
Haynes, Alan, *The White Bear: the Elizabethan Earl of Leicester* (London, 1987)
————*Invisible Power: the Elizabethan Secret Services, 1570–1603* (Stroud, 1992)
————*Sex in Elizabethan England* (Stroud, 1997)
Hayward, Maria, 'Dressed to Impress', in *Tudor Queenship: The Reigns of Mary and Elizabeth*, eds Alice Hunt and Anna Whitelock (Basingstoke, 2010), pp. 81–94
Hearn, Karen, ed., *Dynasties: Painting in Tudor and Jacobean England, 1530–1630* (London, 1995)
————and Croft, Pauline, 'Only Matrimony Maketh Children To Be Certain... Two Elizabethan Pregnancy Portraits', *British Art Journal*, 3.3 (2002), pp. 19–24
Heath, James, *Torture and English Law: An Administrative and Legal History from the Plantagenets to the Stuarts* (London, 1982)
Hibbert, C., *The Virgin Queen: The Personal History of Elizabeth* (London, 1990)
Hicks, Leo, 'The Growth of a Myth: Father Robert Persons SJ, and Leicester's Commonwealth', *Studies: An Irish Quarterly*, 46 (1957), pp. 91–105
———— 'The Strange Case of Dr William Parry: The Career of an Agent-provocateur', *Studies: An Irish Quarterly*, 37 (1984), pp. 343–62
Highley, C., 'A Pestilent and Seditious Book: Nicholas Sander's *Schismatis Anglicano* and Catholic Histories of the Reformation', *Huntington Library Quarterly*, LXVII (2005), pp. 151–72
Holmes, Peter, 'The Authorship and Early Reception of *A Conference about the*

Next Succession to the Crown of England', *Historical Journal*, 23 (1980),
   pp. 415–29
————'The Authorship of Leicester's Commonwealth', *Journal of Ecclesiastical
   History*, 33 (1982), pp. 424–30
————*Resistance and Compromise: the Political Thought of Elizabethan Catholics*
   (Cambridge, 1982)
————'Mary Stewart in England', in *Mary Stewart, Queen in Three Kingdoms*,
   ed. Michael Lynch (Oxford, 1988), pp. 195–215
————'Stafford, William (1554–1612)', *ODNB* (Oxford, 2004; online edn,
   Oct 2007)
Horton-Smith, L. G. H., *Dr Walter Bailey 1529–1592: Physician to Queen
   Elizabeth* (St Albans, 1952)
Hoskins, A., 'Mary Boleyn's Carey Children and Offspring of Henry VIII',
   Genealogists Magazine, 25 (1997), pp. 345–52
Houliston, V., *Catholic Resistance in Elizabethan England: Robert Persons's Jesuit
   Polemic, 1580–1610* (Aldershot, 2007)
Howarth, David, *Images of Rule: Art and Politics in the English Renaissance,
   1485–1649* (Los Angeles, 1997)
Hume, M. A. S., *The Courtships of Queen Elizabeth* (London, 1904)
Hunt, Alice, *The Drama of Coronation: Medieval Ceremony in Early Modern
   England* (Cambridge, 2008)
Hunt, Lynn, ed. *The Invention of Pornography: Obscenity and the Origins of
   Modernity, 1500–1800* (New York, 1993)
Hunter, Joseph, *Hallamshire: the History and Topography of the Parish of Sheffield
   in the Citie of York . . .* (London, 1819)
Hutchinson, Robert, *Elizabeth's Spy Master: Francis Walsingham and the Secret
   War that Saved England* (New York, 2007)
James, Henry and Walker, Greg, 'The Politics of Gorboduc', *English Historical
   Review*, 110 (1995) pp. 109–21
Jenkins, E., *Elizabeth the Great* (London, 1958)
————*Elizabeth and Leicester* (London, 1961)
Jensen, D. L., *Diplomacy and Dogmatism: Bernardino de Mendoza and the French
   Catholic League* (Cambridge, 1988)
———— 'The Spanish Armada: The Worst-kept Secret in Europe', *Sixteenth-
   century Journal*, 19 (1988), pp. 621–41
Johnson, P., *Elizabeth I: A Study in Power and Intellect* (London, 1974)
Jones, Norman, *Faith by Statute: Parliament and the Settlement of Religion 1559*
   (London, 1982)
————*The Birth of the Elizabethan Age: England in the 1560s* (Oxford,
   1993)
————'Defining Superstitions: Treasonous Catholics and the Act Against
   Witchcraft of 1563', in *State, Sovereigns and Society: Essays in Early Modern
   English History in Honour of A.J. Slavin*, eds Charles Carlton et al. (London,
   1998), pp. 187–203
Jones, N. and White, P. W., 'Gorboduc and Royal Marriages', *English Literary
   Renaissance*, 27 (1987), pp. 421–51
Jordan, Constance, 'Women's Rule in Sixteenth-century British Political
   Thought', *Renaissance Quarterly*, 40 (1987), pp. 421–51

Judges, A. V., ed. *The Elizabethan Underworld* (London, 1965)

Kantorowicz, Ernst H., *The King's Two Bodies: A Study in Mediaeval Political Theology* (Princeton, 1957)

Kaplan, M. Lindsay, *The Culture of Slander in Early Modern England* (Cambridge, 1997)

Kassel, Lauren, *Medicine and Magic in Elizabethan London: Simon Forman: Astrologer, Alchemist and Physician,* (Oxford, 2005)

Kay, Dennis, 'She was a Queen, and Therefore Beautiful: Sidney, His Mother and Queen Elizabeth', *Review of English Studies,* 169 (February, 1992), pp. 18–39

Kegl, Rosemary, 'Those Terrible Aproches: Sexuality, Social Mobility and Resisting the Courtliness of Puttenham's *The Arte of English Poesie*', *English Literary Renaissance,* 20 (1990), pp. 179–208

Kendall, A., *Robert Dudley, Earl of Leicester* (London, 1980)

Kenny, R. W., *Elizabeth's Admiral. The Political Career of Charles Howard, Earl of Nottingham, 1536–1624* (Baltimore and London, 1990)

Kesselring, K. J., *The Northern Rebellion of 1569: Faith, Politics and Protest in Elizabethan England* (Basingstoke, 2007)

King, John N., *Tudor Royal Iconography: Literature and Art in an Age of Religious Crisis* (Princeton, 1989)

————'Queen Elizabeth I: Representations of the Virgin Queen', *Renaissance Quarterly,* 43 (1990), pp. 41–84

Kinghorn, Jonathan, 'A Privvie in Perfection: Sir John Harington's Water Closet', *Bath History,* 1 (1986), pp. 173–88

Lake, Peter, 'The Monarchical Republic of Elizabeth I, Revisited (by its Victims) as a Conspiracy', in *Conspiracies and Conspiracy Theory in Early Modern Europe: from the Waldensians to the French Revolution,* eds Barry Coward and Julian Swann (Aldershot, 2004), pp. 87–111

Lawson, J. A., 'This Remembrance of the New Year: Books Given to Queen Elizabeth as New Year's Gifts', in *Elizabeth I and the Culture of Writing,* eds P. Beal and G. Ioppolo (London, 2007), pp. 133–71

Leimon, M. and Parker, G., 'Treason and Plot in Elizabethan Diplomacy: the "Fame of Sir Edward Stafford" Reconsidered', *English Historical Review,* 111 (1996), pp. 1134–58

Levin, Carole, 'Queens and Claimants: Political Insecurity in Sixteenth-century England', in *Gender, Ideology and Action,* ed. Janet Sharistanian (New York, 1986), pp. 41–66

————'We Shall Never Have a Merry World while the Queene lyveth: Gender, Monarchy and the Power of Seditious Words', in *Dissing Elizabeth: Negative Representations of Gloriana,* ed. Julia M. Walker (London, 1988), pp. 77–98

————'Would I Could Give You Help and Succour: Elizabeth I and the Politics of Touch', *Albion,* 21:2 (1989), pp. 191–205

————'Power, Politics, and Sexuality: Images of Elizabeth I', in *The Politics of Gender in Early Modern Europe,* eds Jean R. Brink, Allison P. Coudert and Maryanne C. Horowitz (Kirksville, Missouri, 1989), pp. 95–110

————*The Heart and Stomach of a King: Elizabeth I and the Politics of Sex and Power* (Pennsylvania, 1994)

————'Elizabeth I: Dreams of Danger', in *Queen Elizabeth: Past and Present*, ed. Christa Jansohn (Munster, 2004), pp. 9–28

————and Sullivan, Patricia A., eds, *Political Rhetoric, Power and Renaissance Women* (Albany, 1995)

Levine, Mortimer, *Tudor Dynastic Problems 1460–1571* (London, 1973)

————*The Early Elizabethan Succession Question, 1558–1568* (Stanford, 1966)

————'A "Letter" on the Elizabethan Succession Question, 1566', Huntington Library Quarterly, 19:1 (1995), pp. 13–38

Levy, F. J., 'A Semi-Professional Diplomat, Guido Cavalcanti and the Marriage Negotiations of 1571', *BIHR* 35 (1962), pp. 211–20

Lilly, Joseph, ed., *A Collection of Seventy-nine Black-Letter Ballads and Broadsides Printed in the Reign of Queen Elizabeth Between the Years 1559 and 1597* (London, 1867)

Linden, Stanton J., *Mystical Metal of Gold: Essays on Alchemy and Renaissance Culture* (New York, 2007)

Llewellyn, Nigel, *The Art of Death: Visual Culture in the English Death Ritual, c. 1500–c. 1800* (London, 1991)

————*Funeral Monuments in Post-Reformation England* (Cambridge, 1991)

Loomie, Albert J., *The Spanish Elizabethans: The English Exiles at the Court of Philip II* (London, 1963)

Loomis, Catherine, 'Elizabeth's Southwell's Manuscript Account of the Death of Queen Elizabeth', *English Literary Renaissance*, 26:3 (1996), pp. 482–509

————*The Death of Elizabeth I: Remembering and Reconstructing the Virgin Queen* (Basingstoke, 2010)

Lovell, Mary S., *Bess of Hardwick: First Lady of Chatsworth, 1527–1608* (London, 2005)

Lynch, Michael, 'Queen Mary's Triumph: The Baptismal Celebrations at Stirling in December 1566', *Scottish Historical Review*, 69 (1990), pp. 1–21

————ed., *Mary Stewart: Queen in Three Kingdoms* (London, 1988)

MacCaffrey, Wallace T., *The Shaping of the Elizabethan Regime* (London, 1969)

————'The Anjou Match and the Making of Elizabethan Foreign Policy', in *The English Commonwealth 1547–1640: Essays Presented to Professor Joel Hurtsfield*, eds Peter Clark, Alan G. T. Smith and Nicholas Tyacke (Leicester, 1979), pp. 59–75

————*Queen Elizabeth and the Making of Policy, 1572–1588* (Princeton, 1981)

————*Elizabeth I: War and Politics, 1588–1603* (Princeton, 1992)

————*Queen Elizabeth I* (London, 1993)

————'The Newhaven Expedition, 1562–1563', *Historical Journal*, 40 (1997), pp. 1–21

McCoog, Thomas M., 'The English Jesuit Mission and the French Match, 1579–1581', *Catholic Historical Review*, 87 (2001), pp. 185–212

————'Construing Martyrdom in the English Catholic Community 1582–1602', in Ethan Shagan, ed. *Catholics and the 'Protestant Nation': Religious Politics and Identity in Early Modern England* (Manchester 2005)

————ed., *The Reckoned Expense: Edmund Campion and the English Jesuits* (Rome, 2007)

McCoy, R. C., 'From the Tower to the Tiltyard: Robert Dudley's return to glory', *Historical Journal*, 27 (1984), pp. 425–35

McCullough, P. E., 'Out of Egypt: Richard Fletcher's Sermon before Elizabeth I after the Execution of Mary, Queen of Scots', in *Dissing Elizabeth: Negative Representations of Gloriana*, ed. Julia M. Walker (London, 1988), pp. 118–52

———*Sermons at Court: Politics and Religion in Elizabethan and Jacobean Preaching* (Cambridge, 1997)

McGrath, Patrick, 'The Imprisonment of Catholics for Religion under Elizabeth I', *Recusant History*, 20 (1991), pp. 415–35

McKeen, David, *A Memory of Honour: The Life of William Brooke, Lord Cobham*, 2 vols (Vienna, 1986)

McLaren, A. N., *Political Culture in the Reign of Elizabeth I: Queen and Commonwealth, 1558–1585* (Cambridge, 1999)

———'The Quest for a King: Gender, Marriage and Succession in Elizabethan England', *Journal of British Studies*, 41 (2002), pp. 259–90

———'Gender, Religion and Early Modern Nationalism: Elizabeth I, Mary Queen of Scots, and the Genesis of English Catholicism', *American Historical Review*, 107:3 (2002), pp. 739–67

———'Memorialising Mary and Elizabeth', in *Tudor Queenship: the Reigns of Mary and Elizabeth*, eds Alice Hunt and Anna Whitelock (Basingstoke, 2010), pp. 11–30

Maclean, I., *The Renaissance Notion of Woman* (Cambridge, 1980)

McManus, Caroline, 'Reading the Margins: Female Courtiers in the Portraits of Elizabeth I', *English Literary Renaissance*, 32:2 (2002), pp. 189–213

Marcus, Leah S., 'Erasing the Stigma of Daughterhood: Mary I, Elizabeth I, Henry VIII', in *Daughters and Fathers*, eds Linda E. Boose and Betty S. Flowers (Baltimore, 1989) pp. 400–17

Martin, Colin and Parker, Geoffrey, *The Spanish Armada* (London, 1988)

Mattingly, Garrett, *Renaissance Diplomacy* (Boston, 1955)

Maxwell, Robin, *The Queen's Bastard* (New York, 1999)

Mayer, Jean-Christophe, ed., *The Struggle for the Succession in Late Elizabethan England: Politics, Polemics and Cultural Representations* (Montpellier, 2004)

Mears, Natalie, 'Counsel, Public Debate, and Queenship: John Stubbs's The Discoverie of a Gaping Gulf, 1579', *Historical Journal*, 44 (2001), pp. 629–50

———'Politics in the Elizabethan Privy Chamber: Lady Mary Sidney and Kat Ashley', in *Women and Politics in Early Modern England, 1450–1700*, ed. James Daybell (Burlington, VT, 2004), pp. 67–82

———*Queenship and Political Discourse in the Elizabethan Realms* (Cambridge, 2005)

———'Love-making and Diplomacy: Elizabeth I and the Anjou Marriage Negotiations, c.1578–81', *History*, 86 (2001), pp. 442–66

Mehl, Dieter, 'Edmund Spenser's Gloriana: Elizabeth as "Faerie Queen"', in *Queen Elizabeth I: Past and Present*, ed. Christa Jansohn (Munster, 2004), pp. 89–100

Mendleson, Sara, 'Popular Perceptions of Elizabeth', in *Elizabeth I: Always Her Own Free Woman*, eds Carole Levin, Jo Elridge-Carney and Debra Barrett-Graves (Aldershot, 2003), pp. 192–214

————and Patricia Crawford, *Women in Early Modern England, 1550–1720* (New York, 1998)

Merton, Charlotte, 'Women, Friendship and Memory', in *Tudor Queenship: The Reigns of Mary and Elizabeth*, eds Alice Hunt and Anna Whitelock (Basingstoke, 2010), pp. 239–550

————'Astley, Katherine (d. 1565)', *ODNB* (Oxford, 2004; online edn, Jan 2008)

Mikhaila, Ninya and Malcolm-Davies, Jane, *The Tudor Tailor: Reconstructing Sixteenth-century Dress* (London, 2006)

Montrose, Louis A., '"Shaping Fantasies": Figurations of Gender and Power in Elizabethan Culture', in *Representing the Renaissance*, ed. Stephen Greenblatt (Berkeley, 1988), pp. 31–64

————'Elizabeth through the Looking Glass: Picturing the Queen's Two Bodies', in *The Body of the Queen: Gender and Rule in the Courtly World*, ed. Regina Schulte (New York, 2006), pp. 61–87

————*The Subject of Elizabeth: Authority, Gender and Representation* (Chicago, 2006)

Morey, Adrian, *The Catholic Subjects of Elizabeth I* (Guildford, 1978)

Morison, Margaret, 'A Narrative of the Journey of Cecilia, Princess of Sweden, to the Court of Queen Elizabeth', *Transactions of the Royal Historical Society*, n.s.12 (1898), pp. 181–224

Mortimer, Ian, *Time Traveller's Guide to Elizabethan England* (London, 2012)

Nardizzi, Vincent Joseph, Guy-Bray, Stephen, Stockton, Will, eds, *Queer Renaissance Historiography, Backward Gaze* (Farnham, 2009)

Neale, J. E., 'Parliament and the Succession Question in 1562/3 and 1566', *English Historical Review* (1921), pp. 497–519

————*Queen Elizabeth* (London, 1934)

————*Elizabeth I and her Parliaments*, 2 vols (London, 1953)

————'The Fame of Sir Edward Stafford', *Studies in Elizabethan History* (1959), pp. 146–69

————*Queen Elizabeth I* (London, 1998)

Nederman, C. J. and Langdon, K., eds, *Medieval Political Theory: The Quest for the Body Politic, 1100–1400* (London, 1993)

Norrington, Ruth, *In the Shadow of the Throne: The Lady Arbella Stuart* (London, 2002)

Oakley-Brown, Liz and Wilkinson, Louise J., eds, *The Rituals and Rhetoric of Queenship: Medieval to Early Modern* (Dublin, 2009)

Osterberg, Eva, *Friendship and Love, Ethics and Politics: Studies in Medieval and Early Modern History* (Budapest, 2010)

Oxford Dictionary of National Biography, eds H. C. G. Matthew and B. Harrison, 61 vols (Oxford, 2004), http://www.oxforddnb.com

Parker, Geoffrey, *The Grand Strategy of Philip II* (New Haven and London, 1998)

———— 'The Place of Tudor England in the Messianic Vision of Philip II of Spain', *Transactions of the Royal Historical Society*, sixth series, 12 (2002), pp. 167–221

Parry, Glyn, 'John Dee and the Elizabethan British Empire in its European Context', *Historical Journal*, 49:3 (2006), pp. 643–75

————*The Arch-Conjuror of England, John Dee* (London, 2011)

Peck, D. C., 'The Letter of Estate: An Elizabethan Libel', *Notes and Queries*, 28:1 (1981), pp. 31–4

Peck, G., 'John Hales and the Puritans during the Marian exile', *Church History*, 10 (1941), pp. 159–77

Perry, Maria, *The Word of a Prince: A Life of Elizabeth I from Contemporary Documents* (Woodbridge, 1990)

Petrina, Alessandra and Tosi, Laura, eds, *Representations of Elizabeth I in Early Modern Culture* (Basingstoke, 2011)

Phillips, James E., 'The Background of Spenser's Attitude Towards Women Rulers', *Huntington Library Quarterly*, 5 (1941–2), pp. 5–32

———*Images of a Queen: Mary Stuart in Sixteenth-century Literature* (Berkeley, 1964)

Plowden, Alison, *Danger to Elizabeth: the Catholics under Elizabeth I* (London, 1973)

———*Marriage with My Kingdom: The Courtships of Elizabeth I* (London, 1977)

——— 'Throckmorton, Francis (1554–1584)', *ODNB* (Oxford, 2004; online edn, May 2007)

Pollen, J. H., 'The Question of Queen Elizabeth's Successor', *The Month*, 101 (1903), pp. 517–32

———*The English Catholics during the Reign of Queen Elizabeth: A Study of their Politics, Civil Life and Government 1558–80* (London, 1920)

———ed., *Papal Negotiations with Mary, Queen of Scots during Her Reign in Scotland, 1561–1567* (Edinburgh, 1901)

Pollit, R., 'The Defeat of the Northern Rebellion and the Shaping of Anglo–Scottish Relations', *Scottish Historical Review*, 64 (1985), pp. 1–21

Potter, David, ed., *Foreign Intelligence and Information in Elizabethan England: Two English Treatises on the State of France, 1580–1584*, Camden Society, fifth series 25 (Cambridge, 2004)

Poynter, F. N. L., ed., *Selected Writings of William Clowes* (London, 1948).

Pritchard, Allan, 'Thomas Charnock's Book Dedicated to Queen Elizabeth', *Ambix*, 26:1 (March, 1979), pp. 56–73

Questier, Michael C., 'Loyal to a Fault: Viscount Montague Explains Himself', *BIHR*, 77 (2004), pp. 225–53

———*Catholicism and Community in Early Modern England: Politics, Aristocratic Patronage and Religion, c.1550–1640* (Cambridge, 2006)

Ramsay, G. D., *The City of London in International Politics at the Accession of Elizabeth Tudor* (Manchester, 1975)

Ravelhofer, Barbara, 'Dancing at the Court of Queen Elizabeth', in *Queen Elizabeth I: Past and Present*, ed. Christa Jansohn (Munster, 2004), pp. 101–16

Razell, Peter, ed., *The Journals of Two Travellers in Elizabethan and Stuart England, Thomas Platter and Horatio Busino* (London, 1995)

Read, Conyers, *Mr Secretary Walsingham and the Policy of Queen Elizabeth*, 3 vols (Oxford, 1925)

———*Lord Burghley and Queen Elizabeth* (London, 1960)

———*Mr Secretary Cecil and Queen Elizabeth* (London, 1965)

Reynolds, E. E., *Campion and Persons: The Jesuit Mission of 1580–81* (London, 1980)

Richards, Judith M., 'Love and a Female Monarch: The Case of Elizabeth Tudor', *Journal of British Studies*, 38.2 (1999), pp. 133–60

Richardson, Ruth Elizabeth, *Mistress Blanche: Queen Elizabeth I's Confidante* (Glasgow, 2007)

Ridley, Jasper, *Elizabeth I* (London, 1987)

Riehl, Anna, *The Face of Queenship: Early Modern Representations of Elizabeth I* (New York, 2010)

Ritchie, Pamela E., *Mary of Guise in Scotland, 1548–1560: a Political Career* (East Lothian, 2002)

Roberts, Peter R., 'Parry, Blanche (1507/8–1590)', *ODNB* (Oxford, 2004; online edn, Sept 2012)

Robinson, A. M. F., 'Queen Elizabeth and the Valois Princes', *English Historical Review*, 2 (1887), pp. 40–77

Rodriguez-Salgado, M. J., *The Changing Face of Empire: Charles V, Philip II and Habsburg authority, 1551–1559* (Cambridge, 1989)

Rolls, Albert, *The Theory of the King's Two Bodies in the Age of Shakespeare*, Studies in Renaissance Literature, 19 (Lewiston, Queenston and Lampeter, 2000)

Ross, Josephine, *Suitors to the Queen* (London, 1975)

Rowse, A. L., *Ralegh and the Throckmortons* (London, 1962)

——*The Elizabethan Renaissance: The Life of the Society* (London, 1971)

Rutton, W. L., 'Lady Katherine Grey and Edward Seymour, Earl of Hertford', *English Historical Review*, 13 (April 1898), pp. 302–7

Rye, W. B., *England as Seen by Foreigners in the Days of Elizabeth and James I* (London, 1865)

St John Brooks, Eric, *Sir Christopher Hatton: Queen Elizabeth's Favourite* (London, 1946)

Saleman, Nannette, 'Positioning Women in the Visual Convention: the Case of Elizabeth I', in *Attending to Women in Early Modern England*, eds Betty S. Travitsky and Adele F. Seef (Newark, 1994), pp. 64–95

Salgādo, Gāmini, *The Elizabethan Underworld* (New York, 1992)

Salmon, J. H. M., *Society in Crisis: France in the Sixteenth Century* (London, 1975)

Sargent, Ralph, *The Life and Lyrics of Sir Edward Dyer* (Oxford, 1968)

Scalingi, Paula Louise, 'The Sceptre or the Distaff: The Question of Female Sovereignty, 1515–1607', *The Historian*, 42 (1978), pp. 59–75

Scarisbrick, Diana, 'Elizabeth's Jewellery', in *Elizabeth: The Exhibition at the National Maritime Museum*, eds D. Starkey and S. Doran (London, 2003), pp. 183–88

Schulte, Regina, ed., *The Body of the Queen: Gender and Rule in the Courtly World, 1500–2000* (New York, 2006)

Schutte, K., *A Biography of Margaret Douglas, Countess of Lennox (1515–1578) Niece of Henry VIII and Mother-in-Law of Mary, Queen of Scots* (Lewiston, NY, 2002)

Seaton, Ethel, *Queen Elizabeth and a Swedish Princess* (London, 1926)

Shagan, Ethan H., ed., *Catholics and the 'Protestant Nation': Religious Politics and Identity in Early Modern England* (Manchester, 2005)

Shapiro, James, *1599: A Year in the Life of William Shakespeare* (London, 2005)

Sharpe, Kevin, *Selling the Tudor Monarchy* (London and New Haven, 2009)

Shell, Marc, *Elizabeth's Glass* (Lincoln, NE, 1993)

Shephard, Amanda, *Gender and Authority in Sixteenth-century England* (Keele, 1994)

Shephard, Robert, 'Sexual Rumours in English Politics: The Case of Elizabeth I and James I', in *Desire and Discipline: Sex and Sexuality in the Premodern West*, eds Jacqueline Murray and Konrad Eisenbechler (Toronto, 1996), pp. 101–22

Sherlock, Peter, 'The Monuments of Elizabeth Tudor and Mary Stuart: King James and the Manipulation of memory', *Journal of British Studies*, 46 (2007), pp. 263–89.

———*Monuments and Memory in Early Modern England* (Burlington, 2008)

Skidmore, Chris, *Death and the Virgin: Elizabeth, Dudley and the Mysterious Fate of Amy Robsart* (London, 2010)

Smith, Virginia, *Clean: A History of Personal Hygiene and Purity* (Oxford, 2007)

Smither, L. J., 'Elizabeth I: A Psychological Profile', *Sixteenth-century Journal*, 15 (1984), pp. 47–72

Somerset, A., *Ladies in Waiting from the Tudors to the Present Day* (London, 1984)

———*Elizabeth I* (New York, 1991)

Sommerville, Margaret R., *Sex and Subjection: Attitudes to Women in Early Modern Society* (New York, 1995)

Stallybrass, Peter, 'Patriarchal Territories: The Body Enclosed', in *Rewriting the Renaissance: The Discourses of Sexual Difference in Early Modern Europe*, eds Margaret W. Ferguson, Maureen Quilligan and Nancy J. Vickers (Chicago, 1986), pp. 123–42.

Starkey, David, *Elizabeth: Apprenticeship* (London, 2000)

———et al., eds, *The English Court from the Wars of the Roses to the Civil War* (London, 1987)

———and Susan Doran, eds, *Elizabeth: The Exhibition at the National Maritime Museum* (London, 2003)

Stone, Lawrence, *An Elizabethan: Sir Horatio Palavicino* (Oxford, 1956)

———*The Family, Sex and Marriage in England 1500–1800* (New York, 1979)

Strachey, L., *Elizabeth and Essex: A Tragic History* (London, 1928)

Strickland, Agnes, *Lives of the Queens of England*, 8 vols (London, 1854)

Strong, Roy, *Portraits of Queen Elizabeth I* (Oxford, 1964)

———*The English Icon: Elizabeth and Jacobean Portraiture* (London, 1969)

———*The Cult of Elizabeth: Elizabethan Portraiture and Pageantry* (Berkeley, 1977)

———*Artists of the Tudor Court: The Portrait Miniature Rediscovered 1520–1620* (London, 1983)

———*Gloriana: The Portraits of Queen Elizabeth* (London, 1987)

Stump, Donald and Felch, Susan, eds, *Elizabeth I and her Age* (New York, 2009)

Sutherland, N. M., *The Massacre of St Bartholomew and the European Conflict, 1559–1572* (London, 1973)

———'The Marian Exiles and the Establishment of the Elizabethan Regime', *Archive for Reformation History*, 78 (1987), pp. 253–84

———*The Huguenot Struggle for Recognition* (London, 1980)

Taylor-Smither, Larissa J., 'Elizabeth I: A Psychological Profile', *Sixteenth-century Journal*, 15 (1984), pp. 47–72

Teague, Frances, 'Queen Elizabeth in her Speeches', in *Gloriana's Face: Women*

Public and Private in the English Renaissance, eds S. P. Cerasano and Marion Wynne-Davies (Hemel Hempstead, 1992), pp. 63–78

Thomas, Keith, *Religion and the Decline of Magic: Studies in Popular Beliefs in Sixteenth and Seventeenth-century England* (London, 1971)

Thorp, Malcolm, 'Catholic Conspiracy in Early Elizabethan Foreign Policy', *Sixteenth-century Journal*, 15 (1984), pp. 431–49

Thurley, Simon, *The Royal Palaces of Tudor England* (New Haven and London, 1993)

———*Whitehall Palace: An Architectural History of the Royal Apartments, 1240–1690* (New Haven and London, 1999)

———*Hampton Court: A Social and Architectural History* (New Haven and London, 2003)

Tighe, W. J., 'Country into Court, Court into Country: John Scudamore of Holme Lacy (c.1542–1623) and His Circles', in Dale Hoak, ed., *Tudor Political Culture* (Cambridge, 1995), pp. 157–78

———'*Familia Reginae*. The Privy Court', in Susan Doran and Norman Jones, eds, *The Elizabethan World* (Oxford, 2011), pp. 76–91

Traub, Valerie, *The Renaissance of Lesbianism in Early Modern England* (Cambridge, 2002)

Turrell, J. F., 'The Ritual of Royal Healing in Early Modern England', *Anglican and Episcopal History*, 68:1 (1999), pp. 3–36

Varlow, S., 'Sir Francis Knollys's Latin Dictionary: New Evidence for Katherine Carey', *BIHR*, 80 (2007), pp. 315–23

———'Knollys, Katherine, Lady Knollys (c.1523–1569)', *ODNB* (Oxford, Oct 2006; online edn, Jan 2009)

Von Bulow, Gottfried, trans., 'Journey through England and Scotland made by Lupold von Wedel in the Year 1584 and 1585', *Transactions of the Royal Historical Society*, n.s. 9 (1895), pp. 223–70

Walker, Julia M., ed., *Dissing Elizabeth: Negative Representations of Gloriana* (London, 1988)

——— 'Reading the Tombs of Queen Elizabeth I', *English Literary Renaissance*, 26 (1996), pp. 510–30

———'Bones of Contention: Posthumous Images of Elizabeth and Stuart Politics', in *Dissing Elizabeth: Negative Representations of Gloriana* (London, 1988), pp. 252–76

Walsham, Alexandra, 'Frantick Hacket: Prophecy, Sorcery, Insanity and the Elizabethan Puritan Movement', *Historical Journal*, 41:1 (1988), pp. 27–66

———*Church Papists: Catholicism, Conformity and Confessional Polemic in Early Modern England* (Woodbridge, 2003)

Walton, Kristen Post, *Catholic Queen, Protestant Patriarchy: Mary Queen of Scots and the Politics of Gender and Religion* (Basingstoke, 2007)

———'The Plot of the Devouring Lions: The "Divelish Conspiracy" of Arthur Pole and the Parliament of 1563' (forthcoming)

Ward, Leslie, 'The Treason Act of 1563: A Study of the Enforcement of Anti-Catholic Legislation', *Parliamentary History*, 8:2 (1989), pp. 289–308

Watkins, J., 'Old Bess in the Ruff: Remembering Elizabeth, 1625–60', *English Literary Renaissance*, XXX (2000), pp. 95–116

Watkins, Joan, *Representing Elizabeth in Stuart England: Literature, History and*

Sovereignty (Cambridge, 2002)

Webster, Charles, ed., *Health, Medicine and Mortality in the Sixteenth Century* (Cambridge, 1979)

Weisener, L., *The Youth of Queen Elizabeth, 1533–1558*, 2 vols (London, 1879)

Wernham, R. B., *Before the Armada: The Growth of English Foreign Policy, 1485–1588* (London, 1966)

———*The Making of English Foreign Policy, 1558–1603* (Berkeley, 1980)

———*The Making of Elizabethan Foreign Policy 1558–1603* (Berkeley, 1980)

———*After the Armada: Elizabethan England and the Struggle for Western Europe, 1588–1595* (Oxford, 1984)

Wheeler, E. D., *Ten Remarkable Women of the Tudor Courts and their Influence in Founding the New World, 1530–1630* (Lampeter, 2000)

Whitelock, Anna, *Mary Tudor: England's First Queen* (London, 2009)

———and Hunt, Alice, eds, *Tudor Queenship: The Reigns of Mary and Elizabeth* (Basingstoke, 2009)

Wilks, M., ed., *Mary Queen of Scots and French Public Opinion, 1542–1600* (Basingstoke, 2004)

Willett, C., and Cunnington, Phillis, *The History of Underclothes* (London, 1951)

Williams, Michael E., 'Squire, Edward (*d.* 1598)', *ODNB* (Oxford, 2004)

Williams, Neville, *Powder and Paint: A History of the Englishwoman's Toilet* (London, 1957)

———*Thomas Howard, Fourth Duke of Norfolk* (London, 1964)

———*Elizabeth I: Queen of England* (New York, 1967)

Wilson, D., *Sweet Robin: A Biography of Robert Dudley, Earl of Leicester 1533–1588* (London, 1981)

Wilson, Jean, *Entertainments for Queen Elizabeth I* (Woodbridge, 1980)

Wilson, Violet A., *Queen Elizabeth's Maids of Honour and Ladies of the Privy Chamber* (London, 1922)

Woolf, D. R., 'Two Elizabeths? James I and the Late Queen's Famous Memory', *Canadian Journal of History*, 20 (1985), pp. 167–91

Woolley, Benjamin, *The Queen's Conjuror: The Science and Magic of Dr Dee* (London, 2001)

Wormald, Jenny, *Mary Queen of Scots: A Study in Failure* (London, 1988)

Wright, J., 'Marian Exiles and the Legitimacy of Flight from Persecution', *Journal of Ecclesiastical History*, LII (2001), pp. 220–43

Wright, Pam, 'A Change in Direction: The Ramification of a Female Household, 1558–1603', in *The English Court from the Wars of the Roses to the Civil War*, eds David Starkey et al. (London, 1987), pp. 147–72

Yates, Frances A., 'Elizabethan Chivalry: the Romance of the Accession Day Tilts', *Journal of the Warburg and Courtauld Institutes*, 20 (1957), pp. 4–25

———*Astraea: The Imperial Theme in the Sixteenth Century* (London, 1975)

———*The Occult Philosophy in the Elizabethan Age* (London and Boston, 1979)

Youngs, Frederick A., *The Proclamations of the Tudor Queens* (Cambridge, 1976)

Ziegler, Georgiana, ed., *Elizabeth I: Then and Now* (Washington, 2003)

Acknowledgements

As I have, during the last few years, been an uninvited guest in Elizabeth's Bedchamber so too have I encroached shamelessly on the time, generosity, support and patience of many people during the writing of this book. It has been a test of stamina and endurance all round.

The Department of History at Royal Holloway, University of London has been enthusiastic about my work and very supportive of my research and writing. My undergraduates continually question and challenge me to think and rethink. My PhD students, Mariana Brockmann and Nikki Clark, have assisted with some research. The staff of the Cambridge University Library have proved continuingly helpful, friendly and supportive, as I have piled books on my desk and submitted endless request slips. Similarly helpful have been the staff of the British Library and the National Archives.

A number of scholars and writers have assisted me and been generous with their time and knowledge. Alice Hunt is a constant source of encouragement, friendship and inspiring discussion. Charlotte Merton generously gave her time and expertise to read through the completed manuscript. Jane Eade, Sebastian Edwards, Olivia Fryman, Sasha Handley, Maria Hayward, Carole Levin and Nigel Llewellyn have also responded helpfully to questions and queries. James McConnachie has been a hugely helpful and discerning reader during the book's early stages and Jo Browning Wroe has been a valuable library comrade and supportive friend. Rebecca Stott has remained a great mentor and friend, who continues to ask difficult questions and support my writing. Rebecca and I have hosted regular 'salons' with historical writers and so I have had the benefit and privilege of inspiring conversation with the very best practitioners of their craft, including Sarah Dunant, Philippa Gregory, Stella Tillyard, Tom Holland, Juliet Gardiner, Kate Summerscale, Malcolm Gaskill and David Kynaston.

Bloomsbury has proved once again to have been the friendliest, most supportive, efficient and ambitious publisher that I could have imagined. It is a publishing house full of energy, vision and commitment to books and their authors. Michael Fishwick is a brilliantly inspiring and insightful editor, a wise critic, and a loyal supporter of me and the book. Anna Simpson is a hidden gem – friendly, helpful, organised and efficient; she quite simply makes things happen behind the scenes and curates the transformation from manuscript to printed book. It has been a great pleasure and relief to work with Kate Johnson for the copyediting, and once again she has worked her magic with meticulous care and incisive comment. Ellen Williams and all the publicity team at Bloomsbury continue to do a fantastic job.

Catherine Clarke, my agent at Felicity Bryan Associates, has been all and more than an agent should be – honest, encouraging, supportive, and discerning. She is a very loyal and enthusiastic champion upon whom I rely hugely. My writing career to date has everything to do with her mentoring. Zoe Pagnamenta my US agent has proved equally committed to the book, as has Katie Haines of The Agency. My 'home' literary festival, Cambridge Wordfest, of which I am a proud patron, has been a place of great inspiration and fun during the long months of writing and research and the Festival Director Cathy Moore has been both a loyal supporter and a valued friend. My debts to other friends are equally great: Jim and Kate Godfrey, Rosie Peppin Vaughan, Pedro Ramos Pinto, Maureen Parry, Alice and James McConnachie, Jo Maybin, Emma Spearing, Chris Reynolds, Caelum Spearing, Layla Evans, Max Delderfield, Bluebelle Storm Evans Delderfield, Tiffany, Chris and Joshua Britton, Jacky Hess, Victoria Alcock, Rebecca Edwards Newman, Peter and Isobel Maddison, Nan James, Sandra Swarbrick and family. All have got used to my need for early nights, my preoccupied conversations and the general eccentricity that the process of writing and research brings. Linda and David Downes, Sally Downes and Lucy and Pete Gratton have also been continually interested and supportive of me and my writing. One notable absentee from my book launch will be the late Suzy Oakes who was always a great supporter of mine and a popular Cambridge figure.

My family have remained a constant source of love, support and encouragement. During the writing of the book we lost my grandfather, Eric Nason, whose much repeated refrain, 'Have you finished the book yet?' continues to resound in my head. I hope this book is fitting to his memory. Thanks are owed to my sister Amy and to Martin Inglis, and to my twin sister Emily who remains entirely unselfish in her support and encourage-ment. My niece Lily and nephews Sam and Bailiee have been refreshingly disinterested in the book and forced me to engage with life beyond the sixteenth century. I continue to rely on my parents, Celia and Paul Whitelock, who have been as unfailing in their love, concern and support as they have been in their desire for the book to be finished. Never has a final full stop been so highly anticipated or hard won.

Finally, I would like to thank Kate Downes who has continued to support me with unselfish patience, care and concern and upon whom I have depended enormously.

A shared achievement indeed.

Cambridge, April 2013

Index

A NOTE ON THE AUTHOR

Anne Whitelock gained her PhD in History from Corpus Christi College, Cambridge. She is now a senior lecturer in Early Modern History at Royal Holloway, University of London, and regularly apears on television and radio. She has written for the *Guardian*, *BBC History Magazine* and *History Today*, the *Times Literary Supplement* and *New York Times*. Her bestselling debut, *Mary Tudor*, was published to critical acclaim in 2009; *Elizabeth's Bedfellows* is her second book. She lives in Cambridge.

A NOTE ON THE TYPE

The text of this book is set in Adobe Caslon, named after the English punch-cutter and type-founder William Caslon I (1692–1766). Caslon's rather old-fashioned types were modelled on seventeenth-century Dutch designs, but found wide acceptance throughout the English-speaking world for much of the eighteenth century until being replaced by newer types towards the end of the century. Used in 1776 to print the Declaration of Independence, they were revived in the nineteenth century, and have been popular ever since, particularly amongst fine printers. There are several digital versions, of which Carol Twombly's Adobe Caslon is one.